CONTENTS

NIST Special Publication 800-39

**National Institute of
Standards and Technology**

U.S. Department of Commerce

Managing Information
Security Risk

*Organization, Mission, and Information
System View*

**JOINT TASK FORCE
TRANSFORMATION INITIATIVE**

INFORMATION SECURITY

Computer Security Division
Information Technology Laboratory
National Institute of Standards and Technology
Gaithersburg, MD 20899-8930

March 2011

U.S. Department of Commerce
Gary Locke, Secretary

National Institute of Standards and Technology
Patrick D. Gallagher, Director

Reports on Computer Systems Technology

The Information Technology Laboratory (ITL) at the National Institute of Standards and Technology (NIST) promotes the U.S. economy and public welfare by providing technical leadership for the nation's measurement and standards infrastructure. ITL develops tests, test methods, reference data, proof of concept implementations, and technical analyses to advance the development and productive use of information technology. ITL's responsibilities include the development of management, administrative, technical, and physical standards and guidelines for the cost-effective security and privacy of other than national security-related information in federal information systems. The Special Publication 800-series reports on ITL's research, guidelines, and outreach efforts in information system security, and its collaborative activities with industry, government, and academic organizations.

Authority

This publication has been developed by NIST to further its statutory responsibilities under the Federal Information Security Management Act (FISMA), Public Law (P.L.) 107-347. NIST is responsible for developing information security standards and guidelines, including minimum requirements for federal information systems, but such standards and guidelines shall not apply to national security systems without the express approval of appropriate federal officials exercising policy authority over such systems. This guideline is consistent with the requirements of the Office of Management and Budget (OMB) Circular A-130, Section 8b(3), *Securing Agency Information Systems*, as analyzed in Circular A-130, Appendix IV: *Analysis of Key Sections*. Supplemental information is provided in Circular A-130, Appendix III, *Security of Federal Automated Information Resources*.

Nothing in this publication should be taken to contradict the standards and guidelines made mandatory and binding on federal agencies by the Secretary of Commerce under statutory authority. Nor should these guidelines be interpreted as altering or superseding the existing authorities of the Secretary of Commerce, Director of the OMB, or any other federal official. This publication may be used by nongovernmental organizations on a voluntary basis and is not subject to copyright in the United States. Attribution would, however, be appreciated by NIST.

NIST Special Publication 800-39, 88 pages

(March 2011)

National Institute of Standards and Technology
Attn: Computer Security Division, Information Technology Laboratory
100 Bureau Drive (Mail Stop 8930) Gaithersburg, MD 20899-8930
Electronic mail: sec-cert@nist.gov

Compliance with NIST Standards and Guidelines

In accordance with the provisions of FISMA,[1] the Secretary of Commerce shall, on the basis of standards and guidelines developed by NIST, prescribe standards and guidelines pertaining to federal information systems. The Secretary shall make standards compulsory and binding to the extent determined necessary by the Secretary to improve the efficiency of operation or security of federal information systems. Standards prescribed shall include information security standards that provide minimum information security requirements and are otherwise necessary to improve the security of federal information and information systems.

- Federal Information Processing Standards (FIPS) are approved by the Secretary of Commerce and issued by NIST in accordance with FISMA. FIPS are compulsory and binding for federal agencies.[2] FISMA requires that federal agencies comply with these standards, and therefore, agencies may not waive their use.

- Special Publications (SPs) are developed and issued by NIST as recommendations and guidance documents. For other than national security programs and systems, federal agencies must follow those NIST Special Publications mandated in a Federal Information Processing Standard. FIPS 200 mandates the use of Special Publication 800-53, as amended. In addition, OMB policies (including OMB Reporting Instructions for FISMA and Agency Privacy Management) state that for other than national security programs and systems, federal agencies must follow certain specific NIST Special Publications.[3]

- Other security-related publications, including interagency reports (NISTIRs) and ITL Bulletins, provide technical and other information about NIST's activities. These publications are mandatory only when specified by OMB.

- Compliance schedules for NIST security standards and guidelines are established by OMB in policies, directives, or memoranda (e.g., annual FISMA Reporting Guidance).[4]

---

[1] The E-Government Act (P.L. 107-347) recognizes the importance of information security to the economic and national security interests of the United States. Title III of the E-Government Act, entitled the Federal Information Security Management Act (FISMA), emphasizes the need for organizations to develop, document, and implement an organization-wide program to provide security for the information systems that support its operations and assets.

[2] The term *agency* is used in this publication in lieu of the more general term *organization* only in those circumstances where its usage is directly related to other source documents such as federal legislation or policy.

[3] While federal agencies are required to follow certain specific NIST Special Publications in accordance with OMB policy, there is flexibility in how agencies apply the guidance. Federal agencies apply the security concepts and principles articulated in the NIST Special Publications in accordance with and in the context of the agency's missions, business functions, and environment of operation. Consequently, the application of NIST guidance by federal agencies can result in different security solutions that are equally acceptable, compliant with the guidance, and meet the OMB definition of *adequate security* for federal information systems. Given the high priority of information sharing and transparency within the federal government, agencies also consider reciprocity in developing their information security solutions. When assessing federal agency compliance with NIST Special Publications, Inspectors General, evaluators, auditors, and assessors consider the intent of the security concepts and principles articulated within the specific guidance document and how the agency applied the guidance in the context of its mission/business responsibilities, operational environment, and unique organizational conditions.

[4] Unless otherwise stated, all references to NIST publications in this document (i.e., Federal Information Processing Standards and Special Publications) are to the most recent version of the publication.

Acknowledgements

This publication was developed by the *Joint Task Force Transformation Initiative* Interagency Working Group with representatives from the Civil, Defense, and Intelligence Communities in an ongoing effort to produce a unified information security framework for the federal government. The National Institute of Standards and Technology wishes to acknowledge and thank the senior leaders from the Departments of Commerce and Defense, the Office of the Director of National Intelligence, the Committee on National Security Systems, and the members of the interagency technical working group whose dedicated efforts contributed significantly to the publication. The senior leaders, interagency working group members, and their organizational affiliations include:

U.S. Department of Defense

Teresa M. Takai
Assistant Secretary of Defense for Networks and Information Integration/DoD Chief Information Officer (Acting)

Gus Guissanie
Deputy Assistant Secretary of Defense (Acting)

Dominic Cussatt
Senior Policy Advisor

Barbara Fleming
Senior Policy Advisor

National Institute of Standards and Technology

Cita M. Furlani
Director, Information Technology Laboratory

William C. Barker
Cyber Security Advisor, Information Technology Laboratory

Donna Dodson
Chief, Computer Security Division

Ron Ross
FISMA Implementation Project Leader

Office of the Director of National Intelligence

Adolpho Tarasiuk Jr.
Assistant Director of National Intelligence and Intelligence Community Chief Information Officer

Charlene P. Leubecker
Deputy Intelligence Community Chief Information Officer

Mark J. Morrison
Director, Intelligence Community Information Assurance

Roger Caslow
Chief, Risk Management and Information Security Programs Division

Committee on National Security Systems

Teresa M. Takai
Acting Chair, CNSS

Eustace D. King
CNSS Subcommittee Co-Chair

Peter Gouldmann
CNSS Subcommittee Co-Chair

Lance Dubsky
CNSS Subcommittee Co-Chair

Joint Task Force Transformation Initiative Interagency Working Group

Ron Ross *NIST, JTF Leader*	Gary Stoneburner *Johns Hopkins APL*	Jennifer Fabius-Greene *The MITRE Corporation*	Kelley Dempsey *NIST*
Deborah Bodeau *The MITRE Corporation*	Cheri Caddy *Intelligence Community*	Peter Gouldmann *Department of State*	Arnold Johnson *NIST*
Peter Williams *Booz Allen Hamilton*	Karen Quigg *The MITRE Corporation*	Richard Graubart *The MITRE Corporation*	Christian Enloe *NIST*

In addition to the above acknowledgments, a special note of thanks goes to Peggy Himes and Elizabeth Lennon for their superb technical editing and administrative support and to Bennett Hodge, Cassandra Kelly, Marshall Abrams, Marianne Swanson, Patricia Toth, Kevin Stine, and Matt Scholl for their valuable insights and contributions. The authors also gratefully acknowledge and appreciate the significant contributions from individuals and organizations in the public and private sectors, both nationally and internationally, whose thoughtful and constructive comments improved the overall quality, thoroughness, and usefulness of this publication.

DEVELOPING COMMON INFORMATION SECURITY FOUNDATIONS

COLLABORATION AMONG PUBLIC AND PRIVATE SECTOR ENTITIES

In developing standards and guidelines required by FISMA, NIST consults with other federal agencies and offices as well as the private sector to improve information security, avoid unnecessary and costly duplication of effort, and ensure that NIST publications are complementary with the standards and guidelines employed for the protection of national security systems. In addition to its comprehensive public review and vetting process, NIST is collaborating with the Office of the Director of National Intelligence (ODNI), the Department of Defense (DoD), and the Committee on National Security Systems (CNSS) to establish a common foundation for information security across the federal government. A common foundation for information security will provide the Intelligence, Defense, and Civil sectors of the federal government and their contractors, more uniform and consistent ways to manage the risk to organizational operations and assets, individuals, other organizations, and the Nation that results from the operation and use of information systems. A common foundation for information security will also provide a strong basis for reciprocal acceptance of security assessment results and facilitate information sharing. NIST is also working with public and private sector entities to establish mappings and relationships between the security standards and guidelines developed by NIST and the International Organization for Standardization (ISO) and International Electrotechnical Commission (IEC).

CAUTIONARY NOTE

INTENDED SCOPE AND USE OF THIS PUBLICATION

The guidance provided in this publication is intended to address *only* the management of information security-related risk derived from or associated with the operation and use of information systems or the environments in which those systems operate. The guidance is *not* intended to replace or subsume other risk-related activities, programs, processes, or approaches that organizations have implemented or intend to implement addressing areas of risk management covered by other legislation, directives, policies, programmatic initiatives, or mission/business requirements. Rather, the information security risk management guidance described herein is complementary to and should be used as part of a more comprehensive Enterprise Risk Management (ERM) program.

Table of Contents

Prologue

"... Through the process of risk management, leaders must consider risk to U.S. interests from adversaries using cyberspace to their advantage and from our own efforts to employ the global nature of cyberspace to achieve objectives in military, intelligence, and business operations..."

"... For operational plans development, the combination of threats, vulnerabilities, and impacts must be evaluated in order to identify important trends and decide where effort should be applied to eliminate or reduce threat capabilities; eliminate or reduce vulnerabilities; and assess, coordinate, and deconflict all cyberspace operations..."

"... Leaders at all levels are accountable for ensuring readiness and security to the same degree as in any other domain..."

-- THE NATIONAL STRATEGY FOR CYBERSPACE OPERATIONS
OFFICE OF THE CHAIRMAN, JOINT CHIEFS OF STAFF, U.S. DEPARTMENT OF DEFENSE

CHAPTER ONE

INTRODUCTION

THE NEED FOR INTEGRATED ORGANIZATION-WIDE RISK MANAGEMENT

Information technology is widely recognized as the engine that drives the U.S. economy, giving industry a competitive advantage in global markets, enabling the federal government to provide better services to its citizens, and facilitating greater productivity as a nation. Organizations[5] in the public and private sectors depend on technology-intensive *information systems*[6] to successfully carry out their missions and business functions. Information systems can include diverse entities ranging from high-end supercomputers, workstations, personal computers, cellular telephones, and personal digital assistants to very specialized systems (e.g., weapons systems, telecommunications systems, industrial/process control systems, and environmental control systems). Information systems are subject to serious *threats* that can have adverse effects on organizational operations (i.e., missions, functions, image, or reputation), organizational assets, individuals, other organizations, and the Nation by exploiting both known and unknown vulnerabilities to compromise the confidentiality, integrity, or availability of the information being processed, stored, or transmitted by those systems. Threats to information and information systems can include purposeful attacks, environmental disruptions, and human/machine errors and result in great harm to the national and economic security interests of the United States. Therefore, it is imperative that leaders and managers at all levels understand their responsibilities and are held accountable for managing information security risk—that is, the risk associated with the operation and use of information systems that support the missions and business functions of their organizations.

Organizational risk can include many types of risk (e.g., program management risk, investment risk, budgetary risk, legal liability risk, safety risk, inventory risk, supply chain risk, and security risk). Security risk related to the operation and use of information systems is just one of many components of organizational risk that senior leaders/executives address as part of their ongoing risk management responsibilities. Effective risk management requires that organizations operate in highly complex, interconnected environments using state-of-the-art and legacy information systems—systems that organizations depend on to accomplish their missions and to conduct important business-related functions. Leaders must recognize that explicit, well-informed risk-based decisions are necessary in order to balance the benefits gained from the operation and use of these information systems with the risk of the same systems being vehicles through which purposeful attacks, environmental disruptions, or human errors cause mission or business failure. Managing information security risk, like risk management in general, is not an exact science. It brings together the best collective judgments of individuals and groups within organizations responsible for strategic planning, oversight, management, and day-to-day operations—providing both the necessary and sufficient risk response measures to adequately protect the missions and business functions of those organizations.

---

[5] The term *organization* describes an entity of any size, complexity, or positioning within an organizational structure (e.g., a federal agency or, as appropriate, any of its operational elements) that is charged with carrying out assigned mission/business processes and that uses information systems in support of those processes.

[6] An *information system* is a discrete set of information resources organized for the collection, processing, maintenance, use, sharing, dissemination, or disposition of information. In the context of this publication, the definition includes the environment in which the information system operates (i.e., people, processes, technologies, facilities, and cyberspace).

The complex relationships among missions, mission/business processes, and the information systems supporting those missions/processes require an integrated, organization-wide view for managing risk.[7] Unless otherwise stated, references to *risk* in this publication refer to information security risk from the operation and use of organizational information systems including the processes, procedures, and structures within organizations that influence or affect the design, development, implementation, and ongoing operation of those systems. The role of information security in managing risk from the operation and use of information systems is also critical to the success of organizations in achieving their strategic goals and objectives. Historically, senior leaders/executives have had a very narrow view of information security either as a technical matter or in a stovepipe that was independent of organizational risk and the traditional management and life cycle processes. This extremely limited perspective often resulted in inadequate consideration of how information security risk, like other organizational risks, affects the likelihood of organizations successfully carrying out their missions and business functions. This publication places information security into the broader organizational context of achieving mission/business success. The objective is to:

- Ensure that senior leaders/executives recognize the importance of managing information security risk and establish appropriate *governance* structures for managing such risk;

- Ensure that the organization's risk management process is being effectively conducted across the three tiers of organization, mission/business processes, and information systems;

- Foster an organizational climate where information security risk is considered within the context of the design of mission/business processes, the definition of an overarching enterprise architecture, and system development life cycle processes; and

- Help individuals with responsibilities for information system implementation or operation better understand how information security risk associated with their systems translates into organization-wide risk that may ultimately affect the mission/business success.

To successfully execute organizational missions and business functions with information system-dependent processes, senior leaders/executives must be committed to making risk management a fundamental mission/business requirement. This top-level, executive commitment ensures that sufficient resources are available to develop and implement effective, organization-wide risk management programs. Understanding and addressing risk is a *strategic* capability and an *enabler* of missions and business functions across organizations. Effectively managing information security risk organization-wide requires the following key elements:

- Assignment of risk management responsibilities to senior leaders/executives;

- Ongoing recognition and understanding by senior leaders/executives of the information security risks to organizational operations and assets, individuals, other organizations, and the Nation arising from the operation and use of information systems;

- Establishing the organizational tolerance for risk and communicating the risk tolerance throughout the organization including guidance on how risk tolerance impacts ongoing decision-making activities;[8] and

- Accountability by senior leaders/executives for their risk management decisions and for the implementation of effective, organization-wide risk management programs.

---

[7] The aggregation of different types of risk across the organization is beyond the scope of this publication.

[8] The evaluation of *residual risk* (which changes over time) to determine acceptable risk is dependent on the threshold set by organizational *risk tolerance*.

1.1 PURPOSE AND APPLICABILITY

NIST Special Publication 800-39 is the flagship document in the series of information security standards and guidelines developed by NIST in response to FISMA. The purpose of Special Publication 800-39 is to provide guidance for an integrated, organization-wide program for managing information security risk to organizational operations (i.e., mission, functions, image, and reputation), organizational assets, individuals, other organizations, and the Nation resulting from the operation and use of federal information systems. Special Publication 800-39 provides a structured, yet flexible approach for managing risk that is intentionally broad-based, with the specific details of assessing, responding to, and monitoring risk on an ongoing basis provided by other supporting NIST security standards and guidelines. The guidance provided in this publication is not intended to replace or subsume other risk-related activities, programs, processes, or approaches that organizations have implemented or intend to implement addressing areas of risk management covered by other legislation, directives, policies, programmatic initiatives, or mission/business requirements. Rather, the risk management guidance described herein is complementary to and should be used as part of a more comprehensive Enterprise Risk Management (ERM) program.

This publication satisfies the requirements of FISMA and meets or exceeds the information security requirements established for executive agencies[9] by the Office of Management and Budget (OMB) in Circular A-130, Appendix III, *Security of Federal Automated Information Resources*. The guidelines in this publication are applicable to all federal information systems other than those systems designated as national security systems as defined in 44 U.S.C., Section 3542. The guidelines have been broadly developed from a technical perspective to complement similar guidelines for national security systems and may be used for such systems with the approval of appropriate federal officials exercising policy authority over such systems. State, local, and tribal governments, as well as private sector organizations are encouraged to consider using these guidelines, as appropriate.

1.2 TARGET AUDIENCE

This publication is intended to serve a diverse group of risk management professionals including:

- Individuals with oversight responsibilities for risk management (e.g., heads of agencies, chief executive officers, chief operating officers);

- Individuals with responsibilities for conducting organizational missions/business functions (e.g., mission/business owners, information owners/stewards, authorizing officials);

- Individuals with responsibilities for acquiring information technology products, services, or information systems (e.g., acquisition officials, procurement officers, contracting officers);

- Individuals with information security oversight, management, and operational responsibilities (e.g., chief information officers, senior information security officers,[10] information security managers, information system owners, common control providers);

---

[9] An *executive agency* is: (i) an executive department specified in 5 U.S.C., Section 101; (ii) a military department specified in 5 U.S.C., Section 102; (iii) an independent establishment as defined in 5 U.S.C., Section 104(1); and (iv) a wholly owned government corporation fully subject to the provisions of 31 U.S.C., Chapter 91. In this publication, the term *executive agency* is synonymous with the term *federal agency*.

[10] At the *agency* level, this position is known as the Senior Agency Information Security Officer. Organizations may also refer to this position as the *Chief Information Security Officer*.

- Individuals with information system/security design, development and implementation responsibilities (e.g., program managers, enterprise architects, information security architects, information system/security engineers; information systems integrators); and

- Individuals with information security assessment and monitoring responsibilities (e.g., system evaluators, penetration testers, security control assessors, independent verifiers/validators, inspectors general, auditors).

1.3 RELATED PUBLICATIONS

The risk management approach described in this publication is supported by a series of security standards and guidelines necessary for managing information security risk. In particular, the Special Publications developed by the Joint Task Force Transformation Initiative[11] supporting the unified information security framework for the federal government include:

- Special Publication 800-37, *Guide for Applying the Risk Management Framework to Federal Information Systems: A Security Life Cycle Approach*;

- Special Publication 800-53, *Recommended Security Controls for Federal Information Systems and Organizations*;

- Special Publication 800-53A, *Guide for Assessing the Security Controls in Federal Information Systems and Organizations*; and

- Draft Special Publication 800-30, *Guide for Conducting Risk Assessments*.[12]

In addition to the Joint Task Force publications listed above, the International Organization for Standardization (ISO) and the International Electrotechnical Commission (IEC) publish standards for risk management and information security including:

- ISO/IEC 31000, *Risk management – Principles and guidelines*;

- ISO/IEC 31010, *Risk management – Risk assessment techniques*;

- ISO/IEC 27001, *Information technology – Security techniques – Information security management systems – Requirements*; and

- ISO/IEC 27005, *Information technology – Security techniques – Information security risk management systems*.

NIST's mission includes harmonization of international and national standards where appropriate. The concepts and principles contained in this publication are intended to implement for federal information systems and organizations, an information security management system and a risk management process similar to those described in ISO/IEC standards. This reduces the burden on organizations that must conform to both ISO/IEC standards and NIST standards and guidance.

---

[11] An overview of each Joint Task Force Transformation Initiative publication, similar to an Executive Summary, can be obtained through appropriate NIST ITL Security Bulletins at http://csrc.nist.gov.

[12] Special Publication 800-39 supersedes the original Special Publication 800-30 as the source for guidance on risk management. Special Publication 800-30 is being revised to provide guidance on risk assessment as a supporting document to Special Publication 800-39.

1.4 ORGANIZATION OF THIS SPECIAL PUBLICATION

The remainder of this special publication is organized as follows:

- **Chapter Two** describes: (i) the components of risk management; (ii) the multitiered risk management approach; (iii) risk management at the organization level (Tier 1); (iv) risk management at the mission/business process level (Tier 2); (v) risk management at the information system level (Tier 3); (vi) risk related to trust and trustworthiness; (vii) the effects of organizational culture on risk; and (viii) relationships among key risk management concepts.

- **Chapter Three** describes a life cycle-based process for managing information security risk including: (i) a general overview of the risk management process; (ii) how organizations establish the context for risk-based decisions; (iii) how organizations assess risk; (iv) how organizations respond to risk; and (v) how organizations monitor risk over time.

- **Supporting appendices** provide additional risk management information including: (i) general references; (ii) definitions and terms; (iii) acronyms; (iv) roles and responsibilities; (v) risk management process tasks; (vi) governance models; (vii) trust models; and (viii) risk response strategies.

CHAPTER TWO

THE FUNDAMENTALS

BASIC CONCEPTS ASSOCIATED WITH RISK MANAGEMENT

This chapter describes the fundamental concepts associated with managing information security risk across an organization including: (i) the components of risk management; (ii) the multitiered risk management approach; (iii) risk management at Tier 1 (organization level); (iv) risk management at Tier 2 (mission/business process level); (v) risk management at Tier 3 (information system level); (vi) risk related to trust and trustworthiness; (vii) the effects of organizational culture on risk; and (viii) the relationships among key risk management concepts.

2.1 COMPONENTS OF RISK MANAGEMENT

Managing risk is a complex, multifaceted activity that requires the involvement of the entire organization—from senior leaders/executives providing the strategic vision and top-level goals and objectives for the organization; to mid-level leaders planning, executing, and managing projects; to individuals on the front lines operating the information systems supporting the organization's missions/business functions. Risk management is a comprehensive process that requires organizations to: (i) *frame* risk (i.e., establish the context for risk-based decisions); (ii) *assess* risk; (iii) *respond* to risk once determined; and (iv) *monitor* risk on an ongoing basis using effective organizational communications and a feedback loop for continuous improvement in the risk-related activities of organizations. Risk management is carried out as a holistic, organization-wide activity that addresses risk from the strategic level to the tactical level, ensuring that risk-based decision making is integrated into every aspect of the organization.[13] The following sections briefly describe each of the four risk management components.

The first component of risk management addresses how organizations *frame* risk or establish a risk context—that is, describing the environment in which risk-based decisions are made. The purpose of the risk framing component is to produce a *risk management strategy* that addresses how organizations intend to assess risk, respond to risk, and monitor risk—making explicit and transparent the risk perceptions that organizations routinely use in making both investment and operational decisions. The risk frame establishes a foundation for managing risk and delineates the boundaries for risk-based decisions within organizations. Establishing a realistic and credible risk frame requires that organizations identify: (i) risk assumptions (e.g., assumptions about the threats, vulnerabilities, consequences/impact, and likelihood of occurrence that affect how risk is assessed, responded to, and monitored over time); (ii) risk constraints (e.g., constraints on the risk assessment, response, and monitoring alternatives under consideration); (iii) risk tolerance (e.g., levels of risk, types of risk, and degree of risk uncertainty that are acceptable); and (iv) priorities and trade-offs (e.g., the relative importance of missions/business functions, trade-offs among different types of risk that organizations face, time frames in which organizations must address risk, and any factors of uncertainty that organizations consider in risk responses). The risk framing component and the associated risk management strategy also include any strategic-level decisions on how risk to organizational operations and assets, individuals, other organizations, and the Nation, is to be managed by senior leaders/executives.

---

[13] Integrated, enterprise-wide risk management includes, for example, consideration of: (i) the strategic goals/objectives of organizations; (ii) organizational missions/business functions prioritized as needed; (iii) mission/business processes; (iv) enterprise and information security architectures; and (v) system development life cycle processes.

The second component of risk management addresses how organizations *assess* risk within the context of the organizational risk frame. The purpose of the risk assessment component is to identify: (i) threats to organizations (i.e., operations, assets, or individuals) or threats directed through organizations against other organizations or the Nation; (ii) vulnerabilities internal and external to organizations;[14] (iii) the harm (i.e., consequences/impact) to organizations that may occur given the potential for threats exploiting vulnerabilities; and (iv) the likelihood that harm will occur. The end result is a determination of risk (i.e., the degree of harm and likelihood of harm occurring). To support the risk assessment component, organizations identify: (i) the tools, techniques, and methodologies that are used to assess risk; (ii) the assumptions related to risk assessments; (iii) the constraints that may affect risk assessments; (iv) roles and responsibilities; (v) how risk assessment information is collected, processed, and communicated throughout organizations; (vi) how risk assessments are conducted within organizations; (vii) the frequency of risk assessments; and (viii) how threat information is obtained (i.e., sources and methods).

The third component of risk management addresses how organizations *respond* to risk once that risk is determined based on the results of risk assessments. The purpose of the risk response component is to provide a consistent, organization-wide, response to risk in accordance with the organizational risk frame by: (i) developing alternative courses of action for responding to risk; (ii) evaluating the alternative courses of action; (iii) determining appropriate courses of action consistent with organizational risk tolerance; and (iv) implementing risk responses based on selected courses of action. To support the risk response component, organizations describe the types of risk responses that can be implemented (i.e., accepting, avoiding, mitigating, sharing, or transferring risk). Organizations also identify the tools, techniques, and methodologies used to develop courses of action for responding to risk, how courses of action are evaluated, and how risk responses are communicated across organizations and as appropriate, to external entities (e.g., external service providers, supply chain partners).[15]

The fourth component of risk management addresses how organizations *monitor* risk over time. The purpose of the risk monitoring component is to: (i) verify that planned risk response measures are implemented and information security requirements derived from/traceable to organizational missions/business functions, federal legislation, directives, regulations, policies, and standards, and guidelines, are satisfied; (ii) determine the ongoing effectiveness of risk response measures following implementation; and (iii) identify risk-impacting changes to organizational information systems and the environments in which the systems operate.[16] To support the risk monitoring component, organizations describe how compliance is verified and how the ongoing effectiveness of risk responses is determined (e.g., the types of tools, techniques, and methodologies used to determine the sufficiency/correctness of risk responses and if risk mitigation measures are implemented correctly, operating as intended, and producing the desired effect with regard to reducing risk). In addition, organizations describe how changes that may impact the ongoing effectiveness of risk responses are monitored.

---

[14] Organizational vulnerabilities are not confined to information systems but can include, for example, vulnerabilities in governance structures, mission/business processes, enterprise architecture, information security architecture, facilities, equipment, system development life cycle processes, supply chain activities, and external service providers.

[15] Supply chain risk management guidance is provided in NIST Interagency Report 7622.

[16] Environments of operation include, but are not limited to: the threat space; vulnerabilities; missions/business functions; mission/business processes; enterprise and information security architectures; information technologies; personnel; facilities; supply chain relationships; organizational governance/culture; procurement/acquisition processes; organizational policies/procedures; organizational assumptions, constraints, risk tolerance, and priorities/trade-offs).

As indicated in the four components of risk management described above, organizations also consider external risk relationships, as appropriate. Organizations identify external entities with which there is an actual or potential risk relationship (i.e., organizations which could impose risks on, transfer risks to, or communicate risks to other organizations, as well as those to which organizations could impose, transfer, or communicate risks). External risk relationships include, for example, suppliers, customers or served populations, mission/business partners, and/or service providers. For organizations dealing with advanced persistent threats (i.e., a long-term pattern of targeted, sophisticated attacks) the risk posed by external partners (especially suppliers in the supply chain) may become more pronounced. Organizations establish practices for sharing risk-related information (e.g., threat and vulnerability information) with external entities, including those with which the organizations have a risk relationship as well as those which could supply or receive risk-related information (e.g., Information Sharing and Analysis Centers [ISAC], Computer Emergency Response Teams [CERT]).

Figure 1 illustrates the risk management process and the information and communications flows among components. The black arrows represent the *primary* flows within the risk management process with risk *framing* informing all the sequential step-by-step set of activities moving from risk *assessment* to risk *response* to risk *monitoring*. For example, one of the primary outputs from the risk framing component is a description of the sources and methods that organizations use in acquiring threat information (e.g., open source, classified intelligence community reports). The output regarding threat information is a primary input to the risk assessment component and is communicated accordingly to that component. Another example is illustrated in the primary output from the risk assessment component—that is, a determination of risk. The output from the risk assessment component is communicated to the risk response component and is received as a primary input for that component. Another primary input to the risk response component is an output from the risk framing component—the risk management strategy that defines how the organization should respond to risk. Together, these inputs, along with any additional inputs, are used by decision makers when selecting among potential courses of action for risk responses.

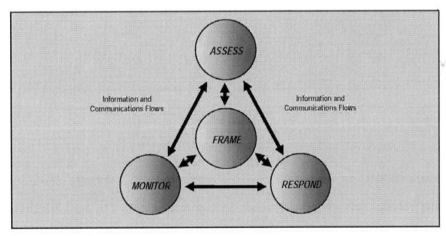

FIGURE 1: RISK MANAGEMENT PROCESS

The bidirectional nature of the arrows indicates that the information and communication flows among the risk management components as well as the execution order of the components, may be flexible and respond to the dynamic nature of the risk management process. For example, new legislation, directives, or policies may require that organizations implement additional risk response measures immediately. This information is communicated directly from the risk framing component to the risk response component where specific activities are carried out to achieve compliance with the new legislation, directives, or policies, illustrating the very dynamic and flexible nature of information as it moves through the risk management process. Chapter Three provides a complete description of the organization-wide risk management process including specifications for inputs/preconditions, activities, and outputs/post conditions.

2.2 MULTITIERED RISK MANAGEMENT

To integrate the risk management process throughout the organization, a three-tiered approach is employed that addresses risk at the: (i) *organization* level; (ii) *mission/business process* level; and (iii) *information system* level. The risk management process is carried out seamlessly across the three tiers with the overall objective of continuous improvement in the organization's risk-related activities and effective inter-tier and intra-tier communication among all stakeholders having a shared interest in the mission/business success of the organization. Figure 2 illustrates the three-tiered approach to risk management along with some of its key characteristics.

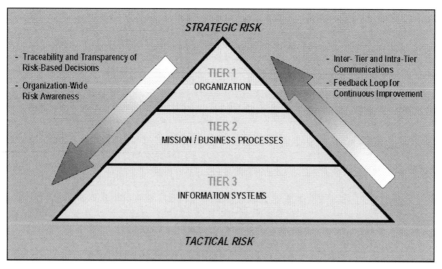

FIGURE 2: MULTITIERED ORGANIZATION-WIDE RISK MANAGEMENT

Tier 1 addresses risk from an *organizational* perspective. Tier 1 implements the first component of risk management (i.e., risk framing), providing the context for all risk management activities carried out by organizations. Tier 1 risk management activities directly affect the activities carried out at Tiers 2 and 3. For example, the missions and business functions defined at Tier 1 influence the design and development of the mission/business processes created at Tier 2 to carry out those missions/business functions. Tier 1 provides a prioritization of missions/business functions which in turn drives investment strategies and funding decisions, thus, affecting the development of enterprise architecture (including embedded information security architecture) at Tier 2 and the allocations and deployment of management, operational, and technical security controls at Tier 3.

Managing Information Security Risk
Organization, Mission, and Information System View

Other examples of Tier 1 activities that affect Tier 2 and Tier 3 activities include the selection of common controls, the provision of guidance from the risk executive (function)[17] to authorizing officials, and the establishment of the order of recovery for information systems supporting critical missions and business operations. Section 2.3 provides a more detailed description of the specific activities associated with Tier 1.

Tier 2 addresses risk from a *mission/business process* perspective and is informed by the risk context, risk decisions, and risk activities at Tier 1. Tier 2 risk management activities include: (i) defining the mission/business processes needed to support the missions and business functions of organizations; (ii) prioritizing the mission/business processes with respect to the strategic goals and objectives of organizations; (iii) defining the types of information needed to successfully execute the mission/business processes, the criticality/sensitivity of the information, and the information flows both internal and external to organizations; (iv) incorporating information security requirements[18] into the mission/business processes; and (v) establishing an enterprise architecture[19] with embedded information security architecture[20] that promotes cost-effective and efficient information technology solutions consistent with the strategic goals and objectives of the organization and measures of performance. Tier 2 activities directly affect the activities carried out at Tier 3. For example, the information security architecture portion of the enterprise architecture developed at Tier 2 influences and guides the allocation of information protection needs which, in turn, influences and guides the allocation of the security controls to specific components of organizational information systems at Tier 3. Enterprise architecture decisions at Tier 2 affect the design of information systems at Tier 3 including the types of information technologies acceptable for use in developing those systems. The activities carried out at Tier 2 can also provide useful feedback to Tier 1, possibly resulting in revisions to the organizational risk frame or affecting risk management activities carried out at Tier 1, for example those performed by the risk executive (function). Section 2.4 provides a more detailed description of the specific activities associated with Tier 2.

Tier 3 addresses risk from an *information system* perspective and is guided by the risk context, risk decisions and risk activities at Tiers 1 and 2. Tier 3 risk management activities include: (i) categorizing organizational information systems; (ii) allocating security controls to organizational information systems and the environments in which those systems operate consistent with the organization's established enterprise architecture and embedded information security architecture; and (iii) managing the selection, implementation, assessment, authorization, and ongoing monitoring of allocated security controls as part of a disciplined and structured system development life cycle process implemented across the organization. At Tier 3, information system owners, common control providers, system and security engineers, and information system security officers make risk-based decisions regarding the implementation, operation, and

---

[17] The risk executive (function) is described in Section 2.3.2.

[18] Information security requirements can be obtained from a variety of sources (e.g., legislation, policies, directives, regulations, standards, and organizational mission/business/operational requirements). Organization-level security requirements are documented in the information security program plan or equivalent document.

[19] Federal Enterprise Architecture Reference Models and Segment and Solution Architectures are defined in the OMB Federal Enterprise Architecture (FEA) Program, *FEA Consolidated Reference Model Document*, Version 2.3, October 2003, and OMB *Federal Segment Architecture Methodology (FSAM)*, January 2009, respectively.

[20] The *information security architecture* describes the security-related aspects of the enterprise architecture that are incorporated into the enterprise architecture definition as an integral part of the architecture development—that is a sub-architecture derived from the enterprise architecture, not a separately defined layer or architecture.

PAGE 10

19

monitoring of organizational information systems. Based on these day-to-day operational risk-based decisions, authorizing officials make follow-on risk-based decisions on whether or not the information systems are initially authorized to operate within the designated environments of operation or continue to receive authorization to operate on an ongoing basis. These ongoing risk-based decisions are informed by the risk management process with guidance from the risk executive (function) and the various architectural considerations supporting the mission/business processes. In addition, the activities at Tier 3 provide essential feedback to Tiers 1 and 2. New vulnerabilities discovered in an organizational information system, for example, may have systemic implications that extend organization-wide. Those same vulnerabilities may trigger changes to the enterprise architecture and embedded information security architecture or may require an adjustment to the organizational risk tolerance. Section 2.5 provides a more detailed description of the specific activities associated with Tier 3.

> *Since mission and business success in organizations depends on information systems, those systems must be dependable. To be dependable in the face of sophisticated threats, the information systems must be used wisely in accordance with the degree of protection and resilience achieved.*

2.3 TIER ONE—ORGANIZATION VIEW

Tier 1 addresses risk from an *organizational* perspective by establishing and implementing *governance* structures that are consistent with the strategic goals and objectives of organizations and the requirements defined by federal laws, directives, policies, regulations, standards, and missions/business functions. Governance structures provide oversight for the risk management activities conducted by organizations and include: (i) the establishment and implementation of a *risk executive (function)*; (ii) the establishment of the organization's risk management strategy including the determination of *risk tolerance*; and (iii) the development and execution of organization-wide *investment strategies* for information resources and information security.

2.3.1 Governance

In general, *governance* is the set of responsibilities and practices exercised by those responsible for an organization (e.g., the board of directors and executive management in a corporation, the head of a federal agency) with the express goal of: (i) providing strategic direction; (ii) ensuring that organizational mission and business objectives are achieved; (iii) ascertaining that risks are managed appropriately; and (iv) verifying that the organization's resources are used responsibly.[21] Risks and resources can be associated with different organizational sectors (e.g., legal, finance, information technology, regulatory compliance, information security). Different sectors require specialized expertise in order to manage the risks associated with that sector. Thus, governance within organizations frequently is organized by sector.[22] The five outcomes of governance related to organization-wide risk management are:

---

[21] This definition is adapted from the IT Governance Institute. The Chartered Institute of Management Accountants and the International Federation of Accountants also adopted this definition in 2004.

[22] While governance is frequently organized by sectors, organizations are well served by establishing a single aligned governance approach. A unified governance approach can coordinate the individual sector governance activities and provide a consistent governance approach, organization-wide.

- Strategic alignment of risk management decisions with missions and business functions consistent with organizational goals and objectives;

- Execution of risk management processes to frame, assess, respond to, and monitor risk to organizational operations and assets, individuals, other organizations, and the Nation;

- Effective and efficient allocation of risk management resources;

- Performance-based outcomes by measuring, monitoring, and reporting risk management metrics to ensure that organizational goals and objectives are achieved; and

- Delivered value by optimizing risk management investments in support of organizational objectives.[23]

As part of organizational governance, senior leaders/executives in consultation and collaboration with the risk executive (function), determine: (i) the types of risk management decisions that are reserved for specific senior leadership roles (e.g., heads of agencies or chief executive officers, chief financial officers, chief information officers, chief information security officers);[24] (ii) the types of risk management decisions that are deemed to be organization-wide and the types of decisions that can be delegated to subordinate organizations or to other roles in the organization (e.g., systems and security engineers, mission/business owners, enterprise architects, information security architects, common infrastructure or service providers, authorizing officials); and (iii) how risk management decisions will be communicated to and by the risk executive (function). Three different types of governance models (i.e., centralized, decentralized, and hybrid) are described in Appendix F. Regardless of the governance model(s) employed, clear assignment and accountability for accepting risk is essential for effective risk management.

> *Strong governance is the best indicator of senior leadership commitment to effective, consistent risk management across the organization to achieve ongoing mission/business success.*

2.3.2 Risk Executive (Function)

The risk executive is a functional role established within organizations to provide a more comprehensive, organization-wide approach to risk management. The *risk executive (function)* serves as the common risk management resource for senior leaders/executives, mission/business owners, chief information officers, chief information security officers, information system owners, common control providers,[25] enterprise architects, information security architects, information systems/security engineers, information system security managers/officers, and any other stakeholders having a vested interest in the mission/business success of organizations. The risk executive (function) coordinates with senior leaders/executives to:

- Establish risk management roles and responsibilities;

---

[23] Information security governance outcomes adapted from *IT Governance Institute, Information Security Governance: Guidance for Boards of Directors and Executive Management*, 2nd Edition, 2006.

[24] There is no implication by listing various titles within an organization of any particular relationship (peer or otherwise) or lines of authority.

[25] A *common control provider* is an organizational official responsible for the development, implementation, assessment, and monitoring of common controls (i.e., security controls inherited by information systems).

- Develop and implement an organization-wide *risk management strategy* that guides and informs organizational risk decisions (including how risk is framed, assessed, responded to, and monitored over time);[26]

- Manage threat and vulnerability information with regard to organizational information systems and the environments in which the systems operate;

- Establish organization-wide forums to consider all types and sources of risk (including aggregated risk);

- Determine organizational risk based on the aggregated risk from the operation and use of information systems and the respective environments of operation;

- Provide oversight for the risk management activities carried out by organizations to ensure consistent and effective risk-based decisions;

- Develop a greater understanding of risk with regard to the strategic view of organizations and their integrated operations;

- Establish effective vehicles and serve as a focal point for communicating and sharing risk-related information among key stakeholders internally and externally to organizations;

- Specify the degree of autonomy for subordinate organizations permitted by parent organizations with regard to framing, assessing, responding to, and monitoring risk;[27]

- Promote cooperation and collaboration among authorizing officials to include security authorization actions requiring shared responsibility (e.g., joint/leveraged authorizations);[28]

- Ensure that security authorization decisions consider all factors necessary for mission and business success; and

- Ensure shared responsibility for supporting organizational missions and business functions using external providers receives the needed visibility and is elevated to appropriate decision-making authorities.

The risk executive (function) presumes neither a specific organizational structure nor formal responsibility assigned to any one individual or group within the organization. Heads of agencies or organizations may choose to retain the risk executive (function) or to delegate the function. The risk executive (function) requires a mix of skills, expertise, and perspectives to understand the strategic goals and objectives of organizations, organizational missions/business functions, technical possibilities and constraints, and key mandates and guidance that shape organizational operations. To provide this needed mixture, the risk executive (function) can be filled by a single individual or office (supported by an expert staff) or by a designated group (e.g., a risk board,

---

[26] Organizational risk decisions include investment decisions (see Section 2.3.4). Organizational *risk tolerance* is determined as part of the risk framing component (see Section 2.3.3) and defined in the risk management strategy.

[27] Because subordinate organizations responsible for carrying out derivative or related missions may have already invested in their own methods of framing, assessing, responding to, and monitoring risk, parent organizations may allow a greater degree of autonomy within parts of the organization or across the entire organization in order to minimize costs. When a diversity of risk management activities is allowed, organizations may choose to employ, when feasible, some means of translation and/or synthesis of the risk-related information produced from those activities to ensure that the output of the different activities can be correlated in a meaningful manner.

[28] NIST Special Publication 800-37 provides guidance on joint and leveraged authorizations.

executive steering committee, executive leadership council).[29] The risk executive (function) fits
into the organizational governance structure in such a way as to facilitate efficiency and to
maximize effectiveness. While the organization-wide scope situates the risk executive (function)
at Tier 1, its role entails ongoing communications with and oversight of the risk management
activities of mission/business owners, authorizing officials, information system owners, common
control providers, chief information officers, chief information security officers, information
system and security engineers, information system security managers/officers, and other
stakeholders at Tiers 2 and 3.

> *To be effective, organization-wide risk management programs require the strong commitment,
> direct involvement, and ongoing support from senior leaders/executives. The objective is to
> institutionalize risk management into the day-to-day operations of organizations as a priority and
> an integral part of how organizations conduct operations in cyberspace—recognizing that this is
> essential in order to successfully carry out missions in threat-laden operational environments.*

2.3.3 Risk Management Strategy

An organizational *risk management strategy*, one of the key outputs of risk framing, addresses
how organizations intend to assess, respond to, and monitor risk—the risk associated with the
operation and use of organizational information systems. The risk management strategy makes
explicit the specific assumptions, constraints, risk tolerances, and priorities/trade-offs used within
organizations for making investment and operational decisions. The risk management strategy
also includes any strategic-level decisions and considerations on how senior leaders/executives
are to manage information security risk to organizational operations and assets, individuals, other
organizations, and the Nation. An organization-wide risk management strategy includes, for
example, an unambiguous expression of the risk tolerance for the organization, acceptable risk
assessment methodologies, risk response strategies, a process for consistently evaluating risk
across the organization with respect to the organization's risk tolerance, and approaches for
monitoring risk over time. The use of a risk executive (function) can facilitate consistent,
organization-wide application of the risk management strategy. The organization-wide risk
management strategy can be informed by risk-related inputs from other sources both internal and
external to the organization to ensure the strategy is both broad-based and comprehensive.

An important Tier 1 risk management activity and also part of risk framing, is the determination
of *risk tolerance*. Risk tolerance is the level of risk or degree of uncertainty that is acceptable to
organizations and is a key element of the organizational risk frame. Risk tolerance affects all
components of the risk management process—having a direct impact on the risk management
decisions made by senior leaders/executives throughout the organization and providing important
constraints on those decisions. For example, risk tolerance affects the nature and extent of risk
management oversight implemented in organizations, the extent and rigor of risk assessments
performed, and the content of organizational strategies for responding to risk. With regard to risk
assessments, more risk-tolerant organizations may be concerned only with those threats that peer
organizations have experienced while less risk-tolerant organizations may expand the list to
include those threats that are theoretically possible, but which have not been observed in
operational environments. With regard to risk response, less risk-tolerant organizations are likely

---

[29] Organizations emphasize the need for inclusiveness within the risk executive (function) by senior leaders/executives
in mission/business areas to help ensure proper information security planning, resourcing, and risk management.

to require additional grounds for confidence in the effectiveness of selected safeguards and countermeasures or prefer safeguards and countermeasures that are more mature and have a proven track record. Such organizations may also decide to employ multiple safeguards and countermeasures from multiple sources (e.g., antivirus software at clients and servers that are provided by different vendors). Another example illustrating the impact of risk tolerance on risk response is that risk tolerance can also affect the organizational requirements for trustworthiness provided by specific information technologies. Two organizations may choose the same information technologies, but their relative degree of risk tolerance may impact the degree of assessment required prior to deployment.

There is no correct level of organizational risk tolerance. Rather, the degree of risk tolerance is: (i) generally indicative of organizational culture; (ii) potentially different for different types of losses/compromises; and (iii) highly influenced by the individual subjective risk tolerance of senior leaders/executives. Yet, the ramifications of risk decisions based on risk tolerance are potentially profound, with less risk-tolerant organizations perhaps failing to achieve needed mission/business capabilities in order to avoid what appears to be unacceptable risk; while more risk-tolerant organizations may focus on near-term mission/business efficiencies at the expense of setting themselves up for future failure. It is important that organizations exercise due diligence in determining risk tolerance—recognizing how fundamental this decision is to the effectiveness of the risk management program.

2.3.4 Investment Strategies

Investment strategies[30] play a significant role in organizational risk management efforts. These strategies generally reflect the long-term strategic goals and objectives of organizations and the associated risk management strategies developed and executed to ensure mission and business success. Underlying all investment strategies is the recognition that there is a finite amount of resources available to invest in helping organizations effectively manage risk—that is, effectively addressing risk to achieve on-going mission/business success.

Mission and Risk Priorities

Organizations generally conduct a variety of missions and are involved in different types of business functions. This is especially true for large and complex organizations that have different organizational components, each of which is typically focused on one or two primary missions. While all of these organizational components and associated missions/business functions are likely to be important and play a key role in the overall success of organizations, in reality they are not of equal importance. The greater the criticality of organizational missions and business functions, the greater the necessity for organizations to ensure that risks are adequately managed. Such missions and business functions are likely to require a greater degree of risk management investments than missions/business functions deemed less critical. The determination of the relative importance of the missions/business functions and hence the level of risk management investment, is something that is decided upon at Tier 1, executed at Tier 2, and influences risk management activities at Tier 3.

Anticipated Risk Response Needs

There is a great variation in the nature of potential threats facing organizations, ranging from hackers attempting to merely deface organizational Web sites (e.g., cyber vandalism), to insider

---

[30] Investment strategies can include organizational approaches to: (i) replacing legacy information systems (e.g., phasing items in gradually, replacing entirely); (ii) outsourcing and using external providers of information systems and services; and (iii) internal development vs. acquisition of commercially available information technology products.

threats, to sophisticated terrorist groups/organized criminal enterprises seeking to exfiltrate sensitive information, to a nation state's military attempting to destroy or disrupt critical missions by attacking organizational information systems.[31] The strategic investments required to address the risk from more traditional adversaries (e.g., hackers conducting small-group activities with limited capabilities) are considerably different than the investments required to address the risk associated with advanced persistent threats consistent with more advanced adversaries (e.g., nation states or terrorist groups with highly sophisticated levels of expertise and resources that seek to establish permanent footholds in organizations for purposes of impeding aspects of the organizational missions). To address less sophisticated threats, organizations can focus their efforts at Tier 3—investing to ensure that needed safeguards and countermeasures (e.g., security controls, security services, and technologies) are obtained, implemented correctly, operating as intended, and producing the desired effect with regard to meeting information security policies and addressing known vulnerabilities. In addition to these basic investments, organizations can also invest in continuous monitoring processes to ensure that the acquired security controls, services, and technologies are operating effectively throughout the system development life cycle.

When organizations need to address advanced persistent threats, it is likely that adequately addressing related risks at Tier 3 is not feasible because necessary security solutions are not currently available in the commercial marketplace. In those instances, organizations must purposefully invest beyond Tier 3 for significant response capabilities at Tier 2, and to some extent at Tier 1. At Tier 3, the nature of investment is likely to change from implementation of existing solutions to an added strategic focus on investing in leading-edge information security technologies (essentially experimenting with innovative security solutions/technologies and being an early adopter) or investing in information security research and development efforts to address specific technology gaps.[32] Information security investments to address advanced persistent threats may require expenditures over the course of several years, as new security solutions and technologies transition from research to development to full deployment. The long-term view of strategic investing in the risk response needs for organizations can help to reduce the continuing focus on near-term vulnerabilities discovered in information systems—vulnerabilities that exist due to the complexity of the information technology products and systems and the inherent weaknesses in those products and systems.

Limitations on Strategic Investments

The ability of organizations to provide strategic information security investments is limited. Where the desired strategic investment funding or strategic resources[33] are not available to address specific needs, organizations may be forced to make compromises. For example, organizations might extend the time frame required for strategic information security objectives to be accomplished. Alternatively, organizations might prioritize risk management investments, opting to provide resources (financial or otherwise) to address some critical strategic needs sooner than other less critical needs. All investment decisions require organizations to prioritize risks and to assess the potential impacts associated with alternative courses of action.

---

[31] The threats described above are a subset of the overarching threat space that also includes errors of omission and commission, natural disasters, and accidents.

[32] This investment strategy is a change from vulnerability and patch management to a longer-term strategy addressing information security gaps such as the lack of information technology products with the trustworthiness necessary to achieve information system resilience in the face of advanced persistent threats.

[33] In some instances, the limitations may not be financial in nature, but limitations in the number of individuals with the appropriate skills/expertise or limitations regarding the state of technology.

2.4 TIER TWO—MISSION/BUSINESS PROCESS VIEW

Tier 2 addresses risk from a *mission/business process* perspective by designing, developing, and implementing mission/business processes that support the missions/business functions defined at Tier 1. Organizational mission/business processes guide and inform the development of an enterprise architecture that provides a disciplined and structured methodology for managing the complexity of the organization's information technology infrastructure. A key component of the enterprise architecture is the embedded information security architecture that provides a roadmap to ensure that mission/business process-driven information security requirements and protection needs are defined and allocated to appropriate organizational information systems and the environments in which those systems operate.

2.4.1 Risk-Aware Mission/Business Processes

The risk management activities at Tier 2 begin with the identification and establishment of *risk-aware mission/business processes* to support the organizational missions and business functions. A risk-aware mission/business process is one that explicitly takes into account the likely risk such a process would cause if implemented. Risk aware processes are designed to manage risk in accordance with the risk management strategy defined at Tier 1 and explicitly account for risk when evaluating the mission/business activities and decisions at Tier 2.[34] Implementing risk-aware mission/business processes requires a thorough understanding of the organizational missions and business functions and the relationships among missions/business functions and supporting processes. This understanding is a prerequisite to building mission/business processes sufficiently resilient to withstand a wide variety of threats including routine and sophisticated cyber attacks, errors/accidents, and natural disasters. An important part of achieving risk-aware processes is the understanding of senior leaders/executives of: (i) the types of threat sources and threat events that can adversely affect the ability of organizations to successfully execute their missions/business functions); (ii) the potential adverse impacts/consequences on organizational operations and assets, individuals, other organizations, or the Nation if the confidentiality, integrity, or availability of information or information systems used in a mission/business process is compromised; and (iii) the likely resilience to such a compromise that can be achieved with a given mission/business process definition, applying realistic expectations for the resilience of information technology.

A key output from the Tier 2 definition of mission/business processes is the selected risk response strategy[35] for these processes within the constraints defined in the risk management strategy. The risk response strategy includes identification of information protection needs and the allocation of those needs across components of the process (e.g., allocation to protections within information systems, protections in the operational environments of those systems, and allocation to alternate mission/business execution paths based on the potential for compromise).

2.4.2 Enterprise Architecture

A significant risk-related issue regarding the ability of organizations to successfully carry out missions and business functions is the complexity of the information technology being used in information systems. To address this complexity and associated potential risk, organizations need a disciplined and structured approach for managing information technology assets supporting

---

[34] The identification of organizational mission/business processes includes defining the types of information that the organization needs to successfully execute those processes, the criticality and/or sensitivity of the information, and the information flows both internal and external to the organization.

[35] Risk response strategies are described in Appendix H.

their mission/business processes. Providing greater clarity and understanding of the information technology infrastructure of organizations including the design and development of the associated information systems is a prerequisite for maximizing the resilience and wise use of these systems in the face of increasingly sophisticated threats. This type of clarity and understanding can be effectively achieved through the development and implementation of enterprise architecture.

Enterprise architecture is a management practice employed by organizations to maximize the effectiveness of mission/business processes and information resources in helping to achieve mission/business success. Enterprise architecture establishes a clear and unambiguous connection from investments (including information security investments) to measurable performance improvements whether for an entire organization or portion of an organization. Enterprise architecture also provides an opportunity to standardize, consolidate, and optimize information technology assets. These activities ultimately produce information systems that are more transparent and therefore, easier to understand and protect. In addition to establishing a roadmap for more efficient and cost-effective usage of information technology throughout organizations, enterprise architecture provides a common language for discussing risk management issues related to missions, business processes, and performance goals—enabling better coordination and integration of efforts and investments across organizational and business activity boundaries. A well-designed enterprise architecture implemented organization-wide, promotes more efficient, cost-effective, consistent, and interoperable information security capabilities to help organizations better protect missions and business functions—and ultimately more effectively manage risk.

The Federal Enterprise Architecture (FEA) defines a collection of interrelated *reference models* including Performance, Business, Service Component, Data, and Technical as well as more detailed *segment* and *solution* architectures that are derived from the *enterprise* architecture.[36] Organizational assets (including programs, processes, information, applications, technology, investments, personnel, and facilities) are mapped to the enterprise-level reference models to create a segment-oriented view of organizations. Segments are elements of organizations describing mission areas, common/shared business services, and organization-wide services. From an investment perspective, segment architecture drives decisions for a business case or group of business cases supporting specific mission areas or common/shared services. The primary stakeholders for segment architecture are mission/business owners. Following closely from segment architecture, solution architecture defines the information technology assets within organizations used to automate and improve mission/business processes. The scope of solution architecture is typically used to develop and implement all or parts of information systems or business solutions, including information security solutions. The primary stakeholders for solution architectures are information system developers and integrators, information system owners, information system/security engineers, and end users.

> *The FEA concepts that define needs-driven, performance-based business processes are applied by organizations, recognizing that effectively managing risk arising from operating in a cyberspace environment with sophisticated, high-end threats is a key need and measure of performance.*

---

[36] The Federal Enterprise Architecture is described in a series of documents published by the OMB FEA Program Management Office. Additional information on the FEA reference models and the segment and solution architectures can be found in the FEA Consolidated Reference Model Document and FEA Practice Guidance, respectively.

Enterprise architecture also promotes the concepts of *segmentation, redundancy*, and elimination of *single points of failure*—all concepts that can help organizations more effectively manage risk. Segmentation is important because it allows organizations to separate missions/business functions and operations and the information systems, system components, or subsystems supporting those missions, functions, and operations from other functions and operations and supporting systems. Segmentation helps to define more manageable components and to potentially reduce the degree of harm from a successful threat exploitation of a vulnerability. Segment architecture supports the concept of segmentation at the highest levels of organizations and the concept is carried forward through solution architecture (including decomposition of information systems and networks into subsystems and subnetworks, as appropriate).

The concept of redundancy is also very important in enterprise architecture. With the high probability of breaches or compromises when threats exploit vulnerabilities in organizational information systems, the failure or degradation of one or more information system components is inevitable. To enhance information system resilience as part of risk response, organizational information systems provide a failover mode that helps to ensure that failed components trigger appropriate backup components with similar capability. This type of capability is essential to address the advanced persistent threat in situations where organizations might be required to operate while under cyber attack in a degraded mode but still providing a sufficient level of capability to achieve mission/business success. Segment and solution architectures support the concept of redundancy by establishing a disciplined and structured approach to developing and implementing key architectural considerations that facilitate replication of critical information system components, where appropriate.

Finally, the concept of single point of failure and the elimination of such failure points is easily supported by enterprise architecture. Having the essential visibility and transparency provided in the architectural design at the organization level exposes potential single points of failure early in the development process. Thus, single points of failure are effectively addressed by segment and solution architectures. Failure to address potential single points of failure early in the architectural design can result in severe or catastrophic effects when those failure points are propagated to information systems and the actual failure causes a loss of mission/business capability.

2.4.3 Information Security Architecture

The *information security architecture* is an integral part of the organization's enterprise architecture. It represents that portion of the enterprise architecture specifically addressing information system resilience and providing architectural information for the implementation of security capabilities.[37] The primary purpose of the information security architecture is to ensure that mission/business process-driven *information security requirements* are consistently and cost-effectively achieved in organizational information systems and the environments in which those systems operate consistent with the organizational risk management strategy.[38] The information security architecture also incorporates security requirements from legislation, directives, policies, regulations, standards, and guidance into the segment architecture. Ultimately, the information security architecture provides a detailed roadmap that allows traceability from the highest-level strategic goals and objectives of organizations, through specific mission/business protection needs, to specific information security solutions provided by people, processes, and technologies.

---

[37] In general, a version of an information security architecture exists for each of the enterprise architecture *reference models;* including Performance, Business, Service Component, Data, and Technical.

[38] Organizations employ sound system and security engineering principles and techniques to ensure that information security requirements are effectively implemented in organizational information systems.

Information security requirements defined in the segment architecture are implemented in the solution architecture in the form of management, operational, and technical *security controls*. The security controls are employed within or inherited by the individual information systems and the environments in which the systems operate. The allocation[39] of security controls is consistent with the information security architecture as well as concepts such as *defense-in-depth* and *defense-in-breadth*. Figure 3 illustrates the process of integrating information security requirements into the enterprise architecture and the associated information systems supporting the mission/business processes of organizations.

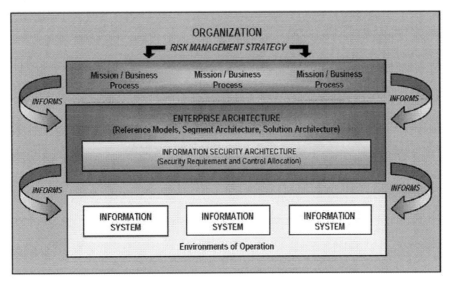

FIGURE 3: INFORMATION SECURITY REQUIREMENTS INTEGRATION

To summarize, risk management considerations can be addressed as an integral part of the enterprise architecture by:

- Developing a segment architecture linked to the strategic goals and objectives of organizations, defined missions/business functions, and associated mission/business processes;

- Identifying where effective risk response is a critical element in the success of organizational missions and business functions;

- Defining the appropriate, architectural-level information security requirements within organization-defined segments based on the organization's risk management strategy;

- Incorporating an information security architecture that implements architectural-level information security requirements;

---

[39] Security control allocation occurs down to the information system component level, employing security controls in selected system components assigned to provide a specific security capability. Specific guidance on how to incorporate information security requirements into enterprise architecture is provided in the FEA Security and Privacy Profile.

- Translating the information security requirements from the segment architecture into specific security controls for information systems/environments of operation as part of the solution architecture;

- Allocating management, operational, and technical security controls to information systems and environments of operation as defined by the information security architecture; and

- Documenting risk management decisions at all levels of the enterprise architecture.[40]

Enterprise architecture provides a disciplined and structured approach to achieving consolidation, standardization, and optimization of information technology assets that are employed within organizations. Risk reduction can be achieved through the full integration of management processes[41] organization-wide, thereby providing greater degrees of security, privacy, reliability, and cost-effectiveness for the missions and business functions being carried out by organizations. This integrated approach of incorporating the organization's risk management strategy into enterprise architecture gives senior leaders/executives the opportunity to make more informed risk-based decisions in dynamic operating environments—decisions based on trade-offs between fulfilling and improving organizational missions and business functions and managing the many types and sources of risk that must be considered in their risk management responsibilities.

> *The use of enterprise architecture can greatly enhance an organization's risk posture by providing greater transparency and clarity in design and development activities—enabling a more consistent application of the principle of 'wise use' of technologies across the organization; optimizing the trade-offs between value gained from and the risk being incurred through the information systems supporting organizational missions/business functions.*

2.5 TIER THREE—INFORMATION SYSTEMS VIEW

All information systems, including operational systems, systems under development, and systems undergoing modification, are in some phase of the system development life cycle.[42] In addition to the risk management activities carried out at Tier 1 and Tier 2 (e.g., reflecting the organization's risk management strategy within the enterprise architecture and embedded information security architecture), risk management activities are also integrated into the system development life cycle of organizational information systems at Tier 3. The risk management activities at Tier 3 reflect the organization's risk management strategy and any risk related to the cost, schedule, and performance requirements for individual information systems supporting the mission/business functions of organizations. Risk management activities take place at every phase in the system development life cycle with the outputs at each phase having an effect on subsequent phases.

---

[40] The activities required to effectively incorporate information security into enterprise architecture are carried out by key stakeholders within organizations including mission/business owners, chief information officers, chief information security officers, authorizing officials, and the risk executive (function).

[41] A management process is a process for planning and controlling the performance or execution of organizational activities (e.g., programs, projects, tasks, processes). Management processes are often referred to as performance measurement and management systems.

[42] There are typically five phases in system development life cycles: (i) *initiation*; (ii) *development/ acquisition*; (iii) *implementation*; (iv) *operation/maintenance*; and (v) *disposal*. Organizations may use a variety of system development life cycle processes including, for example, waterfall, spiral, or agile development.

For example, requirements definition[43] is a critical part of any system development process and begins very early in the life cycle, typically in the *initiation* phase. The latest threat information that is available to organizations, or current organizational assumptions concerning threat, may significantly influence information system requirements and the types of solutions that are deemed by organizations to be acceptable (from a technological and operational perspective) in the face of such threats. Information security requirements are a subset of the functional requirements levied on information systems and are incorporated into the system development life cycle simultaneously with the other requirements. The information security requirements define the needed security functionality[44] for information systems and the level of trustworthiness for that functionality (see Section 2.6 on the trustworthiness of information systems).

Organizations also address risk management issues during the *development/acquisition* phase of the system development life cycle (e.g., system design, system development/integration, and demonstration). Whether in response to specific and credible threat information or assumptions about the threat, potential design-related vulnerabilities in organizational information systems can be mitigated during this phase by choosing less susceptible alternatives. Supply chain risk during the acquisition phase of the information system is also an area of concern for organizations. To address supply chain risk during the development/acquisition phase, organizations implement specific security controls as deemed necessary by the organization. Organizations also consider risk from the standpoint of the environment in which the information systems are intended to operate when selecting the most appropriate security controls. To be effective, controls must be mutually supporting, employed with realistic expectations for effectiveness, and implemented as part of an explicit, information system-level security architecture that is consistent with the security architecture embedded in the organization's enterprise architecture. For example, when certain technical controls are less than effective due to achievable levels of trustworthiness in organizational information systems, management and operational controls are employed as compensating controls—thus providing another opportunity to manage risk.

Subsequent to initiation, development, and acquisition, the *implementation* phase of the system development life cycle provides an opportunity for the organization to determine the effectiveness of the selected security controls employed within or inherited by the information systems under development prior to the commencement of actual operations. Expectations generated during this phase can be compared with actual behavior as information systems are implemented. Given the current threat information that is available to organizations and organizational assumptions about the threat, the information discovered during effectiveness assessments, and the potential adverse impacts on organizational missions/business functions, it may be necessary to modify or change the planned implementation of the information system. Risk-related information can be developed to justify the proposed changes.

Once approved for operation, information systems move into the *operations/maintenance* phase of the system development life cycle. The monitoring of security control effectiveness and any changes to organizational information systems and the environments in which those systems operate ensure that selected risk response measures are operating as intended on an ongoing basis. Ongoing monitoring is paramount to maintaining situational awareness of risk to organizational missions and business functions—an awareness that is critical to making the necessary course

---

[43] Information security requirements can be obtained from a variety of sources (e.g., legislation, policies, directives, regulations, standards, and organizational mission/business/operational requirements).

[44] Security functionality is the set of security controls employed within or inherited by an information system or the environment in which the system operates. The security controls, described in NIST Special Publication 800-53, are implemented by a combination of people, processes, and technologies.

corrections when risk exceeds organizational risk tolerance. During the *disposal* phase of the system development life cycle, it is standard procedure for organizations to verifiably remove prior to disposal, any information from information systems that may cause adverse impacts, if compromised, and also assess any risk associated with these activities.[45]

Early integration of information security requirements into the system development life cycle is the most cost-effective method for implementing the organizational risk management strategy at Tier 3.[46] Incorporating risk management into the system development life cycle ensures that the risk management process is not isolated from the other management processes employed by the organization to develop, acquire, implement, operate, and maintain the information systems supporting organizational missions and business functions. To support system development life cycle integration, risk management (including information security considerations) is also incorporated into program, planning, and budgeting activities to help ensure that appropriate resources are available when needed—thus facilitating the completion of program and project milestones established by organizations. To incorporate risk management into program, planning and budgeting activities, risk and information security professionals are an integral part of the teams and structures used to address information system and organizational requirements.

The overall *resilience* of organizational information systems (i.e., how well systems operate while under stress) is a key factor and performance measure in determining the potential survivability of missions/business functions. The use of certain information technologies may introduce inherent vulnerabilities into these information systems—resulting in risk that may have to be mitigated by reengineering the current mission/business processes. The *wise use* of information technologies during the design, development, and implementation of organizational information systems is of paramount importance in managing risk.

> *Making information security-related requirements and activities an integral part of the system development life cycle ensures that senior leaders/executives consider the risks to organizational operations and assets, individuals, other organizations, and the Nation resulting from the operation and use of information systems and take appropriate actions to exercise the organization's due diligence.*

2.6 TRUST AND TRUSTWORTHINESS

Trust is an important concept related to risk management. How organizations approach trust influences their behaviors and their internal and external trust relationships. This section introduces some conceptual ways of thinking about trust, defines the concept of *trustworthiness*, and shows how the concept of trustworthiness can be used in developing *trust relationships*. Appendix G describes several *trust models* that can be applied in an organizational context, and

---

[45] While the presentation of the system development life cycle is expressed as a linear flow, in reality, the knowledge gained during a later phase of the life cycle or changes in system requirements or operational environments may dictate revisiting an earlier phase. For example, changes in the threat environment during the operation/maintenance phrase may dictate the need to initiate a new or revised system capability.

[46] The Risk Management Framework (RMF), described in NIST Special Publication 800-37, provides a structured process that integrates risk management activities into the system development life cycle. The RMF operates primarily at Tier 3 but also interacts with Tier 1 and Tier 2 (e.g., providing feedback from authorization decisions to the risk executive [function], disseminating updated risk information to authorizing officials, common control providers, and information system owners).

considers how trust can be measured. The importance of organizational governance, culture, and transparency[47] are also considered with regard to trust and its affect on risk management.

Trust is a belief that an entity will behave in a predictable manner in specified circumstances. The entity may be a person, process, object or any combination of such components. The entity can be of any size from a single hardware component or software module, to a piece of equipment identified by make and model, to a site or location, to an organization, to a nation-state. Trust, while inherently a subjective determination, can be based on objective evidence and subjective elements. The objective grounds for trust can include for example, the results of information technology product testing and evaluation. Subjective belief, level of comfort, and experience may supplement (or even replace) objective evidence, or substitute for such evidence when it is unavailable. Trust is usually relative to a specific circumstance or situation (e.g., the amount of money involved in a transaction, the sensitivity or criticality of information, or whether safety is an issue with human lives at stake). Trust is generally not transitive (e.g., you trust a friend but not necessarily a friend of a friend). Finally, trust is generally earned, based on experience or measurement. However, in certain organizations, trust may be mandated by policy (see Appendix G, *mandated trust model*).

Trustworthiness is an attribute of a person or organization that provides confidence to others of the qualifications, capabilities, and reliability of that entity to perform specific tasks and fulfill assigned responsibilities. Trustworthiness is also a characteristic of information technology products and systems (see Section 2.6.2 on *trustworthiness of information systems*). The attribute of trustworthiness, whether applied to people, processes, or technologies, can be measured, at least in relative terms if not quantitatively.[48] The determination of trustworthiness plays a key role in establishing trust relationships among persons and organizations. The trust relationships are key factors in risk decisions made by senior leaders/executives.

2.6.1 Establishing Trust Among Organizations

Parties enter into trust relationships based on mission and business needs.[49] Trust among parties typically exists along a continuum with varying degrees of trust achieved based on a number of factors. Organizations can still share information and obtain information technology services even if their trust relationship falls short of complete trust. The degree of trust required for organizations to establish partnerships can vary widely based on many factors including the organizations involved and the specifics of the situation (e.g., the missions, goals, and objectives of the potential partners, the criticality/sensitivity of activities involved in the partnership, the risk tolerance of the organizations participating in the partnership, and the historical relationship among the participants). Finally, the degree of trust among entities is not a static quality but can vary over time as circumstances change.

---

[47] *Transparency* is achieved by providing *visibility* into the risk management and information security activities carried out by organizations participating in partnerships (e.g., employing common security standards, specification language for security controls including common controls, assessment procedures, risk assessment methodologies; defining common artifacts and bodies of evidence used in making risk-related decisions).

[48] Current state-of-the-practice for measuring *trustworthiness* can reliably differentiate between widely different levels of trustworthiness and is capable of producing a trustworthiness scale that is hierarchical between similar instances of measuring activities (e.g., the results from ISO/IEC 15408 [Common Criteria] evaluations).

[49] Trust relationships can be: (i) formally established, for example, by documenting the trust-related information in contracts, service-level agreements, statements of work, memoranda of agreement/understanding, or interconnection security agreements; (ii) scalable and inter-organizational or intra-organizational in nature; and/or (iii) represented by simple (bilateral) relationships between two partners or more complex many-to many relationships among many diverse partners.

Organizations are becoming increasingly reliant on information system services[50] and information provided by external organizations as well as partnerships to accomplish missions and business functions. This reliance results in the need for *trust relationships* among organizations.[51] In many cases, trust relationships with external organizations, while generating greater productivity and cost efficiencies, can also bring greater risk to organizations. This risk is addressed by the risk management strategies established by organizations that take into account the strategic goals and objectives of organizations.

Effectively addressing the risk associated with the growing dependence on external service providers and partnerships with domestic and international public and private sector participants necessitates that organizations:

- Define the types of services/information to be provided to organizations or the types of information to be shared/exchanged in any proposed partnering arrangements;

- Establish the degree of control or influence organizations have over the external organizations participating in such partnering arrangements;

- Describe how the services/information are to be protected in accordance with the information security requirements of organizations;

- Obtain the relevant information from external organizations to determine trustworthiness and to support and maintain trust (e.g., visibility into business practices and risk/information security decisions to understand risk tolerance);

- Appropriately balance mission/business-based requirements to support information sharing while considering the risk of working with competing or hostile entities and the risk that other organizations, while neither competing or hostile, may be a path through which such entities attack;

- Determine if the ongoing risk to organizational operations and assets, individuals, other organizations, or the Nation resulting from the continuing use of the services/information or the participation in the partnership, is at an acceptable level; and

- Recognize that decisions to establish trust relationships are expressions of acceptable risk.

The degree of trust that an organization places in external organizations can vary widely, ranging from those who are highly trusted (e.g., business partners in a joint venture that share a common business model and common goals) to those who are less trusted and may represent greater sources of risk (e.g., business partners in one endeavor who are also competitors or adversaries). The specifics of establishing and maintaining trust can differ from organization to organization based on mission/business requirements, the participants involved in the trust relationship, the criticality/sensitivity of the information being shared or the types of services being rendered, the history between the organizations, and the overall risk to the organizations participating in the relationship. Appendix G provides several trust models that organizations can use when dealing with external organizations.

In many situations, the trust established between organizations may not allow a full spectrum of information sharing or a complete provision of services. When an organization determines that

---

[50] External information system services are services that are implemented outside of the system's traditional authorization boundary (i.e., services that are used by, but not a part of, the organizational information system).

[51] External providers or mission/business partners can be public or private sector entities, domestic or international.

the trustworthiness of another organization does not permit the complete sharing of information or use of external services, the organization can: (i) mitigate risk, transfer risk, or share risk by employing one or more compensating controls; (ii) accept a greater degree of risk; or (iii) avoid risk by performing missions/business functions with reduced levels of functionality or possibly no functionality at all.

> *Explicit understanding and acceptance of the risk to an organization's operations and assets, individuals, other organizations, and the Nation by senior leaders/executives (reflecting the organization's risk tolerance) are made in accordance with the organization's risk management strategy and a prerequisite for establishing trust relationships among organizations.*

2.6.2 Trustworthiness of Information Systems

The concept of trustworthiness can also be applied to information systems and the information technology products and services that compose those systems. Trustworthiness expresses the degree to which information systems (including the information technology products from which the systems are built) can be expected to preserve the confidentiality, integrity, and availability of the information being processed, stored, or transmitted by the systems across the full range of threats. Trustworthy information systems are systems that have been determined to have the level of trustworthiness necessary to operate within defined levels of *risk* despite the environmental disruptions, human errors, and purposeful attacks that are expected to occur in their environments of operation. Two factors affecting the trustworthiness of information systems are:

- *Security functionality* (i.e., the security features/functions employed within the system); and

- *Security assurance* (i.e., the grounds for confidence that the security functionality is effective in its application).[52]

Security functionality can be obtained by employing within organizational information systems and their environments of operation, a combination of management, operational, and technical security controls from NIST Special Publication 800-53.[53] The development and implementation of needed security controls is guided by and informed by the enterprise architecture established by organizations.

Security assurance is a critical aspect in determining the trustworthiness of information systems. Assurance is the measure of confidence that the security features, practices, procedures, and architecture of an information system accurately mediates and enforces the security policy.[54] Assurance is obtained by: (i) the actions taken by developers and implementers[55] with regard to the design, development, implementation, and operation of the security functionality (i.e., security controls); and (ii) the actions taken by assessors to determine the extent to which the functionality is implemented correctly, operating as intended, and producing the desired outcome

---

[52] Assurance also represents the grounds for confidence that the intended functionality of an information system is correct, always invoked (when needed), and resistant to bypass or tampering.

[53] The employment of appropriate security controls for information systems and environments of operation is guided by the first three steps in the Risk Management Framework (i.e., categorization, selection, and implementation).

[54] A *security policy* is set of criteria for the provision of security services.

[55] In this context, a developer/implementer is an individual or group of individuals responsible for the design, development, implementation, or operation of security controls for an information system or supporting infrastructure.

with respect to meeting the security requirements for information systems and their environments of operation.[56] Developers and implementers can increase the assurance in security functionality by employing well-defined security policies and policy models, structured and rigorous hardware and software development techniques, and sound system/security engineering principles.

Assurance for information technology products and systems is commonly based on the assessments conducted (and associated assessment evidence produced) during the initiation, acquisition/development, implementation, and operations/maintenance phases of the system development life cycle. For example, developmental evidence may include the techniques and methods used to design and develop security functionality. Operational evidence may include flaw reporting and remediation, the results of security incident reporting, and the results of ongoing security control monitoring. Independent assessments by qualified assessors may include analyses of the evidence as well as testing, inspections, and audits of the implementation of the selected security functionality.[57]

The concepts of assurance and trustworthiness are closely related. Assurance contributes to the trustworthiness determination relative to an information technology product or an information system. Developers/implementers of information technology products or systems may provide assurance evidence by generating appropriate artifacts (e.g., the results of independent testing and evaluation, design documentation, high-level or low-level specifications, source code analysis). Organizations using information technology products or systems may perform, or rely on others to perform, some form of assessment on the products or systems. Organizations may also have direct experience with the product or system, or may receive information about the performance of the product or system from third parties. Organizations typically evaluate all of the available assurance evidence, often applying different weighting factors as appropriate, to determine the trustworthiness of the product or system relative to the circumstances.

Information technology products and systems exhibiting a higher degree of trustworthiness (i.e., products/systems having appropriate functionality and assurance) are expected to exhibit a lower rate of latent design and implementation flaws and a higher degree of penetration resistance against a range of threats including sophisticated cyber attacks, natural disasters, accidents, and intentional/unintentional errors. The susceptibility of missions/business functions of organizations to known threats, the environments of operation where information systems are deployed, and the maximum acceptable level of risk to organizational operations and assets, individuals, other organizations, or the Nation, guide the degree of trustworthiness needed.

Trustworthiness is a key factor in the selection and wise use of information technology products used in organizational information systems. Insufficient attention to trustworthiness of information technology products and systems can adversely affect an organization's capability to successfully carry out its assigned missions/business functions.

---

[56] For other than national security systems, organizations meet minimum assurance requirements specified in NIST Special Publication 800-53, Appendix E.

[57] NIST Special Publication 800-53A provides guidance on assessing security controls in federal information systems.

2.7 ORGANIZATIONAL CULTURE

Organizational *culture* refers to the values, beliefs, and norms that influence the behaviors and actions of the senior leaders/executives and individual members of organizations. Culture describes the way things are done in organizations and can explain why certain things occur. There is a direct relationship between organizational culture and how organizations respond to uncertainties and the potential for near-term benefits to be the source for longer-term losses. The organization's culture informs and even, to perhaps a large degree, defines that organization's risk management strategy. At a minimum, when an expressed risk management strategy is not consistent with that organization's culture, then it is likely that the strategy will be difficult if not impossible to implement. Recognizing and addressing the significant influence culture has on risk-related decisions of senior leaders/executives within organizations can therefore, be key to achieving effective management of risk.

Recognizing the impact from organizational culture on the implementation of an organization-wide risk management program is important as this can reflect a major organizational change. This change must be effectively managed and understanding the culture of an organization plays an important part in achieving such organization-wide change. Implementing an effective risk management program may well represent a significant organization-wide change aligning the people, processes, and culture within the organization with the new or revised organizational goals and objectives, the risk management strategy, and communication mechanisms for sharing risk-related information among entities. To effectively manage such change, organizations include cultural considerations as a fundamental component in their strategic-level thinking and decision-making processes (e.g., developing the risk management strategy). If the senior leaders/executives understand the importance of culture, they have a better chance of achieving the organization's strategic goals and objectives by successfully managing risk.

Culture also impacts the degree of risk being incurred. Culture is reflected in an organization's willingness to adopt new and leading edge information technologies. For example, organizations that are engaged in research and development activities may be more likely to push technological boundaries. Such organizations are more prone to be early adopters of new technologies and therefore, more likely to view the new technologies from the standpoint of the potential benefits achieved versus potential harm from use. In contrast, organizations that are engaged in security-related activities may be more conservative by nature and less likely to push technological boundaries—being more suspicious of the new technologies, especially if provided by some entity with which the organization lacks familiarity and trust. These types of organizations are also less likely to be early adopters of new technologies and would be more inclined to look at the potential harm caused by the adoption of the new technologies. Another example is that some organizations have a history of developing proprietary software applications and services, or procuring software applications and services solely for their use. These organizations may be reluctant to use externally-provided software applications and services and this reluctance may result in lower risk being incurred. Other organizations may, on the other hand, seek to maximize advantages achieved by modern net-centric architectures (e.g., service-oriented architectures, cloud computing), where hardware, software, and services are typically provided by external organizations. Since organizations typically do not have direct control over assessment, auditing, and oversight activities of external providers, a greater risk might be incurred.

In addition to the cultural impacts on organizational risk management perspectives, there can also be cultural issues between organizations. Where two or more organizations are operating together toward a common purpose, there is a possibility that cultural differences in each of the respective organizations may result in different risk management strategies, propensity to incur risk, and willingness to accept risk.[58] For example, assume two organizations are working together to create a common security service intended to address the advanced persistent threat. The culture of one of the organizations may result in a focus on preventing unauthorized disclosure of information, while the nature of the other organization may result in an emphasis on mission continuity. The differences in focus and emphasis resulting from organizational culture can generate different priorities and expectations regarding what security services to procure, because the organizations perceive the nature of the threat differently. Such culture-related disconnects do not occur solely between organizations but can also occur within organizations, where different organizational components (e.g., information technology components, operational components) have different values and perhaps risk tolerances. An example of an internal disconnect can be observed in a hospital that emphasizes different cultures between protecting the personal privacy of patients and the availability of medical information to medical professionals for treatment purposes.

Culture both shapes and is shaped by the people within organizations. Cultural influences and impacts can be felt across all three tiers in the multitiered risk management approach. Senior leaders/executives both directly and indirectly in Tier 1 governance structures set the stage for how organizations respond to various approaches to managing risk. Senior leaders/executives establish the risk tolerance for organizations both formally (e.g., through publication of strategy and guidance documents) and informally (e.g., through actions that get rewarded and penalized, the degree of consistency in actions, and the degree of accountability enforced). The direction set by senior leaders/executives and the understanding of existing organizational values and priorities are major factors determining how risk is managed within organizations.

2.8 RELATIONSHIP AMONG KEY RISK CONCEPTS

As indicated by the discussions above, there are a variety of risk-related concepts (e.g., risk tolerance, trust, and culture), all of which have an impact on risk management. The concepts do not operate in a vacuum; rather, there is often a strong interplay among the concepts (e.g., an organization's culture along with its governance structures and processes, often influences the pace of change and the implementation of its risk management strategy). For this reason, the risk executive (function) and other parties involved in organizational risk-based decisions, need to have an awareness and appreciation for all of the concepts. Several examples of the relationships among the risk-related concepts are provided below. The list of relationships is not exhaustive and serves only to illustrate how combining risk-related concepts can produce unintended consequences, both positive and negative in scope.

2.8.1 Governance, Risk Tolerance, and Trust

As part of implementing the organization's risk management strategy at Tier 1, the risk executive (function) establishes practices for sharing risk-related information with external entities. With regard to the demonstration of due diligence for managing risk, organizations that are less risk tolerant are likely to require more supporting evidence than organizations that are more risk tolerant. Such organizations may only trust (and hence partner with) organizations with which they have had a long and successful relationship (see direct historical trust model in Appendix G). The amount of centralization[59] within an organization may be reflective of the organizational risk tolerance and/or its willingness to trust partnering organizations. Some organizations select a

---

[58] A similar situation can exist between subordinate elements of an organization when these elements are afforded a fair amount of autonomy and operational authority.

[59] Additional information on governance models can be found in Appendix F.

decentralized governance structure for reasons such as widely diverging mission/business areas or need for increased separation between mission/business lines due to sensitivity of the work. The reasons for decentralization may reflect and likely will influence risk tolerance. For instance, if there are no partnering organizations meeting the established trust qualifications, less risk-tolerant organizations may require significantly more supporting evidence of due diligence (e.g., access to risk assessments, security plans, security assessment reports, risk acceptance decisions) than is typically required in such situations (see validated trust model in Appendix G).

2.8.2 Trust and Culture

There is also potential interplay between the concepts of risk, trust, and culture. Changes in mission/business requirements (e.g., a new mission or business requirement to interconnect information systems for the purpose of sharing information) may require a greater acceptance of risk than is typical for that organization. In the short term, additional measures may be needed to establish and/or build trust (e.g., increase transparency between interconnecting organizations). Such measures facilitate building trust and evolving organizational beliefs and norms over the longer term. Interaction between trust and culture can also be observed when there are gaps and overlaps in responsibility among an organization's components that may impact the ability for proposed actions (especially new actions) to be carried out quickly. For example, many organizations with decentralized governance structures may be slower to embrace change unless there has been an extensive effort to expand coordination and improve trust among organizational components. Assume that some organizations are directed by higher authorities (see mandated trust model in Appendix G) to share information more freely with peer organizations. If the organizations have a history and culture of tightly controlling information, they may be reluctance to share information with outside entities, even though directed to do so. In such situations, organizations may require that partnering organizations provide concrete evidence of the steps taken to protect the information designated for sharing prior to release.

2.8.3 Investment Strategy and Risk Tolerance

Investment strategies and organizational risk tolerance also have linkages. Organizations may recognize that there is a need to address advanced persistent threats where adversaries have achieved some degree of penetration of and foothold within organizational information systems and the environments in which those systems operate. The strategic investments that are required to address these types of threats may, in part, be influenced by the risk tolerance of organizations. Less risk-tolerant organizations may focus investments on information technologies that prevent adversaries from gaining further access within organizations and/or limiting the damage done to the organizations even if at the expense of achieving some of the many mission/business benefits automation can provide. More risk-tolerant organizations may focus investments on information technologies that provide greater mission/business benefits even if these benefits are achieved at the expense of adversaries gaining some advantage or benefit from compromising the information systems and supporting infrastructure.

2.8.4 Culture and Risk Tolerance

A major part of managing risk within organizations is identifying what the organizational risk tolerance is for a particular type of loss. Risk tolerance can be described as a combination of the cultural willingness to accept certain types of loss within organizations and the subjective risk-related actions of senior leaders/executives. Risk-based decisions within organizations often reflect the blending of the risk tolerance of senior leaders/executives and the risk tolerance that is embedded within the culture of organizations. In establishing organizational risk tolerance, the values, beliefs, and norms of organizations are examined in order to understand why risk trade-offs are made. For some organizations, in particular those organizations that deal with critical and/or sensitive information, personally identifiable information, or classified information, the emphasis is often on preventing unauthorized disclosure. In contrast, in those organizations driven by a combination of organizational culture and the nature of their missions and business functions, the emphasis is on maintaining the availability of information systems to achieve an ongoing operational capability. As part of establishing organizational risk tolerance, a risk assessment identifies the kinds and levels of risk to which organizations may be exposed. This assessment considers both the likelihood and impact of undesired events (see Chapter Three, the risk management process).

CHAPTER THREE

THE PROCESS

APPLYING RISK MANAGEMENT CONCEPTS ACROSS AN ORGANIZATION

This chapter describes a process for managing information security risk including: (i) a general overview of the risk management process; (ii) how organizations establish the context for risk-based decisions; (iii) how organizations assess risk considering threats, vulnerabilities, likelihood, and consequences/impact; (iv) how organizations respond to risk once determined; and (v) how organizations monitor risk over time with changing mission/business needs, operating environments, and supporting information systems . The risk management process, introduced in Chapter Two, is described in this chapter along with its applicability across the three tiers of risk management. Each of the steps in the risk management process (i.e., risk framing, risk assessment, risk response, and risk monitoring) is described in a structured manner focusing on the *inputs* or *preconditions* necessary to initiate the step, the specific *activities* that compose the step, and the *outputs* or *post conditions* resulting from the step.[60] The effect of the risk concepts described in Chapter Two (e.g., risk tolerance, trust, and culture) are also discussed in the context of the risk management process and its multitiered application. Figure 4 illustrates the risk management process as applied across the tiers—organization, mission/business process, and information system. The bidirectional arrows in the figure indicate that the information and communication flows among the risk management components as well as the execution order of the components, may be flexible and respond to the dynamic nature of the risk management process as it is applied across all three tiers.

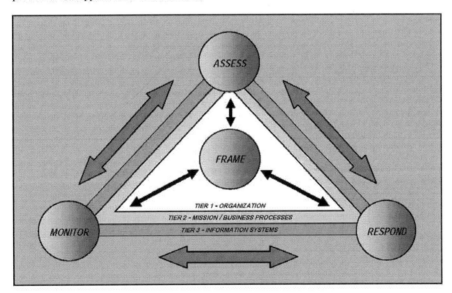

FIGURE 4: RISK MANAGEMENT PROCESS APPLIED ACROSS THE TIERS

---

[60] Additional guidance on selected steps in the risk management process (e.g., risk assessment, risk monitoring) can be found in other NIST Special Publications listed in Appendix A.

The steps in the risk management process are not inherently sequential in nature. The steps are performed in different ways, depending on the particular tier where the step is applied and on prior activities related to each of the steps. What is consistent is that the outputs or post conditions from a particular risk management step directly impact one or more of the other risk management steps in the risk management process. Organizations have significant flexibility in how the risk management steps are performed (e.g., sequence, degree of rigor, formality, and thoroughness of application) and in how the results of each step are captured and shared—both internally and externally. Ultimately, the objective of applying the risk management process and associated risk-related concepts is to develop a better understanding of information security risk in the context of the broader actions and decisions of organizations and in particular, with respect to organizational operations and assets, individuals, other organizations, and Nation.

3.1 FRAMING RISK

Risk framing establishes the context and provides a common perspective on how organizations manage risk. Risk framing, as its principal output, produces a *risk management strategy* that addresses how organizations intend to assess risk, respond to risk, and monitor risk. The risk management strategy makes explicit the specific assumptions, constraints, risk tolerances, and priorities/trade-offs used within organizations for making investment and operational decisions. The risk management strategy also includes any strategic-level decisions and considerations on how risk to organizational operations and assets, individuals, other organizations, and the Nation, is to be managed by senior leaders/executives.

At Tier 1, senior leaders/executives, in consultation and collaboration with the risk executive (function), define the organizational risk frame including the types of risk decisions (e.g., risk responses) supported, how and under what conditions risk is assessed to support those risk decisions, and how risk is monitored (e.g., to what level of detail, in what form, and with what frequency). At Tier 2, mission/business owners apply their understanding of the organizational risk frame to address concerns specific to the organization's missions/business functions (e.g., additional assumptions, constraints, priorities, and trade-offs). At Tier 3, program managers, information system owners, and common control providers apply their understanding of the organizational risk frame based on how decision makers at Tiers 1 and 2 choose to manage risk.

The Risk Management Framework[61] is the primary means for addressing risk at Tier 3. The RMF addresses concerns specific to the design, development, implementation, operation, and disposal of organizational information systems and the environments in which those systems operate. The risk frame can be adapted at Tier 3 based on the current phase of the system development life cycle, which further constrains potential risk responses. Initially, organizational risk frames might not be explicit or might not be defined in terms that correspond to the risk management tiers. In the absence of explicit risk frames (describing assumptions, constraints, risk tolerance, and priorities/trade-offs), mission/business owners can have divergent perspectives on risk or how to manage it. This impedes a common understanding at Tier 1 of how information security risk contributes to organizational risk, and at Tier 2, of how risk accepted for one mission or business function potentially affects risk with respect to other missions/business functions. Differences in risk tolerance and the underlying assumptions, constraints, and priorities/trade-offs are grounded in operational and/or architectural considerations and should be understood and accepted by senior leaders/executives within their respective organizations.

---

[61] The Risk Management Framework (RMF) which operates primarily at Tier 3 is described in NIST Special Publication 800-37.

STEP 1: RISK FRAMING

Inputs and Preconditions

Risk framing is the set of assumptions, constraints, risk tolerances, and priorities/trade-offs that shape an organization's approach for managing risk. Risk framing is informed by the organizational governance structure, financial posture, legal/regulatory environment, investment strategy, culture, and trust relationships established within and among organizations. Inputs to the risk framing step include, for example, laws, policies, directives, regulations, contractual relationships, and financial limitations which impose constraints on potential risk decisions by organizations. Other inputs to risk framing can include, for example, specific information from organizations to make explicit: (i) the identification of trust relationships and trust models (see Appendix G) that derive from existing memoranda of understanding or agreement (MOUs or MOAs); and (ii) the identification of the governance structures and processes that indicate the extent of or limits on decision-making authority for risk decisions that can be delegated to mission or business owners. The key precondition for risk framing is senior leadership commitment to defining an explicit risk management strategy and holding mission/business owners responsible and accountable for implementing the strategy.

The guidance produced by the risk framing step, and the underlying assumptions, constraints, risk tolerances, and priorities/trade-offs used to develop that guidance, may be inappropriate to one or more organizational missions or business functions. In addition, the risk environment has the potential to change over time. Thus, the risk management process allows for feedback to the risk framing step from the other steps in the process, as follows:

- *Risk assessment:* Information generated during the risk assessment may influence the original assumptions, change the constraints regarding appropriate risk responses, identify additional tradeoffs, or shift priorities. For example, the characterization of adversaries (including representative tactics, techniques, and procedures), or sources of vulnerability information may not be consistent with how some organizations conduct their missions/business functions; a source of threat/vulnerability information that is useful for one mission/business function could, in fact, be useful for others; or organizational guidance on assessing risk under uncertainty may be too onerous, or insufficiently defined, to be useful for one or more mission/business functions.

- *Risk response:* Information uncovered during the development of alternative courses of action could reveal that risk framing has removed or failed to uncover some potentially high-payoff alternatives from consideration. This situation may challenge organizations to revisit original assumptions or investigate ways to change established constraints.

- *Risk monitoring:* Security control monitoring by organizations could indicate that a class of controls, or a specific implementation of a control, is relatively ineffective, given investments in people, processes, or technology. This situation could lead to changes in assumptions about which types of risk responses are preferred by organizations. Monitoring of the operational environment could reveal changes in the threat landscape (e.g., changes in the tactics, techniques, and procedures observed across all organizational information systems; increasing frequency and/or intensity of attacks against specific missions/business functions) that cause organizations to revisit original threat assumptions and/or to seek different sources of threat information. Significant advances in defensive or proactive operational and technical solutions could generate the need to revisit the investment strategy identified during the framing step. Monitoring of legal/regulatory environments could also influence changes in assumptions or constraints. Also, monitoring of risk being incurred might result in the need to reconsider the organizational risk tolerance if the existing statement of risk tolerance does not appear to match the operational realities.

Activities

RISK ASSUMPTIONS

TASK 1-1: Identify assumptions that affect how risk is assessed, responded to, and monitored within the organization.

Supplemental Guidance: Organizations that identify, characterize, and provide representative examples of threat sources, vulnerabilities, consequences/impacts, and likelihood determinations promote a common terminology and frame of reference for comparing and addressing risks across disparate mission/business areas. Organizations can also select appropriate risk assessment methodologies, depending on organizational governance, culture, and how divergent the missions/business functions are within the respective organizations. For example, organizations with highly centralized governance structures might elect to use a single risk assessment methodology. Organizations with hybrid governance structures might select multiple risk assessment methodologies for Tier 2, and an additional risk assessment methodology for Tier 1 that assimilates and harmonizes the findings, results, and observations of the Tier 2 risk assessments. Alternatively, when autonomy and diversity are central to the organizational culture, organizations could define requirements for the degree of rigor and the form of results, leaving the choice of specific risk assessment methodologies to mission/business owners.

Threat Sources

Threat sources cause events having undesirable consequences or adverse impacts on organizational operations and assets, individuals, other organizations, and the Nation. Threat sources include: (i) hostile cyber/physical attacks; (ii) human errors of omission or commission; or (iii) natural and man-made disasters. For threats due to hostile cyber attacks or physical attacks, organizations provide a succinct characterization of the types of tactics, techniques, and procedures employed by adversaries that are to be addressed by safeguards and countermeasures (i.e., security controls) deployed at Tier 1 (organization level), at Tier 2 (mission/business process level), and at Tier 3 (information system level)—making explicit the types of threat-sources that are to be addressed as well as making explicit those not being addressed by the safeguards/countermeasures. Adversaries can be characterized in terms of threat levels (based on capabilities, intentions, and targeting) or with additional detail. Organizations make explicit any assumptions about threat source targeting, intentions, and capabilities. Next, organizations identify a set of representative threat events. This set of threat events provides guidance on the level of detail with which the events are described. Organizations also identify conditions for when to consider threat events in risk assessments. For example, organizations can restrict risk assessments to those threat events that have actually been observed (either internally or externally by partners or peer organizations) or alternatively, specify that threat events described by credible researchers can also be considered. Finally, organizations identify the sources of threat information found to be credible and useful (e.g., sector Information Sharing and Analysis Centers [ISACs]). Trust relationships determine from which partners, suppliers, and customers, threat information is obtained as well as the expectations placed on those partners, suppliers and customers in subsequent risk management process steps. By establishing common starting points for identifying threat sources at Tier 1, organizations provide a basis for aggregating and consolidating the results of risk assessments at Tier 2 (including risk assessments conducted for coalitions of missions and business areas or for common control providers) into an overall assessment of risk to the organization as a whole. At Tier 2, mission/business owners may identify additional sources of threat information specific to organizational missions or business functions. These sources are typically based on: (i) a particular business or critical infrastructure sector (e.g., sector ISAC); (ii) operating environments specific to the missions or lines of business (e.g., maritime, airspace); and (iii) external dependencies (e.g., GPS or satellite communications). The characterization of threat sources are refined for the missions/business functions established by organizations—with the results being that some threat sources might not be of concern, while others could be described in greater detail. At Tier 3, program managers, information system owners, and common control providers consider the phase in the system development life cycle to determine the level of detail with which threats can be considered. Greater threat specificity tends to be available later in the life cycle.

Vulnerabilities

Organizations identify approaches used to characterize vulnerabilities, consistent with the characterization of threat sources and events. Vulnerabilities can be associated with exploitable weakness or deficiencies in: (i) the hardware, software, or firmware components that compose organizational information systems (or the security controls employed within or inherited by those systems; (ii) mission/business processes and enterprise architectures (including embedded information security architectures) implemented by organizations; or (iii) organizational governance structures or processes. Vulnerabilities can also be associated with the susceptibility of organizations to adverse impacts, consequences, or harm from external sources (e.g., physical destruction of non-owned infrastructure such as electric power grids). Organizations provide guidance regarding how to consider dependencies on external organizations as vulnerabilities in the risk assessments conducted. The guidance can be informed by the types of trust relationships established by organizations with external providers. Organizations identify the degree of specificity with which vulnerabilities are described (e.g., general terms, Common Vulnerability Enumeration [CVE] identifiers, identification of weak/deficient security controls), giving some representative examples corresponding to representative threats. Organizational governance structures and processes determine how vulnerability information is shared across organizations. Organizations may also identify sources of vulnerability information found to be credible and useful. At Tier 2, mission/business owners may choose to identify additional sources of vulnerability information (e.g., a sector ISAC for information about vulnerabilities specific to that sector). At Tier 3, program managers, information system owners, and common control providers consider the phase in the system development life cycle—and in particular, the technologies included in the system – to determine the level of detail with which vulnerabilities can be considered. Organizations make explicit any assumptions about the degree of organizational or information system vulnerability to specific threat sources (by name or by type).

Consequences and Impact

Organizations provide guidance on how to assess impacts to organizational operations (i.e., mission, functions, image, and reputation), organizational assets, individuals, other organizations, and the Nation (e.g., using FIPS 199, CNSS Instruction 1253, or a more granular approach). Organizations can experience the consequences/impact of adverse events at the information system level (e.g., failing to perform as required), at the mission/business process level (e.g., failing to fully meet mission/business objectives), and at the organizational level (e.g., failing to comply with legal or regulatory requirements, damaging reputation or relationships, or undermining long-term viability). Organizations determine at Tier 1, which consequences and types of impact are to be considered at Tier 2, the mission/business process level. An adverse event can have multiple consequences and different types of impact, at different levels, and in different time frames. For example, the exposure of sensitive information (e.g., personally identifiable information) by a particular mission/business area (e.g., human resources) can have organization-wide consequences and adverse impact with regard to reputation damage; the information system consequence/impact for multiple systems of an attacker more easily overcoming identification and authentication security controls; and the mission/business process consequence/impact (for one or more mission/business areas) of an attacker falsifying information on which future decisions are based. To ensure consistency, organizations determine at Tier 1, how consequences/impacts experienced in different time frames are to be assessed. At Tier 2, mission/business owners may amplify organizational guidance, as appropriate. The types of consequences and impact considered in risk determinations are identified to provide a basis for determining, aggregating, and/or consolidating risk results and to facilitate risk communication. Organizations also provide guidance to Tier 2 and Tier 3 with regard to the extent that risk assessments are to consider the risk to other organizations and the Nation. Organization make explicit any assumptions about the degree of impact/consequences related to specific threat sources (by name or by type) or through specific vulnerabilities (individually or by type).

Likelihood

Organizations can employ a variety of approaches for determining the likelihood of threat events. Some organizations treat the likelihood that a threat event will occur and the likelihood that, if it occurs, it will result in adverse effects as separate factors, while other organizations assess threat likelihood as a combination of these factors. In addition, some organizations prefer quantitative risk assessments while other organizations, particularly when the assessment involves a high degree of uncertainty, prefer qualitative risk assessments. Likelihood determinations can be based on either threat assumptions or actual threat data (e.g., historical data on cyber attacks, historical data on earthquakes, or specific information on adversary capabilities, intentions, and targeting). When specific and credible threat data is available (e.g., types of cyber attacks, cyber attack trends, frequencies of attacks), organizations can use the empirical data and statistical analyses to determine more specific probabilities of threat events occurring. Organizations select a method consistent with organizational culture and risk tolerance. Organizations can also make explicit assumptions concerning the likelihood that a threat event will result in adverse effects as follows: (i) *worst case* (i.e., attack will be successful unless strong, objective reasons to presume otherwise); (ii) *best case* (i.e., attack will not be successful unless specific, credible information to the contrary); or (iii) something in between best and worst cases (e.g., the most probable case). Organizations document any overarching assumptions. Organizations can use empirical data and statistical analyses to help inform any of the approaches used to determine the likelihood of threat events occurring. Organizations select a method consistent with organizational culture, understanding of the operational environment, and risk tolerance.

RISK CONSTRAINTS

TASK 1-2: Identify constraints on the conduct of risk assessment, risk response, and risk monitoring activities within the organization.

Supplemental Guidance: The execution of the risk management process can be constrained in various ways, some of which are direct and obvious, while others are indirect. Financial limitations can constrain the set of risk management activities directly (e.g., by limiting the total resources available for investments in risk assessments or in safeguards or countermeasures) or indirectly (e.g., by eliminating activities which, while involving relatively small investments in risk response, entail curtailing or discarding investments in legacy information systems or information technology). Organizations might also discover that the need to continue to depend on legacy information systems may constrain the risk management options available to the organization. Constraints can also include legal, regulatory, and/or contractual requirements. Such constraints can be reflected in organizational policies (e.g., restrictions on outsourcing, restrictions on and/or requirements for information to be gathered as part of risk monitoring). Organizational culture can impose indirect constraints on governance changes (e.g., precluding a shift from decentralized to hybrid governance structures) and which security controls are considered by organizations as potential common controls. In particular, organizational attitudes toward information technology risk that, for example, favor extensive automation and early adoption of new technologies can constrain the degree of risk avoidance and perhaps risk mitigation that can be achieved. Any cultural constraints that limit senior leader/executive (e.g., chief information officer) visibility into organizational information systems that are beyond their formal authority (e.g. mission-related systems) may impede overall understanding of the complexity of information systems environment and the related risks to the organization. At Tier 2, mission/business owners interpret constraints in light of organizational missions/business functions. Some regulatory constraints may not apply to particular missions/business functions (e.g., regulations that apply to international operations, when mission/business areas are restricted to the United States). Alternately, additional requirements may apply (e.g., mission/business processes performed jointly with another organization, which imposes contractual constraints). At Tier 3, information system owners, common control providers, and/or program managers interpret the organization-wide and mission/business function-specific constraints with respect to their systems and environments of operation (e.g., requirements to provide specific security controls are satisfied through common controls).

RISK TOLERANCE

TASK 1-3: Identify the level of risk tolerance for the organization.

Supplemental Guidance: Risk tolerance is the level of risk that organizations are willing to accept in pursuit of strategic goals and objectives. Organizations define information security-related risk tolerance organization-wide considering all missions/business functions. Organizations can use a variety of techniques for identifying information security risk tolerance (e.g., by establishing zones in a likelihood-impact trade space or by using a set of representative scenarios). Organizations also define tolerance for other types of organizational and operational risks (e.g., financial risk, safety risk, compliance risk, or reputation risk). At Tier 2, mission/business owners may have different risk tolerances from the organization as a whole. The risk executive (function) provides organizations with ways to resolve such differences in risk tolerances at Tier 2. The level of residual risk accepted by authorizing officials for information systems or inherited common controls is within the organizational risk tolerance, and not the individual risk tolerances of those authorizing officials. In addition, organizations provide to Tier 2 and Tier 3, guidance on evaluating risk for specific mission/business processes or information systems and a focus on near-term mission/business effectiveness with the longer-term, strategic focus of the organizational risk tolerance. See Section 2.3.3 for additional information on risk tolerance.

PRIORITIES AND TRADE-OFFS

TASK 1-4: Identify priorities and trade-offs considered by the organization in managing risk.

Supplemental Guidance: Risk is experienced at different levels, in different forms, and in different time frames. At Tier 1, organizations make trade-offs among and establish priorities for responding to such risks. Organizations tend to have multiple priorities that at times conflict, which generates potential risk. Approaches employed by organizations for managing portfolios of risks reflect organizational culture, risk tolerance, as well as risk-related assumptions and constraints. These approaches are typically embodied in the strategic plans, policies, and roadmaps of organizations which may indicate preferences for different forms of risk response. For example, organizations may be willing to accept short-term risk of slightly degraded operations to achieve long-term reduction in information security risk. However, this trade-off could be unacceptable for one particularly critical mission/business function (e.g., real-time requirements in many industrial/process control systems). For that high-priority area, a different approach to improving security may be required including the application of compensating security controls.

Outputs and Post Conditions

The output of the risk framing step is the *risk management strategy* that identifies how organizations intend to assess, respond to, and monitor risk over time. The framing step also produces a set of organizational policies, procedures, standards, guidance, and resources covering the following topics: (i) scope of the organizational risk management process (e.g., organizational entities covered; mission/business functions affected; how risk management activities are applied within the risk management tiers); (ii) risk assessment guidance including, for example, the characterization of threat sources, sources of threat information, representative threat events (in particular, adversary tactics, techniques, and procedures), when to consider and how to evaluate threats, sources of vulnerability information, risk assessment methodologies to be used, and risk assumptions; (iii) risk response guidance including, for example, risk tolerances, risk response concepts to be employed, opportunity costs, trade-offs, consequences of responses, hierarchy of authorities, and priorities; (iv) risk monitoring guidance, including, for example, guidance on analysis of monitored risk factors to determine changes in risk, and monitoring frequency, methods, and reporting; (v) other and risk constraints on executing risk management activities; and (vi) organizational priorities and trade-offs. Outputs from the risk framing step serve as inputs to the risk assessment, risk response, and risk monitoring steps.

3.2 ASSESSING RISK

Risk assessment identifies, prioritizes, and estimates risk to organizational operations (i.e., mission, functions, image, and reputation), organizational assets, individuals, other organizations, and the Nation, resulting from the operation and use of information systems.[62] Risk assessments use the results of threat and vulnerability assessments to identify and evaluate risk in terms of likelihood of occurrence and potential adverse impact (i.e., magnitude of harm) to organizations, assets, and individuals. Risk assessments can be conducted at any of the risk management tiers

---

[62] Draft NIST Special Publication 800-30, Revision 1, provides guidance on conducting risk assessments (including incremental or differential risk assessments) across all three tiers in the multitiered risk management approach.

with different objectives and utility of the information produced. For example, risk assessments conducted at Tier 1 or Tier 2 focus on organizational operations, assets, and individuals—whether comprehensive across mission/business lines or only on those assessments that are cross-cutting to the particular mission/business line. Organization-wide assessments of risk can be based solely on the assumptions, constraints, risk tolerances, priorities, and trade-offs established in the risk framing step (derived primarily from Tier 1 activities) or can be based on risk assessments conducted across multiple mission/business lines (derived primarily from Tier 2 activities). Risk assessments conducted at one tier can be used to refine/enhance threat, vulnerability, likelihood, and impact information used in assessments conducted in other tiers. The degree that information from risk assessments can be reused is shaped by the similarity of missions/business functions and the degree of autonomy that organizational entities or subcomponents have with respect to parent organizations. Organizations that are decentralized can expect to conduct more risk assessment activities at Tier 2 and, as a result, may have a greater need to communicate within Tier 2 to identify cross-cutting threats and vulnerabilities. Decentralized organizations can still benefit from Tier 1 risk assessments and, in particular, the identification of an initial set of threat and vulnerability sources. Organization-wide risk assessments provide some initial prioritization of risks for decision makers to consider when entering the risk response step.

Organizations benefit significantly from conducting risk assessments as part of an organization-wide risk management process. However, once risk assessments are complete, it is prudent for organizations to invest some time in keeping the assessments current. Maintaining currency of risk assessments requires support from the risk monitoring step (e.g., observing changes in organizational information systems and environments of operation or analyzing monitoring results to maintain awareness of the risk). Keeping risk assessments up to date provides many potential benefits such as timely, relevant information that enables senior leaders/executives to perform near real-time risk management. Maintaining risk assessments also reduces future assessment costs and supports ongoing risk monitoring efforts. Organizations may determine that conducting comprehensive risk assessments as a way of maintaining current risk assessments do not provide sufficient value. In such situations, organizations consider conducting incremental and/or differential risk assessments. Incremental risk assessments consider only new information (e.g., the effects of using a new information system on mission/business risk), whereas differential risk assessments consider how changes affect the overall risk determination. Incremental or differential risk assessments are useful if organizations require a more targeted review of risk, seek an expanded understanding of risk, or desire an expanded understanding of the risk in relation to missions/business functions.

STEP 2: RISK ASSESSMENT

Inputs and Preconditions

Inputs to the risk assessment step from the risk framing step include, for example: (i) acceptable risk assessment methodologies; (ii) the breadth and depth of analysis employed during risk assessments; (iii) the level of granularity required for describing threats; (iv) whether/how to assess external service providers; and (v) whether/how to aggregate risk assessment results from different organizational entities or mission/business functions to the organization as a whole. Organizational expectations regarding risk assessment methodologies, techniques, and/or procedures are shaped heavily by governance structures, risk tolerance, culture, trust, and life cycle processes. Prior to conducting risk assessments, organizations understand the fundamental reasons for conducting the assessments and what constitutes adequate depth and breadth for the assessments. Risk assumptions, risk constraints, risk tolerance, and priorities/trade-offs defined during the risk framing step shape how organizations use risk assessments—for example, localized applications of the risk assessments within each of the risk management tiers (i.e., governance, mission/business process, information systems) or global applications of the risk assessments across the entire organization. Risk assessments can be conducted by organizations even when some of the inputs from the risk framing step have not been received or preconditions established. However, in those situations, the quality of the risk assessment results may be affected. In addition to the risk framing step, the risk assessment step can receive inputs from the risk monitoring step, especially during mission operations and the operations/maintenance phase of the system development life cycle (e.g., when organizations discover new threats or vulnerabilities that require an immediate reassessment of risk). The risk assessment step can also receive inputs from the risk response step (e.g., when organizations are considering the risk of employing new technology-based solutions as alternatives for risk reduction measures). As courses of action are developed in the risk response step, a differential risk assessment may be needed to evaluate differences that each course of action makes in the overall risk determination.

Activities

THREAT AND VULNERABILITY IDENTIFICATION

TASK 2-1: Identify threats to and vulnerabilities in organizational information systems and the environments in which the systems operate.

Supplemental Guidance: Threat identification requires an examination of threat sources and events. For examining threat sources and events, organizations identify threat capabilities, intentions, and targeting information from all available sources. Organizations can leverage a number of sources for threat information at strategic or tactical levels. Threat information generated at any tier can be used to inform or refine the risk-related activities in any other tier. For example, specific threats (i.e., tactics, techniques, and procedures) identified during Tier 1 threat assessments may directly affect mission/business process and architectural design decisions at Tier 2. Specific threat information generated at Tiers 2 and 3 can be used by organizations to refine threat information generated during initial threat assessments carried out at Tier 1.

Vulnerability identification occurs at all tiers. Vulnerabilities related to organizational governance (e.g., inconsistent decisions about the relative priorities of mission/business processes, selection of incompatible implementations of security controls) as well as vulnerabilities related to external dependencies (e.g., electrical power, supply chain, telecommunications), are most effectively identified at Tier 1. However, most vulnerability identification occurs at Tiers 2 and 3. At Tier 2, process and architecture-related vulnerabilities (e.g., exploitable weaknesses or deficiencies in mission/business processes, enterprise /information security architectures including embedded information security architectures) are more likely to be identified. At Tier 3, information system vulnerabilities are the primary focus. These vulnerabilities are commonly found in the hardware, software, and firmware components of information systems or in the environments in which the systems operate. Other areas of potential vulnerabilities include vulnerabilities associated with the definition, application/implementation, and monitoring of processes, procedures and services related to management, operational, and technical aspects of information security. Vulnerabilities associated with architectural design and mission/business processes can have a greater impact on the ability of organizations to successfully carry out missions and business functions due to the potential impact across multiple information systems and mission environments. The refined vulnerability assessments conducted at Tiers 2 and 3 are shared with organizational personnel responsible for assessing risks more strategically. Vulnerability assessments conducted at Tier 2 and Tier 3 have the opportunity to evaluate additional related variables such as location, proximity to other high risk assets (physical or logical), and resource considerations related to operational environments. Information specific to operational environments allows for more useful and actionable assessment results. Vulnerability identification can be accomplished at a per-individual weakness/deficiency level or at a root-cause level. When selecting between approaches, organizations consider whether the overall objective is identifying each specific instance or symptom of a problem or understanding the underlying root causes of problems. Understanding specific exploitable weaknesses or deficiencies is helpful when problems are first identified or when quick fixes are required. This specific understanding also provides organizations with necessary sources of information for eventually diagnosing potential root causes of problems, especially those problems that are systemic in nature.

Organizations with more established enterprise architectures (including embedded information security architectures) and mature life cycle processes have outputs that can be used to inform risk assessment processes. Risk assumptions, constraints, tolerances, priorities, and trade-offs used for developing enterprise architectures and embedded information security architectures can be useful sources of information for initial risk assessment activities. Risk assessments conducted to support the development of segment or solution architectures may also serve as information sources for the identification of threats and vulnerabilities. Another factor influencing threat and vulnerability identification is organizational culture. Organizations that promote free and open communications and non-retribution for sharing adverse information tend to foster greater openness from individuals working within those organizations. Frequently, organizational personnel operating at Tiers 2 and 3 have valuable information and can make meaningful contributions in the area of threat and vulnerability identification. The culture of organizations influences the willingness of personnel to communicate potential threat and vulnerability information, which ultimately affects the quality and quantity of the threats/vulnerabilities identified.

RISK DETERMINATION

TASK 2-2: Determine the risk to organizational operations and assets, individuals, other organizations, and the Nation if identified threats exploit identified vulnerabilities.

Supplemental Guidance: Organizations determine risk by considering the likelihood that known threats exploit known vulnerabilities and the resulting consequences or adverse impacts (i.e., magnitude of harm) if such exploitations occur. Organizations use threat and vulnerability information together with likelihood and consequences/impact information to determine risk either qualitatively or quantitatively. Organizations can employ a variety of approaches to determine the likelihood of threats exploiting vulnerabilities. Likelihood determinations can be based on either threat assumptions or actual threat information (e.g., historical data on cyber attacks, historical data on earthquakes, or specific information on adversary capabilities, intentions, and targeting). When specific and credible threat information is available (e.g., types of cyber attacks, cyber attack trends, frequencies of attacks), organizations can use empirical data and statistical analyses to determine more specific probabilities of threats occurring. Assessment of likelihood can also be influenced by whether vulnerability identification occurred at the individual weakness or deficiency level or at the root-cause level. The relative ease/difficulty of vulnerability exploitation, the sophistication of adversaries, and the nature of operational environments all influence the likelihood that threats exploit vulnerabilities. Organizations can characterize adverse impacts by security objective (e.g., loss of confidentiality, integrity, or availability). However, to maximize usefulness, adverse impact is expressed in or translated into terms of organizational missions, business functions, and stakeholders.

Risk Determination and Uncertainty

Risk determinations require analysis of threat, vulnerability, likelihood, and impact-related information. Organizations also need to examine mission/business vulnerabilities and threats where safeguards and/or countermeasures do not exist. The nature of the inputs provided to this step (e.g., general, specific, strategic, tactical) directly affects the type of outputs or risk determinations made. The reliability and accuracy of risk determinations are dependent on the currency, accuracy, completeness, and integrity of information collected to support the risk assessment process. In addition, the components of risk assessment results that affect reliability and accuracy of risk determinations also affect the amount of uncertainty associated with those risk determinations and subsequent determinations. Organizations also consider additional insights related to the anticipated time frames associated with particular risks. Time horizons associated with potential threats can shape future risk responses (e.g., risk may not be a concern if the time horizon for the risk is in the distant future).

Organizational guidance for determining risk under uncertainty indicates how combinations of likelihood and impact are combined into a determination of the risk level or risk score/rating. Organizations need to understand the type and amount of uncertainty surrounding risk decisions so that risk determinations can be understood. During the risk framing step, organizations may have provided guidance on how to analyze risk and how to determine risk when a high degree of uncertainty exists. Uncertainty is particularly a concern when the risk assessment considers advanced persistent threats, for which analysis of interacting vulnerabilities may be needed, the common body of knowledge is sparse, and past behavior may not be predictive.

While threat and vulnerability determinations apply frequently to missions and business functions, the specific requirements associated with the missions/business functions, including the environments of operation, may lead to different assessment results. Different missions, business functions, and environments of operation can lead to differences in the applicability of specific threat information considered and the likelihood of threats causing potential harm. Understanding the threat component of the risk assessment requires insight into the particular threats facing specific missions or business functions. Such awareness of threats includes understanding the capability, intent, and targeting of particular adversaries. The risk tolerance of organizations and underlying beliefs associated with how the risk tolerance is formed (including the culture within organizations) may shape the perception of impact and likelihood in the context of identified threats and vulnerabilities.

Even with the establishment of explicit criteria, risk assessments are influenced by organizational culture and the personal experiences and accumulated knowledge of the individuals conducting the assessments. As a result, assessors of risk can reach different conclusions from the same information. This diversity of perspective can enrich the risk assessment process and provide decision makers with a greater array of information and potentially fewer biases. However, such diversity may also lead to risk assessments that are inconsistent. Organizationally-defined and applied processes provide the means to identify inconsistent practices and include processes to identify and resolve such inconsistencies.

Outputs and Post Conditions

The output of the risk assessment step is a determination of risk to organizational operations (i.e., mission, functions, image, and reputation), organizational assets, individuals, other organizations, and the Nation. Depending on the approach that organizations take, either the overall risk to the organization or the inputs used to determine risk may be communicated to the decision makers responsible for risk response. In certain situations, there are recurring cycles between the risk assessment step and the risk response step until particular objectives are achieved. Based on the course of action selected during the risk response step, some residual risk may remain. Under certain circumstances, the level of residual risk could trigger a reassessment of risk. This reassessment is typically incremental (assessing only the new information) and differential (assessing how the new information changes the overall risk determination).

The aggregation of risk assessment results from all three tiers drives the management of portfolios of risks undertaken by organizations. Identified risks common to more than one mission/business function within organizations may also be the source for future assessment activities at Tier 1, such as root-cause analysis. Gaining a better understanding of the reasons why certain risks are more common or frequent assists decision makers in selecting risk responses that address underlying (or root-cause) problems instead of solely focusing on the surface issues surrounding the existence of the risks. The results of risk assessments can also shape future design and development decisions related to enterprise architecture (including embedded information security architecture), and organizational information systems. The extent to which missions/business functions are vulnerable to a set of identified threats and the relative ease with which those vulnerabilities can be exploited, contribute to the risk-related information provided to senior leaders/executives.

Outputs from the risk assessment step can be useful inputs to the risk framing and risk monitoring steps. For example, risk determinations can result in revisiting the organizational risk tolerance established during the risk framing step. Organizations can also choose to use information from the risk assessment step to inform the risk monitoring step. For example, risk assessments can include recommendations to monitor specific elements of risk (e.g., threat sources) so that if certain thresholds are crossed, previous risk assessment results can be reviewed and updated, as appropriate. Particular thresholds established as part of risk monitoring programs can also serve as the basis for reassessments of risk. If organizations establish criteria as a part of the risk framing step for when risk assessment results do not warrant risk responses, then assessment results could be fed directly to the risk monitoring step as a source of input.

3.3 RESPONDING TO RISK

Risk response identifies, evaluates, decides on, and implements appropriate courses of action to accept, avoid, mitigate, share, or transfer risk to organizational operations and assets, individuals, other organizations, and the Nation, resulting from the operation and use of information systems. Identifying and analyzing alternative courses of action[63] typically occurs at Tier 1 or Tier 2. This is due to the fact that alternative courses of action (i.e., potential risk responses) are evaluated in terms of anticipated organization-wide impacts and the ability of organizations to continue to successfully carry out organizational missions and business functions. Decisions to employ risk response measures organization-wide are typically made at Tier 1, although the decisions are informed by risk-related information from the lower tiers. At Tier 2, alternative courses of action are evaluated in terms of anticipated impacts on organizational missions/business functions, the associated mission/business processes supporting the missions/business functions, and resource requirements. At Tier 3, alternative courses of action tend to be evaluated in terms of the system development life cycle or the maximum amount of time available for implementing the selected course(s) of action. The breadth of potential risk responses is a major factor for whether the activity is carried out at Tier 1, Tier 2, or Tier 3. Risk decisions are influenced by organizational risk tolerance developed as part of risk framing activities at Tier 1. Organizations can implement risk decisions at any of the risk management tiers with different objectives and utility of information produced.

STEP 3: RISK RESPONSE

Inputs and Preconditions

Inputs from the risk assessment and risk framing steps include: (i) identification of threat sources and threat events; (ii) identification of vulnerabilities that are subject to exploitation; (iii) estimates of potential consequences and/or impact if

---

[63] A *course of action* is a time-phased or situation-dependent combination of risk response measures. A *risk response measure* is a specific action taken to respond to an identified risk. Risk response measures can be separately managed and can include, for example, the implementation of security controls to mitigate risk, promulgation of security policies to avoid risk or to accept risk in specific circumstances, and organizational agreements to share or transfer risk.

threats exploit vulnerabilities; (iv) likelihood estimates that threats exploit vulnerabilities; (v) a determination of risk to organizational operations (i.e., mission, functions, image, and reputation), organizational assets, individuals, other organizations, and the Nation; (vi) risk response guidance from the organizational risk management strategy (see Appendix H); and (vii) the general organizational directions and guidance on appropriate responses to risk. In addition to the risk assessment and risk framing steps, the risk response step can receive inputs from the risk monitoring step (e.g., when organizations experience a breach or compromise to their information systems or environments of operation that require an immediate response to address the incident and reduce additional risk that results from the event). The risk response step can also receive inputs from the risk framing step (e.g., when organizations are required to deploy new safeguards and countermeasures in their information systems based on security requirements in new legislation or OMB policies). The risk framing step also directly shapes the resource constraints associated with selecting an appropriate course of action. Additional preconditions established at the risk framing step may include: (i) constraints based on architecture and previous investments; (ii) organizational preferences and tolerances; (iii) the expected effectiveness at mitigating risk (including how effectiveness is measured and monitored); and (iv) the time horizon for the risk (e.g., current risk, projected risk—that is, a risk expected to arise in the future based on the results of threat assessments or a planned changes in missions/business functions, enterprise architecture (including information security architecture), or aspects of legal or regulatory compliance).

Activities

RISK RESPONSE IDENTIFICATION

TASK 3-1: Identify alternative courses of action to respond to risk determined during the risk assessment.

Supplemental Guidance: Organizations can respond to risk in a variety of ways. These include: (i) risk acceptance; (ii) risk avoidance; (iii) risk mitigation; (iv) risk sharing; (v) risk transfer; or (vi) a combination of the above. A course of action is a time-phased or situation-dependent combination of risk response measures. For example, in an emergency situation, organizations might accept the risk associated with unfiltered connection to an external communications provider for a limited time; then avoid risk in the near-term by applying security controls to search for malware or evidence of unauthorized access to information that occurred during the period of unfiltered connection; and finally mitigate risk long-term by applying controls to handle such connections more securely.

Risk Acceptance

Risk acceptance is the appropriate risk response when the identified risk is within the organizational risk tolerance. Organizations can accept risk deemed to be low, moderate, or high depending on particular situations or conditions. For example, organizations with data centers residing in the northeastern portion of the United States may opt to accept the risk of earthquakes based on known likelihood of earthquakes and data center vulnerability to damage by earthquakes. Organizations accept the fact that earthquakes are possible, but given the infrequency of major earthquakes in that region of the country, believe it is not cost-effective to address such risk—that is, the organizations have determined that risk associated with earthquakes is low. Conversely, organizations may accept substantially greater risk (in the moderate/high range) due to compelling mission, business, or operational needs. For example, federal agencies may decide to share very sensitive information with first responders who do not typically have access to such information due to time-sensitive needs to stop pending terrorist attacks, even though the information is not itself perishable with regard to risk through loss of confidentiality. Organizations typically make determinations regarding the general level of acceptable risk and the types of acceptable risk with consideration of organizational priorities and trade-offs between: (i) near-term mission/business needs and potential for longer-term mission/business impacts; and (ii) organizational interests and the potential impacts on individuals, other organizations, and the Nation.

Risk Avoidance

Risk avoidance may be the appropriate risk response when the identified risk exceeds the organizational risk tolerance. Organizations may conduct certain types of activities or employ certain types of information technologies that result in risk that is unacceptable. In such situations, risk avoidance involves taking specific actions to eliminate the activities or technologies that are the basis for the risk or to revise or reposition these activities or technologies in the organizational mission/business processes to avoid the potential for unacceptable risk. For example, organizations planning to employ networked connections between two domains, may determine through risk assessments that there is unacceptable risk in establishing such connections. Organizations may also determine that implementing effective safeguards and countermeasures (e.g., cross-domain solutions) is not practical in the given circumstances. Thus, the organizations decide to avoid the risk by eliminating the electronic or networked connections and employing an "air gap" with a manual connection processes (e.g., data transfers by secondary storage devices).

Risk Mitigation

Risk mitigation, or risk reduction, is the appropriate risk response for that portion of risk that cannot be accepted, avoided, shared, or transferred. The alternatives to mitigate risk depend on: (i) the risk management tier and the scope of risk response decisions assigned or delegated to organizational officials at that tier (defined by the organizational governance structures); and (ii) the organizational risk management strategy and associated risk response strategies. The means used by organizations to mitigate risk can involve a combination of risk response measures across the three tiers. For example, risk mitigation can include common security controls at Tier 1, process re-engineering at Tier 2, and/or new or enhanced management, operational, or technical safeguards or countermeasures (or some combination of all three) at Tier 3. Another example of a potential risk requiring mitigation can be illustrated when adversaries gain access to mobile devices (e.g., laptop computers or personal digital assistants) while users are traveling. Possible risk mitigation measures include, for example, organizational policies prohibiting transport of mobile devices to certain areas of the world or procedures for users to obtain a clean mobile device that is never allowed to connect to the organizational networks.

Risk Sharing or Transfer

Risk sharing or risk transfer is the appropriate risk response when organizations desire and have the means to shift risk liability and responsibility to other organizations. Risk transfer shifts the entire risk responsibility or liability from one organization to another organization (e.g., using insurance to transfer risk from particular organizations to insurance companies). Risk sharing shifts a portion of risk responsibility or liability to other organizations (usually organizations that are more qualified to address the risk). It is important to note that risk transfer reduces neither the likelihood of harmful events occurring nor the consequences in terms of harm to organizational operations and assets, individuals, other organizations, or the Nation. Risk sharing may be a sharing of liability or a sharing of responsibility for other, adequate risk responses such as mitigation. Therefore, the concept of risk transfer is less applicable in the public sector (e.g., federal, state, local governments) than the private sector, as liability of organizations is generally established by legislation or policy. As such, self-initiated transfers of risk by public sector organizations (as typified by purchasing insurance) are generally not possible. Risk sharing often occurs when organizations determine that addressing risk requires expertise or resources that are better provided by other organizations. For example, an identified risk might be the physical penetration of perimeters and kinetic attacks by terrorist groups. The organization decides to partner with another organization sharing the physical facility to take joint responsibility for addressing risk from kinetic attacks.

EVALUATION OF ALTERNATIVES

TASK 3-2: Evaluate alternative courses of action for responding to risk.

Supplemental Guidance: The evaluation of alternative courses of action can include: (i) the expected effectiveness in achieving desired risk response (and how effectiveness is measured and monitored); and (ii) anticipated feasibility of implementation, including, for example, mission/business impact, political, legal, social, financial, technical, and economic considerations. Economic considerations include costs throughout the expected period of time during which the course of action is followed (e.g., cost of procurement, integration into organizational processes at Tier 1 and/or Tier 2, information systems at Tier 3, training, and maintenance). During the evaluation of alternative courses of action, trade-offs can be made explicit between near-term gains in mission/business effectiveness or efficiency and long-term risk of mission/business harm due to compromise of information or information systems that are providing this near-term benefit. For example, organizations concerned about the potential for mobile devices (e.g., laptop computers) being compromised while employees are on travel can evaluate several courses of action including: (i) providing users traveling to high-risk areas with clean laptops; (ii) removing hard drives from laptops and operate from CDs or DVDs; or (iii) having laptops go through a detailed assessment before being allowed to connect to organizational networks. The first option is highly effective as returning laptops are never connected to organizational networks. While the second option ensures that hard drives cannot be corrupted, it is not quite as effective in that it is still possible that hardware devices (e.g., motherboards) could have been compromised. The effectiveness of the third option is limited by the ability of organizations to detect potential insertion of malware into the hardware, firmware, or software. As such, it is the least effective of the three options. From a cost perspective, the first option is potentially the most expensive, depending upon the number of travelers (hence number of travel laptops) required. The second and third options are considerably less expensive. From a mission and operational perspective, the third option is the best alternative as users have access to standard laptop configurations including all applications and supporting data needed to perform tasks supporting missions and business functions. Such applications and data would not be available if the first or second option is selected. Ultimately, the evaluation of courses of action is made based on operational requirements, including information security requirements, needed for near and long term mission/business success. Budgetary constraints, consistency with investment management strategies, civil liberties, and privacy protection, are some of the important elements organizations consider when selecting appropriate courses of action. In those instances where organizations only identify a single course of action, then the evaluation is focused on whether the course of action is adequate. If the course of action is deemed inadequate, then organizations need to refine the identified course of action to address the inadequacies or develop another course of action (see Task 3-1).

In summary, a risk verses risk-response trade-off is conducted for each course of action to provide the information necessary for: (i) selecting between the courses of action; and (ii) evaluating the courses of action in terms of response effectiveness, costs, mission/business impact, and any other factors deemed relevant to organizations. Part of risk versus risk-response trade-off considers the issue of competing resources. From an organizational perspective, this means organizations consider whether the cost (e.g., money, personnel, time) for implementing a given course of action has the potential to adversely impact other missions or business functions, and if so, to what extent. This is necessary because organizations have finite resources to employ and many competing missions/business functions across many organizational elements. Therefore, organizations assess the overall value of alternative courses of action with regard to the missions/business functions and the potential risk to each organizational element. Organizations may determine that irrespective of a particular mission/business function and the validity of the associated risk, there are more important missions/business functions that face more significant risks, and hence have a better claim on the limited resources.

RISK RESPONSE DECISION

TASK 3-3: Decide on the appropriate course of action for responding to risk.

Supplemental Guidance: Decisions on the most appropriate course of action include some form of prioritization. Some risks may be of greater concern than other risks. In that case, more resources may need to be directed at addressing higher-priority risks than at other lower-priority risks. This does not necessarily mean that the lower-priority risks would not be addressed. Rather, it could mean that fewer resources might be directed at the lower-priority risks (at least initially), or that the lower-priority risks would be addressed at a later time. A key part of the risk decision process is the recognition that regardless of the decision, there still remains a degree of residual risk that must be addressed. Organizations determine acceptable degrees of residual risk based on organizational risk tolerance and the specific risk tolerances of particular decision makers. Impacting the decision process are some of the more intangible risk-related concepts (e.g., risk tolerance, trust, and culture). The specific beliefs and approaches that organizations embrace with respect to these risk-related concepts affect the course of action selected by decision-makers.

RISK RESPONSE IMPLEMENTATION

TASK 3-4: Implement the course of action selected to respond to risk.

Supplemental Guidance: Once a course of action is selected, organizations implement the associated risk response. Given the size and complexity of some organizations, the actual implementation of risk response measures may be challenging. Some risk response measures are tactical in nature (e.g., applying patches to identified vulnerabilities in organizational information systems) and may be implemented rather quickly. Other risk response measures may be more strategic in nature and reflect solutions that take much longer to implement. Therefore, organizations apply, and tailor as appropriate to a specific risk response course of action, the risk response implementation considerations in the risk response strategies (part of the risk management strategy developed during the risk framing step). See Appendix H, Risk Response Strategies.

Outputs and Post Conditions

The output of the risk response step is the implementation of the selected courses of action with consideration for: (i) individuals or organizational elements responsible for the selected risk response measures and specifications of effectiveness criteria (i.e., articulation of indicators and thresholds against which the effectiveness of risk response measures can be judged); (ii) dependencies of each selected risk response measure on other risk response measures; (iii) dependencies of selected risk response measures on other factors (e.g., the implementation of other planned information technology measures); (iv) timeline for implementation of risk response measures; (v) plans for monitoring the effectiveness of risk response measures; (vi) identification of risk monitoring triggers; and (vii) interim risk response measures selected for implementation, if appropriate. There are also ongoing communications and sharing of risk-related information with individuals or organizational elements impacted by the risk responses (including potential actions that may need to be taken by the individuals or organizational elements).

In addition to the risk monitoring step, outputs from the risk response step can be useful inputs to the risk framing and risk assessment steps. For example, it is possible that the analysis occurring during the evaluation of alternative courses of action may call into question some aspects of the risk response strategy that is part of the risk management strategy generated during the risk framing step. In such instances, organizations use that information to inform the risk framing step with appropriate actions taken to revisit the risk management strategy and its associated risk response strategy. Organizations might also determine during the evaluation of alternative courses of action for risk response, that some aspects of the risk assessments are incomplete or incorrect. This information can be used to inform the risk assessment step possibly resulting in further analysis or reassessments of risk.

3.4 MONITORING RISK

Risk monitoring provides organizations with the means to: (i) verify *compliance*;[64] (ii) determine the ongoing *effectiveness* of risk response measures; and (iii) identify risk-impacting *changes* to organizational information systems and environments of operation. Analyzing monitoring results gives organizations the capability to maintain awareness of the risk being incurred, highlight the need to revisit other steps in the risk management process, and initiate process improvement activities as needed.[65] Organizations employ risk monitoring tools, techniques, and procedures to increase risk awareness, helping senior leaders/executives develop a better understanding of the ongoing risk to organizational operations and assets, individuals, other organizations, and the Nation. Organizations can implement risk monitoring at any of the risk management tiers with different objectives and utility of information produced. For example, Tier 1 monitoring activities might include ongoing threat assessments and how changes in the threat space may affect Tier 2 and Tier 3 activities, including enterprise architectures (with embedded information security architectures) and organizational information systems. Tier 2 monitoring activities might include, for example, analyses of new or current technologies either in use or considered for future use by organizations to identify exploitable weaknesses and/or deficiencies in those technologies that may affect mission/business success. Tier 3 monitoring activities focus on information systems and might include, for example, automated monitoring of standard configuration settings for information technology products, vulnerability scanning, and ongoing assessments of security controls. In addition to deciding on appropriate monitoring activities across the risk management tiers, organizations also decide how monitoring is to be conducted (e.g., automated or manual approaches) and the frequency of monitoring activities based on, for example, the frequency with which deployed security controls change, critical items on plans of action and milestones, and risk tolerance.

STEP 4: RISK MONITORING

Inputs and Preconditions

Inputs to this step include implementation strategies for selected courses of action for risk responses and the actual implementation of selected courses of action. In addition to the risk response step, the risk monitoring step can receive inputs from the risk framing step (e.g., when organizations become aware of an advanced persistent threat reflecting a change in threat assumptions, this may result in a change in the frequency of follow on monitoring activities). The risk framing step also directly shapes the resource constraints associated with establishing and implementing an organization-wide monitoring strategy. In some instances, outputs from the risk assessment step may be useful inputs to the risk monitoring step. For example, risk assessment threshold conditions (e.g., likelihood of threats exploiting vulnerabilities) could be input to the risk monitoring step. In turn, organizations could monitor to determine if such threshold conditions are met. If threshold conditions are met, such information could be used in the risk assessment step, where it could serve as the basis for an incremental, differential risk assessment or an overall reassessment of risk to the organization.

Activities

RISK MONITORING STRATEGY

TASK 4-1: Develop a risk monitoring strategy for the organization that includes the purpose, type, and frequency of monitoring activities.

[64] Compliance verification ensures that organizations have implemented required risk response measures and that information security requirements derived from and traceable to organizational missions/business functions, federal legislation, directives, regulations, policies, and standards/guidelines are satisfied.

[65] Draft NIST Special Publication 800-137 provides guidance on monitoring organizational information systems and environments of operation.

Supplemental Guidance: Organizations implement risk monitoring programs: (i) to verify that required risk response measures are implemented and that information security requirements derived from and traceable to organizational missions/business functions, federal legislation, directives, regulations, policies, and standards/guidelines, are satisfied (*compliance monitoring*); (ii) to determine the ongoing effectiveness of risk response measures after the measures have been implemented (*effectiveness monitoring*); and (iii) to identify changes to organizational information systems and the environments in which the systems operate that may affect risk (*change monitoring*) including changes in the feasibility of the ongoing implementation of risk response measures). Determining the purpose of risk monitoring programs directly impacts the means used by organizations to conduct the monitoring activities and where monitoring occurs (i.e., at which risk management tiers). Organizations also determine the type of monitoring to be employed, including approaches that rely on automation or approaches that rely on procedural/manual activities with human intervention. Finally, organizations determine how often monitoring activities are conducted, balancing value gained from frequent monitoring with potential for operational disruptions due for example, to interruption of mission/business processes, reduction in operational bandwidth during monitoring, and shift of resources from operations to monitoring. Monitoring strategies developed at Tier 1 influence and provide direction for similar strategies developed at Tier 2 and Tier 3 including the monitoring activities associated with the Risk Management Framework at the information system level.

Monitoring Compliance

Compliance monitoring is employed to ensure that organizations are implementing needed risk response measures. This includes ensuring that the risk response measures selected and implemented by organizations in response to risk determinations produced from risk assessments are implemented correctly and operating as intended. Failure to implement the risk response measures selected by organizations can result in the organizations continuing to be subject to the identified risk. Compliance monitoring also includes ensuring that risk response measures required by federal mandates (e.g., legislation, directives, policies, regulations, standards) or organizational mandates (e.g., local policies, procedures, mission/business requirements) are implemented. Compliance monitoring is the easiest type of monitoring to perform because there are typically a finite set of risk response measures employed by organizations usually in the form of security controls. Such measures are typically well-defined and articulated as an output from the risk response step. The more challenging part of compliance monitoring is evaluating whether the risk response measures are implemented correctly (and in some instances continuously). Compliance monitoring also includes, as feasible, analysis as to why compliance failed. The reason for compliance failure can range from individuals failing to do their jobs correctly to the risk response measure not functioning as intended. If monitoring indicates a failure in compliance, then the response step of the risk management process is revisited. A key element of the feedback to the response step is the finding from compliance monitoring indicating the reason for the compliance failure. In some instances, compliance failures can be fixed by simply re-implementing the same risk response measures with little or no change. But in other instances, compliance failures are more complicated (e.g., the selected risk response measures are too difficult to implement or the measures did not function as expected). In such instances, it may be necessary for organizations to return to the evaluation and decision portions of the risk response step to develop different risk response measures.

Monitoring Effectiveness

Effectiveness monitoring is employed by organizations to determine if implemented risk response measures have actually been effective in reducing identified risk to the desired level. Although effectiveness monitoring is different than compliance monitoring, failure to achieve desired levels of effectiveness may be an indication that risk response measures have been implemented incorrectly or are not operating as intended. Determining the effectiveness of risk response measures is generally more challenging than determining whether the measures have been implemented correctly and are operating as intended (i.e., meeting identified compliance requirements). Risk response measures implemented correctly and operating as intended do not guarantee an effective reduction of risk. This is primarily due to: (i) the complexity of operating environments which may generate unintended consequences; (ii) subsequent changes in levels of risk or associated risk factors (e.g., threats, vulnerabilities, impact, or likelihood); (iii) inappropriate or incomplete criteria established as an output of the risk response step; and (iv) changes in information systems and environments of operation after implementation of risk response measures. This is especially true when organizations try to determine if more strategic outcomes have been achieved and for more dynamic operating environments. For example, if the desired outcome for organizations is to be less susceptible to advanced persistent threats, this may be challenging to measure since these types of threats are, by definition, very difficult to detect. Even when organizations are able to establish effectiveness criteria, it is often difficult to obtain criteria that are quantifiable. Therefore, it may become a matter of subjective judgment as to whether the implemented risk response measures are ultimately effective. Moreover, even if quantifiable effectiveness criteria are provided, it may be difficult to determine if the information provided satisfies the criteria. If organizations determine that risk response measures are not effective, then it may be necessary to return to the risk response step. Generally, for effectiveness failures, organizations cannot simply return to the implementation portion of the risk response step. Therefore, depending on the reason for the lack of effectiveness, organizations revisit all portions of the risk response step (i.e., development, evaluation, decision, and implementation) and potentially the risk assessment step. These activities may result in organizations developing and implementing entirely new risk responses.

Monitoring Changes

In addition to compliance monitoring and effectiveness monitoring, organizations monitor changes to organizational information systems and the environments in which those systems operate. Monitoring changes to information systems and environments of operation is not linked directly to previous risk response measures but it is nonetheless important to detect changes that may affect the risk to organizational operations and assets, individuals, other organizations, and the Nation. Generally, such monitoring detects changes in conditions that may undermine risk assumptions (articulated in the risk framing step).

- *Information System:* Changes can occur in organizational information systems (including hardware, software, and firmware) that can introduce new risk or change existing risk. For example, updates to operating system software can eliminate security capabilities that existed in earlier versions, thus introducing new vulnerabilities into organizational information systems. Another example is the discovery of new system vulnerabilities that fall outside of the scope of the tools and processes available to address such vulnerabilities (e.g., vulnerabilities for which there are no established mitigations).

- *Environments of Operation:* The environments in which information systems operate can also change in ways that introduce new risk or change existing risk. Environmental and operational considerations include, but are not limited to, missions/business functions, threats, vulnerabilities, mission/business processes, facilities, policies, legislation, and technologies. For example, new legislation or regulations could be passed that impose additional requirements on organizations. This change might affect the risk assumptions established by organizations. Another example is a change in the threat environment that reports new tactics, techniques, procedures, or increases in the technical capabilities of adversaries. Organizations might experience reductions in available resources (e.g., personnel or funding), which in turn results in changing priorities. Organizations might also experience changes in the ownership of third-party suppliers which could affect supply chain risk. Mission changes may require that organizations revisit underlying risk assumptions. For example, an organization whose mission is to collect threat information on possible domestic terrorist attacks and share such information with appropriate federal law enforcement and intelligence agencies may have its scope changed so that the organization is responsible for also sharing some of the information with local first responders. Such a change could affect assumptions regarding the security resources such users may have at their disposal. Changes in technology may also affect the underlying risk assumptions established by organizations. Unlike other types of change, technology changes may be totally independent of organizations, but still affect the risk organizations must address. For example, improvements in computing power may undermine assumptions regarding what constitutes sufficiently strong means of authentication (e.g., number of authentication factors) or cryptographic mechanism.

Automated Versus Manual Monitoring

Broadly speaking, organizations can conduct monitoring either by automated or manual methods. Where automated monitoring is feasible, it should be employed because it is generally faster, more efficient, and more cost-effective than manual monitoring. Automated monitoring is also less prone to human error. However, not all monitoring can take advantage of automation. Monitoring conducted at Tier 3 generally lends itself to automation where activities being monitored are information technology-based. Such activities can usually be detected, tracked, and monitored through the installation of appropriate software, hardware and/or firmware. To ensure that automated processes, procedures, and/or mechanisms supporting monitoring activities are providing the information needed, such processes, procedures, and mechanisms should be appropriately validated, updated and monitored. Compliance monitoring can be supported by automation when the risk mitigation measures being validated are information technology-based (e.g., installation of firewalls or testing of configuration settings on desktop computers). Such automated validation can often check whether risk mitigation measures are installed and whether the installations are correct. Similarly, effectiveness monitoring may also be supported by automation. If the threshold conditions for determining the effectiveness of risk response measures are predetermined, then automation can support such effectiveness monitoring. While automation can be a supporting capability for Tiers 1 and 2, generally automation does not provide substantive insight for non-information technology-based activities which are more prevalent at those higher tiers. Activities that are not as likely to benefit from automation include, for example, the use of multiple suppliers within the supply chain, evolving environments of operation, or evaluating the promise of emerging technical capabilities in support of missions/business functions. Where automated monitoring is not available, organizations employ manual monitoring and/or analysis.

Frequency of Monitoring

The frequency of risk monitoring (whether automated or manual) is driven by organizational missions/business functions and the ability of organizations to use the monitoring results to facilitate greater situational awareness. An increased level of situational awareness of the security state of organizational information systems and environments of operation helps organizations develop a better understanding of risk. Monitoring frequency is also driven by other factors, for example: (i) the anticipated frequency of changes in organizational information systems and operating environments; (ii) the potential impact of risk if not properly addressed through appropriate response measures; and (iii) the degree to which the threat space is changing. The frequency of monitoring can also be affected by the type of monitoring conducted (i.e., automated versus procedural approaches). Depending on the frequency of monitoring required by organizations, in most situations, monitoring is most efficient and cost-effective when automation is employed. Monitoring can provide significant benefits, especially in situations where such monitoring limits the opportunities for adversaries to gain a foothold within organizations (either through information systems or the environments in which those systems operate). When manual monitoring is employed by organizations, it is generally not efficient to perform the monitoring with the frequency that automation allows. In some instances, infrequent monitoring is not a major issue. For example, missions/business functions, facilities, legislation, policies, and technologies tend to change on a more gradual basis and as such, do not lend themselves to frequent monitoring. Instead, these types of changes are better suited to condition/event-based monitoring (e.g., if missions and/or business functions change, then monitoring of such changes is appropriate to determine if the changes have any impact on risk).

RISK MONITORING

TASK 4-2: Monitor organizational information systems and environments of operation on an ongoing basis to verify compliance, determine effectiveness of risk response measures, and identify changes.

Supplemental Guidance: Once organizations complete the development of their monitoring strategies, the strategies are implemented organization-wide. Because there are so many diverse aspects of monitoring, not all aspects of monitoring may be performed, or they may be performed at different times. The particular aspects of monitoring that are performed are dictated largely by the assumptions, constraints, risk tolerance, and priorities/trade-offs established by organizations during the risk framing step. For example, while organizations might desire to conduct all forms of monitoring (i.e., compliance, effectiveness, and change), the constraints imposed upon the organizations may allow only compliance monitoring that can be readily automated at Tier 3. If multiple aspects of monitoring can be supported, the output from the risk framing step helps organizations to determine the degree of emphasis and level of effort to place on the various monitoring activities.

As noted above, not all monitoring activities are conducted at the same tiers, for the same purpose, at the same time, or using the same techniques. However, it is important that organizations attempt to coordinate the various monitoring activities. Coordination of monitoring activities facilitates the sharing of risk-related information that may be useful for organizations in providing early warning, developing trend information, or allocating risk response measures in a timely and efficient manner. If monitoring is not coordinated, then the benefit of monitoring may be reduced, and could undermine the overall effort to identify and address risk. As feasible, organizations implement the various monitoring activities in a manner that maximizes the overall goal of monitoring, looking beyond the limited goals of particular monitoring activities. Risk monitoring results are applied in performing incremental risk assessments to maintain awareness of the risk being incurred, to highlight changes in risk, and to indicate the need to revisit other steps in the risk management process, as appropriate.

Outputs and Post Conditions

The output from the risk monitoring step is the information generated by: (i) verifying that required risk response measures are implemented and that information security requirements derived from and traceable to organizational missions/business functions, federal legislation, directives, regulations, policies, and standards/guidelines, are satisfied; (ii) determining the ongoing effectiveness of risk response measures; and (iii) identifying changes to organizational information systems and environments of operation. Outputs from the risk monitoring step can be useful inputs to the risk framing, risk assessment, and risk response steps. For example, compliance monitoring results may require that organizations revisit the implementation portion of the risk response step, while effectiveness monitoring results may require that organizations revisit the entire risk response step. The results of monitoring for changes to information systems and environments of operation may require organizations to revisit the risk assessment step. The results of the risk monitoring step can also serve the risk framing step (e.g., when organizations discover new threats or vulnerabilities that affect changes in organizational risk assumptions, risk tolerance, and/or priorities/trade-offs).

APPENDIX A

REFERENCES

LAWS, POLICIES, DIRECTIVES, INSTRUCTIONS, STANDARDS, AND GUIDELINES

LEGISLATION

1. E-Government Act [includes FISMA] (P.L. 107-347), December 2002.

2. Federal Information Security Management Act (P.L. 107-347, Title III), December 2002.

POLICIES, DIRECTIVES, INSTRUCTIONS

1. Committee on National Security Systems (CNSS) Instruction 4009, *National Information Assurance (IA) Glossary*, April 2010.

2. Committee on National Security Systems (CNSS) Instruction 1253, *Security Categorization and Control Selection for National Security Systems*, October 2009.

3. Office of Management and Budget, Circular A-130, Appendix III, Transmittal Memorandum #4, *Management of Federal Information Resources*, November 2000.

STANDARDS

1. National Institute of Standards and Technology Federal Information Processing Standards Publication 199, *Standards for Security Categorization of Federal Information and Information Systems*, February 2004.

2. National Institute of Standards and Technology Federal Information Processing Standards Publication 200, *Minimum Security Requirements for Federal Information and Information Systems*, March 2006.

3. ISO/IEC 15408:2005, *Common Criteria for Information Technology Security Evaluation*, 2005.

GUIDELINES

1. National Institute of Standards and Technology Special Publication 800-18, Revision 1, *Guide for Developing Security Plans for Federal Information Systems*, February 2006.

2. National Institute of Standards and Technology Special Publication 800-30, Revision 1, *Guide for Conducting Risk Assessments*, (Projected Publication Spring 2011).

3. National Institute of Standards and Technology Special Publication 800-37, Revision 1, *Guide for Applying the Risk Management Framework to Federal Information Systems: A Security Life Cycle Approach*, February 2010.

4. National Institute of Standards and Technology Special Publication 800-53, Revision 3, *Recommended Security Controls for Federal Information Systems and Organizations*, August 2009.

5. National Institute of Standards and Technology Special Publication 800-53A, Revision 1, *Guide for Assessing the Security Controls in Federal Information Systems and Organizations: Building Effective Security Assessment Plans*, June 2010.

6. National Institute of Standards and Technology Special Publication 800-59, *Guideline for Identifying an Information System as a National Security System*, August 2003.

7. National Institute of Standards and Technology Special Publication 800-60, Revision 1, *Guide for Mapping Types of Information and Information Systems to Security Categories*, August 2008.

8. National Institute of Standards and Technology Special Publication 800-70, Revision 1, *National Checklist Program for IT Products--Guidelines for Checklist Users and Developers*, September 2009.

9. National Institute of Standards and Technology Special Publication 800-137, Initial Public Draft, *Information Security Continuous Monitoring for Federal Information Systems and Organizations*, December 2010.

APPENDIX B

GLOSSARY

COMMON TERMS AND DEFINITIONS

This appendix provides definitions for security terminology used within Special Publication 800-39. The terms in the glossary are consistent with the terms used in the suite of FISMA-related security standards and guidelines developed by NIST. Unless otherwise stated, all terms used in this publication are also consistent with the definitions contained in the CNSS Instruction 4009, *National Information Assurance (IA) Glossary*.

Adequate Security [OMB Circular A-130, Appendix III]	Security commensurate with the risk and magnitude of harm resulting from the loss, misuse, or unauthorized access to or modification of information.
Advanced Persistent Threat	An adversary that possesses sophisticated levels of expertise and significant resources which allow it to create opportunities to achieve its objectives by using multiple attack vectors (e.g., cyber, physical, and deception). These objectives typically include establishing and extending footholds within the information technology infrastructure of the targeted organizations for purposes of exfiltrating information, undermining or impeding critical aspects of a mission, program, or organization; or positioning itself to carry out these objectives in the future. The advanced persistent threat: (i) pursues its objectives repeatedly over an extended period of time; (ii) adapts to defenders' efforts to resist it; and (iii) is determined to maintain the level of interaction needed to execute its objectives.
Agency	See *Executive Agency*.
Assessment	See *Security Control Assessment*.
Assessor	See *Security Control Assessor*.
Assurance [CNSSI 4009]	Measure of confidence that the security features, practices, procedures, and architecture of an information system accurately mediates and enforces the security policy.
[NIST SP 800-53]	Grounds for confidence that the set of intended security controls in an information system are effective in their application.
Assurance Case [Software Engineering Institute, Carnegie Mellon University]	A structured set of arguments and a body of evidence showing that an information system satisfies specific claims with respect to a given quality attribute.
Authentication [FIPS 200]	Verifying the identity of a user, process, or device, often as a prerequisite to allowing access to resources in an information system.

Authenticity	The property of being genuine and being able to be verified and trusted; confidence in the validity of a transmission, a message, or message originator. See *Authentication*.
Authorization (to operate)	The official management decision given by a senior organizational official to authorize operation of an information system and to explicitly accept the risk to organizational operations (including mission, functions, image, or reputation), organizational assets, individuals, other organizations, and the Nation based on the implementation of an agreed-upon set of security controls.
Authorization Boundary [NIST SP 800-37]	All components of an information system to be authorized for operation by an authorizing official and excludes separately authorized systems, to which the information system is connected.
Authorizing Official [CNSSI 4009]	Senior (federal) official or executive with the authority to formally assume responsibility for operating an information system at an acceptable level of risk to organizational operations (including mission, functions, image, or reputation), organizational assets, individuals, other organizations, and the Nation.
Availability [44 U.S.C., Sec. 3542]	Ensuring timely and reliable access to and use of information.
Chief Information Officer [PL 104-106, Sec. 5125(b)]	Agency official responsible for: (i) Providing advice and other assistance to the head of the executive agency and other senior management personnel of the agency to ensure that information technology is acquired and information resources are managed in a manner that is consistent with laws, Executive Orders, directives, policies, regulations, and priorities established by the head of the agency; (ii) Developing, maintaining, and facilitating the implementation of a sound and integrated information technology architecture for the agency; and (iii) Promoting the effective and efficient design and operation of all major information resources management processes for the agency, including improvements to work processes of the agency.
Chief Information Security Officer	See *Senior Agency Information Security Officer*.
Classified National Security Information [CNSSI 4009]	Information that has been determined pursuant to Executive Order 13526 or any predecessor order to require protection against unauthorized disclosure and is marked to indicate its classified status when in documentary form.

Common Control [NIST SP 800-37]	A security control that is inherited by one or more organizational information systems. See *Security Control Inheritance.*
Common Control Provider [NIST SP 800-37]	An organizational official responsible for the development, implementation, assessment, and monitoring of common controls (i.e., security controls inherited by information systems).
Compensating Security Control [CNSSI 4009]	A management, operational, and/or technical control (i.e., safeguard or countermeasure) employed by an organization in lieu of a recommended security control in the low, moderate, or high baselines that provides equivalent or comparable protection for an information system.
Confidentiality [44 U.S.C., Sec. 3542]	Preserving authorized restrictions on information access and disclosure, including means for protecting personal privacy and proprietary information.
Course of Action (Risk Response)	A time-phased or situation-dependent combination of risk response measures.
Cyber Attack [CNSSI 4009]	An attack, via cyberspace, targeting an enterprise's use of cyberspace for the purpose of disrupting, disabling, destroying, or maliciously controlling a computing environment/infrastructure; or destroying the integrity of the data or stealing controlled information.
Cyber Security [CNSSI 4009]	The ability to protect or defend the use of cyberspace from cyber attacks.
Cyberspace [CNSSI 4009]	A global domain within the information environment consisting of the interdependent network of information systems infrastructures including the Internet, telecommunications networks, computer systems, and embedded processors and controllers.
Defense-in-Breadth [CNSSI 4009]	A planned, systematic set of multidisciplinary activities that seek to identify, manage, and reduce risk of exploitable vulnerabilities at every stage of the system, network, or subcomponent life cycle (system, network, or product design and development; manufacturing; packaging; assembly; system integration; distribution; operations; maintenance; and retirement).
Defense-in-Depth [CNSSI 4009]	Information security strategy integrating people, technology, and operations capabilities to establish variable barriers across multiple layers and missions of the organization.

Enterprise [CNSSI 4009]	An organization with a defined mission/goal and a defined boundary, using information systems to execute that mission, and with responsibility for managing its own risks and performance. An enterprise may consist of all or some of the following business aspects: acquisition, program management, financial management (e.g., budgets), human resources, security, and information systems, information and mission management. See *Organization*.
Enterprise Architecture [CNSSI 4009]	The description of an enterprise's entire set of information systems: how they are configured, how they are integrated, how they interface to the external environment at the enterprise's boundary, how they are operated to support the enterprise mission, and how they contribute to the enterprise's overall security posture.
Environment of Operation [NIST SP 800-37]	The physical surroundings in which an information system processes, stores, and transmits information.
Executive Agency [41 U.S.C., Sec. 403]	An executive department specified in 5 U.S.C., Sec. 101; a military department specified in 5 U.S.C., Sec. 102; an independent establishment as defined in 5 U.S.C., Sec. 104(1); and a wholly owned Government corporation fully subject to the provisions of 31 U.S.C., Chapter 91.
Federal Agency	See *Executive Agency*.
Federal Information System [40 U.S.C., Sec. 11331]	An information system used or operated by an executive agency, by a contractor of an executive agency, or by another organization on behalf of an executive agency.
Hybrid Security Control [NIST SP 800-53]	A security control that is implemented in an information system in part as a common control and in part as a system-specific control. See *Common Control* and *System-Specific Security Control*.
Individuals	An assessment object that includes people applying specifications, mechanisms, or activities.
Industrial Control System	An information system used to control industrial processes such as manufacturing, product handling, production, and distribution. Industrial control systems include supervisory control and data acquisition systems used to control geographically dispersed assets, as well as distributed control systems and smaller control systems using programmable logic controllers to control localized processes.
Information [CNSSI 4009]	Any communication or representation of knowledge such as facts, data, or opinions in any medium or form, including textual, numerical, graphic, cartographic, narrative, or audiovisual.
[FIPS 199]	An instance of an information type.

Information Owner [CNSSI 4009]	Official with statutory or operational authority for specified information and responsibility for establishing the controls for its generation, classification, collection, processing, dissemination, and disposal. See *Information Steward*.
Information Resources [44 U.S.C., Sec. 3502]	Information and related resources, such as personnel, equipment, funds, and information technology.
Information Security [44 U.S.C., Sec. 3542]	The protection of information and information systems from unauthorized access, use, disclosure, disruption, modification, or destruction in order to provide confidentiality, integrity, and availability.
Information Security Architecture	An embedded, integral part of the enterprise architecture that describes the structure and behavior for an enterprise's security processes, information security systems, personnel and organizational sub-units, showing their alignment with the enterprise's mission and strategic plans.
Information Security Program Plan [NIST SP 800-53]	Formal document that provides an overview of the security requirements for an organization-wide information security program and describes the program management controls and common controls in place or planned for meeting those requirements.
Information Steward [CNSSI 4009]	An agency official with statutory or operational authority for specified information and responsibility for establishing the controls for its generation, collection, processing, dissemination, and disposal.
Information System [44 U.S.C., Sec. 3502]	A discrete set of information resources organized for the collection, processing, maintenance, use, sharing, dissemination, or disposition of information.
Information System Boundary	See *Authorization Boundary*.
Information System Owner (or Program Manager)	Official responsible for the overall procurement, development, integration, modification, or operation and maintenance of an information system.
Information System Resilience	The ability of an information system to continue to: (i) operate under adverse conditions or stress, even if in a degraded or debilitated state, while maintaining essential operational capabilities; and (ii) recover to an effective operational posture in a time frame consistent with mission needs.
Information System Security Officer	Individual assigned responsibility by the senior agency information security officer, authorizing official, management official, or information system owner for maintaining the appropriate operational security posture for an information system or program.

Information Security Risk	The risk to organizational operations (including mission, functions, image, reputation), organizational assets, individuals, other organizations, and the Nation due to the potential for unauthorized access, use, disclosure, disruption, modification, or destruction of information and/or information systems.
Information System-Related Security Risks	Risks that arise through the loss of confidentiality, integrity, or availability of information or information systems and consider impacts to the organization (including assets, mission, functions, image, or reputation), individuals, other organizations, and the Nation. See *Risk*.
Information Technology [40 U.S.C., Sec. 1401]	Any equipment or interconnected system or subsystem of equipment that is used in the automatic acquisition, storage, manipulation, management, movement, control, display, switching, interchange, transmission, or reception of data or information by the executive agency. For purposes of the preceding sentence, equipment is used by an executive agency if the equipment is used by the executive agency directly or is used by a contractor under a contract with the executive agency which: (i) requires the use of such equipment; or (ii) requires the use, to a significant extent, of such equipment in the performance of a service or the furnishing of a product. The term information technology includes computers, ancillary equipment, software, firmware, and similar procedures, services (including support services), and related resources.
Information Type [FIPS 199]	A specific category of information (e.g., privacy, medical, proprietary, financial, investigative, contractor sensitive, security management) defined by an organization or in some instances, by a specific law, Executive Order, directive, policy, or regulation.
Integrity [44 U.S.C., Sec. 3542]	Guarding against improper information modification or destruction, and includes ensuring information non-repudiation and authenticity.
Management Controls [FIPS 200]	The security controls (i.e., safeguards or countermeasures) for an information system that focus on the management of risk and the management of information system security.

Managing Information Security Risk (800-39)
65

National Security System [44 U.S.C., Sec. 3542]	Any information system (including any telecommunications system) used or operated by an agency or by a contractor of an agency, or other organization on behalf of an agency (i) the function, operation, or use of which involves intelligence activities; involves cryptologic activities related to national security; involves command and control of military forces; involves equipment that is an integral part of a weapon or weapons system; or is critical to the direct fulfillment of military or intelligence missions (excluding a system that is to be used for routine administrative and business applications, for example, payroll, finance, logistics, and personnel management applications); or (ii) is protected at all times by procedures established for information that have been specifically authorized under criteria established by an Executive Order or an Act of Congress to be kept classified in the interest of national defense or foreign policy.
Operational Controls [FIPS 200]	The security controls (i.e., safeguards or countermeasures) for an information system that are primarily implemented and executed by people (as opposed to systems).
Organization [FIPS 200, Adapted]	An entity of any size, complexity, or positioning within an organizational structure (e.g., a federal agency or, as appropriate, any of its operational elements). See *Enterprise*.
Plan of Action and Milestones [OMB Memorandum 02-01]	A document that identifies tasks needing to be accomplished. It details resources required to accomplish the elements of the plan, any milestones in meeting the tasks, and scheduled completion dates for the milestones.
Reciprocity	Mutual agreement among participating organizations to accept each other's security assessments in order to reuse information system resources and/or to accept each other's assessed security posture in order to share information.
Resilience	See *Information System Resilience*.
Risk [CNSSI 4009]	A measure of the extent to which an entity is threatened by a potential circumstance or event, and typically a function of: (i) the adverse impacts that would arise if the circumstance or event occurs; and (ii) the likelihood of occurrence. [Note: Information system-related security risks are those risks that arise from the loss of confidentiality, integrity, or availability of information or information systems and reflect the potential adverse impacts to organizational operations (including mission, functions, image, or reputation), organizational assets, individuals, other organizations, and the Nation.]

Risk Assessment	The process of identifying risks to organizational operations (including mission, functions, image, reputation), organizational assets, individuals, other organizations, and the Nation, resulting from the operation of an information system.
	Part of risk management, incorporates threat and vulnerability analyses, and considers mitigations provided by security controls planned or in place. Synonymous with risk analysis.
Risk Executive (Function) [CNSSI 4009]	An individual or group within an organization that helps to ensure that: (i) security risk-related considerations for individual information systems, to include the authorization decisions for those systems, are viewed from an organization-wide perspective with regard to the overall strategic goals and objectives of the organization in carrying out its missions and business functions; and (ii) managing risk from individual information systems is consistent across the organization, reflects organizational risk tolerance, and is considered along with other organizational risks affecting mission/business success.
Risk Management [CNSSI 4009, adapted]	The program and supporting processes to manage information security risk to organizational operations (including mission, functions, image, reputation), organizational assets, individuals, other organizations, and the Nation, and includes: (i) establishing the context for risk-related activities; (ii) assessing risk; (iii) responding to risk once determined; and (iv) monitoring risk over time.
Risk Mitigation [CNSSI 4009]	Prioritizing, evaluating, and implementing the appropriate risk-reducing controls/countermeasures recommended from the risk management process.
Risk Monitoring	Maintaining ongoing awareness of an organization's risk environment, risk management program, and associated activities to support risk decisions.
Risk Response	Accepting, avoiding, mitigating, sharing, or transferring risk to organizational operations (i.e., mission, functions, image, or reputation), organizational assets, individuals, other organizations, or the Nation.
Risk Response Measure	A specific action taken to respond to an identified risk.
Root Cause Analysis	A principle-based, systems approach for the identification of underlying causes associated with a particular set of risks.
Security Authorization (to Operate)	See *Authorization (to operate)*.

Security Categorization	The process of determining the security category for information or an information system. Security categorization methodologies are described in CNSS Instruction 1253 for national security systems and in FIPS 199 for other than national security systems.
Security Control Assessment [CNSSI 4009, Adapted]	The testing and/or evaluation of the management, operational, and technical security controls to determine the extent to which the controls are implemented correctly, operating as intended, and producing the desired outcome with respect to meeting the security requirements for an information system or organization.
Security Control Assessor	The individual, group, or organization responsible for conducting a security control assessment.
Security Control Baseline [CNSSI 4009]	The set of minimum security controls defined for a low-impact, moderate-impact, or high-impact information system.
Security Control Enhancements	Statements of security capability to: (i) build in additional, but related, functionality to a basic control; and/or (ii) increase the strength of a basic control.
Security Control Inheritance [CNSSI 4009]	A situation in which an information system or application receives protection from security controls (or portions of security controls) that are developed, implemented, assessed, authorized, and monitored by entities other than those responsible for the system or application; entities either internal or external to the organization where the system or application resides. See *Common Control*.
Security Controls [FIPS 199, CNSSI 4009]	The management, operational, and technical controls (i.e., safeguards or countermeasures) prescribed for an information system to protect the confidentiality, integrity, and availability of the system and its information.
Security Impact Analysis [NIST SP 800-37]	The analysis conducted by an organizational official to determine the extent to which changes to the information system have affected the security state of the system.
Security Objective [FIPS 199]	Confidentiality, integrity, or availability.
Security Plan [NIST SP 800-18]	Formal document that provides an overview of the security requirements for an information system or an information security program and describes the security controls in place or planned for meeting those requirements. See *System Security Plan* or *Information Security Program Plan*.
Security Policy [CNSSI 4009]	A set of criteria for the provision of security services.

Security Requirements [FIPS 200]	Requirements levied on an information system that are derived from applicable laws, Executive Orders, directives, policies, standards, instructions, regulations, procedures, or organizational mission/business case needs to ensure the confidentiality, integrity, and availability of the information being processed, stored, or transmitted.
Senior Agency Information Security Officer [44 U.S.C., Sec. 3544]	Official responsible for carrying out the Chief Information Officer responsibilities under FISMA and serving as the Chief Information Officer's primary liaison to the agency's authorizing officials, information system owners, and information system security officers. [Note: Organizations subordinate to federal agencies may use the term *Senior Information Security Officer* or *Chief Information Security Officer* to denote individuals filling positions with similar responsibilities to Senior Agency Information Security Officers.]
Senior Information Security Officer	See *Senior Agency Information Security Officer*.
Subsystem	A major subdivision or component of an information system consisting of information, information technology, and personnel that performs one or more specific functions.
Supplementation (Security Controls)	The process of adding security controls or control enhancements to a security control baseline from NIST Special Publication 800-53 or CNSS Instruction 1253 in order to adequately meet the organization's risk management needs.
System	See *Information System*.
System Security Plan [NIST SP 800-18]	Formal document that provides an overview of the security requirements for an information system and describes the security controls in place or planned for meeting those requirements.
System-Specific Security Control [NIST SP 800-37]	A security control for an information system that has not been designated as a common control or the portion of a hybrid control that is to be implemented within an information system.
Tailoring [NIST SP 800-53, CNSSI 4009]	The process by which a security control baseline is modified based on: (i) the application of scoping guidance; (ii) the specification of compensating security controls, if needed; and (iii) the specification of organization-defined parameters in the security controls via explicit assignment and selection statements.
Tailored Security Control Baseline	A set of security controls resulting from the application of tailoring guidance to the security control baseline. See *Tailoring*.

Technical Controls [FIPS 200]	Security controls (i.e., safeguards or countermeasures) for an information system that are primarily implemented and executed by the information system through mechanisms contained in the hardware, software, or firmware components of the system.
Threat [CNSSI 4009]	Any circumstance or event with the potential to adversely impact organizational operations (including mission, functions, image, or reputation), organizational assets, individuals, other organizations, or the Nation through an information system via unauthorized access, destruction, disclosure, modification of information, and/or denial of service.
Threat Assessment [CNSSI 4009]	Process of formally evaluating the degree of threat to an information system or enterprise and describing the nature of the threat.
Threat Source [CNSSI 4009]	The intent and method targeted at the intentional exploitation of a vulnerability or a situation and method that may accidentally exploit a vulnerability.
Trustworthiness [CNSSI 4009]	The attribute of a person or enterprise that provides confidence to others of the qualifications, capabilities, and reliability of that entity to perform specific tasks and fulfill assigned responsibilities.
Vulnerability [CNSSI 4009]	Weakness in an information system, system security procedures, internal controls, or implementation that could be exploited by a threat source.
Vulnerability Assessment [CNSSI 4009]	Systematic examination of an information system or product to determine the adequacy of security measures, identify security deficiencies, provide data from which to predict the effectiveness of proposed security measures, and confirm the adequacy of such measures after implementation.

APPENDIX C

ACRONYMS

COMMON ABBREVIATIONS

APT	Advanced Persistent Threat
CIO	Chief Information Officer
CNSS	Committee on National Security Systems
COTS	Commercial Off-The-Shelf
DoD	Department of Defense
FIPS	Federal Information Processing Standards
FISMA	Federal Information Security Management Act
IA	Information Assurance
ICS	Industrial Control System
IEC	International Electrotechnical Commission
ISO	International Organization for Standardization
NIST	National Institute of Standards and Technology
NSA	National Security Agency
ODNI	Office of the Director of National Intelligence
OMB	Office of Management and Budget
POAM	Plan of Action and Milestones
RMF	Risk Management Framework
SCAP	Security Content Automation Protocol
SP	Special Publication
U.S.C.	United States Code

APPENDIX D

ROLES AND RESPONSIBILITIES

KEY PARTICIPANTS IN THE RISK MANAGEMENT PROCESS

The following sections describe the roles and responsibilities[66] of key participants involved in an organization's risk management process.[67] Recognizing that organizations have widely varying missions and organizational structures, there may be differences in naming conventions for risk management-related roles and how specific responsibilities are allocated among organizational personnel (e.g., multiple individuals filling a single role or one individual filling multiple roles).[68] However, the basic functions remain the same. The application of the risk management process across the three risk management tiers described in this publication is flexible, allowing organizations to effectively accomplish the intent of the specific tasks within their respective organizational structures to best manage risk.

D.1 HEAD OF AGENCY (CHIEF EXECUTIVE OFFICER)

The *head of agency* (or chief executive officer) is the highest-level senior official or executive within an organization with the overall responsibility to provide information security protections commensurate with the risk and magnitude of harm (i.e., impact) to organizational operations and assets, individuals, other organizations, and the Nation resulting from unauthorized access, use, disclosure, disruption, modification, or destruction of: (i) information collected or maintained by or on behalf of the agency; and (ii) information systems used or operated by an agency or by a contractor of an agency or other organization on behalf of an agency. Agency heads are also responsible for ensuring that: (i) information security management processes are integrated with strategic and operational planning processes; (ii) senior officials within the organization provide information security for the information and information systems that support the operations and assets under their control; and (iii) the organization has trained personnel sufficient to assist in complying with the information security requirements in related legislation, policies, directives, instructions, standards, and guidelines. Through the development and implementation of strong policies, the head of agency establishes the organizational commitment to information security and the actions required to effectively manage risk and protect the missions/business functions being carried out by the organization. The head of agency establishes appropriate accountability for information security and provides active support and oversight of monitoring and improvement for the information security program. Senior leadership commitment to information security establishes a level of due diligence within the organization that promotes a climate for mission and business success.

D.2 RISK EXECUTIVE (FUNCTION)

The *risk executive (function)* is an individual or group within an organization that provides a more comprehensive, organization-wide approach to risk management. The risk executive (function) serves as the common risk management resource for senior leaders/executives, mission/business

---

[66] The roles and responsibilities described in this appendix are consistent with the roles and responsibilities associated with the Risk Management Framework in NIST Special Publication 800-37.

[67] Organizations may define other roles (e.g., facilities manager, human resources manager, systems administrator) to support the risk management process.

[68] Caution is exercised when one individual fills multiples roles in the risk management process to ensure that the individual retains an appropriate level of independence and remains free from conflicts of interest.

owners, chief information officers, chief information security officers, information system owners, common control providers, enterprise architects, information security architects, information systems/security engineers, information system security managers/officers, and any other stakeholders having a vested interest in the mission/business success of organizations. The risk executive (function) coordinates with senior leaders/executives to:

- Establish risk management roles and responsibilities;

- Develop and implement an organization-wide *risk management strategy* that guides and informs organizational risk decisions (including how risk is framed, assessed, responded to, and monitored over time);

- Manage threat and vulnerability information with regard to organizational information systems and the environments in which the systems operate;

- Establish organization-wide forums to consider all types and sources of risk (including aggregated risk);

- Determine organizational risk based on the aggregated risk from the operation and use of information systems and the respective environments of operation;

- Provide oversight for the risk management activities carried out by organizations to ensure consistent and effective risk-based decisions;

- Develop a greater understanding of risk with regard to the strategic view of organizations and their integrated operations;

- Establish effective vehicles and serve as a focal point for communicating and sharing risk-related information among key stakeholders internally and externally to organizations;

- Specify the degree of autonomy for subordinate organizations permitted by parent organizations with regard to framing, assessing, responding to, and monitoring risk;

- Promote cooperation and collaboration among authorizing officials to include security authorization actions requiring shared responsibility (e.g., joint/leveraged authorizations);

- Ensure that security authorization decisions consider all factors necessary for mission and business success; and

- Ensure shared responsibility for supporting organizational missions and business functions using external providers receives the needed visibility and is elevated to appropriate decision-making authorities.

The risk executive (function) presumes neither a specific organizational structure nor formal responsibility assigned to any one individual or group within the organization. Heads of agencies or organizations may choose to retain the risk executive (function) or to delegate the function. The risk executive (function) requires a mix of skills, expertise, and perspectives to understand the strategic goals and objectives of organizations, organizational missions/business functions, technical possibilities and constraints, and key mandates and guidance that shape organizational operations. To provide this needed mixture, the risk executive (function) can be filled by a single individual or office (supported by an expert staff) or by a designated group (e.g., a risk board, executive steering committee, executive leadership council). The risk executive (function) fits into the organizational governance structure in such a way as to facilitate efficiency and effectiveness.

D.3 CHIEF INFORMATION OFFICER

The *chief information officer*[69] is an organizational official responsible for: (i) designating a senior information security officer; (ii) developing and maintaining information security policies, procedures, and control techniques to address all applicable requirements; (iii) overseeing personnel with significant responsibilities for information security and ensuring that the personnel are adequately trained; (iv) assisting senior organizational officials concerning their security responsibilities; and (v) in coordination with other senior officials, reporting annually to the head of the federal agency on the overall effectiveness of the organization's information security program, including progress of remedial actions. The chief information officer, with the support of the risk executive (function) and the senior information security officer, works closely with authorizing officials and their designated representatives to help ensure that:

- An organization-wide information security program is effectively implemented resulting in adequate security for all organizational information systems and environments of operation for those systems;

- Information security considerations are integrated into programming/planning/budgeting cycles, enterprise architectures, and acquisition/system development life cycles;

- Information systems are covered by approved security plans and are authorized to operate;

- Information security-related activities required across the organization are accomplished in an efficient, cost-effective, and timely manner; and

- There is centralized reporting of appropriate information security-related activities.

The chief information officer and authorizing officials also determine, based on organizational priorities, the appropriate allocation of resources dedicated to the protection of the information systems supporting the organization's missions and business functions. For selected information systems, the chief information officer may be designated as an authorizing official or a co-authorizing official with other senior organizational officials. The role of chief information officer has inherent U.S. Government authority and is assigned to government personnel only.

D.4 INFORMATION OWNER/STEWARD

The *information owner/steward* is an organizational official with statutory, management, or operational authority for specified information and the responsibility for establishing the policies and procedures governing its generation, collection, processing, dissemination, and disposal.[70] In information-sharing environments, the information owner/steward is responsible for establishing the rules for appropriate use and protection of the subject information (e.g., rules of behavior) and retains that responsibility when the information is shared with or provided to other organizations. The owner/steward of the information processed, stored, or transmitted by an information system

---

[69] When an organization has not designated a formal chief information officer position, FISMA requires the associated responsibilities to be handled by a comparable organizational official.

[70] Federal information is an asset of the Nation, not of a particular federal agency or its subordinate organizations. In that spirit, many federal agencies are developing policies, procedures, processes, and training needed to end the practice of *information ownership* and implement the practice of *information stewardship*. Information stewardship is the careful and responsible management of federal information belonging to the Nation as a whole, regardless of the entity or source that may have originated, created, or compiled the information. Information stewards provide maximum access to federal information to elements of the federal government and its customers, balanced by the obligation to protect the information in accordance with the provisions of FISMA and any associated security-related federal policies, directives, regulations, standards, and guidance.

may or may not be the same as the system owner. A single information system may contain information from multiple information owners/stewards. Information owners/stewards provide input to information system owners regarding the security requirements and security controls for the systems where the information is processed, stored, or transmitted.

D.5 SENIOR INFORMATION SECURITY OFFICER

The *senior information security officer* is an organizational official responsible for: (i) carrying out the chief information officer security responsibilities under FISMA; and (ii) serving as the primary liaison for the chief information officer to the organization's authorizing officials, information system owners, common control providers, and information system security officers. The senior information security officer: (i) possesses professional qualifications, including training and experience, required to administer the information security program functions; (ii) maintains information security duties as a primary responsibility; and (iii) heads an office with the mission and resources to assist the organization in achieving more secure information and information systems in accordance with the requirements in FISMA. The senior information security officer (or supporting staff members) may also serve as authorizing official designated representatives or security control assessors. The role of senior information security officer has inherent U.S. Government authority and is assigned to government personnel only.

D.6 AUTHORIZING OFFICIAL

The *authorizing official* is a senior official or executive with the authority to formally assume responsibility for operating an information system at an acceptable level of risk to organizational operations and assets, individuals, other organizations, and the Nation.[71] Authorizing officials typically have budgetary oversight for an information system *or* are responsible for the mission and/or business operations supported by the system. Through the security authorization process, authorizing officials are *accountable* for the security risks associated with information system operations. Accordingly, authorizing officials are in management positions with a level of authority commensurate with understanding and accepting such information system-related security risks. Authorizing officials also approve security plans, memorandums of agreement or understanding, and plans of action and milestones and determine whether significant changes in the information systems or environments of operation require reauthorization. Authorizing officials can deny authorization to operate an information system or if the system is operational, halt operations, if unacceptable risks exist. Authorizing officials coordinate their activities with the risk executive (function), chief information officer, senior information security officer, common control providers, information system owners, information system security officers, security control assessors, and other interested parties during the security authorization process. With the increasing complexity of mission/business processes, partnership arrangements, and the use of external/shared services, it is possible that a particular information system may involve multiple authorizing officials. If so, agreements are established among the authorizing officials and documented in the security plan. Authorizing officials are responsible for ensuring that all activities and functions associated with security authorization that are delegated to authorizing official designated representatives are carried out. The role of authorizing official has inherent U.S. Government authority and is assigned to government personnel only.

---

[71] The responsibility of authorizing officials described in FIPS 200, was extended in NIST Special Publication 800-53 to include risks to other organizations and the Nation.

D.7 AUTHORIZING OFFICIAL DESIGNATED REPRESENTATIVE

The *authorizing official designated representative* is an organizational official that acts on behalf of an authorizing official to coordinate and conduct the required day-to-day activities associated with the security authorization process. Authorizing official designated representatives can be empowered by authorizing officials to make certain decisions with regard to the planning and resourcing of the security authorization process, approval of the security plan, approval and monitoring the implementation of plans of action and milestones, and the assessment and/or determination of risk. The designated representative may also be called upon to prepare the final authorization package, obtain the authorizing official's signature on the authorization decision document, and transmit the authorization package to appropriate organizational officials. The only activity that cannot be delegated to the designated representative by the authorizing official is the authorization decision and signing of the associated authorization decision document (i.e., the acceptance of risk to organizational operations and assets, individuals, other organizations, and the Nation).

D.8 COMMON CONTROL PROVIDER

The *common control provider* is an individual, group, or organization responsible for the development, implementation, assessment, and monitoring of common controls (i.e., security controls inherited by information systems).[72] Common control providers are responsible for: (i) documenting the organization-identified common controls in a *security plan* (or equivalent document prescribed by the organization); (ii) ensuring that required assessments of common controls are carried out by qualified assessors with an appropriate level of independence defined by the organization; (iii) documenting assessment findings in a *security assessment report*; and (iv) producing a *plan of action and milestones* for all controls having weaknesses or deficiencies. Security plans, security assessment reports, and plans of action and milestones for common controls (or a summary of such information) is made available to information system owners *inheriting* those controls after the information is reviewed and approved by the senior official or executive with oversight responsibility for those controls.

D.9 INFORMATION SYSTEM OWNER

The *information system owner* is an organizational official responsible for the procurement, development, integration, modification, operation, maintenance, and disposal of an information system.[73] The information system owner is responsible for addressing the operational interests of the user community (i.e., individuals who depend upon the information system to satisfy mission, business, or operational requirements) and for ensuring compliance with information security requirements. In coordination with the information system security officer, the information system owner is responsible for the development and maintenance of the security plan and ensures that the system is deployed and operated in accordance with the agreed-upon security controls. In coordination with the information owner/steward, the information system owner is

---

[72] Organizations can have multiple common control providers depending on how information security responsibilities are allocated organization-wide. Common control providers may also be *information system owners* when the common controls are resident within an information system.

[73] The *information system owner* serves as the focal point for the information system. In that capacity, the information system owner serves both as an owner and as the central point of contact between the authorization process and the owners of components of the system including, for example: (i) applications, networking, servers, or workstations; (ii) owners/stewards of information processed, stored, or transmitted by the system; and (iii) owners of the missions and business functions supported by the system. Some organizations may refer to information system owners as program managers or business/asset owners.

also responsible for deciding who has access to the system (and with what types of privileges or access rights)[74] and ensures that system users and support personnel receive the requisite security training (e.g., instruction in rules of behavior). Based on guidance from the authorizing official, the information system owner informs appropriate organizational officials of the need to conduct the security authorization, ensures that the necessary resources are available for the effort, and provides the required information system access, information, and documentation to the security control assessor. The information system owner receives the security assessment results from the security control assessor. After taking appropriate steps to reduce or eliminate vulnerabilities, the information system owner assembles the authorization package and submits the package to the authorizing official or the authorizing official designated representative for adjudication.[75]

D.10 INFORMATION SYSTEM SECURITY OFFICER

The *information system security officer*[76] is an individual responsible for ensuring that the appropriate operational security posture is maintained for an information system and as such, works in close collaboration with the information system owner. The information system security officer also serves as a principal advisor on all matters, technical and otherwise, involving the security of an information system. The information system security officer has the detailed knowledge and expertise required to manage the security aspects of an information system and, in many organizations, is assigned responsibility for the day-to-day security operations of a system. This responsibility may also include, but is not limited to, physical and environmental protection, personnel security, incident handling, and security training and awareness. The information system security officer may be called upon to assist in the development of the security policies and procedures and to ensure compliance with those policies and procedures. In close coordination with the information system owner, the information system security officer often plays an active role in the monitoring of a system and its environment of operation to include developing and updating the security plan, managing and controlling changes to the system, and assessing the security impact of those changes.

D.11 INFORMATION SECURITY ARCHITECT

The *information security architect* is an individual, group, or organization responsible for ensuring that the information security requirements necessary to protect the organizational missions/business functions are adequately addressed in all aspects of enterprise architecture including reference models, segment and solution architectures, and the resulting information systems supporting those missions and business processes. The information security architect serves as the liaison between the enterprise architect and the information system security engineer and also coordinates with information system owners, common control providers, and information system security officers on the allocation of security controls as system-specific, hybrid, or common controls. In addition, information security architects, in close coordination with information system security officers, advise authorizing officials, chief information officers,

---

[74] The responsibility for deciding who has access to specific information within an information system (and with what types of privileges or access rights) may reside with the information owner/steward.

[75] Depending on how the organization has organized its security authorization activities, the authorizing official may choose to designate an individual other than the information system owner to compile and assemble the information for the security authorization package. In this situation, the designated individual must coordinate the compilation and assembly activities with the information system owner.

[76] Organizations may also define an *information system security manager* or *information security manager* role with similar responsibilities as an information system security officer or with oversight responsibilities for an information security program. In these situations, information system security officers may, at the discretion of the organization, report directly to information system security managers or information security managers.

senior information security officers, and the risk executive (function), on a range of security-related issues including, for example, establishing information system boundaries, assessing the severity of weaknesses and deficiencies in the information system, plans of action and milestones, risk mitigation approaches, security alerts, and potential adverse effects of vulnerabilities.

D.12 INFORMATION SYSTEM SECURITY ENGINEER

The *information system security engineer* is an individual, group, or organization responsible for conducting information system security engineering activities. Information system security engineering is a process that captures and refines information security requirements and ensures that the requirements are effectively integrated into information technology component products and information systems through purposeful security architecting, design, development, and configuration. Information system security engineers are an integral part of the development team (e.g., integrated project team) designing and developing organizational information systems or upgrading legacy systems. Information system security engineers employ best practices when implementing security controls within an information system including software engineering methodologies, system/security engineering principles, secure design, secure architecture, and secure coding techniques. System security engineers coordinate their security-related activities with information security architects, senior information security officers, information system owners, common control providers, and information system security officers.

D.13 SECURITY CONTROL ASSESSOR

The *security control assessor* is an individual, group, or organization responsible for conducting a comprehensive assessment of the management, operational, and technical security controls employed within or inherited by an information system to determine the overall effectiveness of the controls (i.e., the extent to which the controls are implemented correctly, operating as intended, and producing the desired outcome with respect to meeting the security requirements for the system). Security control assessors also provide an assessment of the severity of weaknesses or deficiencies discovered in the information system and its environment of operation and recommend corrective actions to address identified vulnerabilities. In addition to the above responsibilities, security control assessors prepare the final security assessment report containing the results and findings from the assessment. Prior to initiating the security control assessment, an assessor conducts an assessment of the security plan to help ensure that the plan provides a set of security controls for the information system that meet the stated security requirements.

The required level of assessor independence is determined by the specific conditions of the security control assessment. For example, when the assessment is conducted in support of an authorization decision or ongoing authorization, the authorizing official makes an explicit determination of the degree of independence required in accordance with federal policies, directives, standards, and guidelines. Assessor independence is an important factor in: (i) preserving the impartial and unbiased nature of the assessment process; (ii) determining the credibility of the security assessment results; and (iii) ensuring that the authorizing official receives the most objective information possible in order to make an informed, risk-based, authorization decision. The information system owner and common control provider rely on the security expertise and the technical judgment of the assessor to: (i) assess the security controls employed within and inherited by the information system using assessment procedures specified in the security assessment plan; and (ii) provide specific recommendations on how to correct weaknesses or deficiencies in the controls and address identified vulnerabilities.

APPENDIX E

RISK MANAGEMENT PROCESS TASKS
SUMMARY OF TASKS FOR STEPS IN THE RISK MANAGEMENT PROCESS

TASK	TASK DESCRIPTION
Step 1: Risk Framing	
TASK 1-1 RISK ASSUMPTIONS	Identify assumptions that affect how risk is assessed, responded to, and monitored within the organization.
TASK 1-2 RISK CONSTRAINTS	Identify constraints on the conduct of risk assessment, risk response, and risk monitoring activities within the organization.
TASK 1-3 RISK TOLERANCE	Identify the level of risk tolerance for the organization.
TASK 1-4 PRIORITIES AND TRADE-OFFS	Identify priorities and trade-offs considered by the organization in managing risk.
Step 2: Risk Assessment	
TASK 2-1 THREAT AND VULNERABILITY IDENTIFICATION	Identify threats to and vulnerabilities in organizational information systems and the environments in which the systems operate.
TASK 2-2 RISK DETERMINATION	Determine the risk to organizational operations and assets, individuals, other organizations, and the Nation if identified threats exploit identified vulnerabilities.
Step 3: Risk Response	
TASK 3-1 RISK RESPONSE IDENTIFICATION	Identify alternative courses of action to respond to risk determined during the risk assessment.
TASK 3-2 EVALUATION OF ALTERNATIVES	Evaluate alternative courses of action for responding to risk.
TASK 3-3 RISK RESPONSE DECISION	Decide on the appropriate course of action for responding to risk.
TASK 3-4 RISK RESPONSE IMPLEMENTATION	Implement the course of action selected to respond to risk.
Step 4: Risk Monitoring	
TASK 4-1 RISK MONITORING STRATEGY	Develop a risk monitoring strategy for the organization that includes the purpose, type, and frequency of monitoring activities.
TASK 4-2 RISK MONITORING	Monitor organizational information systems and environments of operation on an ongoing basis to verify compliance, determine effectiveness of risk response measures, and identify changes.

APPENDIX F

GOVERNANCE MODELS

APPROACHES TO INFORMATION SECURITY GOVERNANCE

Three approaches to information security governance can be used to meet organizational needs: (i) a *centralized* approach; (ii) a *decentralized* approach; or (iii) a *hybrid* approach. The authority, responsibility, and decision-making power related to information security and risk management differ in each governance approach. The appropriate governance structure for an organization varies based on many factors (e.g., mission/business needs; culture and size of the organization; geographic distribution of organizational operations, assets, and individuals; and risk tolerance). The information security governance structure is aligned with other governance structures (e.g., information technology governance) to ensure compatibility with the established management practices within the organization and to increase its overall effectiveness.

Centralized Governance

In centralized governance structures, the authority, responsibility, and decision-making power are vested solely within central bodies. These centralized bodies establish the appropriate policies, procedures, and processes for ensuring organization-wide involvement in the development and implementation of risk management and information security strategies, risk, and information security decisions, and the creation inter-organizational and intra-organizational communication mechanisms. A centralized approach to governance requires strong, well-informed central leadership and provides consistency throughout the organization. Centralized governance structures also provide less autonomy for subordinate organizations that are part of the parent organization.

Decentralized Governance

In decentralized information security governance structures, the authority, responsibility, and decision-making power are vested in and delegated to individual subordinate organizations within the parent organization (e.g., bureaus/components within an executive department of the federal government or business units within a corporation). Subordinate organizations establish their own policies, procedures, and processes for ensuring (sub) organization-wide involvement in the development and implementation of risk management and information security strategies, risk and information security decisions, and the creation of mechanisms to communicate within the organization. A decentralized approach to information security governance accommodates subordinate organizations with divergent mission/business needs and operating environments at the cost of consistency throughout the organization as a whole. The effectiveness of this approach is greatly increased by the sharing of risk-related information among subordinate organizations so that no subordinate organization is able to transfer risk to another without the latter's informed consent. It is also important to share risk-related information with parent organizations as the risk decisions by subordinate organizations may have an effect on the organization as a whole.

Hybrid Governance

In hybrid information security governance structures, the authority, responsibility, and decision-making power are distributed between a central body and individual subordinate organizations. The central body establishes the policies, procedures, and processes for ensuring organization-wide involvement in the portion of the risk management and information security strategies and decisions affecting the entire organization (e.g., decisions related to shared infrastructure or common security services). Subordinate organizations, in a similar manner, establish appropriate policies, procedures, and processes for ensuring their involvement in the portion of the risk management and information security strategies and decisions that are specific to their mission/business needs and environments of operation. A hybrid approach to governance requires strong, well-informed leadership for the organization as a whole and for subordinate organizations, and provides consistency throughout the organization for those aspects of risk and information security that affect the entire organization.

APPENDIX G

TRUST MODELS

APPROACHES TO ESTABLISHING TRUST RELATIONSIPS

The following trust models describe ways in which organizations can obtain the levels of trust needed to form partnerships, collaborate with other organizations, share information, or receive information system/security services. No single trust model is inherently better than any other model. Rather, each model provides organizations with certain advantages and disadvantages based on their circumstances (e.g., governance structure, risk tolerance, and criticality/sensitivity of organizational missions and business processes).

Validated Trust

In the *validated trust model*, one organization obtains a body of evidence regarding the actions of another organization (e.g., the organization's information security policies, activities, and risk-related decisions) and uses that evidence to establish a level of trust with the other organization. An example of validated trust is where one organization develops an application or information system and provides evidence (e.g., security plan, assessment results) to a second organization that supports the claims by the first organization that the application/system meets certain security requirements and/or addresses the appropriate security controls in NIST Special Publication 800-53. Validated trust may not be sufficient—that is, the evidence offered by the first organization to the second organization may not fully satisfy the second organization's trust requirements or trust expectations. The more evidence provided between organizations as well as the quality of such evidence, the greater the degree of trust that can be achieved. Trust is linked to the degree of transparency between the two organizations with regard to risk and information security-related activities and decisions.

Direct Historical Trust

In the *direct historical trust model*, the track record exhibited by an organization in the past, particularly in its risk and information security-related activities and decisions, can contribute to and help establish a level of trust with other organizations. While validated trust models assume that an organization provides the required level of evidence needed to establish trust, obtaining such evidence may not always be possible. In such instances, trust may be based on other deciding factors, including the organization's historical relationship with the other organization or its recent experience in working with the other organization. For example, if one organization has worked with a second organization for years doing some activity and has not had any negative experiences, the first organization may be willing to trust the second organization in working on another activity, even though the organizations do not share any common experience for that particular activity. Direct historical trust tends to build up over time with the more positive experiences contributing to increased levels of trust between organizations. Conversely, negative experiences may cause trust levels to decrease among organizations.

Mediated Trust

In the *mediated trust model*, an organization establishes a level of trust with another organization based on assurances provided by some mutually trusted third party. There are several types of mediated trust models that can be employed. For example, two organizations attempting to establish a trust relationship may not have a direct trust history between the two organizations, but do have a trust relationship with a third organization. The third party that is trusted by both organizations, brokers the trust relationship between the two organizations, thus helping to establish the required level of trust. Another type of mediated trust involves the concept of transitivity of trust. In this example, one organization establishes a trust relationship with a second organization. Independent of the first trust relationship, the second organization establishes a trust relationship with a third organization. Since the first organization trusts the second organization and the second organization trusts the third organization, a trust relationship is now established between the first and third organizations (illustrating the concept of transitive trust among organizations).[77]

Mandated Trust

In the *mandated trust model*, an organization establishes a level of trust with another organization based on a specific mandate issued by a third party in a position of authority.[78] This mandate can be established by the respective authority through Executive Orders, directives, regulations, or policies (e.g., a memorandum from an agency head directing that all subordinate organizations accept the results of security assessments conducted by any subordinate organization within the agency). Mandated trust can also be established when some organizational entity is decreed to be the authoritative source for the provision of information resources including information technology products, systems, or services. For example, an organization may be given the responsibility and the authority to issue Public Key Infrastructure (PKI) certificates for a group of organizations.

Hybrid Trust

In general, the trust models described above are not mutually exclusive. Each of the trust models may be used independently as a stand-alone model or in conjunction with another model. Several trust models may be used at times within the organization (e.g., at various phases in the system development life cycle). Also, since organizations are often large and diverse, it is possible that subordinate organizations within a parent organization might independently employ different trust models in establishing trust relationships with potential partnering organizations (including subordinate organizations). The organizational governance structure may establish the specific terms and conditions for how the various trust models are employed in a complementary manner within the organization.

Suitability of Various Trust Models

The trust models can be employed at various tiers in the risk management approach described in this publication. None of the trust models is inherently better or worse than the others. However, some models may be better suited to some situations than others. For example, the validated trust model, because it requires evidence of a technical nature (e.g., tests completed successfully), is probably best suited for application at Tier 3. In contrast, the direct historical trust model, with a significant emphasis on past experiences, is more suited for application at Tiers 1 or 2. The mediated and mandated trust models are typically more oriented toward governance and consequently are best suited for application at Tier 1. However, some implementations of the mandated trust model, for example, being required to trust the source of a PKI certificate, are more oriented toward Tier 3. Similarly, although the mediated trust model is primarily oriented toward Tier 1, there can be implementations of it that are more information system-, or Tier 3-

---

[77] In the mediated trust model, the first organization typically has no insight into the nature of the trust relationship between the second and third organizations.

[78] The authoritative organization explicitly accepts the risks to be incurred by all organizations covered by the mandate and is accountable for the risk-related decisions imposed by the organization.

oriented. An example of this application might be the use of authentication services that validate the authenticity or identity of an information system component or service.

The nature of a particular information technology service can also impact the suitability and the applicability of the various trust models. The validated trust model is the more traditional model for validating the trust of an information technology product, system, or service. However, this trust model works best in situations where there is a degree of control between parties (e.g., a contract between the government and an external service provider) or where there is sufficient time to obtain and validate the evidence needed to establish a trust relationship. Validated trust is a suboptimal model for situations where the two parties are peers and/or where the trust decisions regarding shared/supplied services must occur quickly due to the very dynamic and rapid nature of the service being requested/provided (e.g., service-oriented architectures).

APPENDIX H

RISK RESPONSE STRATEGIES

FROM BOUNDARY PROTECTION TO AGILE DEFENSES

O rganizations develop *risk management strategies* as part of the risk framing step in the risk management process described in Chapter Three. The risk management strategies address how organizations intend to assess risk, respond to risk, and monitor risk— making explicit and transparent the risk perceptions that organizations routinely use in making both investment and operational decisions. As part of organizational risk management strategies, organizations also develop *risk response strategies*. The practical realities facing organizations today make risk response strategies essential—the realities of needing the mission/business effectiveness offered by information technology, the lack of trustworthiness in the technologies available, and the growing awareness by adversaries of the potential to achieve their objectives to cause harm by compromising organizational information systems and the environments in which those systems operate. Senior leaders/executives in modern organizations are faced with an almost intractable dilemma—that is, the information technologies needed for mission/business success may be the same technologies through which adversaries cause mission/business failure. The risk response strategies developed and implemented by organizations provide these senior leaders/executives (i.e., decision makers within organizations) with practical, pragmatic paths for dealing with this dilemma. Clearly defined and articulated risk response strategies help to ensure that senior leaders/executives take ownership of organizational risk responses and are ultimately *responsible* and *accountable* for risk decisions—understanding, acknowledging, and explicitly accepting the resulting mission/business risk.

As described in Chapter Two, there are five basic types of responses to risk: (i) accept; (ii) avoid; (iii) mitigate; (iv) share; and (v) transfer.[79] While each type of response can have an associated strategy, there should be an overall strategy for selecting from among the basic response types. This overall risk response strategy and a strategy for each type of response are discussed below. In addition, specific *risk mitigation strategies* are presented, including a description of how such strategies can be implemented within organizations.

H.1 OVERALL RISK RESPONSE STRATEGIES

Risk response strategies specify: (i) individuals or organizational subcomponents that are responsible for the selected risk response measures and specifications of effectiveness criteria (i.e., articulation of indicators and thresholds against which the effectiveness of risk response measures can be judged); (ii) dependencies of the selected risk response measures on other risk response measures; (iii) dependencies of selected risk response measures on other factors (e.g., implementation of other planned information technology measures); (iv) implementation timeline for risk responses; (v) plans for monitoring the effectiveness of the risk response measures; (vi) identification of risk monitoring triggers; and (vii) interim risk response measures selected for implementation, if appropriate. Risk response implementation strategies may include interim measures that organizations choose to implement. An overall risk response strategy provides an organizational approach to selecting between the basic risk responses for a given risk situation. A decision to *accept* risk must be consistent with the stated organizational tolerance for risk. Yet

---

[79] There is overlap between the basic risk responses. For example, a shared risk is one that is being accepted by each party in the sharing arrangement, and avoiding risk can be thought of as mitigating risk to zero. Nonetheless, with this understanding of overlap, there is value in addressing each of the five types of risk responses separately.

there is still need for a well-defined, established organizational path for selecting one or a combination of the risk responses of acceptance, avoidance, mitigation, sharing, or transfer. Organizations are often placed in situations where there is greater risk than the designated senior leaders/executives desire to accept. Some risk acceptance will likely be necessary. It might be possible to avoid risk or to share or transfer risk, and some risk mitigation is probably feasible. Avoiding risk may require selective reengineering of organizational mission/business processes and forgoing some of the benefits being accrued by the use of information technology organization-wide, perhaps even what organizations perceive as *necessary* benefits. Mitigating risk requires expenditure of limited resources and may quickly become cost-ineffective due to the pragmatic realities of the degree of mitigation that can actually be achieved. Lastly, risk sharing and transfer have ramifications as well, some of which if not unacceptable, may be undesirable. The risk response strategies of organizations empower senior leaders/executives to make risk-based decisions compliant with the goals, objectives, and broader organizational perspectives.

H.2 RISK ACCEPTANCE STRATEGIES

Organizational *risk acceptance strategies* are essential companions to organizational statements of risk tolerance. The objective of establishing an organizational risk tolerance is to state in clear and unambiguous terms, a limit for risk—that is, how far organizations are willing to go with regard to accepting risk to organizational operations (including missions, functions, image, and reputation), organizational assets, individuals, other organizations, and the Nation. Real-world operations, however, are seldom so simple as to make such risk tolerance statements the end-statement for risk acceptance decisions. Organizational risk acceptance strategies place the acceptance of risk into a framework of organizational perspectives on dealing with the practical realities of operating with risk and provide the guidance necessary to ensure that the extent of the risk being accepted in specific situations is compliant with organizational direction.

H.3 RISK AVOIDANCE STRATEGIES

Of all the risk response strategies, organizational *risk avoidance strategies* may be the key to achieving adequate risk response. The pragmatic realities of the trustworthiness of information technologies available for use within common resource constraints, make wise use of those technologies arguably a significant, if not *the* most significant risk response. Wise use of the information technologies that compose organizational information systems is fundamentally a form of risk avoidance—that is, organizations modify how information technologies are used to change the nature of the risk being incurred (i.e., avoid the risk). Yet such approaches can be in great tension with organizational desires and in some cases, the mandate to fully automate mission/business processes. Organizations proactively address this dilemma so that: (i) senior leaders/executives (and other organizational officials making risk-based decisions) are held accountable for only that which is within their ability to affect; and (ii) decision makers can make the difficult risk decisions that may, in fact, be in the best interests of organizations.

H.4 RISK SHARING AND TRANSFER STRATEGIES

Organizational *risk sharing strategies* and *risk transfer strategies* are key elements in enabling risk decisions for specific organizational missions/business functions at Tier 2 or organizational information systems at Tier 3. Risk sharing and transfer strategies both consider and take full advantage of a lessening of risk by sharing/transferring the potential impact across other internal organizational elements or with other external organizations—making the case that some other entities are, in fact, wholly (transfer) or partly (share) responsible and accountable for risk. For risk sharing or risk transfer to be effective risk responses, the impact on the local environment (e.g., mission/business processes or information systems) must be addressed by the sharing or transfer (i.e., the focus must be on mission/business success, not assigning blame). In addition, risk sharing and risk transfer activities must be carried out in accordance with intra- and inter-organizational dynamics and realities (e.g., organizational culture, governance, risk tolerance). This explains why risk sharing/transfer strategies are particularly important for the sharing and/or transfer to be a viable risk response option.

H.5 RISK MITIGATION STRATEGIES

Organizational *risk mitigation strategies* reflect an organizational perspective on what mitigations are to be employed and where the mitigations are to be applied, to reduce information security risks to organizational operations and assets, individuals, other organizations, and the Nation. Risk mitigation strategies are the primary link between organizational risk management programs and information security programs—with the former covering all aspects of managing risk and the latter being primarily a part of the risk response component of the risk management process. Effective *risk mitigation strategies* consider the general placement and allocation of mitigations, the degree of intended mitigation, and cover mitigations at Tier 1 (e.g., common controls), at Tier 2 (e.g., enterprise architecture including embedded information security architecture, and risk-aware mission/business processes), and at Tier 3 (security controls in individual information systems). Organizational risk mitigation strategies reflect the following:

- Mission/business processes are designed with regard to information protection needs and information security requirements;[80]

- Enterprise architectures (including embedded information security architectures) are designed with consideration for realistically achievable risk mitigations;

- Risk mitigation measures are implemented within organizational information systems and environments of operation by safeguards/countermeasure (i.e., security controls) consistent with information security architectures; and

- Information security programs, processes, and safeguards/countermeasures are highly *flexible* and *agile* with regard to implementation, recognizing the diversity in organizational missions and business functions and the dynamic environments in which the organizations operate.[81]

Organizations develop risk mitigation strategies based on strategic goals and objectives, mission and business requirements, and organizational priorities. The strategies provide the basis for making risk-based decisions on the information security solutions associated with and applied to information systems within the organization. Risk mitigation strategies are necessary to ensure that organizations are adequately protected against the growing threats to information processed, stored, and transmitted by organizational information systems. The nature of the threats and the dynamic environments in which organizations operate, demand flexible and scalable defenses as well as solutions that can be tailored to meet rapidly changing conditions. These conditions include, for example, the emergence of new threats and vulnerabilities, the development of new technologies, changes in missions/business requirements, and/or changes to environments of operation. Effective risk mitigation strategies support the goals and objectives of organizations and established mission/business priorities, are tightly coupled to enterprise architectures and information security architectures, and can operate throughout the system development life cycle.

---

[80] In addition to mission/business-driven information protection needs, information security requirements are obtained from a variety of sources (e.g., federal legislation, policies, directives, regulations, and standards).

[81] Dynamic environments of operation are characterized, for example, by ongoing changes in people, processes, technologies, physical infrastructure, and threats.

Traditional risk mitigation strategies with regard to threats from cyber attacks at first relied almost exclusively on monolithic *boundary protection*. These strategies assumed adversaries were outside of some established defensive perimeter, and the objective of organizations was to repel the attack. The primary focus of static boundary protection was penetration resistance of the information technology products and information systems employed by the organization as well as any additional safeguards and countermeasures implemented in the environments in which the products and systems operated. Recognition that information system boundaries were permeable or porous led to defense-in-depth as part of the mitigation strategy, relying on detection and response mechanisms to address the threats within the protection perimeter. In today's world characterized by *advanced persistent threats*,[82] a more comprehensive risk mitigation strategy is needed—a strategy that combines traditional boundary protection with *agile defense*.

Agile defense assumes that a small percentage of threats from purposeful cyber attacks will be successful by compromising organizational information systems through the supply chain[83] by defeating the initial safeguards and countermeasures (i.e., security controls) implemented by organizations, or by exploiting previously unidentified vulnerabilities for which protections are not in place. In this scenario, adversaries are operating inside the defensive perimeters established by organizations and may have substantial or complete control of organizational information systems. Agile defense employs the concept of *information system resilience*—that is, the ability of systems to operate while under attack, even in a degraded or debilitated state, and to rapidly recover operational capabilities for essential functions after a successful attack. The concept of information system resilience can also be applied to the other classes of threats including threats from environmental disruptions and/or human errors of omission/commission. The most effective risk mitigation strategies employ a combination of boundary protection and agile defenses depending on the characteristics of the threat.[84] This dual protection strategy illustrates two important information security concepts known as defense-in-depth[85] and defense-in-breadth.[86]

> *Information has value and must be protected. Information systems (including people, processes, and technologies) are the primary vehicles employed to process, store, and transmit such information— allowing organizations to carry out their missions in a variety of environments of operation and to ultimately be successful.*

---

[82] An *advanced persistent threat* is an adversary that possesses sophisticated levels of expertise and significant resources which allow it to create opportunities to achieve its objectives by using multiple attack vectors (e.g., cyber, physical, and deception). These objectives typically include establishing/extending footholds within the information technology infrastructure of the targeted organizations for purposes of exfiltrating information, undermining or impeding critical aspects of a mission, program, or organization; or positioning itself to carry out these objectives in the future. The advanced persistent threat: (i) pursues its objectives repeatedly over an extended period of time; (ii) adapts to defenders' efforts to resist it; and (iii) is determined to maintain the level of interaction needed to execute its objectives.

[83] Draft NIST Interagency Report 7622 provides guidance on managing supply chain risk.

[84] Threat characteristics include capabilities, intentions, and targeting information.

[85] *Defense-in-depth* is an information security strategy integrating people, technology, and operations capabilities to establish variable barriers across multiple layers and missions of the organization.

[86] *Defense-in-breadth* is a planned, systematic set of multidisciplinary activities that seek to identify, manage, and reduce risk of exploitable vulnerabilities at every stage of the system, network, or subcomponent life cycle (system, network, or product design and development; manufacturing; packaging; assembly; system integration; distribution; operations; maintenance; and retirement).

NIST Special Publication 800-30
Revision 1

Guide for Conducting
Risk Assessments

NIST

**National Institute of
Standards and Technology**

U.S. Department of Commerce

**JOINT TASK FORCE
TRANSFORMATION INITIATIVE**

INFORMATION   SECURITY

Computer Security Division
Information Technology Laboratory
National Institute of Standards and Technology
Gaithersburg, MD 20899-8930

September 2012

U.S. Department of Commerce
Rebecca M. Blank, Acting Secretary

National Institute of Standards and Technology
*Patrick D. Gallagher, Under Secretary for Standards and Technology
and Director*

Reports on Computer Systems Technology

The Information Technology Laboratory (ITL) at the National Institute of Standards and Technology (NIST) promotes the U.S. economy and public welfare by providing technical leadership for the nation's measurement and standards infrastructure. ITL develops tests, test methods, reference data, proof of concept implementations, and technical analyses to advance the development and productive use of information technology. ITL's responsibilities include the development of management, administrative, technical, and physical standards and guidelines for the cost-effective security and privacy of other than national security-related information in federal information systems. The Special Publication 800-series reports on ITL's research, guidelines, and outreach efforts in information system security, and its collaborative activities with industry, government, and academic organizations.

Authority

This publication has been developed by NIST to further its statutory responsibilities under the Federal Information Security Management Act (FISMA), Public Law (P.L.) 107-347. NIST is responsible for developing information security standards and guidelines, including minimum requirements for federal information systems, but such standards and guidelines shall not apply to national security systems without the express approval of appropriate federal officials exercising policy authority over such systems. This guideline is consistent with the requirements of the Office of Management and Budget (OMB) Circular A-130, Section 8b(3), *Securing Agency Information Systems*, as analyzed in Circular A-130, Appendix IV: *Analysis of Key Sections*. Supplemental information is provided in Circular A-130, Appendix III, *Security of Federal Automated Information Resources*.

Nothing in this publication should be taken to contradict the standards and guidelines made mandatory and binding on federal agencies by the Secretary of Commerce under statutory authority. Nor should these guidelines be interpreted as altering or superseding the existing authorities of the Secretary of Commerce, Director of the OMB, or any other federal official. This publication may be used by nongovernmental organizations on a voluntary basis and is not subject to copyright in the United States. Attribution would, however, be appreciated by NIST.

NIST Special Publication 800-30, 95 pages

(September 2012)

CODEN: NSPUE2

Comments on this publication may be submitted to:

National Institute of Standards and Technology
Attn: Computer Security Division, Information Technology Laboratory
100 Bureau Drive (Mail Stop 8930) Gaithersburg, MD 20899-8930
Electronic mail: sec-cert@nist.gov

PAGE iii

Compliance with NIST Standards and Guidelines

In accordance with the provisions of FISMA,[1] the Secretary of Commerce shall, on the basis of standards and guidelines developed by NIST, prescribe standards and guidelines pertaining to federal information systems. The Secretary shall make standards compulsory and binding to the extent determined necessary by the Secretary to improve the efficiency of operation or security of federal information systems. Standards prescribed shall include information security standards that provide minimum information security requirements and are otherwise necessary to improve the security of federal information and information systems.

- Federal Information Processing Standards (FIPS) are approved by the Secretary of Commerce and issued by NIST in accordance with FISMA. FIPS are compulsory and binding for federal agencies.[2] FISMA requires that federal agencies comply with these standards, and therefore, agencies may not waive their use.

- Special Publications (SPs) are developed and issued by NIST as recommendations and guidance documents. For other than national security programs and systems, federal agencies must follow those NIST Special Publications mandated in a Federal Information Processing Standard. FIPS 200 mandates the use of Special Publication 800-53, as amended. In addition, OMB policies (including OMB Reporting Instructions for FISMA and Agency Privacy Management) state that for other than national security programs and systems, federal agencies must follow certain specific NIST Special Publications.[3]

- Other security-related publications, including interagency reports (NISTIRs) and ITL Bulletins, provide technical and other information about NIST's activities. These publications are mandatory only when specified by OMB.

- Compliance schedules for NIST security standards and guidelines are established by OMB in policies, directives, or memoranda (e.g., annual FISMA Reporting Guidance).[4]

---

[1] The E-Government Act (P.L. 107-347) recognizes the importance of information security to the economic and national security interests of the United States. Title III of the E-Government Act, entitled the Federal Information Security Management Act (FISMA), emphasizes the need for organizations to develop, document, and implement an organization-wide program to provide security for the information systems that support its operations and assets.

[2] The term *agency* is used in this publication in lieu of the more general term *organization* only in those circumstances where its usage is directly related to other source documents such as federal legislation or policy.

[3] While federal agencies are required to follow certain specific NIST Special Publications in accordance with OMB policy, there is flexibility in how agencies apply the guidance. Federal agencies apply the security concepts and principles articulated in the NIST Special Publications in accordance with and in the context of the agency's missions, business functions, and environment of operation. Consequently, the application of NIST guidance by federal agencies can result in different security solutions that are equally acceptable, compliant with the guidance, and meet the OMB definition of *adequate security* for federal information systems. Given the high priority of information sharing and transparency within the federal government, agencies also consider reciprocity in developing their information security solutions. When assessing federal agency compliance with NIST Special Publications, Inspectors General, evaluators, auditors, and assessors consider the intent of the security concepts and principles articulated within the specific guidance document and how the agency applied the guidance in the context of its mission/business responsibilities, operational environment, and unique organizational conditions.

[4] Unless otherwise stated, all references to NIST publications in this document (i.e., Federal Information Processing Standards and Special Publications) are to the most recent version of the publication.

Acknowledgements

This publication was developed by the *Joint Task Force Transformation Initiative* Interagency Working Group with representatives from the Civil, Defense, and Intelligence Communities in an ongoing effort to produce a unified information security framework for the federal government. The National Institute of Standards and Technology wishes to acknowledge and thank the senior leaders from the Departments of Commerce and Defense, the Office of the Director of National Intelligence, the Committee on National Security Systems, and the members of the interagency technical working group whose dedicated efforts contributed significantly to the publication. The senior leaders, interagency working group members, and their organizational affiliations include:

Department of Defense

Teresa M. Takai
DoD Chief Information Officer

Richard Hale
Deputy Chief Information Officer for Cybersecurity

Paul Grant
Director, Cybersecurity Policy

Dominic Cussatt
Deputy Director, Cybersecurity Policy

Kurt Eleam
Policy Advisor

National Institute of Standards and Technology

Charles H. Romine
Director, Information Technology Laboratory

Donna Dodson
Cybersecurity Advisor, Information Technology Laboratory

Donna Dodson
Chief, Computer Security Division

Ron Ross
FISMA Implementation Project Leader

Office of the Director of National Intelligence

Adolpho Tarasiuk Jr.
Assistant DNI and Intelligence Community Chief Information Officer

Charlene Leubecker
Deputy Intelligence Community Chief Information Officer

Catherine A. Henson
Director, Data Management

Greg Hall
Chief, Risk Management and Information Security Programs Division

Committee on National Security Systems

Teresa M. Takai
Chair, CNSS

Richard Spires
Co-Chair, CNSS

Dominic Cussatt
CNSS Subcommittee Co-Chair

Jeffrey Wilk
CNSS Subcommittee Co-Chair

Joint Task Force Transformation Initiative Interagency Working Group

Ron Ross *NIST, JTF Leader*	Gary Stoneburner *Johns Hopkins APL*	Jennifer Fabius *The MITRE Corporation*	Kelley Dempsey *NIST*
Deborah Bodeau *The MITRE Corporation*	Steve Rodrigo *Tenacity Solutions, Inc.*	Peter Gouldmann *Department of State*	Arnold Johnson *NIST*
Peter Williams *Booz Allen Hamilton*	Karen Quigg *The MITRE Corporation*	Christina Sames *TASC*	Christian Enloe *NIST*

In addition to the above acknowledgments, a special note of thanks goes to Peggy Himes and Elizabeth Lennon of NIST for their superb technical editing and administrative support. The authors also gratefully acknowledge and appreciate the significant contributions from individuals and organizations in the public and private sectors, both nationally and internationally, whose thoughtful and constructive comments improved the overall quality, thoroughness, and usefulness of this publication.

Guide for Conducting Risk Assessments (800-30 rev 1)

DEVELOPING COMMON INFORMATION SECURITY FOUNDATIONS

COLLABORATION AMONG PUBLIC AND PRIVATE SECTOR ENTITIES

In developing standards and guidelines required by FISMA, NIST consults with other federal agencies and offices as well as the private sector to improve information security, avoid unnecessary and costly duplication of effort, and ensure that NIST publications are complementary with the standards and guidelines employed for the protection of national security systems. In addition to its comprehensive public review and vetting process, NIST is collaborating with the Office of the Director of National Intelligence (ODNI), the Department of Defense (DoD), and the Committee on National Security Systems (CNSS) to establish a common foundation for information security across the federal government. A common foundation for information security will provide the Intelligence, Defense, and Civil sectors of the federal government and their contractors, more uniform and consistent ways to manage the risk to organizational operations and assets, individuals, other organizations, and the Nation that results from the operation and use of information systems. A common foundation for information security will also provide a strong basis for reciprocal acceptance of security authorization decisions and facilitate information sharing. NIST is also working with public and private sector entities to establish specific mappings and relationships between the security standards and guidelines developed by NIST and the International Organization for Standardization and International Electrotechnical Commission (ISO/IEC).

Table of Contents

Prologue

"... Through the process of risk management, leaders must consider risk to U.S. interests from adversaries using cyberspace to their advantage and from our own efforts to employ the global nature of cyberspace to achieve objectives in military, intelligence, and business operations..."

"... For operational plans development, the combination of threats, vulnerabilities, and impacts must be evaluated in order to identify important trends and decide where effort should be applied to eliminate or reduce threat capabilities; eliminate or reduce vulnerabilities; and assess, coordinate, and deconflict all cyberspace operations..."

"... Leaders at all levels are accountable for ensuring readiness and security to the same degree as in any other domain..."

-- THE NATIONAL STRATEGY FOR CYBERSPACE OPERATIONS
   OFFICE OF THE CHAIRMAN, JOINT CHIEFS OF STAFF, U.S. DEPARTMENT OF DEFENSE

CAUTIONARY NOTES

SCOPE AND APPLICABILITY OF RISK ASSESSMENTS

- Risk assessments are a key part of effective risk management and facilitate decision making at all three tiers in the risk management hierarchy including the organization level, mission/business process level, and information system level.

- Because risk management is ongoing, risk assessments are conducted throughout the system development life cycle, from pre-system acquisition (i.e., material solution analysis and technology development), through system acquisition (i.e., engineering/manufacturing development and production/deployment), and on into sustainment (i.e., operations/support).

- There are no specific requirements with regard to: (i) the formality, rigor, or level of detail that characterizes any particular risk assessment; (ii) the methodologies, tools, and techniques used to conduct such risk assessments; or (iii) the format and content of assessment results and any associated reporting mechanisms. Organizations have maximum flexibility on how risk assessments are conducted and are encouraged to apply the guidance in this document so that the various needs of organizations can be addressed and the risk assessment activities can be integrated into broader organizational risk management processes.

- Organizations are also cautioned that risk assessments are often not precise instruments of measurement and reflect: (i) the limitations of the specific assessment methodologies, tools, and techniques employed; (ii) the subjectivity, quality, and trustworthiness of the data used; (iii) the interpretation of assessment results; and (iv) the skills and expertise of those individuals or groups conducting the assessments.

- Since cost, timeliness, and ease of use are a few of the many important factors in the application of risk assessments, organizations should attempt to reduce the level of effort for risk assessments by sharing risk-related information, whenever possible.

CHAPTER ONE

INTRODUCTION

THE NEED FOR RISK ASSESSMENTS TO SUPPORT ENTERPRISE-WIDE RISK MANAGEMENT

Organizations[5] in the public and private sectors depend on information technology[6] and information systems[7] to successfully carry out their missions and business functions. Information systems can include very diverse entities ranging from office networks, financial and personnel systems to very specialized systems (e.g., industrial/process control systems, weapons systems, telecommunications systems, and environmental control systems). Information systems are subject to serious *threats* that can have adverse effects on organizational operations and assets, individuals, other organizations, and the Nation by exploiting both known and unknown *vulnerabilities* to compromise the confidentiality, integrity, or availability of the information being processed, stored, or transmitted by those systems. Threats to information systems can include purposeful attacks, environmental disruptions, human/machine errors, and structural failures, and can result in harm to the national and economic security interests of the United States. Therefore, it is imperative that leaders and managers at all levels understand their responsibilities and are held accountable for managing information security risk—that is, the risk associated with the operation and use of information systems that support the missions and business functions of their organizations.

Risk assessment is one of the fundamental components of an organizational risk management process as described in NIST Special Publication 800-39. Risk assessments are used to identify, estimate, and prioritize risk to organizational operations (i.e., mission, functions, image, and reputation), organizational assets, individuals, other organizations, and the Nation, resulting from the operation and use of information systems. The purpose of risk assessments is to inform decision makers and support risk responses by identifying: (i) relevant threats to organizations or threats directed through organizations against other organizations; (ii) vulnerabilities both internal and external to organizations; (iii) impact (i.e., harm) to organizations that may occur given the potential for threats exploiting vulnerabilities; and (iv) likelihood that harm will occur. The end result is a determination of risk (i.e., typically a function of the degree of harm and likelihood of harm occurring). Risk assessments can be conducted at all three tiers in the risk management hierarchy—including Tier 1 (organization level), Tier 2 (mission/business process level), and Tier 3 (information system level). At Tiers 1 and 2, organizations use risk assessments to evaluate, for example, systemic information security-related risks associated with organizational governance and management activities, mission/business processes, enterprise architecture, or the funding of information security programs. At Tier 3, organizations use risk assessments to more effectively support the implementation of the *Risk Management Framework* (i.e., security categorization; security control selection, implementation, and assessment; information system and common control authorization; and security control monitoring).[8]

---

[5] The term *organization* describes an entity of any size, complexity, or positioning within an organizational structure (e.g., a federal agency or, as appropriate, any of its operational elements) that is charged with carrying out assigned mission/business processes and that uses information systems in support of those processes.

[6] Organizations also manage information technology in the form of common infrastructures, sets of shared services, and sets of common controls.

[7] An *information system* is a discrete set of information resources organized for the collection, processing, maintenance, use, sharing, dissemination, or disposition of information.

[8] The Risk Management Framework is described in NIST Special Publication 800-37.

1.1 PURPOSE AND APPLICABILITY

The purpose of Special Publication 800-30 is to provide guidance for conducting risk assessments of federal information systems and organizations, amplifying the guidance in Special Publication 800-39. Risk assessments, carried out at all three tiers in the risk management hierarchy, are part of an overall risk management process—providing senior leaders/executives with the information needed to determine appropriate courses of action in response to identified risks. In particular, this document provides guidance for carrying out each of the steps in the *risk assessment process* (i.e., preparing for the assessment, conducting the assessment, communicating the results of the assessment, and maintaining the assessment) and how risk assessments and other organizational risk management processes complement and inform each other. Special Publication 800-30 also provides guidance to organizations on identifying specific risk factors to monitor on an ongoing basis, so that organizations can determine whether risks have increased to unacceptable levels (i.e., exceeding organizational risk tolerance) and different courses of action should be taken.

This publication satisfies the requirements of FISMA and meets or exceeds the information security requirements established for executive agencies[9] by the Office of Management and Budget (OMB) in Circular A-130, Appendix III, *Security of Federal Automated Information Resources*. The guidelines in this publication are applicable to all federal information systems other than those systems designated as national security systems as defined in 44 U.S.C., Section 3542. The guidelines have been broadly developed from a technical perspective to complement similar guidelines for national security systems and may be used for such systems with the approval of appropriate federal officials exercising policy authority over such systems. State, local, and tribal governments, as well as private sector organizations are encouraged to consider using these guidelines, as appropriate.

1.2 TARGET AUDIENCE

This publication is intended to serve a diverse group of risk management professionals including:

- Individuals with oversight responsibilities for risk management (e.g., heads of agencies, chief executive officers, chief operating officers, risk executive [function]);

- Individuals with responsibilities for conducting organizational missions/business functions (e.g., mission/business owners, information owners/stewards, authorizing officials);

- Individuals with responsibilities for acquiring information technology products, services, or information systems (e.g., acquisition officials, procurement officers, contracting officers);

- Individuals with information system/security design, development, and implementation responsibilities (e.g., program managers, enterprise architects, information security architects, information system/security engineers, information systems integrators);

- Individuals with information security oversight, management, and operational responsibilities (e.g., chief information officers, senior information security officers,[10] information security managers, information system owners, common control providers); and

---

[9] An *executive agency* is: (i) an executive department specified in 5 U.S.C., Section 101; (ii) a military department specified in 5 U.S.C., Section 102; (iii) an independent establishment as defined in 5 U.S.C., Section 104(1); and (iv) a wholly owned government corporation fully subject to the provisions of 31 U.S.C., Chapter 91. In this publication, the term *executive agency* is synonymous with the term *federal agency*.

[10] At the *agency* level, this position is known as the Senior Agency Information Security Officer. Organizations may also refer to this position as the *Chief Information Security Officer*.

- Individuals with information security/risk assessment and monitoring responsibilities (e.g., system evaluators, penetration testers, security control assessors, risk assessors, independent verifiers/validators, inspectors general, auditors).

1.3 RELATED PUBLICATIONS

The risk assessment approach described in this publication is supported by a series of security standards and guidelines necessary for managing information security risk. In addition to this publication, the Special Publications developed by the Joint Task Force Transformation Initiative supporting the unified information security framework for the federal government include:

- Special Publication 800-39, *Managing Information Security Risk: Organization, Mission, and Information System View*;[11]

- Special Publication 800-37, *Guide for Applying the Risk Management Framework to Federal Information Systems: A Security Life Cycle Approach*;

- Special Publication 800-53, *Recommended Security Controls for Federal Information Systems and Organizations*; and

- Special Publication 800-53A, *Guide for Assessing the Security Controls in Federal Information Systems and Organizations: Building Effective Security Assessment Plans*.

The concepts and principles associated with the risk assessment processes and approaches contained in this publication are intended to be similar to and consistent with the processes and approaches described in International Organization for Standardization (ISO) and International Electrotechnical Commission (IEC) standards. Extending the concepts and principles of these international standards for the federal government and its contractors and promoting the reuse of risk assessment results, reduces the burden on organizations that must conform to ISO/IEC and NIST standards.

1.4 ORGANIZATION OF THIS SPECIAL PUBLICATION

The remainder of this special publication is organized as follows:

- **Chapter Two** describes: (i) the risk management process and how risk assessments are an integral part of that process; (ii) the basic terminology used in conducting risk assessments; and (iii) how risk assessments can be applied across the organization's risk management tiers (i.e., organization level, mission/business process level, and information system level).

- **Chapter Three** describes the process of assessing information security risk including: (i) a high-level overview of the risk assessment process; (ii) the activities necessary to prepare for a risk assessment; (iii) the activities necessary to conduct a risk assessment; (iv) the activities necessary to communicate risk assessment results and share risk-related information across the organization; and (v) the activities necessary to maintain the results of a risk assessment.

- **Supporting appendices** provide additional risk assessment information including: (i) general references; (ii) a glossary of terms; (iii) acronyms; (iv) threat sources; (v) threat events; (vi) vulnerabilities and predisposing conditions; (vii) likelihood of threat event occurrence; (viii) organizational impact; (ix) risk determination; (x) informing risk response; (xi) essential information for risk assessment reports; and (xii) a summary of risk assessment tasks.

---

[11] Special Publication 800-39 supersedes Special Publication 800-30 as the primary source for guidance on information security risk management.

CHAPTER TWO

THE FUNDAMENTALS

BASIC CONCEPTS ASSOCIATED WITH RISK ASSESSMENTS

This chapter describes the fundamental concepts associated with assessing information security risk within an organization including: (i) a high-level overview of the risk management process and the role risk assessments play in that process; (ii) the basic concepts used in conducting risk assessments; and (iii) how risk assessments can be applied across the organization's risk management tiers.[12]

2.1 RISK MANAGEMENT PROCESS

Risk assessment is a key component of a holistic, organization-wide *risk management process* as defined in NIST Special Publication 800-39, *Managing Information Security Risk: Organization, Mission, and Information System View*. Risk management processes include: (i) framing risk; (ii) assessing risk; (iii) responding to risk; and (iv) monitoring risk. Figure 1 illustrates the four steps in the risk management process—including the risk assessment step and the information and communications flows necessary to make the process work effectively.[13]

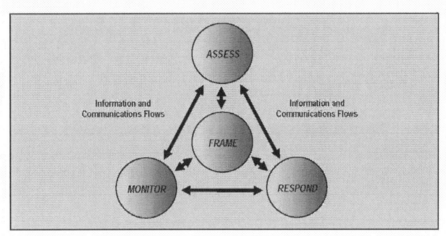

FIGURE 1: RISK ASSESSMENT WITHIN THE RISK MANAGEMENT PROCESS

The first component of risk management addresses how organizations *frame* risk or establish a risk context—that is, describing the environment in which risk-based decisions are made. The purpose of the risk framing component is to produce a *risk management strategy* that addresses how organizations intend to assess risk, respond to risk, and monitor risk—making explicit and

---

[12] NIST Special Publication 800-39 provides guidance on the three tiers in the risk management hierarchy including Tier 1 (organization), Tier 2 (mission/business process), and Tier 3 (information system).

[13] Many of the outputs from the risk framing step provide essential inputs to the risk assessment step and the associated risk assessment process. These include, for example, the risk management strategy, organizational risk tolerance, risk assessment methodology, assumptions, constraints, and mission/business priorities.

transparent the risk perceptions that organizations routinely use in making both investment and operational decisions. The risk management strategy establishes a foundation for managing risk and delineates the boundaries for risk-based decisions within organizations.[14]

The second component of risk management addresses how organizations *assess* risk within the context of the organizational risk frame. The purpose of the risk assessment component is to identify: (i) threats to organizations (i.e., operations, assets, or individuals) or threats directed through organizations against other organizations or the Nation; (ii) vulnerabilities internal and external to organizations;[15] (iii) the harm (i.e., adverse impact) that may occur given the potential for threats exploiting vulnerabilities; and (iv) the likelihood that harm will occur. The end result is a determination of risk (i.e., typically a function of the degree of harm and likelihood of harm occurring).

The third component of risk management addresses how organizations *respond* to risk once that risk is determined based on the results of a risk assessment. The purpose of the risk response component is to provide a consistent, organization-wide response to risk in accordance with the organizational risk frame by: (i) developing alternative courses of action for responding to risk; (ii) evaluating the alternative courses of action; (iii) determining appropriate courses of action consistent with organizational risk tolerance; and (iv) implementing risk responses based on selected courses of action.

The fourth component of risk management addresses how organizations *monitor* risk over time. The purpose of the risk monitoring component is to: (i) determine the ongoing effectiveness of risk responses (consistent with the organizational risk frame); (ii) identify risk-impacting changes to organizational information systems and the environments in which the systems operate;[16] and (iii) verify that planned risk responses are implemented and information security requirements derived from and traceable to organizational missions/business functions, federal legislation, directives, regulations, policies, standards, and guidelines are satisfied.

2.2 RISK ASSESSMENT

This publication focuses on the risk assessment component of risk management—providing a step-by-step process for organizations on: (i) how to prepare for risk assessments; (ii) how to conduct risk assessments; (iii) how to communicate risk assessment results to key organizational personnel; and (iv) how to maintain the risk assessments over time. Risk assessments are not simply one-time activities that provide permanent and definitive information for decision makers to guide and inform responses to information security risks. Rather, organizations employ risk assessments on an ongoing basis throughout the system development life cycle and across all of the tiers in the risk management hierarchy—with the frequency of the risk assessments and the resources applied during the assessments, commensurate with the expressly defined purpose and scope of the assessments.

---

[14] In the absence of an explicit or formal organizational risk management strategy, organizational resources (e.g., tools, data repositories) and references (e.g., exemplary risk assessment reports) can be used to discern those aspects of the organization's approach to risk management that affect risk assessment.

[15] Organizational vulnerabilities are not confined to information systems but can include, for example, vulnerabilities in governance structures, mission/business processes, enterprise architecture, information security architecture, facilities, equipment, system development life cycle processes, supply chain activities, and external service providers.

[16] Environments of operation include, but are not limited to: the threat space; vulnerabilities; missions/business functions; mission/business processes; enterprise and information security architectures; information technologies; personnel; facilities; supply chain relationships; organizational governance/culture; procurement/acquisition processes; organizational policies/procedures; organizational assumptions, constraints, risk tolerance, and priorities/trade-offs).

Risk assessments address the potential adverse impacts to organizational operations and assets, individuals, other organizations, and the economic and national security interests of the United States, arising from the operation and use of information systems and the information processed, stored, and transmitted by those systems. Organizations conduct risk assessments to determine risks that are common to the organization's core missions/business functions, mission/business processes, mission/business segments, common infrastructure/support services, or information systems. Risk assessments can support a wide variety of risk-based decisions and activities by organizational officials across all three tiers in the risk management hierarchy including, but not limited to, the following:

- Development of an information security architecture;

- Definition of interconnection requirements for information systems (including systems supporting mission/business processes and common infrastructure/support services);

- Design of security solutions for information systems and environments of operation including selection of security controls, information technology products, suppliers/supply chain, and contractors;

- Authorization (or denial of authorization) to operate information systems or to use security controls inherited by those systems (i.e., common controls);

- Modification of missions/business functions and/or mission/business processes permanently, or for a specific time frame (e.g., until a newly discovered threat or vulnerability is addressed, until a compensating control is replaced);

- Implementation of security solutions (e.g., whether specific information technology products or configurations for those products meet established requirements); and

- Operation and maintenance of security solutions (e.g., continuous monitoring strategies and programs, ongoing authorizations).

Because organizational missions and business functions, supporting mission/business processes, information systems, threats, and environments of operation tend to change over time, the validity and usefulness of any risk assessment is bounded in time.

2.3 KEY RISK CONCEPTS

Risk is a measure of the extent to which an entity is threatened by a potential circumstance or event, and is typically a function of: (i) the adverse impacts that would arise if the circumstance or event occurs; and (ii) the likelihood of occurrence. Information security risks are those risks that arise from the loss of confidentiality, integrity, or availability of information or information systems and reflect the potential adverse impacts to organizational operations (i.e., mission, functions, image, or reputation), organizational assets, individuals, other organizations, and the Nation. *Risk assessment* is the process of identifying, estimating, and prioritizing information security risks. Assessing risk requires the careful analysis of threat and vulnerability information to determine the extent to which circumstances or events could adversely impact an organization and the likelihood that such circumstances or events will occur.

A *risk assessment methodology* typically includes: (i) a risk assessment process (as described in Chapter Three); (ii) an explicit *risk model*, defining key terms and assessable risk factors and the relationships among the factors; (iii) an *assessment approach* (e.g., quantitative, qualitative, or semi-qualitative), specifying the range of values those risk factors can assume during the risk assessment and how combinations of risk factors are identified/analyzed so that values of those factors can be functionally combined to evaluate risk; and (iv) an *analysis approach* (e.g., threat-oriented, asset/impact-oriented, or vulnerability-oriented), describing how combinations of risk factors are identified/analyzed to ensure adequate coverage of the problem space at a consistent level of detail. Risk assessment methodologies are defined by organizations and are a component of the risk management strategy developed during the risk framing step of the risk management process.[17] Figure 2 illustrates the fundamental components in organizational risk frames and the relationships among those components.

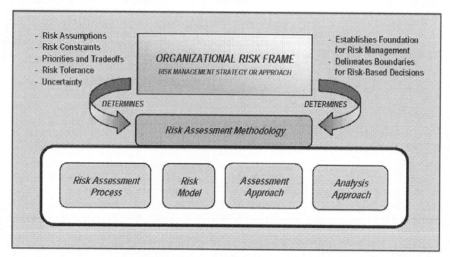

FIGURE 2: RELATIONSHIP AMONG RISK FRAMING COMPONENTS

Organizations can use a single risk assessment methodology or can employ multiple assessment methodologies, with the selection of a specific methodology depending on, for example: (i) the time frame for investment planning or for planning policy changes; (ii) the complexity/maturity of organizational mission/business processes (by enterprise architecture segments); (iii) the phase of the information systems in the system development life cycle; or (iv) the criticality/sensitivity[18] of the information and information systems supporting the core organizational missions/business functions. By making explicit the risk model, the assessment approach, and the analysis approach employed, and requiring as part of the assessment process, a rationale for the assessed values of risk factors, organizations can increase the *reproducibility* and *repeatability* of risk assessments.[19]

---

[17] Risk assessment methodologies are influenced in large measure by the organizational risk management strategy. However, risk assessment methodologies can be customized for each risk assessment based on the purpose and scope of the assessment and the specific inputs organizations choose to make regarding the risk assessment process, risk model, assessment approach, and analysis approach.

[18] NIST Special Publication 800-60 discusses the concepts of *criticality* and *sensitivity* of information with respect to security categorization.

[19] *Reproducibility* refers to the ability of different experts to produce the same results from the same data. *Repeatability* refers to the ability to repeat the assessment in the future, in a manner that is consistent with and hence comparable to prior assessments—enabling the organization to identify trends.

2.3.1 Risk Models

Risk models define the *risk factors* to be assessed and the relationships among those factors.[20] Risk factors are characteristics used in risk models as inputs to determining levels of risk in risk assessments. Risk factors are also used extensively in risk communications to highlight what strongly affects the levels of risk in particular situations, circumstances, or contexts. Typical risk factors include threat, vulnerability, impact, likelihood, and predisposing condition. Risk factors can be decomposed into more detailed characteristics (e.g., threats decomposed into threat sources and threat events).[21] These definitions are important for organizations to document prior to conducting risk assessments because the assessments rely upon well-defined attributes of threats, vulnerabilities, impact, and other risk factors to effectively determine risk.

Threats

A *threat* is any circumstance or event with the potential to adversely impact organizational operations and assets, individuals, other organizations, or the Nation through an information system via unauthorized access, destruction, disclosure, or modification of information, and/or denial of service.[22] Threat events are caused by threat sources. A *threat source* is characterized as: (i) the intent and method targeted at the exploitation of a vulnerability; or (ii) a situation and method that may accidentally exploit a vulnerability. In general, types of threat sources include: (i) hostile cyber or physical attacks; (ii) human errors of omission or commission; (iii) structural failures of organization-controlled resources (e.g., hardware, software, environmental controls); and (iv) natural and man-made disasters, accidents, and failures beyond the control of the organization. Various taxonomies of threat sources have been developed.[23] Some taxonomies of threat sources use the type of adverse impacts as an organizing principle. Multiple threat sources can initiate or cause the same threat event—for example, a provisioning server can be taken off-line by a denial-of-service attack, a deliberate act by a malicious system administrator, an administrative error, a hardware fault, or a power failure.

Risk models differ in the degree of detail and complexity with which threat events are identified. When threat events are identified with great specificity, *threat scenarios* can be modeled, developed, and analyzed.[24] Threat events for cyber or physical attacks are characterized by the tactics, techniques, and procedures (TTPs) employed by adversaries. Understanding adversary-based threat events gives organizations insights into the capabilities associated with certain threat sources. In addition, having greater knowledge about who is carrying out the attacks gives organizations a better understanding of what adversaries desire to gain by the attacks. Knowing

---

[20] Documentation of a risk model includes: (i) identification of risk factors (definitions, descriptions, value scales); and (ii) identification of the relationships among those risk factors (both conceptual relationships, presented descriptively, and algorithms for combining values). The risk model presented in this section (and described in Appendices D-I) does not specify algorithms for combining values.

[21] A risk factor can have a single assessable characteristic (e.g., impact severity) or multiple characteristics, some of which may be assessable and some of which may not be assessable. Characteristics which are not assessable typically help determine what lower-level characteristics are relevant. For example, a threat source has a (characteristic) threat type (using a taxonomy of threat types, which are nominal rather than assessable). The threat type determines which of the more detailed characteristics are relevant (e.g., a threat source of type *adversary* has associated characteristics of capabilities, intent, and targeting, which are directly assessable characteristics).

[22] Organizations can choose to specify threat events as: (i) single events, actions, or circumstances; or (ii) sets and/or sequences of related actions, activities, and/or circumstances.

[23] Appendix D provides an exemplary taxonomy of threat sources and associated threat characteristics.

[24] A *threat scenario* is a set of discrete threat events, attributed to a specific threat source or multiple threat sources, ordered in time, that result in adverse effects.

the intent and targeting aspects of a potential attack helps organizations narrow the set of threat events that are most relevant to consider.

Threat shifting is the response of adversaries to perceived safeguards and/or countermeasures (i.e., security controls), in which adversaries change some characteristic of their intent/targeting in order to avoid and/or overcome those safeguards/countermeasures. Threat shifting can occur in one or more domains including: (i) the time domain (e.g., a delay in an attack or illegal entry to conduct additional surveillance); (ii) the target domain (e.g., selecting a different target that is not as well protected); (iii) the resource domain (e.g., adding resources to the attack in order to reduce uncertainty or overcome safeguards and/or countermeasures); or (iv) the attack planning/attack method domain (e.g., changing the attack weapon or attack path). Threat shifting is a natural consequence of a dynamic set of interactions between threat sources and types of organizational assets targeted. With more sophisticated threat sources, it also tends to default to the path of least resistance to exploit particular vulnerabilities, and the responses are not always predictable. In addition to the safeguards and/or countermeasures implemented and the impact of a successful exploit of an organizational vulnerability, another influence on threat shifting is the benefit to the attacker. That perceived benefit on the attacker side can also influence how much and when threat shifting occurs.

Vulnerabilities and Predisposing Conditions

A *vulnerability* is a weakness in an information system, system security procedures, internal controls, or implementation that could be exploited by a threat source.[25] Most information system vulnerabilities can be associated with security controls that either have not been applied (either intentionally or unintentionally), or have been applied, but retain some weakness. However, it is also important to allow for the possibility of emergent vulnerabilities that can arise naturally over time as organizational missions/business functions evolve, environments of operation change, new technologies proliferate, and new threats emerge. In the context of such change, existing security controls may become inadequate and may need to be reassessed for effectiveness. The tendency for security controls to potentially degrade in effectiveness over time reinforces the need to maintain risk assessments during the entire system development life cycle and also the importance of continuous monitoring programs to obtain ongoing situational awareness of the organizational security posture.

Vulnerabilities are not identified only within information systems. Viewing information systems in a broader context, vulnerabilities can be found in organizational governance structures (e.g., the lack of effective risk management strategies and adequate risk framing, poor intra-agency communications, inconsistent decisions about relative priorities of missions/business functions, or misalignment of enterprise architecture to support mission/business activities). Vulnerabilities can also be found in external relationships (e.g., dependencies on particular energy sources, supply chains, information technologies, and telecommunications providers), mission/business processes (e.g., poorly defined processes or processes that are not risk-aware), and enterprise/information security architectures (e.g., poor architectural decisions resulting in lack of diversity or resiliency in organizational information systems).[26]

---

[25] The *severity* of a vulnerability is an assessment of the relative importance of mitigating/remediating the vulnerability. The severity can be determined by the extent of the potential adverse impact if such a vulnerability is exploited by a threat source. Thus, the severity of vulnerabilities, in general, is context-dependent.

[26] NIST Special Publication 800-39 provides guidance on vulnerabilities at all three tiers in the risk management hierarchy and the potential adverse impact that can occur if threats exploit such vulnerabilities.

In general, risks materialize as a result of a series of threat events, each of which takes advantage of one or more vulnerabilities. Organizations define *threat scenarios* to describe how the events caused by a threat source can contribute to or cause harm. Development of threat scenarios is analytically useful, since some vulnerabilities may not be exposed to exploitation unless and until other vulnerabilities have been exploited. Analysis that illuminates how a set of vulnerabilities, taken together, could be exploited by one or more threat events is therefore more useful than the analysis of individual vulnerabilities. In addition, a threat scenario tells a story, and hence is useful for risk communication as well as for analysis.

In addition to vulnerabilities as described above, organizations also consider predisposing conditions. A *predisposing condition* is a condition that exists within an organization, a mission or business process, enterprise architecture, information system, or environment of operation, which affects (i.e., increases or decreases) the likelihood that threat events, once initiated, result in adverse impacts to organizational operations and assets, individuals, other organizations, or the Nation.[27] Predisposing conditions include, for example, the location of a facility in a hurricane- or flood-prone region (increasing the likelihood of exposure to hurricanes or floods) or a stand-alone information system with no external network connectivity (decreasing the likelihood of exposure to a network-based cyber attack). Vulnerabilities resulting from predisposing conditions that cannot be easily corrected could include, for example, gaps in contingency plans, use of outdated technologies, or weaknesses/deficiencies in information system backup and failover mechanisms. In all cases, these types of vulnerabilities create a predisposition toward threat events having adverse impacts on organizations. Vulnerabilities (including those attributed to predisposing conditions) are part of the overall security posture of organizational information systems and environments of operation that can affect the likelihood of occurrence of a threat event.

Likelihood

The *likelihood of occurrence* is a weighted risk factor based on an analysis of the probability that a given threat is capable of exploiting a given vulnerability (or set of vulnerabilities). The likelihood risk factor combines an estimate of the likelihood that the threat event will be initiated with an estimate of the likelihood of impact (i.e., the likelihood that the threat event results in adverse impacts). For adversarial threats, an assessment of likelihood of occurrence is typically based on: (i) adversary *intent*; (ii) adversary *capability*; and (iii) adversary *targeting*. For other than adversarial threat events, the likelihood of occurrence is estimated using historical evidence, empirical data, or other factors. Note that the likelihood that a threat event will be initiated or will occur is assessed with respect to a specific time frame (e.g., the next six months, the next year, or the period until a specified milestone is reached). If a threat event is almost certain to be initiated or occur in the (specified or implicit) time frame, the risk assessment may take into consideration the estimated frequency of the event. The likelihood of threat occurrence can also be based on the state of the organization (including for example, its core mission/business processes, enterprise architecture, information security architecture, information systems, and environments in which those systems operate)—taking into consideration predisposing conditions and the presence and effectiveness of deployed security controls to protect against unauthorized/undesirable behavior, detect and limit damage, and/or maintain or restore mission/business capabilities. The likelihood of impact addresses the probability (or possibility) that the threat event will result in an adverse impact, regardless of the magnitude of harm that can be expected.

---

[27] The concept of predisposing condition is also related to the term *susceptibility* or *exposure*. Organizations are not susceptible to risk (or exposed to risk) if a threat cannot exploit a vulnerability to cause adverse impact. For example, organizations that do not employ database management systems are not vulnerable to the threat of SQL injections and therefore, are not susceptible to such risk.

Organizations typically employ a three-step process to determine the overall likelihood of threat events. First, organizations assess the likelihood that threat events will be initiated (for adversarial threat events) or will occur (for non-adversarial threat events). Second, organizations assess the likelihood that the threat events once initiated or occurring, will result in adverse impacts or harm to organizational operations and assets, individuals, other organizations, or the Nation. Finally, organizations assess the overall likelihood as a combination of likelihood of initiation/occurrence and likelihood of resulting in adverse impact.

Threat-vulnerability pairing (i.e., establishing a one-to-one relationship between threats and vulnerabilities) may be undesirable when assessing likelihood at the mission/business function level, and in many cases, can be problematic even at the information system level due to the potentially large number of threats and vulnerabilities. This approach typically drives the level of detail in identifying threat events and vulnerabilities, rather than allowing organizations to make effective use of threat information and/or to identify threats at a level of detail that is meaningful. Depending on the level of detail in threat specification, a given threat event could exploit multiple vulnerabilities. In assessing likelihoods, organizations examine vulnerabilities that threat events could exploit and also the mission/business function susceptibility to events for which no security controls or viable implementations of security controls exist (e.g., due to functional dependencies, particularly external dependencies). In certain situations, the most effective way to reduce mission/business risk attributable to information security risk is to redesign the mission/business processes so there are viable work-arounds when information systems are compromised. Using the concept of threat scenarios described above, may help organizations overcome some of the limitations of threat-vulnerability pairing.

Impact

The level of *impact* from a threat event is the magnitude of harm that can be expected to result from the consequences of unauthorized disclosure of information, unauthorized modification of information, unauthorized destruction of information, or loss of information or information system availability. Such harm can be experienced by a variety of organizational and non-organizational stakeholders including, for example, heads of agencies, mission and business owners, information owners/stewards, mission/business process owners, information system owners, or individuals/groups in the public or private sectors relying on the organization—in essence, anyone with a vested interest in the organization's operations, assets, or individuals, including other organizations in partnership with the organization, or the Nation.[28] Organizations make explicit: (i) the process used to conduct impact determinations; (ii) assumptions related to impact determinations; (iii) sources and methods for obtaining impact information; and (iv) the rationale for conclusions reached with regard to impact determinations.

Organizations may explicitly define how established priorities and values guide the identification of high-value assets and the potential adverse impacts to organizational stakeholders. If such information is not defined, priorities and values related to identifying targets of threat sources and associated organizational impacts can typically be derived from strategic planning and policies. For example, security categorization levels indicate the organizational impacts of compromising different types of information. Privacy Impact Assessments and criticality levels (when defined as part of contingency planning or Mission/Business Impact Analysis) indicate the adverse impacts of destruction, corruption, or loss of accountability for information resources to organizations.

---

[28] The term *organizational assets* can have a very wide scope of applicability to include, for example, high-impact programs, physical plant, mission-critical information systems, personnel, equipment, or a logically related group of systems. More broadly, organizational assets represent any resource or set of resources which the organization values, including intangible assets such as image or reputation.

Strategic plans and policies also assert or imply the relative priorities of immediate or near-term mission/business function accomplishment and long-term organizational viability (which can be undermined by the loss of reputation or by sanctions resulting from the compromise of sensitive information). Organizations can also consider the range of effects of threat events including the relative size of the set of resources affected, when making final impact determinations. Risk tolerance assumptions may state that threat events with an impact below a specific value do not warrant further analysis.

Risk

Figure 3 illustrates an example of a risk model including the key risk factors discussed above and the relationship among the factors. Each of the risk factors is used in the risk assessment process in Chapter Three.

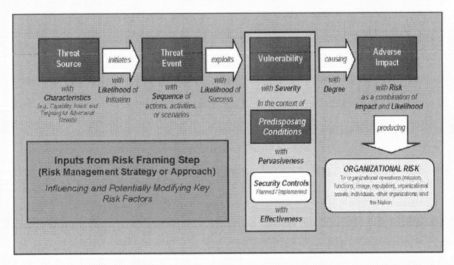

FIGURE 3: GENERIC RISK MODEL WITH KEY RISK FACTORS

As noted above, *risk* is a function of the likelihood of a threat event's occurrence and potential adverse impact should the event occur. This definition accommodates many types of adverse impacts at all tiers in the risk management hierarchy described in Special Publication 800-39 (e.g., damage to image or reputation of the organization or financial loss at Tier 1; inability to successfully execute a specific mission/business process at Tier 2; or the resources expended in responding to an information system incident at Tier 3). It also accommodates relationships among impacts (e.g., loss of current or future mission/business effectiveness due to the loss of data confidentiality; loss of confidence in critical information due to loss of data or system integrity; or unavailability or degradation of information or information systems). This broad definition also allows risk to be represented as a single value or as a vector (i.e., multiple values), in which different types of impacts are assessed separately. For purposes of risk communication, risk is generally grouped according to the types of adverse impacts (and possibly the time frames in which those impacts are likely to be experienced).

Aggregation

Organizations may use risk *aggregation* to roll up several discrete or lower-level risks into a more general or higher-level risk. Organizations may also use risk aggregation to efficiently manage the scope and scale of risk assessments involving multiple information systems and multiple mission/business processes with specified relationships and dependencies among those systems and processes. Risk aggregation, conducted primarily at Tiers 1 and 2 and occasionally at Tier 3, assesses the overall risk to organizational operations, assets, and individuals given the set of discrete risks. In general, for discrete risks (e.g., the risk associated with a single information system supporting a well-defined mission/business process), the worst-case impact establishes an upper bound for the overall risk to organizational operations, assets, and individuals.[29] One issue for risk aggregation is that this upper bound for risk may fail to apply. For example, it may be advantageous for organizations to assess risk at the organization level when multiple risks materialize concurrently or when the same risk materializes repeatedly over a period of time. In such situations, there is the possibility that the amount of overall risk incurred is beyond the risk capacity of the organization, and therefore the overall impact to organizational operations and assets (i.e., mission/business impact) goes beyond that which was originally assessed for each specific risk.

When aggregating risk, organizations consider the relationship among various discrete risks. For example, there may be a cause and effect relationship in that if one risk materializes, another risk is more or less likely to materialize. If there is a direct or inverse relationship among discrete risks, then the risks can be coupled (in a qualitative sense) or correlated (in a quantitative sense) either in a positive or negative manner. Risk coupling or correlation (i.e., finding relationships among risks that increase or decrease the likelihood of any specific risk materializing) can be done at Tiers 1, 2, or 3.

Uncertainty

Uncertainty is inherent in the evaluation of risk, due to such considerations as: (i) limitations on the extent to which the future will resemble the past; (ii) imperfect or incomplete knowledge of the threat (e.g., characteristics of adversaries including tactics, techniques, and procedures); (iii) undiscovered vulnerabilities in technologies or products; and (iv) unrecognized dependencies, which can lead to unforeseen impacts. Uncertainty about the value of specific risk factors can also be due to the step in the RMF or phase in the system development life cycle at which a risk assessment is performed. For example, at early phases in the system development life cycle, the presence and effectiveness of security controls may be unknown, while at later phases in the life cycle, the cost of evaluating control effectiveness may outweigh the benefits in terms of more fully informed decision making. Finally, uncertainty can be due to incomplete knowledge of the risks associated with other information systems, mission/ business processes, services, common infrastructures, and/or organizations. The degree of uncertainty in risk assessment results, due to these different reasons, can be communicated in the form of the results (e.g., by expressing results qualitatively, by providing ranges of values rather than single values for identified risks, or by using a visual representations of fuzzy regions rather than points).

---

[29] Security categorizations conducted in accordance with FIPS Publication 199 provide examples of *worst-case* impact analyses (using the high water mark concept). This type of impact analysis provides an upper bound for risk when applied to discrete situations within organizations.

2.3.2 Assessment Approaches

Risk, and its contributing factors, can be assessed in a variety of ways, including quantitatively, qualitatively, or semi-quantitatively. Each risk assessment approach considered by organizations has advantages and disadvantages. A preferred approach (or situation-specific set of approaches) can be selected based on organizational culture and, in particular, attitudes toward the concepts of uncertainty and risk communication. *Quantitative* assessments typically employ a set of methods, principles, or rules for assessing risk based on the use of numbers—where the meanings and proportionality of values are maintained inside and outside the context of the assessment. This type of assessment most effectively supports cost-benefit analyses of alternative risk responses or courses of action. However, the meaning of the quantitative results may not always be clear and may require interpretation and explanation—particularly to explain the assumptions and constraints on using the results. For example, organizations may typically ask if the numbers or results obtained in the risk assessments are reliable or if the differences in the obtained values are meaningful or insignificant. Additionally, the rigor of quantification is significantly lessened when subjective determinations are buried within the quantitative assessments, or when significant uncertainty surrounds the determination of values. The benefits of quantitative assessments (in terms of the rigor, repeatability, and reproducibility of assessment results) can, in some cases, be outweighed by the costs (in terms of the expert time and effort and the possible deployment and use of tools required to make such assessments).

In contrast to quantitative assessments, *qualitative* assessments typically employ a set of methods, principles, or rules for assessing risk based on nonnumerical categories or levels (e.g., very low, low, moderate, high, very high). This type of assessment supports communicating risk results to decision makers. However, the range of values in qualitative assessments is comparatively small in most cases, making the relative prioritization or comparison within the set of reported risks difficult. Additionally, unless each value is very clearly defined or is characterized by meaningful examples, different experts relying on their individual experiences could produce significantly different assessment results. The repeatability and reproducibility of qualitative assessments are increased by the annotation of assessed values (e.g., this value is high because of the following reasons) and by the use of tables or other well-defined functions to combine qualitative values.

Finally, *semi-quantitative* assessments typically employ a set of methods, principles, or rules for assessing risk that uses bins, scales, or representative numbers whose values and meanings are not maintained in other contexts. This type of assessment can provide the benefits of quantitative and qualitative assessments. The bins (e.g., 0-15, 16-35, 36-70, 71-85, 86-100) or scales (e.g., 1-10) translate easily into qualitative terms that support risk communications for decision makers (e.g., a score of 95 can be interpreted as very high), while also allowing relative comparisons between values in different bins or even within the same bin (e.g., the difference between risks scored 70 and 71 respectively is relatively insignificant, while the difference between risks scored 36 and 70 is relatively significant). The role of expert judgment in assigning values is more evident than in a purely quantitative approach. Moreover, if the scales or sets of bins provide sufficient granularity, relative prioritization among results is better supported than in a purely qualitative approach. As in a quantitative approach, rigor is significantly lessened when subjective determinations are buried within assessments, or when significant uncertainty surrounds a determination of value. As with the nonnumeric categories or levels used in a well-founded qualitative approach, each bin or range of values needs to be clearly defined and/or characterized by meaningful examples.

Independent of the type of value scale selected, assessments make explicit the *temporal* element of risk factors. For example, organizations can associate a specific time period with assessments of likelihood of occurrence and assessments of impact severity.

2.3.3 Analysis Approaches

Analysis approaches differ with respect to the orientation or starting point of the risk assessment, level of detail in the assessment, and how risks due to similar threat scenarios are treated. An analysis approach can be: (i) *threat-oriented*; (ii) *asset/impact-oriented*; or (iii) *vulnerability-oriented*.[30] A threat-oriented approach starts with the identification of threat sources and threat events, and focuses on the development of threat scenarios; vulnerabilities are identified in the context of threats, and for adversarial threats, impacts are identified based on adversary intent. An asset/impact-oriented approach starts with the identification of impacts or consequences of concern and critical assets, possibly using the results of a mission or business impact analyses[31] and identifying threat events that could lead to and/or threat sources that could seek those impacts or consequences. A vulnerability-oriented approach starts with a set of predisposing conditions or exploitable weaknesses/deficiencies in organizational information systems or the environments in which the systems operate, and identifies threat events that could exercise those vulnerabilities together with possible consequences of vulnerabilities being exercised. Each analysis approach takes into consideration the same risk factors, and thus entails the same set of risk assessment activities, albeit in different order. Differences in the starting point of the risk assessment can potentially bias the results, causing some risks not to be identified. Therefore, identification of risks from a second orientation (e.g., complementing a threat-oriented analysis approach with an asset/impact-oriented analysis approach) can improve the rigor and effectiveness of the analysis.

In addition to the orientation of the analysis approach, organizations can apply more rigorous analysis techniques (e.g., graph-based analyses) to provide an effective way to account for the many-to-many relationships between: (i) threat sources and threat events (i.e., a single threat event can be caused by multiple threat sources and a single threat source can cause multiple threat events); (ii) threat events and vulnerabilities (i.e., a single threat event can exploit multiple vulnerabilities and a single vulnerability can be exploited by multiple threat events); and (iii) threat events and impacts/assets (i.e., a single threat event can affect multiple assets or have multiple impacts, and a single asset can be affected by multiple threat events).[32] Rigorous analysis approaches also provide a way to account for whether, in the time frame for which risks are assessed, a specific adverse impact could occur (or a specific asset could be harmed) at most once, or perhaps repeatedly, depending on the nature of the impacts and on how organizations (including mission/business processes or information systems) recover from such adverse impacts.

---

[30] Organizations have great flexibility in choosing a particular analysis approach. The specific approach taken is driven by different organizational considerations (e.g., the quality and quantity of information available with respect to threats, vulnerabilities, and impacts/assets; the specific orientation carrying the highest priority for organizations; availability of analysis tools emphasizing certain orientations; or a combination of the above).

[31] A *Business Impact Analysis* (BIA) identifies high-value assets and adverse impacts with respect to the loss of integrity or availability. DHS Federal Continuity Directive 2 provides guidance on BIAs at the organization and mission/business process levels of the risk management hierarchy, respectively. NIST Special Publication 800-34 provides guidance on BIAs at the information system level of the risk management hierarchy.

[32] For example, graph-based analysis techniques (e.g., functional dependency network analysis, attack tree analysis for adversarial threats, fault tree analysis for other types of threats) provide ways to use specific threat events to generate threat scenarios. Graph-based analysis techniques can also provide ways to account for situations in which one event can change the likelihood of occurrence for another event. Attack and fault tree analyses, in particular, can generate multiple threat scenarios that are nearly alike, for purposes of determining the levels of risk. With automated modeling and simulation, large numbers of threat scenarios (e.g., attack/fault trees, traversals of functional dependency networks) can be generated. Thus, graph-based analysis techniques include ways to restrict the analysis to define a reasonable subset of all possible threat scenarios.

2.3.4 Effects of Organizational Culture on Risk Assessments

Organizations can differ in the risk models, assessment approaches, and analysis approaches that they prefer for a variety of reasons. For example, cultural issues[33] can predispose organizations to employ risk models that assume a constant value for one or more possible risk factors, so that some factors that are present in other organizations' models are not represented. Culture can also predispose organizations to employ risk models that require detailed analyses using quantitative assessments (e.g., nuclear safety). Alternately, organizations may prefer qualitative or semi-quantitative assessment approaches. In addition to differences among organizations, differences can also exist within organizations. For example, organizations can use coarse or high-level risk models early in the system development life cycle to select security controls, and subsequently, more detailed models to assess risk to given missions or business functions. Organizational risk frames[34] determine which risk models, assessment approaches, and analysis approaches to use under varying circumstances.

THE USE OF RISK MODELS

A single risk model (consisting of a fixed set of factors, a fixed assessment scale for each factor, and a fixed algorithm for combining factors) cannot meet the diverse needs of the organizations in the public and private sectors that rely on Special Publication 800-30. For example, while some organizations may emphasize adversarial threats and provide detailed information about such threats, other organizations may choose instead to focus on non-adversarial threats, providing greater detail for those types of threats and lesser detail for adversarial threats. Therefore, the risk models developed by organizations with different assumptions regarding threats will involve different factors as well as different levels of detail.

Similarly, within a single organization or community of interest, different assessment scales may be appropriate for different missions/business functions, different categories of information systems, and/or for systems at different stages in the system development life cycle. For example, during an initial risk assessment performed when an information system is first being considered, the information available about threats and vulnerabilities may be nonspecific and highly uncertain. For such risk assessments, a qualitative assessment, using only a few factors, may be appropriate. By contrast, a risk assessment informed by a security controls assessment can be far more specific, and estimates can be made with greater fidelity. For such assessments, a semi-quantitative assessment using the 0-100 value scales may be more appropriate.

The expectation set forth in Special Publications 800-39 and 800-30 is that each organization or community will define a risk model appropriate to its view of risk (i.e., formulas that reflect organizational or community views of which risk factors must be considered, which factors can be combined, which factors must be further decomposed, and how assessed values should be combined algorithmically). Special Publication 800-30 does identify risk factors that are common across a wide spectrum of risk models. In addition, by defining multiple aligned value scales, this publication provides a foundation for a consistent approach to estimating information security risk across the system development life cycle, without forcing assessments early in the life cycle to be more detailed than can be justified by available information.

---

[33] NIST Special Publication 800-39 describes how organizational culture affects risk management.

[34] NIST Special Publication 800-39 defines an organization's risk frame as the set of assumptions, constraints, risk tolerances, priorities, and trade-offs that underpin the organization's risk management strategy—establishing a solid foundation for managing risk and bounding its risk-based decisions.

2.4 APPLICATION OF RISK ASSESSMENTS

As stated previously, risk assessments can be conducted at all three tiers in the risk management hierarchy—*organization level, mission/business process level,* and *information system level.* Figure 4 illustrates the risk management hierarchy defined in NIST Special Publication 800-39, which provides multiple risk perspectives from the strategic level to the tactical level. Traditional risk assessments generally focus at the Tier 3 level (i.e., information system level) and as a result, tend to overlook other significant risk factors that may be more appropriately assessed at the Tier 1 or Tier 2 levels (e.g., exposure of a core mission/business function to an adversarial threat based on information system interconnections).

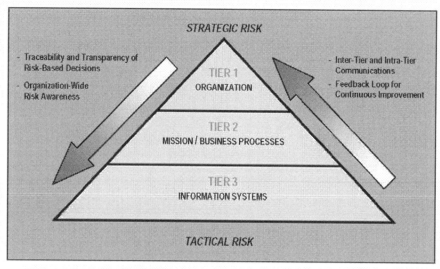

FIGURE 4: RISK MANAGEMENT HIERARCHY

Risk assessments support risk response decisions at the different tiers of the risk management hierarchy. At Tier 1, risk assessments can affect, for example: (i) organization-wide information security programs, policies, procedures, and guidance; (ii) the types of appropriate risk responses (i.e., risk acceptance, avoidance, mitigation, sharing, or transfer); (iii) investment decisions for information technologies/systems; (iv) procurements; (v) minimum organization-wide security controls; (vi) conformance to enterprise/security architectures; and (vii) monitoring strategies and ongoing authorizations of information systems and common controls. At Tier 2, risk assessments can affect, for example: (i) enterprise architecture/security architecture design decisions; (ii) the selection of common controls; (iii) the selection of suppliers, services, and contractors to support organizational missions/business functions; (iv) the development of risk-aware mission/business processes; and (v) the interpretation of information security policies with respect to organizational information systems and environments in which those systems operate. Finally, at Tier 3, risk assessments can affect, for example: (i) design decisions (including the selection, tailoring, and supplementation of security controls and the selection of information technology products for organizational information systems); (ii) implementation decisions (including whether specific information technology products or product configurations meet security control requirements); and (iii) operational decisions (including the requisite level of monitoring activity, the frequency of ongoing information system authorizations, and system maintenance decisions).

Risk assessments can also inform other risk management activities across the three tiers that are not security-related. For example, at Tier 1, risk assessments can provide useful inputs to: (i) operational risk determinations (including business continuity for organizational missions and business functions); (ii) organizational risk determinations (including financial risk, compliance risk, regulatory risk, reputation risk, and cumulative acquisition risk across large-scale projects); and (iii) multiple-impact risk (including supply chain risk and risk involving partnerships). At Tier 2, risk assessments can provide the same useful inputs to operational, organizational, and multiple-impact risks, specific to mission/business processes. At Tier 3, risk assessments can inform assessments of cost, schedule, and performance risks associated with information systems, with information security experts coordinating with program managers, information system owners, and authorizing officials. This type of coordination is essential within organizations in order to eliminate silos and/or stove-piped activities that produce less than optimal or inefficient information technology and security solutions—thus affecting the ability of organizations to carry out assigned missions/business functions with maximum efficiency and cost-effectiveness.

It is important to note that information security risk contributes to non-security risks at each tier. Thus, the results of a risk assessment at a given tier serve as inputs to, and are aligned with, non-security risk management activities at that tier.[35] In addition, the results of risk assessments at lower tiers serve as inputs to risk assessments at higher tiers. Risks can arise on different time scales (e.g., the disclosure of information about current organizational operations can compromise the effectiveness of those operations immediately, while the disclosure of strategic planning information can compromise future operational capabilities). Risk response decisions can also take effect in different time frames (e.g., changes in organizational policies or investment strategies can sometimes require years to take effect, while configuration changes in an individual system can often be implemented immediately). In general, the risk management process tends to move more slowly at Tiers 1 and 2 than at Tier 3. This is due to how organizations typically respond to risks that potentially affect widespread organizational operations and assets—where such risk responses may need to address systemic or institutional issues. However, some Tier 1 decisions (e.g., newly discovered threats or vulnerabilities requiring the implementation of an organization-wide mandate for mitigation) can involve immediate action.

2.4.1   Risk Assessments at the Organizational Tier

At Tier 1, risk assessments support organizational strategies, policies, guidance, and processes for managing risk. Risk assessments conducted at Tier 1 focus on organizational operations, assets, and individuals—comprehensive assessments across mission/business lines. For example, Tier 1 risk assessments may address: (i) the specific types of threats directed at organizations that may be different from other organizations and how those threats affect policy decisions; (ii) systemic weaknesses or deficiencies discovered in multiple organizational information systems capable of being exploited by adversaries; (iii) the potential adverse impact on organizations from the loss or compromise of organizational information (either intentionally or unintentionally); and (iv) the use of new information and computing technologies such as mobile and cloud and the potential effect on the ability of organizations to successfully carry out their missions/business operations while using those technologies. Organization-wide assessments of risk can be based solely on the assumptions, constraints, risk tolerances, priorities, and trade-offs established in the risk framing step (i.e., derived primarily from Tier 1 activities). However, more realistic and meaningful risk assessments are based on assessments conducted across multiple mission/business lines (i.e., derived primarily from Tier 2 activities). The ability of organizations to effectively use Tier 2 risk

---

[35] In particular, risk assessment results support investment risk management. NIST Special Publication 800-65 provides guidance on integrating information security into the Capital Planning and Investment Control (CPIC) process.

assessments as inputs to Tier 1 risk assessments is shaped by such considerations as: (i) the similarity of organizational missions/business functions and mission/business processes; and (ii) the degree of autonomy that organizational entities or subcomponents have with respect to parent organizations. In decentralized organizations or organizations with varied missions/business functions and/or environments of operation, expert analysis may be needed to normalize the results from Tier 2 risk assessments. Finally, risk assessments at Tier 1 take into consideration the identification of mission-essential functions from Continuity of Operations Plans (COOP)[36] prepared by organizations when determining the contribution of Tier 2 risks. Risk assessment results at Tier 1 are communicated to organizational entities at Tier 2 and Tier 3.

2.4.2 Risk Assessments at the Mission/Business Process Tier

At Tier 2, risk assessments support the determination of mission/business process protection and resiliency requirements, and the allocation of those requirements to the enterprise architecture as part of mission/business segments (that support mission/business processes). This allocation is accomplished through an information security architecture embedded within the enterprise architecture. Tier 2 risk assessments also inform and guide decisions on whether, how, and when to use information systems for specific mission/business processes, in particular for alternative mission/business processing in the face of compromised information systems. Risk management and associated risk assessment activities at Tier 2 are closely aligned with the development of Business Continuity Plans (BCPs). Tier 2 risk assessments focus on mission/business segments, which typically include multiple information systems, with varying degrees of criticality and/or sensitivity with regard to core organizational missions/business functions.[37] Risk assessments at Tier 2 can also focus on information security architecture as a critical component of enterprise architecture to help organizations select common controls inherited by organizational information systems at Tier 3. Risk assessment results produced at Tier 2 are communicated to and shared with organizational entities at Tier 3 to help inform and guide the allocation of security controls to information systems and environments in which those systems operate. Tier 2 risk assessments also provide assessments of the security and risk posture of organizational mission/business processes, which inform assessments of organizational risks at Tier 1. Thus, risk assessment results at Tier 2 are routinely communicated to organizational entities at Tier 1 and Tier 3.

2.4.3 Risk Assessments at the Information System Tier

The Tier 2 context and the system development life cycle determine the purpose and define the scope of risk assessment activities at Tier 3. While initial risk assessments (i.e., risk assessments performed for the first time, rather than updating prior risk assessments) can be performed at any phase in the system development life cycle, ideally these assessments should be performed in the Initiation phase.[38] In the Initiation phase, risk assessments evaluate the anticipated vulnerabilities and predisposing conditions affecting the confidentiality, integrity, and availability of information systems in the context of the planned environments of operation. Such assessments inform risk response, enabling information system owners/program managers, together with mission/business owners to make the final decisions about the security controls necessary based on the security categorization and the environment of operation. Risk assessments are also conducted at later phases in the system development life cycle, updating risk assessment results from earlier phases. These risk assessment results for as-built or as-deployed information systems typically include

---

[36] NIST Special Publication 800-34 provides guidance on Information System Contingency Planning (ISCP).

[37] The criticality of information systems to organizational missions/business functions may be identified in Business Impact Analyses.

[38] NIST Special Publication 800-64 provides guidance for security considerations in the system development life cycle.

descriptions of vulnerabilities in the systems, an assessment of the risks associated with each vulnerability (thereby updating the assessment of vulnerability severity), and corrective actions that can be taken to mitigate the risks. The risk assessment results also include an assessment of the overall risk to the organization and the information contained in the information systems by operating the systems as evaluated. Risk assessment results at Tier 3 are communicated to organizational entities at Tier 1 and Tier 2.

Risk assessment activities can be integrated with the steps in the Risk Management Framework (RMF), as defined in NIST Special Publication 800-37. The RMF, in its system development life cycle approach, operates primarily at Tier 3 with some application at Tiers 1 and 2, for example, in the selection of common controls. Risk assessments can be tailored to each step in the RMF as reflected in the purpose and scope of the assessments described in Section 3.1. Risk assessments can also help determine the type of security assessments conducted during various phases of the system development life cycle, the frequency of such assessments, the level of rigor applied during the assessments, the assessment methods used, and the types/number of objects assessed. The benefit of risk assessments conducted as part of the RMF can be realized from both initial assessments and from updated assessments, as described below.

RMF Step 1 – Categorize

Organizations can use initial risk assessments to make security categorization decisions consistent with the risk management strategy provided by the risk executive (function) and as a preparatory step to security control selection. Conducting initial risk assessments brings together the available information on threat sources, threat events, vulnerabilities, and predisposing conditions—thus enabling organizations to use such information to categorize information and information systems based on known and potential threats to and vulnerabilities in organizational information systems and environments in which those systems operate.[39] Security categorization decisions inform the selection of initial baseline security controls. Baseline security controls serve as the starting point for organizational tailoring and supplementation activities described in the RMF Select step.

RMF Step 2 – Select

Organizations can use risk assessments to inform and guide the selection of security controls for organizational information systems and environments of operation. After the initial security control baseline is selected based on the security categorization process, the risk assessment results help organizations: (i) apply appropriate tailoring guidance to adjust the controls based on specific mission/business requirements, assumptions, constraints, priorities, trade-offs, or other organization-defined conditions; and (ii) supplement the controls based on specific and credible threat information.[40] Threat data from risk assessments provide critical information on adversary capabilities, intent, and targeting that may affect the decisions by organizations regarding the selection of additional security controls including the associated costs and benefits. Organizations also consider risk assessment results when selecting common controls (typically a Tier 1 and Tier 2 activity). Risk is introduced if the implementation of a common control results in a single point of failure because the control provides a security capability potentially inherited by multiple information systems. As risk assessments are updated and refined, organizations use the results to modify current security control selections based on the most recent threat and vulnerability information available.

---

[39] Even when an initial risk assessment is performed prior to the existence of an information system, vulnerabilities may be present in certain technologies that will be used in the system, in common controls that will be inherited by the system, or in the environment in which the system will operate.

[40] Supplementation will be incorporated into the tailoring process in NIST Special Publication 800-53, Revision 4.

RMF Step 3 — Implement

Organizations can use risk assessment results to identify alternative implementations of selected security controls (e.g., considering vulnerabilities inherent in one security control implementation versus another). Some information technology products, system components, or architectural configurations may be more susceptible to certain types of threat sources; these susceptibilities are subsequently addressed during security control development and implementation. In addition, the strength of security mechanisms selected for implementation can take into consideration the threat data from risk assessments. Individual configuration settings for information technology products and system components can eliminate vulnerabilities identified during the analysis of threat events. Risk assessment results also help inform decisions regarding the cost, benefit, and risk trade-offs in using one type of technology versus another or how security controls are effectively implemented in particular operational environments (e.g., when compensating controls must be used due to the unavailability of certain technologies). As risk assessments are updated and refined, organizations use the results to help determine if current security control implementations remain effective given changes to the threat space.

RMF Step 4 — Assess

Organizations can use the results from security control assessments to inform risk assessments. Security control assessments (documented in security assessment reports) identify vulnerabilities in organizational information systems and the environments in which those systems operate. Partial or complete failure of deployed security controls or the absence of planned controls represents potential vulnerabilities that can be exploited by threat sources. Organizations use the results from risk assessments to help determine the severity of such vulnerabilities which in turn, can guide and inform organizational risk responses (e.g., prioritizing risk response activities, establishing milestones for corrective actions).

RMF Step 5 — Authorize

Organizations can use risk assessment results to provide risk-related information to authorizing officials. The risk responses carried out by organizations based on the risk assessments result in a known security posture of organizational information systems and environments of operation. Risk assessment results provide essential information to enable authorizing officials to make risk-based decisions on whether to operate those systems in the current security posture or take actions to provide additional security controls, thereby further reducing risk to organizational operations and assets, individuals, other organizations, or the Nation.

RMF Step 6 — Monitor

Organizations can update risk assessments on an ongoing basis using security-related information from organizational continuous monitoring processes.[41] Continuous monitoring processes evaluate: (i) the *effectiveness* of security controls; (ii) *changes* to information systems and environments of operation; and (iii) *compliance* to federal legislation, regulations, directives, policies, standards, and guidance. As risk assessments are updated and refined, organizations use the results to update the risk management strategy, thereby incorporating lessons learned into risk management processes, improving responses to risk, and building a solid foundation of threat and vulnerability information tailored to organizational missions/business functions.

---

[41] NIST Special Publication 800-137 provides guidance on information security continuous monitoring for information systems and organizations.

2.4.4   Risk Communications and Information Sharing

The risk assessment process entails ongoing communications and information sharing among stakeholders to ensure that: (i) the inputs to such assessments are as accurate as possible; (ii) intermediate assessment results can be used, for example, to support risk assessments at other tiers; and (iii) the results are meaningful and useful inputs to the risk response step in the risk management process. The manner and form in which risks are communicated are an expression of organizational culture as well as legal, regulatory, and contractual constraints. To be effective, communication of information security risks and other risk-related information produced during the risk assessment is consistent with other forms of risk communication within organizations. To maximize the benefit of risk assessments, organizations should establish policies, procedures, and implementing mechanisms to ensure that the information produced during such assessments is effectively communicated and shared across all three risk management tiers.[42] To reinforce the importance of risk communication and information sharing within organizations, the input tables in Appendices D, E, F, G, H, and I (i.e., threat sources, threat events, vulnerabilities, predisposing conditions, likelihood, impact, and risk) and the recommended elements of a risk assessment report (Appendix K) provide recommendations for risk communication/sharing among the tiers.

TARGETED RISK ASSESSMENTS

Organizations can use *targeted* risk assessments, in which the scope is narrowly defined, to produce answers to specific questions (e.g., what is the risk associated with relying on a given technology, how should prior assessments of risk be revised based on incidents that have occurred, what new risks can be identified based on knowledge about a newly discovered threat or vulnerability) or to inform specific decisions (e.g., which risks should be managed at Tier 1 rather than Tier 2 or 3). Organizations may consider assessing risk at Tier 1 and Tier 2 arising from a set of common threats and vulnerabilities applicable to a wide range of organizational information systems. Assessing risk at Tiers 1 and 2 allows organizations to reduce the number of threats and vulnerabilities considered at the individual information system level and develop common risk responses for such organization-wide risks. This approach can support the common control selection process for organizations and increase the efficiency and cost-effectiveness of risk assessments across the organization.

With respect to all three tiers in the risk management hierarchy, there are *no specific requirements* with regard to: (i) the formality, rigor, or level of detail that characterizes any particular risk assessment; (ii) the methodologies, tools, and techniques used to conduct such risk assessments; or (iii) the format and content of assessment results and any associated reporting mechanisms. Organizations have *maximum flexibility* on how risk assessments are conducted, where such assessments are applied, and how the results will be used. Organizations are encouraged to use the guidance in a manner that most effectively and cost-effectively provides the information necessary to senior leaders/executives to facilitate informed risk management decisions.

---

[42] NIST Special Publications 800-117 and 800-126 provide guidance on the Security Content Automation Protocol (SCAP) program. The SCAP program provides a standard, consistent way to communicate threat and vulnerability information.

CHAPTER THREE

THE PROCESS
CONDUCTING RISK ASSESSMENTS WITHIN ORGANIZATIONS

This chapter describes the process of assessing information security risk including: (i) a high-level overview of the risk assessment process; (ii) the activities necessary to prepare for risk assessments; (iii) the activities necessary to conduct effective risk assessments; (iv) the activities necessary to communicate the assessment results and share risk-related information; and (v) the activities necessary to maintain the results of risk assessments on an ongoing basis. The risk assessment process[43] is composed of four steps: (i) *prepare* for the assessment; (ii) *conduct* the assessment; (iii) *communicate* assessment results; and (iv) *maintain* the assessment.[44] Each step is divided into a set of tasks. For each task, supplemental guidance provides additional information for organizations conducting risk assessments. Risk tables and exemplary assessment scales are listed in appropriate tasks and cross-referenced to additional, more detailed information in the supporting appendices. Figure 5 illustrates the basic steps in the risk assessment process and highlights the specific tasks for conducting the assessment.

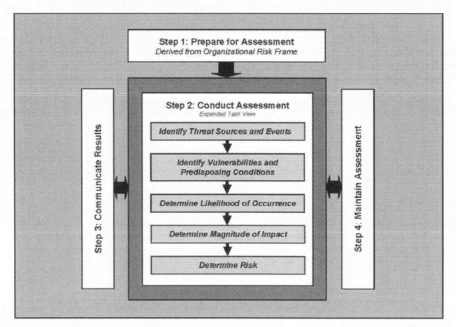

FIGURE 5: RISK ASSESSMENT PROCESS

---

[43] The intent of the process description in Chapter Three is to provide a common expression of the essential elements of an effective risk assessment. It is not intended to limit organizational flexibility in conducting those assessments. Other procedures can be implemented if organizations choose to do so, consistent with the intent of the process description.

[44] The four-step risk assessment process described in this publication is consistent with the general risk assessment process described in NIST Special Publication 800-39. The additional steps and tasks result from the need to provide more detailed guidance to effectively carry out the specific activities associated with risk assessments.

3.1 PREPARING FOR THE RISK ASSESSMENT

The first step in the risk assessment process is to *prepare* for the assessment. The objective of this step is to establish a context for the risk assessment. This context is established and informed by the results from the risk framing step of the risk management process. Risk framing identifies, for example, organizational information regarding policies and requirements for conducting risk assessments, specific assessment methodologies to be employed, procedures for selecting risk factors to be considered, scope of the assessments, rigor of analyses, degree of formality, and requirements that facilitate consistent and repeatable risk determinations across the organization. Organizations use the risk management strategy to the extent practicable to obtain information to prepare for the risk assessment. Preparing for a risk assessment includes the following tasks:

- Identify the purpose of the assessment;

- Identify the scope of the assessment;

- Identify the assumptions and constraints associated with the assessment;

- Identify the sources of information to be used as inputs to the assessment; and

- Identify the risk model and analytic approaches (i.e., assessment and analysis approaches) to be employed during the assessment.

STEP 1: PREPARE FOR THE ASSESSMENT

IDENTIFY PURPOSE

TASK 1-1: Identify the purpose of the risk assessment in terms of the information that the assessment is intended to produce and the decisions the assessment is intended to support.

Supplemental Guidance: The purpose of the risk assessment is explicitly stated in sufficient detail to ensure that the assessment produces the appropriate information and supports the intended decisions. Organizations can provide guidance on how to capture and present information produced during the risk assessment (e.g., using a defined organizational template). Appendix K provides an exemplary template for a risk assessment report or the preferred vehicle for risk communication. At Tier 3, risk assessments support: (i) authorization-related decisions throughout the system development life cycle; (ii) reciprocity, particularly for reuse of assessment information; (iii) risk management activities at Tier 2; and (iv) programmatic risk management activities throughout the system development life cycle. At Tier 2, risk assessments enable organizations to: (i) understand dependencies and ways in which risks are accepted, rejected, shared, transferred, or mitigated among information systems that support organizational mission/business processes; (ii) support architectural and operational decisions for organizational risk responses (e.g., reducing dependencies, limiting connectivity, enhancing or focusing monitoring, and enhancing information/system resiliency); (iii) identify trends, so that proactive risk response strategies and courses of action for mission/business processes can be defined; and (iv) support reciprocity, particularly to enable information sharing. At Tier 1, risk assessments: (i) support the risk executive (function); and (ii) serve as a key input to the risk management strategy. In addition to these common purposes, risk assessments may have a very specific purpose, to answer a specific question (e.g., What are the risk implications of a newly discovered vulnerability or class of vulnerabilities, allowing new connectivity, outsourcing a specific function, or adopting a new technology?). Risk assessment results from all tiers can be used by organizations to inform the acquisition process by helping to ensure information security requirements are clearly specified.

The purpose of the risk assessment is influenced by whether the assessment is: (i) an initial assessment; or (ii) a subsequent assessment initiated from the risk response or monitoring steps in the risk management process. For initial assessments, the purpose can include, for example: (i) establishing a baseline assessment of risk; or (ii) identifying threats and vulnerabilities, impacts to organizational operations and assets, individuals, other organizations, and the Nation, and other risk factors to be tracked over time as part of risk monitoring. For a reassessment initiated from the risk response step, the purpose can include, for example, providing a comparative analysis of alternative risk responses or answering a specific question (see discussion of *targeted risk assessments* above). Alternatively, for a reassessment initiated from the risk monitoring step, the purpose can include, for example, updating the risk assessment based on: (i) ongoing determinations of the effectiveness of security controls in organizational information systems or environments of operation; (ii) changes to information systems or environments of operation (e.g., changes to hardware, firmware, software; changes to system-specific, hybrid, or common controls; changes to mission/business processes, common infrastructure and support services, threats, vulnerabilities, or facilities); and (iii) results from compliance verification activities. Reassessments can also be initiated by organizations due to incidents that have occurred (e.g., cyber attacks compromising organizational information or information systems).

IDENTIFY SCOPE

TASK 1-2: Identify the scope of the risk assessment in terms of organizational applicability, time frame supported, and architectural/technology considerations.

Supplemental Guidance: The scope of the risk assessment determines what will be considered in the assessment. Risk assessment scope affects the range of information available to make risk-based decisions and is determined by the organizational official requesting the assessment and the risk management strategy. Establishing the scope of the risk assessment helps organizations to determine: (i) what tiers are addressed in the assessment; (ii) what parts of organizations are affected by the assessment and how they are affected; (iii) what decisions the assessment results support; (iv) how long assessment results are relevant; and (v) what influences the need to update the assessment. Establishing the scope of the risk assessment helps to determine the form and content of the risk assessment report, as well as the information to be shared as a result of conducting the assessment. At Tier 3, the scope of a risk assessment can depend on the authorization boundary for the information system. Appendix K provides an example of the type of information that may be included in a risk assessment report or the preferred vehicle for risk communication.

Organizational Applicability

Organizational applicability describes which parts of the organization or suborganizations are affected by the risk assessment and the risk-based decisions resulting from the assessment (including the parts of the organization or suborganizations responsible for implementing the activities and tasks related to the decisions). For example, the risk assessment can inform decisions regarding information systems supporting a particular organizational mission/business function or mission/business process. This can include decisions regarding the selection, tailoring, or supplementation of security controls for specific information systems or the selection of common controls. Alternatively, the risk assessment can inform decisions regarding a set of closely related missions/business functions or mission/business processes. The scope of the risk assessment can include not only the missions/business functions, mission/business processes, common infrastructure, or shared services on which the organization currently depends, but also those which the organization might use under specific operational conditions.

Effectiveness Time Frame

Organizations determine how long the results of particular risk assessments can be used to legitimately inform risk-based decisions. The time frame is usually related to the purpose of the assessment. For example, a risk assessment to inform Tier 1 policy-related decisions needs to be relevant for an extended period of time since the governance process for policy changes can be time-consuming in many organizations. A risk assessment conducted to inform a Tier 3 decision on the use of a compensating security control for an information system may be relevant only until the next release of the information technology product providing the required security capability. Organizations determine the useful life of risk assessment results and under what conditions the current assessment results become ineffective or irrelevant. Risk monitoring can be used to help determine the effectiveness of time frames for risk assessments. In addition to risk assessment results, organizations also consider the currency/timeliness (i.e., latency or age) of all types of information/data used in assessing risk. This is of particular concern in information reuse and evaluating the validity of assessment results.

Architectural/Technology Considerations

Organizations use architectural and technology considerations to clarify the scope of the risk assessment. For example, at Tier 3, the scope of the risk assessment can be an organizational information system in its environment of operations. This entails placing the information system in its architectural context, so that vulnerabilities in inherited controls can be taken into consideration. Alternately, the scope of the assessment can be limited solely to the information system, without consideration of inherited vulnerabilities. At Tier 2, the scope of the risk assessment can be defined in terms of the mission/business segment architecture (e.g., including all systems, services, and infrastructures that support a specific mission/function). For a targeted risk assessment at any tier, the specific question to be answered can restrict the scope to a specific technology.

IDENTIFY ASSUMPTIONS AND CONSTRAINTS

TASK 1-3: Identify the specific assumptions and constraints under which the risk assessment is conducted.

Supplemental Guidance: As part of the risk framing step in the risk management process, organizations make explicit the specific assumptions, constraints, risk tolerance, and priorities/trade-offs used within organizations to make investment and operational decisions. This information guides and informs organizational risk assessments. When an organizational risk management strategy cannot be cited, risk assessments identify and document assumptions and constraints. Assumptions and constraints identified by organizations during the risk framing step and included as part of the organizational risk management strategy need not be repeated in each individual risk assessment. By making assumptions and constraints explicit, there is greater clarity in the risk model selected for the risk assessment, increased reproducibility/repeatability of assessment results, and an increased opportunity for reciprocity among organizations. Organizations identify assumptions in key areas relevant to the risk assessment including, for example: (i) threat sources; (ii) threat events; (iii) vulnerabilities and predisposing conditions; (iv) potential impacts; (v) assessment and analysis approaches; and (vi) which missions/business functions are primary. Organizations also identify constraints in key areas relevant to the risk assessment including, for example: (i) resources available for the assessment; (ii) skills and expertise required for the assessment; and (iii) operational considerations related to mission/business activities. For example, organizational assumptions about how threats and impacts should be assessed can range from using worst-case projections to using best-case projections or anything in between those endpoints. Finally, organizations consider the uncertainty with regard to assumptions made or other information used in the risk assessment. Uncertainty in assumptions can affect organizational risk tolerance. For example, assumptions based on a lack of specific or credible information may reduce an organization's risk tolerance because of the uncertainty influencing the assumptions. The following sections provide some representative examples of areas where assumptions/constraints for risk assessments may be identified.

Threat Sources

Organizations determine which types of threat sources are to be considered during risk assessments. Organizations make explicit the process used to identify threats and any assumptions related to the threat identification process. If such information is identified during the risk framing step and included as part of the organizational risk management strategy, the information need not be repeated in each individual risk assessment. Risk assessments can address all types of threat sources, a single broad threat source (e.g., adversarial), or a specific threat source (e.g., trusted insider). Table D-2 provides a sample taxonomy of threat sources that can be considered by organizations in identifying assumptions for risk assessments. Organizational assumptions about threat sources to consider inform Task 2-1.

Threat Events

Organizations determine which type of threat events are to be considered during risk assessments and the level of detail needed to describe such events. Descriptions of threat events can be expressed in highly general terms (e.g., phishing, distributed denial-of-service), in more descriptive terms using tactics, techniques, and procedures, or in highly specific terms (e.g., the names of specific information systems, technologies, organizations, roles, or locations). In addition, organizations consider: (i) what representative set of threat events can serve as a starting point for the identification of the specific threat events in the risk assessment; and (ii) what degree of confirmation is needed for threat events to be considered relevant for purposes of the risk assessment. For example, organizations may consider only those threat events that have been observed (either internally or by organizations that are peers/partners) or all possible threat events. Table E-2 and Table E-3 provide representative examples of adversarial and non-adversarial threat events at a level of detail that can be used for risk assessments at all tiers. Greater detail can be found in multiple sources (e.g., Common Attack Pattern Enumeration and Classification [CAPEC]). Organizational assumptions about threat events to consider and level of detail, inform Task 2-2.

Vulnerabilities and Predisposing Conditions

Organizations determine the types of vulnerabilities that are to be considered during risk assessments and the level of detail provided in the vulnerability descriptions. Organizations make explicit the process used to identify vulnerabilities and any assumptions related to the vulnerability identification process. If such information is identified during the risk framing step and included as part of the organizational risk management strategy, the information need not be repeated in each individual risk assessment. Vulnerabilities can be associated with organizational information systems (e.g., hardware, software, firmware, internal controls, and security procedures) or the environments in which those systems operate (e.g., organizational governance, external relationships, mission/business processes, enterprise architectures, information security architectures). Organizations also determine the types of predisposing conditions that are to be considered during risk assessments including, for example, architectures and technologies employed, environments of operation, and personnel. Table F-4 provides representative examples of such predisposing conditions. Organizational assumptions about vulnerabilities and predisposing conditions to consider and level of detail, inform Task 2-3.

Likelihood

Organizations make explicit the process used to conduct likelihood determinations and any assumptions related to the likelihood determination process. If such information is identified during the risk framing step and included as part of the organizational risk management strategy, the information need not be repeated in each individual risk assessment. Organizational assumptions about how to determine likelihood inform Task 2-4.

Impacts

Organizations determine potential adverse impacts in terms of organizational operations (i.e., missions, functions, image, and reputation), organizational assets, individuals, other organizations, and the Nation. Organizations make explicit the process used to conduct impact determinations and any assumptions related to the impact determination process. If such information is identified during the risk framing step and included as part of the organizational risk management strategy, the information need not be repeated in each individual risk assessment. Organizations address impacts at a level of detail that includes, for example, specific mission/business processes or information resources (e.g., information, personnel, equipment, funds, and information technology). Organizations may include information from Business Impact Analyses with regard to providing impact information for risk assessments. Table H-2 provides representative examples of types of impacts (i.e., harm) that can be considered by organizations. Organizational assumptions about how to determine impacts and at what level of detail, inform Task 2-5.

Risk Tolerance and Uncertainty

Organizations determine the levels and types of risk that are acceptable. Risk tolerance is determined as part of the organizational risk management strategy to ensure consistency across the organization. Organizations also provide guidance on how to identify reasons for uncertainty when risk factors are assessed, since uncertainty in one or more factors will propagate to the resulting evaluation of level of risk, and how to compensate for incomplete, imperfect, or assumption-dependent estimates. Consideration of uncertainty is especially important when organizations consider advanced persistent threats (APT) since assessments of the likelihood of threat event occurrence can have a great degree of uncertainty. To compensate, organizations can take a variety of approaches to determine likelihood, ranging from assuming the worst-case likelihood (certain to happen sometime in the foreseeable future) to assuming that if an event has not been observed, it is unlikely to happen. Organizations also determine what levels of risk (combination of likelihood and impact) indicate that no further analysis of any risk factors is needed.

Analytic Approach

Risk assessments include both assessment approaches (i.e., quantitative, qualitative, semi-quantitative) and analysis approaches (i.e., threat-oriented, asset/impact-oriented, vulnerability-oriented). Together, the assessment and analysis approaches form the *analytic approach* for the risk assessment. Organizations determine the level of detail and in what form, threats are analyzed including the level of granularity to describe threat events or threat scenarios. Different analysis approaches can lead to different levels of detail in characterizing adverse events for which likelihoods are determined. For example, an adverse event could be characterized in several ways (with increasing levels of detail): (i) a threat event (for which the likelihood is determined by taking the maximum overall threat sources); (ii) a pairing of a threat event and a threat source; or (iii) a detailed threat scenario/attack tree. In general, organizations can be expected to require more detail for highly critical missions/business functions, common infrastructures, or shared services on which multiple missions or business functions depend (as common points of failure), and information systems with high criticality or sensitivity. Mission/business owners may amplify this guidance for risk *hot spots* (information systems, services, or critical infrastructure components of particular concern) in mission/business segments.

IDENTIFY INFORMATION SOURCES

TASK 1-4: Identify the sources of descriptive, threat, vulnerability, and impact information to be used in the risk assessment.

Supplemental Guidance: Descriptive information enables organizations to be able to determine the relevance of threat and vulnerability information. At Tier 1, descriptive information can include, for example, the type of risk management and information security governance structures in place within organizations and how the organization identifies and prioritizes critical missions/business functions. At Tier 2, descriptive information can include, for example, information about: (i) organizational mission/business processes, functional management processes, and information flows; (ii) enterprise architecture, information security architecture, and the technical/process flow architectures of the systems, common infrastructures, and shared services that fall within the scope of the risk assessment; and (iii) the external environments in which organizations operate including, for example, the relationships and dependencies with external providers. Such information is typically found in architectural documentation (particularly documentation of high-level operational views), business continuity plans, and risk assessment reports for organizational information systems, common infrastructures, and shared services that fall within the scope of the risk assessment. At Tier 3, descriptive information can include, for example, information about: (i) the design of and technologies used in organizational information systems; (ii) the environment in which the systems operate; (iii) connectivity to and dependency on other information systems; and (iv) dependencies on common infrastructures or shared services. Such information is found in system documentation, contingency plans, and risk assessment reports for other information systems, infrastructures, and services.

Sources of information as described in Tables D-1, E-1, F-1, H-1, and I-1 can be either internal or external to organizations. Internal sources of information that can provide insights into both threats and vulnerabilities can include, for example, risk assessment reports, incident reports, security logs, trouble tickets, and monitoring results. Note that internally, information from risk assessment reports at one tier can serve as input to risk assessments at other tiers. Mission/business owners are encouraged to identify not only common infrastructure and/or support services they depend on, but also those they might use under specific operational circumstances. External sources of threat information can include cross-community organizations (e.g., US Computer Emergency Readiness Team [US-CERT], sector partners (e.g., Defense Industrial Base [DIB] using the DoD-Defense Industrial Base Collaborative Information

Sharing Environment [DCISE], Information Sharing and Analysis Centers [ISACs] for critical infrastructure sectors), research and nongovernmental organizations (e.g. Carnegie Mellon University, Software Engineering Institute-CERT), and security service providers). Organizations using external sources, consider the timeliness, specificity, and relevance of threat information. Similar to sources of threat information, sources of vulnerability information can also be either internal or external to organizations (see Table F-1). Internal sources can include, for example, vulnerability assessment reports. External sources of vulnerability information are similar to the sources identified above for threat information. As described in Table F-1, information about predisposing conditions can be found in a variety of sources including, for example, descriptions of information systems, environments of operation, shared services, common infrastructures, and enterprise architecture. As described in Table H-1, sources of impact information can include, for example, mission/business impact analyses, information system component inventories, and security categorizations. Security categorization constitutes a determination of the potential impacts should certain events occur which jeopardize the information and information systems needed by the organization to accomplish its assigned missions, protect its assets, fulfill its legal responsibilities, maintain its day-to-day functions, and protect individuals. Security categories are to be used in conjunction with vulnerability and threat information in assessing the risk to organizational operations and assets, individuals, other organizations, and the Nation. Security categories constitute an initial summary of impact in terms of failures to meet the security objectives of confidentiality, integrity, and availability, and are informed by the types of harm presented in Table H-2.

IDENTIFY RISK MODEL AND ANALYTIC APPROACH

TASK 1-5: Identify the risk model and analytic approach to be used in the risk assessment.

Supplemental Guidance: Organizations define one or more risk models for use in conducting risk assessments (see Section 2.3.1) and identify which model is to be used for the risk assessment. To facilitate reciprocity of assessment results, organization-specific risk models include, or can be translated into, the risk factors (i.e., threat, vulnerability, impact, likelihood, and predisposing condition) defined in the appendices. Organizations also identify the specific analytic approach to be used for the risk assessment including the assessment approach (i.e., quantitative, qualitative, semi-quantitative) and the analysis approach (i.e., threat-oriented, asset/impact-oriented, vulnerability-oriented). For each assessable risk factor, the appendices include three assessment scales (one qualitative and two semi-quantitative scales) with correspondingly different representations. Organizations typically define (or select and tailor from the appendices) the assessment scales to be used in their risk assessments, annotating with organizationally-meaningful examples for specific values and defining break points between bins for semi-quantitative approaches. In addition, mission/business owners can provide further annotations with mission/business-specific examples. Organizations can identify different assessment scales to be used in different circumstances. For example, for low-impact information systems, organizations could use qualitative values, while for moderate- and high-impact systems, the most granular semi-quantitative values (0-100) could be used. As discussed in Special Publication 800-39, Task 1-1, Risk Assumptions, organizations vary in the relative weights applied to risk factors. Therefore, this guideline does not specify algorithms for combining semi-quantitative values. Organization-specific risk models include algorithms (e.g., formulas, tables, rules) for combining risk factors. If an organization-specific risk model is not provided in the risk management strategy as part of the risk framing step, then part of this task is to specify the algorithms for combining values. Algorithms for combining risk factors reflect organizational risk tolerance (see the supplemental guidance to Task 2-4 for examples). Organization-specific risk models are refined as part of preparation for a risk assessment by: (i) identifying the risk model and the rationale for using it (when multiple organization-specific risk models are provided); (ii) providing additional examples for values of risk factors; and (iii) identifying any assessment-specific algorithms (e.g., algorithms specific to the use of an attack graph analysis technique). In the absence of pre-existing organization-specific risk models or analytic approaches defined in the organizational risk management strategy, the risk model and analytic approaches to be used in the risk assessment are defined and documented in this task.

Summary of Key Activities – Preparing for Risk Assessments

- Identify the *purpose* of the risk assessment.
- Identify the *scope* of the risk assessment.
- Identify the *assumptions* and *constraints* under which the risk assessment is conducted.
- Identify *sources* of threat, vulnerability, and impact information to be used in the risk assessment (see Tables D-1, E-1, F-1, H-1, and I-1 as tailored by the organization).
- Define or refine the *risk model, assessment approach,* and *analysis approach* to be used in the risk assessment.

3.2   CONDUCTING THE RISK ASSESSMENT

The second step in the risk assessment process is to *conduct* the assessment. The objective of this step is to produce a list of information security risks that can be prioritized by risk level and used to inform risk response decisions. To accomplish this objective, organizations analyze threats and vulnerabilities, impacts and likelihood, and the uncertainty associated with the risk assessment process. This step also includes the gathering of essential information as a part of each task and is conducted in accordance with the assessment context established in the Prepare step of the risk assessment process. The expectation for risk assessments is to adequately cover the entire threat space in accordance with the specific definitions, guidance, and direction established during the Prepare step. However, in practice, adequate coverage within available resources may dictate generalizing threat sources, threat events, and vulnerabilities to ensure full coverage and assessing specific, detailed sources, events, and vulnerabilities only as necessary to accomplish risk assessment objectives. Conducting risk assessments includes the following specific tasks:

* Identify threat sources that are relevant to organizations;

* Identify threat events that could be produced by those sources;

* Identify vulnerabilities within organizations that could be exploited by threat sources through specific threat events and the predisposing conditions that could affect successful exploitation;

* Determine the likelihood that the identified threat sources would initiate specific threat events and the likelihood that the threat events would be successful;

* Determine the adverse impacts to organizational operations and assets, individuals, other organizations, and the Nation resulting from the exploitation of vulnerabilities by threat sources (through specific threat events); and

* Determine information security risks as a combination of likelihood of threat exploitation of vulnerabilities and the impact of such exploitation, including any uncertainties associated with the risk determinations.

The specific tasks are presented in a sequential manner for clarity. However, in practice, some iteration among the tasks is both necessary and expected.[45] Depending on the purpose of the risk assessment, organizations may find reordering the tasks advantageous.[46] Whatever adjustments organizations make to the tasks described below, risk assessments should meet the stated purpose, scope, assumptions, and constraints established by the organizations initiating the assessments. To assist organizations in executing the individual tasks in the risk assessment process, a set of templates is provided in Appendices D through I. These appendices provide useful information for organizations in assessing risk and can also be used to record assessment results produced during essential calculations and analyses. The templates are exemplary and can be tailored by organizations in accordance with specific organizational mission/business requirements. The use of the templates is not required in order to conduct risk assessments.

---

[45] For example, as vulnerabilities are identified, additional threat events might be identified by asking how the newly identified vulnerabilities could be exploited. If organizations identify vulnerabilities first and then define threat events, there may be some events that do not map cleanly to vulnerabilities but do map to predisposing conditions.

[46] For example, the risk assessment could start with an identification of mission/business impacts at Tiers 1 and 2 using common techniques such as Mission Impact Analyses, Business Impact Analyses, Mission/Business Thread Analyses, or Business Continuity Analyses. The results of such analyses could enable risk assessors to focus attention on, and perform more detailed analysis of, potential threats to critical information systems, databases, communications links, or other assets.

STEP 2: CONDUCT THE ASSESSMENT

IDENTIFY THREAT SOURCES

TASK 2-1: Identify and characterize threat sources of concern, including capability, intent, and targeting characteristics for adversarial threats and range of effects for non-adversarial threats.

Supplemental Guidance: Organizations identify threat sources of concern and determine the characteristics associated with those threat sources. For adversarial threat sources, assess the capabilities, intentions, and targeting associated with the threat sources. For non-adversarial threat sources, assess the potential range of effects from the threat sources. The risk management strategy and the results of the Prepare step provide organizational direction and guidance for conducting threat source identification and characterization including, for example: (i) sources for obtaining threat information; (ii) threat sources to consider (by type/name); (iii) threat taxonomy to be used; and (iv) the process for identifying which threat sources are of concern for the risk assessment. As identified in Task 1-3, organizations make explicit any assumptions concerning threat sources including decisions regarding the identification of threat sources when specific and credible threat information is unavailable. Organizations can also view adversarial threat sources from a broad-based perspective, considering the time such threat sources may have to exploit identified organizational vulnerabilities, the scale of the attack, and the potential use of multiple attack vectors. The identification and characterization of Advanced Persistent Threats (APTs) can involve considerable uncertainty. Organizations annotate such threat sources with appropriate rationale and references (and providing classifications as necessary).

Appendix D provides a set of exemplary tables for use in identifying threat sources.

- Table D-1 provides a set of exemplary inputs to the threat source identification task;
- Table D-2 provides an exemplary taxonomy that can be used to identify and characterize threat sources;
- Tables D-3, D-4, and D-5 provide exemplary assessment scales to assess the risk factors (i.e., characteristics) of adversarial threat sources with regard to capability, intent, and targeting;
- Table D-6 provides an exemplary assessment scale for assessing the ranges of effects from threat events initiated by non-adversarial threat sources; and
- Tables D-7 and D-8 provide templates for summarizing and documenting the results of threat source identification and characterization.

If a particular type of threat source is outside the scope of the risk assessment or not relevant to the organization, the information in Tables D-7 and D-8 can be truncated accordingly. The information produced in Task 2-1 provides threat source inputs to the risk tables in Appendix I.

Summary of Key Activities – Task 2-1

- Identify threat source inputs (see **Table D-1**, as tailored by the organization).
- Identify threat sources (see **Table D-2**, as tailored by the organization).
- Determine if threat sources are relevant to the organization and in scope (see **Table D-1**, as tailored by the organization).
- Create or update the assessment of threat sources (see **Table D-7** for adversarial threat sources and **Table D-8** for non-adversarial threat sources, as tailored by the organization).
    - For relevant adversarial threat sources:
        - Assess adversary capability (see **Table D-3**, as tailored by the organization).
        - Assess adversary intent (see **Table D-4**, as tailored by the organization).
        - Assess adversary targeting (see **Table D-5**, as tailored by the organization).
    - For relevant non-adversarial threat sources:
        - Assess the range of effects from threat sources (see **Table D-6**, as tailored by the organization).

IDENTIFY THREAT EVENTS

TASK 2-2: Identify potential threat events, relevance of the events, and the threat sources that could initiate the events.

Supplemental Guidance: Threat events are characterized by the threat sources that could initiate the events, and for adversarial events, the TTPs used to carry out attacks. Organizations define these threat events with sufficient detail to accomplish the purpose of the risk assessment. At Tier 1, threat events that could affect the organizational level are of particular interest. At Tier 2, threat events that cross or span information system boundaries, exploit functional dependencies or connectivity among systems, or affect mission/business owners, are of particular interest. At Tier 3, threat events that can be described in terms of specific information systems, technologies, or environments of operation are of particular interest. Multiple threat sources can initiate a single threat event. Conversely, a single threat source can potentially initiate any of multiple threat events. Therefore, there can be a many-to-many relationship among threat events and threat sources that can potentially increase the complexity of the risk assessment. To enable effective use and communication of risk assessment results, organizations tailor the general descriptions of threat events in Tables E-2 and E-3 to identify how each event could potentially harm organizational operations (including mission, functions, image, or reputation) and assets, individuals, other organizations, or the Nation. For each threat event identified, organizations determine the relevance of the event. Table E-4 provides a range of values for relevance of threat events. The values selected by organizations have a direct linkage to organizational risk tolerance. The more risk averse, the greater the range of values considered. Organizations accepting greater risk or having a greater risk tolerance are more likely to require substantive evidence before giving serious consideration to threat events. If a threat event is deemed to be irrelevant, no further consideration is given. For relevant threat events, organizations identify all potential threat sources that could initiate the events. For use in Task 2-4, organizations can identify each pairing of threat source and threat event separately since the likelihood of threat initiation and success could be different for each pairing. Alternatively, organizations can identify the set of all possible threat sources that could potentially initiate a threat event.

Appendix E provides a set of exemplary tables for use in identifying threat events:

- Table E-1 provides a set of exemplary inputs to the threat event identification task;
- Table E-2 provides representative examples of adversarial threat events expressed as TTPs;
- Table E-3 provides representative examples of non-adversarial threat events;
- Table E-4 provides exemplary values for the relevance of threat events to organizations; and
- Table E-5 provides a template for summarizing and documenting the results of threat event identification.

The information produced in Task 2-2 provides threat event inputs to the risk tables in Appendix I.

Summary of Key Activities – Task 2-2

- Identify threat event inputs (see **Table E-1**, as tailored by the organization).
- Identify threat events (see **Table E-2** for adversarial threat events and **Table E-3** for non-adversarial threat events, as tailored by the organization); create or update **Table E-5**.
- Identify threat sources that could initiate the threat events (see **Table D-7** and **Table D-8**, as tailored by the organization); update **Table E-5**.
- Assess the relevance of threat events to the organization (see **Table E-4**, as tailored by the organization); update **Table E-5**.
- Update Columns 1-6 in **Table I-5** for adversarial risk (see **Table E-5** and **Table D-7**); or update Columns 1-4 in **Table I-7** for non-adversarial risk (see **Table E-5** and **Table D-8**).

IDENTIFY VULNERABILITIES AND PREDISPOSING CONDITIONS

TASK 2-3: Identify vulnerabilities and predisposing conditions that affect the likelihood that threat events of concern result in adverse impacts.

Supplemental Guidance: The primary purpose of vulnerability assessments is to understand the nature and degree to which organizations, mission/business processes, and information systems are vulnerable to threat sources identified in Task 2-1 and the threat events identified in Task 2-2 that can be initiated by those threat sources. Vulnerabilities at Tier 1 can be pervasive across organizations and can have wide-ranging adverse impacts if exploited by threat events. For example, organizational failure to consider supply chain activities can result in organizations acquiring subverted components that adversaries could exploit to disrupt organizational missions/business functions or to obtain sensitive organizational information. Vulnerabilities at Tier 2 can be described in terms of organizational mission/business processes, enterprise architecture, the use of multiple information systems, or common infrastructures/shared services. At Tier 2, vulnerabilities typically cross or span information system boundaries. Vulnerabilities at Tier 3 can be described in terms of the information technologies employed within organizational information systems, the environments in which those systems operate, and/or the lack of or weaknesses in system-specific security controls. There is potentially a many-to-many relationship between threat events and vulnerabilities. Multiple threat events can exploit a single vulnerability, and conversely, multiple vulnerabilities can be exploited by a single threat event. The severity of a vulnerability is an assessment of the relative importance of mitigating such a vulnerability. Initially, the extent to which mitigation is unplanned can serve as a surrogate for vulnerability severity. Once the risks associated with a particular vulnerability have been assessed, the impact severity and exposure of the vulnerability given the security controls implemented and other vulnerabilities can be taken into consideration in assessing vulnerability severity. Assessments of vulnerability severity support risk response. Vulnerabilities can be identified at varying degrees of granularity and specificity. The level of detail provided in any particular vulnerability assessment is consistent with the purpose of the risk assessment and the type of inputs needed to support follow-on likelihood and impact determinations.

Due to the ever-increasing size and complexity of organizations, mission/business processes, and the information systems supporting those processes, the number of vulnerabilities tends to be large and can increase the overall complexity of the analysis. Therefore, organizations have the option of using the vulnerability identification task to understand the general nature of the vulnerabilities (including scope, number, and type) relevant to the assessment (see Task 1-3) and performing a cataloging of specific vulnerabilities as necessary to do so. Organizations determine which vulnerabilities are relevant to which threat events in order to reduce the space of potential risks to be assessed. In addition to identifying vulnerabilities, organizations also identify any predisposing conditions which may affect susceptibility to certain vulnerabilities. Predisposing conditions that exist within organizations (including mission/business processes, information systems, and environments of operation) can contribute to (i.e., increase or decrease) the likelihood that one or more threat events, once initiated by threat sources, result in adverse impacts to organizational operations, organizational assets, individuals, other organizations, or the Nation. Organizations determine which predisposing conditions are relevant to which threat events in order to reduce the space of potential risks to be assessed. Organizations assess the pervasiveness of predisposing conditions to support determination of the tier(s) at which risk response could be most effective.

Appendix F provides a set of exemplary tables for use in identifying vulnerabilities and predisposing conditions:

- Table F-1 provides a set of exemplary inputs to the vulnerability and predisposing condition identification task;
- Table F-2 provides an exemplary assessment scale for assessing the severity of identified vulnerabilities;
- Table F-3 provides a template for summarizing/documenting the results of vulnerability identification;
- Table F-4 provides an exemplary taxonomy that can be used to identify and characterize predisposing conditions;
- Table F-5 provides an exemplary assessment scale for assessing the pervasiveness of predisposing conditions; and
- Table F-6 provides a template for summarizing/documenting the results of identifying predisposing conditions.

The information produced in Task 2-3 provides vulnerability and predisposing condition inputs to the risk tables in Appendix I.

Summary of Key Activities – Task 2-3

- Identify vulnerability and predisposing condition inputs (see **Table F-1**, as tailored by the organization).
- Identify vulnerabilities using organization-defined information sources; create or update **Table F-3**.
- Assess the severity of identified vulnerabilities (see **Table F-2**, as tailored by the organization); update **Table F-3**.
- Identify predisposing conditions (see **Table F-4**, as tailored by the organization); create or update **Table F-6**.
- Assess the pervasiveness of predisposing conditions (see **Table F-5**, as tailored by the organization); update **Table F-6**.
- Update Column 8 in **Table I-5** for adversarial risk; or update Column 6 in **Table I-7** for non-adversarial risk (see **Table F-3** and **Table F-6**).
- Update Column 9 in **Table I-5** for adversarial risk; or update Column 7 in **Table I-7** for non-adversarial risk (see **Table F-2** and **Table F-5**).

DETERMINE LIKELIHOOD

TASK 2-4: Determine the likelihood that threat events of concern result in adverse impacts, considering: (i) the characteristics of the threat sources that could initiate the events; (ii) the vulnerabilities/predisposing conditions identified; and (iii) the organizational susceptibility reflecting the safeguards/countermeasures planned or implemented to impede such events.

Supplemental Guidance: Organizations employ a three-step process to determine the overall likelihood of threat events. First, organizations assess the likelihood that threat events will be initiated (for adversarial threat events) or will occur (for non-adversarial threat events). Second, organizations assess the likelihood that threat events once initiated or occurring, will result in adverse impacts to organizational operations and assets, individuals, other organizations, or the Nation. Finally, organizations assess the overall likelihood as a combination of likelihood of initiation/occurrence and likelihood of resulting in adverse impact.

Organizations assess the likelihood of threat event initiation by taking into consideration the characteristics of the threat sources of concern including capability, intent, and targeting (see Task 2-1 and Appendix D). If threat events require more capability than adversaries possess (and adversaries are cognizant of this fact), then the adversaries are not expected to initiate the events. If adversaries do not expect to achieve intended objectives by executing threat events, then the adversaries are not expected to initiate the events. And finally, if adversaries are not actively targeting specific organizations or their missions/business functions, adversaries are not expected to initiate threat events. Organizations use the assessment scale in Table G-2 and provide a rationale for the assessment allowing explicit consideration of deterrence and threat shifting. Organizations can assess the likelihood of threat event occurrence (non-adversarial) using Table G-3 and provide a similar rationale for the assessment.

Organizations assess the likelihood that threat events result in adverse impacts by taking into consideration the set of identified vulnerabilities and predisposing conditions (see Task 2-3 and Appendix F). For threat events initiated by adversaries, organizations consider characteristics of associated threat sources. For non-adversarial threat events, organizations take into account the anticipated severity and duration of the event (as included in the description of the event). Organizations use the assessment scale in Table G-4 and provide a rationale for the assessment allowing explicit consideration as stated above. Threat events for which no vulnerabilities or predisposing conditions are identified, have a very low likelihood of resulting in adverse impacts. Such threat events can be highlighted and moved to the end of the table (or to a separate table), so that they can be tracked for consideration in follow-on risk assessments. However, no further consideration during the current assessment is warranted.

The *overall likelihood* of a threat event is a combination of: (i) the likelihood that the event will occur (e.g., due to human error or natural disaster) or be initiated by an adversary; and (ii) the likelihood that the initiation/occurrence will result in adverse impacts. Organizations assess the overall likelihood of threat events by using inputs from Tables G-2, G-3, and G-4. Any specific algorithm or rule for combining the determined likelihood values depends on: (i) general organizational attitudes toward risk, including overall risk tolerance and tolerance for uncertainty; (ii) specific tolerances toward uncertainty in different risk factors; and (iii) organizational weighting of risk factors. For example, organizations could use any of the following rules (or could define a different rule): (i) use the maximum of the two likelihood values; (ii) use the minimum of the two likelihood values; (iii) consider likelihood of initiation/occurrence only, assuming that if threat events are initiated or occur, the events will result in adverse impacts; (iv) consider likelihood of impact only, assuming that if threat events could result in adverse impacts, adversaries will initiate the events; or (v) take a weighted average of the two likelihood values. Organizations make explicit the rules used.

Appendix G provides a set of exemplary tables for use in determining likelihood of threat events:

- Table G-1 provides a set of exemplary inputs to the likelihood determination task;
- Table G-2 provides an exemplary assessment scale for assessing the likelihood of initiation for adversarial threat events;
- Table G-3 provides an exemplary assessment scale for assessing the likelihood of non-adversarial threat events occurring;
- Table G-4 provides an exemplary assessment scale for assessing the likelihood of threat events having adverse impacts if the events are initiated (adversarial) or occur (non-adversarial); and
- Table G-5 provides an exemplary assessment scale for assessing the overall likelihood of threat events (i.e., a combination of the likelihood of initiation/occurrence and the likelihood of impact).

The information produced in Task 2-4 provides threat event likelihood inputs to the risk tables in Appendix I.

Summary of Key Activities – Task 2-4

- Identify likelihood determination inputs (see **Table G-1**, as tailored by the organization).
- Identify likelihood determination factors using organization-defined information sources (e.g., threat source characteristics, vulnerabilities, predisposing conditions).
- Assess the likelihood of threat event initiation for adversarial threats and the likelihood of threat event occurrence for non-adversarial threats (see **Table G-2** and **Table G-3**, as tailored by the organization).
- Assess the likelihood of threat events resulting in adverse impacts, given likelihood of initiation or occurrence (see **Table G-4**, as tailored by the organization).
- Assess the overall likelihood of threat event initiation/occurrence and likelihood of threat events resulting in adverse impacts (see **Table G-5**, as tailored by the organization).
- Update Columns 7, 10, and 11 in **Table I-5** for adversarial risk (see **Table G-2**, **Table G-4**, and **Table G-5**); or update Columns 5, 8, and 9 in **Table I-7** for non-adversarial risk (see **Table G-3**, **Table G-4**, and **Table G-5**).

DETERMINE IMPACT

TASK 2-5: Determine the adverse impacts from threat events of concern considering: (i) the characteristics of the threat sources that could initiate the events; (ii) the vulnerabilities/predisposing conditions identified; and (iii) the susceptibility reflecting the safeguards/countermeasures planned or implemented to impede such events.

Supplemental Guidance: Organizations describe adverse impacts in terms of the potential harm caused to organizational operations and assets, individuals, other organizations, or the Nation. Where the threat event occurs and whether the effects of the event are contained or spread, influences the severity of the impact. Assessing impact can involve identifying assets or potential targets of threat sources, including information resources (e.g., information, data repositories, information systems, applications, information technologies, communications links), people, and physical resources (e.g., buildings, power supplies), which could be affected by threat events. Organizational impacts are defined and prioritized at Tiers 1 and 2, and communicated to Tier 3 as part of risk framing. At Tier 3, impacts are associated with information system capabilities (e.g., processing, display, communications, storage, and retrieval) and resources (e.g., databases, services, components) that could be compromised.

Appendix H provides a set of exemplary tables for use in determining adverse impacts:

- Table H-1 provides a set of exemplary inputs to the impact determination task;
- Table H-2 provides representative examples of adverse impacts to organizations focusing on harm to organizational operations and assets, individuals, other organizations, and the Nation;
- Table H-3 provides an exemplary assessment scale for assessing the impact of threat events; and
- Table H-4 provides a template for summarizing/documenting adverse impacts.

The information produced in Task 2-5 provides adverse impact inputs to the risk tables in Appendix I.

Summary of Key Activities – Task 2-5

- Identify impact determination inputs (see **Table H-1** as tailored by the organization).
- Identify impact determination factors using organization-defined information sources.
- Identify adverse impacts and affected assets (see **Table H-2**, as tailored by the organization); create or update **Table H-4**.
- Assess the maximum impact associated with the affected assets (see **Table H-3**, as tailored by the organization); update **Table H-4**.
- Update Column 12 in **Table I-5** for adversarial risk; or update Column 10 in **Table I-7** for non-adversarial risk.

DETERMINE RISK

TASK 2-6: Determine the risk to the organization from threat events of concern considering: (i) the impact that would result from the events; and (ii) the likelihood of the events occurring.

Supplemental Guidance: Organizations assess the risks from threat events as a combination of likelihood and impact. The level of risk associated with identified threat events represents a determination of the degree to which organizations are threatened by such events. Organizations make explicit the uncertainty in the risk determinations, including, for example, organizational assumptions and subjective judgments/decisions. Organizations can order the list of threat events of concern by the level of risk determined during the risk assessment—with the greatest attention going to high-risk events. Organizations can further prioritize risks at the same level or with similar scores (see Appendix J). Each risk corresponds to a specific threat event with a level of impact if that event occurs. In general, the risk level is typically not higher than the impact level, and likelihood can serve to reduce risk below that impact level. However, when addressing organization-wide risk management issues with a large number of missions/business functions, mission/business processes, and supporting information systems, impact as an upper bound on risk may not hold. For example, when multiple risks materialize, even if each risk is at the moderate level, the set of those moderate-level risks could aggregate to a higher level of risk for organizations. To address situations where harm occurs multiple times, organizations can define a threat event as multiple occurrences of harm and an impact level associated with the cumulative degree of harm. During the execution of Tasks 2-1 through 2-5, organizations capture key information related to uncertainties in risk assessments. These uncertainties arise from sources such as missing information, subjective determinations, and assumptions made. The effectiveness of risk assessment results is in part determined by the ability of decision makers to be able to determine the continued applicability of assumptions made as part of the assessment. Information related to uncertainty is compiled and presented in a manner that readily supports informed risk management decisions.

Appendix I provides a set of exemplary tables for use in determining risk:

- Table I-1 provides a set of exemplary inputs to the risk and uncertainty determination task;
- Tables I-2 and I-3 provide exemplary assessment scales for assessing levels of risk;

- Tables I-4 and I-6 provide descriptions of column headings for key data elements used in risk determinations for adversarial and non-adversarial threat events, respectively; and

- Tables I-5 and I-7 provide templates for summarizing/documenting key data elements used in risk determinations for adversarial and non-adversarial threat events, respectively.

The information produced in Task 2-6 provides risk inputs to the risk tables in Appendix I.

Summary of Key Activities – Task 2-6

- Identify risk and uncertainty determination inputs (see **Table I-1**, as tailored by the organization).
- Determine risk (see **Table I-2** and **Table I-3**, as tailored by the organization); update Column 13 in **Table I-5** for adversarial risk and Column 11 in **Table I-7** for non-adversarial risk.

3.3 COMMUNICATING AND SHARING RISK ASSESSMENT INFORMATION

The third step in the risk assessment process is to *communicate* the assessment results and *share* risk-related information.[47] The objective of this step is to ensure that decision makers across the organization have the appropriate risk-related information needed to inform and guide risk decisions. Communicating and sharing information consists of the following specific tasks:

- Communicate the risk assessment results; and

- Share information developed in the execution of the risk assessment, to support other risk management activities.

STEP 3: COMMUNICATE AND SHARE RISK ASSESSMENT RESULTS

COMMUNICATE RISK ASSESSMENT RESULTS

TASK 3-1: Communicate risk assessment results to organizational decision makers to support risk responses.

Supplemental Guidance: Organizations can communicate risk assessment results in a variety of ways (e.g., executive briefings, risk assessment reports, dashboards). Such risk communications can be formal or informal with the content and format determined by organizations initiating and conducting the assessments. Organizations provide guidance on specific risk communication and reporting requirements, included as part of preparing for the risk assessment (if not provided in the risk management strategy as part of the risk framing task). Organizations prioritize risks at the same level or with similar scores (see Appendix J). Appendix K provides an example of type of information that may be included in a risk assessment report or the preferred vehicle for risk communication.

SHARE RISK-RELATED INFORMATION

TASK 3-2: Share risk-related information produced during the risk assessment with appropriate organizational personnel.

Supplemental Guidance: Organizations share source information and intermediate results and provide guidance on sharing risk-related information. Information sharing occurs primarily within organizations, via reports and briefings, and by updating risk-related data repositories with supporting evidence for the risk assessment results. Information sharing is also supported by documenting the sources of information, analytical processes, and intermediate results (e.g., the completed tables in Appendices D-I), so that risk assessments can be easily maintained. Information sharing may also occur with other organizations.

> ### *Summary of Key Activities – Communicating and Sharing Information*
>
> - Determine the appropriate method (e.g., executive briefing, risk assessment report, or dashboard) to communicate risk assessment results.
> - Communicate risk assessment *results* to designated organizational stakeholders.
> - Share the *risk assessment results* and supporting evidence in accordance with organizational policies and guidance.

---

[47] The risk assessment process entails ongoing communications and information sharing between those personnel performing assessment activities, subject matter experts, and key organizational stakeholders (e.g., mission/business owners, risk executive [function], chief information security officers, information system owners/program managers). This communication and information sharing ensures that: (i) the inputs to risk assessments are as accurate as possible; (ii) intermediate results can be used (e.g., to support risk assessments at other tiers); and (iii) results are meaningful and useful inputs to risk response.

3.4 MAINTAINING THE RISK ASSESSMENT

The fourth step in the risk assessment process is to *maintain* the assessment. The objective of this step is to keep current, the specific knowledge of the risk organizations incur. The results of risk assessments inform risk management decisions and guide risk responses. To support the ongoing review of risk management decisions (e.g., acquisition decisions, authorization decisions for information systems and common controls, connection decisions), organizations maintain risk assessments to incorporate any changes detected through risk monitoring.[48] Risk monitoring provides organizations with the means to, on an ongoing basis: (i) determine the *effectiveness* of risk responses; (ii) identify risk-impacting *changes* to organizational information systems and the environments in which those systems operate;[49] and (iii) verify *compliance*.[50] Maintaining risk assessments includes the following specific tasks:

- Monitor risk factors identified in risk assessments on an ongoing basis and understanding subsequent changes to those factors; and

- Update the components of risk assessments reflecting the monitoring activities carried out by organizations.

STEP 4: MAINTAIN THE ASSESSMENT

MONITOR RISK FACTORS

TASK 4-1: Conduct ongoing monitoring of the risk factors that contribute to changes in risk to organizational operations and assets, individuals, other organizations, or the Nation.

Supplemental Guidance: Organizations monitor risk factors of importance on an ongoing basis to ensure that the information needed to make credible, risk-based decisions continues to be available over time. Monitoring risk factors (e.g., threat sources and threat events, vulnerabilities and predisposing conditions, capabilities and intent of adversaries, targeting of organizational operations, assets, or individuals) can provide critical information on changing conditions that could potentially affect the ability of organizations to conduct core missions and business functions. Information derived from the ongoing monitoring of risk factors can be used to refresh risk assessments at whatever frequency deemed appropriate. Organizations can also attempt to capture changes in the effectiveness of risk response measures in order to maintain the currency of risk assessments. The objective is to maintain an ongoing situational awareness of the organizational governance structures and activities, mission/business processes, information systems, and environments of operation, and thereby all of the risk factors that may affect the risk being incurred by organizations. Therefore, in applying the risk assessment context or risk frame (i.e., scope, purpose, assumptions, constraints, risk tolerances, priorities, and trade-offs), organizations consider the part risk factors play in the risk response plan executed. For example, it is expected to be quite common for the security posture of information systems (that is, the risk factors measured within those systems) to reflect only a part of the organizational risk response, with response actions at the organization level or mission/business process level providing a significant portion of that response. In

---

[48] *Risk monitoring*, the fourth step in the risk management process, is described in NIST Special Publication 800-39. The step in the risk assessment process to maintain the assessment results over time overlaps to some degree with the risk monitoring step in the risk management process and the continuous monitoring step in the RMF. This overlap reinforces the important concept that many of the activities in the risk management process are complementary and mutually reinforcing. For example, the continuous monitoring step in the RMF can be used to monitor the ongoing effectiveness of deployed security controls with the results used to inform and guide a more extensive organizational risk monitoring process. At the organization level, risk monitoring may include monitoring key risk factors that are necessary to conduct subsequent risk assessments. Organizations use the risk management strategy to convey key requirements for maintaining risk assessments including, for example, risk factors to monitor and the frequency of such monitoring.

[49] NIST Special Publication 800-137 provides guidance on the ongoing monitoring of organizational information systems and environments of operation.

[50] Compliance verification ensures that organizations have implemented required risk response measures and that information security requirements derived from and traceable to organizational missions/business functions, federal legislation, directives, regulations, policies, and standards/guidelines are satisfied.

such situations, monitoring only the security posture of information systems would likely not provide sufficient information to determine the overall risk being incurred by organizations. Highly capable, well-resourced, and purpose-driven threat sources can be expected to defeat commonly available protection mechanisms (e.g., by bypassing or tampering with such mechanisms). Thus, process-level risk response measures such as reengineering mission/business processes, wise use of information technology, or the use of alternate execution processes, in the event of compromised information systems, can be major elements of organizational risk response plans.

UPDATE RISK ASSESSMENT

TASK 4-2: Update existing risk assessment using the results from ongoing monitoring of risk factors.

Supplemental Guidance: Organizations determine the frequency and the circumstances under which risk assessments are updated. Such determinations can include, for example, the current level of risk to and/or the importance of, core organizational missions/business functions. If significant changes (as defined by organizational policies, direction, or guidance) have occurred since the risk assessment was conducted, organizations can revisit the purpose, scope, assumptions, and constraints of the assessment to determine whether all tasks in the risk assessment process need to be repeated. Otherwise, the updates constitute subsequent risk assessments, identifying and assessing only how selected risk factors have changed, for example: (i) the identification of new threat events, vulnerabilities, predisposing conditions, undesirable consequences and/or affected assets; and (ii) the assessments of threat source characteristics (e.g., capability, intent, targeting, range of effects), likelihoods, and impacts. Organizations communicate the results of subsequent risk assessments to entities across all risk management tiers to ensure that responsible organizational officials have access to critical information needed to make ongoing risk-based decisions.

Summary of Key Activities – Maintaining Risk Assessments

- Identify key **risk factors** that have been identified for ongoing monitoring.
- Identify the **frequency** of risk factor monitoring activities and the **circumstances** under which the risk assessment needs to be updated.
- Reconfirm the **purpose, scope,** and **assumptions** of the risk assessment.
- Conduct the appropriate risk assessment **tasks**, as needed.
- Communicate the subsequent risk assessment **results** to specified organizational personnel.

APPENDIX A

REFERENCES
LAWS, POLICIES, DIRECTIVES, INSTRUCTIONS, STANDARDS, AND GUIDELINES

LEGISLATION

1. E-Government Act [includes FISMA] (P.L. 107-347), December 2002.

2. Federal Information Security Management Act (P.L. 107-347, Title III), December 2002.

POLICIES, DIRECTIVES, INSTRUCTIONS

1. Office of Management and Budget, Circular A-130, Appendix III, Transmittal Memorandum #4, *Management of Federal Information Resources*, November 2000.

2. Committee on National Security Systems Instruction (CNSSI) No. 4009, *National Information Assurance (IA) Glossary*, April 2010.

3. Committee on National Security Systems Instruction (CNSSI) No. 1253, *Security Categorization and Control Selection for National Security Systems*, March 2012.

4. Department of Homeland Security Federal Continuity Directive 2 (FCD 2), *Federal Executive Branch Mission Essential Function and Primary Mission Essential Function Identification and Submission Process*, February 2008.

STANDARDS

1. National Institute of Standards and Technology Federal Information Processing Standards Publication 199, *Standards for Security Categorization of Federal Information and Information Systems*, February 2004.

2. National Institute of Standards and Technology Federal Information Processing Standards Publication 200, *Minimum Security Requirements for Federal Information and Information Systems*, March 2006.

3. ISO/IEC 31000:2009, *Risk management – Principles and guidelines*.

4. ISO/IEC 30101:2009, *Risk management – Risk assessment techniques*.

5. ISO/IEC Guide 73, *Risk management – Vocabulary*.

6. ISO/IEC 27005:2011, *Information technology – Security techniques – Information security risk management*.

GUIDELINES

1. National Institute of Standards and Technology Special Publication 800-18, Revision 1, *Guide for Developing Security Plans for Federal Information Systems*, February 2006.

2. National Institute of Standards and Technology Special Publication 800-34, Revision 1, *Contingency Planning Guide for Federal Information Systems*, May 2010.

3. National Institute of Standards and Technology Special Publication 800-37, Revision 1, *Guide for Applying the Risk Management Framework to Federal Information Systems: A Security Life Cycle Approach*, February 2010.

4. National Institute of Standards and Technology Special Publication 800-39, *Managing Information Security Risk: Organization, Mission, and Information System View*, March 2011.

5. National Institute of Standards and Technology Special Publication 800-53, Revision 3, *Recommended Security Controls for Federal Information Systems and Organizations*, August 2009.

6. National Institute of Standards and Technology Special Publication 800-53A, Revision 1, *Guide for Assessing the Security Controls in Federal Information Systems and Organizations: Building Effective Security Assessment Plans*, June 2010.

7. National Institute of Standards and Technology Special Publication 800-59, *Guideline for Identifying an Information System as a National Security System*, August 2003.

8. National Institute of Standards and Technology Special Publication 800-60, Revision 1, *Guide for Mapping Types of Information and Information Systems to Security Categories*, August 2008.

9. National Institute of Standards and Technology Special Publication 800-64, Revision 2, *Security Considerations in the System Development Life Cycle*, October 2008.

10. National Institute of Standards and Technology Special Publication 800-65, *Integrating IT Security into the Capital Planning and Investment Control Process*, January 2005.

11. National Institute of Standards and Technology Special Publication 800-70, Revision 2, *National Checklist Program for IT Products--Guidelines for Checklist Users and Developers*, February 2011.

12. National Institute of Standards and Technology Special Publication 800-117, Version 1.0, *Guide to Adopting and Using the Security Content Automation Protocol (SCAP)*, July 2010.

13. National Institute of Standards and Technology Special Publication 800-126, *The Technical Specification for the Security Content Automation Protocol (SCAP): SCAP Version 1.0*, November 2009.

14. National Institute of Standards and Technology Special Publication 800-137, *Information Security Continuous Monitoring for Federal Information Systems and Organizations*, September 2011.

APPENDIX B

GLOSSARY
COMMON TERMS AND DEFINITIONS

This appendix provides definitions for security terminology used within Special Publication 800-30. The terms in the glossary are consistent with the terms used in the suite of FISMA-related security standards and guidelines developed by NIST. Unless otherwise stated, all terms used in this publication are also consistent with the definitions contained in the CNSSI No. 4009, *National Information Assurance (IA) Glossary*.

Adequate Security [OMB Circular A-130, Appendix III]	Security commensurate with the risk and magnitude of harm resulting from the loss, misuse, or unauthorized access to or modification of information.
Advanced Persistent Threat [NIST SP 800-39]	An adversary with sophisticated levels of expertise and significant resources, allowing it through the use of multiple different attack vectors (e.g., cyber, physical, and deception), to generate opportunities to achieve its objectives which are typically to establish and extend its presence within the information technology infrastructure of organizations for purposes of continually exfiltrating information and/or to undermine or impede critical aspects of a mission, program, or organization, or place itself in a position to do so in the future; moreover, the advanced persistent threat pursues its objectives repeatedly over an extended period of time, adapting to a defender's efforts to resist it, and with determination to maintain the level of interaction needed to execute its objectives.
Adversary [DHS Risk Lexicon]	Individual, group, organization, or government that conducts or has the intent to conduct detrimental activities.
Agency	See *Executive Agency*.
Analysis Approach	The approach used to define the orientation or starting point of the risk assessment, the level of detail in the assessment, and how risks due to similar threat scenarios are treated.
Assessment	See *Security Control Assessment* or *Risk Assessment*.
Assessment Approach	The approach used to assess risk and its contributing risk factors, including quantitatively, qualitatively, or semi-quantitatively.
Assessor	See *Security Control Assessor* or *Risk Assessor*.
Attack [CNSSI No. 4009]	Any kind of malicious activity that attempts to collect, disrupt, deny, degrade, or destroy information system resources or the information itself.

Authentication [FIPS 200]	Verifying the identity of a user, process, or device, often as a prerequisite to allowing access to resources in an information system.
Authenticity [CNSSI No. 4009]	The property of being genuine and being able to be verified and trusted; confidence in the validity of a transmission, a message, or message originator. See *Authentication*.
Authorization (to operate) [CNSSI No. 4009]	The official management decision given by a senior organizational official to authorize operation of an information system and to explicitly accept the risk to organizational operations (including mission, functions, image, or reputation), organizational assets, individuals, other organizations, and the Nation based on the implementation of an agreed-upon set of security controls.
Authorization Boundary [CNSSI No. 4009]	All components of an information system to be authorized for operation by an authorizing official and excludes separately authorized systems, to which the information system is connected.
Authorizing Official [CNSSI No. 4009]	Senior (federal) official or executive with the authority to formally assume responsibility for operating an information system at an acceptable level of risk to organizational operations (including mission, functions, image, or reputation), organizational assets, individuals, other organizations, and the Nation.
Availability [44 U.S.C., Sec. 3542]	Ensuring timely and reliable access to and use of information.
Chief Information Officer [PL 104-106, Sec. 5125(b)]	Agency official responsible for: (i) Providing advice and other assistance to the head of the executive agency and other senior management personnel of the agency to ensure that information technology is acquired and information resources are managed in a manner that is consistent with laws, Executive Orders, directives, policies, regulations, and priorities established by the head of the agency; (ii) Developing, maintaining, and facilitating the implementation of a sound and integrated information technology architecture for the agency; and (iii) Promoting the effective and efficient design and operation of all major information resources management processes for the agency, including improvements to work processes of the agency.
Chief Information Security Officer	See *Senior Agency Information Security Officer*.
Common Control [NIST SP 800-37]	A security control that is inherited by one or more organizational information systems. See *Security Control Inheritance*.

Common Control Provider [CNSSI No. 4009]	An organizational official responsible for the development, implementation, assessment, and monitoring of common controls (i.e., security controls inherited by information systems).
Compensating Security Control [CNSSI No. 4009]	A management, operational, and/or technical control (i.e., safeguard or countermeasure) employed by an organization in lieu of a recommended security control in the low, moderate, or high baselines that provides equivalent or comparable protection for an information system.
Confidentiality [44 U.S.C., Sec. 3542]	Preserving authorized restrictions on information access and disclosure, including means for protecting personal privacy and proprietary information.
Course of Action [NIST SP 800-39]	A time-phased or situation-dependent combination of risk response measures. See *Risk Response*.
Critical Infrastructure	System and assets, whether physical or virtual, so vital to the United States that the incapacity or destruction of such systems and assets would have a debilitating impact on security, national economic security, national public health or safety, or any combination of those matters.
Critical Infrastructure Sectors [HSPD-7]	Information technology; telecommunications; chemical; transportation systems, including mass transit, aviation, maritime, ground/surface, and rail and pipeline systems; emergency services; and postal and shipping.
Criticality [NIST SP 800-60]	A measure of the degree to which an organization depends on the information or information system for the success of a mission or of a business function.
Cyber Attack [CNSSI No. 4009]	An attack, via cyberspace, targeting an enterprise's use of cyberspace for the purpose of disrupting, disabling, destroying, or maliciously controlling a computing environment/infrastructure; or destroying the integrity of the data or stealing controlled information.
Cyber Security [CNSSI No. 4009]	The ability to protect or defend the use of cyberspace from cyber attacks.
Cyberspace [CNSSI No. 4009]	A global domain within the information environment consisting of the interdependent network of information systems infrastructures including the Internet, telecommunications networks, computer systems, and embedded processors and controllers.

Defense-in-Breadth [CNSSI No. 4009]	A planned, systematic set of multidisciplinary activities that seek to identify, manage, and reduce risk of exploitable vulnerabilities at every stage of the system, network, or subcomponent life cycle (system, network, or product design and development; manufacturing; packaging; assembly; system integration; distribution; operations; maintenance; and retirement).
Defense-in-Depth [CNSSI No. 4009]	Information security strategy integrating people, technology, and operations capabilities to establish variable barriers across multiple layers and missions of the organization.
Enterprise [CNSSI No. 4009]	An organization with a defined mission/goal and a defined boundary, using information systems to execute that mission, and with responsibility for managing its own risks and performance. An enterprise may consist of all or some of the following business aspects: acquisition, program management, financial management (e.g., budgets), human resources, security, and information systems, information and mission management. See *Organization*.
Enterprise Architecture [CNSSI No. 4009]	The description of an enterprise's entire set of information systems: how they are configured, how they are integrated, how they interface to the external environment at the enterprise's boundary, how they are operated to support the enterprise mission, and how they contribute to the enterprise's overall security posture.
Environment of Operation	The physical, technical, and organizational setting in which an information system operates, including but not limited to: missions/business functions; mission/business processes; threat space; vulnerabilities; enterprise and information security architectures; personnel; facilities; supply chain relationships; information technologies; organizational governance and culture; acquisition and procurement processes; organizational policies and procedures; organizational assumptions, constraints, risk tolerance, and priorities/trade-offs).
Executive Agency [41 U.S.C., Sec. 403]	An executive department specified in 5 U.S.C., Sec. 101; a military department specified in 5 U.S.C., Sec. 102; an independent establishment as defined in 5 U.S.C., Sec. 104(1); and a wholly owned Government corporation fully subject to the provisions of 31 U.S.C., Chapter 91.

Fault Tree Analysis	A top-down, deductive failure analysis in which an undesired state of a system (top event) is analyzed using Boolean logic to combine a series of lower-level events.
	An analytical approach whereby an undesired state of a system is specified and the system is then analyzed in the context of its environment of operation to find all realistic ways in which the undesired event (top event) can occur.
Federal Agency	See *Executive Agency.*
Federal Information System [40 U.S.C., Sec. 11331]	An information system used or operated by an executive agency, by a contractor of an executive agency, or by another organization on behalf of an executive agency.
Hybrid Security Control [NIST SP 800-53]	A security control that is implemented in an information system in part as a common control and in part as a system-specific control. See *Common Control* and *System-Specific Security Control.*
Impact Level [CNSSI No. 4009]	The magnitude of harm that can be expected to result from the consequences of unauthorized disclosure of information, unauthorized modification of information, unauthorized destruction of information, or loss of information or information system availability.
Impact Value [CNSSI No. 1253]	The assessed potential impact resulting from a compromise of the confidentiality, integrity, or availability of an information type, expressed as a value of low, moderate, or high.
Industrial Control System [NIST SP 800-39]	An information system used to control industrial processes such as manufacturing, product handling, production, and distribution. Industrial control systems include supervisory control and data acquisition systems used to control geographically dispersed assets, as well as distributed control systems and smaller control systems using programmable logic controllers to control localized processes.
Information [CNSSI No. 4009]	Any communication or representation of knowledge such as facts, data, or opinions in any medium or form, including textual, numerical, graphic, cartographic, narrative, or audiovisual.
[FIPS 199]	An instance of an information type.
Information Owner [CNSSI No. 4009]	Official with statutory or operational authority for specified information and responsibility for establishing the controls for its generation, classification, collection, processing, dissemination, and disposal. See *Information Steward.*
Information Resources [44 U.S.C., Sec. 3502]	Information and related resources, such as personnel, equipment, funds, and information technology.

Information Security [44 U.S.C., Sec. 3542]	The protection of information and information systems from unauthorized access, use, disclosure, disruption, modification, or destruction in order to provide confidentiality, integrity, and availability.
Information Security Architecture [NIST SP 800-39]	A description of the structure and behavior for an enterprise's security processes, information security systems, personnel and organizational sub-units, showing their alignment with the enterprise's mission and strategic plans.
Information Security Program Plan [NIST SP 800-53]	Formal document that provides an overview of the security requirements for an organization-wide information security program and describes the program management controls and common controls in place or planned for meeting those requirements.
Information Security Risk	The risk to organizational operations (including mission, functions, image, reputation), organizational assets, individuals, other organizations, and the Nation due to the potential for unauthorized access, use, disclosure, disruption, modification, or destruction of information and/or information systems. See *Risk*.
Information Steward [CNSSI No. 4009]	An agency official with statutory or operational authority for specified information and responsibility for establishing the controls for its generation, collection, processing, dissemination, and disposal.
Information System [44 U.S.C., Sec. 3502]	A discrete set of information resources organized for the collection, processing, maintenance, use, sharing, dissemination, or disposition of information.
Information System Boundary	See *Authorization Boundary*.
Information System Owner (or Program Manager)	Official responsible for the overall procurement, development, integration, modification, or operation and maintenance of an information system.
Information System Resilience	The ability of an information system to continue to operate while under attack, even if in a degraded or debilitated state, and to rapidly recover operational capabilities for essential functions after a successful attack.
Information System Security Officer	Individual assigned responsibility by the senior agency information security officer, authorizing official, management official, or information system owner for maintaining the appropriate operational security posture for an information system or program.

Information System-Related Security Risk	Risk that arises through the loss of confidentiality, integrity, or availability of information or information systems considering impacts to organizational operations and assets, individuals, other organizations, and the Nation. A subset of *Information Security Risk*. See *Risk*.
Information Technology [40 U.S.C., Sec. 1401]	Any equipment or interconnected system or subsystem of equipment that is used in the automatic acquisition, storage, manipulation, management, movement, control, display, switching, interchange, transmission, or reception of data or information by the executive agency. For purposes of the preceding sentence, equipment is used by an executive agency if the equipment is used by the executive agency directly or is used by a contractor under a contract with the executive agency which: (i) requires the use of such equipment; or (ii) requires the use, to a significant extent, of such equipment in the performance of a service or the furnishing of a product. The term information technology includes computers, ancillary equipment, software, firmware, and similar procedures, services (including support services), and related resources.
Information Type [FIPS 199]	A specific category of information (e.g., privacy, medical, proprietary, financial, investigative, contractor sensitive, security management) defined by an organization or in some instances, by a specific law, Executive Order, directive, policy, or regulation.
Integrity [44 U.S.C., Sec. 3542]	Guarding against improper information modification or destruction, and includes ensuring information non-repudiation and authenticity.
Likelihood of Occurrence [CNSSI No. 4009, adapted]	A weighted factor based on a subjective analysis of the probability that a given threat is capable of exploiting a given vulnerability or a set of vulnerabilities.
Management Controls [FIPS 200]	The security controls (i.e., safeguards or countermeasures) for an information system that focus on the management of risk and the management of information system security.
Mission/Business Segment	Elements of organizations describing mission areas, common/shared business services, and organization-wide services. Mission/business segments can be identified with one or more information systems which collectively support a mission/business process.

National Security System [44 U.S.C., Sec. 3542]	Any information system (including any telecommunications system) used or operated by an agency or by a contractor of an agency, or other organization on behalf of an agency (i) the function, operation, or use of which involves intelligence activities; involves cryptologic activities related to national security; involves command and control of military forces; involves equipment that is an integral part of a weapon or weapons system; or is critical to the direct fulfillment of military or intelligence missions (excluding a system that is to be used for routine administrative and business applications, for example, payroll, finance, logistics, and personnel management applications); or (ii) is protected at all times by procedures established for information that have been specifically authorized under criteria established by an Executive Order or an Act of Congress to be kept classified in the interest of national defense or foreign policy.
Operational Controls [FIPS 200]	The security controls (i.e., safeguards or countermeasures) for an information system that are primarily implemented and executed by people (as opposed to systems).
Organization [FIPS 200, Adapted]	An entity of any size, complexity, or positioning within an organizational structure (e.g., a federal agency or, as appropriate, any of its operational elements). See *Enterprise*.
Plan of Action and Milestones [OMB Memorandum 02-01]	A document that identifies tasks needing to be accomplished. It details resources required to accomplish the elements of the plan, any milestones in meeting the tasks, and scheduled completion dates for the milestones.
Predisposing Condition	A condition that exists within an organization, a mission/business process, enterprise architecture, or information system including its environment of operation, which contributes to (i.e., increases or decreases) the likelihood that one or more threat events, once initiated, will result in undesirable consequences or adverse impact to organizational operations and assets, individuals, other organizations, or the Nation.
Qualitative Assessment [DHS *Risk Lexicon*]	Use of a set of methods, principles, or rules for assessing risk based on nonnumerical categories or levels.
Quantitative Assessment [DHS *Risk Lexicon*]	Use of a set of methods, principles, or rules for assessing risks based on the use of numbers where the meanings and proportionality of values are maintained inside and outside the context of the assessment.
Repeatability	The ability to repeat an assessment in the future, in a manner that is consistent with, and hence comparable to, prior assessments.

Reproducibility	The ability of different experts to produce the same results from the same data.
Residual Risk [CNSSI No. 4009]	Portion of risk remaining after security measures have been applied.
Risk [CNSSI No. 4009]	A measure of the extent to which an entity is threatened by a potential circumstance or event, and typically a function of: (i) the adverse impacts that would arise if the circumstance or event occurs; and (ii) the likelihood of occurrence. See *Information System-Related Security Risk.*
Risk Assessment [NIST SP 800-39]	The process of identifying, estimating, and prioritizing risks to organizational operations (including mission, functions, image, reputation), organizational assets, individuals, other organizations, and the Nation, resulting from the operation of an information system. Part of risk management, incorporates threat and vulnerability analyses, and considers mitigations provided by security controls planned or in place. Synonymous with risk analysis.
Risk Assessment Methodology	A risk assessment process, together with a risk model, assessment approach, and analysis approach.
Risk Assessment Report	The report which contains the results of performing a risk assessment or the formal output from the process of assessing risk.
Risk Assessor	The individual, group, or organization responsible for conducting a risk assessment.
Risk Executive (Function) [CNSSI No. 4009]	An individual or group within an organization that helps to ensure that: (i) security risk-related considerations for individual information systems, to include the authorization decisions for those systems, are viewed from an organization-wide perspective with regard to the overall strategic goals and objectives of the organization in carrying out its missions and business functions; and (ii) managing risk from individual information systems is consistent across the organization, reflects organizational risk tolerance, and is considered along with other organizational risks affecting mission/business success.
Risk Factor	A characteristic used in a risk model as an input to determining the level of risk in a risk assessment.

Risk Management [NIST SP 800-39] [CNSSI No. 4009, adapted]	The program and supporting processes to manage information security risk to organizational operations (including mission, functions, image, reputation), organizational assets, individuals, other organizations, and the Nation, and includes: (i) establishing the context for risk-related activities; (ii) assessing risk; (iii) responding to risk once determined; and (iv) monitoring risk over time.
Risk Mitigation [CNSSI No. 4009]	Prioritizing, evaluating, and implementing the appropriate risk-reducing controls/countermeasures recommended from the risk management process. A subset of *Risk Response.*
Risk Model	A key component of a risk assessment methodology (in addition to assessment approach and analysis approach) that defines key terms and assessable risk factors.
Risk Monitoring [NIST SP 800-39]	Maintaining ongoing awareness of an organization's risk environment, risk management program, and associated activities to support risk decisions.
Risk Response [NIST SP 800-39]	Accepting, avoiding, mitigating, sharing, or transferring risk to organizational operations (i.e., mission, functions, image, or reputation), organizational assets, individuals, other organizations, or the Nation. See *Course of Action.*
Risk Response Measure [NIST SP 800-39]	A specific action taken to respond to an identified risk.
Root Cause Analysis	A principle-based, systems approach for the identification of underlying causes associated with a particular set of risks.
Security Authorization (to Operate)	See *Authorization (to operate).*
Security Categorization	The process of determining the security category for information or an information system. Security categorization methodologies are described in CNSSI No.1253 for national security systems and in FIPS 199 for other than national security systems.
Security Control Assessment [NIST SP 800-39] [CNSSI No. 4009, Adapted]	The testing and/or evaluation of the management, operational, and technical security controls to determine the extent to which the controls are implemented correctly, operating as intended, and producing the desired outcome with respect to meeting the security requirements for an information system or organization.
Security Control Assessor	The individual, group, or organization responsible for conducting a security control assessment.

Security Control Baseline [CNSSI No. 4009]	The set of minimum security controls defined for a low-impact, moderate-impact, or high-impact information system.
[CNSSI No. 1253]	A set of information security controls that has been established through information security strategic planning activities to address one or more specified security categorizations; this set of security controls is intended to be the initial security control set selected for a specific system once that system's security categorization is determined.
Security Control Enhancement [NIST SP 800-39, adapted]	Statement of security capability to: (i) build in additional, but related, functionality to a basic security control; and/or (ii) increase the strength of a basic control.
Security Control Inheritance [CNSSI No. 4009]	A situation in which an information system or application receives protection from security controls (or portions of security controls) that are developed, implemented, assessed, authorized, and monitored by entities other than those responsible for the system or application; entities either internal or external to the organization where the system or application resides. See *Common Control*.
Security Controls [FIPS 199, CNSSI No. 4009]	The management, operational, and technical controls (i.e., safeguards or countermeasures) prescribed for an information system to protect the confidentiality, integrity, and availability of the system and its information.
Security Impact Analysis [NIST SP 800-37]	The analysis conducted by an organizational official to determine the extent to which changes to the information system have affected the security state of the system.
Security Objective [FIPS 199]	Confidentiality, integrity, or availability.
Security Plan [NIST SP 800-18]	Formal document that provides an overview of the security requirements for an information system or an information security program and describes the security controls in place or planned for meeting those requirements. See *System Security Plan* or *Information Security Program Plan*.
Security Policy [CNSSI No. 4009]	A set of criteria for the provision of security services.
Security Posture [CNSSI No. 4009]	The security status of an enterprise's networks, information, and systems based on information assurance resources (e.g., people, hardware, software, policies) and capabilities in place to manage the defense of the enterprise and to react as the situation changes.

Security Requirements [FIPS 200]	Requirements levied on an information system that are derived from applicable laws, Executive Orders, directives, policies, standards, instructions, regulations, procedures, or organizational mission/business case needs to ensure the confidentiality, integrity, and availability of the information being processed, stored, or transmitted.
Semi-Quantitative Assessment [Department of Homeland Security (DHS) *Risk Lexicon*]	Use of a set of methods, principles, or rules for assessing risk based on bins, scales, or representative numbers whose values and meanings are not maintained in other contexts.
Senior Agency Information Security Officer [44 U.S.C., Sec. 3544]	Official responsible for carrying out the Chief Information Officer responsibilities under FISMA and serving as the Chief Information Officer's primary liaison to the agency's authorizing officials, information system owners, and information system security officers. [Note: Organizations subordinate to federal agencies may use the term *Senior Information Security Officer* or *Chief Information Security Officer* to denote individuals filling positions with similar responsibilities to Senior Agency Information Security Officers.]
Senior Information Security Officer	See *Senior Agency Information Security Officer*.
Sensitivity [NIST SP 800-60]	A measure of the importance assigned to information by its owner, for the purpose of denoting its need for protection.
Subsystem [NIST SP 800-39]	A major subdivision or component of an information system consisting of information, information technology, and personnel that performs one or more specific functions.
Supplementation (Security Controls) [NIST SP 800-39]	The process of adding security controls or control enhancements to a security control baseline from NIST Special Publication 800-53 or CNSSI No. 1253 in order to adequately meet the organization's risk management needs.
System	See *Information System*.
System Security Plan [NIST SP 800-18]	Formal document that provides an overview of the security requirements for an information system and describes the security controls in place or planned for meeting those requirements.
System-Specific Security Control [NIST SP 800-37]	A security control for an information system that has not been designated as a common control or the portion of a hybrid control that is to be implemented within an information system.

Tailoring [NIST SP 800-53, CNSSI No. 4009]	The process by which a security control baseline is modified based on: (i) the application of scoping guidance; (ii) the specification of compensating security controls, if needed; and (iii) the specification of organization-defined parameters in the security controls via explicit assignment and selection statements.
Tailored Security Control Baseline [NIST SP 800-39]	A set of security controls resulting from the application of tailoring guidance to the security control baseline. See *Tailoring*.
Technical Controls [FIPS 200]	Security controls (i.e., safeguards or countermeasures) for an information system that are primarily implemented and executed by the information system through mechanisms contained in the hardware, software, or firmware components of the system.
Threat [CNSSI No.4009]	Any circumstance or event with the potential to adversely impact organizational operations (including mission, functions, image, or reputation), organizational assets, individuals, other organizations, or the Nation through an information system via unauthorized access, destruction, disclosure, or modification of information, and/or denial of service.
Threat Assessment [CNSSI No. 4009]	Process of formally evaluating the degree of threat to an information system or enterprise and describing the nature of the threat.
Threat Event	An event or situation that has the potential for causing undesirable consequences or impact.
Threat Scenario	A set of discrete threat events, associated with a specific threat source or multiple threat sources, partially ordered in time. Synonym for *Threat Campaign*.
Threat Shifting	Response from adversaries to perceived safeguards and/or countermeasures (i.e., security controls), in which the adversaries change some characteristic of their intent to do harm in order to avoid and/or overcome those safeguards/countermeasures.
Threat Source [CNSSI No. 4009]	The intent and method targeted at the intentional exploitation of a vulnerability or a situation and method that may accidentally exploit a vulnerability.
Vulnerability [CNSSI No. 4009]	Weakness in an information system, system security procedures, internal controls, or implementation that could be exploited by a threat source.
Vulnerability Assessment [CNSSI No. 4009]	Systematic examination of an information system or product to determine the adequacy of security measures, identify security deficiencies, provide data from which to predict the effectiveness of proposed security measures, and confirm the adequacy of such measures after implementation.

APPENDIX C

ACRONYMS
COMMON ABBREVIATIONS

APT	Advanced Persistent Threat
BCP	Business Continuity Plan
BIA	Business Impact Analysis
CNSS	Committee on National Security Systems
COOP	Continuity of Operations
DoD	Department of Defense
DHS	Department of Homeland Security
DNI	Director of National Intelligence
EA	Enterprise Architecture
FIPS	Federal Information Processing Standards
FISMA	Federal Information Security Management Act
ICS	Industrial Control System
IEC	International Electrotechnical Commission
ISO	International Organization for Standardization
IT	Information Technology
JTF	Joint Task Force
NIST	National Institute of Standards and Technology
NOFORN	Not Releasable to Foreign Nationals
ODNI	Office of the Director of National Intelligence
OMB	Office of Management and Budget
RAR	Risk Assessment Report
RMF	Risk Management Framework
SCAP	Security Content Automation Protocol
SP	Special Publication
TTP	Tactic Technique Procedure
U.S.C.	United States Code

APPENDIX D

THREAT SOURCES

TAXONOMY OF THREATS SOURCES CAPABLE OF INITIATING THREAT EVENTS

This appendix provides: (i) a description of potentially useful inputs to the *threat source* identification task; (ii) an exemplary taxonomy of threat sources by type, description, and risk factors (i.e., characteristics) used to assess the likelihood and/or impact of such threat sources initiating threat events; (iii) an exemplary set of tailorable assessment scales for assessing those risk factors; and (iv) templates for summarizing and documenting the results of the threat source identification Task 2-1. The taxonomy and assessment scales in this appendix can be used by organizations as a starting point with appropriate tailoring to adjust for organization-specific conditions. Tables D-7 and D-8, outputs from Task 2-1, provide relevant inputs to the risk tables in Appendix I.

TABLE D-1: INPUTS – THREAT SOURCE IDENTIFICATION

Description	Provided To		
	Tier 1	Tier 2	Tier 3

From Tier 1: (Organization level)
- Sources of threat information deemed to be credible (e.g., open source and/or classified threat reports, previous risk/threat assessments). (Section 3.1, Task 1-4)
- Threat source information and guidance specific to Tier 1 (e.g., threats related to organizational governance, core missions/business functions, management/operational policies, procedures, and structures, external mission/business relationships).
- Taxonomy of threat sources, annotated by the organization, if necessary. (Table D-2)
- Characterization of adversarial and non-adversarial threat sources.
  - Assessment scales for assessing adversary capability, intent, and targeting, annotated by the organization, if necessary. (Table D-3, Table D-4, Table D-5)
  - Assessment scale for assessing the range of effects, annotated by the organization, if necessary. (Table D-6)
- Threat sources identified in previous risk assessments, if appropriate.
	No	Yes	Yes
			if not provided by Tier 2

From Tier 2: (Mission/business process level) - Threat source information and guidance specific to Tier 2 (e.g., threats related to mission/business processes, EA segments, common infrastructure, support services, common controls, and external dependencies). - Mission/business process-specific characterization of adversarial and non-adversarial threat sources.	Yes *via RAR*	Yes *via peer sharing*	Yes
From Tier 3: (Information system level) - Threat source information and guidance specific to Tier 3 (e.g., threats related to information systems, information technologies, information system components, applications, networks, environments of operation). - Information system-specific characterization of adversarial and non-adversarial threat sources.	Yes *via RAR*	Yes *via RAR*	Yes *via peer sharing*

TABLE D-2: TAXONOMY OF THREAT SOURCES

Type of Threat Source	Description	Characteristics

ADVERSARIAL
- Individual
  - Outsider
  - Insider
  - Trusted Insider
  - Privileged Insider
- Group
  - Ad hoc
  - Established
- Organization
  - Competitor
  - Supplier
  - Partner
  - Customer
- Nation-State
	Individuals, groups, organizations, or states that seek to exploit the organization's dependence on cyber resources (i.e., information in electronic form, information and communications technologies, and the communications and information-handling capabilities provided by those technologies).	Capability, Intent, Targeting

ACCIDENTAL - User - Privileged User/Administrator	Erroneous actions taken by individuals in the course of executing their everyday responsibilities.	Range of effects

STRUCTURAL
- Information Technology (IT) Equipment
  - Storage
  - Processing
  - Communications
  - Display
  - Sensor
  - Controller
- Environmental Controls
  - Temperature/Humidity Controls
  - Power Supply
- Software
  - Operating System
  - Networking
  - General-Purpose Application
  - Mission-Specific Application
	Failures of equipment, environmental controls, or software due to aging, resource depletion, or other circumstances which exceed expected operating parameters.	Range of effects

ENVIRONMENTAL
- Natural or man-made disaster
  - Fire
  - Flood/Tsunami
  - Windstorm/Tornado
  - Hurricane
  - Earthquake
  - Bombing
  - Overrun
- Unusual Natural Event (e.g., sunspots)
- Infrastructure Failure/Outage
  - Telecommunications
  - Electrical Power
	Natural disasters and failures of critical infrastructures on which the organization depends, but which are outside the control of the organization.
	Note: Natural and man-made disasters can also be characterized in terms of their severity and/or duration. However, because the threat source and the threat event are strongly identified, severity and duration can be included in the description of the threat event (e.g., Category 5 hurricane causes extensive damage to the facilities housing mission-critical systems, making those systems unavailable for three weeks).
		Range of effects

TABLE D-3: ASSESSMENT SCALE – CHARACTERISTICS OF ADVERSARY CAPABILITY

Qualitative Values	Semi-Quantitative Values		Description
Very High	96-100	10	The adversary has a very sophisticated level of expertise, is well-resourced, and can generate opportunities to support multiple successful, continuous, and coordinated attacks.
High	80-95	8	The adversary has a sophisticated level of expertise, with significant resources and opportunities to support multiple successful coordinated attacks.
Moderate	21-79	5	The adversary has moderate resources, expertise, and opportunities to support multiple successful attacks.
Low	5-20	2	The adversary has limited resources, expertise, and opportunities to support a successful attack.
Very Low	0-4	0	The adversary has very limited resources, expertise, and opportunities to support a successful attack.

TABLE D-4: ASSESSMENT SCALE – CHARACTERISTICS OF ADVERSARY INTENT

Qualitative Values	Semi-Quantitative Values		Description
Very High	96-100	10	The adversary seeks to undermine, severely impede, or destroy a core mission or business function, program, or enterprise by exploiting a presence in the organization's information systems or infrastructure. The adversary is concerned about disclosure of tradecraft only to the extent that it would impede its ability to complete stated goals.
High	80-95	8	The adversary seeks to undermine/impede critical aspects of a core mission or business function, program, or enterprise, or place itself in a position to do so in the future, by maintaining a presence in the organization's information systems or infrastructure. The adversary is very concerned about minimizing attack detection/disclosure of tradecraft, particularly while preparing for future attacks.
Moderate	21-79	5	The adversary seeks to obtain or modify specific critical or sensitive information or usurp/disrupt the organization's cyber resources by establishing a foothold in the organization's information systems or infrastructure. The adversary is concerned about minimizing attack detection/disclosure of tradecraft, particularly when carrying out attacks over long time periods. The adversary is willing to impede aspects of the organization's missions/business functions to achieve these ends.
Low	5-20	2	The adversary actively seeks to obtain critical or sensitive information or to usurp/disrupt the organization's cyber resources, and does so without concern about attack detection/disclosure of tradecraft.
Very Low	0-4	0	The adversary seeks to usurp, disrupt, or deface the organization's cyber resources, and does so without concern about attack detection/disclosure of tradecraft.

TABLE D-5: ASSESSMENT SCALE – CHARACTERISTICS OF ADVERSARY TARGETING

Qualitative Values	Semi-Quantitative Values		Description
Very High	96-100	10	The adversary analyzes information obtained via reconnaissance and attacks to target persistently a specific organization, enterprise, program, mission or business function, focusing on specific high-value or mission-critical information, resources, supply flows, or functions; specific employees or positions; supporting infrastructure providers/suppliers; or partnering organizations.
High	80-95	8	The adversary analyzes information obtained via reconnaissance to target persistently a specific organization, enterprise, program, mission or business function, focusing on specific high-value or mission-critical information, resources, supply flows, or functions, specific employees supporting those functions, or key positions.
Moderate	21-79	5	The adversary analyzes publicly available information to target persistently specific high-value organizations (and key positions, such as Chief Information Officer), programs, or information.
Low	5-20	2	The adversary uses publicly available information to target a class of high-value organizations or information, and seeks targets of opportunity within that class.
Very Low	0-4	0	The adversary may or may not target any specific organizations or classes of organizations.

TABLE D-6: ASSESSMENT SCALE – RANGE OF EFFECTS FOR NON-ADVERSARIAL THREAT SOURCES

Qualitative Values	Semi-Quantitative Values		Description
Very High	96-100	10	The effects of the error, accident, or act of nature are sweeping, involving almost all of the cyber resources of the [Tier 3: information systems; Tier 2: mission/business processes or EA segments, common infrastructure, or support services; Tier 1: organization/governance structure].
High	80-95	8	The effects of the error, accident, or act of nature are extensive, involving most of the cyber resources of the [Tier 3: information systems; Tier 2: mission/business processes or EA segments, common infrastructure, or support services; Tier 1: organization/governance structure], including many critical resources.
Moderate	21-79	5	The effects of the error, accident, or act of nature are wide-ranging, involving a significant portion of the cyber resources of the [Tier 3: information systems; Tier 2: mission/business processes or EA segments, common infrastructure, or support services; Tier 1: organization/governance structure], including some critical resources.
Low	5-20	2	The effects of the error, accident, or act of nature are limited, involving some of the cyber resources of the [Tier 3: information systems; Tier 2: mission/business processes or EA segments, common infrastructure, or support services; Tier 1: organization/governance structure], but involving no critical resources.
Very Low	0-4	0	The effects of the error, accident, or act of nature are minimal, involving few if any of the cyber resources of the [Tier 3: information systems; Tier 2: mission/business processes or EA segments, common infrastructure, or support services; Tier 1: organization/governance structure], and involving no critical resources.

TABLE D-7: TEMPLATE – IDENTIFICATION OF ADVERSARIAL THREAT SOURCES

Identifier	Threat Source Source of Information	In Scope	Capability	Intent	Targeting
Organization -defined	Table D-2 and Task 1-4 or Organization-defined	Yes / No	Table D-3 or Organization -defined	Table D-4 or Organization -defined	Table D-5 or Organization -defined

TABLE D-8: TEMPLATE – IDENTIFICATION OF NON-ADVERSARIAL THREAT SOURCES

Identifier	Threat Source Source of Information	In Scope	Range of Effects
Organization -defined	Table D-2 and Task 1-4 or Organization-defined	Yes / No	Table D-6 or Organization-defined

APPENDIX E

THREAT EVENTS

REPRESENTATIVE THREAT EVENTS INITIATED BY THREAT SOURCES

This appendix provides: (i) a description of potentially useful inputs to the *threat event* identification task; (ii) representative examples of adversarial threat events expressed as tactics, techniques, and procedures (TTPs) and non-adversarial threat events; (iii) an exemplary assessment scale for the relevance of those threat events; and (iv) templates for summarizing and documenting the results of the threat identification Task 2-2. Organizations can eliminate certain threat events from further consideration if no adversary with the necessary capability has been identified.[51] Organizations can also modify the threat events provided to describe specific TTPs with sufficient detail[52] and at the appropriate classification level.[53] Organizations can use the representative threat events and predicated/expected values for the relevance of those events as a starting point with tailoring to adjust for any organization-specific conditions. Table E-5, an output from Task 2-2, provides relevant inputs to the risk tables in Appendix I.

TABLE E-1: INPUTS – THREAT EVENT IDENTIFICATION

Description	Provided To		
	Tier 1	Tier 2	Tier 3
From Tier 1: (Organization level) - Sources of threat information deemed to be credible (e.g., open source and/or classified threat reports, previous risk/threat assessments. (Section 3.1, Task 1-4.) - Threat event information and guidance specific to Tier 1 (e.g., threats related to organizational governance, core missions/business functions, external mission/business relationships, management/operational policies, procedures, and structures). - Exemplary adversarial threat events, annotated by the organization, if necessary. (Table E-2) - Exemplary non-adversarial threat events, annotated by the organization, if necessary. (Table E-3) - Assessment scale for assessing the relevance of threat events, annotated by the organization, if necessary. (Table E-4) - Threat events identified in previous risk assessments, if appropriate.	No	Yes	Yes *If not provided by Tier 2*
From Tier 2: (Mission/business process level) - Threat event information and guidance specific to Tier 2 (e.g., threats related to mission/business processes, EA segments, common infrastructure, support services, common controls, and external dependencies). - Mission/business process-specific characterization of adversarial and non-adversarial threat events.	Yes *Via RAR*	Yes *Via Peer Sharing*	Yes
From Tier 3: (Information system level) - Threat event information and guidance specific to Tier 3 (e.g., threats related to information systems, information technologies, information system components, applications, networks, environments of operation). - Information system-specific characterization of adversarial and non-adversarial threat events. - Incident reports.	Yes *Via RAR*	Yes *Via RAR*	Yes *Via Peer Sharing*

[51] Each entry in Table E-2 implicitly assumes a level of adversary capability, intent, and targeting. Depending on the results of threat source identification, some entries could be determined to be irrelevant, while other entries could be combined. In addition, some entries could be rewritten in terms of an organization's enterprise architecture.

[52] The level of detail of TTPs is established as part of the organizational risk frame. The level of detail in Table E-2 is intended to support risk assessments at all three tiers, and to be tailorable to include additional details, as necessary. More detailed descriptions of threat events that exploit software, for example, can be found in the Common Attack Pattern Enumeration and Classification (CAPEC) site at http://capec.mitre.org.

[53] The threat events in Table E-2 are provided at the *unclassified* level. Additional threat events at the *classified* level are available from selected federal agencies to individuals with appropriate security clearances and need to know.

TABLE E-2: REPRESENTATIVE EXAMPLES – ADVERSARIAL THREAT EVENTS[54]

Threat Events (Characterized by TTPs)	Description
Perform reconnaissance and gather information.	
Perform perimeter network reconnaissance/scanning.	Adversary uses commercial or free software to scan organizational perimeters to obtain a better understanding of the information technology infrastructure and improve the ability to launch successful attacks.
Perform network sniffing of exposed networks.	Adversary with access to exposed wired or wireless data channels used to transmit information, uses network sniffing to identify components, resources, and protections.
Gather information using open source discovery of organizational information.	Adversary mines publically accessible information to gather information about organizational information systems, business processes, users or personnel, or external relationships that the adversary can subsequently employ in support of an attack.
Perform reconnaissance and surveillance of targeted organizations.	Adversary uses various means (e.g., scanning, physical observation) over time to examine and assess organizations and ascertain points of vulnerability.
Perform malware-directed internal reconnaissance.	Adversary uses malware installed inside the organizational perimeter to identify targets of opportunity. Because the scanning, probing, or observation does not cross the perimeter, it is not detected by externally placed intrusion detection systems.
Craft or create attack tools.	
Craft phishing attacks.	Adversary counterfeits communications from a legitimate/trustworthy source to acquire sensitive information such as usernames, passwords, or SSNs. Typical attacks occur via email, instant messaging, or comparable means; commonly directing users to websites that appear to be legitimate sites, while actually stealing the entered information.
Craft spear phishing attacks.	Adversary employs phishing attacks targeted at high value targets (e.g., senior leaders/executives).
Craft attacks specifically based on deployed information technology environment.	Adversary develops attacks (e.g., crafts targeted malware) that take advantage of adversary knowledge of the organizational information technology environment.
Create counterfeit/spoof website.	Adversary creates duplicates of legitimate websites; when users visit a counterfeit site, the site can gather information or download malware.
Craft counterfeit certificates.	Adversary counterfeits or compromises a certificate authority, so that malware or connections will appear legitimate.
Create and operate false front organizations to inject malicious components into the supply chain.	Adversary creates false front organizations with the appearance of legitimate suppliers in the critical life-cycle path that then inject corrupted/malicious information system components into the organizational supply chain.
Deliver/insert/install malicious capabilities.	
Deliver known malware to internal organizational information systems (e.g., virus via email).	Adversary uses common delivery mechanisms (e.g., email) to install/insert known malware (e.g., malware whose existence is known) into organizational information systems.
Deliver modified malware to internal organizational information systems.	Adversary uses more sophisticated delivery mechanisms than email (e.g., web traffic, instant messaging, FTP) to deliver malware and possibly modifications of known malware to gain access to internal organizational information systems.
Deliver targeted malware for control of internal systems and exfiltration of data.	Adversary installs malware that is specifically designed to take control of internal organizational information systems, identify sensitive information, exfiltrate the information back to adversary, and conceal these actions.
Deliver malware by providing removable media.	Adversary places removable media (e.g., flash drives) containing malware in locations external to organizational physical perimeters but where employees are likely to find the media (e.g., facilities parking lots, exhibits at conferences attended by employees) and use it on organizational information systems.

---

[54] While not restricted to the APT as a threat source, the threat events in Table E-2 generally follow the flow of an APT campaign. Within each stage in a campaign, similar events are listed in order of adversary capability.

Guide for Conducting Risk Assessments (800-30 rev 1)

158

Threat Events (Characterized by TTPs)	Description
Insert untargeted malware into downloadable software and/or into commercial information technology products.	Adversary corrupts or inserts malware into common freeware, shareware or commercial information technology products. Adversary is not targeting specific organizations, simply looking for entry points into internal organizational information systems. Note that this is particularly a concern for mobile applications.
Insert targeted malware into organizational information systems and information system components.	Adversary inserts malware into organizational information systems and information system components (e.g., commercial information technology products), specifically targeted to the hardware, software, and firmware used by organizations (based on knowledge gained via reconnaissance).
Insert specialized malware into organizational information systems based on system configurations.	Adversary inserts specialized, non-detectable, malware into organizational information systems based on system configurations, specifically targeting critical information system components based on reconnaissance and placement within organizational information systems.
Insert counterfeit or tampered hardware into the supply chain.	Adversary intercepts hardware from legitimate suppliers. Adversary modifies the hardware or replaces it with faulty or otherwise modified hardware.
Insert tampered critical components into organizational systems.	Adversary replaces, though supply chain, subverted insider, or some combination thereof, critical information system components with modified or corrupted components.
Install general-purpose sniffers on organization-controlled information systems or networks.	Adversary installs sniffing software onto internal organizational information systems or networks.
Install persistent and targeted sniffers on organizational information systems and networks.	Adversary places within internal organizational information systems or networks software designed to (over a continuous period of time) collect (sniff) network traffic.
Insert malicious scanning devices (e.g., wireless sniffers) inside facilities.	Adversary uses postal service or other commercial delivery services to deliver to organizational mailrooms a device that is able to scan wireless communications accessible from within the mailrooms and then wirelessly transmit information back to adversary.
Insert subverted individuals into organizations.	Adversary places individuals within organizations who are willing and able to carry out actions to cause harm to organizational missions/business functions.
Insert subverted individuals into privileged positions in organizations.	Adversary places individuals in privileged positions within organizations who are willing and able to carry out actions to cause harm to organizational missions/business functions. Adversary may target privileged functions to gain access to sensitive information (e.g., user accounts, system files, etc.) and may leverage access to one privileged capability to get to another capability.
Exploit and compromise.	
Exploit physical access of authorized staff to gain access to organizational facilities.	Adversary follows ("tailgates") authorized individuals into secure/controlled locations with the goal of gaining access to facilities, circumventing physical security checks.
Exploit poorly configured or unauthorized information systems exposed to the Internet.	Adversary gains access through the Internet to information systems that are not authorized for Internet connectivity or that do not meet organizational configuration requirements.
Exploit split tunneling.	Adversary takes advantage of external organizational or personal information systems (e.g., laptop computers at remote locations) that are simultaneously connected securely to organizational information systems or networks and to nonsecure remote connections.
Exploit multi-tenancy in a cloud environment.	Adversary, with processes running in an organizationally-used cloud environment, takes advantage of multi-tenancy to observe behavior of organizational processes, acquire organizational information, or interfere with the timely or correct functioning of organizational processes.
Exploit known vulnerabilities in mobile systems (e.g., laptops, PDAs, smart phones).	Adversary takes advantage of fact that transportable information systems are outside physical protection of organizations and logical protection of corporate firewalls, and compromises the systems based on known vulnerabilities to gather information from those systems.
Exploit recently discovered vulnerabilities.	Adversary exploits recently discovered vulnerabilities in organizational information systems in an attempt to compromise the systems before mitigation measures are available or in place.

Guide for Conducting Risk Assessments (800-30 rev 1)
159

Threat Events (Characterized by TTPs)	Description
Exploit vulnerabilities on internal organizational information systems.	Adversary searches for known vulnerabilities in organizational internal information systems and exploits those vulnerabilities.
Exploit vulnerabilities using zero-day attacks.	Adversary employs attacks that exploit as yet unpublicized vulnerabilities. Zero-day attacks are based on adversary insight into the information systems and applications used by organizations as well as adversary reconnaissance of organizations.
Exploit vulnerabilities in information systems timed with organizational mission/business operations tempo.	Adversary launches attacks on organizations in a time and manner consistent with organizational needs to conduct mission/business operations.
Exploit insecure or incomplete data deletion in multi-tenant environment.	Adversary obtains unauthorized information due to insecure or incomplete data deletion in a multi-tenant environment (e.g., in a cloud computing environment).
Violate isolation in multi-tenant environment.	Adversary circumvents or defeats isolation mechanisms in a multi-tenant environment (e.g., in a cloud computing environment) to observe, corrupt, or deny service to hosted services and information/data.
Compromise critical information systems via physical access.	Adversary obtains physical access to organizational information systems and makes modifications.
Compromise information systems or devices used externally and reintroduced into the enterprise.	Adversary installs malware on information systems or devices while the systems/devices are external to organizations for purposes of subsequently infecting organizations when reconnected.
Compromise software of organizational critical information systems.	Adversary inserts malware or otherwise corrupts critical internal organizational information systems.
Compromise organizational information systems to facilitate exfiltration of data/information.	Adversary implants malware into internal organizational information systems, where the malware over time can identify and then exfiltrate valuable information.
Compromise mission-critical information.	Adversary compromises the integrity of mission-critical information, thus preventing or impeding ability of organizations to which information is supplied, from carrying out operations.
Compromise design, manufacture, and/or distribution of information system components (including hardware, software, and firmware).	Adversary compromises the design, manufacture, and/or distribution of critical information system components at selected suppliers.
Conduct an attack (i.e., direct/coordinate attack tools or activities).	
Conduct communications interception attacks.	Adversary takes advantage of communications that are either unencrypted or use weak encryption (e.g., encryption containing publically known flaws), targets those communications, and gains access to transmitted information and channels.
Conduct wireless jamming attacks.	Adversary takes measures to interfere with wireless communications so as to impede or prevent communications from reaching intended recipients.
Conduct attacks using unauthorized ports, protocols and services.	Adversary conducts attacks using ports, protocols, and services for ingress and egress that are not authorized for use by organizations.
Conduct attacks leveraging traffic/data movement allowed across perimeter.	Adversary makes use of permitted information flows (e.g., email communication, removable storage) to compromise internal information systems, which allows adversary to obtain and exfiltrate sensitive information through perimeters.
Conduct simple Denial of Service (DoS) attack.	Adversary attempts to make an Internet-accessible resource unavailable to intended users, or prevent the resource from functioning efficiently or at all, temporarily or indefinitely.
Conduct Distributed Denial of Service (DDoS) attacks.	Adversary uses multiple compromised information systems to attack a single target, thereby causing denial of service for users of the targeted information systems.
Conduct targeted Denial of Service (DoS) attacks.	Adversary targets DoS attacks to critical information systems, components, or supporting infrastructures, based on adversary knowledge of dependencies.
Conduct physical attacks on organizational facilities.	Adversary conducts a physical attack on organizational facilities (e.g., sets a fire).
Conduct physical attacks on infrastructures supporting organizational facilities.	Adversary conducts a physical attack on one or more infrastructures supporting organizational facilities (e.g., breaks a water main, cuts a power line).
Conduct cyber-physical attacks on organizational facilities.	Adversary conducts a cyber-physical attack on organizational facilities (e.g., remotely changes HVAC settings).

Guide for Conducting Risk Assessments (800-30 rev 1)

160

Threat Events (Characterized by TTPs)	Description
Conduct data scavenging attacks in a cloud environment.	Adversary obtains data used and then deleted by organizational processes running in a cloud environment.
Conduct brute force login attempts/password guessing attacks.	Adversary attempts to gain access to organizational information systems by random or systematic guessing of passwords, possibly supported by password cracking utilities.
Conduct nontargeted zero-day attacks.	Adversary employs attacks that exploit as yet unpublicized vulnerabilities. Attacks are not based on any adversary insights into specific vulnerabilities of organizations.
Conduct externally-based session hijacking.	Adversary takes control of (hijacks) already established, legitimate information system sessions between organizations and external entities (e.g., users connecting from off-site locations).
Conduct internally-based session hijacking.	Adversary places an entity within organizations in order to gain access to organizational information systems or networks for the express purpose of taking control (hijacking) an already established, legitimate session either between organizations and external entities (e.g., users connecting from remote locations) or between two locations within internal networks.
Conduct externally-based network traffic modification (man in the middle) attacks.	Adversary, operating outside organizational systems, intercepts/eavesdrops on sessions between organizational and external systems. Adversary then relays messages between organizational and external systems, making them believe that they are talking directly to each other over a private connection, when in fact the entire communication is controlled by the adversary. Such attacks are of particular concern for organizational use of community, hybrid, and public clouds.
Conduct internally-based network traffic modification (man in the middle) attacks.	Adversary operating within the organizational infrastructure intercepts and corrupts data sessions.
Conduct outsider-based social engineering to obtain information.	Externally placed adversary takes actions (e.g., using email, phone) with the intent of persuading or otherwise tricking individuals within organizations into revealing critical/sensitive information (e.g., personally identifiable information).
Conduct insider-based social engineering to obtain information.	Internally placed adversary takes actions (e.g., using email, phone) so that individuals within organizations reveal critical/sensitive information (e.g., mission information).
Conduct attacks targeting and compromising personal devices of critical employees.	Adversary targets key organizational employees by placing malware on their personally owned information systems and devices (e.g., laptop/notebook computers, personal digital assistants, smart phones). The intent is to take advantage of any instances where employees use personal information systems or devices to handle critical/sensitive information.
Conduct supply chain attacks targeting and exploiting critical hardware, software, or firmware.	Adversary targets and compromises the operation of software (e.g., through malware injections), firmware, and hardware that performs critical functions for organizations. This is largely accomplished as supply chain attacks on both commercial off-the-shelf and custom information systems and components.
Achieve results (i.e., cause adverse impacts, obtain information)	
Obtain sensitive information through network sniffing of external networks.	Adversary with access to exposed wired or wireless data channels that organizations (or organizational personnel) use to transmit information (e.g., kiosks, public wireless networks) intercepts communications.
Obtain sensitive information via exfiltration.	Adversary directs malware on organizational systems to locate and surreptitiously transmit sensitive information.
Cause degradation or denial of attacker-selected services or capabilities.	Adversary directs malware on organizational systems to impair the correct and timely support of organizational mission/business functions.
Cause deterioration/destruction of critical information system components and functions.	Adversary destroys or causes deterioration of critical information system components to impede or eliminate organizational ability to carry out missions or business functions. Detection of this action is not a concern.
Cause integrity loss by creating, deleting, and/or modifying data on publicly accessible information systems (e.g., web defacement).	Adversary vandalizes, or otherwise makes unauthorized changes to, organizational websites or data on websites.
Cause integrity loss by polluting or corrupting critical data.	Adversary implants corrupted and incorrect data in critical data, resulting in suboptimal actions or loss of confidence in organizational data/services.

Guide for Conducting Risk Assessments (800-30 rev 1)

161

Threat Events (Characterized by TTPs)	Description
Cause integrity loss by injecting false but believable data into organizational information systems.	Adversary injects false but believable data into organizational information systems, resulting in suboptimal actions or loss of confidence in organizational data/services.
Cause disclosure of critical and/or sensitive information by authorized users.	Adversary induces (e.g., via social engineering) authorized users to inadvertently expose, disclose, or mishandle critical/sensitive information.
Cause unauthorized disclosure and/or unavailability by spilling sensitive information.	Adversary contaminates organizational information systems (including devices and networks) by causing them to handle information of a classification/sensitivity for which they have not been authorized. The information is exposed to individuals who are not authorized access to such information, and the information system, device, or network is unavailable while the spill is investigated and mitigated.
Obtain information by externally located interception of wireless network traffic.	Adversary intercepts organizational communications over wireless networks. Examples include targeting public wireless access or hotel networking connections, and drive-by subversion of home or organizational wireless routers.
Obtain unauthorized access.	Adversary with authorized access to organizational information systems, gains access to resources that exceeds authorization.
Obtain sensitive data/information from publicly accessible information systems.	Adversary scans or mines information on publically accessible servers and web pages of organizations with the intent of finding sensitive information.
Obtain information by opportunistically stealing or scavenging information systems/components.	Adversary steals information systems or components (e. g., laptop computers or data storage media) that are left unattended outside of the physical perimeters of organizations, or scavenges discarded components.
Maintain a presence or set of capabilities.	
Obfuscate adversary actions.	Adversary takes actions to inhibit the effectiveness of the intrusion detection systems or auditing capabilities within organizations.
Adapt cyber attacks based on detailed surveillance.	Adversary adapts behavior in response to surveillance and organizational security measures.
Coordinate a campaign.	
Coordinate a campaign of multi-staged attacks (e.g., hopping).	Adversary moves the source of malicious commands or actions from one compromised information system to another, making analysis difficult.
Coordinate a campaign that combines internal and external attacks across multiple information systems and information technologies.	Adversary combines attacks that require both physical presence within organizational facilities and cyber methods to achieve success. Physical attack steps may be as simple as convincing maintenance personnel to leave doors or cabinets open.
Coordinate campaigns across multiple organizations to acquire specific information or achieve desired outcome.	Adversary does not limit planning to the targeting of one organization. Adversary observes multiple organizations to acquire necessary information on targets of interest.
Coordinate a campaign that spreads attacks across organizational systems from existing presence.	Adversary uses existing presence within organizational systems to extend the adversary's span of control to other organizational systems including organizational infrastructure. Adversary thus is in position to further undermine organizational ability to carry out missions/business functions.
Coordinate a campaign of continuous, adaptive, and changing cyber attacks based on detailed surveillance.	Adversary attacks continually change in response to surveillance and organizational security measures.
Coordinate cyber attacks using external (outsider), internal (insider), and supply chain (supplier) attack vectors.	Adversary employs continuous, coordinated attacks, potentially using all three attack vectors for the purpose of impeding organizational operations.

TABLE E-3: REPRESENTATIVE EXAMPLES – NON-ADVERSARIAL THREAT EVENTS

Threat Event	Description
Spill sensitive information	Authorized user erroneously contaminates a device, information system, or network by placing on it or sending to it information of a classification/sensitivity which it has not been authorized to handle. The information is exposed to access by unauthorized individuals, and as a result, the device, system, or network is unavailable while the spill is investigated and mitigated.
Mishandling of critical and/or sensitive information by authorized users	Authorized privileged user inadvertently exposes critical/sensitive information.
Incorrect privilege settings	Authorized privileged user or administrator erroneously assigns a user exceptional privileges or sets privilege requirements on a resource too low.
Communications contention	Degraded communications performance due to contention.
Unreadable display	Display unreadable due to aging equipment.
Earthquake at primary facility	Earthquake of organization-defined magnitude at primary facility makes facility inoperable.
Fire at primary facility	Fire (not due to adversarial activity) at primary facility makes facility inoperable.
Fire at backup facility	Fire (not due to adversarial activity) at backup facility makes facility inoperable or destroys backups of software, configurations, data, and/or logs.
Flood at primary facility	Flood (not due to adversarial activity) at primary facility makes facility inoperable.
Flood at backup facility	Flood (not due to adversarial activity) at backup facility makes facility inoperable or destroys backups of software, configurations, data, and/or logs.
Hurricane at primary facility	Hurricane of organization-defined strength at primary facility makes facility inoperable.
Hurricane at backup facility	Hurricane of organization-defined strength at backup facility makes facility inoperable or destroys backups of software, configurations, data, and/or logs.
Resource depletion	Degraded processing performance due to resource depletion.
Introduction of vulnerabilities into software products	Due to inherent weaknesses in programming languages and software development environments, errors and vulnerabilities are introduced into commonly used software products.
Disk error	Corrupted storage due to a disk error.
Pervasive disk error	Multiple disk errors due to aging of a set of devices all acquired at the same time, from the same supplier.
Windstorm/tornado at primary facility	Windstorm/tornado of organization-defined strength at primary facility makes facility inoperable.
Windstorm/tornado at backup facility	Windstorm/tornado of organization-defined strength at backup facility makes facility inoperable or destroys backups of software, configurations, data, and/or logs.

TABLE E-4: RELEVANCE OF THREAT EVENTS

Value	Description
Confirmed	The threat event or TTP has been seen by the organization.
Expected	The threat event or TTP has been seen by the organization's peers or partners.
Anticipated	The threat event or TTP has been reported by a trusted source.
Predicted	The threat event or TTP has been predicted by a trusted source.
Possible	The threat event or TTP has been described by a somewhat credible source.
N/A	The threat event or TTP is not currently applicable. For example, a threat event or TTP could assume specific technologies, architectures, or processes that are not present in the organization, mission/business process, EA segment, or information system; or predisposing conditions that are not present (e.g., location in a flood plain). Alternately, if the organization is using detailed or specific threat information, a threat event or TTP could be deemed inapplicable because information indicates that no adversary is expected to initiate the threat event or use the TTP.

TABLE E-5: TEMPLATE – IDENTIFICATION OF THREAT EVENTS

Identifier	Threat Event Source of Information	Threat Source	Relevance
Organization -defined	Table E-2, Table E-3, Task 1-4 or Organization-defined	Table D-7, Table D-8 or Organization-defined	Table E-4 or Organization-defined

APPENDIX F

VULNERABILITIES AND PREDISPOSING CONDITIONS
RISK FACTORS AFFECTING THE LIKELIHOOD OF SUCCESSFUL THREAT EXPLOITATION

This appendix provides: (i) a description of potentially useful inputs to the *vulnerability* and *predisposing condition* identification task; (ii) an exemplary taxonomy of predisposing conditions; (iii) exemplary assessment scales for assessing the severity of vulnerabilities and the pervasiveness of predisposing conditions; and (iv) a set of templates for summarizing and documenting the results of the vulnerability and predisposing condition identification task. The taxonomy and assessment scales in this appendix can be used by organizations as a starting point with appropriate tailoring to adjust for any organization-specific conditions. Tables F-3 and F-6, outputs from Task 2-3, provide relevant inputs to the risk tables in Appendix I.

TABLE F-1: INPUTS – VULNERABILITIES AND PREDISPOSING CONDITIONS

Description	Provided To		
	Tier 1	Tier 2	Tier 3

From Tier 1 (Organization level)
 	
- Sources of vulnerability information deemed to be credible (e.g., open source and/or classified vulnerabilities, previous risk/vulnerability assessments, Mission and/or Business Impact Analyses). (Section 3.1, Task 1-4.)
- Vulnerability information and guidance specific to Tier 1 (e.g., vulnerabilities related to organizational governance, core missions/business functions, management/operational policies, procedures, and structures, external mission/business relationships).
- Taxonomy of predisposing conditions, annotated by the organization, if necessary. (Table F-4)
- Characterization of vulnerabilities and predisposing conditions.
  - Assessment scale for assessing the severity of vulnerabilities, annotated by the organization, if necessary. (Table F-2)
  - Assessment scale for assessing the pervasiveness of predisposing conditions, annotated by the organization, if necessary. (Table F-5)
  - Business Continuity Plan, Continuity of Operations Plan for the organization, if such plans are defined for the entire organization.
	No	Yes	Yes
			if not provided by Tier 2

From Tier 2: (Mission/business process level) - Vulnerability information and guidance specific to Tier 2 (e.g., vulnerabilities related to organizational mission/business processes, EA segments, common infrastructure, support services, common controls, and external dependencies). - Business Continuity Plans, Continuity of Operations Plans for mission/business processes, if such plans are defined for individual processes or business units.	Yes *Via RAR*	Yes *Via Peer Sharing*	Yes
From Tier 3: (Information system level) - Vulnerability information and guidance specific to Tier 3 (e.g., vulnerabilities related to information systems, information technologies, information system components, applications, networks, environments of operation). - Security assessment reports (i.e., deficiencies in assessed controls identified as vulnerabilities). - Results of monitoring activities (e.g., automated and nonautomated data feeds). - Vulnerability assessments, Red Team reports, or other reports from analyses of information systems, subsystems, information technology products, devices, networks, or applications. - Contingency Plans, Disaster Recovery Plans, Incident Reports. - Vendor/manufacturer vulnerability reports.	Yes *Via RAR*	Yes *Via RAR*	Yes *Via Peer Sharing*

TABLE F-2: ASSESSMENT SCALE – VULNERABILITY SEVERITY

Qualitative Values	Semi-Quantitative Values		Description
Very High	96-100	10	The vulnerability is exposed and exploitable, and its exploitation could result in severe impacts. Relevant security control or other remediation is not implemented and not planned; or no security measure can be identified to remediate the vulnerability.
High	80-95	8	The vulnerability is of high concern, based on the exposure of the vulnerability and ease of exploitation and/or on the severity of impacts that could result from its exploitation. Relevant security control or other remediation is planned but not implemented; compensating controls are in place and at least minimally effective.
Moderate	21-79	5	The vulnerability is of moderate concern, based on the exposure of the vulnerability and ease of exploitation and/or on the severity of impacts that could result from its exploitation. Relevant security control or other remediation is partially implemented and somewhat effective.
Low	5-20	2	The vulnerability is of minor concern, but effectiveness of remediation could be improved. Relevant security control or other remediation is fully implemented and somewhat effective.
Very Low	0-4	0	The vulnerability is not of concern. Relevant security control or other remediation is fully implemented, assessed, and effective.

TABLE F-3: TEMPLATE – IDENTIFICATION OF VULNERABILITIES

Identifier	Vulnerability Source of Information	Vulnerability Severity
Organization-defined	Task 2-3, Task 1-4 or Organization-defined	Table F-2 or Organization-defined

TABLE F-4: TAXONOMY OF PREDISPOSING CONDITIONS

Type of Predisposing Condition	Description

INFORMATION-RELATED
- Classified National Security Information
- Compartments
- Controlled Unclassified Information
- Personally Identifiable Information
- Special Access Programs
- Agreement-Determined
  - NOFORN
  - Proprietary
	Needs to handle information (as it is created, transmitted, stored, processed, and/or displayed) in a specific manner, due to its sensitivity (or lack of sensitivity), legal or regulatory requirements, and/or contractual or other organizational agreements.

TECHNICAL
- Architectural
  - Compliance with technical standards
  - Use of specific products or product lines
  - Solutions for and/or approaches to user-based collaboration and information sharing
  - Allocation of specific security functionality to common controls
- Functional
  - Networked multiuser
  - Single-user
  - Stand-alone / nonnetworked
  - Restricted functionality (e.g., communications, sensors, embedded controllers)
	Needs to use technologies in specific ways.

OPERATIONAL / ENVIRONMENTAL
- Mobility
  - Fixed-site (specify location)
  - Semi-mobile
    - Land-based, Airborne, Sea-based, Space-based
  - Mobile (e.g., handheld device)
- Population with physical and/or logical access to components of the information system, mission/business process, EA segment
  - Size of population
  - Clearance/vetting of population
	Ability to rely upon physical, procedural, and personnel controls provided by the operational environment.

TABLE F-5: ASSESSMENT SCALE – PERVASIVENESS OF PREDISPOSING CONDITIONS

Qualitative Values	Semi-Quantitative Values		Description
Very High	96-100	10	Applies to all organizational missions/business functions (Tier 1), mission/business processes (Tier 2), or information systems (Tier 3).
High	80-95	8	Applies to most organizational missions/business functions (Tier 1), mission/business processes (Tier 2), or information systems (Tier 3).
Moderate	21-79	5	Applies to many organizational missions/business functions (Tier 1), mission/business processes (Tier 2), or information systems (Tier 3).
Low	5-20	2	Applies to some organizational missions/business functions (Tier 1), mission/business processes (Tier 2), or information systems (Tier 3).
Very Low	0-4	0	Applies to few organizational missions/business functions (Tier 1), mission/business processes (Tier 2), or information systems (Tier 3).

TABLE F-6: TEMPLATE – IDENTIFICATION OF PREDISPOSING CONDITIONS

Identifier	Predisposing Condition Source of Information	Pervasiveness of Condition
Organization-defined	Table F-4, Task 1-4 or Organization-defined	Table F-5 or Organization-defined

APPENDIX G

LIKELIHOOD OF OCCURRENCE

DETERMINING THE LIKELIHOOD OF THREAT EVENTS CAUSING ADVERSE IMPACTS

This appendix provides: (i) a description of potentially useful inputs to the *likelihood*[55] determination task; and (ii) exemplary assessment scales for assessing the likelihood of threat event initiation/occurrence, the likelihood of threat events resulting in adverse impacts, and the overall likelihood of threat events being initiated or occurring and doing damage to organizational operations, assets, or individuals. The assessment scales in this appendix can be used by organizations as a starting point with appropriate tailoring to adjust for any organization-specific conditions. Tables G-2, G-3, G-4, and G-5, outputs from Task 2-4, provide relevant inputs to the risk tables in Appendix I.

TABLE G-1: INPUTS – DETERMINATION OF LIKELIHOOD

Description	Provided To		
	Tier 1	Tier 2	Tier 3
From Tier 1 (Organization level) - Likelihood information and guidance specific to Tier 1 (e.g., likelihood information related to organizational governance, core missions/business functions, management/operational policies, procedures, and structures, external mission/business relationships). - Guidance on organization-wide levels of likelihood needing no further consideration. - Assessment scale for assessing the likelihood of threat event initiation (adversarial threat events), annotated by the organization, if necessary. (Table G-2) - Assessment scale for assessing the likelihood of threat event occurrence (non-adversarial threat events), annotated by the organization, if necessary. (Table G-3) - Assessment scale for assessing the likelihood of threat events resulting in adverse impacts, annotated by the organization, if necessary. (Table G-4) - Assessment scale for assessing the overall likelihood of threat events being initiated or occurring and resulting in adverse impacts, annotated by the organization, if necessary. (Table G-5)	No	Yes	Yes *If not provided by Tier 2*
From Tier 2: (Mission/business process level) - Likelihood information and guidance specific to Tier 2 (e.g., likelihood information related to mission/business processes, EA segments, common infrastructure, support services, common controls, and external dependencies).	Yes *Via RAR*	Yes *Via Peer Sharing*	Yes
From Tier 3: (Information system level) - Likelihood information and guidance specific to Tier 3 (e.g., likelihood information related to information systems, information technologies, information system components, applications, networks, environments of operation). - Historical data on successful and unsuccessful cyber attacks; attack detection rates. - Security assessment reports (i.e., deficiencies in assessed controls identified as vulnerabilities). - Results of monitoring activities (e.g., automated and nonautomated data feeds). - Vulnerability assessments, Red Team reports, or other reports from analyses of information systems, subsystems, information technology products, devices, networks, or applications. - Contingency Plans, Disaster Recovery Plans, Incident Reports. - Vendor/manufacturer vulnerability reports.	Yes *Via RAR*	Yes *Via RAR*	Yes *Via Peer Sharing*

---

[55] The term *likelihood*, as discussed in this guideline, is not likelihood in the strict sense of the term; rather, it is a likelihood score. Risk assessors do not define a likelihood function in the statistical sense. Instead, risk assessors assign a score (or likelihood assessment) based on available evidence, experience, and expert judgment. Combinations of factors such as targeting, intent, and capability thus can be used to produce a score representing the likelihood of threat initiation; combinations of factors such as capability and vulnerability severity can be used to produce a score representing the likelihood of adverse impacts; and combinations of these scores can be used to produce an overall likelihood score.

TABLE G-2: ASSESSMENT SCALE – LIKELIHOOD OF THREAT EVENT INITIATION (ADVERSARIAL)

Qualitative Values	Semi-Quantitative Values		Description
Very High	96-100	10	Adversary is almost certain to initiate the threat event.
High	80-95	8	Adversary is highly likely to initiate the threat event.
Moderate	21-79	5	Adversary is somewhat likely to initiate the treat event.
Low	5-20	2	Adversary is unlikely to initiate the threat event.
Very Low	0-4	0	Adversary is highly unlikely to initiate the threat event.

TABLE G-3: ASSESSMENT SCALE – LIKELIHOOD OF THREAT EVENT OCCURRENCE (NON-ADVERSARIAL)

Qualitative Values	Semi-Quantitative Values		Description
Very High	96-100	10	Error, accident, or act of nature is almost certain to occur; or occurs more than 100 times a year.
High	80-95	8	Error, accident, or act of nature is highly likely to occur; or occurs between 10-100 times a year.
Moderate	21-79	5	Error, accident, or act of nature is somewhat likely to occur; or occurs between 1-10 times a year.
Low	5-20	2	Error, accident, or act of nature is unlikely to occur; or occurs less than once a year, but more than once every 10 years.
Very Low	0-4	0	Error, accident, or act of nature is highly unlikely to occur; or occurs less than once every 10 years.

TABLE G-4: ASSESSMENT SCALE – LIKELIHOOD OF THREAT EVENT RESULTING IN ADVERSE IMPACTS

Qualitative Values	Semi-Quantitative Values		Description
Very High	96-100	10	If the threat event is initiated or occurs, it is almost certain to have adverse impacts.
High	80-95	8	If the threat event is initiated or occurs, it is highly likely to have adverse impacts.
Moderate	21-79	5	If the threat event is initiated or occurs, it is somewhat likely to have adverse impacts.
Low	5-20	2	If the threat event is initiated or occurs, it is unlikely to have adverse impacts.
Very Low	0-4	0	If the threat event is initiated or occurs, it is highly unlikely to have adverse impacts.

TABLE G-5: ASSESSMENT SCALE – OVERALL LIKELIHOOD

Likelihood of Threat Event Initiation or Occurrence	Likelihood Threat Events Result in Adverse Impacts				
	Very Low	Low	Moderate	High	Very High
Very High	Low	Moderate	High	Very High	Very High
High	Low	Moderate	Moderate	High	Very High
Moderate	Low	Low	Moderate	Moderate	High
Low	Very Low	Low	Low	Moderate	Moderate
Very Low	Very Low	Very Low	Low	Low	Low

Guide for Conducting Risk Assessments (800-30 rev 1)
170

APPENDIX H

IMPACT
EFFECTS OF THREAT EVENTS ON ORGANIZATIONS, INDIVIDUALS, AND THE NATION

This appendix provides: (i) a description of useful inputs to the impact determination task; (ii) representative examples of adverse impacts to organizational operations and assets, individuals, other organizations, or the Nation; (iii) exemplary assessment scales for assessing the impact of threat events and the range of effect of threat events; and (iv) a template for summarizing and documenting the results of the impact determination Task 2-5. The assessment scales in this appendix can be used as a starting point with appropriate tailoring to adjust for any organization-specific conditions. Table H-4, an output from Task 2-5, provides relevant inputs to the risk tables in Appendix I.

TABLE H-1: INPUTS – DETERMINATION OF IMPACT

Description	Provided To		
	Tier 1	Tier 2	Tier 3
From Tier 1 (Organization level) - Impact information and guidance specific to Tier 1 (e.g., impact information related to organizational governance, core missions/business functions, management and operational policies, procedures, and structures, external mission/business relationships). - Guidance on organization-wide levels of impact needing no further consideration. - Identification of critical missions/business functions. - Exemplary set of impacts, annotated by the organization, if necessary. (Table H-2) - Assessment scale for assessing the impact of threat events, annotated by the organization, if necessary. (Table H-3)	No	Yes	Yes *If not provided by Tier 2*
From Tier 2: (Mission/business process level) - Impact information and guidance specific to Tier 2 (e.g., impact information related to mission/business processes, EA segments, common infrastructure, support services, common controls, and external dependencies). - Identification of high-value assets.	Yes *Via RAR*	Yes *Via Peer Sharing*	Yes
From Tier 3: (Information system level) - Impact information and guidance specific to Tier 3 (e.g., likelihood information affecting information systems, information technologies, information system components, applications, networks, environments of operation). - Historical data on successful and unsuccessful cyber attacks; attack detection rates. - Security assessment reports (i.e., deficiencies in assessed controls identified as vulnerabilities). - Results of continuous monitoring activities (e.g., automated and nonautomated data feeds). - Vulnerability assessments, Red Team reports, or other reports from analyses of information systems, subsystems, information technology products, devices, networks, or applications. - Contingency Plans, Disaster Recovery Plans, Incident Reports.	Yes *Via RAR*	Yes *Via RAR*	Yes *Via Peer Sharing*

TABLE H-2: EXAMPLES OF ADVERSE IMPACTS

Type of Impact	Impact

HARM TO OPERATIONS	- Inability to perform current missions/business functions.
	  - In a sufficiently timely manner.
	  - With sufficient confidence and/or correctness.
	  - Within planned resource constraints.
	- Inability, or limited ability, to perform missions/business functions in the future.
	  - Inability to restore missions/business functions.
	  - In a sufficiently timely manner.
	  - With sufficient confidence and/or correctness.
	  - Within planned resource constraints.
	- Harms (e.g., financial costs, sanctions) due to noncompliance.
	  - With applicable laws or regulations.
	  - With contractual requirements or other requirements in other binding agreements (e.g., liability).
	- Direct financial costs.
	- Relational harms.
	  - Damage to trust relationships.
	  - Damage to image or reputation (and hence future or potential trust relationships).

HARM TO ASSETS	- Damage to or loss of physical facilities. - Damage to or loss of information systems or networks. - Damage to or loss of information technology or equipment. - Damage to or loss of component parts or supplies. - Damage to or loss of information assets. - Loss of intellectual property.
HARM TO INDIVIDUALS	- Injury or loss of life. - Physical or psychological mistreatment. - Identity theft. - Loss of Personally Identifiable Information. - Damage to image or reputation.

HARM TO OTHER ORGANIZATIONS	- Harms (e.g., financial costs, sanctions) due to noncompliance.
	  - With applicable laws or regulations.
	  - With contractual requirements or other requirements in other binding agreements.
	- Direct financial costs.
	- Relational harms.
	  - Damage to trust relationships.
	  - Damage to reputation (and hence future or potential trust relationships).

HARM TO THE NATION	- Damage to or incapacitation of a critical infrastructure sector.
	- Loss of government continuity of operations.
	- Relational harms.
	  - Damage to trust relationships with other governments or with nongovernmental entities.
	  - Damage to national reputation (and hence future or potential trust relationships).
	- Damage to current or future ability to achieve national objectives.
	  - Harm to national security.

TABLE H-3: ASSESSMENT SCALE – IMPACT OF THREAT EVENTS

Qualitative Values	Semi-Quantitative Values		Description
Very High	96-100	10	The threat event could be expected to have multiple severe or catastrophic adverse effects on organizational operations, organizational assets, individuals, other organizations, or the Nation.
High	80-95	8	The threat event could be expected to have a severe or catastrophic adverse effect on organizational operations, organizational assets, individuals, other organizations, or the Nation. A severe or catastrophic adverse effect means that, for example, the threat event might: (i) cause a severe degradation in or loss of mission capability to an extent and duration that the organization is not able to perform one or more of its primary functions; (ii) result in major damage to organizational assets; (iii) result in major financial loss; or (iv) result in severe or catastrophic harm to individuals involving loss of life or serious life-threatening injuries.
Moderate	21-79	5	The threat event could be expected to have a serious adverse effect on organizational operations, organizational assets, individuals other organizations, or the Nation. A serious adverse effect means that, for example, the threat event might: (i) cause a significant degradation in mission capability to an extent and duration that the organization is able to perform its primary functions, but the effectiveness of the functions is significantly reduced; (ii) result in significant damage to organizational assets; (iii) result in significant financial loss; or (iv) result in significant harm to individuals that does not involve loss of life or serious life-threatening injuries.
Low	5-20	2	The threat event could be expected to have a limited adverse effect on organizational operations, organizational assets, individuals other organizations, or the Nation. A limited adverse effect means that, for example, the threat event might: (i) cause a degradation in mission capability to an extent and duration that the organization is able to perform its primary functions, but the effectiveness of the functions is noticeably reduced; (ii) result in minor damage to organizational assets; (iii) result in minor financial loss; or (iv) result in minor harm to individuals.
Very Low	0-4	0	The threat event could be expected to have a negligible adverse effect on organizational operations, organizational assets, individuals other organizations, or the Nation.

TABLE H-4: TEMPLATE – IDENTIFICATION OF ADVERSE IMPACTS

Type of Impact	Impact Affected Asset	Maximum Impact
Table H-2 or Organization-defined	Table H-2 or Organization-defined	Table H-3 or Organization-defined

APPENDIX I

RISK DETERMINATION

ASSESSING RISK TO ORGANIZATIONS, INDIVIDUALS, AND THE NATION

This appendix provides: (i) a description of potentially useful inputs to the risk determination task including considerations for uncertainty of determinations; (ii) exemplary assessment scales for assessing the levels of risk; (iii) tables for describing content (i.e., data inputs) for adversarial and non-adversarial risk determinations; and (iv) templates for summarizing and documenting the results of the risk determination Task 2-6. The assessment scales in this appendix can be used as a starting point with appropriate tailoring to adjust for any organization-specific conditions. Table I-5 (adversarial risk) and Table I-7 (non-adversarial risk) are outputs from Task 2-6.

TABLE I-1: INPUTS – RISK

Description	Provided To		
	Tier 1	Tier 2	Tier 3
From Tier 1 (Organization level) - Sources of risk and uncertainty information identified for organization-wide use (e.g., specific information that may be useful in determining likelihoods such as adversary capabilities, intent, and targeting objectives). - Guidance on organization-wide levels of risk (including uncertainty) needing no further consideration. - Criteria for uncertainty determinations. - List of high-risk events from previous risk assessments. - Assessment scale for assessing the level of risk as a combination of likelihood and impact, annotated by the organization, if necessary. (Table I-2) - Assessment scale for assessing level of risk, annotated by the organization, if necessary. (Table I-3)	No	Yes	Yes *If not provided by Tier 2*
From Tier 2: (Mission/business process level) - Risk-related information and guidance specific to Tier 2 (e.g., risk and uncertainty information related to mission/business processes, EA segments, common infrastructure, support services, common controls, and external dependencies).	Yes *Via RAR*	Yes *Via Peer Sharing*	Yes
From Tier 3: (Information system level) - Risk-related information and guidance specific to Tier 3 (e.g., likelihood information affecting information systems, information technologies, information system components, applications, networks, environments of operation).	Yes *Via RAR*	Yes *Via RAR*	Yes *Via Peer Sharing*

TABLE I-2: ASSESSMENT SCALE – LEVEL OF RISK (COMBINATION OF LIKELIHOOD AND IMPACT)

Likelihood (Threat Event Occurs and Results in Adverse Impact)	Level of Impact				
	Very Low	Low	Moderate	High	Very High
Very High	Very Low	Low	Moderate	High	Very High
High	Very Low	Low	Moderate	High	Very High
Moderate	Very Low	Low	Moderate	Moderate	High
Low	Very Low	Low	Low	Low	Moderate
Very Low	Very Low	Very Low	Very Low	Low	Low

TABLE I-3: ASSESSMENT SCALE – LEVEL OF RISK

Qualitative Values	Semi-Quantitative Values		Description
Very High	96-100	10	**Very high risk** means that a threat event could be expected to have **multiple severe or catastrophic** adverse effects on organizational operations, organizational assets, individuals, other organizations, or the Nation.
High	80-95	8	**High risk** means that a threat event could be expected to have a **severe or catastrophic** adverse effect on organizational operations, organizational assets, individuals, other organizations, or the Nation.
Moderate	21-79	5	**Moderate risk** means that a threat event could be expected to have a **serious** adverse effect on organizational operations, organizational assets, individuals, other organizations, or the Nation.
Low	5-20	2	**Low risk** means that a threat event could be expected to have a **limited** adverse effect on organizational operations, organizational assets, individuals, other organizations, or the Nation.
Very Low	0-4	0	**Very low risk** means that a threat event could be expected to have a **negligible** adverse effect on organizational operations, organizational assets, individuals, other organizations, or the Nation.

TABLE I-4: COLUMN DESCRIPTIONS FOR ADVERSARIAL RISK TABLE

Column	Heading	Content
1	Threat Event	Identify threat event. (Task 2-2; Table E-1; Table E-2; Table E-5; Table I-5.)
2	Threat Sources	Identify threat sources that could initiate the threat event. (Task 2-1; Table D-1; Table D-2; Table D-7; Table I-5.)
3	Capability	Assess threat source capability. (Task 2-1; Table D-3; Table D-7; Table I-5.)
4	Intent	Assess threat source intent. (Task 2-1; Table D-4; Table D-7; Table I-5.)
5	Targeting	Assess threat source targeting. (Task 2-1; Table D-5; Table D-7; Table I-5.)
6	Relevance	Determine relevance of threat event. (Task 2-2; Table E-1; Table E-4; Table E-5; Table I-5.) If the relevance of the threat event does not meet the organization's criteria for further consideration, do not complete the remaining columns.
7	Likelihood of Attack Initiation	Determine likelihood that one or more of the threat sources initiates the threat event, taking into consideration capability, intent, and targeting. (Task 2-4; Table G-1; Table G-2; Table I-5.)
8	Vulnerabilities and Predisposing Conditions	Identify vulnerabilities which could be exploited by threat sources initiating the threat event and the predisposing conditions which could increase the likelihood of adverse impacts. (Task 2-5; Table F-1; Table F-3; Table F-4; Table F-6; Table I-5.)
9	Severity Pervasiveness	Assess severity of vulnerabilities and pervasiveness of predisposing conditions. (Task 2-5; Table F-1; Table F-2; Table F-5; Table F-6; Table I-5.)
10	Likelihood Initiated Attack Succeeds	Determine the likelihood that the threat event, once initiated, will result in adverse impact, taking into consideration threat source capability, vulnerabilities, and predisposing conditions. (Task 2-4; Table G-1; Table G-4; Table I-5.)
11	Overall Likelihood	Determine the likelihood that the threat event will be initiated and result in adverse impact (i.e., combination of likelihood of attack initiation and likelihood that initiated attack succeeds). (Task 2-4; Table G-1; Table G-5; Table I-5.)
12	Level of Impact	Determine the adverse impact (i.e., potential harm to organizational operations, organizational assets, individuals, other organizations, or the Nation) from the threat event. (Task 2-5; Table H-1; Table H-2; Table H-3; Table H-4; Table I-5.)
13	Risk	Determine the level of risk as a combination of likelihood and impact. (Task 2-6; Table I-1; Table I-2; Table I-3; Table I-5.)

TABLE I-5: TEMPLATE – ADVERSARIAL RISK

1	2	3	4	5	6	7	8	9	10	11	12	13
		Threat Source Characteristics										
Threat Event	Threat Sources	Capability	Intent	Targeting	Relevance	Likelihood of Attack Initiation	Vulnerabilities and Predisposing Conditions	Severity and Pervasiveness	Likelihood Initiated Attack Succeeds	Overall Likelihood	Level of Impact	Risk

Guide for Conducting Risk Assessments (800-30 rev 1)
176

TABLE I-6: COLUMN DESCRIPTIONS FOR NON-ADVERSARIAL RISK TABLE

Column	Heading	Content
1	Threat Event	Identify threat event. (Task 2-2; Table E-1; Table E-3; Table E-5; Table I-7.)
2	Threat Sources	Identify threat sources that could initiate the threat event. (Task 2-1; Table D-1; Table D-2; Table D-8; Table I-7.)
3	Range of Effects	Identify the range of effects from the threat source. (Task 2-1; Table D-1; Table D-6; Table I-7.)
4	Relevance	Determine relevance of threat event. (Task 2-2; Table E-1; Table E-4; Table E-5; Table I-7.) If the relevance of the threat event does not meet the organization's criteria for further consideration, do not complete the remaining columns.
5	Likelihood of Threat Event Occurring	Determine the likelihood that the threat event will occur. (Task 2-4; Table G-1; Table G-3; Table I-7.)
6	Vulnerabilities and Predisposing Conditions	Identify vulnerabilities which could be exploited by threat sources initiating the threat event and the predisposing conditions which could increase the likelihood of adverse impacts. (Task 2-5; Table F-1; Table F-3; Table F-4; Table F-6; Table I-7.)
7	Severity Pervasiveness	Assess severity of vulnerabilities and pervasiveness of predisposing conditions. (Task 2-5; Table F-1; Table F-2; Table F-5; Table F-6; Table I-5.)
8	Likelihood Threat Event Results in Adverse Impact	Determine the likelihood that the threat event, once initiated, will result in adverse impact, taking into consideration vulnerabilities and predisposing conditions. (Task 2-4; Table G-1; Table G-4; Table I-7.)
9	Overall Likelihood	Determine the likelihood that the threat event will occur and result in adverse impacts (i.e., combination of likelihood of threat occurring and likelihood that the threat event results in adverse impact). (Task 2-4; Table G-1; Table G-5; Table I-7.)
10	Level of Impact	Determine the adverse impact (i.e., potential harm to organizational operations, organizational assets, individuals, other organizations, or the Nation) from the threat event. (Task 2-5; Table H-1, Table H-2; Table H-3; Table H-4; Table I-7.)
11	Risk	Determine the level of risk as a combination of likelihood and impact. (Task 2-6; Table I-1; Table I-2; Table I-3; Table I-7.)

TABLE I-7: TEMPLATE – NON-ADVERSARIAL RISK

1	2	3	4	5	6	7	8	9	10	11
Threat Event	Threat Sources	Range of Effects	Relevance	Likelihood of Event Occurring	Vulnerabilities and Predisposing Conditions	Severity and Pervasiveness	Likelihood Event Results in Adverse Impact	Overall Likelihood	Level of Impact	Risk

APPENDIX J

INFORMING RISK RESPONSE
APPROACHES TO REFINING RISK ASSESSMENT RESULTS

A risk assessment may identify a number of risks that have similar scores (e.g., 78, 82, 83) or levels (e.g., moderate, high). When too many risks are clustered at or about the same value, organizations need a method to refine the presentation of risk assessment results, prioritizing within sets of risks with similar values, to better inform the risk response component of the risk management process.[56] Such a method should be associated with the mission/business requirements of the organization, consistent with the organizational risk tolerance, and maximize the use of available resources. Prioritization is a key component of risk-based protection and becomes necessary when requirements cannot be fully satisfied or when resources do not allow all risks to be mitigated within a reasonable time frame. To facilitate informed risk response decisions by senior leaders/executives (e.g., why certain risks were or were not mitigated), the risk assessment results are annotated to enable those decision makers to know or obtain the answers to the following questions about each risk in a set with similar scores:

Time Frame

In the event the identified risk materialized—

- How high would the *immediate* impact be to organizational operations (including mission, functions, image, or reputation), organizational assets, individuals, other organizations, or the Nation?

- How high would the *future* impact be to organizational operations (including mission, functions, image, or reputation), organizational assets, individuals, other organizations, or the Nation?

The answers to the above questions, together with the risk tolerance of the organization, provide the basis for a risk prioritization that is based on current and future organizational needs. When weighing immediate impacts versus future impacts, senior leaders must decide whether a critical mission/business need today warrants jeopardizing the future capabilities of the organization. Mission/business owners and mission/business subject matter experts can be consulted to obtain the most complete and up-to-date information on mission/business impacts. Other subject matter experts or stakeholder representatives can be consulted to obtain information on immediate versus future impacts (e.g., consulting the Privacy Office for impacts to individuals).

Total Cumulative Impact

- What is the expected impact from a single occurrence of the threat?

- If the risk can materialize more than once, what is the overall expected impact (i.e., cumulative loss) for the time period of concern?

Note that one aspect of the total impact to organizations is the cost of recovery from a loss of confidentiality, integrity, or availability.

---

[56] The *risk executive (function)* provides policy-level guidance on organizational risk tolerance and other factors that inform and guide the risk-based decisions of authorizing officials. This guidance can also influence the prioritization of risk responses including for example, mitigation activities.

Synergies Among Risks

If a risk materializes that is closely related to multiple risks, it is likely that a cluster of risks will materialize at or near the same time. Managing the adverse impact from one risk materializing may be possible; managing multiple risks of high impact that materialize at the same time may challenge the capacity of the organization and therefore needs to be managed much more closely. The following questions address relationships among risks.

Will the materialization of a particular risk result in:

- A high likelihood or virtual certainty of other identified risks materializing?

- A high likelihood or virtual certainty of other identified risks *not* materializing?

- No particular effect on other identified risks materializing?

If a risk is highly coupled to other risks or seen as likely to lead to other risks materializing (whether the risk is the cause or materializes concurrently), the risk should be given higher priority than a risk that has no particular effect on other risks. If a risk materializing actually decreases the likelihood of other risks materializing, then further analysis is warranted to determine which risks become a lower priority to mitigate.

In conclusion, organizations can benefit significantly by refining risk assessment results in preparation for the risk response step in the risk management process. During the risk response step, which is described in NIST Special Publication 800-39, organizations: (i) analyze different courses of action; (ii) conduct cost-benefit analyses; (iii) address scalability issues for large-scale implementations; (iv) examine the interactions/dependencies among risk mitigation approaches (e.g., dependencies among security controls); and (v) assess other factors affecting organizational missions/business functions. In addition, organizations address cost, schedule, and performance issues associated with information systems and information technology infrastructure supporting organizational missions/business functions.

CAUTIONARY NOTE

Organizations are cautioned that risk assessments are often not precise instruments of measurement and reflect the limitations of the specific assessment methodologies, tools, and techniques employed—as well as the subjectivity, quality, and trustworthiness of the data used. Risk determinations may be very coarse due to the assessment approach selected, the uncertainty in the likelihood of occurrence and impact values, and the potential mischaracterization of threats. Risks that are on the borderline between bins using the organization-defined binning scales, must ultimately be assigned to one bin. This determination could have a significant effect on the risk prioritization process. Thus, organizations should incorporate as much information as practical on particular risks during the prioritization process to ensure that the values for risks are appropriately determined (e.g., very low, low, moderate, high, very high).

APPENDIX K

RISK ASSESSMENT REPORTS
ESSENTIAL ELEMENTS OF INFORMATION

This appendix provides the essential elements of information that organizations can use to communicate the results of risk assessments.[57] Risk assessment results provide decision makers with an understanding of the information security risk to organizational operations and assets, individuals, other organizations, or the Nation that derive from the operation and use of organizational information systems and the environments in which those systems operate. The essential elements of information in a risk assessment can be described in three sections of the risk assessment report (or whatever vehicle is chosen by organizations to convey the results of the assessment): (i) an executive summary; (ii) the main body containing detailed risk assessment results; and (iii) supporting appendices.

Executive Summary

- List the date of the risk assessment.

- Summarize the purpose of the risk assessment.

- Describe the scope of the risk assessment.

  - For Tier 1 and Tier 2 risk assessments, identify: organizational governance structures or processes associated with the assessment (e.g., risk executive [function], budget process, acquisition process, systems engineering process, enterprise architecture, information security architecture, organizational missions/business functions, mission/business processes, information systems supporting the mission/business processes).

  - For Tier 3 risk assessments, identify: the information system name and location(s), security categorization, and information system (i.e., authorization) boundary.

- State whether this is an initial or subsequent risk assessment. If a subsequent risk assessment, state the circumstances that prompted the update and include a reference to the previous Risk Assessment Report.

- Describe the overall level of risk (e.g., Very Low, Low, Moderate, High, or Very High).

- List the number of risks identified for each level of risk (e.g., Very Low, Low, Moderate, High, or Very High).

Body of the Report

- Describe the purpose of the risk assessment, including questions to be answered by the assessment. For example:

---

[57] The essential elements of information described in this appendix are informative and exemplary only and are not intended to require or promote a specific template for documenting risk assessment results. Organizations have maximum flexibility in determining the type and the level of detail of information included in organizational risk assessments and the associated reports. For example, Tier 1 and Tier 2 risk assessment results may be conveyed via an executive briefing or dashboard, whereas Tier 3 risk assessment results may be conveyed via a risk assessment report (formal or informal depending on organizational preference). The essential elements of information for communicating risk assessment results can be modified accordingly to meet the needs of organizations conducting the assessments.

- How the use of a specific information technology would potentially change the risk to organizational missions/business functions if employed in information systems supporting those missions/business functions; or

- How the risk assessment results are to be used in the context of the RMF (e.g., an initial risk assessment to be used in tailoring security control baselines and/or to guide and inform other decisions and serve as a starting point for subsequent risk assessments; subsequent risk assessment to incorporate results of security control assessments and inform authorization decisions; subsequent risk assessment to support the analysis of alternative courses of action for risk responses; subsequent risk assessment based on risk monitoring to identify new threats or vulnerabilities; subsequent risk assessments to incorporate knowledge gained from incidents or attacks).

- Identify assumptions and constraints.

- Describe risk tolerance inputs to the risk assessment (including the range of consequences to be considered).

- Identify and describe the risk model and analytic approach; provide a reference or include as an appendix, identifying risk factors, value scales, and algorithms for combining values.

- Provide a rationale for any risk-related decisions during the risk assessment process.

- Describe the uncertainties within the risk assessment process and how those uncertainties influence decisions.

- If the risk assessment includes organizational missions/business functions, describe the missions/functions (e.g., mission/business processes supporting the missions/functions, interconnections and dependencies among related missions/business functions, and information technology that supports the missions/business functions).

- If the risk assessment includes organizational information systems, describe the systems (e.g., missions/business functions the system is supporting, information flows to/from the systems, and dependencies on other systems, shared services, or common infrastructures).

- Summarize risk assessment results (e.g., using tables or graphs), in a form that enables decision makers to quickly understand the risk (e.g., number of threat events for different combinations of likelihood and impact, the relative proportion of threat events at different risk levels).

- Identify the time frame for which the risk assessment is valid (i.e., time frame for which the assessment is intended to support decisions).

- List the risks due to adversarial threats (see Table F-1).

- List the risks due to non-adversarial threats (see Table F-2).

Appendices

- List references and sources of information.

- List the team or individuals conducting the risk assessment including contact information.

- List risk assessment details and any supporting evidence (e.g., Tables D-7, D-8, E-5, F-3, F-6, H-4), as needed to understand and enable reuse of results (e.g., for reciprocity, for subsequent risk assessments, to serve as input to Tier 1 and Tier 2 risk assessments).

APPENDIX L

SUMMARY OF TASKS
RISK ASSESSMENT TASKS AND ASSOCIATED RISK TABLES

TABLE L-1: SUMMARY OF RISK ASSESSMENT TASKS

TASK	TASK DESCRIPTION
Step 1: Prepare for Risk Assessment	
TASK 1-1 IDENTIFY PURPOSE Section 3.1	Identify the purpose of the risk assessment in terms of the information that the assessment is intended to produce and the decisions the assessment is intended to support.
TASK 1-2 IDENTIFY SCOPE Section 3.1	Identify the scope of the risk assessment in terms of organizational applicability, time frame supported, and architectural/technology considerations.
TASK 1-3 IDENTIFY ASSUMPTIONS AND CONSTRAINTS Section 3.1	Identify the specific assumptions and constraints under which the risk assessment is conducted.
TASK 1-4 IDENTIFY INFORMATION SOURCES Section 3.1	Identify the sources of descriptive, threat, vulnerability, and impact information to be used in the risk assessment.
TASK 1-5 IDENTIFY RISK MODEL AND ANALYTIC APPROACH Section 3.1	Identify the risk model and analytic approach to be used in the risk assessment.
Step 2: Conduct Risk Assessment	
TASK 2-1 IDENTIFY THREAT SOURCES Section 3.2, Appendix D	Identify and characterize threat sources of concern, including capability, intent, and targeting characteristics for adversarial threats and range of effects for non-adversarial threats.
TASK 2-2 IDENTIFY THREAT EVENTS Section 3.2, Appendix E	Identify potential threat events, relevance of the events, and the threat sources that could initiate the events.
TASK 2-3 IDENTIFY VULNERABILITIES AND PREDISPOSING CONDITIONS Section 3.2, Appendix F	Identify vulnerabilities and predisposing conditions that affect the likelihood that threat events of concern result in adverse impacts.

TASK	TASK DESCRIPTION
TASK 2-4 DETERMINE LIKELIHOOD Section 3.2, Appendix G	Determine the likelihood that threat events of concern result in adverse impacts, considering: (i) the characteristics of the threat sources that could initiate the events; (ii) the vulnerabilities/predisposing conditions identified; and (iii) the organizational susceptibility reflecting the safeguards/countermeasures planned or implemented to impede such events.
TASK 2-5 DETERMINE IMPACT Section 3.2, Appendix H	Determine the adverse impacts from threat events of concern, considering: (i) the characteristics of the threat sources that could initiate the events; (ii) the vulnerabilities/predisposing conditions identified; and (iii) the organizational susceptibility reflecting the safeguards/countermeasures planned or implemented to impede such events.
TASK 2-6 DETERMINE RISK Section 3.2, Appendix I	Determine the risk to the organization from threat events of concern considering: (i) the impact that would result from the events; and (ii) the likelihood of the events occurring.
Step 3: Communicate and Share Risk Assessment Results	
TASK 3-1 COMMUNICATE RISK ASSESSMENT RESULTS Section 3.3, Appendix K	Communicate risk assessment results to organizational decision makers to support risk responses.
TASK 3-2 SHARE RISK-RELATED INFORMATION Section 3.3	Share risk-related information produced during the risk assessment with appropriate organizational personnel.
Step 4: Maintain Risk Assessment	
TASK 4-1 MONITOR RISK FACTORS Section 3.4	Conduct ongoing monitoring of the risk factors that contribute to changes in risk to organizational operations and assets, individuals, other organizations, or the Nation.
TASK 4-2 UPDATE RISK ASSESSMENT Section 3.4	Update existing risk assessment using the results from ongoing monitoring of risk factors.

NIST Special Publication 800-37
Revision 2

Risk Management Framework for Information Systems and Organizations

A System Life Cycle Approach for Security and Privacy

This publication contains comprehensive updates to the *Risk Management Framework*. The updates include an alignment with the constructs in the NIST Cybersecurity Framework; the integration of privacy risk management processes; an alignment with system life cycle security engineering processes; and the incorporation of supply chain risk management processes. Organizations can use the frameworks and processes in a complementary manner within the RMF to effectively manage security and privacy risks to organizational operations and assets, individuals, other organizations, and the Nation. Revision 2 includes a set of organization-wide RMF tasks that are designed to prepare information system owners to conduct system-level risk management activities. The intent is to increase the effectiveness, efficiency, and cost-effectiveness of the RMF by establishing a closer connection to the organization's missions and business functions and improving the communications among senior leaders, managers, and operational personnel.

JOINT TASK FORCE

This publication is available free of charge from:
https://doi.org/10.6028/NIST.SP.800-37r2

**National Institute of
Standards and Technology**
U.S. Department of Commerce

NIST Special Publication 800-37
Revision 2

Risk Management Framework for Information Systems and Organizations

A System Life Cycle Approach for Security and Privacy

JOINT TASK FORCE

This publication is available free of charge from:
https://doi.org/10.6028/NIST.SP.800-37r2

December 2018

U.S. Department of Commerce
Wilbur L. Ross, Jr., Secretary

National Institute of Standards and Technology
Walter Copan, NIST Director and Under Secretary of Commerce for Standards and Technology

Authority

This publication has been developed by NIST to further its statutory responsibilities under the Federal Information Security Modernization Act (FISMA), 44 U.S.C. § 3551 *et seq.*, Public Law (P.L.) 113-283. NIST is responsible for developing information security standards and guidelines, including minimum requirements for federal information systems, but such standards and guidelines shall not apply to national security systems without the express approval of the appropriate federal officials exercising policy authority over such systems. This guideline is consistent with requirements of the Office of Management and Budget (OMB) Circular A-130.

Nothing in this publication should be taken to contradict the standards and guidelines made mandatory and binding on federal agencies by the Secretary of Commerce under statutory authority. Nor should these guidelines be interpreted as altering or superseding the existing authorities of the Secretary of Commerce, OMB Director, or any other federal official. This publication may be used by nongovernmental organizations on a voluntary basis and is not subject to copyright in the United States. Attribution would, however, be appreciated by NIST.

National Institute of Standards and Technology Special Publication 800-37, Revision 2
Natl. Inst. Stand. Technol. Spec. Publ. 800-37, Rev. 2, **183 pages** (December 2018)

CODEN: NSPUE2

This publication is available free of charge from:
https://doi.org/10.6028/NIST.SP.800-37r2

Comments on this publication may be submitted to:

National Institute of Standards and Technology
Attn: Computer Security Division, Information Technology Laboratory
100 Bureau Drive (Mail Stop 8930) Gaithersburg, MD 20899-8930
Email: sec-cert@nist.gov

All comments are subject to release under the Freedom of Information Act (FOIA) [FOIA96].

PAGE i

Reports on Computer Systems Technology

The National Institute of Standards and Technology (NIST) Information Technology Laboratory (ITL) promotes the U.S. economy and public welfare by providing technical leadership for the Nation's measurement and standards infrastructure. ITL develops tests, test methods, reference data, proof of concept implementations, and technical analyses to advance the development and productive use of information technology (IT). ITL's responsibilities include the development of management, administrative, technical, and physical standards and guidelines for the cost-effective security of other than national security-related information in federal information systems. The Special Publication 800-series reports on ITL's research, guidelines, and outreach efforts in information systems security and privacy and its collaborative activities with industry, government, and academic organizations.

Abstract

This publication describes the Risk Management Framework (RMF) and provides guidelines for applying the RMF to information systems and organizations. The RMF provides a disciplined, structured, and flexible process for managing security and privacy risk that includes information security categorization; control selection, implementation, and assessment; system and common control authorizations; and continuous monitoring. The RMF includes activities to prepare organizations to execute the framework at appropriate risk management levels. The RMF also promotes near real-time risk management and ongoing information system and common control authorization through the implementation of continuous monitoring processes; provides senior leaders and executives with the necessary information to make efficient, cost-effective, risk management decisions about the systems supporting their missions and business functions; and incorporates security and privacy into the system development life cycle. Executing the RMF tasks links essential risk management processes at the system level to risk management processes at the organization level. In addition, it establishes responsibility and accountability for the controls implemented within an organization's information systems and inherited by those systems.

Keywords

assess; authorization to operate; authorization to use; authorizing official; categorize; common control; common control authorization; common control provider; continuous monitoring; control assessor; control baseline; cybersecurity framework profile; hybrid control; information owner or steward; information security; monitor; ongoing authorization; plan of action and milestones; privacy; privacy assessment report; privacy control; privacy plan; privacy risk; risk assessment; risk executive function; risk management; risk management framework; security; security assessment report; security control; security engineering; security plan; security risk; senior agency information security officer; senior agency official for privacy; supply chain risk management; system development life cycle; system owner; system privacy officer; system security officer; system-specific control.

Guide for Applying the Risk Management Framework to Federal Information Systems (800-37 rev 2)

Acknowledgements

This publication was developed by the *Joint Task Force* Interagency Working Group. The group includes representatives from the Civil, Defense, and Intelligence Communities. The National Institute of Standards and Technology wishes to acknowledge and thank the senior leaders from the Departments of Commerce and Defense, the Office of the Director of National Intelligence, the Committee on National Security Systems, and the members of the interagency working group whose dedicated efforts contributed significantly to the publication.

Department of Defense

Dana Deasy
Chief Information Officer

Essye B. Miller
Principal Deputy CIO and DoD Senior Information Security Officer

Thomas P. Michelli
Acting Deputy Chief Information Officer for Cybersecurity

Vicki Michetti
Director, Cybersecurity Policy, Strategy, International, and Defense Industrial Base Directorate

National Institute of Standards and Technology

Charles H. Romine
Director, Information Technology Laboratory

Donna Dodson
Cybersecurity Advisor, Information Technology Laboratory

Matt Scholl
Chief, Computer Security Division

Kevin Stine
Chief, Applied Cybersecurity Division

Ron Ross
FISMA Implementation Project Leader

Office of the Director of National Intelligence

John Sherman
Chief Information Officer

Vacant
Deputy Chief Information Officer

Susan Dorr
Director, Cybersecurity Division and Chief Information Security Officer

Wallace Coggins
Director, Security Coordination Center

Committee on National Security Systems

Thomas Michelli
Chair—Defense Community

Susan Dorr—Intelligence Community
Co-Chair

Vicki Michetti
Tri-Chair—Defense Community

Chris Johnson
Tri-Chair—Intelligence Community

Paul Cunningham
Tri-Chair—Civil Agencies

Joint Task Force Working Group

Ron Ross *NIST, JTF Leader*	Kevin Dulany *DoD*	Peter Duspiva *Intelligence Community*	Kelley Dempsey *NIST*
Taylor Roberts *OMB*	Ellen Nadeau *NIST*	Victoria Pillitteri *NIST*	Naomi Lefkovitz *NIST*
Jordan Burris *OMB*	Charles Cutshall *OMB*	Kevin Herms *OMB*	Carol Bales *OMB*
Jeff Marron *NIST*	Kaitlin Boeckl *NIST*	Kirsten Moncada *OMB*	Jon Boyens *NIST*
Dorian Pappas *CNSS*	Dominic Cussatt *Veterans Affairs*	Esten Porter *The MITRE Corporation*	Celia Paulsen *NIST*
Daniel Faigin *The Aerospace Corporation*	Christina Sames *The MITRE Corporation*	Julie Snyder *The MITRE Corporation*	Martin Stanley *Homeland Security*

Guide for Applying the Risk Management Framework to Federal Information Systems (800-37 rev 2)

NIST SP 800-37, REVISION 2

RISK MANAGEMENT FRAMEWORK FOR INFORMATION SYSTEMS AND ORGANIZATIONS
A System Life Cycle Approach for Security and Privacy

The authors also wish to recognize Matt Barrett, Kathleen Coupe, Jeff Eisensmith, Chris Enloe, Ned Goren, Matthew Halstead, Jody Jacobs, Ralph Jones, Martin Kihiko, Raquel Leone, and the scientists, engineers, and research staff from the Computer Security Division and the Applied Cybersecurity Division for their exceptional contributions in helping to improve the content of the publication. A special note of thanks to Jim Foti and the NIST web team for their outstanding administrative support.

In addition, the authors wish to acknowledge the United States Air Force and the "RMF Next" initiative, facilitated by Air Force CyberWorx, that provided the inspiration for some of the new ideas in this update to the RMF. The working group, led by Lauren Knausenberger, Bill Bryant, and Venice Goodwine, included government and industry representatives Jake Ames, Chris Bailey, James Barnett, Steve Bogue, Wes Chiu, Kurt Danis, Shane Deichman; Joe Erskine, Terence Goodman, Jason Howe, Brandon Howell, Todd Jacobs, Peter Klabe, William Kramer, Bryon Kroger, Kevin LaSalle, Dinh Le, Noam Liran, Sam Miles, Michael Morrison, Raymond Tom Nagley, Wendy Nather, Jasmine Neal, Ryan Perry, Eugene Peterson, Lawrence Rampaul, Jessica Rheinschmidt, Greg Roman, Susanna Scarveles, Justin Schoenthal, Christian Sorenson, Stacy Studstill, Charles Wade, Shawn Whitney, David Wilcox, and Thomas Woodring.

Finally, the authors also gratefully acknowledge the significant contributions from individuals and organizations in both the public and private sectors, nationally and internationally, whose thoughtful and constructive comments improved the overall quality, thoroughness, and usefulness of this publication.

HISTORICAL CONTRIBUTIONS TO NIST SPECIAL PUBLICATION 800-37

The authors acknowledge the many individuals who contributed to previous versions of Special Publication 800-37 since its inception in 2005. They include Marshall Abrams, William Barker, Beckie Koonge, Roger Caslow, John Gilligan, Peter Gouldmann, Richard Graubart, John Grimes, Gus Guissanie, Priscilla Guthrie, Jennifer Fabius, Cita Furlani, Richard Hale, Peggy Himes, William Hunteman, Arnold Johnson, Donald Jones, Stuart Katzke, Eustace King, Mark Morrison, Sherrill Nicely, Karen Quigg, George Rogers, Cheryl Roby, Gary Stoneburner, Marianne Swanson, Glenda Turner, and Peter Williams.

Executive Summary

As we push computers to "the edge," building a complex world of interconnected information systems and devices, security and privacy risks (including supply chain risks) continue to be a large part of the national conversation and topics of great importance. The significant increase in the complexity of the hardware, software, firmware, and systems within the public and private sectors (including the U.S. critical infrastructure) represents a significant increase in attack surface that can be exploited by adversaries. Moreover, adversaries are using the supply chain as an attack vector and effective means of penetrating our systems, compromising the integrity of system elements, and gaining access to critical assets.

The Defense Science Board Report, *Resilient Military Systems and the Advanced Cyber Threat* [DSB 2013], provides a sobering assessment of the vulnerabilities in the United States Government, the U.S. critical infrastructure, and the systems supporting the mission-essential operations and assets in the public and private sectors.

> *"...The Task Force notes that the cyber threat to U.S. critical infrastructure is outpacing efforts to reduce pervasive vulnerabilities, so that for the next decade at least the United States must lean significantly on deterrence to address the cyber threat posed by the most capable U.S. adversaries. It is clear that a more proactive and systematic approach to U.S. cyber deterrence is urgently needed..."*

There is an urgent need to further strengthen the underlying information systems, component products, and services that we depend on in every sector of the critical infrastructure—ensuring that the systems, products, and services are sufficiently trustworthy throughout the system development life cycle (SDLC) and can provide the necessary resilience to support the economic and national security interests of the United States. System modernization, the increased use of automation, and the consolidation, standardization, and optimization of federal systems and networks to strengthen the protection for high value assets [OMB M-19-03], are key objectives for the federal government.

Executive Order (E.O.) 13800, *Strengthening the Cybersecurity of Federal Networks and Critical Infrastructure* [EO 13800] recognizes the increasing interconnectedness of Federal information systems and requires heads of agencies to ensure appropriate risk management not only for the Federal agency's enterprise, but also for the Executive Branch as a whole. The E.O. states:

> *"...The executive branch operates its information technology (IT) on behalf of the American people. Its IT and data should be secured responsibly using all United States Government capabilities..."*

> *"...Cybersecurity risk management comprises the full range of activities undertaken to protect IT and data from unauthorized access and other cyber threats, to maintain awareness of cyber threats, to detect anomalies and incidents adversely affecting IT and data, and to mitigate the impact of, respond to, and recover from incidents..."*

OMB Memorandum M-17-25, *Reporting Guidance for Executive Order on Strengthening the Cybersecurity of Federal Networks and Critical Infrastructure* [OMB M-17-25] provides implementation guidance to Federal agencies for E.O. 13800. The memorandum states:

> *"... An effective enterprise risk management program promotes a common understanding for recognizing and describing potential risks that can impact an agency's mission and the delivery of services to the public. Such risks include, but are not limited to, strategic, market, cyber, legal,*

Guide for Applying the Risk Management Framework to Federal Information Systems (800-37 rev 2)

191

reputational, political, and a broad range of operational risks such as information security, human capital, business continuity, and related risks..."

"... Effective management of cybersecurity risk requires that agencies align information security management processes with strategic, operational, and budgetary planning processes..."

OMB Circular A-130, *Managing Information as a Strategic Resource* [OMB A-130], addresses responsibilities for protecting federal information resources and for managing personally identifiable information (PII). Circular A-130 requires agencies to implement the RMF that is described in this guideline and requires agencies to integrate privacy into the RMF process. In establishing requirements for information security programs and privacy programs, the OMB circular emphasizes the need for both programs to collaborate on shared objectives:

"While security and privacy are independent and separate disciplines, they are closely related, and it is essential for agencies to take a coordinated approach to identifying and managing security and privacy risks and complying with applicable requirements...."

This update to NIST Special Publication 800-37 (Revision 2) responds to the call by the Defense Science Board, the Executive Order, and the OMB policy memorandum to develop the next-generation Risk Management Framework (RMF) for information systems, organizations, and individuals.

There are seven major objectives for this update:

- To provide closer linkage and communication between the risk management processes and activities at the C-suite or governance level of the organization and the individuals, processes, and activities at the system and operational level of the organization;

- To institutionalize critical risk management preparatory activities at all risk management levels to facilitate a more effective, efficient, and cost-effective execution of the RMF;

- To demonstrate how the NIST Cybersecurity Framework [NIST CSF] can be aligned with the RMF and implemented using established NIST risk management processes;

- To integrate privacy risk management processes into the RMF to better support the privacy protection needs for which privacy programs are responsible;

- To promote the development of trustworthy secure software and systems by aligning life cycle-based systems engineering processes in NIST Special Publication 800-160, Volume 1 [SP 800-160 v1], with the relevant tasks in the RMF;

- To integrate security-related, supply chain risk management (SCRM) concepts into the RMF to address untrustworthy suppliers, insertion of counterfeits, tampering, unauthorized production, theft, insertion of malicious code, and poor manufacturing and development practices throughout the SDLC; and

- To allow for an organization-generated control selection approach to complement the traditional baseline control selection approach and support the use of the consolidated control catalog in NIST Special Publication 800-53, Revision 5.

The addition of the *Prepare* step is one of the key changes to the RMF—incorporated to achieve more effective, efficient, and cost-effective security and privacy risk management processes. The primary objectives for institutionalizing organization-level and system-level preparation are:

- To facilitate effective communication between senior leaders and executives at the organization and mission/business process levels and system owners at the operational level;

- To facilitate organization-wide identification of common controls and the development of organizationally-tailored control baselines, reducing the workload on individual system owners and the cost of system development and asset protection;

- To reduce the complexity of the information technology (IT) and operations technology (OT) infrastructure using Enterprise Architecture concepts and models to consolidate, optimize, and standardize organizational systems, applications, and services;

- To reduce the complexity of systems by eliminating unnecessary functions and security and privacy capabilities that do not address security and privacy risk; and

- To identify, prioritize, and focus resources on the organization's high value assets (HVA) that require increased levels of protection—taking measures commensurate with the risk to such assets.

By achieving the above objectives, organizations can **simplify** RMF execution, employ **innovative** approaches for managing risk, and increase the level of **automation** when carrying out specific tasks. Organizations implementing the RMF will be able to:

- Use the tasks and outputs of the Organization-Level and System-Level *Prepare* step to promote a consistent starting point within organizations to execute the RMF;

- Maximize the use of common controls at the organization level to promote standardized, consistent, and cost-effective security and privacy capability inheritance;

- Maximize the use of shared or cloud-based systems, services, and applications to reduce the number of authorizations needed across the organization;

- Employ organizationally-tailored control baselines to increase the speed of security and privacy plan development and the consistency of security and privacy plan content;

- Employ organization-defined controls based on security and privacy requirements generated from a systems security engineering process;

- Maximize the use of automated tools to manage security categorization; control selection, assessment, and monitoring; and the authorization process;

- Decrease the level of effort and resource expenditures for low-impact systems if those systems cannot adversely affect higher-impact systems through system connections;

- Maximize the reuse of RMF artifacts (e.g., security and privacy assessment results) for standardized hardware/software deployments, including configuration settings;

- Reduce the complexity of the IT/OT infrastructure by eliminating unnecessary systems, system components, and services — employing the least functionality principle; and

- Make the transition to ongoing authorization a priority and use continuous monitoring approaches to reduce the cost and increase the efficiency of security and privacy programs.

Recognizing that the preparation for RMF execution may vary from organization to organization, achieving the above objectives can reduce the overall IT/OT footprint and attack surface of organizations, promote IT modernization objectives, conserve resources, prioritize security activities to focus protection strategies on the most critical assets and systems, and promote privacy protections for individuals.

COMMON SECURITY AND PRIVACY RISK FOUNDATIONS

In developing standards and guidelines, NIST consults with federal agencies, state, local, and tribal governments, and private sector organizations; avoids unnecessary and costly duplication of effort; and ensures that its publications are complementary with the standards and guidelines used for the protection of national security systems. In addition to implementing a transparent public review process for its publications, NIST collaborates with the Office of Management and Budget, the Office of the Director of National Intelligence, the Department of Defense, and the Committee on National Security Systems, and has established a unified risk management framework for the federal government. This common foundation provides the Civil, Defense, and Intelligence Communities of the federal government and their contractors, cost-effective, flexible, and consistent methods and techniques to manage security and privacy risks to organizational operations and assets, individuals, other organizations, and the Nation. The unified framework also provides a strong basis for reciprocal acceptance of assessment results and authorization decisions and facilitates information sharing and collaboration. NIST continues to work with public and private sector entities to establish mappings and relationships between its security and privacy standards and guidelines and those developed by external organizations.

ACCEPTANCE OF SECURITY AND PRIVACY RISK

The Risk Management Framework addresses security and privacy risk from two perspectives—an information system perspective and a common controls perspective. For an information system, authorizing officials issue an *authorization to operate* or *authorization to use* for the system, accepting the security and privacy risks to the organization's operations and assets, individuals, other organizations, and the Nation. For common controls, authorizing officials issue a *common control authorization* for a specific set of controls that can be inherited by designated organizational systems, accepting the security and privacy risks to the organization's operations and assets, individuals, other organizations, and the Nation. Authorizing officials also consider the risk of inheriting common controls as part of their system authorizations. The different types of authorizations are described in Appendix F.

Guide for Applying the Risk Management Framework to Federal Information Systems (800-37 rev 2)

196

THE RMF IS TECHNOLOGY NEUTRAL

The RMF is purposefully designed to be technology neutral so that the methodology can be applied to any type of information system* without modification. While the specific controls selected, control implementation details, and control assessment methods and objects may vary with different types of IT resources, there is no need to adjust the RMF process to accommodate specific technologies.

All information systems process, store, or transmit some type of information. For example, information about the temperature in a remote facility collected and transmitted by a sensor to a monitoring station, location coordinates transmitted by radio to a controller on a weapons system, photographic images transmitted by a remote camera (land/satellite-based) to a server, or health IT devices transmitting patient information via a hospital network, require protection. This information can be protected by: categorizing the information to determine the impact of loss; assessing whether the processing of the information could impact individuals' privacy; and selecting and implementing controls that are applicable to the IT resources in use. Therefore, cloud-based systems, industrial/process control systems, weapons systems, cyber-physical systems, applications, IoT devices, or mobile devices/systems, do not require a separate risk management process but rather a tailored set of controls and specific implementation details determined by applying the existing RMF process.

The RMF is applied iteratively, as applicable, during the system development life cycle for any type of system development approach (including *Agile* and *DevOps* approaches). The security and privacy requirements and controls are implemented, verified, and validated as development progresses throughout the life cycle. This flexibility allows the RMF to support rapid technology cycles, innovation, and the use of current best practices in system and system component development.

* **Note:** The publication pertains to information systems, which are discrete sets of information resources organized for the collection, processing, maintenance, use, sharing, dissemination, or disposition of information, whether such information is in digital or non-digital form. Information resources include information and related resources, such as personnel, equipment, funds, and information technology. Therefore, information systems may or may not include hardware, firmware, and software.

USE OF AUTOMATION IN THE EXECUTION OF THE RMF

Organizations should maximize the use of *automation*, wherever possible, to increase the speed, effectiveness, and efficiency of executing the steps in the Risk Management Framework (RMF). Automation is particularly useful in the assessment and continuous monitoring of controls, the preparation of authorization packages for timely decision-making, and the implementation of ongoing authorization approaches—together facilitating a real-time or near real-time risk-based decision-making process for senior leaders. Organizations have significant flexibility in deciding when, where, and how to use automation or automated support tools for their security and privacy programs. In some situations, automated assessments and monitoring of controls may not be possible or feasible.

Guide for Applying the Risk Management Framework to Federal Information Systems (800-37 rev 2)
198

SCOPE AND APPLICABILITY

This publication is intended to help organizations manage security and privacy risk, and to satisfy the requirements in the Federal Information Security Modernization Act of 2014 (FISMA), the Privacy Act of 1974, OMB policies, and Federal Information Processing Standards, among other laws, regulations, and policies. The scope of this publication pertains to federal information systems, which are discrete sets of information resources organized for the collection, processing, maintenance, use, sharing, dissemination, or disposition of information, whether such information is in digital or non-digital form. Information resources include information and related resources, such as personnel, equipment, funds, and information technology.

While mandatory for federal government use, the RMF can be applied to any type of nonfederal organization (e.g., business, industry, academia). As such, State, local, and tribal governments, as well as private sector organizations are encouraged to use these guidelines on a voluntary basis, as appropriate. In addition, nonfederal organizations that have adopted and implemented the Cybersecurity Framework might find value in using the RMF as a risk management process for execution of the Framework—providing the essential tasks for control implementation, assessment, and monitoring, as well as system authorizations (for risk-based decision making).

Guide for Applying the Risk Management Framework to Federal Information Systems (800-37 rev 2)

MANAGING RISK
Using the Cybersecurity Framework

Executive Order (E.O.) 13800 requires federal agencies to modernize their IT infrastructure and systems and recognizes the increasing interconnectedness of federal information systems and networks. The E.O. also requires heads of agencies to manage risk at the agency level and across the Executive Branch using the *Framework for Improving Critical Infrastructure Cybersecurity* (i.e., Cybersecurity Framework). And finally, the E.O. reinforces the Federal Information Security Modernization Act (FISMA) of 2014 by holding heads of agencies responsible and accountable for managing the cybersecurity risk to their organizations.

The Cybersecurity Framework is adaptive to provide a flexible and risk-based implementation that can be used with a broad array of cybersecurity risk management processes. Therefore, consistent with OMB Memorandum M-17-25, the federal implementation of the Cybersecurity Framework fully supports the use of and is consistent with the risk management processes and approaches defined in [SP 800-39] and NIST Special Publication 800-37. This allows agencies to meet their concurrent obligations to comply with the requirements of FISMA and E.O. 13800.

Each task in the RMF includes references to specific sections in the Cybersecurity Framework. For example, Task P-2, *Risk Management Strategy*, aligns with the Cybersecurity Framework Core [Identify Function]; Task P-4, *Organizationally-Tailored Control Baselines and Cybersecurity Framework Profiles*, aligns with the Cybersecurity Framework Profile construct; and Task R-5, *Authorization Reporting*, and Task M-5, *Security and Privacy Reporting*, support OMB reporting and risk management requirements organization-wide by using the Cybersecurity Framework constructs of Functions, Categories, and Subcategories. The Subcategory mappings to the [SP 800-53] controls are available at: https://www.nist.gov/cyberframework/federal-resources.

NIST SP 800-37, REVISION 2

RISK MANAGEMENT FRAMEWORK FOR INFORMATION SYSTEMS AND ORGANIZATIONS
A System Life Cycle Approach for Security and Privacy

SECURITY AND PRIVACY IN THE RMF

Organizations are encouraged to collaborate on the plans, assessments, and plans of action and milestones (POAM) for security and privacy issues to maximize efficiency and reduce duplication of effort. The objective is to ensure that security and privacy requirements derived from laws, executive orders, directives, regulations, policies, standards, or missions and business functions are adequately addressed, and the appropriate controls are selected, implemented, assessed, and monitored on an ongoing basis. The authorization decision, a key step in the RMF, depends on the development of credible and actionable security and privacy evidence generated for the authorization package. Creating such evidence in a cost-effective and efficient manner is important.

The unified and collaborative approach to bring security and privacy evidence together in a single authorization package will support authorizing officials with critical information from security and privacy professionals to help inform the authorization decision. In the end, it is not about generating additional paperwork, artifacts, or documentation. Rather, it is about ensuring greater visibility into the implementation of security and privacy controls which will promote more informed, risk-based authorization decisions.

Guide for Applying the Risk Management Framework to Federal Information Systems (800-37 rev 2)
201

Table of Contents

Errata

This table contains changes that have been incorporated into Special Publication 800-37. Errata updates can include corrections, clarifications, or other minor changes in the publication that are either *editorial* or *substantive* in nature.

DATE	TYPE	CHANGE	PAGE

CHAPTER ONE

INTRODUCTION

THE NEED TO MANAGE SECURITY AND PRIVACY RISK

O rganizations depend on information systems[1] to carry out their missions and business functions. The success of the missions and business functions depends on protecting the confidentiality, integrity, availability of information processed, stored, and transmitted by those systems and the privacy of individuals. The threats to information systems include equipment failure, environmental disruptions, human or machine errors, and purposeful attacks that are often sophisticated, disciplined, well-organized, and well-funded.[2] When successful, attacks on information systems can result in serious or catastrophic damage to organizational operations[3] and assets, individuals, other organizations, and the Nation.[4] Therefore, it is imperative that organizations remain vigilant and that senior executives, leaders, and managers throughout the organization understand their responsibilities and are accountable for protecting organizational assets and for managing risk.[5]

In addition to the responsibility to protect organizational assets from the threats that exist in today's environment, organizations have a responsibility to consider and manage the risks to individuals when information systems process personally identifiable information (PII).[6] [7] The information security and privacy programs implemented by organizations have complementary objectives with respect to managing the confidentiality, integrity, and availability of PII. While many privacy risks arise from unauthorized activities that lead to the loss of confidentiality, integrity, or availability of PII, other privacy risks result from authorized activities involving the creation, collection, use, processing, storage, maintenance, dissemination, disclosure, or disposal of PII that enables an organization to meet its mission or business objectives. For example, organizations could fail to provide appropriate notice of PII processing depriving an individual of knowledge of such processing or an individual could be embarrassed or stigmatized

---

[1] An *information system* is a discrete set of information resources organized for the collection, processing, maintenance, use, sharing, dissemination, or disposition of information [44 USC 3502]. The term information system includes, for example, general-purpose computing systems; industrial/process control systems; cyber-physical systems; weapons systems; super computers; command, control, and communications systems; devices such as smart phones and tablets; environmental control systems; embedded devices/sensors; and paper-based systems.

[2] Defense Science Board Task Force Report, *Resilient Military Systems and the Advanced Cyber Threat* [DSB 2013].

[3] Organizational operations include mission, functions, image, and reputation.

[4] Adverse impacts include, for example, compromises to systems supporting critical infrastructure applications or that are paramount to government continuity of operations as defined by the Department of Homeland Security.

[5] Risk is a measure of the extent to which an entity is threatened by a potential circumstance or event. Risk is also a function of the adverse impacts that arise if the circumstance or event occurs, and the likelihood of occurrence. Types of risk include program risk; compliance/regulatory risk; financial risk; legal risk; mission/business risk; political risk; security and privacy risk (including supply chain risk); project risk; reputational risk; safety risk; strategic planning risk.

[6] [OMB A-130] defines PII as "information that can be used to distinguish or trace an individual's identity, either alone or when combined with other information that is linked or linkable to a specific individual."

[7] Organizations may also choose to consider risks to individuals that may arise from interactions with information systems, where the processing of PII may be less impactful than the effect the system has on individuals' behavior or activities. Such effects would constitute risks to individual autonomy and organizations may need to take steps to manage those risks in addition to information security and privacy risks.

by the authorized disclosure of PII. While managing privacy risk requires close coordination between information security and privacy programs due to the complementary nature of the programs' objectives around the confidentiality, integrity, and availability of PII, privacy risks also raise distinct concerns that require specialized expertise and approaches. Therefore, it is critical that organizations also establish and maintain robust privacy programs to ensure compliance with applicable privacy requirements and to manage the risk to individuals associated with the processing of PII.

Closely related to, and a part of security and privacy risks, supply chain risk[8] is also of growing concern to organizations. Because of the increased reliance on third-party or external providers and commercial-off-the-shelf products, systems, and services, attacks or disruptions in the supply chain which impact an organization's systems are increasing. Such attacks can be difficult to trace or manage and can result in serious, severe, or catastrophic consequences for an organization's systems. Supply chain risk management (SCRM) overlaps and works in harmony with security and privacy risk management. This publication integrates security and privacy risk management practices associated with SCRM into the RMF to help promote a comprehensive approach to managing security and privacy risk. While the publication is principally focused on managing information security and privacy risk, SCRM concepts that support security and privacy risk management are specifically called out in several areas to add emphasis and to clarify how they can be addressed using the RMF.

1.1 BACKGROUND

NIST in its partnership with the Department of Defense, the Office of the Director of National Intelligence, and the Committee on National Security Systems, developed a *Risk Management Framework* (RMF) to improve information security, strengthen risk management processes, and encourage reciprocity[9] among organizations. In July 2016, the Office of Management and Budget (OMB) revised Circular A-130 to include responsibilities for privacy programs under the RMF.

The RMF emphasizes risk management by promoting the development of security and privacy capabilities into information systems throughout the system development life cycle (SDLC);[10] by maintaining situational awareness of the security and privacy posture of those systems on an ongoing basis through continuous monitoring processes; and by providing information to senior leaders and executives to facilitate decisions regarding the acceptance of risk to organizational operations and assets, individuals, other organizations, and the Nation arising from the use and operation of their systems. The RMF:

- Provides a repeatable process designed to promote the protection of information and information systems commensurate with risk;

- Emphasizes organization-wide preparation necessary to manage security and privacy risks;

[8] SCRM requirements are promulgated in [OMB A-130], [DODI 5200.44], and for national security systems in [CNSSD 505]. SCRM requirements have also been addressed by the Federal SCRM Policy Coordinating Committee.
[9] Reciprocity is an agreement between organizations to accept one another's security assessment results in order to reuse system resources or to accept each other's assessed security posture in order to share information.
[10] [SP 800-64] and [SP 800-160 v1] provide guidance on security considerations in the SDLC.

- Facilitates the categorization of information and systems, the selection, implementation, assessment, and monitoring of controls, and the authorization of information systems and common controls;[11]

- Promotes the use of automation for near real-time risk management and ongoing system and control authorization through the implementation of continuous monitoring processes;

- Encourages the use of correct and timely metrics to provide senior leaders and managers with the necessary information to make cost-effective, risk-based decisions for information systems supporting their missions and business functions;

- Facilitates the integration of security and privacy requirements[12] and controls into enterprise architecture,[13] SDLC, acquisition processes, and systems engineering processes;

- Connects risk management processes at the organization and mission/business process levels to risk management processes at the information system level through a senior accountable official for risk management and risk executive (function);[14] and

- Establishes responsibility and accountability for controls implemented within information systems and inherited by those systems.

The RMF provides a dynamic and flexible approach to effectively manage security and privacy risks in diverse environments with complex and sophisticated threats, evolving missions and business functions, and changing system and organizational vulnerabilities. The framework is policy and technology neutral, which facilitates ongoing upgrades to IT resources[15] and to IT modernization efforts—to support and help ensure essential missions and services are provided during such transition periods.

1.2 PURPOSE AND APPLICABILITY

This publication describes the RMF and provides guidelines for managing security and privacy risks and applying the RMF to information systems and organizations. The guidelines have been developed:

- To ensure that managing system-related security and privacy risk is consistent with the mission and business objectives of the organization and risk management strategy established by the senior leadership through the risk executive (function);

- To achieve privacy protections for individuals and security protections for information and information systems through the implementation of appropriate risk response strategies;

- To support consistent, informed, and ongoing authorization decisions,[16] reciprocity, and the transparency and traceability of security and privacy information;

---

[11] Chapter 3 describes the seven steps and associated tasks in the RMF.

[12] Section 2.6 describes the relationship between requirements and controls with respect to RMF execution.

[13] [OMB FEA] provides guidance on the Federal Enterprise Architecture.

[14] [OMB M-17-25] provides guidance on risk management roles and responsibilities.

[15] IT resources refer to the information technology component of *information resources* defined in [OMB A-130].

[16] [SP 800-137] provides guidance on information security continuous monitoring supporting ongoing authorization. Future publications will address privacy continuous monitoring.

- To facilitate the integration of security and privacy requirements and controls into the enterprise architecture, SDLC processes, acquisition processes, and systems engineering processes;[17] and

- To facilitate the implementation of the *Framework for Improving Critical Infrastructure Cybersecurity* [NIST CSF] within federal agencies.[18]

This publication is intended to help organizations[19] manage security and privacy risk and to satisfy the requirements in the Federal Information Security Modernization Act of 2014 [FISMA], the Privacy Act of 1974 [PRIVACT], OMB policies, and designated Federal Information Processing Standards, among other laws, regulations, and policies.

The scope of this publication pertains to federal information systems, which are discrete sets of information resources organized for the collection, processing, maintenance, use, sharing, dissemination, or disposition of information, whether such information is in digital or non-digital form. Information resources include information and related resources, such as personnel, equipment, funds, and information technology. The guidelines have been developed from a technical perspective to complement guidelines for national security systems and may be used for such systems with the approval of appropriate federal officials with policy authority over such systems. State, local, and tribal governments, as well as private sector organizations are encouraged to use these guidelines, as appropriate.

1.3 TARGET AUDIENCE

This publication serves individuals associated with the design, development, implementation, assessment, operation, maintenance, and disposition of information systems including:

- Individuals with mission or business ownership responsibilities or fiduciary responsibilities (e.g., and heads of federal agencies);

- Individuals with information system, information security, or privacy management, oversight, or governance responsibilities (e.g., senior leaders, risk executives, authorizing officials, chief information officers, senior agency information security officers, and senior agency officials for privacy);

- Individuals responsible for conducting security or privacy assessments and for monitoring information systems, for example, control assessors, auditors, and system owners;

- Individuals with security or privacy implementation and operational responsibilities, for example, system owners, common control providers, information owners/stewards, mission or business owners, security or privacy architects, and systems security or privacy engineers;

- Individuals with information system development and acquisition responsibilities (e.g., program managers, procurement officials, component product and system developers, systems integrators, and enterprise architects); and

---

[17] [SP 800-160 v1] provides guidance on systems security engineering and building trustworthy, secure systems.

[18] [EO 13800] directs federal agencies to use the [NIST CSF] to manage cybersecurity risk.

[19] The term organization is used in this publication to describe an entity of any size, complexity, or positioning within an organizational structure (e.g., a federal agency or, as appropriate, any of its operational elements).

- Individuals with logistical or disposition-related responsibilities (e.g., program managers, procurement officials, system integrators, and property managers).

For a comprehensive list and description of roles and responsibilities associated with the RMF, see Appendix D.

1.4 ORGANIZATION OF THIS PUBLICATION

The remainder of this special publication is organized as follows:

- Chapter Two describes the concepts associated with managing information system-related security and privacy risk. This includes an organization-wide view of risk management; the RMF steps and task structure; the relationship between information security and privacy programs and how these programs are addressed in the RMF; information resources as system and system elements; authorization boundaries; security and privacy posture; and security and privacy considerations related to supply chain risk management.

- Chapter Three describes the tasks required to implement the steps in the RMF including: organization-level and information system-level preparation; categorization of information and information systems; control selection, tailoring, and implementation; assessment of control effectiveness; information system and common control authorization; the ongoing monitoring of controls; and maintaining awareness of the security and privacy posture of information systems and the organization.

- Supporting Appendices provide additional information and guidance for the application of the RMF including:

  - References;

  - Glossary of Terms;

  - Acronyms;

  - Roles and Responsibilities;

  - Summary of RMF Tasks;

  - System and Common Control Authorizations;

  - Authorization Boundary Considerations; and

  - System Life Cycle Considerations.

CHAPTER TWO

THE FUNDAMENTALS

HOW TO MANAGE SECURITY AND PRIVACY RISK

This chapter describes the basic concepts associated with managing information system-related security and privacy risk in organizations. These concepts include the RMF steps and task structure; information security and privacy programs in the RMF; information system, system elements, and how authorization boundaries are established; security and privacy posture; and security and privacy risk management practices associated with the supply chain.

2.1 ORGANIZATION-WIDE RISK MANAGEMENT

Managing information system-related security and privacy risk is a complex undertaking that requires the involvement of the entire organization—from senior leaders providing the strategic vision and top-level goals and objectives for the organization, to mid-level leaders planning, executing, and managing projects, to individuals developing, implementing, operating, and maintaining the systems supporting the organization's missions and business functions. Risk management is a holistic activity that affects every aspect of the organization including the mission and business planning activities, the enterprise architecture, the SDLC processes, and the systems engineering activities that are integral to those system life cycle processes. Figure 1 illustrates a multi-level approach to risk management described in [SP 800-39] that addresses security and privacy risk at the *organization* level, the *mission/business process* level, and the *information system* level. Communication and reporting are bi-directional information flows across the three levels to ensure that risk is addressed throughout the organization.

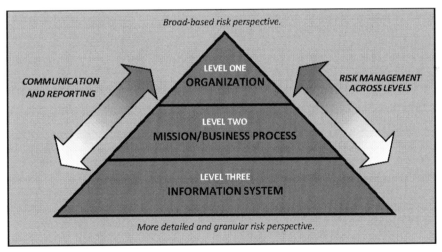

FIGURE 1: ORGANIZATION-WIDE RISK MANAGEMENT APPROACH

The activities conducted at Levels 1 and 2 are critical to preparing the organization to execute the RMF. Such preparation involves a wide range of activities that go beyond simply managing the security and privacy risk associated with operating or using specific systems and includes activities that are essential to managing security and privacy risk appropriately throughout the organization. Decisions about how to manage such risk at the system level cannot be made in isolation. Such decisions are closely linked to the:

- Mission or business objectives of organizations;
- Modernization initiatives for systems, components, and services;
- Enterprise architecture and the need to manage and reduce the complexity[20] of systems through consolidation, optimization, and standardization;[21] and
- Allocation of resources to ensure the organization can conduct its missions and business operations effectively, efficiently, and in a cost-effective manner.

Preparing the organization to execute the RMF can include:

- Assigning roles and responsibilities for organizational risk management processes;
- Establishing a risk management strategy and organizational risk tolerance;
- Identifying the missions, business functions, and mission/business processes the information system is intended to support;
- Identifying key stakeholders (internal and external to the organization) that have an interest in the information system;
- Identifying and prioritizing assets (including information assets);
- Understanding threats to information systems and organizations;
- Understanding the potential adverse effects on individuals;
- Conducting organization- and system-level risk assessments;
- Identifying and prioritizing security and privacy requirements;[22]
- Determining authorization boundaries for information systems and common controls;[23]
- Defining information systems in terms of the enterprise architecture;
- Developing the security and privacy architectures that include controls suitable for inheritance by information systems;

---

[20] Managing complexity of systems through consolidation, optimization, and standardization reduces the attack surface and technology footprint exploitable by adversaries.

[21] *Enterprise architecture* defines the mission, information, and the technologies necessary to perform the mission, and transitional processes for implementing new technologies in response to changing mission needs. It also includes a baseline architecture, a target architecture, and a sequencing plan. [OMB FEA] provides guidance for implementing enterprise architectures.

[22] Security and privacy requirements can be obtained from many sources (e.g., laws, executive orders, directives, regulations, policies, standards, and mission/business/operational requirements).

[23] Authorization boundaries determine the scope of authorizations for information systems and common controls (i.e., the system elements that define the system or the set of common controls available for inheritance).

- Identifying, aligning, and deconflicting security and privacy requirements; and

- Allocating security and privacy requirements to information systems, system elements, and organizations.

In contrast to the Level 1 and 2 activities that prepare the organization for the execution of the RMF, Level 3 addresses risk from an *information system* perspective and is guided and informed by the risk decisions at the organization and mission/business process levels. The risk decisions at Levels 1 and 2 can impact the selection and implementation of controls at the system level. Controls are designated by the organization as system-specific, hybrid, or common (inherited) controls in accordance with the enterprise architecture, security or privacy architecture, and any tailored control baselines or overlays that have been developed by the organization.[24]

Organizations establish *traceability* of controls to the security and privacy requirements that the controls are intended to satisfy. Establishing such traceability ensures that all requirements are addressed during system design, development, implementation, operations, maintenance, and disposition.[25] Each level of the risk management hierarchy is a beneficiary of a successful RMF execution—reinforcing the iterative nature of the risk management process where security and privacy risks are framed, assessed, responded to, and monitored at various organizational levels.

Without adequate risk management preparation at the organizational level, security and privacy activities can become too costly, demand too many skilled security and privacy professionals, and produce ineffective solutions. For example, organizations that fail to implement an effective enterprise architecture will have difficulty in consolidating, optimizing, and standardizing their information technology infrastructures. Additionally, the effect of architectural and design decisions can adversely affect the ability of organizations to implement effective security and privacy solutions. A lack of adequate preparation by organizations could result in unnecessary redundancy as well as inefficient, costly and vulnerable systems, services, and applications.

2.2 RISK MANAGEMENT FRAMEWORK STEPS AND STRUCTURE

There are seven steps in the RMF; a preparatory step to ensure that organizations are ready to execute the process and six main steps. All seven steps are essential for the successful execution of the RMF. The steps are:

- Prepare to execute the RMF from an organization- and a system-level perspective by establishing a context and priorities for managing security and privacy risk.

- Categorize the system and the information processed, stored, and transmitted by the system based on an analysis of the impact of loss.[26]

---

[24] Controls can be allocated at all three levels in the risk management hierarchy. For example, common controls may be allocated at the organization, mission/business process, or information system level.

[25] [SP 800-160 v1] provides guidance on requirements engineering and traceability.

[26] Impact of loss is one of four risk factors considered during risk assessment activities—the other three factors being threats, vulnerabilities, and likelihood of occurrence [SP 800-30]. Organizations leverage risk assessment results when categorizing information and systems. For national security systems, it may be important to consider specific issues affecting risk factors as part of categorization, such as, whether the system processes, stores, or transmits classified or intelligence information; whether the system will be accessed directly or indirectly by non-U.S. personnel; and whether the information processed, stored, or transmitted by the system will cross security domains. [CNSSI 1253] provides additional information on categorizing national security systems.

- <u>Select</u> an initial set of controls for the system and tailor the controls as needed to reduce risk to an acceptable level based on an assessment of risk.

- <u>Implement</u> the controls and describe how the controls are employed within the system and its environment of operation.

- <u>Assess</u> the controls to determine if the controls are implemented correctly, operating as intended, and producing the desired outcomes with respect to satisfying the security and privacy requirements.

- <u>Authorize</u> the system or common controls based on a determination that the risk to organizational operations and assets, individuals, other organizations, and the Nation is acceptable.

- <u>Monitor</u> the system and the associated controls on an ongoing basis to include assessing control effectiveness, documenting changes to the system and environment of operation, conducting risk assessments and impact analyses, and reporting the security and privacy posture of the system.

Figure 2 illustrates the steps in the RMF. The RMF operates at all levels in the risk management hierarchy illustrated in <u>Figure 1</u>. <u>Chapter Three</u> provides a detailed description of each of the tasks necessary to carry out the steps in the RMF.

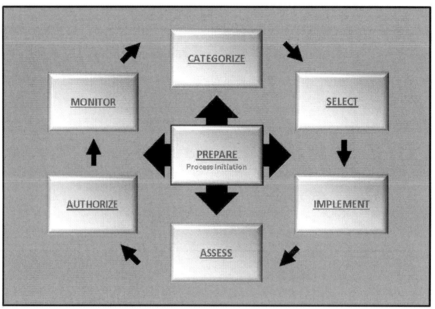

FIGURE 2: RISK MANAGEMENT FRAMEWORK

While the RMF steps are listed in sequential order above and in Chapter Three, the steps following the *Prepare* step can be carried out in a nonsequential order. After completing the tasks in the *Prepare* step, organizations executing the RMF for the first time for a system or set of common controls typically carry out the remaining steps in sequential order. However, there could be many points in the risk management process where there is a need to diverge from the sequential order due to the type of system, risk decisions made by senior leadership, or to allow for iterative cycles between tasks or revisiting of tasks (e.g., during agile development). Once the organization is in the *Monitor* step, events may dictate a nonsequential execution of steps. For example, changes in risk or in system functionality may necessitate revisiting one or more of the steps in the RMF to address the change.

FLEXIBILITY IN RMF IMPLEMENTATION

Organizations are expected to execute all steps and tasks in the RMF (apart from tasks labeled as optional). However, organizations have significant flexibility in how each of the RMF steps and tasks are carried out, as long as organizations are meeting all applicable requirements and effectively managing security and privacy risk. The intent is to allow organizations to implement the RMF in the most efficient, effective, and cost-effective manner to support mission and business needs in a way that promotes effective security and privacy. Flexible implementation may include executing tasks in a different (potentially nonsequential) order, emphasizing certain tasks over other tasks, or combining certain tasks where appropriate. It can also include the use of the Cybersecurity Framework to enhance RMF task execution.

Flexibility of implementation can also be applied to control *selection*, control *tailoring* to meet organizational security and privacy needs, or conducting control assessments throughout the SDLC. For example, the selection, tailoring, implementation, and assessments of controls can be done incrementally as a system is being developed. The implementation of control tailoring helps to ensure that security and privacy solutions are customized for the specific missions, business functions, risks, and operating environments of the organization. In the end, the flexibility inherent in RMF execution promotes effective security and privacy that helps to protect the systems that organizations depend on for mission and business success and the individuals whose information is processed by those systems.

Note: Since the RMF is an SDLC process that emphasizes ongoing authorization, organizations have the flexibility to determine which RMF step to enter (or reenter) based on an assessment of risk and the tasks described in the *Prepare—System Level* step. Determination of the appropriate RMF step requires an assessment of the current state of the system, a review of the activities that have already been completed for the system, identification of a proposed step and task entry into the RMF, a gap analysis to ensure that the risk is acceptable, documenting decisions, notifying stakeholders, and approval from the Authorizing Official (or other relevant decision maker).

Although the risk management approach in Figure 1 is conveyed as hierarchical, project and organization dynamics are typically more complex. The risk management approach selected by an organization may vary on a continuum from top-down command to decentralized consensus among peers. However, in all cases, organizations use a consistent approach that is applied to risk management processes organization-wide from the *organization* level to the *information system* level. Organizational officials identify and secure the needed resources to complete the risk management tasks described in this publication and ensure that those resources are made available to the appropriate personnel. Resource allocation includes funding to conduct risk management tasks and assigning qualified personnel that are needed to accomplish the tasks.

Each step in the RMF has a *purpose* statement, a defined set of *outcomes*, and a set of *tasks* that are carried out to achieve those outcomes. The outcomes can be achieved by different risk management levels—that is, some of the outcomes are universal to the entire organization, while others are system-focused or mission/business unit-focused. Figure 3 provides an example of the purpose statement and outcomes for the RMF *Prepare* step—Organization-Level.

3.1 PREPARE

Purpose

The purpose of the **Prepare** step is to carry out essential activities at the organization, mission and business process, and information system levels of the organization to help prepare the organization to manage its security and privacy risks using the *Risk Management Framework*.

PREPARE TASKS—ORGANIZATION LEVEL

Table 1 provides a summary of tasks and expected outcomes for the RMF *Prepare* step at the *organization* level. Applicable Cybersecurity Framework constructs are also provided.

TABLE 1: PREPARE TASKS AND OUTCOMES—ORGANIZATION LEVEL

Tasks	Outcomes
TASK P-1 RISK MANAGEMENT ROLES	• Individuals are identified and assigned key roles for executing the Risk Management Framework. [*Cybersecurity Framework*: ID.AM-6; ID.GV-2]
TASK P-2 RISK MANAGEMENT STRATEGY	• A risk management strategy for the organization that includes a determination and expression of organizational risk tolerance is established. [*Cybersecurity Framework*: ID.RM; ID.SC]
TASK P-3 RISK ASSESSMENT—ORGANIZATION	• An organization-wide risk assessment is completed or an existing risk assessment is updated. [*Cybersecurity Framework*: ID.RA; ID.SC-2]
TASK P-4 ORGANIZATIONALLY-TAILORED CONTROL BASELINES AND CYBERSECURITY FRAMEWORK PROFILES (OPTIONAL)	• Organizationally-tailored control baselines and/or Cybersecurity Framework Profiles are established and made available. [*Cybersecurity Framework*: **Profile**]
TASK P-5 COMMON CONTROL IDENTIFICATION	• Common controls that are available for inheritance by organizational systems are identified, documented, and published.
TASK P-6 IMPACT-LEVEL PRIORITIZATION (OPTIONAL)	• A prioritization of organizational systems with the same impact level is conducted. [*Cybersecurity Framework*: ID.AM-5]
TASK P-7 CONTINUOUS MONITORING STRATEGY—ORGANIZATION	• An organization-wide strategy for monitoring control effectiveness is developed and implemented. [*Cybersecurity Framework*: DE.CM; ID.SC-4]

Quick link to summary table for RMF tasks, responsibilities, and supporting roles.

FIGURE 3: RISK MANAGEMENT FRAMEWORK TASK STRUCTURE

Each task contains a set of potential inputs needed to execute the task and a set of expected outputs generated from task execution.[27] In addition, each task describes the risk management roles and responsibilities associated with the task and the phase of the SDLC where task execution occurs.[28] A discussion section provides information related to the task to facilitate understanding and to promote effective task execution. Finally, completing the RMF task description, there is a list of references to provide organizations with supplemental information for each task. Where applicable, the references also identify systems security engineering tasks that correlate with the RMF task.[29] Figure 4 illustrates the structure of a typical RMF task.

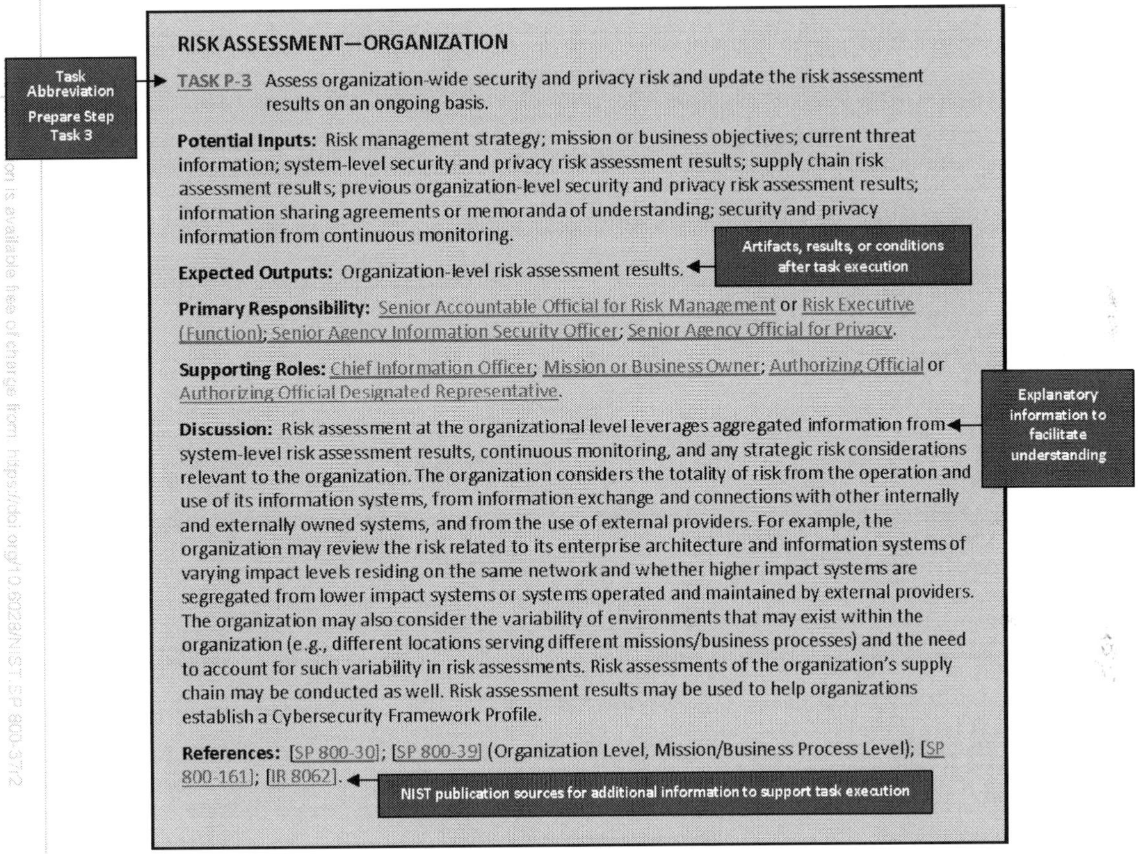

RISK ASSESSMENT—ORGANIZATION

Task Abbreviation
Prepare Step
Task 3

TASK P-3 Assess organization-wide security and privacy risk and update the risk assessment results on an ongoing basis.

Potential Inputs: Risk management strategy; mission or business objectives; current threat information; system-level security and privacy risk assessment results; supply chain risk assessment results; previous organization-level security and privacy risk assessment results; information sharing agreements or memoranda of understanding; security and privacy information from continuous monitoring.

Artifacts, results, or conditions after task execution

Expected Outputs: Organization-level risk assessment results.

Primary Responsibility: Senior Accountable Official for Risk Management or Risk Executive (Function); Senior Agency Information Security Officer; Senior Agency Official for Privacy.

Supporting Roles: Chief Information Officer; Mission or Business Owner; Authorizing Official or Authorizing Official Designated Representative.

Explanatory information to facilitate understanding

Discussion: Risk assessment at the organizational level leverages aggregated information from system-level risk assessment results, continuous monitoring, and any strategic risk considerations relevant to the organization. The organization considers the totality of risk from the operation and use of its information systems, from information exchange and connections with other internally and externally owned systems, and from the use of external providers. For example, the organization may review the risk related to its enterprise architecture and information systems of varying impact levels residing on the same network and whether higher impact systems are segregated from lower impact systems or systems operated and maintained by external providers. The organization may also consider the variability of environments that may exist within the organization (e.g., different locations serving different missions/business processes) and the need to account for such variability in risk assessments. Risk assessments of the organization's supply chain may be conducted as well. Risk assessment results may be used to help organizations establish a Cybersecurity Framework Profile.

References: [SP 800-30]; [SP 800-39] (Organization Level, Mission/Business Process Level); [SP 800-161]; [IR 8062].

NIST publication sources for additional information to support task execution

FIGURE 4: RISK MANAGEMENT FRAMEWORK TASK STRUCTURE

---

[27] The *potential inputs* for a task may not always be derived from the *expected outputs* from the previous task. This can occur because the RMF steps are not always executed in sequential order, breaking the sequential dependencies.

[28] Appendix D provides a description of each of the roles and responsibilities identified in the tasks.

[29] [SP 800-160 v1] describes life cycle-based systems security engineering processes.

2.3 INFORMATION SECURITY AND PRIVACY IN THE RMF

OMB CIRCULAR A-130: INTEGRATION OF INFORMATION SECURITY AND PRIVACY

In 2016, OMB revised Circular A-130, the circular establishing general policy for the planning, budgeting, governance, acquisition, and management of federal information, personnel, equipment, funds, information technology resources, and supporting infrastructure and services. The circular addresses responsibilities for protecting federal information resources and managing personally identifiable information (PII). In establishing requirements for information security programs and privacy programs, the circular emphasizes the need for both programs to collaborate on shared objectives:

While security and privacy are independent and separate disciplines, they are closely related, and it is essential for agencies to take a coordinated approach to identifying and managing security and privacy risks and complying with applicable requirements.

[OMB A-130] requires organizations to implement the RMF that is described in this guideline. With the 2016 revision to the circular, OMB also requires organizations to integrate privacy into the RMF process:

The RMF provides a disciplined and structured process that integrates information security, privacy, and risk management activities into the SDLC. This Circular requires organizations to use the RMF to manage privacy risks beyond those that are typically included under the "confidentiality" objective of the term "information security." While many privacy risks relate to the unauthorized access or disclosure of PII, privacy risks may also result from other activities, including the creation, collection, use, and retention of PII; the inadequate quality or integrity of PII; and the lack of appropriate notice, transparency, or participation.

This section of the guideline describes the *relationship* between information security programs and privacy programs under the RMF. However, subject to OMB policy, organizations retain the flexibility to undertake the integration of privacy into the RMF in the most effective manner, considering the organization's mission and circumstances.

Executing the RMF requires close collaboration between information security programs and privacy programs. While information security programs and privacy programs have different objectives, those objectives are overlapping and complementary. Information security programs are responsible for protecting information and information systems from unauthorized access, use, disclosure, disruption, modification, or destruction (i.e., unauthorized system activity or behavior) in order to provide confidentiality, integrity, and availability. Privacy programs are responsible for ensuring compliance with applicable privacy requirements and for managing the risks to individuals associated with the creation, collection, use, processing, dissemination, storage, maintenance, disclosure, or disposal (collectively referred to as "processing") of PII.[30] When preparing to execute the steps of the RMF, organizations consider how to best promote and institutionalize collaboration between the two programs to ensure that the objectives of both disciplines are met at every step of the process.

---

[30] Privacy programs may also choose to consider the risks to individuals that may arise from their interactions with information systems, where the processing of PII may be less impactful than the effect the system has on individuals' behavior or activities. Such effects would constitute risks to individual autonomy and organizations may need to take steps to manage those risks in addition to information security and privacy risks.

When an information system processes PII, the organization's information security program and privacy program have a shared responsibility for managing the risks to individuals that may arise from unauthorized system activity or behavior. This requires the two programs to collaborate when selecting, implementing, assessing, and monitoring security controls.[31] However, while information security programs and privacy programs have complementary objectives with respect to managing the confidentiality, integrity, and availability of PII, protecting individuals' privacy cannot be achieved solely by securing PII.

Not all privacy risks arise from unauthorized system activity or behavior, such as unauthorized access or disclosure of PII. Some privacy risks may result from authorized activity that is beyond the scope of information security. For example, privacy programs are responsible for managing the risks to individuals that may result from the creation, collection, use, and retention of PII; the inadequate quality or integrity of PII; and the lack of appropriate notice, transparency, or participation. Therefore, to help ensure compliance with applicable privacy requirements and to manage privacy risks from authorized and unauthorized processing of PII, organizations' privacy programs also select, implement, assess, and monitor privacy controls.[32]

[OMB A-130] defines a *privacy control* as an administrative, technical, or physical safeguard employed within an agency to ensure compliance with applicable privacy requirements and to manage privacy risks. A privacy control is different from a *security control*, which the Circular defines as a safeguard or countermeasure prescribed for an information system or an organization to protect the confidentiality, integrity, and availability of the system and its information. Due to the shared responsibility that organizations' information security programs and privacy programs have to manage the risks to individuals arising from unauthorized system activity or behavior, controls that achieve both security and privacy objectives are both privacy and security controls. This guideline refers to such controls that achieve both sets of objectives simply as "controls." When this guideline uses the descriptors "privacy" and "security" with the term *control*, it is referring to those controls in circumstances where the controls are selected, implemented, and assessed for particular objectives.

The risk management processes described in this publication are equally applicable to security and privacy programs. However, the risks that security and privacy programs are required to manage are overlapping in some areas, but not in others. Consequently, it is important that organizations understand the interplay between privacy and security to promote effective collaboration between privacy and security officials at every level of the organization.

---

[31] For example, in Task C-2 of the *Categorize* step, privacy and security programs work together to consider potential adverse impacts to organizational operations, organizational assets, individuals, other organizations, and the Nation resulting from the loss of confidentiality, integrity, or availability of PII in order to determine the impact level for the information system. The resulting impact level drives the selection of a security control baseline in Task S-1 of the *Select* step.

[32] Different controls may need to be selected to mitigate the privacy risks associated with authorized processing of PII. For example, there may be a risk that individuals would be embarrassed or stigmatized if certain information is disclosed about them. While encryption could prevent unauthorized disclosure of PII, it would not address any privacy risks related to disclosures to parties that are authorized to decrypt and access the PII. To mitigate this privacy risk, organizations would need to assess the risk of allowing authorized parties to decrypt the information and potentially select controls that would mitigate that risk. In such an example, an organization might select controls to enable individuals to understand the organization's disclosure practices and exercise choices about this access or use differential privacy or privacy-enhancing cryptographic techniques to disassociate the information from an individual.

2.4 SYSTEM AND SYSTEM ELEMENTS

This publication uses the statutory definition of information system for RMF execution. It is important, however, to describe information systems in the context of the SDLC process and how security and privacy capabilities are implemented within the components of those systems. Therefore, organizations executing the RMF take a broad view of the life cycle of information system development to provide a contextual relationship and linkage to architectural and engineering concepts that allow security and privacy risks (including supply chain risks) to be addressed throughout the life cycle and at the appropriate level of detail to help ensure that such capabilities are achieved. [ISO 15288] provides an engineering view of an information system and the entities with which the system interacts in its environment of operation.[33]

Similar to how federal law defines information system as a discrete set of information resources organized for the collection, processing, maintenance, use, sharing, dissemination, or disposition of information. [ISO 15288] defines a *system* as a set of interacting elements that are organized to achieve one or more stated purposes. Just as the information resources that comprise an information system include information and other resources (e.g., personnel, equipment, funds, and information technology), system elements include technology or machine elements, human elements, and physical or environmental elements. Each of the *system elements*[34] within the system fulfills specified requirements and may be implemented via hardware, software, or firmware;[35] physical structures or devices; or people, processes, policies, and procedures. Individual system elements or a combination of system elements may satisfy stated system requirements. Interconnections between system elements allow those elements to interact as necessary to produce a capability as specified by the system requirements. Finally, every system operates within an environment that influences the system and its operation.

The authorization boundary defines the system[36] for RMF execution to facilitate risk management and accountability. The system may be supported by one or more *enabling systems* that provide support during the system life cycle. Enabling systems are not contained within the authorization boundary of the system and do not necessarily exist in the system's environment of operation. An enabling system may provide common (i.e., inherited) controls for the system or may include any type of service or functionality used by the system such as identification and authentication services, network services, or monitoring functionality. Finally, there are *other systems* the system interacts with in the operational environment. The other systems are also outside of the authorization boundary and may be the beneficiaries of services provided by the system or may simply have some general interaction.[37]

---

[33] [SP 800-160 v1] addresses system security engineering as part of the SDLC.

[34] The terms *system element* and *information resource* are used interchangeably in this publication. Information resources as defined in 44 U.S.C. Sec. 3502 include information and related resources, such as personnel, equipment, funds, and information technology. By law, a system is composed of a discrete set of information resources.

[35] The term *system component* refers to a *system element* that is implemented via hardware, software, or firmware.

[36] Historically, NIST has used the terms *authorization boundary* and *system boundary* interchangeably. In the interest of clarity, accuracy, and use of standardized terminology, the term authorization boundary is now used exclusively to refer to the set of system elements comprising the system to be authorized for operation or authorized for use by an authorizing official (i.e., the scope of the authorization). Authorization boundary can also refer to the set of common controls to be authorized for inheritance purposes.

[37] Risk management and accountability for enabling systems and other systems are addressed within their respective authorization boundaries.

NIST SP 800-37, REVISION 2

RISK MANAGEMENT FRAMEWORK FOR INFORMATION SYSTEMS AND ORGANIZATIONS
A System Life Cycle Approach for Security and Privacy

Figure 5 illustrates the conceptual view of the system and the relationships among the system, system elements, enabling systems, other systems, and the environment of operation.[38]

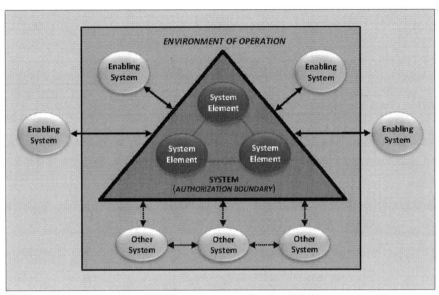

FIGURE 5: CONCEPTUAL VIEW OF THE SYSTEM

Certain parts of the environment of operation may be included in the authorization boundary (i.e., determined to be "in scope" for the authorization) while other parts may be excluded. For example, if the facility (i.e., environment of operation) that provides protection for the system elements is determined to be in scope for the authorization of the system, the physical and environmental protection controls (e.g., physical access controls at entry points, perimeter protection devices) are included in the authorization boundary and therefore, are included in the system security plan. If the facility provides physical and environmental protections as common controls to be inherited by the system, the environment of operation is out of scope for the system and is not included in the authorization boundary for the system.[39]

The system may also communicate or have other interactions with enabling systems and other systems that are part of the extended environment of operation but are outside of the scope of authorization for the system.[40] Organizations determine which parts of the environment of operation are within the authorization boundary. These determinations are typically specific to the system and are context-driven.

---

[38] The terms *system, system element, enabling system, other systems,* and the *environment of operation* are agnostic with respect to information technology (IT) and operations technology (OT).

[39] *Common controls* are referenced in the security and privacy plans for the system inheriting the controls.

[40] For connections and information exchange between the system and the enabling or other systems outside of the authorization boundary, organizations consider the risks introduced by such connections and information exchange.

2.5 AUTHORIZATION BOUNDARIES

The authorization boundary establishes the scope of protection for an information system (i.e., what the organization agrees to protect under its direct management or within the scope of its responsibilities).[41] The authorization boundary includes the people, processes, and information technologies (i.e., system elements) that are part of each system supporting the organization's missions and business functions. Authorization boundaries that are too expansive (i.e., include too many system elements or components) make the risk management process unnecessarily complex. Conversely, authorization boundaries that are too limited (i.e., include too few system elements or components) increase the number of systems that must be separately managed and therefore, may unnecessarily inflate the information security and privacy costs for the organization.

The authorization boundary for a system is established during the RMF *Prepare Task – System level*, Task P-11. Organizations have flexibility in determining what constitutes the authorization boundary for a system. The set of system elements included within an authorization boundary defines the system (i.e., the scope of the authorization). When a set of system elements is identified as an authorization boundary for a system, the elements are generally under the same direct management.[42] Other considerations for determining the authorization boundary include identifying system elements that:

- Support the same mission or business functions;
- Have similar operating characteristics and security and privacy requirements;
- Process, store, and transmit similar types of information (e.g., categorized at the same impact level);[43] or
- Reside in the same environment of operation (or in the case of a distributed system, reside in various locations with similar operating environments).

The scope of the authorization boundary is revisited periodically as part of the continuous monitoring process carried out by the organization. While the above considerations may be useful to organizations in determining authorization boundaries for purposes of managing risk, the considerations are not intended to limit the organization's flexibility in establishing authorization boundaries that promote effective security and privacy with the available resources of the organization.

The process of establishing authorization boundaries carries significant risk management implications and is therefore an organization-wide activity that requires coordination among key participants. The process considers mission and business requirements, security and privacy

[41] Information systems are discrete sets of information resources organized for the collection, processing, use, sharing, maintenance, dissemination, or disposition of information, whether such information is in digital or non-digital form. Information resources include information and related resources, such as personnel, equipment, funds, and information technology. Information systems may or may not include hardware, firmware, and software.

[42] For information systems, direct management control involves budgetary, programmatic, or operational authority and associated *responsibility* and *accountability*. Direct management control does not necessarily imply that there is no intervening management.

[43] If a system contains information at multiple impact levels, the system is categorized at the highest impact level. See [FIPS 199] and [FIPS 200].

requirements, and the costs to the organization. Appendix G provides additional information and considerations for determining authorization boundaries, including boundaries for complex systems and software applications.

EFFECTIVE AUTHORIZATION BOUNDARIES

Establishing meaningful authorization boundaries for *systems* and *common controls* is one of the most important risk management activities carried out by an organization. The authorization boundary defines the specific scope of an authorizing official's responsibility and accountability for protecting information resources and individuals' privacy—including the use of systems, components, and services from external providers. Establishment of meaningful authorization boundaries is a foundation for assuring mission and business success for the organization.

2.6 REQUIREMENTS AND CONTROLS

Before executing the RMF, it is important to understand the concept of security and privacy requirements and the relationship between requirements and controls. The term *requirements* can be used in different contexts. In the context of federal information security and privacy policies, the term is generally used to refer to information security and privacy obligations imposed on organizations. For example, OMB Circular A-130 imposes a series of information security and privacy requirements with which federal agencies must comply when managing information resources. In addition to the use of the term requirements in the context of federal policy, the term *requirements* is used in this guideline in a broader sense to refer to an expression of the set of stakeholder protection needs for a particular system or organization. Stakeholder protection needs and corresponding security and privacy requirements may be derived from many sources (e.g., laws, executive orders, directives, regulations, policies, standards, mission and business needs, or risk assessments). The term *requirements*, as used in this guideline, includes both legal and policy requirements, as well as an expression of the broader set of stakeholder protection needs that may be derived from other sources. All of these requirements, when applied to a system, help determine the required characteristics of the system—encompassing security, privacy, and assurance.

Organizations may choose to divide security and privacy requirements into more granular categories depending on where the requirements are employed in the SDLC and for what purpose. Organizations may use the term *capability requirement* to describe a capability that the system or organization must provide to satisfy a stakeholder protection need. In addition, organizations may refer to system requirements that pertain to particular hardware, software, and firmware components of a system as *specification requirements*—that is, capabilities that implement all or part of a control and that may be assessed (i.e., as part of the verification, validation, testing, and evaluation processes). Finally, organizations may use the term *statement of work* requirements to refer to actions that must be performed operationally or during system development.

Controls can be viewed as descriptions of the safeguards and protection capabilities appropriate for achieving the particular security and privacy objectives of the organization and reflecting the protection needs of organizational stakeholders. Controls are selected and implemented by the organization in order to satisfy the system requirements. Controls can include technical aspects, administrative aspects, and physical aspects. In some cases, the selection and implementation of a control may necessitate additional specification by the organization in the form of *derived requirements* or instantiated control parameter values. The derived requirements and control parameter values may be necessary to provide the appropriate level of implementation detail for particular controls within the SDLC.

CONTEXT-DEPENDENT REQUIREMENTS

Security and privacy requirements and risks identified by the organization, lead to the need for security and privacy controls to respond to the risk. The controls selected by the organization subsequently lead to both specification requirements and statement of work requirements in the systems engineering context. This is an important aspect of how systems engineers develop, derive, and decompose requirements as part of the SDLC process. Thus, organizations manage security and privacy requirements at various levels of granularity and specificity during the life cycle of the system. Controls play an important part in the life cycle by providing high-level statements of protection capability that can be refined and expanded upon by the organization.

2.7 SECURITY AND PRIVACY POSTURE

The purpose of the RMF is to help ensure that, throughout the SDLC, information systems, organizations, and individuals are adequately protected, and that authorizing officials have the information needed to make credible, risk-based decisions regarding the operation or use of systems or the provision of common controls. A key aspect of risk-based decision making for authorizing officials is understanding the security and privacy posture of information systems and the common controls that are available for inheritance by those systems. The security and privacy posture represents the status of information systems and information resources (e.g., personnel, equipment, funds, and information technology) within an organization based on information assurance resources (e.g., people, hardware, software, policies, procedures) and the capabilities in place to manage the defense of the organization in its operation or use of systems; comply with applicable privacy requirements and manage privacy risks; and react as the situation changes.

The security and privacy posture of information systems and organizations is determined on an ongoing basis by assessing and continuously monitoring system-specific, hybrid, and common controls.[44] The control assessments and monitoring activities provide evidence that the controls selected by the organization are implemented correctly, operating as intended, and satisfying the security and privacy requirements in response to laws, executive orders, regulations, directives, policies, standards, or mission and business requirements. Authorizing officials use the security and privacy posture to determine if the risk to organizational operations and assets,

---

[44] Monitoring of controls is part of an organization-wide risk management approach defined in [SP 800-39].

individuals, other organizations, or the Nation are acceptable based on the organization's risk management strategy and organizational risk tolerance.[45]

2.8 SUPPLY CHAIN RISK MANAGEMENT

Organizations are becoming increasingly reliant on products, systems, and services provided by external providers to carry out missions and business functions. Organizations are responsible and accountable for the risk incurred when using such component products, systems, and services.[46] Relationships with external providers can be established in a variety of ways, for example, through joint ventures, business partnerships, various types of formal agreements (e.g., contracts, interagency agreements, lines of business arrangements, licensing agreements), or outsourcing arrangements.

The growing dependence on products, systems, and services from external providers, along with the nature of the relationships with those providers, present an increasing amount of risk to an organization. Risk may increase based on the likelihood of occurrence and adverse impact from threat events such as the insertion of counterfeits, unauthorized production, tampering, theft, insertion of malicious software and hardware, as well as poor manufacturing and development practices in the supply chain, including the failure to build in security or privacy capabilities that enable an organization to better manage risk in its environment.

Supply chain risks can be endemic or systemic within a system element, system, organization, sector, or nation. While the singular use of a system element or service within a system may present an acceptable risk to an organization, its common or extended use throughout a system, organization, sector or nation can raise the risk to an unacceptable level. These risks are often associated with the global and distributed nature of product and service supply chains and an organization's decreased visibility into, and understanding of, how the technology that they acquire is developed, integrated, and deployed. This includes the processes, procedures, and practices used to assure the integrity, security, resilience, privacy capabilities, and quality of the acquired products, systems, and services.

To address supply chain risks, organizations develop an SCRM policy, which is an important vehicle for directing SCRM activities. Guided and informed by applicable laws, executive orders, directives, policies, and regulations, the SCRM policy supports applicable organizational policies (e.g., acquisition and procurement, information security and privacy, logistics, quality, and supply chain). The policy addresses the goals and objectives in the organization's strategic plan, missions and business functions, and the internal and external customer requirements. It also defines the integration points for SCRM with the risk management and the SDLC processes for the organization. Finally, the SCRM policy defines the SCRM roles and responsibilities within the organization, any dependencies among those roles, and the interaction among the roles. SCRM roles specify the responsibilities for procurement, conducting risk assessments, collecting supply chain threat intelligence, identifying and implementing risk-based mitigations, and performing monitoring functions.

---

[45] See RMF *Prepare-Organization Level* step, Task P-2.

[46] [OMB A-130] defines supply chain risk and requires federal agencies to consider supply chain security issues for all resource planning and management activities throughout the SDLC so that risks are appropriately managed.

[FISMA] and [OMB A-130] require external providers handling federal information or operating systems on behalf of the federal government to meet the same security and privacy requirements as federal agencies. Security and privacy requirements for external providers including the controls for systems processing, storing, or transmitting federal information are expressed in contracts or other formal agreements. The RMF can be effectively used to manage supply chain risk.[47] The conceptual view of the system in Figure 5 can guide and inform security, privacy, and risk management activities for all elements of the supply chain. Every step in the RMF can be executed by nonfederal external providers except for the *Authorize* step—that is, the acceptance of risk is an inherent federal responsibility for which senior executives are held responsible and accountable. The authorization decision is directly linked to the management of risk related to the acquisition and use of component products, systems, and services from external providers.[48] [OMB A-130] also requires organizations to develop and implement SCRM plans.[49]

Managing supply chain risk is a complex, multifaceted undertaking requiring a coordinated effort across an organization—building trust relationships and communicating with both internal and external stakeholders. SCRM activities involve identifying and assessing applicable risks, determining appropriate mitigating actions, developing appropriate SCRM plans to document selected mitigating actions, and monitoring performance against SCRM plans. Because supply chains differ across and within organizations, SCRM plans are tailored to the individual program, organizational, and operational contexts. Tailored plans provide the basis for determining whether a system is "fit for purpose" and as such, the controls need to be tailored accordingly. Tailored SCRM plans help organizations to focus their resources on the most critical missions and business functions based on mission and business requirements and their risk environment.

The determination that the risk from acquiring products, systems, or services from external providers is acceptable depends on the level of assurance[50] that the organization can gain from the providers. The level of assurance is based on the degree of control the organization can exert on the external provider regarding the controls needed for the protection of the product, system, or service and the evidence brought forth by the provider as to the effectiveness of those controls.

The degree of control is established by the specific terms and conditions of the contract or service-level agreement. Some organizations have extensive control through contract vehicles or other agreements that specify the security and privacy requirements for the external provider. Other organizations, in contrast, have limited control because they are purchasing commodity

---

[47] *Supply chain risk* means risks that arise from the loss of confidentiality, integrity, or availability of information or information systems and reflect the potential adverse impacts to organizational operations (including mission, functions, image, or reputation), organizational assets, individuals, other organizations, and the Nation [OMB A-130]. When system elements process PII, SCRM practices address both information security and privacy risk.

[48] While *authorization* (i.e., the acceptance of risk) of federal information systems is an inherent federal responsibility, it is a foundational concept that can be used by senior executives in nonfederal organizations at all levels in the supply chain to manage security and privacy risk.

[49] [SP 800-161] provides guidance on SCRM plans.

[50] The level of assurance provided by an external provider can vary, ranging from those who provide high assurance (e.g., business partners in a joint venture that share a common business model and goals) to those who provide less assurance and represent greater sources of risk (e.g., business partners in one endeavor who are also competitors in another market sector).

services or commercial off-the-shelf products. The level of assurance can also be based on many other factors that convince the organization that the requisite controls have been implemented and that a credible determination of control effectiveness exists. For example, an authorized external cloud service provided to an organization through a well-established line-of-business relationship may provide a level of trust in the service that is within the risk tolerance of the organization. Ultimately, the responsibility for responding to risks from the use of component products, systems, and services from external providers remains with the organization and the authorizing official. Organizations require that an appropriate *chain of trust* be established with external providers when dealing with the issues associated with system security or privacy risks.

SUPPLY CHAIN RISK MANAGEMENT STRATEGIES AND PLANS

Organizations have flexibility on how the details of SCRM strategies and plans are documented. SCRM strategy details for Levels 1 and 2 (organization and mission/business process levels), can be documented in the information security program plan for the organization or in a separate organization-level and/or mission/business process-level SCRM strategy. SCRM plan details for Level 3 (information system level) can be documented in the information system security plan or in a separate system-level SCRM plan. An SCRM strategy template is provided in [SP 800-161].

Guide for Applying the Risk Management Framework to Federal Information Systems (800-37 rev 2)

225

CHAPTER THREE

THE PROCESS

EXECUTING THE RISK MANAGEMENT FRAMEWORK TASKS

This chapter describes the steps and associated tasks that comprise the RMF and the selected individuals or groups (defined organizational roles) that carry out such tasks.[51] Organizations align their risk management roles with complementary or similar roles defined for the SDLC whenever possible, and consistent with missions and business functions. RMF tasks are executed concurrently with, or as part of, the SDLC processes in the organization. Executing RMF tasks concurrently with SDLC processes helps to ensure that organizations are effectively integrating the process of managing information security and privacy risks into SDLC processes. Moreover, the expected outputs required by the RMF (e.g., security and privacy plans, assessment reports, plans of action and milestones), can be routinely obtained from the SDLC processes in place within organizations and may not need to be developed solely for RMF implementation.

RMF ALIGNMENT WITH THE SDLC

The best RMF implementation is one that is indistinguishable from the routine SDLC processes carried out by organizations. That is, RMF tasks are closely aligned with the ongoing activities in the SDLC processes, ensuring the seamless integration of security and privacy protections into organizational systems—and taking maximum advantage of the artifacts generated by the SDLC processes to produce the necessary evidence in authorization packages to facilitate credible, risk-based decision making by senior leaders in organizations.

The process of implementing RMF tasks may vary from organization to organization. While the tasks appear in sequential order, there can be many points in the risk management process that require divergence from the sequential order, including the need for iterative cycles between initial task execution and revisiting tasks. For example, control assessment results can trigger a set of remediation actions by system owners and common control providers, which can in turn require the reassessment of selected controls. Monitoring controls can generate a cycle of tracking changes to the system and its environment of operation; assessing the information security and privacy impact; reassessing controls, taking remediation actions, and reporting the security and privacy posture of the system and the organization.

There may be other opportunities to diverge from the sequential nature of the tasks when it is more effective, efficient, or cost-effective to do so. For example, while the control assessment tasks are listed after the control implementation tasks, organizations may begin the assessment of controls as soon as they are implemented but prior to the complete implementation of all

---

[51] Appendix D describes the roles and responsibilities of key participants involved in organizational risk management and the execution of the RMF. Many risk management roles defined in this publication have counterpart roles defined in the SDLC process.

controls described in the system security plans and privacy plans. Assessing controls as soon as they are implemented may result in organizations assessing the physical and environmental protection controls within a facility prior to assessing the controls implemented in the hardware, firmware, or software components of the system (which may be implemented later). Regardless of the task ordering, the final action before a system is placed into operation is the explicit acceptance of risk by the authorizing official.

The RMF steps and associated tasks can be applied to new development systems and existing systems at appropriate phases in the SDLC. For new and existing systems, organizations ensure that the designated tasks have been completed to prepare for the execution of the RMF. For existing systems, organizations confirm that the security categorization and (for information systems processing PII) a privacy risk assessment have been completed and are appropriate; and that the needed controls have been selected, tailored, and implemented.

Applying the RMF steps and associated tasks to existing systems can serve as a gap analysis to determine if the organization's security and privacy risks have been effectively managed. Deficiencies in controls can be addressed in the RMF steps for implementation, assessment, authorization, and monitoring in the same manner as in new development systems. If no deficiencies are discovered during the gap analysis and there is a current authorization in effect, the organization can move directly to the continuous monitoring step in the RMF. If a current authorization is not in effect, the organization continues in the usual sequence with the assessment, authorization, and monitoring steps.

TASK DELEGATION

The roles specified in the *Primary Responsibility* section for each RMF task are responsible for ensuring that the task is completed. The roles with primary responsibility may complete a task or may delegate completion of a task to one or more *supporting* roles except where delegation is specifically prohibited or disallowed in the task *Discussion* section or Appendix D. If completion of a task is delegated, the role with primary responsibility for that task remains accountable for task completion.

TIPS FOR STREAMLINING RMF IMPLEMENTATION

- Use the tasks and outputs of the Organization-Level and System-Level *Prepare* Step to promote a consistent starting point within organizations to execute the RMF.

- Maximize the use of *common controls* to promote standardized, consistent, and cost-effective security and privacy capability inheritance.

- Maximize the use of *shared* or *cloud-based* systems, services, and applications where applicable, to reduce the number of organizational authorizations.

- Employ *organizationally-tailored control baselines* to increase the speed of security and privacy plan development, promote consistency of security and privacy plan content, and address organization-wide threats.

- Employ *organization-defined controls* based on security and privacy requirements generated from a systems security engineering process.

- Maximize the use of *automated tools* to manage security categorization; control selection, assessment, and monitoring; and the authorization process.

- Decrease the level of effort and resource expenditures for *low-impact* systems if those systems cannot adversely affect higher-impact systems through system connections.

- Maximize the *reuse* of RMF artifacts (e.g., security and privacy assessment results) for standardized hardware/software deployments, including configuration settings.

- Reduce the *complexity* of the IT/OT infrastructure by eliminating unnecessary systems, system elements, and services — employ *least functionality* principle.

- Make the transition to *ongoing authorization* and use *continuous monitoring* approaches to reduce the cost and increase the efficiency of security and privacy programs.

DEVELOPING WELL-DEFINED SECURITY AND PRIVACY REQUIREMENTS

The RMF is an SDLC-based process that can be effectively used to help ensure that security and privacy requirements are satisfied for information systems or organizations. Defining clear, consistent, and unambiguous security and privacy requirements is an important element in the successful execution of the RMF. The requirements are defined early in the SDLC in collaboration with the senior leaders and are integrated into the acquisition and procurement processes. For example, organizations can use the [SP 800-160 v1] life cycle-based systems engineering process to define an initial set of security and privacy requirements, which in turn, can be used to select a set of controls* to satisfy the requirements. The requirements or the controls can be stated in the Request for Proposal or other contractual agreement when organizations acquire systems, system components, or services. Requirements can also be added throughout the life cycle, such as with the agile development methodology where new features are continuously deployed.

The NIST *Cybersecurity Framework* [NIST CSF] (i.e., Core, Profiles) can also be used to identify, align, and deconflict security requirements and to subsequently inform the selection of security controls for an organization. Cybersecurity Framework Profiles can provide a link between cybersecurity activities and organizational mission/business objectives, which supports risk-based decision-making throughout the RMF. While Profiles may be used as a starting point to inform control selection and tailoring activities, further evaluation is needed to ensure the appropriate controls are selected. Some organizations may choose to use the Cybersecurity Framework in concert with the NIST *Systems Security Engineering* publications—identifying, aligning, and deconflicting requirements across a sector, an industry, or an organization—and subsequently employing a systems engineering approach to further refine the requirements and obtain trustworthy secure solutions to help protect the organization's operations, assets, individuals.

* See Section 2.3 for specific guidance on privacy control selection and managing privacy risk.

ORGANIZATION AND SYSTEM PREPARATION

Preparation can achieve effective, efficient, and cost-effective execution of risk management processes. The primary objectives of the *Prepare* step include:

- Facilitate better communication between senior leaders and executives in the C-suite and system owners and operators—
  - aligning organizational priorities with resource allocation and prioritization at the system level; and
  - conveying acceptable limits regarding the selection and implementation of controls within the established organizational risk tolerance.
- Promote organization-wide identification of common controls and the development of organizationally-tailored control baselines, to reduce the workload on individual system owners and the cost of system development and protection.
- Reduce the complexity of the IT infrastructure by consolidating, standardizing, and optimizing systems, applications, and services through the application of enterprise architecture concepts and models.
- Identify, prioritize, and focus resources on high value assets (as defined in [OMB M-19-03]), that require increased levels of protection.
- Facilitate system readiness for system-specific tasks.

These objectives, if achieved, significantly reduce the information technology footprint and the attack surface of organizations, promote IT modernization objectives, and prioritize security and privacy activities to focus protection strategies on the most critical assets and systems.

Finally, certain tasks in the *Prepare* step at the organization level are designated as *optional*. These tasks are included to provide organizations additional options to help make their RMF implementations more effective, efficient, and cost-effective.

Guide for Applying the Risk Management Framework to Federal Information Systems (800-37 rev 2)
230

3.1 PREPARE [52]

<table>
<tr><td>

Purpose

The purpose of the **Prepare** step is to carry out essential activities at the organization, mission and business process, and information system levels of the organization to help prepare the organization to manage its security and privacy risks using the *Risk Management Framework*.

</td></tr>
</table>

PREPARE TASKS—ORGANIZATION LEVEL [53]

Table 1 provides a summary of tasks and expected outcomes for the RMF *Prepare* step at the *organization* level. Applicable Cybersecurity Framework constructs are also provided.

TABLE 1: PREPARE TASKS AND OUTCOMES—ORGANIZATION LEVEL

Tasks	Outcomes
TASK P-1 RISK MANAGEMENT ROLES	• Individuals are identified and assigned key roles for executing the Risk Management Framework. [*Cybersecurity Framework*: ID.AM-6; ID.GV-2]
TASK P-2 RISK MANAGEMENT STRATEGY	• A risk management strategy for the organization that includes a determination and expression of organizational risk tolerance is established. [*Cybersecurity Framework*: ID.RM; ID.SC]
TASK P-3 RISK ASSESSMENT—ORGANIZATION	• An organization-wide risk assessment is completed or an existing risk assessment is updated. [*Cybersecurity Framework*: ID.RA; ID.SC-2]
TASK P-4 ORGANIZATIONALLY-TAILORED CONTROL BASELINES AND CYBERSECURITY FRAMEWORK PROFILES (OPTIONAL)	• Organizationally-tailored control baselines and/or Cybersecurity Framework Profiles are established and made available. [*Cybersecurity Framework*: Profile]
TASK P-5 COMMON CONTROL IDENTIFICATION	• Common controls that are available for inheritance by organizational systems are identified, documented, and published.
TASK P-6 IMPACT-LEVEL PRIORITIZATION (OPTIONAL)	• A prioritization of organizational systems with the same impact level is conducted. [*Cybersecurity Framework*: ID.AM-5]
TASK P-7 CONTINUOUS MONITORING STRATEGY—ORGANIZATION	• An organization-wide strategy for monitoring control effectiveness is developed and implemented. [*Cybersecurity Framework*: DE.CM; ID.SC-4]

<u>Quick link to summary table for RMF tasks, responsibilities, and supporting roles.</u>

---

[52] The *Prepare* step is intended to leverage activities already being conducted within security, privacy, and supply chain programs to emphasize the importance of having organization-wide governance and the appropriate resources in place to enable the execution of cost-effective and consistent risk management processes across the organization.

[53] For ease of use, the preparatory activities are grouped into organization-level preparation and information system-level preparation.

RISK MANAGEMENT ROLES

TASK P-1   Identify and assign individuals to specific roles associated with security and privacy risk management.

Potential Inputs: Organizational security and privacy policies and procedures; organizational charts.

Expected Outputs: Documented Risk Management Framework role assignments.

Primary Responsibility: Head of Agency; Chief Information Officer; Senior Agency Official for Privacy.

Supporting Roles: Authorizing Official or Authorizing Official Designated Representative; Senior Accountable Official for Risk Management or Risk Executive (Function); Senior Agency Information Security Officer.

Discussion: The roles and responsibilities of key participants in risk management processes are described in Appendix D. The roles and responsibilities may include personnel that are internal or external to the organization, as appropriate. Since organizations have different missions, functions, and organizational structures, there may be differences in naming conventions for risk management roles and how specific responsibilities are allocated among organizational personnel (e.g., multiple individuals filling a single role or one individual filling multiple roles). In either situation, the basic risk management functions remain the same. Organizations ensure that there are no conflicts of interest when assigning the same individual to multiple risk management roles. For example, authorizing officials cannot occupy the role of system owner or common control provider for systems or common controls they are authorizing. In addition, combining multiple roles for security and privacy requires care because the two disciplines may require different expertise, and in some circumstances, the priorities may be competing. Some roles may be allocated to a group or an office rather than to an individual, for example, control assessor, risk executive (function), or system administrator.

References: [SP 800-160 v1] (Human Resource Management Process); [SP 800-181]; [NIST CSF] (Core [Identify Function]).

RISK MANAGEMENT STRATEGY

TASK P-2   Establish a risk management strategy for the organization that includes a determination of risk tolerance.

Potential Inputs: Organizational mission statement; organizational policies; organizational risk assumptions, constraints, priorities and trade-offs.

Expected Outputs: Risk management strategy and statement of risk tolerance inclusive of information security and privacy risk.

Primary Responsibility: Head of Agency.

Supporting Roles: Senior Accountable Official for Risk Management or Risk Executive (Function); Chief Information Officer; Senior Agency Information Security Officer; Senior Agency Official for Privacy.

Discussion: Risk tolerance is the degree of risk or uncertainty that is acceptable to an organization. Risk tolerance affects all parts of the organization's risk management process, having a direct impact on the risk management decisions made by senior leaders or executives throughout the organization and providing important constraints on those decisions. The risk management strategy guides and informs risk-based decisions including how security and privacy risk is framed, assessed, responded to, and monitored. The risk management strategy may be composed of a single document, or separate security and privacy risk management documents.[54] The risk management strategy makes explicit the threats, assumptions, constraints, priorities, trade-offs, and risk tolerance used for making investment and

---

[54] A separate supply chain risk management strategy document is called a *supply chain risk management plan*.

Guide for Applying the Risk Management Framework to Federal Information Systems (800-37 rev 2)

operational decisions. This strategy includes the strategic-level decisions and considerations for how senior leaders and executives are to manage security and privacy risks (including supply chain risks) to organizational operations, organizational assets, individuals, other organizations, and the Nation. The risk management strategy includes an expression of organizational risk tolerance; acceptable risk assessment methodologies and risk response strategies; a process for consistently evaluating security and privacy risks organization-wide; and approaches for monitoring risk over time. As organizations define and implement the risk management strategies, policies, procedures, and processes, it is important that they include SCRM considerations. The risk management strategy for security and privacy connects security and privacy programs with the management control systems established in the organization's Enterprise Risk Management strategy. [55]

References: [SP 800-30]; [SP 800-39] (Organization Level); [SP 800-160 v1] (Risk Management, Decision Management, Quality Assurance, Quality Management, Project Assessment and Control Processes); [SP 800-161]; [IR 8062]; [IR 8179] (Criticality Analysis Process B); [NIST CSF] (Core [Identify Function]).

RISK ASSESSMENT—ORGANIZATION

TASK P-3   Assess organization-wide security and privacy risk and update the risk assessment results on an ongoing basis.

Potential Inputs: Risk management strategy; mission or business objectives; current threat information; system-level security and privacy risk assessment results; supply chain risk assessment results; previous organization-level security and privacy risk assessment results; information sharing agreements or memoranda of understanding; security and privacy information from continuous monitoring.

Expected Outputs: Organization-level risk assessment results.

Primary Responsibility: Senior Accountable Official for Risk Management or Risk Executive (Function); Senior Agency Information Security Officer; Senior Agency Official for Privacy.

Supporting Roles: Chief Information Officer; Mission or Business Owner; Authorizing Official or Authorizing Official Designated Representative.

Discussion: Risk assessment at the organizational level leverages aggregated information from system-level risk assessment results, continuous monitoring, and any strategic risk considerations relevant to the organization. The organization considers the totality of risk from the operation and use of its information systems, from information exchange and connections with other internally and externally owned systems, and from the use of external providers. For example, the organization may review the risk related to its enterprise architecture and information systems of varying impact levels residing on the same network and whether higher impact systems are segregated from lower impact systems or systems operated and maintained by external providers. The organization may also consider the variability of environments that may exist within the organization (e.g., different locations serving different missions/business processes) and the need to account for such variability in risk assessments. Risk assessments of the organization's supply chain may be conducted as well. Risk assessment results may be used to help organizations establish a Cybersecurity Framework Profile.

References: [SP 800-30]; [SP 800-39] (Organization Level, Mission/Business Process Level); [SP 800-161]; [IR 8062].

---

[55] See [OMB A-123].

ORGANIZATIONALLY-TAILORED CONTROL BASELINES AND CYBERSECURITY FRAMEWORK PROFILES (Optional)

<u>TASK P-4</u> Establish, document, and publish organizationally-tailored control baselines and/or Cybersecurity Framework Profiles.

Potential Inputs: Documented security and privacy requirements directing the use of organizationally-tailored control baselines; mission or business objectives; enterprise architecture; security architecture; privacy architecture; organization- and system-level risk assessment results; list of common control providers and common controls available for inheritance; NIST Special Publication 800-53B control baselines.[56]

Expected Outputs: List of approved or directed organizationally-tailored control baselines; [NIST CSF] Profiles.

Primary Responsibility: <u>Mission or Business Owner</u>; <u>Senior Accountable Official for Risk Management</u> or <u>Risk Executive (Function)</u>.

Supporting Roles: <u>Chief Information Officer</u>; <u>Authorizing Official</u> or <u>Authorizing Official Designated Representative</u>; <u>Senior Agency Information Security Officer</u>; <u>Senior Agency Official for Privacy</u>.

Discussion: To address the organizational mission or business need for specialized sets of controls to reduce risk, organizationally-tailored control baselines may be developed for organization-wide use.[57] An organizationally-tailored baseline provides a fully specified set of controls, control enhancements, and supplemental guidance derived from established control baselines described in [SP 800-53B]. The tailoring process can also be guided and informed by the requirements engineering process described in [SP 800-160 v1]. Organizations can use the tailored control baseline concept when there is divergence from the specific assumptions used to create the initial control baselines in [SP 800-53B]. This would include, for example, situations when the organization has specific security or privacy risks, has specific mission or business needs, or plans to operate in environments that are not addressed in the initial baselines.

Organizationally-tailored baselines and overlays complement the NIST control baselines by providing an opportunity to add or eliminate controls to accommodate organizational requirements while continuing to protect information commensurate with risk. Organizations can use tailored baselines and overlays to customize control baselines by describing control applicability and by providing interpretations for specific technologies; types of missions or business functions, operations, systems, environments of operation, and operating modes; and statutory or regulatory requirements. Multiple customized baselines may be useful for organizations with heterogeneous systems (e.g., organizations that maintain systems with different operating or processing characteristics, or mission or business characteristics).

Organizationally-tailored baselines can establish organization-defined control parameter values for assignment or selection statements in controls and control enhancements that are agreeable to specific communities of interest and can also extend the supplemental guidance where necessary. Tailored baselines may be more stringent or less stringent than the baselines identified in [SP 800-53B] and are applied to multiple systems.

Tailored baselines developed outside the organization may also be mandated for use by certain laws, executive orders, directives, regulations, policies, or standards. In some situations, tailoring actions may

---

[56] NIST Special Publication 800-53 (Revision 5), separates the control catalog from the control baselines that have been included historically in that publication. A new companion publication, NIST Special Publication 800-53B, *Control Baselines and Tailoring Guidance for Federal Information Systems and Organizations* defines the recommended baselines. NIST Special Publication 800-53B is referenced throughout the RMF in the relevant tasks.

[57] Tailored control baselines may also be referred to as *overlays*. An organizationally-tailored control baseline is analogous to an organization-wide overlay since an overlay is a tailored baseline that services a community of interest, in this case, the organization.

be restricted or limited by the developer of the tailored baseline or by the issuing authority for the tailored baseline. Tailored baselines (or overlays) have been developed by communities of interest for cloud and shared systems, services, and applications; industrial control systems; privacy; national security systems; weapons and space-based systems; high value assets;[58] mobile device management; federal public key infrastructure; and privacy risks.

Organizations may also benefit from developing one or more Cybersecurity Framework *Profiles*. A Cybersecurity Framework Profile uses the Subcategories in the Framework Core to align cybersecurity outcomes with mission or business requirements, risk tolerance, and resources of the organization.[59] The prioritized list of cybersecurity outcomes developed at the organization and mission/business process levels can be helpful in facilitating consistent, risk-based decisions at the system level. The Subcategories identified in the applicable Cybersecurity Framework Profiles can also be used to guide and inform the development of the tailored control baselines described above.

References: [SP 800-53]; [SP 800-53B]; [SP 800-160 v1] (Business or Mission Analysis and Stakeholder Needs and Requirements Definition Processes); [NIST CSF] (Core, Profiles).

COMMON CONTROL IDENTIFICATION

TASK P-5   Identify, document, and publish organization-wide common controls that are available for inheritance by organizational systems.

Potential Inputs: Documented security and privacy requirements; existing common control providers and associated security and privacy plans; information security and privacy program plans; organization- and system-level security and privacy risk assessment results.

Expected Outputs: List of common control providers and common controls available for inheritance; security and privacy plans (or equivalent documents) providing a description of the common control implementation (including inputs, expected behavior, and expected outputs).

Primary Responsibility: Senior Agency Information Security Officer; Senior Agency Official for Privacy.

Supporting Roles: Mission or Business Owner; Senior Accountable Official for Risk Management or Risk Executive (Function); Chief Information Officer; Authorizing Official or Authorizing Official Designated Representative; Common Control Provider; System Owner.

Discussion: Common controls are controls that can be inherited by one or more information systems.[60] Common controls can include controls from any [SP 800-53] control family, for example, physical and environmental protection controls, system boundary and monitoring controls, personnel security controls, policies and procedures, acquisition controls, account and identity management controls, audit log and accountability controls, or complaint management controls for receiving privacy inquiries from the public. Organizations identify and select the set of common controls and allocate those controls to the organizational entities designated as common control providers. Common controls may differ based upon a variety of factors, such as hosting location, system architecture, and the structure of the organization. The organization-wide list of common controls takes these factors into account. Common controls can also be identified at different levels of the organization (e.g., corporate, department, or agency level; bureau or subcomponent level; or individual program level). Organizations may establish one or more lists of common controls that can be inherited by information systems. A requirement may not be fully met by a common control. In such cases, the control is considered a hybrid control and is noted as such by the organization, including specifying which parts of the control requirement are provided for inheritance by the common control and which parts are to be provided at the system level.

---

[58] See [OMB M-19-03].

[59] See [NIST CSF], Section 2.3.

[60] Common controls are *authorized* by designated authorizing officials before the controls are made available for inheritance by organizational systems. See Appendix F for a description of the different types of authorizations.

When there are multiple sources of common controls, organizations specify the common control provider (i.e., who is providing the controls and through what venue, for example, shared services, specific systems, or within a specific type of architecture) and which systems or types of systems can inherit the controls. Common control listings are communicated to system owners, so they are aware of the security and privacy capabilities that are available from the organization through inheritance. System owners are not required to assess common controls that are inherited by their systems or document common control implementation details; that is the responsibility of the common control providers. Likewise, common control providers are not required to have visibility into the system-level details of those systems that are inheriting the common controls they are providing.

Risk assessment results can be used when identifying common controls to determine if the controls available for inheritance satisfy the security and privacy requirements for organizational systems and the environments in which those systems operate (including the identification of potential single points of failure). When the common controls provided by the organization are determined to be insufficient for the information systems inheriting those controls, system owners can supplement the common controls with system-specific or hybrid controls to achieve the required protection for their systems or accept greater risk with the acknowledgement and approval of the organization.

Common control providers execute the RMF steps to implement, assess, and monitor the controls designated as common controls. Common control providers may also be system owners when the common controls are resident within an information system. Organizations select senior officials or executives to serve as authorizing officials for common controls. The senior agency official for privacy is responsible for designating common privacy controls and for documenting them in the organization's privacy program plan. Authorizing officials are responsible for accepting security and privacy risk resulting from the use of common controls inherited by organizational systems.

Common control providers are responsible for documenting common controls in security and privacy plans (or equivalent documents prescribed by the organization); ensuring that the common controls are implemented and assessed for effectiveness by qualified assessors and that assessment findings are documented in assessment reports; producing a plan of action and milestones for common controls determined to have unacceptable deficiencies and targeted for remediation; receiving authorization for the common controls from the designated authorizing official; and monitoring control effectiveness on an ongoing basis. Plans, assessment reports, and plans of action and milestones for common controls (or a summary of such information) are made available to system owners and can be used by authorizing officials to guide and inform authorization decisions for systems inheriting common controls. For information about the authorization of common controls, see Task R-4 and Appendix F.

References: [SP 800-53].

IMPACT-LEVEL PRIORITIZATION (Optional) [61]

TASK P-6   Prioritize organizational systems with the same impact level.

Potential Inputs: Security categorization information for organizational systems; system descriptions; organization- and system-level risk assessment results; mission or business objectives; Cybersecurity Framework Profiles.

Expected Outputs: Organizational systems prioritized into low-, moderate-, and high-impact sub-categories.

Primary Responsibility: Senior Accountable Official for Risk Management or Risk Executive (Function).

---

[61] Organizations can use this task in conjunction with the optional RMF *Prepare-Organization Level* step, Task P4, to develop organizationally-tailored baselines for the more granular impact designations, for example, organizationally-tailored baselines for low-moderate systems and high-moderate systems.

Supporting Roles: Senior Agency Information Security Officer; Senior Agency Official for Privacy; Mission or Business Owner; System Owner; Chief Information Officer; Authorizing Official or Authorizing Official Designated Representative.

Discussion: This task is carried out *only* after organizational systems have been categorized (see Task C1). This task requires organizations to first apply the high-water mark concept to each of their information systems categorized in accordance with [FIPS 199] and [FIPS 200].[62] The application of the high-water mark concept results in systems designated as low impact, moderate impact, or high impact. Organizations desiring additional granularity in their impact designations for risk-based decision making can use this task to prioritize their systems within each impact level.[63] For example, an organization may decide to prioritize its moderate-impact systems by assigning each moderate system to one of three new subcategories: *low-moderate* systems, *moderate-moderate* systems, and *high-moderate* systems. The high-moderate systems assume a higher priority than the moderate-moderate systems and low-moderate systems assume a lower priority than the moderate-moderate systems. The prioritization of its moderate systems gives organizations an opportunity to make more informed decisions regarding control selection and the tailoring of control baselines when responding to identified risks.

Impact-level prioritization can also be used to determine those systems that are critical or essential to organizational missions and business operations and therefore, organizations can focus on the factors of complexity, aggregation, and system interconnections. Such systems can be identified, for example, by prioritizing high-impact systems into *low-high* systems, *moderate-high* systems, and *high-high* systems. Impact-level prioritizations can be conducted at any level of the organization and are based on security categorization data reported by individual system owners. Impact-level prioritization may necessitate the development of organizationally-tailored baselines to designate the appropriate set of controls for the additional, more granular impact levels.

Cybersecurity Framework *Profiles* can be used by organizations to support the impact-level prioritization task. The mission and business objectives and prioritized outcomes defined in applicable Cybersecurity Framework Profiles can help distinguish relative priority between systems with the same impact level. Cybersecurity Framework Profiles can be organized around the priority of mission/business objectives of an organization, and those objectives are assigned a relative priority among them. For example, human and environmental safety objectives may be the two most important objectives relevant to a Profile's context. In this example, when performing Task P-6, a system that relates to a human safety objective may be prioritized higher than a system that has the same impact levels but does not relate to the human safety objective.

References: [FIPS 199]; [FIPS 200]; [SP 800-30]; [SP 800-39] (Organization and System Levels); [SP 800-59]; [SP 800-60 v1]; [SP 800-60 v2]; [SP 800-160 v1] (System Requirements Definition Process); [IR 8179] (Criticality Analysis Process B); [CNSSI 1253]; [NIST CSF] (Core [Identify Function]; Profiles).

CONTINUOUS MONITORING STRATEGY—ORGANIZATION

TASK P-7 Develop and implement an organization-wide strategy for continuously monitoring control effectiveness.

Potential Inputs: Risk management strategy; organization- and system-level risk assessment results; organizational security and privacy policies.

Expected Outputs: An implemented organizational continuous monitoring strategy.

Primary Responsibility: Senior Accountable Official for Risk Management or Risk Executive (Function).

---

[62] Organizations operating National Security Systems follow the categorization guidance in [CNSSI 1253] which does not apply the *high-water mark* concept.
[63] Organizations can also elect to use an alternative, organization-defined categorization approach to add additional granularity to the impact levels defined in [FIPS 199].

Supporting Roles: Chief Information Officer; Senior Agency Information Security Officer; Senior Agency Official for Privacy; Mission or Business Owner; System Owner; Authorizing Official or Authorizing Official Designated Representative.

Discussion: An important aspect of risk management is the ability to monitor the security and privacy posture across the organization and the effectiveness of controls implemented within or inherited by organizational systems on an ongoing basis.[64] An effective organization-wide continuous monitoring strategy is essential to efficiently and cost-effectively carry out such monitoring. Continuous monitoring strategies can also include supply chain risk considerations, for example, regularly reviewing supplier foreign ownership, control, or influence (FOCI), monitoring inventory forecasts, or requiring on-going audits of suppliers. The implementation of a robust and comprehensive continuous monitoring program helps an organization understand the security and privacy posture of its information systems. It also facilitates ongoing authorization after the initial system or common control authorizations. This includes the potential for changing missions or business functions, stakeholders, technologies, vulnerabilities, threats, risks, and suppliers of systems, components, or services.

The organizational continuous monitoring strategy addresses monitoring requirements at the organization, mission/business process, and information system levels. The continuous monitoring strategy identifies the minimum monitoring frequency for implemented controls across the organization; defines the ongoing control assessment approach; and describes how ongoing assessments are to be conducted (e.g., addressing the use and management of automated tools, and instructions for ongoing assessment of controls for which monitoring cannot be automated). The continuous monitoring strategy may also define security and privacy reporting requirements including recipients of the reports. The criteria for determining the minimum frequency for control monitoring is established in collaboration with organizational officials (e.g., senior accountable official for risk management or risk executive [function]; senior agency information security officer; senior agency official for privacy; chief information officer; system owners; common control providers; and authorizing officials or their designated representatives). An organizational risk assessment can be used to guide and inform the frequency of monitoring.

The use of automation facilitates a greater frequency and volume of control assessments as part of the monitoring process. The ongoing monitoring of controls using automated tools and supporting databases facilitates near real-time risk management for information systems and supports ongoing authorization and efficient use of resources. The senior accountable official for risk management or the risk executive (function) approves the continuous monitoring strategy including the minimum frequency with which controls are to be monitored.

References: [SP 800-30]; [SP 800-39] (Organization, Mission or Business Process, System Levels); [SP 800-53]; [SP 800-53A]; [SP 800-137]; [SP 800-161]; [IR 8011 v1]; [IR 8062]; [NIST CSF] (Core [Identify, Detect Functions]); [CNSSI 1253].

MISSION/BUSINESS PROCESS (LEVEL 2) CONSIDERATIONS

Mission/business process considerations are addressed in the RMF *Prepare-Organization Level* step and the RMF *Prepare-System Level* step by specifying mission/business process concerns; by identifying the mission or business owners in primary or supporting roles; and by identifying the mission or business objectives. Task P-8 and Task P-9 from the RMF *Prepare-System Level* step are mission/business process level tasks conducted with a system-level specific focus.

---

[64] Monitoring for control effectiveness is a form of control assessment. [SP 800-53A], [SP 800-137], and [IR 8011 v1] provide additional information on monitoring, conducting control effectiveness assessments, and automating control effectiveness assessments respectively.

PREPARE TASKS—SYSTEM LEVEL

Table 2 provides a summary of tasks and expected outcomes for the RMF *Prepare* step at the *system* level. Applicable Cybersecurity Framework constructs are also provided.

TABLE 2: PREPARE TASKS AND OUTCOMES—SYSTEM LEVEL

Tasks	Outcomes
TASK P-8 MISSION OR BUSINESS FOCUS	• Missions, business functions, and mission/business processes that the system is intended to support are identified. [*Cybersecurity Framework*: Profile; Implementation Tiers; ID.BE]
TASK P-9 SYSTEM STAKEHOLDERS	• The stakeholders having an interest in the system are identified. [*Cybersecurity Framework*: ID.AM; ID.BE]
TASK P-10 ASSET IDENTIFICATION	• Stakeholder assets are identified and prioritized. [*Cybersecurity Framework*: ID.AM]
TASK P-11 AUTHORIZATION BOUNDARY	• The authorization boundary (i.e., system) is determined.
TASK P-12 INFORMATION TYPES	• The types of information processed, stored, and transmitted by the system are identified. [*Cybersecurity Framework*: ID.AM-5]
TASK P-13 INFORMATION LIFE CYCLE	• All stages of the information life cycle are identified and understood for each information type processed, stored, or transmitted by the system. [*Cybersecurity Framework*: ID.AM-3; ID.AM-4]
TASK P-14 RISK ASSESSMENT—SYSTEM	• A system-level risk assessment is completed or an existing risk assessment is updated. [*Cybersecurity Framework*: ID.RA; ID.SC-2]
TASK P-15 REQUIREMENTS DEFINITION	• Security and privacy requirements are defined and prioritized. [*Cybersecurity Framework*: ID.GV; PR.IP]
TASK P-16 ENTERPRISE ARCHITECTURE	• The placement of the system within the enterprise architecture is determined.
TASK P-17 REQUIREMENTS ALLOCATION	• Security and privacy requirements are allocated to the system and to the environment in which the system operates. [*Cybersecurity Framework*: ID.GV]
TASK P-18 SYSTEM REGISTRATION	• The system is registered for purposes of management, accountability, coordination, and oversight. [*Cybersecurity Framework*: ID.GV]

Quick link to summary table for RMF tasks, responsibilities, and supporting roles.

MISSION OR BUSINESS FOCUS

TASK P-8   Identify the missions, business functions, and mission/business processes that the system is intended to support.

Potential Inputs: Organizational mission statement; organizational policies; mission/business process information; system stakeholder information; Cybersecurity Framework Profiles; requests for proposal or other acquisition documents; concept of operations.

Expected Outputs: Missions, business functions, and mission/business processes that the system will support.

Primary Responsibility: Mission or Business Owner.

This publication is available free of charge from: https://doi.org/10.6028/NIST.SP.800-37r2

Supporting Roles: Authorizing Official or Authorizing Official Designated Representative; System Owner; Information Owner or Steward; Chief Information Officer; Senior Agency Information Security Officer; Senior Agency Official for Privacy.

System Development Life Cycle Phase: New – Initiation (concept/requirements definition).
Existing – Operations/Maintenance.

Discussion: Organizational missions and business functions influence the design and development of the mission or business processes that are created to carry out those missions and business functions. The prioritization of missions and business functions drives investment strategies, funding decisions, resource prioritization, and risk decisions—and thus affects the existing enterprise architecture and development of the associated security and privacy architectures. Information is elicited from stakeholders to acquire a more thorough understanding of the missions, business functions, and mission/business processes of the organization from a system security and privacy perspective.

References: [SP 800-39] (Organization and Mission/Business Process Levels); [SP 800-64]; [SP 800-160 v1] (Business or Mission Analysis, Portfolio Management, and Project Planning Processes); [NIST CSF] (Core [Identify Function]); [IR 8179] (Criticality Analysis Process B).

SYSTEM STAKEHOLDERS

TASK P-9   Identify stakeholders who have an interest in the design, development, implementation, assessment, operation, maintenance, or disposal of the system.

Potential Inputs: Organizational mission statement; mission or business objectives; missions, business functions, and mission/business processes that the system will support; other mission/business process information; organizational security and privacy policies and procedures; organizational charts; information about individuals or groups (internal and external) that have an interest in and decision-making responsibility for the system.

Expected Outputs: List of system stakeholders.

Primary Responsibility: Mission or Business Owner; System Owner.

Supporting Roles: Chief Information Officer; Authorizing Official or Authorizing Official Designated Representative; Information Owner or Steward; Senior Agency Information Security Officer; Senior Agency Official for Privacy; Chief Acquisition Officer.

System Development Life Cycle Phase: New – Initiation (concept/requirements definition).
Existing – Operations/Maintenance.

Discussion: Stakeholders include individuals, organizations, or representatives that have an interest in the system throughout the system life cycle—for design, development, implementation, delivery, operation, and sustainment of the system. It also includes all aspects of the supply chain. Stakeholders may reside in the same organization or they may reside in different organizations in situations when there is a common interest by those organizations in the information system. For example, this may occur during the development, operation, and maintenance of cloud-based systems, shared service systems, or any system where organizations may be adversely impacted by a breach or a compromise to the system or for a variety of considerations related to the supply chain. Communication among stakeholders is important during every step in the RMF and throughout the SDLC to ensure that security and privacy requirements are satisfied, concerns and issues are addressed expeditiously, and risk management processes are carried out effectively.

References: [SP 800-39] (Organization Level); [SP 800-64]; [SP 800-160 v1] (Stakeholder Needs and Requirements Definition and Portfolio Management Processes); [SP 800-161]; [NIST CSF] (Core [Identify Function]).

ASSET IDENTIFICATION

TASK P-10   Identify assets that require protection.

Potential Inputs: Missions, business functions, and mission/business processes the information system will support; business impact analyses; internal stakeholders; system stakeholder information; system information; information about other systems that interact with the system.

Expected Outputs: Set of assets to be protected.

Primary Responsibility: System Owner.

Supporting Roles: Authorizing Official or Authorizing Official Designated Representative; Mission or Business Owner; Information Owner or Steward; Senior Agency Information Security Officer; Senior Agency Official for Privacy; System Administrator.

System Development Life Cycle Phase: New – Initiation (concept/requirements definition).
                                                     Existing – Operations/Maintenance.

Discussion: Assets are tangible and intangible items that are of value to achievement of mission or business objectives. Tangible assets are physical in nature and include physical/environmental elements (e.g., non-digital information, structures, facilities), human elements, and technology/machine elements (e.g., hardware elements, mechanisms, and networks). In contrast, intangible assets are not physical in nature and include mission and business processes, functions, digital information and data, firmware, software, and services. Information assets can be tangible or intangible assets, and can include the information needed to carry out missions or business functions, to deliver services, and for system management/operation; controlled unclassified information and classified information; and all forms of documentation associated with the information system. Intangible assets can also include the image or reputation of an organization, and the privacy interests of the individuals whose information will be processed by the system. The organization defines the scope of stakeholder assets to be considered for protection. The assets that require protection are identified based on stakeholder concerns and the contexts in which the assets are used. This includes the missions or business functions of the organization; the other systems that interact with the system; and stakeholders whose assets are utilized by the mission or business functions or by the system. Assets can be documented in the system security and privacy plans.

References: [SP 800-39] (Organization Level); [SP 800-64]; [SP 800-160 v1] (Stakeholder Needs and Requirements Definition Process); [IR 8179] (Criticality Analysis Process C); [NIST CSF] (Core [Identify Function]); [NARA CUI].

AUTHORIZATION BOUNDARY

TASK P-11   Determine the authorization boundary of the system.

Potential Inputs: System design documentation; network diagrams; system stakeholder information; asset information; network and/or enterprise architecture diagrams; organizational structure (charts, information).

Expected Outputs: Documented authorization boundary.

Primary Responsibility: Authorizing Official.

Supporting Roles: Chief Information Officer; System Owner; Mission or Business Owner; Senior Agency Information Security Officer; Senior Agency Official for Privacy; Enterprise Architect.

System Development Life Cycle Phase: New – Initiation (concept/requirements definition).
                                                     Existing – Operations/Maintenance.

Discussion: Authorization boundaries establish the scope of protection for information systems (i.e., what the organization agrees to protect under its management control or within the scope of its responsibilities). Authorization boundaries are determined by authorizing officials with input from the system owner based on mission, management, or budgetary responsibility (see Appendix F). A clear delineation of authorization boundaries is important for accountability and for security categorization, especially in situations where lower-impact systems are connected to higher-impact systems, or when external providers are responsible for the operation or maintenance of a system. Each system includes a set of elements (i.e., information resources)[65] organized to achieve one or more purposes and to support the organization's missions and business processes. Each system element is implemented in a way that allows the organization to satisfy specified security and privacy requirements. System elements include human elements, technology/machine elements, and physical/environmental elements.

The term system is used to define the set of system elements, system element interconnections, and the environment that is the focus of the RMF implementation (see Figure 5). The system is included in a single authorization boundary to ensure accountability. For systems processing PII, the privacy and security programs collaborate to develop a common understanding of authorization boundaries. To conduct effective risk assessments and select appropriate controls, privacy and security programs provide a clear and consistent understanding of what constitutes the authorization boundary. Understanding the authorization boundary and what will occur beyond it may influence controls selected and how they are implemented. For example, if a function of the system includes sharing PII externally, robust encryption controls may be selected for PII transmitted from the system.

Similarly, for systems either partially or wholly managed, maintained, or operated by external providers, an agreement clearly describing authorization boundaries ensures accountability. Privacy and security programs collaborate with providers to develop a common understanding of authorization boundaries. Formal agreements with external providers (e.g. contracts) may be used to delineate what constitutes authorization boundaries. Understanding such boundaries facilitates the selection of appropriate controls to manage supply chain risk.

References: [SP 800-18]; [SP 800-39] (System Level); [SP 800-47]; [SP 800-64]; [SP 800-160 v1] (System Requirements Definition Process); [NIST CSF] (Core [Identify Function]).

INFORMATION TYPES

TASK P-12   Identify the types of information to be processed, stored, and transmitted by the system.

Potential Inputs: System design documentation; assets to be protected; mission/business process information; system design documentation.

Expected Outputs: A list of information types for the system.

Primary Responsibility: System Owner; Information Owner or Steward.

Supporting Role: Mission or Business Owner; System Security Officer; System Privacy Officer.[66]

System Development Life Cycle Phase: New – Initiation (concept/requirements definition).
Existing – Operations/Maintenance.

Discussion: Identifying the types of information needed to support organizational missions, business functions, and mission/business processes is an important step in developing security and privacy plans for the system and a precondition for determining the security categorization. [NARA CUI] defines the information types that require protection as part of its Controlled Unclassified Information (CUI) program, in accordance with laws, regulations, or governmentwide policies. Organizations may define additional information types needed to support organizational missions, business functions, and mission/business

---

[65] System elements are implemented via hardware, software, or firmware; physical structures or devices; or people, processes, and procedures. The term *system component* is used to indicate system elements that are implemented specifically via hardware, software, and firmware.

[66] System Privacy Officer is only a primary role when the information system processes PII.

processes that are not defined in the CUI Registry or in [SP 800-60 v2]. Identified information types are confirmed by the information owners or stewards and documented in the system security and privacy plans.

References: [OMB A-130]; [NARA CUI]; [SP 800-39] (System Level); [SP 800-60 v1]; [SP 800-60 v2]; [NIST CSF] (Core [Identify Function]).

INFORMATION LIFE CYCLE

TASK P-13   Identify and understand all stages of the information life cycle for each information type processed, stored, or transmitted by the system.

Potential Inputs: Missions, business functions, and mission/business processes the system will support; system stakeholder information; authorization boundary information; information about other systems that interact with the system (e.g., information exchange/connection agreements); system design documentation; system element information; list of system information types.

Expected Outputs: Documentation of the stages through which information passes in the system, such as a data map or model illustrating how information is structured or is processed by the system throughout its life cycle. Such documentation includes, for example, data flow diagrams, entity relationship diagrams, database schemas, and data dictionaries.

Primary Responsibility: Senior Agency Official for Privacy; System Owner; Information Owner or Steward.

Supporting Roles: Chief Information Officer; Mission or Business Owner; Security Architect; Privacy Architect; Enterprise Architect; Systems Security Engineer; Privacy Engineer.

System Development Life Cycle Phase: New – Initiation (concept/requirements definition).
Existing – Operations/Maintenance.

Discussion: The information life cycle describes the stages through which information passes, typically characterized as creation or collection, processing, dissemination, use, storage, and disposition, to include destruction and deletion [OMB A-130]. Identifying and understanding how each information type is processed during all stages of the life cycle helps organizations identify considerations for protecting the information, informs the organization's security and privacy risk assessments, and informs the selection and implementation of controls. Identification and understanding of the information life cycle facilitates the employment of practices to help ensure, for example, that organizations have the authority to collect or create information, develop rules related to the processing of information in accordance with its impact level, create agreements for information sharing, and follow retention schedules for the storage and disposition of information.

Using tools such as a data map enables organizations to understand how information is being processed so that organizations can better assess where security and privacy risks could arise and where controls could be applied most effectively. It is important for organizations to consider the appropriate delineation of the authorization boundary and the information system's interaction with other systems because the way information enters and leaves the system can affect the security and privacy risk assessments. The elements of the system are identified with sufficient granularity to support such risk assessments.

Identifying and understanding the information life cycle is particularly relevant for the assessment of security and privacy risks since information may be processed by a system in any of the SDLC phases. For example, in the testing and integration phase of the SDLC, processing actual (i.e., live) data would likely raise security and privacy risks, but using substitute (i.e., synthetic) data may allow an equivalent benefit in terms of system testing while reducing risk.

References: [OMB A-130]; [OMB M-13-13]; [NARA RECM]; [NIST CSF] (Core [Identify Function]); [IR 8062].

NIST SP 800-37, REVISION 2

RISK MANAGEMENT FRAMEWORK FOR INFORMATION SYSTEMS AND ORGANIZATIONS
A System Life Cycle Approach for Security and Privacy

RISK ASSESSMENT—SYSTEM

TASK P-14   Conduct a system-level risk assessment and update the risk assessment results on an ongoing basis.

Potential Inputs: Assets to be protected; missions, business functions, and mission/business processes the system will support; business impact analyses or criticality analyses; system stakeholder information; information about other systems that interact with the system; provider information; threat information; data map; system design documentation; Cybersecurity Framework Profiles; risk management strategy; organization-level risk assessment results.

Expected Outputs: Security and privacy risk assessment reports.

Primary Responsibility: System Owner; System Security Officer; System Privacy Officer.

Supporting Roles: Senior Accountable Official for Risk Management or Risk Executive (Function); Authorizing Official or Authorizing Official Designated Representative; Mission or Business Owner; Information Owner or Steward; Control Assessor.

System Development Life Cycle Phase: New – Initiation (concept/requirements definition).
Existing – Operations/Maintenance.

Discussion: This task may require that organizations conduct security and privacy risk assessments to ensure that each type of risk is fully assessed. Assessment of security risk includes identification of threat sources[67] and threat events affecting assets, whether and how the assets are vulnerable to the threats, the likelihood that an asset vulnerability will be exploited by a threat, and the impact (or consequence) of loss of the assets. As a key part of the risk assessment, assets are prioritized based on the adverse impact or consequence of asset loss. The meaning of loss is defined for each asset type to enable a determination of the loss consequence (i.e., the adverse impact of the loss). Loss consequences may be tangible (e.g., monetary, industrial casualties) or intangible (e.g., reputation) and constitute a continuum that spans from partial loss to total loss relative to the asset. Interpretations of information loss may include, for example, loss of possession, destruction, or loss of precision or accuracy. The loss of a function or service may be interpreted as a loss of control, loss of accessibility, loss of the ability to deliver normal function, performance, or behavior, or a limited loss of capability resulting in a level of degradation of function, performance, or behavior. Physical consequences of compromise can include unscheduled production downtime, industrial equipment damage, casualties at the site, environmental disasters and public safety threats. Prioritization of assets is based on asset value, physical consequences, cost of replacement, criticality, impact on image or reputation, or trust by users, by collaborating organizations, or by mission or business partners. The asset priority translates to precedence in allocating resources, determining strength of mechanisms, and defining levels of assurance.

Privacy risk assessments are conducted to determine the likelihood that a given operation the system is taking when processing PII could create an adverse effect on individuals—and the potential impact on individuals.[68] These adverse effects can arise from unauthorized activities that lead to the loss of confidentiality, integrity, or availability in information systems processing PII, or may arise as a byproduct of authorized activities. Privacy risk assessments are influenced by contextual factors. Contextual factors can include, but are not limited to, the sensitivity level of the PII, including specific elements or in aggregate; the types of organizations using or interacting with the system and individuals' perceptions about the organizations with respect to privacy; individuals' understanding about the nature and purpose of the processing; and the privacy interests of individuals, technological expertise or demographic characteristics that influence their understanding or behavior. The privacy risks to individuals may affect

---

[67] In addition, the use of threat intelligence, threat analysis, and threat modelling can help organizations develop the security capabilities necessary to reduce organizational susceptibility to a variety of threats including hostile cyber-attacks, equipment failures, natural disasters, and errors of omission and commission.

[68] [IR 8062] introduces privacy risk management and a privacy risk model for conducting privacy risk assessments.

individuals' decisions to engage with the system thereby impacting mission or business objectives, or create legal liability, reputational risks, or other types of risks for the organization. Impacts to the organization are not privacy risks. However, these impacts can guide and inform organizational decision-making and influence prioritization and resource allocation for risk response.

Risk assessments are also conducted to determine the potential that the use of an external provider for the development, implementation, maintenance, management, operation, or disposition of a system, system element, or service could create a loss, and the potential impact of that loss. The impact may be immediate (e.g., physical theft) or on-going (e.g., the ability of adversaries to replicate critical equipment because of theft). The impact may be endemic (e.g., limited to a single system) or systemic (e.g., including any system that uses a specific type of system component). Supply chain risk assessments consider vulnerabilities which may arise related to the disposition of a system or system element and from the use of external providers. Vulnerabilities in the supply chain may include a lack of traceability or accountability leading to the potential use of counterfeits, insertion of malware, or poor-quality systems. The use of external providers may result in a loss of visibility and control over how systems, system elements, and services are developed, deployed, and maintained. A clear understanding of the threats, vulnerabilities, and potential impacts of an adverse supply chain event can help organizations appropriately balance supply chain risk with risk tolerance. Supply chain risk assessments can include information from supplier audits, reviews, and supply chain intelligence. Organizations develop a strategy for collecting information, including a strategy for collaborating with providers on supply chain risk assessments. Such collaboration helps organizations leverage information from providers, reduce redundancy, identify potential courses of action for risk responses, and reduce the burden on providers.

Risk assessments are conducted throughout the SDLC and support various RMF steps and tasks. Risk assessment results are used to inform security and privacy requirements definition; categorization decisions; the selection, tailoring, implementation, and assessment of controls; authorization decisions; potential courses of action and prioritization for risk responses; and continuous monitoring strategy. Organizations determine the form of risk assessment conducted (including the scope, rigor, and formality of such assessments) and method of reporting results.

References: [FIPS 199]; [FIPS 200]; [SP 800-30]; [SP 800-39] (Organization Level); [SP 800-59]; [SP 800-60 v1]; [SP 800-60 v2]; [SP 800-64]; [SP 800-160 v1] (Stakeholder Needs and Requirements Definition and Risk Management Processes); [SP 800-161] (Assess); [IR 8062]; [IR 8179]; [NIST CSF] (Core [Identify Function]); [CNSSI 1253].

REQUIREMENTS DEFINITION

TASK P-15   Define the security and privacy requirements for the system and the environment of operation.

Potential Inputs: System design documentation; organization- and system-level risk assessment results; known set of stakeholder assets to be protected; missions, business functions, and mission/business processes the system will support; business impact analyses or criticality analyses; system stakeholder information; data map of the information life cycle for PII; Cybersecurity Framework Profiles; information about other systems that interact with the system; supply chain information; threat information; laws, executive orders, directives, regulations, or policies that apply to the system; risk management strategy.

Expected Outputs: Documented security and privacy requirements.

Primary Responsibility: Mission or Business Owner; System Owner; Information Owner or Steward; System Privacy Officer.[69]

---

[69] The system privacy officer is a primary role only when the information system processes PII.

Supporting Roles: Authorizing Official or Authorizing Official Designated Representative; System Security Officer; Senior Agency Information Security Officer; Senior Agency Official for Privacy; Chief Acquisition Officer; Security Architect; Privacy Architect; Enterprise Architect.

System Development Life Cycle Phase: New – Initiation (concept/requirements definition).
Existing – Operations/Maintenance.

Discussion: Protection needs are an expression of the protection capability required for the system in order to reduce security and privacy risk to an acceptable level while supporting mission or business needs. Protection needs include the security characteristics[70] of the system and the security behavior of the system in its intended operational environment and across all system life cycle phases. The protection needs reflect the priorities of stakeholders, results of negotiations among stakeholders in response to conflicts, opposing priorities, contradictions, and stated objectives, and thus, are inherently subjective. The protection needs are documented to help ensure that the reasoning, assumptions, and constraints associated with those needs are available for future reference and to provide traceability to the security and privacy requirements. Security and privacy requirements[71] constitute a formal, more granular expression of protection needs across all SDLC phases, the associated life cycle processes, and protections for the assets associated with the system. Security and privacy requirements are obtained from many sources (e.g., laws, executive orders, directives, regulations, policies, standards, mission and business needs, or risk assessments). Security and privacy requirements are an important part of the formal expression of the required characteristics of the system.[72] The security and privacy requirements guide and inform the selection of controls for a system and the tailoring activities associated with those controls.

Organizations can use the Cybersecurity Framework to manage security and privacy requirements and express those requirements in Cybersecurity Framework *Profiles* defined for the organization. For instance, multiple requirements can be aligned and even deconflicted using the *Function-Category-Subcategory* structure of the Framework Core. The Profiles can then be used to inform the development of organizationally-tailored control baselines described in the RMF *Prepare-Organization Level* step, Task P-4.

References: [SP 800-39] (Organization Level); [SP 800-64]; [SP 800-160 v1] (Stakeholder Needs and Requirements Definition Process); [SP 800-161] (Multi-Tiered Risk Management); [IR 8179]; [NIST CSF] (Core [Protect, Detect, Respond, Recover Functions]; Profiles).

ENTERPRISE ARCHITECTURE

TASK P-16   Determine the placement of the system within the enterprise architecture.

Potential Inputs: Security and privacy requirements; organization- and system-level risk assessment results; enterprise architecture information; security architecture information; privacy architecture information; asset information.

Expected Outputs: Updated enterprise architecture; updated security architecture; updated privacy architecture; plans to use cloud-based systems and shared systems, services, or applications.

---

[70] For example, a fundamental security characteristic is that the system exhibits only specified behaviors, interactions, and outcomes.

[71] The term *requirements* can have discrete meanings. For example, legal and policy requirements impose obligations to which organizations must adhere. Security and privacy requirements, however, are derived from the protection needs for the system and those protection needs can derive from legal or policy requirements, mission or business needs, risk assessments, or other sources.

[72] Security and privacy requirements can also include *assurance* requirements. Assurance is having confidence about the ability of the system to remain trustworthy with respect to security and privacy across all forms of adversity resulting from malicious or non-malicious intent.

Primary Responsibility: Mission or Business Owner; Enterprise Architect; Security Architect; Privacy Architect.

Supporting Roles: Chief Information Officer; Authorizing Official or Authorizing Official Designated Representative; Senior Agency Information Security Officer; Senior Agency Official for Privacy; System Owner; Information Owner or Steward.

System Development Life Cycle Phase: New – Initiation (concept/requirements definition).
Existing – Operations/Maintenance.

Discussion: Enterprise architecture is a management practice used to maximize the effectiveness of mission/business processes and information resources and to achieve mission and business success. An enterprise architecture can provide greater understanding of information and operational technologies included in the initial design and development of information systems and is a prerequisite for achieving resilience and survivability of those systems in an environment of increasingly sophisticated threats. Enterprise architecture also provides an opportunity for organizations to consolidate, standardize, and optimize information and technology assets. An effectively implemented architecture produces systems that are more transparent and therefore, easier to understand and protect. Enterprise architecture also establishes an unambiguous connection from investments to measurable performance improvements. The placement of a system within the enterprise architecture is important as it provides greater visibility and understanding about the other systems (internal and external) that are connected to the system and can also be used to establish security domains for increased levels of protection for the system.

The security architecture and the privacy architecture are integral parts of the enterprise architecture. These architectures represent the parts of the enterprise architecture related to the implementation of security and privacy requirements. The primary purpose of the security and privacy architectures is to ensure that security and privacy requirements are consistently and cost-effectively met in organizational systems and are aligned with the risk management strategy. The security and privacy architectures provide a roadmap that facilitates traceability from the strategic goals and objectives of organizations, through protection needs and security and privacy requirements, to specific security and privacy solutions provided by people, processes, and technologies.

References: [SP 800-39] (Mission/Business Process Level); [SP 800-64]; [SP 800-160 v1] (System Requirements Definition Process); [NIST CSF] (Core [Identify Function]; Profiles); [OMB FEA].

REQUIREMENTS ALLOCATION

TASK P-17   Allocate security and privacy requirements to the system and to the environment of operation.

Potential Inputs: Organization- and system-level risk assessment results; documented security and privacy requirements; organization- and system-level risk assessment results; list of common control providers and common controls available for inheritance; system description; system element information; system component inventory; relevant laws, executive orders, directives, regulations, and policies.

Expected Outputs: List of security and privacy requirements allocated to the system, system elements, and the environment of operation.

Primary Responsibility: Security Architect; Privacy Architect; System Security Officer; System Privacy Officer.

Supporting Roles: Chief Information Officer; Authorizing Official or Authorizing Official Designated Representative; Mission or Business Owner; Senior Agency Information Security Officer; Senior Agency Official for Privacy; System Owner.

System Development Life Cycle Phase: New – Initiation (concept/requirements definition).
Existing – Operations/Maintenance.

Discussion: Security and privacy requirements are allocated to guide and inform control selection and implementation for the organization, system, system elements, and/or environment of operation.[73] Requirements allocation identifies where controls will be implemented. The allocation of requirements conserves resources and helps to streamline the risk management process by ensuring that requirements are not implemented on multiple systems or system elements when implementation of a common control or a system-level control on a specific system element provides the needed protection capability.

References: [SP 800-39] (Organization, Mission/Business Process, and System Levels); [SP 800-64]; [SP 800-160 v1] (System Requirements Definition Process); [NIST CSF] (Core [Identify Function]; Profiles); [OMB FEA].

SYSTEM REGISTRATION

TASK P-18   Register the system with organizational program or management offices.

Potential Inputs: Organizational policy on system registration; system information.

Expected Outputs: Registered system in accordance with organizational policy.

Primary Responsibility: System Owner.

Supporting Role: Mission or Business Owner; Chief Information Officer; System Security Officer; System Privacy Officer.

System Development Life Cycle Phase: New – Initiation (concept/requirements definition).
Existing – Operations/Maintenance.

Discussion: System registration, in accordance with organizational policy, serves to inform the governing organization of plans to develop the system or the existence of the system; the key characteristics of the system; and the expected security and privacy implications for the organization due to the operation and use of the system. System registration provides organizations with a management and tracking tool to facilitate bringing the system into the enterprise architecture, implementation of protections that are commensurate with risk, and security and privacy posture reporting in accordance with applicable laws, executive orders, directives, regulations, policies, or standards. As part of the system registration process, organizations add the system to the organization-wide system inventory. System registration information is updated with security categorization and system characterization information upon completion of the *Categorize* step.

References: None.

---

[73] The environment of operation for an information system refers to the physical surroundings in which the system processes, stores, and transmits information. For example, *security requirements* are allocated to the facilities where the system is located and operates. Those security requirements can be satisfied by the physical security controls in [SP 800-53]

3.2 CATEGORIZE[74]

Purpose

The purpose of the **Categorize** step is to inform organizational risk management processes and tasks by determining the adverse impact to organizational operations and assets, individuals, other organizations, and the Nation with respect to the loss of confidentiality, integrity, and availability of organizational systems and the information processed, stored, and transmitted by those systems.

CATEGORIZE TASKS

Table 3 provides a summary of tasks and expected outcomes for the RMF *Categorize* step. Applicable Cybersecurity Framework constructs are also provided.

TABLE 3: CATEGORIZE TASKS AND OUTCOMES

Tasks	Outcomes
TASK C-1 SYSTEM DESCRIPTION	• The characteristics of the system are described and documented. [*Cybersecurity Framework:* **Profile**]
TASK C-2 SECURITY CATEGORIZATION	• A security categorization of the system, including the information processed by the system represented by the organization-identified information types, is completed. [*Cybersecurity Framework:* **ID.AM-1; ID.AM-2; ID.AM-3; ID.AM-4; ID.AM-5**] • Security categorization results are documented in the security, privacy, and SCRM plans. [*Cybersecurity Framework:* **Profile**] • Security categorization results are consistent with the enterprise architecture and commitment to protecting organizational missions, business functions, and mission/business processes. [*Cybersecurity Framework:* **Profile**] • Security categorization results reflect the organization's risk management strategy.
TASK C-3 SECURITY CATEGORIZATION REVIEW AND APPROVAL	• The security categorization results are reviewed and the categorization decision is approved by senior leaders in the organization.

Quick link to summary table for RMF tasks, responsibilities, and supporting roles.

SYSTEM DESCRIPTION

TASK C-1   Document the characteristics of the system.

Potential Inputs: System design and requirements documentation; authorization boundary information; list of security and privacy requirements allocated to the system, system elements, and the environment

---

[74] The RMF *Categorize* step is a precondition for the selection of security controls. However, for privacy, there are other factors considered by organizations that guide and inform the selection of privacy controls. These factors are described in the RMF *Prepare-System Level* step, Task P-15.

of operation; physical or other processes controlled by system elements; system element information; system component inventory; system element supply chain information, including inventory and supplier information; security categorization; data map of the information life cycle for information types processed, stored, and transmitted by the system; information on system use, users, and roles.

Expected Outputs: Documented system description.

Primary Responsibility: System Owner.

Supporting Roles: Authorizing Official or Authorizing Official Designated Representative; Information Owner or Steward; System Security Officer; System Privacy Officer.

System Development Life Cycle Phase: New – Initiation (concept/requirements definition).
Existing – Operations/Maintenance.

Discussion: A description of the system characteristics is documented in the security and privacy plans, included in attachments to the plans, or referenced in other standard sources for the information generated as part of the SDLC. Duplication of information is avoided, whenever possible. The level of detail in the security and privacy plans is determined by the organization and is commensurate with the security categorization and the security and privacy risk assessments of the system. Information may be added to or updated in the system description as it becomes available during the system life cycle, during the execution of the RMF steps, and as any system characteristics change.

Examples of different types of descriptive information that organizations can include in security and privacy plans include: descriptive name of the system and system identifier; system version or release number; manufacturer and supplier information; individual responsible for the system; system contact information; organization that manages, owns, or controls the system; system location; purpose of the system and missions/business processes supported; how the system is integrated into the enterprise architecture; SDLC phase; results of the categorization process and privacy risk assessment; authorization boundary; laws, directives, policies, regulations, or standards affecting individuals' privacy and the security of the system; architectural description of the system including network topology; information types; hardware, firmware, and software components that are part of the system; hardware, software, and system interfaces (internal and external); information flows within the system; network connection rules for communicating with external systems; interconnected systems and identifiers for those systems; physical or other processes, components and equipment controlled by system elements; system users (including affiliations, access rights, privileges, citizenship); system provenance in the supply chain; maintenance or other relevant agreements; potential suppliers for replacement components for the system; alternative compatible system components; number and location in inventory of replacement system components; ownership or operation of the system (government-owned, government-operated; government-owned, contractor-operated; contractor-owned, contractor-operated; nonfederal [state and local governments, grantees]); incident response points of contact; authorization date and authorization termination date; and ongoing authorization status. System registration information is updated with the system characterization information (see Task P-18).

References: [SP 800-18]; [NIST CSF] (Core [Identify Function]).

SECURITY CATEGORIZATION

TASK C-2 Categorize the system and document the security categorization results.

Potential Inputs: Risk management strategy; organizational risk tolerance; authorization boundary (i.e., system) information; organization- and system-level risk assessment results; information types processed, stored, or transmitted by the system; list of security and privacy requirements allocated to the system, system elements, and environment of operation; organizational authority or purpose for operating the system; business impact analyses or criticality analyses; information about missions, business functions, and mission/business processes supported by the system.

Expected Outputs: Impact levels determined for each information type and for each security objective (confidentiality, integrity, availability); security categorization based on high-water mark of information type impact levels.

Primary Responsibility: System Owner; Information Owner or Steward.

Supporting Roles: Senior Accountable Official for Risk Management or Risk Executive (Function); Chief Information Officer; Senior Agency Information Security Officer; Senior Agency Official for Privacy; Authorizing Official or Authorizing Official Designated Representative; System Security Officer; System Privacy Officer.

System Development Life Cycle Phase: New – Initiation (concept/requirements definition).
Existing – Operations/Maintenance.

Discussion: Security categorization determinations consider potential adverse impacts to organizational operations, organizational assets, individuals, other organizations, and the Nation resulting from the loss of confidentiality, integrity, or availability of information. Organizations have flexibility in conducting a security categorization using either [FIPS 200] to establish a single impact level for a system based on the high-water mark concept (for other than national security systems), or [CNSSI 1253] to establish three impact values that may vary for each of the security objectives of confidentiality, integrity, and availability (for national security systems). The security categorization process is carried out by the system owner and the information owner or steward in cooperation and collaboration with senior leaders and executives with mission, business function, or risk management responsibilities. Cooperation and collaboration helps to ensure that individual systems are categorized based on the mission and business objectives of the organization. The system owner and information owner or steward consider the results from the security risk assessment (and the privacy risk assessment when the system processes PII) as a part of the security categorization decision. The decision is consistent with the risk management strategy. The results of the categorization process influence the selection of security controls for the system. Security categorization information is documented in the system security plan or included as an attachment to the plan and can be cross-referenced in a privacy plan when the system processes PII.

The security categorization results for the system can be further refined by the organization to facilitate an impact-level prioritization of systems with the same impact level (see Task P-6). Results from the impact-level prioritization conducted by the organization can be used to help system owners in control selection and tailoring decisions.

References: [FIPS 199]; [FIPS 200]; [SP 800-30]; [SP 800-39] (System Level); [SP 800-59]; [SP 800-60 v1]; [SP 800-60 v2]; [SP 800-160 v1] (Stakeholder Needs and Requirements Definition and System Requirements Definition Processes); [IR 8179]; [CNSSI 1253]; [NIST CSF] (Core [Identify Function]).

SECURITY CATEGORIZATION REVIEW AND APPROVAL

TASK C-3   Review and approve the security categorization results and decision.

Potential Inputs: Impact levels determined for each information type and for each security objective (confidentiality, integrity, availability); security categorization based on high-water mark of information type impact levels; list of high value assets for the organization.

Expected Outputs: Approval of security categorization for the system.

Primary Responsibility: Authorizing Official or Authorizing Official Designated Representative; Senior Agency Official for Privacy.[75]

---

[75] The senior agency official for privacy participates in determining whether the information processed by the information system is considered PII, and is involved in reviewing and approving the categorization for such systems.

Supporting Roles: Senior Accountable Official for Risk Management or Risk Executive (Function); Chief Information Officer; Senior Agency Information Security Officer.

System Development Life Cycle Phase: New – Initiation (concept/requirements definition).
Existing – Operations/Maintenance.

Discussion: For information systems that process PII, the senior agency official for privacy reviews and approves the security categorization results and decision prior to the authorizing official's review.[76] Security categorization results and decisions are reviewed by the authorizing official or a designated representative to ensure that the security category selected for the information system is consistent with the mission and business functions of the organization and the need to adequately protect those missions and functions. The authorizing official or designated representative reviews the categorization results and decision from an organization-wide perspective, including how the decision aligns with the categorization decisions for all other organizational systems. The authorizing official collaborates with the senior accountable official for risk management or the risk executive (function) to ensure that the categorization decision for the system is consistent with the organizational risk management strategy and satisfies requirements for high value assets. As part of the approval process, the authorizing official can provide specific guidance to the system owner with respect to any limitations on baseline tailoring activities for the system that occur at the RMF *Select* step (see Task S-2). If the security categorization decision is not approved, the system owner initiates steps to repeat the categorization process and resubmits the adjusted results to the authorizing official or designated representative. System registration information is subsequently updated with the approved security categorization information (see Task P-18).

References: [FIPS 199]; [SP 800-30]; [SP 800-39] (Organization Level); [SP 800-160 v1] (Stakeholder Needs and Requirements Definition Process); [CNSSI 1253]; [NIST CSF] (Core [Identify Function]).

---

[76] The responsibilities of the senior agency official for privacy are detailed in [OMB A-130].

3.3 SELECT

Purpose

The purpose of the *Select* step is to select, tailor, and document the controls necessary to protect the information system and organization commensurate with risk to organizational operations and assets, individuals, other organizations, and the Nation.

SELECT TASKS

Table 4 provides a summary of tasks and expected outcomes for the RMF *Select* step. Applicable Cybersecurity Framework constructs are also provided.

TABLE 4: SELECT TASKS AND OUTCOMES

Tasks	Outcomes
TASK S-1 CONTROL SELECTION	• Control baselines necessary to protect the system commensurate with risk are selected. [Cybersecurity Framework: Profile]
TASK S-2 CONTROL TAILORING	• Controls are tailored producing tailored control baselines. [Cybersecurity Framework: Profile]
TASK S-3 CONTROL ALLOCATION	• Controls are designated as system-specific, hybrid, or common controls. • Controls are allocated to the specific system elements (i.e., machine, physical, or human elements). [Cybersecurity Framework: Profile; PR.IP]
TASK S-4 DOCUMENTATION OF PLANNED CONTROL IMPLEMENTATIONS	• Controls and associated tailoring actions are documented in security and privacy plans or equivalent documents. [Cybersecurity Framework: Profile]
TASK S-5 CONTINUOUS MONITORING STRATEGY—SYSTEM	• A continuous monitoring strategy for the system that reflects the organizational risk management strategy is developed. [Cybersecurity Framework: ID.GV; DE.CM]
TASK S-6 PLAN REVIEW AND APPROVAL	• Security and privacy plans reflecting the selection of controls necessary to protect the system and the environment of operation commensurate with risk are reviewed and approved by the authorizing official.

Quick link to summary table for RMF tasks, responsibilities, and supporting roles.

CONTROL SELECTION

TASK S-1   Select the controls for the system and the environment of operation.

Potential Inputs: Security categorization; organization- and system-level risk assessment results; system element information; system component inventory; list of security and privacy requirements allocated to the system, system elements, and environment of operation; list of contractual requirements allocated to external providers of the system or system element; business impact analysis or criticality analysis; risk management strategy; organizational security and privacy policy; federal or organization-approved or mandated baselines or overlays; Cybersecurity Framework Profiles.

Expected Outputs: Controls selected for the system and the environment of operation.

Primary Responsibility: System Owner; Common Control Provider.

Supporting Roles: Authorizing Official or Authorizing Official Designated Representative; Information Owner or Steward; Systems Security Engineer; Privacy Engineer; System Security Officer; System Privacy Officer.

System Development Life Cycle Phase: New – Development/Acquisition.
                                        Existing – Operations/Maintenance.

Discussion: There are two approaches that can be used for the initial selection of controls: a *baseline* control selection approach, or an *organization-generated* control selection approach. The baseline control selection approach uses control baselines, which are pre-defined sets of controls specifically assembled to address the protection needs of a group, organization, or community of interest. Control baselines serve as a starting point for the protection of individuals' privacy, information, and information systems. Federal control baselines are provided in [SP 800-53B]. The system security categorization (see Task C-2) and the security requirements derived from stakeholder protection needs, laws, executive orders, regulations, policies, directives, instructions, and standards (see Task P-15) can help inform the selection of security control baselines. A privacy risk assessment (see Task P-14) and privacy requirements derived from stakeholder protection needs, laws, executive orders, regulations, policies, directives, instructions, and standards (see Task P-15) can help inform the selection of privacy control baselines. Privacy programs use security and privacy control baselines to manage the privacy risks arising from both unauthorized system activity or behavior, as well as from authorized activities. After the pre-defined control baseline is selected, organizations tailor the baseline in accordance with the guidance provided (see Task S-2). The baseline control selection approach can provide consistency across a broad community of interest.

The organization-generated control selection approach differs from the baseline selection approach because the organization does not start with a pre-defined set of controls. Rather, the organization uses its own selection process to select controls. This may be necessary when the system is highly specialized (e.g., a weapons system or a medical device) or has limited purpose or scope (e.g., a smart meter). In these situations, it may be more efficient and cost-effective for an organization to select a specific set of controls for the system (i.e., a bottom-up approach) instead of starting with a pre-defined set of controls from a broad-based control baseline and subsequently eliminating controls through the tailoring process (i.e., top-down approach).

In both the baseline control selection approach and organization-generated control selection approach, organizations develop a well-defined set of security and privacy requirements using a life cycle-based systems engineering process (e.g., [ISO 15288] and [SP 800-160 v1] as described in the RMF *Prepare-System Level* step, Task P-15. This process generates a set of requirements that can be used to guide and inform the selection of a set of controls to satisfy the requirements (whether the organization starts with a control baseline or generates the set of controls from its own selection process). Similarly, organizations can use the [NIST CSF] to develop Cybersecurity Framework *Profiles* representing a set of organization-specific security and privacy requirements—and thus, guiding and informing control selection from [SP 800-53]. Tailoring may also be required in the organization-generated control selection approach (see Task S-2). Organizations do not need to choose one approach for the selection of controls for each of their systems, but instead, may use different approaches as circumstances dictate.

References: [FIPS 199]; [FIPS 200]; [SP 800-30]; [SP 800-53]; [SP 800-53B]; [SP 800-160 v1] (System Requirements Definition, Architecture Definition, and Design Definition Processes); [SP 800-161] (Respond and Chapter 3); [IR 8062]; [IR 8179]; [CNSSI 1253]; [NIST CSF] (Core [Identify, Protect, Detect, Respond, Recover Functions]; Profiles).

CONTROL TAILORING

TASK S-2   Tailor the controls selected for the system and the environment of operation.

Potential Inputs: Initial control baselines; organization- and system-level risk assessment results; system element information; system component inventory; list of security and privacy requirements allocated to the system, system elements, and environment of operation; business impact analysis or criticality analysis; risk management strategy; organizational security and privacy policies; federal or organization-approved or mandated overlays.

Expected Outputs: List of tailored controls for the system and environment of operation (i.e., tailored control baselines).

Primary Responsibility: System Owner; Common Control Provider.

Supporting Roles: Authorizing Official or Authorizing Official Designated Representative; Information Owner or Steward; Systems Security Engineer; Privacy Engineer; System Security Officer; System Privacy Officer.

System Development Life Cycle Phase: New – Development/Acquisition.
Existing – Operations/Maintenance.

Discussion: After selecting the applicable control baselines, organizations tailor the controls based on various factors (e.g., missions or business functions, threats, security and privacy risks (including supply chain risks), type of system, or risk tolerance). The tailoring process includes identifying and designating common controls in the control baselines (see Task P-5); applying scoping considerations to the remaining baseline controls; selecting compensating controls, if needed; assigning values to organization-defined control parameters using either assignment or selection statements; supplementing baselines with additional controls; and providing specification information for control implementation.[77] Organizations determine the amount of detail to include in justifications or supporting rationale required for tailoring decisions. For example, the justification or supporting rationale for scoping decisions related to a high-impact system or high value asset[78] may necessitate greater specificity than similar decisions for a low-impact system. Such determinations are consistent with the organization's missions and business functions; stakeholder needs; and any relevant laws, executive orders, regulations, directives, or policies. Controls related to the SDLC and SCRM provide the basis for determining whether an information system is fit-for-purpose[79] and need to be tailored accordingly.

Organizations use risk assessments to inform and guide the tailoring process. Threat information from security risk assessments provides information on adversary capabilities, intent, and targeting that may affect organizational decisions regarding the selection of security controls, including the associated costs and benefits. Privacy risk assessments, including the contextual factors therein, will also influence tailoring when an information system processes PII.[80] Risk assessment results are also leveraged when identifying common controls to determine if the controls available for inheritance meet the security and privacy requirements for the system and its environment of operation. When common controls provided by the organization do not provide adequate protection for the systems inheriting the controls, system owners can either supplement the common controls with system-specific or hybrid controls to achieve the required level of protection or recommend a greater acceptance of risk to the authorizing official. Organizations may also consider federally or organizationally directed or approved overlays, tailored baselines, or Cybersecurity Framework Profiles when tailoring controls (see Task P-4).

References: [FIPS 199]; [FIPS 200]; [SP 800-30]; [SP 800-53]; [SP 800-53B]; [SP 800-160 v1] (System Requirements Definition, Architecture Definition, and Design Definition Processes); [SP 800-161] (Respond

---

[77] The tailoring process is fully described in [SP 800-53B].

[78] For more information on high value assets, see [OMB M-19-03] and [OCIO HVA].

[79] [ISO 15288] describes *fit-for-purpose* as an outcome from the validation process in the SDLC that demonstrates, through assessment of the services presented to the stakeholders, that the "right" system has been created and satisfies the customer need.

[80] [IR 8062] provides a discussion of context and its function in a privacy risk model.

and Chapter 3); [IR 8179]; [CNSSI 1253]; [NIST CSF] (Core [Identify, Protect, Detect, Respond, Recover Functions]; Profiles).

CONTROL ALLOCATION

TASK S-3 Allocate security and privacy controls to the system and to the environment of operation.

Potential Inputs: Security categorization; organization- and system-level risk assessment results; organizational policy on system registration; enterprise architecture; security and privacy architectures; security and privacy requirements; list of security and privacy requirements allocated to the system, system elements, and the environment of operation; list of common control providers and common controls available for inheritance; system description; system element information; system component inventory; relevant laws, executive orders, directives, regulations, and policies.

Expected Outputs: List of security and privacy controls allocated to the system, system elements, and the environment of operation.

Primary Responsibility: Security Architect; Privacy Architect; System Security Officer; System Privacy Officer.

Supporting Roles: Chief Information Officer; Authorizing Official or Authorizing Official Designated Representative; Mission or Business Owner; Senior Agency Information Security Officer; Senior Agency Official for Privacy; System Owner.

System Development Life Cycle Phase: New – Initiation (concept/requirements definition).
                                       Existing – Operations/Maintenance.

Discussion: The organization designates controls as system-specific, hybrid, or common, and allocates the controls to the system elements (i.e, machine, physical, or human elements) responsible for providing a security or privacy capability. Controls are allocated to a system or an organization consistent with the organization's enterprise architecture and security or privacy architecture and the allocated security and privacy requirements. Not all controls need to be allocated to every system element. Controls providing a specific security or privacy capability are only allocated to system elements that require that capability. The security categorization, privacy risk assessment, security and privacy architectures, and the allocation of controls work together to help achieve a suitable balance between security and privacy protections and the mission-based function of the system.

Security and privacy requirements allocated to the system, system elements, and the environment of operation (see Task P-17) guide and inform control allocation to system elements. Common controls that are made available by the organization during the RMF *Prepare-Organization Level* step (see Task P-5), are selected for inheritance; hybrid controls are also selected. Common controls satisfy security and privacy requirements allocated to the organization and provide a protection capability that is inherited by one or more systems. Hybrid controls satisfy security and privacy requirements allocated to the system and to the organization and provide a protection capability that is partially inherited by one or more systems. And finally, system-specific controls satisfy security and privacy requirements allocated to the system and provide a protection capability for that system. Controls can be allocated to specific system elements rather than to every element within a system. For example, system-specific controls associated with management of audit logs may be allocated to a log management server and need not be implemented on every system element.

References: [SP 800-39] (Organization, Mission/Business Process, and System Levels); [SP 800-64]; [SP 800-160 v1] (System Requirements Definition, Architecture Definition, and Design Definition Processes); [NIST CSF] (Core [Identify Function]; Profiles); [OMB FEA].

DOCUMENTATION OF PLANNED CONTROL IMPLEMENTATIONS

<u>TASK S-4</u> Document the controls for the system and environment of operation in security and privacy plans.

Potential Inputs: Security categorization; organization- and system-level risk assessment results (security, privacy, and/or supply chain); system element information; system component inventory; business impact or criticality analysis; list of security and privacy requirements allocated to the system, system elements, and environment of operation; risk management strategy; list of selected controls for the system and environment of operation; organizational security, privacy, and SCRM policies.

Expected Outputs: Security and privacy plans for the system.

Primary Responsibility: <u>System Owner</u>; <u>Common Control Provider</u>.

Supporting Roles: <u>Authorizing Official</u> or <u>Authorizing Official Designated Representative</u>; <u>Information Owner or Steward</u>; <u>Systems Security Engineer</u>; <u>Privacy Engineer</u>; <u>System Security Officer</u>; <u>System Privacy Officer</u>.

System Development Life Cycle Phase: New – Development/Acquisition.
Existing – Operations/Maintenance.

Discussion: Security and privacy plans contain an overview of the security and privacy requirements for the system and the controls selected to satisfy the requirements. The plans describe the intended application of each selected control in the context of the system with a sufficient level of detail to correctly implement the control and to subsequently assess the effectiveness of the control. The control documentation describes how system-specific and hybrid controls are implemented and the plans and expectations regarding the functionality of the system. The description includes planned inputs, expected behavior, and expected outputs where appropriate, typically for those controls implemented in the hardware, software, or firmware components of the system. Common controls are also identified in the plans. There is no requirement to provide implementation details for inherited common controls. Rather, those details are provided in the plans for common control providers and are made available to system owners. For hybrid controls, the organization specifies in the system-level plans the parts of the control that are provided by the common control provider and the parts of the control that are implemented at the system level.

Organizations may develop a consolidated plan that incorporates security and privacy plans or maintain separate plans. If developing a consolidated plan, privacy programs collaborate with security programs to ensure that the plan reflects the selection of controls that provide protections with respect to managing the confidentiality, integrity, and availability of PII; and delineates roles and responsibilities for control implementation, assessment, and monitoring. For separate system security plans and privacy plans, organizations cross-reference the controls in all plans to help maintain accountability and awareness. The senior agency official for privacy reviews and approves the privacy plan (or integrated plan) before the plan is provided to the authorizing official or designated representative for review (see <u>Task S-6</u>). Organizations may document the control selection and tailoring information in documents equivalent to security and privacy plans, for example, in systems engineering or system life cycle artifacts or documents.

Documentation of planned control implementations allows for traceability of decisions prior to and after the deployment of the system. To the extent possible, organizations reference existing documentation (either by vendors or other organizations that have employed the same or similar systems or system elements), use automated support tools, and coordinate across the organization to reduce redundancy and increase the efficiency and cost-effectiveness of control documentation. The documentation also addresses platform dependencies and includes any additional information necessary to describe how the capability required is to be achieved at the level of detail sufficient to support control implementation and assessment. Documentation for control implementations follows best practices for hardware and software development and for systems security and privacy engineering disciplines and is also consistent with established policies and procedures for documenting activities in the SDLC. In certain situations, security controls can be implemented in ways that create privacy risks. The privacy program supports documentation of privacy risk considerations and the implementations intended to mitigate them.

For controls that are mechanism-based, organizations take advantage of the functional specifications provided by or obtainable from manufacturers, vendors, and systems integrators. This includes any documentation that may assist the organization during the development, implementation, assessment, and monitoring of controls. For certain controls, organizations obtain control implementation information from the appropriate organizational entities (e.g., physical security offices, facilities offices, records management offices, and human resource offices). Since the enterprise architecture and the security and privacy architectures established by the organization guide and inform the organizational approach used to plan for and implement controls, documenting the process helps to ensure traceability in meeting the security and privacy requirements.

References: [FIPS 199]; [FIPS 200]; [SP 800-18]; [SP 800-30]; [SP 800-53]; [SP 800-64]; [SP 800-160 v1] (System Requirements Definition, Architecture Definition, and Design Definition Processes); [SP 800-161] (Respond and Chapter 3); [IR 8179]; [CNSSI 1253]; [NIST CSF] (Core [Identify, Protect, Detect, Respond, Recover Functions]; Profiles).

CONTINUOUS MONITORING STRATEGY—SYSTEM

<u>TASK S-5</u> Develop and implement a system-level strategy for monitoring control effectiveness that is consistent with and supplements the organizational continuous monitoring strategy.

Potential Inputs: Organizational risk management strategy; organizational continuous monitoring strategy; organization- and system-level risk assessment results; security and privacy plans; organizational security and privacy policies.

Expected Outputs: Continuous monitoring strategy for the system including time-based trigger for ongoing authorization.

Primary Responsibility: System Owner; Common Control Provider.

Supporting Roles: Senior Accountable Official for Risk Management or Risk Executive (Function); Chief Information Officer; Senior Agency Information Security Officer; Senior Agency Official for Privacy; Authorizing Official or Authorizing Official Designated Representative; Information Owner or Steward; Security Architect; Privacy Architect; Systems Security Engineer; Privacy Engineer; System Security Officer; System Privacy Officer.

System Development Life Cycle Phase: New – Development/Acquisition.
Existing – Operations/Maintenance.

Discussion: An important aspect of risk management is the ongoing monitoring of controls implemented within or inherited by an information system. An effective continuous monitoring strategy at the system level is developed and implemented in coordination with the organizational continuous monitoring strategy early in the SDLC (i.e., during initial system design or procurement decision). The system-level continuous monitoring strategy is consistent with and supplements the continuous monitoring strategy for the organization. The system-level strategy addresses monitoring those controls for which monitoring is not provided as part of the continuous monitoring strategy and implementation for the organization. The system-level strategy identifies the frequency of monitoring for controls not addressed by the organization-level strategy and defines the approach to be used for assessing those controls. The system-level continuous monitoring strategy, consistent with the organizational monitoring strategy, defines how changes to the system and the environment of operation[81] are to be monitored; how risk assessments are

---

[81] Changes to the operating environment (including the supply chain) may create vulnerabilities (e.g., availability of software patches, changes in supplier ownership providing services, maintenance, repair parts or other support).

to be conducted; and the security and privacy posture reporting requirements including recipients of the reports. The system-level continuous monitoring strategy can be included in security and privacy plans.[82]

For controls that are not addressed by the organizational continuous monitoring strategy, the system-level continuous monitoring strategy identifies the criteria for determining the frequency with which controls are monitored post-implementation and the plan for the ongoing assessment of those controls. The criteria are established by the system owner or common control provider in collaboration with other organizational officials (e.g., the authorizing official or designated representative; senior accountable official for risk management or risk executive [function]; senior agency information security officer; senior agency official for privacy; and chief information officer). The frequency criteria at the system level reflect organizational priorities and the importance of the system to the organization's operations and assets, individuals, other organizations, and the Nation. Controls that are volatile (i.e., where the control or the control implementation is most likely to change over time),[83] critical to certain aspects of the protection needs for the organization, or identified in plans of action and milestones, may require more frequent assessment. The approach to control assessments during continuous monitoring may include reuse of assessment procedures and results that supported the initial authorization decision; detection of the status of system elements; and analysis of historical and operational data.

The authorizing official or designated representative approves the continuous monitoring strategy and the minimum frequency with which each control is to be monitored. The approval of the strategy can be obtained in conjunction with the security and privacy plan approval. The monitoring of controls begins at the start of the operational phase of the SDLC and continues through the disposal phase.

References: [SP 800-30]; [SP 800-39] (Organization, Mission or Business Process, System Levels); [SP 800-53]; [SP 800-53A]; [SP 800-137]; [SP 800-161]; [IR 8011 v1]; [CNSSI 1253]; [NIST CSF] (Core [Detect Function]).

PLAN REVIEW AND APPROVAL

TASK S-6   Review and approve the security and privacy plans for the system and the environment of operation.

Potential Inputs: Security and privacy plans; organization- and system-level risk assessment results.

Expected Outputs: Security and privacy plans approved by the authorizing official.

Primary Responsibility: Authorizing Official or Authorizing Official Designated Representative.

Supporting Roles: Senior Accountable Official for Risk Management or Risk Executive (Function); Chief Information Officer; Chief Acquisition Officer; Senior Agency Information Security Officer; Senior Agency Official for Privacy.

System Development Life Cycle Phase: New – Development/Acquisition.
         Existing – Operations/Maintenance.

---

[82] The Privacy Continuous Monitoring (PCM) strategy includes all of the available privacy controls implemented throughout the organization at all risk management levels (i.e., organization, mission/business process, and system). The strategy ensures that the controls are monitored on an ongoing basis by assigning an organization-defined assessment frequency to each control that is sufficient to ensure compliance with applicable privacy requirements and to manage privacy risks. If, during the development of a new system, there is a need to create or use a privacy control not included in the PCM strategy, the senior agency official for privacy is consulted to determine whether it is appropriate for the proposed use case. If there is a decision to implement a new privacy control, the organization's PCM strategy is updated to include the new control with an organization-defined monitoring frequency.

[83] Volatility is most prevalent in those controls implemented in the hardware, software and firmware elements of the system. For example, replacing or upgrading an operating system, a database system, application, or a network router may change the security controls provided by the vendor or original equipment manufacturer. Configuration settings may also require adjustments as organizational missions, business functions, threats, risks, and risk tolerance change.

Discussion: The security and privacy plan review by the authorizing official or designated representative with support from the senior accountable official for risk management or risk executive (function), chief information officer, senior agency information security officer, and senior agency official for privacy, determines if the plans are complete, consistent, and satisfy the stated security and privacy requirements for the system. Based on the results from this review, the authorizing official or designated representative may recommend changes to the security and privacy plans. If the plans are unacceptable, the system owner or common control provider make appropriate changes to the plans. If the plans are acceptable, the authorizing official or designated representative approves the plans.

The acceptance of the security and privacy plans represents an important milestone in the SDLC and risk management process. The authorizing official or designated representative, by approving the plans, agrees to the set of controls (i.e., system-specific, hybrid, or common controls) and the description of the proposed implementation of the controls to meet the security and privacy requirements for the system and the environment in which the system operates.[84] The approval of the plans allows the risk management process to proceed to the RMF *Implement* step. The approval of the plans also establishes the level of effort required to successfully complete the remainder of the RMF steps and provides the basis of the security and privacy specifications for the acquisition of the system or individual system elements.

References: [SP 800-30]; [SP 800-53]; [SP 800-160 v1] (System Requirements Definition, Architecture Definition, and Design Definition Processes).

---

[84] After the initial review and approval of the system security plan by the authorizing official, any subsequent authorization-related actions (e.g., reauthorizations or ongoing authorizations) provide an inherent review and approval of the system security plan since it is included in the authorization package.

3.4 IMPLEMENT

<table>
<tr><td>Purpose</td></tr>
<tr><td>The purpose of the Implement step is to implement the controls in the security and privacy plans for the system and for the organization and to document in a baseline configuration, the specific details of the control implementation.</td></tr>
</table>

IMPLEMENT TASKS

Table 5 provides a summary of tasks and expected outcomes for the RMF *Implement* step. Applicable Cybersecurity Framework constructs are also provided.

TABLE 5: IMPLEMENT TASKS AND OUTCOMES

Tasks	Outcomes
TASK I-1 CONTROL IMPLEMENTATION	• Controls specified in the security and privacy plans are implemented. [*Cybersecurity Framework*: PR.IP-1] • Systems security and privacy engineering methodologies are used to implement the controls in the system security and privacy plans. [*Cybersecurity Framework*: PR.IP-2]
TASK I-2 UPDATE CONTROL IMPLEMENTATION INFORMATION	• Changes to the planned implementation of controls are documented. [*Cybersecurity Framework*: PR.IP-1] • The security and privacy plans are updated based on information obtained during the implementation of the controls. [*Cybersecurity Framework*: Profile]

<u>Quick link to summary table for RMF tasks, responsibilities, and supporting roles.</u>

CONTROL IMPLEMENTATION

<u>TASK I-1</u>   Implement the controls in the security and privacy plans.

Potential Inputs: Approved security and privacy plans; system design documents; organizational security and privacy policies and procedures; business impact or criticality analyses; enterprise architecture information; security architecture information; privacy architecture information; list of security and privacy requirements allocated to the system, system elements; and environment of operation; system element information; system component inventory; organization- and system-level risk assessment results.

Expected Outputs: Implemented controls.

Primary Responsibility: System Owner; Common Control Provider.

Supporting Roles: Information Owner or Steward; Security Architect; Privacy Architect; Systems Security Engineer; Privacy Engineer; System Security Officer; System Privacy Officer; Enterprise Architect; System Administrator.

System Development Life Cycle Phase: New – Development/Acquisition; Implementation/Assessment.
Existing – Operations/Maintenance.

Discussion: Organizations implement the controls as described in the security and privacy plans. The control implementation is consistent with the organization's enterprise architecture and associated security and privacy architectures. Organizations use best practices when implementing controls, including systems security and privacy engineering methodologies, concepts, and principles. Risk assessments guide and inform decisions regarding the cost, benefit, and risk trade-offs in using different technologies or policies for control implementation. Organizations also ensure that mandatory configuration settings are established and implemented on system elements in accordance with federal and organizational policies. When organizations have no direct control over what controls are implemented in a system element, for example, in commercial off-the-shelf products, organizations consider the use of system elements that have been tested, evaluated, or validated by approved, independent, third-party assessment facilities (e.g., NIST Cryptographic Module Validation Program Testing Laboratories, National Information Assurance Partnership Common Criteria Testing Laboratories). The tests, evaluations, and validations consider products in specific configurations and in isolation; control implementation addresses how the product is integrated into the system while preserving security functionality and assurance.

Organizations also address, where applicable, assurance requirements when implementing controls. Assurance requirements are directed at the activities that control developers and implementers carry out to increase the level of confidence that the controls are implemented correctly, operating as intended, and producing the desired outcome with respect to meeting the security and privacy requirements for the system. The assurance requirements address quality of the design, development, and implementation of the controls.[85]

For the common controls inherited by the system, systems security and privacy engineers with support from system security and privacy officers, coordinate with the common control provider to determine the most appropriate way to implement common controls. System owners can refer to the authorization packages prepared by common control providers when making determinations regarding the adequacy of common controls inherited by their systems. During implementation, it may be determined that common controls previously selected to be inherited by the system do not meet the specified security or privacy requirements for the system. For common controls that do not meet the requirements for the system inheriting the controls or when common controls have unacceptable deficiencies, the system owners identify compensating or supplementary controls to be implemented. System owners can supplement the common controls with system-specific or hybrid controls to achieve the required protection for their systems or they can accept greater risk with the acknowledgement and approval of the organization. Risk assessments may determine how gaps in security or privacy requirements between systems and common controls affect the risk associated with the system, and how to prioritize the need for compensating or supplementary controls to mitigate specific risks.

Consistent with the flexibility allowed in applying the tasks in the RMF, organizations conduct initial control assessments during system development and implementation. Conducting such assessments in parallel with the development and implementation phases of the SDLC facilitates early identification of deficiencies and provides a cost-effective method for initiating corrective actions. Issues discovered during these assessments can be referred to authorizing officials for resolution. The results of the initial control assessments can also be used during the authorize step to avoid delays or costly repetition of assessments. Assessment results that are subsequently reused in other phases of the SDLC meet the reuse requirements established by the organization.[86]

---

[85] [SP 800-53] provides a list of assurance-related security and privacy controls.

[86] See the RMF *Assess* step and [SP 800-53A] for information on assessments and reuse of assessment results.

References: [FIPS 200]; [SP 800-30]; [SP 800-53]; [SP 800-53A]; [SP 800-160 v1] (Implementation, Integration, Verification, and Transition Processes); [SP 800-161]; [IR 8062]; [IR 8179].

UPDATE CONTROL IMPLEMENTATION INFORMATION

TASK I-2 Document changes to planned control implementations based on the "as-implemented" state of controls.

Potential Inputs: Security and privacy plans; information from control implementation efforts.

Expected Outputs: Security and privacy plans updated with implementation detail sufficient for use by assessors; system configuration baseline.

Primary Responsibility: System Owner; Common Control Provider.

Supporting Roles: Information Owner or Steward; Security Architect; Privacy Architect; Systems Security Engineer; Privacy Engineer; System Security Officer; System Privacy Officer; Enterprise Architect; System Administrator.

System Development Life Cycle Phase: New – Development/Acquisition; Implementation/Assessment. Existing – Operations/Maintenance.

Discussion: Despite the control implementation details in the security and privacy plans and the system design documents, it is not always feasible to implement controls as planned. Therefore, as control implementations are carried out, the security and privacy plans are updated with as-implemented control implementation details. The updates include revised descriptions of implemented controls including changes to planned inputs, expected behavior, and expected outputs with sufficient detail to support control assessments. Documenting the "as implemented" control information is essential to providing the capability to determine when there are changes to the controls, whether those changes are authorized, and the impact of the changes on the security and privacy posture of the system and the organization.

References: [SP 800-53]; [SP 800-128]; [SP 800-160 v1] (Implementation, Integration, Verification, and Transition, Configuration Management Processes).

3.5 ASSESS

Purpose

The purpose of the *Assess* step is to determine if the controls selected for implementation are implemented correctly, operating as intended, and producing the desired outcome with respect to meeting the security and privacy requirements for the system and the organization.

ASSESS TASKS

Table 6 provides a summary of tasks and expected outcomes for the RMF *Assess* step. Applicable Cybersecurity Framework constructs are also provided.

TABLE 6: ASSESS TASKS AND OUTCOMES

Tasks	Outcomes
TASK A-1 ASSESSOR SELECTION	• An assessor or assessment team is selected to conduct the control assessments. • The appropriate level of independence is achieved for the assessor or assessment team selected.
TASK A-2 ASSESSMENT PLAN	• Documentation needed to conduct the assessments is provided to the assessor or assessment team. • Security and privacy assessment plans are developed and documented. • Security and privacy assessment plans are reviewed and approved to establish the expectations for the control assessments and the level of effort required.
TASK A-3 CONTROL ASSESSMENTS	• Control assessments are conducted in accordance with the security and privacy assessment plans. • Opportunities to reuse assessment results from previous assessments to make the risk management process timely and cost-effective are considered. • Use of automation to conduct control assessments is maximized to increase speed, effectiveness, and efficiency of assessments.
TASK A-4 ASSESSMENT REPORTS	• Security and privacy assessment reports that provide findings and recommendations are completed.
TASK A-5 REMEDIATION ACTIONS	• Remediation actions to address deficiencies in the controls implemented in the system and environment of operation are taken. • Security and privacy plans are updated to reflect control implementation changes made based on the assessments and subsequent remediation actions. *[Cybersecurity Framework: Profile]*
TASK A-6 PLAN OF ACTION AND MILESTONES	• A plan of action and milestones detailing remediation plans for unacceptable risks identified in security and privacy assessment reports is developed. *[Cybersecurity Framework: ID.RA-6]*

Quick link to summary table for RMF tasks, responsibilities, and supporting roles.

Guide for Applying the Risk Management Framework to Federal Information Systems (800-37 rev 2)
264

ASSESSOR SELECTION

<u>TASK A-1</u> Select the appropriate assessor or assessment team for the type of control assessment to be conducted.

Potential Inputs: Security, privacy, and SCRM plans; program management control information; common control documentation; organizational security and privacy program plans; SCRM strategy; system design documentation; enterprise, security, and privacy architecture information; security, privacy, and SCRM policies and procedures applicable to the system.

Expected Outputs: Selection of assessor or assessment team responsible for conducting the control assessment.

Primary Responsibility: <u>Authorizing Official</u> or <u>Authorizing Official Designated Representative</u>.

Supporting Roles: <u>Chief Information Officer</u>; <u>Senior Agency Information Security Officer</u>; <u>Senior Agency Official for Privacy</u>.

System Development Life Cycle Phase: New – Development/Acquisition; Implementation/Assessment. Existing – Operations/Maintenance.

Discussion: Organizations consider both the technical expertise and level of independence[87] required in selecting control assessors.[88] Organizations ensure that control assessors possess the required skills and technical expertise to develop effective assessment plans and to conduct assessments of program management, system-specific, hybrid, and common controls, as appropriate. This includes general knowledge of risk management concepts and approaches as well as comprehensive knowledge of and experience with the hardware, software, and firmware components implemented. In organizations where the assessment capability is centrally managed, the senior agency information security officer may have the responsibility of selecting and managing the security control assessors or assessment teams for organizational systems. As controls may be implemented to achieve security and privacy objectives, organizations consider the degree of collaboration between security control and privacy control assessors that is necessary.

Organizations can conduct self-assessments of controls or obtain the services of an independent control assessor. An independent assessor is an individual or group that can conduct an impartial assessment. Impartiality means that assessors are free from perceived or actual conflicts of interest with respect to the determination of control effectiveness or the development, operation, or management of the system, common controls, or program management controls. The authorizing official determines the level of assessor independence based on applicable laws, executive orders, directives, regulations, policies, or standards. The authorizing official consults with the Office of the Inspector General, chief information officer, senior agency official for privacy, and senior agency information security officer to help guide and inform decisions regarding assessor independence.

The system privacy officer is responsible for identifying assessment methodologies and metrics to determine if privacy controls are implemented correctly, operating as intended, and sufficient to ensure compliance with applicable privacy requirements and manage privacy risks. The senior agency official for privacy is responsible for conducting assessments of privacy controls and documenting the results of the assessments. At the discretion of the organization, privacy controls may be assessed by an independent assessor. However, in all cases, the senior agency official for privacy is responsible and accountable for

---

[87] In accordance with [OMB A-130], an independent evaluation of privacy program and practices is not required. However, an organization may choose to employ independent privacy assessments at the organization's discretion.

[88] Some organizations may select control assessors prior to the RMF *Assess* step to support control assessments at the earliest opportunity during the system life cycle. Early identification and selection of assessors allows organizations to plan for the assessment activities, including agreeing on the scope of the assessment. Organizations implementing a systems security engineering approach may also benefit from early selection of assessors to support verification and validation activities that occur throughout the system life cycle.

the organization's privacy program, including any privacy functions performed by independent assessors. The senior agency official for privacy is responsible for providing privacy information to the authorizing official.

References: [FIPS 199]; [SP 800-30]; [SP 800-53A]; [SP 800-55].

ASSESSMENT PLAN

TASK A-2   Develop, review, and approve plans to assess implemented controls.

Potential Inputs: Security, privacy, and SCRM plans; program management control information; common control documentation; organizational security and privacy program plans; SCRM strategy; system design documentation; supply chain information; enterprise, security, and privacy architecture information; security, privacy, and SCRM policies and procedures applicable to the system.

Expected Outputs: Security and privacy assessment plans approved by the authorizing official.

Primary Responsibility: Authorizing Official or Authorizing Official Designated Representative; Control Assessor.

Supporting Roles: Senior Agency Information Security Officer; Senior Agency Official for Privacy; System Owner; Common Control Provider; Information Owner or Steward; System Security Officer; System Privacy Officer.

System Development Life Cycle Phase: New – Development/Acquisition; Implementation/Assessment. Existing – Operations/Maintenance.

Discussion: Security and privacy assessment plans are developed by control assessors based on the implementation information contained in security and privacy plans, program management control documentation, and common control documentation. Organizations may choose to develop a single, integrated security and privacy assessment plan for the system or the organization. An integrated assessment plan delineates roles and responsibilities for control assessment. Assessment plans also provide the objectives for control assessments and specific assessment procedures for each control. Assessment plans reflect the type of assessment the organization is conducting, including for example: developmental testing and evaluation; independent verification and validation; audits, including supply chain; assessments supporting system and common control authorization or reauthorization; program management control assessments; continuous monitoring; and assessments conducted after remediation actions.

Assessment plans are reviewed and approved by the authorizing official or the designated representative of the authorizing official to help ensure that the plans are consistent with the security and privacy objectives of the organization; employ procedures, methods, techniques, tools, and automation to support continuous monitoring and near real-time risk management; and are cost-effective. Approved assessment plans establish expectations for the control assessments and the level of effort for the assessment. Approved assessment plans help to ensure that appropriate resources are applied toward determining control effectiveness while providing the necessary level of assurance in making such determinations. When controls are provided by an external provider through contracts, interagency agreements, lines of business arrangements, licensing agreements, or supply chain arrangements, the organization can request security and privacy assessment plans and assessments results or evidence from the provider.

References: [SP 800-53A]; [SP 800-160 v1] (Verification and Validation Processes); [SP 800-161]; [IR 8011 v1].

CONTROL ASSESSMENTS

TASK A-3 Assess the controls in accordance with the assessment procedures described in assessment plans.

Potential Inputs: Security and privacy assessment plans; security and privacy plans; external assessment or audit results (if applicable).

Expected Outputs: Completed control assessments and associated assessment evidence.

Primary Responsibility: Control Assessor.

Supporting Roles: Authorizing Official or Authorizing Official Designated Representative; System Owner; Common Control Provider; Information Owner or Steward; Senior Agency Information Security Officer; Senior Agency Official for Privacy; System Security Officer; System Privacy Officer.

System Development Life Cycle Phase: New – Development/Acquisition; Implementation/Assessment. Existing – Operations/Maintenance.

Discussion: Control assessments determine the extent to which the selected controls are implemented correctly, operating as intended, and producing the desired outcome with respect to meeting security and privacy requirements for the system and the organization. The system owner, common control provider, and/or organization rely on the technical skills and expertise of assessors to assess implemented controls using the assessment procedures specified in assessment plans and provide recommendations on how to respond to control deficiencies to reduce or eliminate identified vulnerabilities or unacceptable risks. The senior agency official for privacy serves as the control assessor for the privacy controls and is responsible for conducting an initial assessment of the privacy controls prior to system operation, and for assessing the controls periodically thereafter at a frequency sufficient to ensure compliance with privacy requirements and to manage privacy risks.[89] Controls implemented to achieve both security and privacy objectives may require a degree of collaboration between security and privacy control assessors. The assessor findings are a factual reporting of whether the controls are operating as intended and whether any deficiencies[90] in the controls are discovered during the assessment.

Control assessments occur as early as practicable in the SDLC, preferably during the development phase. These types of assessments are referred to as developmental testing and evaluation, and validate that the controls are implemented correctly and are consistent with the established information security and privacy architectures. Developmental testing and evaluation activities include, for example, design and code reviews, regression testing, and application scanning. Deficiencies identified early in the SDLC can be resolved in a more cost-effective manner. Assessments may be needed prior to source selection during the procurement process to assess potential suppliers or providers before the organization enters into agreements or contracts to begin the development phase. The results of control assessments conducted during the SDLC can also be used (consistent with reuse criteria established by the organization) during the authorization process to avoid unnecessary delays or costly repetition of assessments. Organizations can maximize the use of automation to conduct control assessments to increase the speed, effectiveness, and efficiency of the assessments, and to support continuous monitoring of the security and privacy posture of organizational systems.

Applying and assessing controls throughout the development process may be appropriate for iterative development processes. When iterative development processes (e.g., agile development) are employed, an iterative assessment may be conducted as each cycle is completed. A similar process is employed for assessing controls in commercial IT products that are used in the system. Organizations may choose to begin assessing controls prior to the complete implementation of all controls in the security and privacy plans. This type of incremental assessment is appropriate if it is more efficient or cost-effective to do so.

---

[89] The senior agency official for privacy can delegate the assessment functions, consistent with applicable policies.

[90] Only deficiencies in controls that can be exploited by threat agents are considered vulnerabilities.

Common controls (i.e., controls that are inherited by the system) are assessed separately (by assessors chosen by common control providers or the organization) and need not be assessed as part of a system-level assessment.

Organizations ensure that assessors have access to the information system and environment of operation where the controls are implemented and to the documentation, records, artifacts, test results, and other materials needed to assess the controls. This includes the controls implemented by external providers through contracts, interagency agreements, lines of business arrangements, licensing agreements, or supply chain arrangements. Assessors have the required degree of independence as determined by the authorizing official.[91] Assessor independence during the continuous monitoring process facilitates reuse of assessment results to support ongoing authorization and reauthorization.

To make the risk management process more efficient and cost-effective, organizations may choose to establish reasonable and appropriate criteria for reusing assessment results as part of organization-wide assessment policy or in the security and privacy program plans. For example, a recent audit of a system may have produced information about the effectiveness of selected controls. Another opportunity to reuse previous assessment results may come from external programs that test and evaluate security and privacy features of commercial information technology products (e.g., Common Criteria Evaluation and Validation Program and NIST Cryptographic Module Validation Program,). If prior assessment results from the system developer or vendor are available, the control assessor, under appropriate circumstances, may incorporate those results into the assessment. In addition, if a control implementation was assessed during other forms of assessment at previous stages of the SDLC (e.g., unit testing, functional testing, acceptance testing), organizations may consider potential reuse of those results to reduce duplication of efforts. And finally, assessment results can be reused to support reciprocity, for example, assessment results supporting an authorization to use (see Appendix F). Additional information on assessment result reuse is available in [SP 800-53A].

References: [SP 800-53A]; [SP 800-160 v1] (Verification and Validation Processes); [IR 8011 v1].

ASSESSMENT REPORTS

TASK A-4   Prepare the assessment reports documenting the findings and recommendations from the control assessments.

Potential Inputs: Completed control assessments and associated assessment evidence.

Expected Outputs: Completed security and privacy assessment reports detailing the assessor findings and recommendations.

Primary Responsibility: Control Assessor.

Supporting Roles: System Owner; Common Control Provider; System Security Officer; System Privacy Officer.

System Development Life Cycle Phase: New – Development/Acquisition; Implementation/Assessment. Existing – Operations/Maintenance.

Discussion: The results of the security and privacy control assessments, including recommendations for correcting deficiencies in the implemented controls, are documented in the assessment reports[92] by control assessors. Organizations may develop a single, integrated security and privacy assessment report. Assessment reports are key documents in the system or common control authorization package that is developed for authorizing officials. The assessment reports include information based on assessor

---

[91] In accordance with [OMB A-130], an independent evaluation of privacy program and practices is not required. However, an organization may choose to employ independent privacy assessments at the organization's discretion.
[92] If a comparable report meets the requirements of what is to be included in an assessment report, then the comparable report would itself constitute the assessment report.

findings, necessary to determine the effectiveness of the controls implemented within or inherited by the information system. Assessment reports are an important factor in a determining risk to organizational operations and assets, individuals, other organizations, and the Nation by the authorizing official. The format and the level of detail provided in assessment reports are appropriate for the type of control assessment conducted, for example, developmental testing and evaluation; independent verification and validation; independent assessments supporting information system or common control authorizations or reauthorizations; self-assessments; assessments after remediation actions; independent evaluations or audits; and assessments during continuous monitoring. The reporting format may also be prescribed by the organization.

Control assessment results obtained during the system development lifecycle are documented in an interim report and included in the final security and privacy assessment reports. Development of interim reports that document assessment results from relevant phases of the SDLC reinforces the concept that assessment reports are evolving documents. Interim reports are used, as appropriate, to inform the final assessment report. Organizations may choose to develop an executive summary from the control assessment findings. The executive summary provides authorizing officials and other interested individuals in the organization with an abbreviated version of the assessment reports that includes a synopsis of the assessment, findings, and the recommendations for addressing deficiencies in the controls.

References: [SP 800-53A]; [SP 800-160 v1] (Verification and Validation Processes).

REMEDIATION ACTIONS

TASK A-5   Conduct initial remediation actions on the controls and reassess remediated controls.

Potential Inputs: Completed security and privacy assessment reports with findings and recommendations; security and privacy plans; security and privacy assessment plans; organization- and system-level risk assessment results.

Expected Outputs: Completed initial remediation actions based on the security and privacy assessment reports; changes to implementations reassessed by the assessment team; updated security and privacy assessment reports; updated security and privacy plans including changes to the control implementations.

Primary Responsibility: System Owner; Common Control Provider; Control Assessor.

Supporting Roles: Authorizing Official or Authorizing Official Designated Representative; Senior Agency Information Security Officer; Senior Agency Official for Privacy; Senior Accountable Official for Risk Management or Risk Executive (Function); Information Owner or Steward; Systems Security Engineer; Privacy Engineer; System Security Officer; System Privacy Officer.

System Development Life Cycle Phase: New – Development/Acquisition; Implementation/Assessment. Existing – Operations/Maintenance.

Discussion: The security and privacy assessment reports describe deficiencies in the controls that could not be resolved during the development of the system or that are discovered post-development. Such control deficiencies may result in security and privacy risks (including supply chain risks). The findings generated during control assessments, provide information that facilitates risk responses based on organizational risk tolerance and priorities. The authorizing official, in consultation and coordination with system owners and other organizational officials, may decide that certain findings represent significant, unacceptable risk and require immediate remediation actions. Additionally, it may be possible and practical to conduct initial remediation actions for assessment findings that can be quickly and easily remediated with existing resources.

If initial remediation actions are taken, assessors reassess the controls. The control reassessments determine the extent to which remediated controls are implemented correctly, operating as intended, and producing the desired outcome with respect to meeting the security and privacy requirements for the system and the organization. The assessors update the assessment reports with the findings from the reassessment, but do not change the original assessment results. The security and privacy plans are updated based on the findings of the control assessments and any remediation actions taken. The updated plans reflect the state of the controls after the initial assessment and any modifications by the system owner or common control provider in addressing recommendations for corrective actions. At the completion of the control assessments, security and privacy plans contain an accurate description of implemented controls, including compensating controls.

Organizations can prepare an addendum to the security and privacy assessment reports that provides an opportunity for system owners and common control providers to respond to initial assessment findings. The addendum may include, for example, information regarding initial remediation actions taken by system owners or common control providers in response to assessor findings. The addendum can also provide the system owner or common control provider perspective on the findings. This may include providing additional explanatory material, rebutting certain findings, and correcting the record. The addendum does not change or influence the initial assessor findings provided in the reports. Information provided in the addendum is considered by authorizing officials when making risk-based authorization decisions. Organizations implement a process to determine the initial actions to take regarding the control deficiencies identified during the assessment. This process can address vulnerabilities and risks, false positives, and other factors that provide useful information to authorizing officials regarding the security and privacy posture of the system and organization including the ongoing effectiveness of system-specific, hybrid, and common controls. The issue resolution process can also ensure that only substantive items are identified and transferred to the plan of actions and milestones.

Findings from a system-level control assessment may necessitate an update to the system risk assessment and the organizational risk assessment.[93] The updated risk assessments and any inputs from the senior accountable official for risk management or risk executive (function) determines the initial remediation actions and the prioritization of those actions. System owners and common control providers may decide, based on a system or organizational risk assessment, that certain findings are inconsequential and present no significant security or privacy risk. Such findings are retained in the security and privacy assessment reports and monitored during the monitoring step. The authorizing official is responsible for reviewing and understanding the assessor findings and for accepting the security and privacy risks (including any supply chain risks) that result from the operation the system or the use of common controls.

In all cases, organizations review assessor findings to determine the significance of the findings and whether the findings warrant any further investigation or remediation. Senior leadership involvement in the mitigation process is necessary to ensure that the organization's resources are effectively allocated in accordance with organizational priorities—providing resources to the systems that are supporting the most critical missions and business functions or correcting the deficiencies that pose the greatest risk.

References: [SP 800-53A]; [SP 800-160 v1] (Verification and Validation Processes).

PLAN OF ACTION AND MILESTONES

TASK A-6   Prepare the plan of action and milestones based on the findings and recommendations of the assessment reports.

Potential Inputs: Updated security and privacy assessment reports; updated security and privacy plans; organization- and system-level risk assessment results; organizational risk management strategy and risk tolerance.

---

[93] Risk assessments are conducted as needed at the organizational level, mission/business level, and at the system level throughout the SDLC. Risk assessment is specified as part of the RMF *Prepare-Organization Level* step, Task P-3 and RMF *Prepare-System Level* step, Task P-14.

Expected Outputs: A plan of action and milestones detailing the findings from the security and privacy assessment reports that are to be remediated.

Primary Responsibility: System Owner; Common Control Provider.

Supporting Roles: Information Owner or Steward; System Security Officer; System Privacy Officer; Senior Agency Information Security Officer; Senior Agency Official for Privacy; Control Assessor; Chief Acquisition Officer.

System Development Life Cycle Phase: New – Implementation/Assessment.
Existing – Operations/Maintenance.

Discussion: The plan of action and milestones is included as part of the authorization package. The plan of action and milestones describes the actions that are planned to correct deficiencies in the controls identified during the assessment of the controls and during continuous monitoring. The plan of action and milestones includes tasks to be accomplished with a recommendation for completion before or after system authorization; resources required to accomplish the tasks; milestones established to meet the tasks; and the scheduled completion dates for the milestones and tasks. The plan of action and milestones is reviewed by the authorizing official to ensure there is agreement with the remediation actions planned to correct the identified deficiencies. It is subsequently used to monitor progress in completing the actions. Deficiencies are accepted by the authorizing official as residual risk or are remediated during the assessment or prior to submission of the authorization package to the authorizing official. Plan of action and milestones entries are not necessary when deficiencies are accepted by the authorizing official as residual risk. However, deficiencies identified during assessment and monitoring are documented in the assessment reports, which can be retained within an automated security/privacy management and reporting tool to maintain an effective audit trail. Organizations develop plans of action and milestones based on assessment results obtained from control assessments, audits, and continuous monitoring and in accordance with applicable laws, executive orders, directives, policies, regulations, standards, or guidance.

Organizations implement a consistent process for developing plans of action and milestones that uses a prioritized approach to risk mitigation that is uniform across the organization. A risk assessment guides the prioritization process for items included in the plan of action and milestones. The process ensures that plans of action and milestones are informed by the security categorization of the system and security, privacy, and supply chain risk assessments; the specific deficiencies in the controls; the criticality of the identified control deficiencies (i.e., the direct or indirect effect that the deficiencies may have on the security and privacy posture of the system, and therefore, on the risk exposure of the organization; or the ability of the organization to perform its mission or business functions); and the proposed risk mitigation approach to address the identified deficiencies in the controls (e.g., prioritization of risk mitigation actions and allocation of risk mitigation resources). Risk mitigation resources include, for example, personnel, new hardware or software, and tools.

References: [SP 800-30]; [SP 800-53A]; [SP 800-160 v1] (Verification and Validation Processes); [IR 8062].

3.6 AUTHORIZE

Purpose

The purpose of the *Authorize* step is to provide organizational accountability by requiring a senior management official to determine if the security and privacy risk (including supply chain risk) to organizational operations and assets, individuals, other organizations, or the Nation based on the operation of a system or the use of common controls, is acceptable.

AUTHORIZE TASKS

Table 7 provides a summary of tasks and expected outcomes for the RMF *Authorize* step. Applicable Cybersecurity Framework constructs are also provided.

TABLE 7: AUTHORIZE TASKS AND OUTCOMES

Tasks	Outcomes
TASK R-1 AUTHORIZATION PACKAGE	• An authorization package is developed for submission to the authorizing official.
TASK R-2 RISK ANALYSIS AND DETERMINATION	• A risk determination by the authorizing official that reflects the risk management strategy including risk tolerance, is rendered.
TASK R-3 RISK RESPONSE	• Risk responses for determined risks are provided. [*Cybersecurity Framework*: ID.RA-6]
TASK R-4 AUTHORIZATION DECISION	• The authorization for the system or the common controls is approved or denied.
TASK R-5 AUTHORIZATION REPORTING	• Authorization decisions, significant vulnerabilities, and risks are reported to organizational officials.

<u>Quick link to summary table for RMF tasks, responsibilities, and supporting roles.</u>

AUTHORIZATION PACKAGE

TASK R-1   Assemble the authorization package and submit the package to the authorizing official for an authorization decision.

Potential Inputs: Security and privacy plans; security and privacy assessment reports; plan of action and milestones; supporting assessment evidence or other documentation, as required.

Expected Outputs: Authorization package (with an executive summary), which may be generated from a security or privacy management tool[94] for submission to the authorizing official.

Primary Responsibility: <u>System Owner</u>; <u>Common Control Provider</u>; <u>Senior Agency Official for Privacy</u>.[95]

---

[94] Organizations are encouraged to maximize the use of automated tools in the preparation, assembly, and transmission of authorization packages and security and privacy information supporting the authorization process. Many commercially available governance, risk, and compliance (GRC) tools can be employed to reduce or eliminate hard copy documentation.

[95] The senior agency official for privacy is active for information systems processing PII.

NIST SP 800-37, REVISION 2

RISK MANAGEMENT FRAMEWORK FOR INFORMATION SYSTEMS AND ORGANIZATIONS
A System Life Cycle Approach for Security and Privacy

Supporting Roles: System Security Officer; System Privacy Officer; Senior Agency Information Security Officer; Control Assessor.

System Development Life Cycle Phase: New – Implementation/Assessment.
Existing – Operations/Maintenance.

Discussion: Authorization packages[96] include security and privacy plans, security and privacy assessment reports, plans of action and milestones, and an executive summary. Additional information can be included in the authorization package at the request of the authorizing official. Organizations maintain version and change control as the information in the authorization package is updated. Providing timely updates to the plans, assessment reports, and plans of action and milestones on an ongoing basis supports the concept of near real-time risk management and ongoing authorization, and can be used for reauthorization actions, if required.

The senior agency official for privacy reviews the authorization package for systems that process PII to ensure compliance with applicable privacy requirements and to manage privacy risks, prior to authorizing officials making risk determination and acceptance decisions.

The information in the authorization package is used by authorizing officials to make informed, risk-based decisions. When controls are implemented by an external provider through contracts, interagency agreements, lines of business arrangements, licensing agreements, or supply chain arrangements, the organization ensures that the information needed to make risk-based decisions is made available by the provider.

The authorization package may be provided to the authorizing official in hard copy or electronically or may be generated using an automated security/privacy management and reporting tool. Organizations can use automated support tools in preparing and managing the content of the authorization package. Automated support tools provide an effective vehicle for maintaining and updating information for authorizing officials regarding the ongoing security and privacy posture of information systems within the organization.

When an information system is under ongoing authorization, the authorization package is presented to the authorizing official via automated reports to provide information in the most efficient and timely manner possible.[97] Information to be presented to the authorizing official in assessment reports is generated in the format and with the frequency determined by the organization using information from the information security and privacy continuous monitoring programs.

The assessment reports presented to the authorizing official include information about deficiencies in system-specific, hybrid, and common controls (i.e., other than satisfied findings determined by assessors). The authorizing official uses automated security/privacy management and reporting tools or other automated methods, whenever practicable, to access the security and privacy plans and the plans of action and milestones. The authorization documents are updated at an organization-defined frequency using automated or manual processes in accordance with the risk management objectives of the organization.[98]

---

[96] If a comparable report meets the requirements of what is to be included in an authorization package, then the comparable report would itself constitute the authorization package.

[97] While the objective is to fully automate all components of the authorization package, organizations may be in various states of transition to a fully automated state—that is, with certain sections of the authorization package available via automated means and other sections available only through manual means.

[98] Organizations decide on the level of detail and the presentation format of security and privacy information that is made available to authorizing officials through automation. Decisions about level of detail and format are based on organizational needs with the automated presentation of security and privacy information tailored to the decision-making needs of the authorizing officials. For example, detailed security and privacy information may be generated and collected at the operational level of the organization with information subsequently analyzed, distilled, and presented to authorizing officials in a summarized or highlighted format using automation.

References: [OMB A-130]; [SP 800-18]; [SP 800-160 v1] (Risk Management Process); [SP 800-161] (SCRM Plans).

RISK ANALYSIS AND DETERMINATION

TASK R-2   Analyze and determine the risk from the operation or use of the system or the provision of common controls.

Potential Inputs: Authorization package; supporting assessment evidence or other documentation as required; information provided by the senior accountable official for risk management or risk executive (function); organizational risk management strategy and risk tolerance; organization- and system-level risk assessment results.

Expected Outputs: Risk determination.

Primary Responsibility: Authorizing Official or Authorizing Official Designated Representative.

Supporting Roles: Senior Accountable Official for Risk Management or Risk Executive (Function); Senior Agency Information Security Officer; Senior Agency Official for Privacy.

System Development Life Cycle Phase: New – Implementation/Assessment.
Existing – Operations/Maintenance.

Discussion: The authorizing official or designated representative, in collaboration with the senior agency information security officer and the senior agency official for privacy (for information systems processing PII), analyzes the information in the authorization package provided by the control assessor, system owner, or common control provider, and finalizes the determination of risk. Further discussion with the control assessor, system owner, or common control provider may be necessary to help ensure a thorough understanding of risk by the authorizing official.

Risk assessments are employed to provide information[99] that may influence the risk analysis and determination. The senior accountable official for risk management or risk executive (function) may provide additional information to the authorizing official that is considered in the final determination of risk to organizational operations and assets, individuals, other organizations, and the Nation resulting from either the operation or use of the system or the provision of common controls. The additional information may include, for example, organizational risk tolerance, dependencies among systems and controls, mission and business requirements, the criticality of the missions or business functions supported by the system, or the risk management strategy.

The authorizing official analyzes the information provided by the senior accountable official for risk management or risk executive (function) and information provided by the system owner or common control provider in the authorization package when making a risk determination. Any additional information provided by the senior accountable official for risk management or risk executive (function) is documented and included, to the extent it is relevant, as part of the authorization decision (see Task R-4). The authorizing official may also use an automated security/privacy management and reporting tool to annotate senior accountable official for risk management or risk executive (function) input.

When the system is operating under an ongoing authorization, the risk determination task is effectively unchanged. The authorizing official analyzes the relevant security and privacy information provided by the automated security/privacy management and reporting tool to determine the current security and privacy posture of the system.

References: [OMB A-130]; [SP 800-30]; [SP 800-39] (Organization, Mission/Business Process, and System Levels); [SP 800-137]; [SP 800-160 v1] (Risk Management Process); [IR 8062].

---

[99] [SP 800-30] provides guidance on conducting security risk assessments. [IR 8062] provides information about privacy risk assessments and associated risk factors.

RISK RESPONSE

TASK R-3 Identify and implement a preferred course of action in response to the risk determined.

Potential Inputs: Authorization package; risk determination; organization- and system-level risk assessment results.

Expected Outputs: Risk responses for determined risks.

Primary Responsibility: Authorizing Official or Authorizing Official Designated Representative.

Supporting Roles: Senior Accountable Official for Risk Management or Risk Executive (Function); Senior Agency Information Security Officer; Senior Agency Official for Privacy; System Owner or Common Control Provider; Information Owner or Steward; Systems Security Engineer; Privacy Engineer; System Security Officer; System Privacy Officer.

System Development Life Cycle Phase: New — Implementation/Assessment.
Existing — Operations/Maintenance.

Discussion: After risk is analyzed and determined, organizations can respond to risk in a variety of ways, including acceptance of risk and mitigation of risk. Existing risk assessment results and risk assessment techniques may be used to help determine the preferred course of action for the risk response.[100] When the response to risk is mitigation, the planned mitigation actions are included in and tracked using the plan of action and milestones. Once mitigated, assessors reassess the controls. Control reassessments determine the extent to which remediated controls are implemented correctly, operating as intended, and producing the desired outcome with respect to meeting the security and privacy requirements for the system and the organization. The assessors update the assessment reports with the findings from the reassessment, but do not change the original assessment results. The security and privacy plans are updated based on the findings of the control assessments and any remediation actions taken. The updated plans reflect the state of the controls after the initial assessment and any modifications by the system owner or common control provider in addressing recommendations for corrective actions.

At the completion of the control reassessments, security and privacy plans contain an accurate description of implemented controls, including compensating controls. When the response to risk is acceptance, the deficiencies found during the assessment process remain documented in the security and privacy assessment reports and are monitored for changes to the risk factors.[101] Because the authorizing official is the only person who can accept risk, the authorizing official is responsible for reviewing the assessment reports and plans of action and milestones and determining whether the identified risks need to be mitigated prior to authorization. Decisions on the most appropriate course of action for responding to risk may include some form of prioritization. Some risks may be of greater concern to organizations than other risks. In that case, more resources may need to be directed at addressing higher-priority risks versus lower-priority risks. Prioritizing risk response does not necessarily mean that the lower-priority risks are ignored. Rather, it could mean that fewer resources are directed at addressing the lower-priority risks, or that the lower-priority risks are addressed later. A key part of the risk-based decision process is the recognition that regardless of the risk response, there remains a degree of residual risk. Organizations determine acceptable degrees of residual risk based on organizational risk tolerance.

References: [SP 800-30]; [SP 800-39] (Organization, Mission/Business Process, and System Levels); [SP 800-160 v1] (Risk Management Process); [IR 8062]; [IR 8179]; [NIST CSF] (Core [Identify Function]).

---

[100] [SP 800-39] provides additional information on risk response.

[101] The four security risk factors are threat, vulnerability, likelihood, and impact. [SP 800-30] and [SP 800-39] provide information about security risk assessments and associated risk factors. [IR 8062] and Section 2.3 provide additional information on privacy risk factors and conducting privacy risk assessments.

AUTHORIZATION DECISION

<u>TASK R-4</u> Determine if the risk from the operation or use of the information system or the provision or use of common controls is acceptable.

Potential Inputs: Risk responses for determined risks.

Expected Outputs: Authorization to operate, authorization to use, common control authorization; denial of authorization to operate, denial of authorization to use, denial of common control authorization.

Primary Responsibility: Authorizing Official.

Supporting Roles: Senior Accountable Official for Risk Management or Risk Executive (Function); Chief Information Officer; Senior Agency Information Security Officer; Senior Agency Official for Privacy; Authorizing Official Designated Representative.

System Development Life Cycle Phase: New – Implementation/Assessment.
Existing – Operations/Maintenance.

Discussion: The explicit acceptance of risk is the responsibility of the authorizing official and cannot be delegated to other officials within the organization. The authorizing official considers many factors when deciding if the risk to the organization's operations (including mission, functions, image, and reputation) and assets, individuals, other organizations, or the Nation, is acceptable. Balancing security and privacy considerations with mission and business needs is paramount to achieving an acceptable risk-based authorization decision.[102] The authorizing official issues an authorization decision for the system or for organization-designated common controls after reviewing the information in the authorization package, input from other organizational officials (see Task R-2), and other relevant information that may affect the authorization decision. The authorization package provides the most current information on the security and privacy posture of the system or the common controls.

The authorizing official consults with the Senior Accountable Official for Risk Management or the Risk Executive (Function) prior to making the final authorization decision for the information system or the common controls. Because there are potentially significant dependencies among organizational systems and with external systems, the authorization decisions for individual systems consider the current residual risk, organizational plans of action and milestones, and the risk tolerance of the organization.

The authorization decision is conveyed by the authorizing official to the system owner or common control provider, and other organizational officials, as appropriate.[103] The authorization decision also conveys the terms and conditions for the authorization to operate; the authorization termination date or time-driven authorization frequency; input from the senior accountable official for risk management or risk executive (function), if provided; and for common control authorizations, the system impact level supported by the common controls.

For systems, the authorization decision indicates to the system owner whether the system is authorized to operate or authorized to use, or not authorized to operate or not authorized to use. For common controls, the authorization decision indicates to the common control provider and to the system owners of inheriting systems, whether the common controls are authorized to be provided or not authorized to

---

[102] While balancing security and privacy considerations with mission and business needs is paramount to achieving an acceptable risk-based authorization decision, there may be instances when the authorizing official and senior agency official for privacy cannot reach a final resolution regarding the appropriate protection for PII and the information systems that process PII. [OMB A-130] provides guidance on how to resolve such instances.

[103] Organizations are encouraged to employ automated security/privacy management and reporting tools whenever feasible, to develop the authorization packages for systems and common controls and to maintain those packages during ongoing authorization. Automated tools can significantly reduce documentation costs, provide increased speed and efficiency in generating important information for decision makers, and provide more effective means for updating critical risk management information. It is recognized that certain controls are not conducive to the use of automated tools and therefore, manual methods are acceptable in those situations.

be provided. The terms and conditions for the common control authorization provide a description of any specific limitations or restrictions placed on the operation of the system or the controls that must be followed by the system owner or common control provider.

The authorization termination date is established by the authorizing official and indicates when the authorization expires. Organizations may eliminate the authorization termination date if the system is operating under an ongoing authorization—that is, the continuous monitoring program is sufficiently robust and mature to provide the authorizing official with the needed information to conduct ongoing risk determination and risk acceptance activities regarding the security and privacy posture of the system and the ongoing effectiveness of the controls employed within and inherited by the system.

The authorization decision is included with the authorization package and is transmitted to the system owner or common control provider. Upon receipt of the authorization decision and the authorization package, the system owner or common control provider acknowledges and implements the terms and conditions of the authorization. The organization ensures that the authorization package, including the authorization decision for systems and common controls, is made available to organizational officials (e.g., system owners inheriting common controls; chief information officers; senior accountable officials for risk management or risk executive [function]; senior agency information security officers; senior agency officials for privacy; and system security and privacy officers). The authorizing official verifies on an ongoing basis as part of continuous monitoring (see Task M-2) that the established terms and conditions for authorization are being followed by the system owner or common control provider.

When the system is operating under ongoing authorization, the authorizing official continues to be responsible and accountable for explicitly understanding and accepting the risk of continuing to operate or use the system or continuing to provide common controls for inheritance. For ongoing authorization, the authorization frequency is specified in lieu of an authorization termination date. The authorizing official reviews the information with the specific time-driven authorization frequency defined by the organization as part of the continuous monitoring strategy and determines if the risk of continued system operation or the provision of common controls remains acceptable. If the risk remains acceptable, the authorizing official acknowledges the acceptance in accordance with organizational processes. If not, the authorizing official indicates that the risk is no longer acceptable and requires further risk response or a full denial of the authorization.

The organization determines the level of formality for the process of communicating and acknowledging continued risk acceptance by the authorizing official. The authorizing official may continue to establish and convey the specific terms and conditions to be followed by the system owner or common control provider for continued authorization to operate, continued common control authorization, or continued authorization to use. The terms and conditions of the authorization may be conveyed through an automated management and reporting tool as part of an automated authorization decision.

If control assessments are conducted by qualified assessors with the level of independence[104] required, the assessment results support ongoing authorization and may be applied to a reauthorization. Organizational policies regarding ongoing authorization and reauthorization are consistent with laws, executive orders, directives, regulations, and policies.

Appendix F provides additional guidance on authorization decisions, the types of authorizations, and the preparation of the authorization packages.

References: [SP 800-39] (Organization, Mission/Business Process, and System Levels); [SP 800-160 v1] (Risk Management Process).

---

[104] In accordance with [OMB A-130], an independent evaluation of privacy program and practices is not required. However, an organization may choose to employ independent privacy assessments at the organization's discretion.

AUTHORIZATION REPORTING

<u>TASK R-5</u> Report the authorization decision and any deficiencies in controls that represent significant security or privacy risk.

Potential Inputs: Authorization decision.

Expected Outputs: A report indicating the authorization decision for a system or set of common controls; annotation of authorization status in the organizational system registry.

Primary Responsibility: <u>Authorizing Official</u> or <u>Authorizing Official Designated Representative</u>.

Supporting Roles: <u>System Owner</u> or <u>Common Control Provider</u>; <u>Information Owner or Steward</u>; <u>System Security Officer</u>; <u>System Privacy Officer</u>; <u>Senior Agency Information Security Officer</u>; <u>Senior Agency Official for Privacy</u>.

System Development Life Cycle Phase: New – Implementation/Assessment.
Existing – Operations/Maintenance.

Discussion: Authorizing officials report authorization decisions for systems and common controls to designated organizational officials so the individual risk decisions can be viewed in the context of organization-wide security and privacy risk to organizational operations and assets, individuals, other organizations, and the Nation. Reporting occurs only in situations where organizations have delegated the authorization functions to levels of the organization below the head of agency. Authorizing officials also report exploitable deficiencies (i.e., vulnerabilities) in the system or controls noted during the assessment and continuous monitoring that represent significant security or privacy risk. Organizations determine, and the organizational policy reflects, what constitutes a significant security or privacy risk for reporting. Deficiencies that represent significant vulnerabilities and risk can be reported using the Subcategories, Categories, and Functions in the [NIST CSF]. Authorization decisions may be tracked and reflected as part of the organization-wide system registration process at the organization's discretion (see Task P-18).

References: [SP 800-39] (Organization, Mission/Business Process, and System Levels); [SP 800-160 v1] (Decision Management and Project Assessment and Control Processes); [NIST CSF] (Core [Identify, Protect, Detect, Respond, Recover Functions]).

3.7 MONITOR

Purpose

The purpose of the **Monitor** step is to maintain an ongoing situational awareness about the security and privacy posture of the information system and the organization in support of risk management decisions.

MONITOR TASKS

Table 8 provides a summary of tasks and expected outcomes for the RMF *Monitor* step. Applicable Cybersecurity Framework constructs are also provided.

TABLE 8: MONITOR TASKS AND OUTCOMES

Tasks	Outcomes
TASK M-1 SYSTEM AND ENVIRONMENT CHANGES	• The information system and environment of operation are monitored in accordance with the continuous monitoring strategy. [*Cybersecurity Framework*: DE.CM; ID.GV]
TASK M-2 ONGOING ASSESSMENTS	• Ongoing assessments of control effectiveness are conducted in accordance with the continuous monitoring strategy. [*Cybersecurity Framework*: ID.SC-4]
TASK M-3 ONGOING RISK RESPONSE	• The output of continuous monitoring activities is analyzed and responded to appropriately. [*Cybersecurity Framework*: RS.AN]
TASK M-4 AUTHORIZATION PACKAGE UPDATES	• Risk management documents are updated based on continuous monitoring activities. [*Cybersecurity Framework*: RS.IM]
TASK M-5 SECURITY AND PRIVACY REPORTING	• A process is in place to report the security and privacy posture to the authorizing official and other senior leaders and executives.
TASK M-6 ONGOING AUTHORIZATION	• Authorizing officials conduct ongoing authorizations using the results of continuous monitoring activities and communicate changes in risk determination and acceptance decisions.
TASK M-7 SYSTEM DISPOSAL	• A system disposal strategy is developed and implemented, as needed.

Quick link to summary table for RMF tasks, responsibilities, and supporting roles.

SYSTEM AND ENVIRONMENT CHANGES

TASK M-1   Monitor the information system and its environment of operation for changes that impact the security and privacy posture of the system.

Potential Inputs: Organizational continuous monitoring strategy; organizational configuration management policy and procedures; organizational policy and procedures for handling unauthorized system changes; security and privacy plans; configuration change requests/approvals; system design documentation; security and privacy assessment reports; plans of action and milestones; information from automated and manual monitoring tools.

Expected Outputs: Updated security and privacy plans; updated plans of action and milestones; updated security and privacy assessment reports.

Primary Responsibility: System Owner or Common Control Provider; Senior Agency Information Security Officer; Senior Agency Official for Privacy.

Supporting Roles: Senior Accountable Official for Risk Management or Risk Executive (Function); Authorizing Official or Authorizing Official Designated Representative; Information Owner or Steward; System Security Officer; System Privacy Officer.

System Development Life Cycle Phase: New – Operations/Maintenance.
Existing – Operations/Maintenance.

Discussion: Systems and environments of operation are in a constant state of change with changes occurring in the technology or machine elements, human elements, and physical or environmental elements. Changes to the technology or machine elements include for example, upgrades to hardware, software, or firmware; changes to the human elements include for example, staff turnover or a reduction in force; and modifications to the surrounding physical and environmental elements include for example, changes in the location of the facility or the physical access controls protecting the facility. Changes made by external providers can be difficult to detect. A disciplined and structured approach to managing, controlling, and documenting changes to systems and environments of operation, and adherence with terms and conditions of the authorization, is an essential element of security and privacy programs. Organizations establish configuration management and control processes to support configuration and change management.[105]

Common activities within organizations can cause changes to systems or the environments of operation and can have a significant impact on the security and privacy posture of systems. Examples include installing or disposing of hardware, making changes to configurations, and installing patches outside of the established configuration change control process. Unauthorized changes may occur because of purposeful attacks by adversaries or inadvertent errors by authorized personnel. In addition to adhering to the established configuration management process, organizations monitor for unauthorized changes to systems and analyze information about unauthorized changes that have occurred to determine the root cause of the unauthorized change. In addition to monitoring for unauthorized changes, organizations continuously monitor systems and environments of operation for any authorized changes that impact the privacy posture of systems.[106]

Once the root cause of an unauthorized change (or an authorized change that impacts the privacy posture of the system) has been determined, organizations respond accordingly (see Task M-3). For example, if the root cause of an unauthorized change is determined to be an adversarial attack, multiple actions could be taken such as invoking incident response processes, adjusting intrusion detection and prevention tools and firewall configurations, or implementing additional or stronger controls to reduce the risk of future attacks. If the root cause of an unauthorized change is determined to be a failure of staff to adhere to established configuration management processes, remedial training for certain individuals may be warranted.

References: [SP 800-30]; [SP 800-128]; [SP 800-137]; [IR 8062].

---

[105] [SP 800-128] provides guidance on security-focused configuration management (SecCM). Note that the SecCM process described in [SP 800-128] includes a related monitoring step.

[106] For information about the distinction between authorized and unauthorized system behavior, see the discussion of security and privacy in Section 2.3.

ONGOING ASSESSMENTS

<u>Task M-2</u> Assess the controls implemented within and inherited by the system in accordance with the continuous monitoring strategy.

Potential Inputs: Organizational continuous monitoring strategy and system level continuous monitoring strategy (if applicable); security and privacy plans; security and privacy assessment plans; security and privacy assessment reports; plans of action and milestones; information from automated and manual monitoring tools; organization- and system-level risk assessment results; external assessment or audit results (if applicable).

Expected Outputs: Updated security and privacy assessment reports.

Primary Responsibility: Control Assessor.

Supporting Roles: Authorizing Official or Authorizing Official Designated Representative; System Owner or Common Control Provider; Information Owner or Steward; System Security Officer; System Privacy Officer; Senior Agency Information Security Officer; Senior Agency Official for Privacy.

System Development Life Cycle Phase: New – Operations/Maintenance.
Existing – Operations/Maintenance.

Discussion: After an initial system or common control authorization, the organization assesses all controls on an ongoing basis. Ongoing assessment of the control effectiveness is part of the continuous monitoring activities of the organization. The monitoring frequency for each control is based on the organizational continuous monitoring strategy (see Task P-7) and can be supplemented by the system-level continuous monitoring strategy (see Task S-5). Adherence to the terms and conditions specified by the authorizing official as part of the authorization decision are also monitored (see Task M-1). Ongoing control assessment continues as the information generated as part of continuous monitoring is correlated, analyzed, and reported to senior leaders.

For ongoing control assessments, assessors have the required degree of independence as determined by the authorizing official.[107] Assessor independence during continuous monitoring introduces efficiencies into the process and may allow for reuse of assessment results in support of ongoing authorization and when reauthorization is required.

To satisfy the annual FISMA security assessment requirement, organizations can use assessment results from control assessments that occurred during authorization, ongoing authorization, or reauthorization; during continuous monitoring; or the during testing and evaluation of systems as part of the SDLC or an audit (provided the assessment results are current, relevant to the determination of control effectiveness, and obtained by assessors with the required degree of independence). Existing assessment results are reused consistent with the reuse policy established by the organization and are supplemented with additional assessments as needed. The reuse of assessment results is helpful in achieving a cost-effective, security program capable of producing the evidence necessary to determine the security posture of information systems and the organization. Finally, the use of automation to support control assessments facilitates a greater frequency, volume, and coverage of assessments.

References: [SP 800-53A]; [SP 800-137]; [SP 800-160 v1] (Verification, Validation, Operation, and Maintenance Processes); [IR 8011 v1].

ONGOING RISK RESPONSE

<u>Task M-3</u> Respond to risk based on the results of ongoing monitoring activities, risk assessments, and outstanding items in plans of action and milestones.

---

[107] In accordance with [OMB A-130], an independent evaluation of privacy programs and practices is not required. However, an organization may choose to employ independent privacy assessments at the organization's discretion.

Potential Inputs: Security and privacy assessment reports; organization- and system-level risk assessment results; security and privacy plans; plans of action and milestones.

Expected Outputs: Mitigation actions or risk acceptance decisions; updated security and privacy assessment reports.

Primary Responsibility: Authorizing Official; System Owner; Common Control Provider.

Supporting Roles: Senior Accountable Official for Risk Management or Risk Executive (Function); Senior Agency Official for Privacy; Authorizing Official Designated Representative; Information Owner or Steward; System Security Officer; System Privacy Officer; Systems Security Engineer; Privacy Engineer; Security Architect; Privacy Architect.

System Development Life Cycle Phase: New – Operations/Maintenance.
　　　　　　　　　　　　　　　　　　　　Existing – Operations/Maintenance.

Discussion: Assessment information produced by an assessor during continuous monitoring is provided to the system owner and the common control provider in updated assessment reports or via reports from automated security/privacy management and reporting tools. The authorizing official determines the appropriate risk response to the assessment findings or approves responses proposed by the system owner and common control provider. The system owner and common control provider subsequently implement the appropriate risk response. When the risk response is acceptance, the findings remain documented in the security and privacy assessment reports and are monitored for changes to risk factors. When the risk response is mitigation, the planned mitigation actions are included in and tracked using the plans of action and milestones. If requested by the authorizing official, control assessors may provide recommendations for remediation actions. Recommendations for remediation actions may also be provided by an automated security/privacy management and reporting tool. An organizational assessment of risk (Task P-3) and system-level risk assessment results (Task P-14) guide and inform the decisions regarding ongoing risk response. Controls that are modified, enhanced, or added as part of ongoing risk response are reassessed by assessors to ensure that the new, modified, or enhanced controls have been implemented correctly, are operating as intended, and producing the desired outcome with respect to meeting the security and privacy requirements of the system.

References: [SP 800-30]; [SP 800-53]; [SP 800-53A]; [SP 800-137]; [SP 800-160 v1] (Risk Management Process); [IR 8011 v1]; [IR 8062]; [NIST CSF] (Core [Respond Function]).

AUTHORIZATION PACKAGE UPDATES

Task M-4　Update plans, assessment reports, and plans of action and milestones based on the results of the continuous monitoring process.

Potential Inputs: Security and privacy assessment reports; organization- and system-level risk assessment results; security and privacy plans; plans of action and milestones.

Expected Outputs: Updated security and privacy assessment reports;[108] updated plans of action and milestones; updated risk assessment results; updated security and privacy plans.

Primary Responsibility: System Owner; Common Control Provider.

Supporting Roles: Information Owner or Steward; System Security Officer; System Privacy Officer; Senior Agency Official for Privacy; Senior Agency Information Security Officer.

System Development Life Cycle Phase: New – Operations/Maintenance.
　　　　　　　　　　　　　　　　　　　　Existing – Operations/Maintenance.

---

[108] If a comparable report meets the requirements of what is to be included in an assessment report (e.g., a report generated from a security or privacy management and reporting tool), then the comparable report would constitute the assessment report.

Discussion: To achieve near real-time risk management, the organization updates security and privacy plans, security and privacy assessment reports, and plans of action and milestones on an ongoing basis. Updates to the plans reflect modifications to controls based on risk mitigation activities carried out by system owners or common control providers. Updates to control assessment reports reflect additional assessment activities carried out to determine control effectiveness based on implementation details in the plans. Plans of action and milestones are updated based on progress made on the current outstanding items; address security and privacy risks discovered as part of control effectiveness monitoring; and describe how the system owner or common control provider intends to address those risks. The updated information raises awareness of the security and privacy posture of the system and the common controls inherited by the system, thereby, supporting near real-time risk management and the ongoing authorization process.

The frequency of updates to risk management information is at the discretion of the system owner, common control provider, and authorizing officials in accordance with federal and organizational policies and is consistent with the organizational and system-level continuous monitoring strategies. The updates to information regarding the security and privacy posture of the system and the common controls inherited by the system are accurate and timely since the information provided influences ongoing actions and decisions by authorizing officials and other senior leaders within the organization. The use of automated support tools and organization-wide security and privacy program management practices ensure that authorizing officials can readily access the current security and privacy posture of the system. Ready access to the current security and privacy posture supports continuous monitoring and ongoing authorization and promotes the near real-time management of risk to organizational operations and assets, individuals, other organizations, and the Nation.

Organizations ensure that information needed for oversight, management, and auditing purposes is not modified or destroyed when updating security and privacy plans, assessment reports, and plans of action and milestones. Providing an effective method to track changes to systems through configuration management procedures is necessary to achieve transparency and traceability in the security and privacy activities of the organization; to obtain individual accountability for any security or privacy actions; and to understand emerging trends in the security and privacy programs of the organization.

References: [SP 800-30]; [SP 800-53A].

SECURITY AND PRIVACY REPORTING

Task M-5   Report the security and privacy posture of the system to the authorizing official and other organizational officials on an ongoing basis in accordance with the organizational continuous monitoring strategy.

Potential Inputs: Security and privacy assessment reports; plans of action and milestones; organization- and system-level risk assessment results; organization- and system-level continuous monitoring strategy; security and privacy plans; Cybersecurity Framework Profile.

Expected Outputs: Security and privacy posture reports.[109]

Primary Responsibility: System Owner; Common Control Provider; Senior Agency Information Security Officer; Senior Agency Official for Privacy.

Supporting Roles: System Security Officer; System Privacy Officer.

System Development Life Cycle Phase: New – Operations/Maintenance.
Existing – Operations/Maintenance.

---

[109] If a comparable report meets the requirements of what is to be included in a security or privacy posture report (e.g., a report generated from a security or privacy management and reporting tool), then the comparable report would constitute the posture report.

Discussion: The results of monitoring activities are documented and reported to the authorizing official and other selected organizational officials on an ongoing basis in accordance with the organizational continuous monitoring strategy. Other organizational officials who may receive security and privacy posture reports include, for example, chief information officer, senior agency information security officer, senior agency official for privacy, senior accountable official for risk management or risk executive (function), information owner or steward, incident response roles, and contingency planning roles. Security and privacy posture reporting can be event-driven, time-driven, or event- and time-driven.[110] The reports provide the authorizing official and other organizational officials with information regarding the security and privacy posture of the systems including the effectiveness of implemented controls. Security and privacy posture reports describe the ongoing monitoring activities employed by system owners or common control providers. The reports also include information about security and privacy risks in the systems and environments of operation discovered during control assessments, auditing, and continuous monitoring and how system owners or common control providers plan to address those risks.

Organizations have flexibility in the breadth, depth, formality, form, and format of security and privacy posture reports. The goal is efficient ongoing communication with the authorizing official and other organizational officials as necessary, conveying the current security and privacy posture of systems and environments of operation and how the current posture affects individuals, organizational missions, and business functions. At a minimum, security and privacy posture reports summarize changes to the security and privacy plans, security and privacy assessment reports, and plans of action and milestones that have occurred since the last report. The use of automated security and privacy management and reporting tools (e.g., a dashboard) by the organization facilitates the effectiveness and timeliness of security and privacy posture reporting.

The frequency of security and privacy posture reports is at the discretion of the organization and in compliance with federal and organizational policies. Reports occur at appropriate intervals to transmit security and privacy information about systems or common controls but not so frequently as to generate unnecessary work or expense. Authorizing officials use the security and privacy posture reports and consult with the senior accountable official for risk management or risk executive (function), senior agency information security officer, and senior agency official for privacy to determine if a reauthorization action is necessary.

Security and privacy posture reports are marked, protected, and handled in accordance with federal and organizational policies. Security and privacy posture reports can be used to satisfy FISMA reporting requirements for documenting remediation actions for security and privacy weaknesses or deficiencies. Reporting on security and privacy posture is intended to be ongoing and should not be interpreted as requiring the time, expense, and formality associated with the information provided for the initial authorization. Rather, reporting is conducted in a cost-effective manner consistent with achieving the reporting objectives.

References: [SP 800-53A]; [SP 800-137]; [NIST CSF] (Core [Identify, Protect, Detect, Respond, Recover Functions]).

ONGOING AUTHORIZATION

Task M-6   Review the security and privacy posture of the system on an ongoing basis to determine whether the risk remains acceptable.

Potential Inputs: Risk tolerance; security and privacy posture reports; plans of action and milestones; organization- and system-level risk assessment results; security and privacy plans.

Expected Outputs: A determination of risk; ongoing authorization to operate, ongoing authorization to use, ongoing common control authorization; denial of ongoing authorization to operate, denial of ongoing authorization to use, denial of ongoing common control authorization.

---

[110] See Appendix F for additional information about time- and event-driven authorizations and reporting.

Primary Responsibility: Authorizing Official.

Supporting Roles: Senior Accountable Official for Risk Management or Risk Executive (Function); Chief Information Officer; Senior Agency Information Security Officer; Senior Agency Official for Privacy; Authorizing Official Designated Representative.

System Development Life Cycle Phase: New – Operations/Maintenance.
Existing – Operations/Maintenance.

Discussion: To employ an ongoing authorization approach, organizations have in place an organization-level and system-level continuous monitoring process to assess implemented controls on an ongoing basis.[111] The findings or results from the continuous monitoring process provides useful information to authorizing officials to support near-real time risk-based decision making. In accordance with the guidance in Task R-4, the authorizing official or designated representative reviews the security and privacy posture of the system (including the effectiveness of the implemented controls) on an ongoing basis to determine the current risk to organizational operations and assets, individuals, other organizations, and the Nation. The authorizing official determines whether the current risk is acceptable and provides appropriate direction to the system owner or common control provider. The authorizing official may determine that the risk remains at an acceptable level for continued operation or that the risk is no longer at an acceptable level for continued operation, and may issue a denial of authorization to operate, authorization to use, or common control authorization.

The risks may change based on the information provided in the security and privacy posture reports because the reports may indicate changes to the security or privacy risk factors. Determining how changing conditions affect organizational and individual risk is essential for managing privacy risk and maintaining adequate security. By carrying out ongoing risk determination and risk acceptance, authorizing officials can maintain system and common control authorizations over time and transition to ongoing authorization. Reauthorization actions occur only in accordance with federal or organizational policies. The authorizing official conveys updated risk determination and acceptance results to the senior accountable official for risk management or the risk executive (function).

The use of automated support tools to capture, organize, quantify, visually display, and maintain security and privacy posture information promotes near real-time risk management regarding the risk posture of the organization. The use of metrics and dashboards increases an organization's capability to make risk-based decisions by consolidating data in an automated fashion and providing the data to decision makers at different levels within the organization in an easy-to-understand format.

References: [SP 800-30]; [SP 800-39] (Organization, Mission/Business Process, and System Levels); [SP 800-55]; [SP 800-160 v1] (Risk Management Process); [IR 8011 v1]; [IR 8062].

SYSTEM DISPOSAL

Task M-7 Implement a system disposal strategy and execute required actions when a system is removed from operation.

Potential Inputs: Security and privacy plans; organization- and system-level risk assessment results; system component inventory.

Expected Outputs: Disposal strategy; updated system component inventory; updated security and privacy plans.

Primary Responsibility: System Owner.

Supporting Roles: Authorizing Official or Authorizing Official Designated Representative; Information Owner or Steward; System Security Officer; System Privacy Officer; Senior Accountable Official for Risk

---

[111] See Appendix F for additional information on ongoing authorization and continuous monitoring.

Management or Risk Executive (Function); Senior Agency Information Security Officer; Senior Agency Official for Privacy.

System Development Life Cycle Phase: New – Not Applicable.
                                         Existing – Disposal.

Discussion: When a system is removed from operation, several risk management actions are required. Organizations ensure that controls addressing system disposal are implemented. Examples include media sanitization; configuration management and control; component authenticity; and record retention. Organizational tracking and management systems (including inventory systems) are updated to indicate the system that is being removed from service. Security and privacy posture reports reflect the security and privacy status of the system. Users and application owners hosted on the disposed system are notified as appropriate, and any control inheritance relationships are reviewed and assessed for impact. This task also applies to system elements that are removed from operation. Organizations removing a system from operation update the inventory of information systems to reflect the removal. System owners and security personnel ensure that disposed systems comply with relevant federal laws, regulations, directives, policies, and standards.

References: [SP 800-30]; [SP 800-88]; [IR 8062].

This publication is available free of charge from: https://doi.org/10.6028/NIST.SP.800-37r2

Guide for Applying the Risk Management Framework to Federal Information Systems (800-37 rev 2)
286

APPENDIX A

REFERENCES

LAWS, POLICIES, DIRECTIVES, REGULATIONS, STANDARDS, AND GUIDELINES

LAWS AND EXECUTIVE ORDERS	
[32 CFR 2002.4]	Title 32 Code of Federal Regulations, Sec. 2002.4, *Definitions*. 2018 ed. https://www.govinfo.gov/app/details/CFR-2018-title32-vol6/CFR-2018-title32-vol6-sec2002-4
[40 USC 11331]	Title 40 U.S. Code, Sec. 11331, *Responsibilities for Federal information systems standards*. 2017 ed. https://www.govinfo.gov/app/details/USCODE-2017-title40/USCODE-2017-title40-subtitleIII-chap113-subchapIII-sec11331
[44 USC 3301]	Title 44 U.S. Code, Sec. 3301, *Definition of records*. 2017 ed. https://www.govinfo.gov/app/details/USCODE-2017-title44/USCODE-2017-title44-chap33-sec3301
[44 USC 3502]	Title 44 U.S. Code, Sec. 3502, *Definitions*. 2017 ed. https://www.govinfo.gov/app/details/USCODE-2017-title44/USCODE-2017-title44-chap35-subchapI-sec3502
[44 USC 3552]	Title 44 U.S. Code, Sec. 3552, *Definitions*. 2017 ed. https://www.govinfo.gov/app/details/USCODE-2017-title44/USCODE-2017-title44-chap35-subchapII-sec3552
[44 USC 3554]	Title 44 U.S. Code, Sec. 3554, *Federal agency responsibilities*. 2017 ed. https://www.govinfo.gov/app/details/USCODE-2017-title44/USCODE-2017-title44-chap35-subchapII-sec3554
[44 USC 3601]	Title 44 U.S. Code, Sec. 3601, *Definitions*. 2017 ed. https://www.govinfo.gov/app/details/USCODE-2017-title44/USCODE-2017-title44-chap36-sec3601
[PRIVACT]	Privacy Act (P.L. 93-579), December 1974. https://www.govinfo.gov/app/details/STATUTE-88/STATUTE-88-Pg1896
[FOIA96]	Freedom of Information Act (FOIA), 5 U.S.C. § 552, As Amended By Public Law No. 104-231, 110 Stat. 3048, Electronic Freedom of Information Act Amendments of 1996. https://www.govinfo.gov/app/details/PLAW-104publ231
[FISMA]	Federal Information Security Modernization Act (P.L. 113-283), December 2014. https://www.govinfo.gov/app/details/PLAW-113publ283
[EO 13800]	Executive Order 13800, *Strengthening the Cybersecurity of Federal Networks and Critical Infrastructure*, May 2017. https://www.govinfo.gov/app/details/FR-2017-05-16/2017-10004

POLICIES, REGULATIONS, DIRECTIVES, AND INSTRUCTIONS	
[OMB A-123]	Office of Management and Budget Circular No. A-123, *Management's Responsibility for Enterprise Risk Management and Internal Control*, July 2016. https://www.whitehouse.gov/sites/whitehouse.gov/files/omb/memoranda/2016/m-16-17.pdf
[OMB A-130]	Office of Management and Budget Circular A-130, *Managing Information as a Strategic Resource*, July 2016. https://www.whitehouse.gov/sites/whitehouse.gov/files/omb/circulars/A130/a130revised.pdf
[OMB M-13-13]	Office of Management and Budget Memorandum M-13-13, *Open Data Policy-Managing Information as an Asset*, May 2013. https://obamawhitehouse.archives.gov/sites/default/files/omb/memoranda/2013/m-13-13.pdf
[OMB M-17-25]	Office of Management and Budget Memorandum M-17-25, *Reporting Guidance for Executive Order on Strengthening the Cybersecurity of Federal Networks and Critical Infrastructure*, May 2017. https://www.whitehouse.gov/sites/whitehouse.gov/files/omb/memoranda/2017/M-17-25.pdf
[OMB M-19-03]	Office of Management and Budget Memorandum M-19-03, *Strengthening the Cybersecurity of Federal Agencies by enhancing the High Value Asset Program*, December 2018. https://www.whitehouse.gov/wp-content/uploads/2018/12/M-19-03.pdf
[CNSSI 1253]	Committee on National Security Systems Instruction 1253, *Security Categorization and Control Selection for National Security Systems*, March 2014. https://www.cnss.gov/CNSS/issuances/Instructions.cfm
[CNSSI 4009]	Committee on National Security Systems Instruction 4009, *Committee on National Security Systems (CNSS) Glossary*, April 2015. https://www.cnss.gov/CNSS/issuances/Instructions.cfm
[CNSSD 505]	Committee on National Security Systems Directive 505, *Supply Chain Risk Management*, August 2017. https://www.cnss.gov/CNSS/issuances/Directives.cfm
[OCIO HVA]	Office of the Federal Chief Information Officer, *The Agency HVA Process*. https://policy.cio.gov/hva/process
[DODI 5200.44]	Department of Defense Instruction 5200.44, *Protection of Mission Critical Functions to Achieve Trusted Systems and Networks* (TSN), July 2017. http://www.esd.whs.mil/Portals/54/Documents/DD/issuances/dodi/520044p.pdf
STANDARDS, GUIDELINES, AND REPORTS	
[IEEE 610.12]	Institute of Electrical and Electronics Engineers (IEEE) Std. 610.12-1990, *IEEE Standard Glossary of Software Engineering Terminology*, December 1990. https://ieeexplore.ieee.org/iel1/2238/4148/00159342.pdf

[ISO 15026-1] International Organization for Standardization/International
Electrotechnical Commission/Institute of Electrical and Electronics
Engineers (ISO/IEC/IEEE) 15026-1:2013, *Systems and software
engineering—Systems and software assurance—Part 1: Concepts and
vocabulary*, May 2015.
https://www.iso.org/standard/62526.html

[ISO 15288] International Organization for Standardization/International
Electrotechnical Commission/Institute of Electrical and Electronics
Engineers (ISO/IEC/IEEE) 15288:2015, *Systems and software engineering—
Systems life cycle processes*, May 2015.
https://www.iso.org/standard/63711.html

[ISO 15408-1] International Organization for Standardization/International
Electrotechnical Commission 15408-1:2009, *Information technology—
Security techniques— Evaluation criteria for IT security—Part 1:
Introduction and general model*.
https://www.commoncriteriaportal.org/files/ccfiles/CCPART1V3.1R5.pdf

[ISO 15408-2] International Organization for Standardization/International
Electrotechnical Commission 15408-2:2008, *Information technology—
Security techniques— Evaluation criteria for IT security—Part 2: Security
functional requirements*.
https://www.commoncriteriaportal.org/files/ccfiles/CCPART2V3.1R5.pdf

[ISO 15408-3] International Organization for Standardization/International
Electrotechnical Commission 15408-3:2008, *Information technology—
Security techniques— Evaluation criteria for IT security—Part 3: Security
assurance requirements*.
https://www.commoncriteriaportal.org/files/ccfiles/CCPART3V3.1R5.pdf

[ISO 27001] International Organization for Standardization/International
Electrotechnical Commission 27001:2013, *Information Technology—
Security techniques— Information security management systems—
Requirements*.
https://www.iso.org/standard/54534.html

[ISO 29148] International Organization for Standardization/International
Electrotechnical Commission/Institute of Electrical and Electronics
Engineers (ISO/IEC/IEEE) 29148:2011, *Systems and software engineering—
Life cycle processes—Requirements engineering*, December 2011.
https://www.iso.org/standard/45171.html

[FIPS 199] National Institute of Standards and Technology Federal Information
Processing Standards Publication 199, *Standards for Security Categorization
of Federal Information and Information Systems*, February 2004.
https://doi.org/10.6028/NIST.FIPS.199

[FIPS 200] National Institute of Standards and Technology Federal Information
Processing Standards Publication 200, *Minimum Security Requirements for
Federal Information and Information Systems*, March 2006.
https://doi.org/10.6028/NIST.FIPS.200

[SP 800-18]   National Institute of Standards and Technology Special Publication 800-18,
Revision 1, *Guide for Developing Security Plans for Federal Information
Systems*, February 2006.
https://doi.org/10.6028/NIST.SP.800-18r1

[SP 800-30]   National Institute of Standards and Technology Special Publication 800-30,
Revision 1, *Guide for Conducting Risk Assessments*, September 2012.
https://doi.org/10.6028/NIST.SP.800-30r1

[SP 800-39]   National Institute of Standards and Technology Special Publication 800-39,
*Managing Information Security Risk: Organization, Mission, and
Information System View*, March 2011.
https://doi.org/10.6028/NIST.SP.800-39

[SP 800-47]   National Institute of Standards and Technology Special Publication 800-47,
Security Guide for Interconnecting Information Technology Systems, August
2002.
https://doi.org/10.6028/NIST.SP.800-47

[SP 800-53]   National Institute of Standards and Technology Special Publication 800-53,
Revision 4, *Security and Privacy Controls for Federal Information Systems
and Organizations*, April 2013.
https://doi.org/10.6028/NIST.SP.800-53r4

[SP 800-53A]   National Institute of Standards and Technology Special Publication 800-53A,
Revision 4, *Assessing Security and Privacy Controls in Federal Information
Systems and Organizations: Building Effective Security Assessment Plans*,
July 2008.
https://doi.org/10.6028/NIST.SP.800-53Ar4

[SP 800-55]   National Institute of Standards and Technology Special Publication 800-55,
Revision 1, *Performance Measurement Guide for Information Security*,
December 2014.
https://doi.org/10.6028/NIST.SP.800-55r1

[SP 800-59]   National Institute of Standards and Technology Special Publication 800-59,
*Guideline for Identifying an Information System as a National Security
System*, August 2003.
https://doi.org/10.6028/NIST.SP.800-59

[SP 800-60 v1]   National Institute of Standards and Technology Special Publication 800-60,
Volume 1, Revision 1, *Guide for Mapping Types of Information and
Information Systems to Security Categories*, August 2008.
https://doi.org/10.6028/NIST.SP.800-60v1r1

[SP 800-60 v2]   National Institute of Standards and Technology Special Publication 800-60,
Volume 2, Revision 1, *Guide for Mapping Types of Information and
Information Systems to Security Categories: Appendices*, August 2008.
https://doi.org/10.6028/NIST.SP.800-60v2r1

[SP 800-61]   National Institute of Standards and Technology Special Publication 800-61,
Revision 2, *Computer Security Incident Handling Guide*, August 2012.
https://doi.org/10.6028/NIST.SP.800-61r2

[SP 800-64]   National Institute of Standards and Technology Special Publication 800-64,
                  Revision 2, *Security Considerations in the System Development Life Cycle*,
                  October 2008.
                  https://doi.org/10.6028/NIST.SP.800-64r2

[SP 800-82]   National Institute of Standards and Technology Special Publication 800-82,
                  Revision 2, *Guide to Industrial Control Systems (ICS) Security*, May 2015.
                  https://doi.org/10.6028/NIST.SP.800-82r2

[SP 800-88]   National Institute of Standards and Technology Special Publication 800-88,
                  Guidelines for Media Sanitization, December 2014.
                  https://doi.org/10.6028/NIST.SP.800-88r1

[SP 800-128]   National Institute of Standards and Technology Special Publication 800-128,
                  *Guide for Security-Focused Configuration Management of Information
                  Systems*, August 2011.
                  https://doi.org/10.6028/NIST.SP.800-128

[SP 800-137]   National Institute of Standards and Technology Special Publication 800-137,
                  *Information Security Continuous Monitoring for Federal Information
                  Systems and Organizations*, September 2011.
                  https://doi.org/10.6028/NIST.SP.800-137

[SP 800-160 v1]   National Institute of Standards and Technology Special Publication 800-160,
                  Volume 1, *Systems Security Engineering: Considerations for a
                  Multidisciplinary Approach in the Engineering of Trustworthy Secure
                  Systems*, November 2016.
                  https://doi.org/10.6028/NIST.SP.800-160v1

[SP 800-161]   National Institute of Standards and Technology Special Publication 800-161,
                  *Supply Chain Risk Management Practices for Federal Information Systems
                  and Organizations*, April 2015.
                  https://doi.org/10.6028/NIST.SP.800-161

[SP 800-181]   National Institute of Standards and Technology Special Publication 800-181,
                  *National Initiative for Cybersecurity Education (NICE) Cybersecurity
                  Workforce Framework*, August 2017.
                  https://doi.org/10.6028/NIST.SP.800-181

[IR 8011 v1]   National Institute of Standards and Technology Interagency Report 8011,
                  Volume 1, *Automation Support for Security Control Assessments: Overview*,
                  June 2017.
                  https://doi.org/10.6028/NIST.IR.8011-1

[IR 8062]   National Institute of Standards and Technology Internal Report 8062, *An
                  Introduction to Privacy Engineering and Risk Management in Federal
                  Systems*, January 2017.
                  https://doi.org/10.6028/NIST.IR.8062

[IR 8179]   National Institute of Standards and Technology Internal Report 8179,
                  Criticality Analysis Process Model: Prioritizing Systems and Components,
                  April 2018.
                  https://doi.org/10.6028/NIST.IR.8179

Guide for Applying the Risk Management Framework to Federal Information Systems (800-37 rev 2)

MISCELLANEOUS PUBLICATIONS AND WEBSITES	
[DSB 2013]	Department of Defense, Defense Science Board, *Task Force Report: Resilient Military Systems and the Advanced Cyber Threat*, January 2013. https://www.acq.osd.mil/dsb/reports/2010s/ResilientMilitarySystemsCyberThreat.pdf
[NARA CUI]	National Archives and Records Administration, *Controlled Unclassified Information (CUI) Registry*. https://www.archives.gov/cui
[NARA RECM]	National Archives and Records Administration, *NARA Records Management Guidance and Regulations*. https://www.archives.gov/records-mgmt/policy/guidance-regulations.html
[NIST CSF]	National Institute of Standards and Technology *Framework for Improving Critical Infrastructure Cybersecurity* (Cybersecurity Framework), Version 1.1, April 2018. https://www.nist.gov/cyberframework
[OMB FEA]	Office of Management and Budget, *Federal Enterprise Architecture (FEA)*. https://obamawhitehouse.archives.gov/omb/e-gov/fea

Guide for Applying the Risk Management Framework to Federal Information Systems (800-37 rev 2)
292

NIST SP 800-37, REVISION 2

RISK MANAGEMENT FRAMEWORK FOR INFORMATION SYSTEMS AND ORGANIZATIONS
A System Life Cycle Approach for Security and Privacy

APPENDIX B

GLOSSARY
COMMON TERMS AND DEFINITIONS

Appendix B provides definitions for terminology used within Special Publication 800-37. Sources for terms used in this publication are cited as applicable. Where no citation is noted, the source of the definition is Special Publication 800-37.

adequate security [OMB A-130]	Security protections commensurate with the risk resulting from the unauthorized access, use, disclosure, disruption, modification, or destruction of information. This includes ensuring that information hosted on behalf of an agency and information systems and applications used by the agency operate effectively and provide appropriate confidentiality, integrity, and availability protections through the application of cost-effective security controls.
agency [OMB A-130]	Any executive agency or department, military department, Federal Government corporation, Federal Government-controlled corporation, or other establishment in the Executive Branch of the Federal Government, or any independent regulatory agency.
allocation	The process an organization employs to assign security or privacy requirements to an information system or its environment of operation; or to assign controls to specific system elements responsible for providing a security or privacy capability (e.g., router, server, remote sensor).
application	A software program hosted by an information system.
assessment	See *control assessment* or *risk assessment*.
assessment plan	The objectives for the control assessments and a detailed roadmap of how to conduct such assessments.
assessor	The individual, group, or organization responsible for conducting a security or privacy assessment.
assignment statement	A control parameter that allows an organization to assign a specific, organization-defined value to the control or control enhancement (e.g., assigning a list of roles to be notified or a value for the frequency of testing). See *organization-defined control parameters* and *selection statement*.

assurance [ISO 15026, Adapted]	Grounds for justified confidence that a [security or privacy] claim has been or will be achieved. *Note 1:* Assurance is typically obtained relative to a set of specific claims. The scope and focus of such claims may vary (e.g., security claims, safety claims) and the claims themselves may be interrelated. *Note 2:* Assurance is obtained through techniques and methods that generate credible evidence to substantiate claims.
audit log [CNSSI 4009]	A chronological record of system activities, including records of system accesses and operations performed in a given period.
audit trail	A chronological record that reconstructs and examines the sequence of activities surrounding or leading to a specific operation, procedure, or event in a security-relevant transaction from inception to result.
authentication [FIPS 200]	Verifying the identity of a user, process, or device, often as a prerequisite to allowing access to resources in a system.
authenticity	The property of being genuine and being able to be verified and trusted; confidence in the validity of a transmission, a message, or message originator. See *authentication*.
authorization boundary [OMB A-130]	All components of an information system to be authorized for operation by an authorizing official. This excludes separately authorized systems to which the information system is connected.
authorization package [OMB A-130]	The essential information that an authorizing official uses to determine whether to authorize the operation of an information system or the provision of a designated set of common controls. At a minimum, the authorization package includes an executive summary, system security plan, privacy plan, security control assessment, privacy control assessment, and any relevant plans of action and milestones.
authorization to operate [OMB A-130]	The official management decision given by a senior Federal official or officials to authorize operation of an information system and to explicitly accept the risk to agency operations (including mission, functions, image, or reputation), agency assets, individuals, other organizations, and the Nation based on the implementation of an agreed-upon set of security and privacy controls. Authorization also applies to common controls inherited by agency information systems.

Guide for Applying the Risk Management Framework to Federal Information Systems (800-37 rev 2)

294

NIST SP 800-37, REVISION 2

RISK MANAGEMENT FRAMEWORK FOR INFORMATION SYSTEMS AND ORGANIZATIONS
A System Life Cycle Approach for Security and Privacy

| **authorization to use** | The official management decision given by an authorizing official to authorize the use of an information system, service, or application based on the information in an existing authorization package generated by another organization, and to explicitly accept the risk to agency operations (including mission, functions, image, or reputation), agency assets, individuals, other organizations, and the Nation based on the implementation of an agreed-upon set of controls in the system, service, or application.

Note: An authorization to use typically applies to cloud and shared systems, services, and applications and is employed when an organization (referred to as the customer organization) chooses to accept the information in an existing authorization package generated by another organization (referred to as the provider organization). |
|---|---|
| **authorizing official**
[OMB A-130] | A senior Federal official or executive with the authority to authorize (i.e., assume responsibility for) the operation of an information system or the use of a designated set of common controls at an acceptable level of risk to agency operations (including mission, functions, image, or reputation), agency assets, individuals, other organizations, and the Nation. |
| **authorizing official designated representative** | An organizational official acting on behalf of an authorizing official in carrying out and coordinating the required activities associated with the authorization process. |
| **availability**
[44 USC 3552] | Ensuring timely and reliable access to and use of information. |
| **baseline** | See *control baseline.* |
| **baseline configuration**
[SP 800-128, Adapted] | A documented set of specifications for a system, or a configuration item within a system, that has been formally reviewed and agreed on at a given point in time, and which can be changed only through change control procedures. |
| **capability** | A combination of mutually reinforcing controls implemented by technical means, physical means, and procedural means. Such controls are typically selected to achieve a common information security or privacy purpose. |
| **capability requirement** | A type of requirement describing the capability that the organization or system must provide to satisfy a stakeholder need.

Note: Capability requirements related to information security and privacy are derived from stakeholder protection needs and the corresponding security and privacy requirements. |
| **chain of trust**
(supply chain) | A certain level of trust in supply chain interactions such that each participant in the consumer-provider relationship provides adequate protection for its component products, systems, and services. |

chief information officer [OMB A-130]	The senior official that provides advice and other assistance to the head of the agency and other senior management personnel of the agency to ensure that IT is acquired and information resources are managed for the agency in a manner that achieves the agency's strategic goals and information resources management goals; and is responsible for ensuring agency compliance with, and prompt, efficient, and effective implementation of, the information policies and information resources management responsibilities, including the reduction of information collection burdens on the public.
chief information security officer	See *Senior Agency Information Security Officer.*
classified information	See classified national security information.
classified national security information [CNSSI 4009]	Information that has been determined pursuant to Executive Order (E.O.) 13526 or any predecessor order to require protection against unauthorized disclosure and is marked to indicate its classified status when in documentary form.
commodity service	A system service provided by a commercial service provider to a large and diverse set of consumers. The organization acquiring or receiving the commodity service possesses limited visibility into the management structure and operations of the provider, and while the organization may be able to negotiate service-level agreements, the organization is typically not able to require that the provider implement specific controls.
common control [OMB A-130]	A security or privacy control that is inherited by multiple information systems or programs.
common control provider	An organizational official responsible for the development, implementation, assessment, and monitoring of common controls (i.e., controls inheritable by organizational systems).
common criteria [CNSSI 4009]	Governing document that provides a comprehensive, rigorous method for specifying security function and assurance requirements for products and systems.
compensating controls	The security and privacy controls implemented in lieu of the controls in the baselines described in NIST Special Publication 800-53 that provide equivalent or comparable protection for a system or organization.
component	See *system component.*
confidentiality [44 USC 3552]	Preserving authorized restrictions on information access and disclosure, including means for protecting personal privacy and proprietary information.

configuration control [CNSSI 4009]	Process for controlling modifications to hardware, firmware, software, and documentation to protect the information system against improper modifications before, during, and after system implementation.
configuration item [SP 800-128]	An aggregation of system components that is designated for configuration management and treated as a single entity in the configuration management process.
configuration management [SP 800-128]	A collection of activities focused on establishing and maintaining the integrity of information technology products and systems, through control of processes for initializing, changing, and monitoring the configurations of those products and systems throughout the system development life cycle.
configuration settings [SP 800-128]	The set of parameters that can be changed in hardware, software, or firmware that affect the security posture and/or functionality of the system.
continuous monitoring	Maintaining ongoing awareness to support organizational risk decisions.
continuous monitoring program	A program established to collect information in accordance with preestablished metrics, utilizing information readily available in part through implemented security controls. *Note:* Privacy and security continuous monitoring strategies and programs can be the same or different strategies and programs.
control	See *security control* and *privacy control*.
control assessment	The testing or evaluation of the controls in an information system or an organization to determine the extent to which the controls are implemented correctly, operating as intended, and producing the desired outcome with respect to meeting the security or privacy requirements for the system or the organization.
control assessor	The individual, group, or organization responsible for conducting a control assessment. See *assessor*.
control baseline	The set of controls that are applicable to information or an information system to meet legal, regulatory, or policy requirements, as well as address protection needs for the purpose of managing risk.
control designation	The process of assigning a control to one of three control types: common, hybrid, or system-specific.
control effectiveness	A measure of whether a given control is contributing to the reduction of information security or privacy risk.
control enhancement	Augmentation of a control to build in additional, but related, functionality to the control; increase the strength of the control; or add assurance to the control.

Guide for Applying the Risk Management Framework to Federal Information Systems (800-37 rev 2)

297

control inheritance	A situation in which a system or application receives protection from controls (or portions of controls) that are developed, implemented, assessed, authorized, and monitored by entities other than those responsible for the system or application; entities either internal or external to the organization where the system or application resides. See *common control*.
control parameter	See *organization-defined control parameter*.
controlled unclassified information [32 CFR 2002.4]	Information that the Government creates or possesses, or that an entity creates or possesses for or on behalf of the Government, that a law, regulation, or Government-wide policy requires or permits an agency to handle using safeguarding or dissemination controls. However, CUI does not include classified information or information a non-executive branch entity possesses and maintains in its own systems that did not come from, or was not created or possessed by or for, an executive branch agency or an entity acting for an agency.
countermeasures [FIPS 200]	Actions, devices, procedures, techniques, or other measures that reduce the vulnerability of a system. Synonymous with *security controls* and *safeguards*.
cybersecurity [OMB A-130]	Prevention of damage to, protection of, and restoration of computers, electronic communications systems, electronic communications services, wire communication, and electronic communication, including information contained therein, to ensure its availability, integrity, authentication, confidentiality, and nonrepudiation.
cybersecurity framework [NIST CSF]	A risk-based approach to reducing cybersecurity risk composed of three parts: the Framework Core, the Framework Profile, and the Framework Implementation Tiers.
cybersecurity framework category [NIST CSF]	The subdivision of a Function into groups of cybersecurity outcomes, closely tied to programmatic needs and particular activities.
cybersecurity framework core [NIST CSF]	A set of cybersecurity activities and references that are common across critical infrastructure sectors and are organized around particular outcomes. The Framework Core comprises four types of elements: Functions, Categories, Subcategories, and Informative References.
cybersecurity framework function [NIST CSF]	One of the main components of the Framework. Functions provide the highest level of structure for organizing basic cybersecurity activities into Categories and Subcategories. The five functions are Identify, Protect, Detect, Respond, and Recover.

cybersecurity framework profile [NIST CSF]	A representation of the outcomes that a particular system or organization has selected from the Framework Categories and Subcategories.
cybersecurity framework subcategory [NIST CSF]	The subdivision of a Category into specific outcomes of technical and/or management activities.
derived requirements [SP 800-160 V1]	A requirement that is implied or transformed from a higher-level requirement. *Note 1*: Implied requirements cannot be assessed since they are not contained in any requirements baseline. The decomposition of requirements throughout the engineering process makes implicit requirements explicit, allowing them to be stated and captured in appropriate baselines and allowing associated assessment criteria to be stated. *Note 2*: A derived requirement must trace back to at least one higher-level requirement.
detect (CSF function) [NIST CSF]	Develop and implement the appropriate activities to identify the occurrence of a cybersecurity event.
developer	A general term that includes developers or manufacturers of systems, system components, or system services; systems integrators; vendors; and product resellers. Development of systems, components, or services can occur internally within organizations or through external entities.
enterprise [CNSSI 4009]	An organization with a defined mission/goal and a defined boundary, using systems to execute that mission, and with responsibility for managing its own risks and performance. An enterprise may consist of all or some of the following business aspects: acquisition, program management, human resources, financial management, security, and systems, information and mission management. See *organization*.
enterprise architecture [44 USC 3601]	A strategic information asset base, which defines the mission; the information necessary to perform the mission; the technologies necessary to perform the mission; and the transitional processes for implementing new technologies in response to changing mission needs; and includes a baseline architecture; a target architecture; and a sequencing plan.
environment of operation [OMB A-130]	The physical surroundings in which an information system processes, stores, and transmits information.
event [SP 800-61, Adapted]	Any observable occurrence in a network or information system.
executive agency [OMB A-130]	An executive department specified in 5 U.S.C. Sec. 101; a military department specified in 5 U.S.C. Sec. 102; an independent establishment as defined in 5 U.S.C. Sec. 104(1); and a wholly owned Government corporation fully subject to the provisions of 31 U.S.C. Chapter 91.

Guide for Applying the Risk Management Framework to Federal Information Systems (800-37 rev 2)
299

external system (or component)	A system or system element that is outside of the authorization boundary established by the organization and for which the organization typically has no direct control over the application of required controls or the assessment of control effectiveness.
external system service	A system service that is implemented outside of the authorization boundary of the organizational system (i.e., a service that is used by, but not a part of, the organizational system) and for which the organization typically has no direct control over the application of required controls or the assessment of control effectiveness.
external system service provider	A provider of external system services to an organization through a variety of consumer-producer relationships including but not limited to: joint ventures; business partnerships; outsourcing arrangements (i.e., through contracts, interagency agreements, lines of business arrangements); licensing agreements; and/or supply chain exchanges.
external network	A network not controlled by the organization.
federal agency	See *executive agency*.
federal enterprise architecture [OMB FEA]	A business-based framework for governmentwide improvement developed by the Office of Management and Budget that is intended to facilitate efforts to transform the federal government to one that is citizen-centered, results-oriented, and market-based.
federal information system [40 USC 11331]	An information system used or operated by an executive agency, by a contractor of an executive agency, or by another organization on behalf of an executive agency.
firmware [CNSSI 4009]	Computer programs and data stored in hardware - typically in read-only memory (ROM) or programmable read-only memory (PROM) - such that the programs and data cannot be dynamically written or modified during execution of the programs. See *hardware* and *software*.
hardware [CNSSI 4009]	The material physical components of a system. See *software* and *firmware*.
high-impact system [FIPS 200]	A system in which at least one security objective (i.e., confidentiality, integrity, or availability) is assigned a FIPS Publication 199 potential impact value of high.
hybrid control [OMB A-130]	A security or privacy control that is implemented for an information system in part as a common control and in part as a system-specific control. See *common control* and *system-specific control*.
identify (CSF function) [NIST CSF]	Develop and implement the appropriate activities to identify the occurrence of a cybersecurity event.

impact	With respect to security, the effect on organizational operations, organizational assets, individuals, other organizations, or the Nation (including the national security interests of the United States) of a loss of confidentiality, integrity, or availability of information or a system. With respect to privacy, the adverse effects that individuals could experience when an information system processes their PII.
impact level	See *impact value*.
impact value [FIPS 199]	The assessed worst-case potential impact that could result from a compromise of the confidentiality, integrity, or availability of information expressed as a value of low, moderate or high.
incident [44 USC 3552]	An occurrence that actually or imminently jeopardizes, without lawful authority, the confidentiality, integrity, or availability of information or an information system; or constitutes a violation or imminent threat of violation of law, security policies, security procedures, or acceptable use policies.
independent verification and validation [CNSSI 4009]	A comprehensive review, analysis, and testing, (software and/or hardware) performed by an objective third party to confirm (i.e., verify) that the requirements are correctly defined, and to confirm (i.e., validate) that the system correctly implements the required functionality and security requirements.
industrial control system [SP 800-82]	General term that encompasses several types of control systems, including supervisory control and data acquisition (SCADA) systems, distributed control systems (DCS), and other control system configurations such as programmable logic controllers (PLC) often found in the industrial sectors and critical infrastructures. An ICS consists of combinations of control components (e.g., electrical, mechanical, hydraulic, pneumatic) that act together to achieve an industrial objective (e.g., manufacturing, transportation of matter or energy).
information [OMB A-130]	Any communication or representation of knowledge such as facts, data, or opinions in any medium or form, including textual, numerical, graphic, cartographic, narrative, electronic, or audiovisual forms.
information life cycle [OMB A-130]	The stages through which information passes, typically characterized as creation or collection, processing, dissemination, use, storage, and disposition, to include destruction and deletion.
information owner	Official with statutory or operational authority for specified information and responsibility for establishing the controls for its generation, collection, processing, dissemination, and disposal.
information resources [44 USC 3502]	Information and related resources, such as personnel, equipment, funds, and information technology.

information security [44 USC 3552]	The protection of information and systems from unauthorized access, use, disclosure, disruption, modification, or destruction in order to provide confidentiality, integrity, and availability.
information security architecture [OMB A-130]	An embedded, integral part of the enterprise architecture that describes the structure and behavior of the enterprise security processes, security systems, personnel and organizational subunits, showing their alignment with the enterprise's mission and strategic plans. See *security architecture*.
information security program plan [OMB A-130]	Formal document that provides an overview of the security requirements for an organization-wide information security program and describes the program management controls and common controls in place or planned for meeting those requirements.
information security risk [SP 800-30]	The risk to organizational operations (including mission, functions, image, reputation), organizational assets, individuals, other organizations, and the Nation due to the potential for unauthorized access, use, disclosure, disruption, modification, or destruction of information and/or systems.
information steward	An agency official with statutory or operational authority for specified information and responsibility for establishing the controls for its generation, collection, processing, dissemination, and disposal.
information system [44 USC 3502]	A discrete set of information resources organized for the collection, processing, maintenance, use, sharing, dissemination, or disposition of information.
information system boundary	See *authorization boundary*.
information system security officer [CNSSI 4009]	Individual with assigned responsibility for maintaining the appropriate operational security posture for an information system or program.
information system security plan [OMB A-130]	A formal document that provides an overview of the security requirements for an information system and describes the security controls in place or planned for meeting those requirements.

NIST SP 800-37, REVISION 2

RISK MANAGEMENT FRAMEWORK FOR INFORMATION SYSTEMS AND ORGANIZATIONS
A System Life Cycle Approach for Security and Privacy

information technology
[OMB A-130]

Any services, equipment, or interconnected system(s) or subsystem(s) of equipment, that are used in the automatic acquisition, storage, analysis, evaluation, manipulation, management, movement, control, display, switching, interchange, transmission, or reception of data or information by the agency. For purposes of this definition, such services or equipment if used by the agency directly or is used by a contractor under a contract with the agency that requires its use; or to a significant extent, its use in the performance of a service or the furnishing of a product. Information technology includes computers, ancillary equipment (including imaging peripherals, input, output, and storage devices necessary for security and surveillance), peripheral equipment designed to be controlled by the central processing unit of a computer, software, firmware and similar procedures, services (including cloud computing and help-desk services or other professional services which support any point of the life cycle of the equipment or service), and related resources. Information technology does not include any equipment that is acquired by a contractor incidental to a contract which does not require its use.

information technology product

See *system component*.

information type
[FIPS 199]

A specific category of information (e.g., privacy, medical, proprietary, financial, investigative, contractor-sensitive, security management) defined by an organization or in some instances, by a specific law, executive order, directive, policy, or regulation.

interface
[CNSSI 4009]

Common boundary between independent systems or modules where interactions take place.

integrity
[44 USC 3552]

Guarding against improper information modification or destruction, and includes ensuring information non-repudiation and authenticity.

joint authorization

Authorization involving multiple authorizing officials.

low-impact system
[FIPS 200]

A system in which all three security objectives (i.e., confidentiality, integrity, and availability) are assigned a FIPS Publication 199 potential impact value of low.

media
[FIPS 200]

Physical devices or writing surfaces including, but not limited to, magnetic tapes, optical disks, magnetic disks, Large-Scale Integration memory chips, and printouts (but excluding display media) onto which information is recorded, stored, or printed within a system.

moderate-impact system [FIPS 200]	A system in which at least one security objective (i.e., confidentiality, integrity, or availability) is assigned a FIPS Publication 199 potential impact value of moderate and no security objective is assigned a potential impact value of high.
national security system [44 USC 3552]	Any system (including any telecommunications system) used or operated by an agency or by a contractor of an agency, or other organization on behalf of an agency—(i) the function, operation, or use of which involves intelligence activities; involves cryptologic activities related to national security; involves command and control of military forces; involves equipment that is an integral part of a weapon or weapons system; or is critical to the direct fulfillment of military or intelligence missions (excluding a system that is to be used for routine administrative and business applications, for example, payroll, finance, logistics, and personnel management applications); or (ii) is protected at all times by procedures established for information that have been specifically authorized under criteria established by an Executive Order or an Act of Congress to be kept classified in the interest of national defense or foreign policy.
network	A system implemented with a collection of interconnected components. Such components may include routers, hubs, cabling, telecommunications controllers, key distribution centers, and technical control devices.
network access	Access to a system by a user (or a process acting on behalf of a user) communicating through a network (e.g., a local area network, a wide area network, and Internet).
operational technology	Programmable systems or devices that interact with the physical environment (or manage devices that interact with the physical environment). These systems/devices detect or cause a direct change through the monitoring and/or control of devices, processes, and events. Examples include industrial control systems, building management systems, fire control systems, and physical access control mechanisms.
operations technology	See *operational technology*.
organization [FIPS 200, Adapted]	An entity of any size, complexity, or positioning within an organizational structure (e.g., federal agencies, private enterprises, academic institutions, state, local, or tribal governments, or as appropriate, any of their operational elements).
organizationally-tailored control baseline	A control baseline tailored for a defined notional (type of) information system using overlays and/or system-specific control tailoring, and intended for use in selecting controls for multiple systems within one or more organizations.

Guide for Applying the Risk Management Framework to Federal Information Systems (800-37 rev 2)

304

organization-defined control parameter	The variable part of a control or control enhancement that can be instantiated by an organization during the tailoring process by either assigning an organization-defined value or selecting a value from a pre-defined list provided as part of the control or control enhancement.
overlay [OMB A-130]	A specification of security or privacy controls, control enhancements, supplemental guidance, and other supporting information employed during the tailoring process, that is intended to complement (and further refine) security control baselines. The overlay specification may be more stringent or less stringent than the original security control baseline specification and can be applied to multiple information systems.
personally identifiable information [OMB A-130]	Information that can be used to distinguish or trace an individual's identity, either alone or when combined with other information that is linked or linkable to a specific individual.
plan of action and milestones	A document that identifies tasks needing to be accomplished. It details resources required to accomplish the elements of the plan, any milestones in meeting the tasks, and scheduled completion dates for the milestones.
potential impact [FIPS 199]	The loss of confidentiality, integrity, or availability could be expected to have a limited adverse effect (FIPS Publication 199 low); a serious adverse effect (FIPS Publication 199 moderate); or a severe or catastrophic adverse effect (FIPS Publication 199 high) on organizational operations, organizational assets, or individuals.
privacy architect	Individual, group, or organization responsible for ensuring that the system privacy requirements necessary to protect individuals' privacy are adequately addressed in all aspects of enterprise architecture including reference models, segment and solution architectures, and information systems processing PII.
privacy architecture	An embedded, integral part of the enterprise architecture that describes the structure and behavior for an enterprise's privacy protection processes, technical measures, personnel and organizational sub-units, showing their alignment with the enterprise's mission and strategic plans.
privacy control [OMB A-130]	The administrative, technical, and physical safeguards employed within an agency to ensure compliance with applicable privacy requirements and manage privacy risks. *Note:* Controls can be selected to achieve multiple objectives; those controls that are selected to achieve both security and privacy objectives require a degree of collaboration between the organization's information security program and privacy program.

NIST SP 800-37, REVISION 2

RISK MANAGEMENT FRAMEWORK FOR INFORMATION SYSTEMS AND ORGANIZATIONS
A System Life Cycle Approach for Security and Privacy

privacy control assessment [OMB A-130]	The assessment of privacy controls to determine whether the controls are implemented correctly, operating as intended, and sufficient to ensure compliance with applicable privacy requirements and manage privacy risks. A privacy control assessment is both an assessment and a formal document detailing the process and the outcome of the assessment.
privacy control baseline	A collection of controls specifically assembled or brought together by a group, organization, or community of interest to address the privacy protection needs of individuals.
privacy impact assessment [OMB A-130]	An analysis of how information is handled to ensure handling conforms to applicable legal, regulatory, and policy requirements regarding privacy; to determine the risks and effects of creating, collecting, using, processing, storing, maintaining, disseminating, disclosing, and disposing of information in identifiable form in an electronic information system; and to examine and evaluate protections and alternate processes for handling information to mitigate potential privacy concerns. A privacy impact assessment is both an analysis and a formal document detailing the process and the outcome of the analysis.
privacy plan [OMB A-130]	A formal document that details the privacy controls selected for an information system or environment of operation that are in place or planned for meeting applicable privacy requirements and managing privacy risks, details how the controls have been implemented, and describes the methodologies and metrics that will be used to assess the controls.
privacy posture	The privacy posture represents the status of the information systems and information resources (e.g., personnel, equipment, funds, and information technology) within an organization based on information assurance resources (e.g., people, hardware, software, policies, procedures) and the capabilities in place to comply with applicable privacy requirements and manage privacy risks and to react as the situation changes.
privacy program plan [OMB A-130]	A formal document that provides an overview of an agency's privacy program, including a description of the structure of the privacy program, the resources dedicated to the privacy program, the role of the Senior Agency Official for Privacy and other privacy officials and staff, the strategic goals and objectives of the privacy program, and the program management controls and common controls in place or planned for meeting applicable privacy requirements and managing privacy risks.

Guide for Applying the Risk Management Framework to Federal Information Systems (800-37 rev 2)

306

NIST SP 800-37, REVISION 2

RISK MANAGEMENT FRAMEWORK FOR INFORMATION SYSTEMS AND ORGANIZATIONS
A System Life Cycle Approach for Security and Privacy

privacy requirement	A requirement that applies to an information system or an organization that is derived from applicable laws, executive orders, directives, policies, standards, regulations, procedures, and/or mission/business needs with respect to privacy. *Note:* The term *privacy requirement* can be used in a variety of contexts from high-level policy activities to low-level implementation activities in system development and engineering disciplines.
privacy information	Information that describes the privacy posture of an information system or organization.
protect (CSF function) [NIST CSF]	Develop and implement the appropriate safeguards to ensure delivery of critical infrastructure services.
provenance	The chronology of the origin, development, ownership, location, and changes to a system or system component and associated data. It may also include personnel and processes used to interact with or make modifications to the system, component, or associated data.
reciprocity	Agreement among participating organizations to accept each other's security assessments to reuse system resources and/or to accept each other's assessed security posture to share information.
records [44 USC 3301]	All recorded information, regardless of form or characteristics, made or received by a Federal agency under Federal law or in connection with the transaction of public business and preserved or appropriate for preservation by that agency or its legitimate successor as evidence of the organization, functions, policies, decisions, procedures, operations, or other activities of the United States Government or because of the informational value of data in them.
recover (CSF function) [NIST CSF]	Develop and implement the appropriate activities to maintain plans for resilience and to restore any capabilities or services that were impaired due to a cybersecurity event.
resilience [CNSSI 4009]	The ability to prepare for and adapt to changing conditions and withstand and recover rapidly from disruptions. Resilience includes the ability to withstand and recover from deliberate attacks, accidents, or naturally occurring threats or incidents.
respond (CSF function) [NIST CSF]	Develop and implement the appropriate activities to take action regarding a detected cybersecurity event.
risk [OMB A-130]	A measure of the extent to which an entity is threatened by a potential circumstance or event, and typically is a function of: (i) the adverse impact, or magnitude of harm, that would arise if the circumstance or event occurs; and (ii) the likelihood of occurrence.

risk assessment
[SP 800-30]

The process of identifying risks to organizational operations (including mission, functions, image, reputation), organizational assets, individuals, other organizations, and the Nation, resulting from the operation of a system.

risk executive (function)
[SP 800-39]

An individual or group within an organization, led by the senior accountable official for risk management, that helps to ensure that security risk considerations for individual systems, to include the authorization decisions for those systems, are viewed from an organization-wide perspective with regard to the overall strategic goals and objectives of the organization in carrying out its missions and business functions; and managing risk from individual systems is consistent across the organization, reflects organizational risk tolerance, and is considered along with other organizational risks affecting mission/business success.

risk management
[OMB A-130]

The program and supporting processes to manage risk to agency operations (including mission, functions, image, reputation), agency assets, individuals, other organizations, and the Nation, and includes: establishing the context for risk-related activities; assessing risk; responding to risk once determined; and monitoring risk over time.

risk mitigation
[CNSSI 4009]

Prioritizing, evaluating, and implementing the appropriate risk-reducing controls/countermeasures recommended from the risk management process.

risk response
[OMB A-130]

Accepting, avoiding, mitigating, sharing, or transferring risk to agency operations, agency assets, individuals, other organizations, or the Nation.

sanitization
[SP 800-88]

A process to render access to target data on the media infeasible for a given level of effort. Clear, purge, and destroy are actions that can be taken to sanitize media.

scoping considerations

A part of tailoring guidance providing organizations with specific considerations on the applicability and implementation of controls in the control baselines. Considerations include policy/regulatory, technology, physical infrastructure, system element allocation, operational/environmental, public access, scalability, common control, and security objective.

security
[CNSSI 4009]

A condition that results from the establishment and maintenance of protective measures that enable an organization to perform its mission or critical functions despite risks posed by threats to its use of systems. Protective measures may involve a combination of deterrence, avoidance, prevention, detection, recovery, and correction that should form part of the organization's risk management approach.

security architect	Individual, group, or organization responsible for ensuring that the information security requirements necessary to protect the organization's core missions and business processes are adequately addressed in all aspects of enterprise architecture including reference models, segment and solution architectures, and the resulting information systems supporting those missions and business processes.
security architecture [SP 800-39]	An embedded, integral part of the enterprise architecture that describes the structure and behavior for an enterprise's security processes, information security systems, personnel and organizational sub-units, showing their alignment with the enterprise's mission and strategic plans. See *information security architecture*.
[SP 800-160 v1]	A set of physical and logical security-relevant representations (i.e., views) of system architecture that conveys information about how the system is partitioned into security domains and makes use of security-relevant elements to enforce security policies within and between security domains based on how data and information must be protected. *Note:* The security architecture reflects security domains, the placement of security-relevant elements within the security domains, the interconnections and trust relationships between the security-relevant elements, and the behavior and interactions between the security-relevant elements. The security architecture, similar to the system architecture, may be expressed at different levels of abstraction and with different scopes.
security categorization	The process of determining the security category for information or a system. Security categorization methodologies are described in CNSS Instruction 1253 for national security systems and in FIPS Publication 199 for other than national security systems. See *security category*.
security category [OMB A-130]	The characterization of information or an information system based on an assessment of the potential impact that a loss of confidentiality, integrity, or availability of such information or information system would have on agency operations, agency assets, individuals, other organizations, and the Nation.
security control [OMB A-130]	The safeguards or countermeasures prescribed for an information system or an organization to protect the confidentiality, integrity, and availability of the system and its information.
security control assessment [OMB A-130]	The testing or evaluation of security controls to determine the extent to which the controls are implemented correctly, operating as intended, and producing the desired outcome with respect to meeting the security requirements for an information system or organization.

security control baseline [OMB A-130]	The set of minimum security controls defined for a low-impact, moderate-impact, or high-impact information system. See also *control baseline*.
security objective [FIPS 199]	Confidentiality, integrity, or availability.
security plan	See *information system security plan*.
security posture [CNSSI 4009]	The security status of an enterprise's networks, information, and systems based on information assurance resources (e.g., people, hardware, software, policies) and capabilities in place to manage the defense of the enterprise and to react as the situation changes. Synonymous with *security status*.
security requirement [FIPS 200, Adapted]	A requirement levied on an information system or an organization that is derived from applicable laws, executive orders, directives, policies, standards, instructions, regulations, procedures, and/or mission/business needs to ensure the confidentiality, integrity, and availability of information that is being processed, stored, or transmitted. *Note:* Security requirements can be used in a variety of contexts from high-level policy activities to low-level implementation activities in system development and engineering disciplines.
security information	Information within the system that can potentially impact the operation of security functions or the provision of security services in a manner that could result in failure to enforce the system security policy or maintain isolation of code and data.
selection statement	A control parameter that allows an organization to select a value from a list of pre-defined values provided as part of the control or control enhancement (e.g., selecting to either restrict an action or prohibit an action). See *assignment statement* and *organization-defined control parameter*.
senior agency information security officer [44 USC 3544]	Official responsible for carrying out the Chief Information Officer responsibilities under FISMA and serving as the Chief Information Officer's primary liaison to the agency's authorizing officials, information system owners, and information system security officers.
senior agency official for privacy [OMB A-130]	The senior official, designated by the head of each agency, who has agency-wide responsibility for privacy, including implementation of privacy protections; compliance with Federal laws, regulations, and policies relating to privacy; management of privacy risks at the agency; and a central policy-making role in the agency's development and evaluation of legislative, regulatory, and other policy proposals.

senior accountable official for risk management [OMB M-17-25]	The senior official, designated by the head of each agency, who has vision into all areas of the organization and is responsible for alignment of information security management processes with strategic, operational, and budgetary planning processes.
software [CNSSI 4009]	Computer programs and associated data that may be dynamically written or modified during execution.
specification [IEEE 610.12]	A document that specifies, in a complete, precise, verifiable manner, the requirements, design, behavior, or other characteristics of a system or component and often the procedures for determining whether these provisions have been satisfied. See *specification requirement*.
specification requirement	A type of requirement that provides a specification for a specific capability that implements all or part of a control and that may be assessed (i.e., as part of the verification, validation, testing, and evaluation processes).
statement of work requirement	A type of requirement that represents an action that is performed operationally or during system development.
subsystem	A major subdivision or element of an information system consisting of information, information technology, and personnel that performs one or more specific functions.
supply chain [OMB A-130]	Linked set of resources and processes between multiple tiers of developers that begins with the sourcing of products and services and extends through the design, development, manufacturing, processing, handling, and delivery of products and services to the acquirer.
supply chain risk [OMB A-130]	Risks that arise from the loss of confidentiality, integrity, or availability of information or information systems and reflect the potential adverse impacts to organizational operations (including mission, functions, image, or reputation), organizational assets, individuals, other organizations, and the Nation.
supply chain risk management [OMB A-130]	The process of identifying, assessing, and mitigating the risks associated with the global and distributed nature of information and communications technology product and service supply chains.

Guide for Applying the Risk Management Framework to Federal Information Systems (800-37 rev 2)
311

system [CNSSI 4009]	Any organized assembly of resources and procedures united and regulated by interaction or interdependence to accomplish a set of specific functions. See *information system*.
	Note: Systems also include specialized systems such as industrial/process controls systems, telephone switching and private branch exchange (PBX) systems, and environmental control systems.
[ISO 15288]	Combination of interacting elements organized to achieve one or more stated purposes.
	Note 1: There are many types of systems. Examples include: general and special-purpose information systems; command, control, and communication systems; crypto modules; central processing unit and graphics processor boards; industrial/process control systems; flight control systems; weapons, targeting, and fire control systems; medical devices and treatment systems; financial, banking, and merchandising transaction systems; and social networking systems.
	Note 2: The interacting elements in the definition of system include hardware, software, data, humans, processes, facilities, materials, and naturally occurring physical entities.
	Note 3: System of systems is included in the definition of system.
system boundary	See *authorization boundary*.
system component [SP 800-128]	A discrete identifiable information technology asset that represents a building block of a system and may include hardware, software, and firmware.
system element [ISO 15288]	Member of a set of elements that constitute a system.
	Note 1: A system element can be a discrete component, product, service, subsystem, system, infrastructure, or enterprise.
	Note 2: Each element of the system is implemented to fulfill specified requirements.
	Note 3: The recursive nature of the term allows the term *system* to apply equally when referring to a discrete component or to a large, complex, geographically distributed system-of-systems.
	Note 4: System elements are implemented by: hardware, software, and firmware that perform operations on data/information; physical structures, devices, and components in the environment of operation; and the people, processes, and procedures for operating, sustaining, and supporting the system elements.
	Note 5: System elements and *information resources* (as defined at 44 U.S.C. Sec. 3502 and in this document) are interchangeable terms as used in this document.
system development life cycle	The scope of activities associated with a system, encompassing the system's initiation, development and acquisition, implementation, operation and maintenance, and ultimately its disposal that instigates another system initiation.
system privacy officer	Individual with assigned responsibility for maintaining the appropriate operational privacy posture for a system or program.
systems privacy engineer	Individual assigned responsibility for conducting systems privacy engineering activities.

systems privacy engineering	Process that captures and refines privacy requirements and ensures their integration into information technology component products and information systems through purposeful privacy design or configuration.
systems security engineer	Individual assigned responsibility for conducting systems security engineering activities.
systems security engineering	Process that captures and refines security requirements and ensures their integration into information technology component products and information systems through purposeful security design or configuration.
system security officer	Individual with assigned responsibility for maintaining the appropriate operational security posture for an information system or program.
system security plan	See *information system security plan.*
system-related privacy risk [OMB A-130]	Risk to an individual or individuals associated with the agency's creation, collection, use, processing, storage, maintenance, dissemination, disclosure, and disposal of their PII. See *risk.*
system-related security risk [SP 800-30]	Risk that arises through the loss of confidentiality, integrity, or availability of information or systems and that considers impacts to the organization (including assets, mission, functions, image, or reputation), individuals, other organizations, and the Nation. See *risk.*
system-specific control [OMB A-130]	A security or privacy control for an information system that is implemented at the system level and is not inherited by any other information system.
tailored control baseline	A set of controls resulting from the application of tailoring guidance to a control baseline. See *tailoring.*
tailoring [OMB A-130]	The process by which security control baselines are modified by identifying and designating common controls; applying scoping considerations; selecting compensating controls; assigning specific values to agency-defined control parameters; supplementing baselines with additional controls or control enhancements; and providing additional specification information for control implementation. The tailoring process may also be applied to privacy controls.
threat [SP 800-30]	Any circumstance or event with the potential to adversely impact organizational operations, organizational assets, individuals, other organizations, or the Nation through a system via unauthorized access, destruction, disclosure, modification of information, and/or denial of service.

threat source [FIPS 200]	The intent and method targeted at the intentional exploitation of a vulnerability or a situation and method that may accidentally trigger a vulnerability. See *threat agent*.
trustworthiness [CNSSI 4009]	The attribute of a person or enterprise that provides confidence to others of the qualifications, capabilities, and reliability of that entity to perform specific tasks and fulfill assigned responsibilities.
trustworthiness (system)	The degree to which an information system (including the information technology components that are used to build the system) can be expected to preserve the confidentiality, integrity, and availability of the information being processed, stored, or transmitted by the system across the full range of threats and individuals' privacy.
trustworthy information system [OMB A-130]	An information system that is believed to be capable of operating within defined levels of risk despite the environmental disruptions, human errors, structural failures, and purposeful attacks that are expected to occur in its environment of operation.
system user	Individual, or (system) process acting on behalf of an individual, authorized to access a system.
vulnerability [CNSSI 4009]	Weakness in an information system, system security procedures, internal controls, or implementation that could be exploited or triggered by a threat source. *Note:* The term *weakness* is synonymous for *deficiency*. Weakness may result in security and/or privacy risks.
vulnerability assessment [CNSSI 4009]	Systematic examination of an information system or product to determine the adequacy of security measures, identify security deficiencies, provide data from which to predict the effectiveness of proposed security measures, and confirm the adequacy of such measures after implementation.

APPENDIX C

ACRONYMS
COMMON ABBREVIATIONS

CIO	Chief Information Officer
CNSS	Committee on National Security Systems
CNSSI	Committee on National Security Systems Instruction
CNSSP	Committee on National Security Systems Policy
CUI	Controlled Unclassified Information
DoD	Department of Defense
EO	Executive Order
FedRAMP	Federal Risk and Authorization Management Program
FIPS	Federal Information Processing Standards
FISMA	Federal Information Security Modernization Act
FOCI	Foreign Ownership, Control, or Influence
GRC	Governance Risk Compliance
GSA	General Services Administration
IEC	International Electrotechnical Commission
IEEE	Institute of Electrical and Electronics Engineers
ISCM	Information Security Continuous Monitoring
IT	Information Technology
IR	Internal Report or Interagency Report
ISO	International Organization for Standardization
NARA	National Archives and Records Administration
NIST	National Institute of Standards and Technology
NSA	National Security Agency
ODNI	Office of the Director of National Intelligence
OMB	Office of Management and Budget
OT	Operations Technology
PCM	Privacy Continuous Monitoring
PII	Personally Identifiable Information
PL	Public Law
RMF	Risk Management Framework

Guide for Applying the Risk Management Framework to Federal Information Systems (800-37 rev 2)

SCRM	Supply Chain Risk Management
SDLC	System Development Life Cycle
SecCM	Security-focused Configuration Management
SP	Special Publication

Guide for Applying the Risk Management Framework to Federal Information Systems (800-37 rev 2)
316

APPENDIX D

ROLES AND RESPONSIBILITIES

KEY PARTICIPANTS IN THE RISK MANAGEMENT PROCESS

The following sections describe the roles and responsibilities of key participants involved in an organization's risk management process.[112] Recognizing that organizations have varying missions, business functions, and organizational structures, there may be differences in naming conventions for risk management roles and how risk management responsibilities are allocated among organizational personnel (e.g., multiple individuals filling a single role or one individual filling multiple roles).[113] However, the basic functions remain the same. The application of the RMF described in this publication is flexible, allowing organizations to effectively accomplish the intent of the specific tasks within their respective organizational structures to best manage security and privacy risks. Many risk management roles defined in this publication have counterpart roles in the SDLC processes carried out by organizations. Organizations align their risk management roles with similar (or complementary) roles defined for the SDLC whenever possible.[114]

AUTHORIZING OFFICIAL

The *authorizing official* is a senior official or executive with the authority to formally assume responsibility and accountability for operating a system; providing common controls inherited by organizational systems; or using a system, service, or application from an external provider. The authorizing official is the only organizational official who can accept the security and privacy risk to organizational operations, organizational assets, and individuals.[115] Authorizing officials typically have budgetary oversight for the system or are responsible for the mission and/or business operations supported by the system. Accordingly, authorizing officials are in management positions with a level of authority commensurate with understanding and accepting such security and privacy risks. Authorizing officials approve plans, memorandums of agreement or understanding, plans of action and milestones, and determine whether significant changes in the information systems or environments of operation require reauthorization.

Authorizing officials coordinate their activities with common control providers, system owners, chief information officers, senior agency information security officers, senior agency officials for privacy, system security and privacy officers, control assessors, senior accountable officials for risk management/risk executive (function), and other interested parties during the authorization process. With the increasing complexity of the mission/business processes in an organization, partnership arrangements, and the use of shared services, it is possible that a system may

---

[112] Organizations may define other roles to support the risk management process.

[113] Organizations ensure that there are no conflicts of interest when assigning the same individual to multiple risk management roles. See RMF *Prepare-Organization Level* step, Task P-1.

[114] For example, the SDLC role of system developer or program manager can be aligned with the role of system owner; and the role of mission or business owner can be aligned with the role of authorizing official. [SP 800-64] provides guidance on information security in the SDLC.

[115] The responsibility and accountability of authorizing officials described in [FIPS 200] was extended in [SP 800-53] to include risks to other organizations and the Nation.

involve co-authorizing officials.[116] If so, agreements are established between the co-authorizing officials and documented in the security and privacy plans. Authorizing officials are responsible and accountable for ensuring that authorization activities and functions that are delegated to authorizing official designated representatives are carried out as specified. For federal agencies, the role of authorizing official is an inherent U.S. Government function and is assigned to government personnel only.

AUTHORIZING OFFICIAL DESIGNATED REPRESENTATIVE

The *authorizing official designated representative* is an organizational official designated by the authorizing official who is empowered to act on behalf of the authorizing official to coordinate and conduct the day-to-day activities associated with managing risk to information systems and organizations. This includes carrying out many of the activities related to the execution of the RMF. The only activity that cannot be delegated by the authorizing official to the designated representative is the authorization decision and signing of the associated authorization decision document (i.e., the acceptance of risk).

CHIEF ACQUISITION OFFICER

The *chief acquisition officer* is an organizational official designated by the head of an agency to advise and assist the head of agency and other agency officials to ensure that the mission of the agency is achieved through the management of the agency's acquisition activities. The chief acquisition officer monitors the performance of acquisition activities and programs; establishes clear lines of authority, accountability, and responsibility for acquisition decision making within the agency; manages the direction and implementation of acquisition policy for the agency; and establishes policies, procedures, and practices that promote full and open competition from responsible sources to fulfill best value requirements considering the nature of the property or service procured. The Chief Acquisition Officer coordinates with mission or business owners, authorizing officials, senior accountable official for risk management, system owners, common control providers, senior agency information security officer, senior agency official for privacy, and risk executive (function) to ensure that security and privacy requirements are defined in organizational procurements and acquisitions.

CHIEF INFORMATION OFFICER

The *chief information officer*[117] is an organizational official responsible for designating a senior agency information security officer; developing and maintaining security policies, procedures, and control techniques to address security requirements; overseeing personnel with significant responsibilities for security and ensuring that the personnel are adequately trained; assisting senior organizational officials concerning their security responsibilities; and reporting to the head of the agency on the effectiveness of the organization's security program, including progress of remedial actions. The chief information officer, with the support of the senior accountable official for risk management, the risk executive (function), and the senior agency information security officer, works closely with authorizing officials and their designated representatives to help ensure that:

---

[116] [OMB A-130] provides additional information about authorizing officials and co-authorizing officials.

[117] When an organization has not designated a formal chief information officer position, [FISMA] requires that the associated responsibilities be handled by a comparable organizational official.

- An organization-wide security program is effectively implemented resulting in adequate security for all organizational systems and environments of operation;

- Security and privacy (including supply chain) risk management considerations are integrated into programming/planning/budgeting cycles, enterprise architectures, the SDLC, and acquisitions;

- Organizational systems and common controls are covered by approved system security plans and possess current authorizations;

- Security activities required across the organization are accomplished in an efficient, cost-effective, and timely manner; and

- There is centralized reporting of security activities.

The chief information officer and authorizing officials determine the allocation of resources dedicated to the protection of systems supporting the organization's missions and business functions based on organizational priorities. For information systems that process personally identifiable information, the chief information officer and authorizing officials coordinate any determination about the allocation of resources dedicated to the protection of those systems with the senior agency official for privacy. For selected systems, the chief information officer may be designated as an authorizing official or a co-authorizing official with other senior organizational officials. The role of chief information officer is an inherent U.S. Government function and is assigned to government personnel only.

COMMON CONTROL PROVIDER

The *common control provider* is an individual, group, or organization that is responsible for the implementation, assessment, and monitoring of common controls (i.e., controls inherited by organizational systems).[118] Common control providers also are responsible for ensuring the documentation of organization-defined common controls in security and privacy plans (or equivalent documents prescribed by the organization); ensuring that required assessments of the common controls are conducted by qualified assessors with an appropriate level of independence; documenting assessment findings in control assessment reports; and producing plans of action and milestones for controls having deficiencies. Security and privacy plans, security and privacy assessment reports, and plans of action and milestones for common controls (or summary of such information) are made available to the system owners of systems inheriting common controls after the information is reviewed and approved by the authorizing officials accountable for those common controls.

The senior agency official for privacy is responsible for designating which privacy controls may be treated as common controls. Privacy controls that are designated as common controls are documented in the organization's privacy program plan.[119] The senior agency official for privacy

---

[118] Organizations can have multiple common control providers depending on how security and privacy responsibilities are allocated organization-wide. Common control providers may be *system owners* when the common controls are resident within an organizational system.

[119] A privacy program plan is a formal document that provides an overview of an agency's privacy program, including a description of the structure of the privacy program; the role of the senior agency official for privacy and other privacy officials and staff; the strategic goals and objectives of the privacy program; the resources dedicated to the privacy program; and the program management controls and common controls in place or planned for meeting applicable privacy requirements and managing privacy risks.

has oversight responsibility for common controls in place or planned for meeting applicable privacy requirements and managing privacy risks and is responsible for assessing those controls. At the discretion of the organization, privacy controls that are designated as common controls may be assessed by an independent assessor. In all cases, however, the senior agency official for privacy retains responsibility and accountability for the organization's privacy program, including any privacy functions performed by independent assessors. Privacy plans and privacy control assessment reports are made available to systems owners whose systems inherit privacy controls that are designated as common controls.

CONTROL ASSESSOR

The *control assessor* is an individual, group, or organization responsible for conducting a comprehensive assessment of implemented controls and control enhancements to determine the effectiveness of the controls (i.e., the extent to which the controls are implemented correctly, operating as intended, and producing the desired outcome with respect to meeting the security and privacy requirements for the system and the organization). For systems, implemented system-specific controls and system-implemented parts of hybrid controls are assessed. For common controls, implemented common controls and common control-implemented parts of hybrid controls are assessed. The system owner and common control provider rely on the security and privacy expertise and judgment of the assessor to assess the implemented controls using the assessment procedures specified in the security and privacy assessment plans. Multiple control assessors who are differentiated by their expertise in specific control requirements or technologies may be required to conduct the assessment effectively. Prior to initiating the control assessment, assessors review the security and privacy plans to facilitate development of the assessment plans. Control assessors provide an assessment of the severity of the deficiencies discovered in the system, environment of operation, and common controls and can recommend corrective actions to address the identified vulnerabilities. For system-level control assessments, control assessors do not assess inherited controls, and only assess the system-implemented portions of hybrid controls. Control assessors prepare security and privacy assessment reports containing the results and findings from the assessment.

The required level of assessor independence is determined by the authorizing official based on laws, executive orders, directives, regulations, policies, standards, or guidelines. When a control assessment is conducted in support of an authorization decision or ongoing authorization, the authorizing official makes an explicit determination of the degree of independence required. Assessor independence is a factor in preserving an impartial and unbiased assessment process; determining the credibility of the assessment results; and ensuring that the authorizing official receives objective information to make an informed, risk-based authorization decision.

The senior agency official for privacy is responsible for assessing privacy controls and for providing privacy information to the authorizing official. At the discretion of the organization, privacy controls may be assessed by an independent assessor. However, in all cases, the senior agency official for privacy retains responsibility and accountability for the privacy program of the organization, including any privacy functions performed by the independent assessors.

ENTERPRISE ARCHITECT

The *enterprise architect* is an individual or group responsible for working with the leadership and subject matter experts in an organization to build a holistic view of the organization's missions and business functions, mission/business processes, information, and information technology assets. With respect to information security and privacy, enterprise architects:

- Implement an enterprise architecture strategy that facilitates effective security and privacy solutions;

- Coordinate with security and privacy architects to determine the optimal placement of systems/system elements within the enterprise architecture and to address security and privacy issues between systems and the enterprise architecture;

- Assist in reducing complexity within the IT infrastructure to facilitate security;

- Assist with determining appropriate control implementations and initial configuration baselines as they relate to the enterprise architecture;

- Collaborate with system owners and authorizing officials to facilitate authorization boundary determinations and allocation of controls to system elements;

- Serve as part of the Risk Executive (function); and

- Assist with integration of the organizational risk management strategy and system-level security and privacy requirements into program, planning, and budgeting activities, the SDLC, acquisition processes, security and privacy (including supply chain) risk management, and systems engineering processes.

HEAD OF AGENCY

The *head of agency* is responsible and accountable for providing information security protections commensurate with the risk to organizational operations and assets, individuals, other organizations, and the Nation—that is, risk resulting from unauthorized access, use, disclosure, disruption, modification, or destruction of information collected or maintained by or on behalf of the agency; and the information systems used or operated by an agency or by a contractor of an agency or other organization on behalf of an agency. The head of agency is also the senior official in an organization with the responsibility for ensuring that privacy interests are protected and that PII is managed responsibly within the organization. The heads of agencies ensure that:

- Information security and privacy management processes are integrated with strategic and operational planning processes;

- Senior officials within the organization provide information security for the information and systems supporting the operations and assets under their control;

- Senior agency officials for privacy are designated who are responsible and accountable for ensuring compliance with applicable privacy requirements, managing privacy risk, and the organization's privacy program; and

- The organization has adequately trained personnel to assist in complying with security and privacy requirements in legislation, executive orders, policies, directives, instructions, standards, and guidelines.

The head of agency establishes the organizational commitment and the actions required to effectively manage security and privacy risk and protect the missions and business functions being carried out by the organization. The head of agency establishes security and privacy accountability and provides active support and oversight of monitoring and improvement for the security and privacy programs. Senior leadership commitment to security and privacy establishes a level of due diligence within the organization that promotes a climate for mission and business success.

INFORMATION OWNER OR STEWARD

The *information owner or steward* is an organizational official with statutory, management, or operational authority for specified information and the responsibility for establishing the policies and procedures governing its generation, collection, processing, dissemination, and disposal. In information-sharing environments, the information owner/steward is responsible for establishing the rules for appropriate use and protection of the information and retains that responsibility even when the information is shared with or provided to other organizations. The owner/steward of the information processed, stored, or transmitted by a system may or may not be the same individual as the system owner. An individual system may contain information from multiple information owners/stewards. Information owners/stewards provide input to system owners regarding the security and privacy requirements and controls for the systems where the information is processed, stored, or transmitted.

MISSION OR BUSINESS OWNER

The *mission or business owner* is the senior official or executive within an organization with specific mission or line of business responsibilities and that has a security or privacy interest in the organizational systems supporting those missions or lines of business. Mission or business owners are key stakeholders that have a significant role in establishing organizational mission and business processes and the protection needs and security and privacy requirements that ensure the successful conduct of the organization's missions and business operations. Mission and business owners provide essential inputs to the risk management strategy, play an active part in the SDLC, and may also serve in the role of authorizing official.

RISK EXECUTIVE (FUNCTION)

The *risk executive (function)* is an individual or group within an organization that provides a comprehensive, organization-wide approach to risk management. The risk executive (function) is led by the senior accountable official for risk management and serves as the common risk management resource for senior leaders, executives, and managers, mission/business owners, chief information officers, senior agency information security officers, senior agency officials for privacy, system owners, common control providers, enterprise architects, security architects, systems security or privacy engineers, system security or privacy officers, and any other stakeholders having a vested interest in the mission/business success of organizations. The risk executive (function) is an inherent U.S. Government function and is assigned to government personnel only.

The risk executive (function) ensures that risk considerations for systems (including authorization decisions for those systems and the common controls inherited by those systems), are viewed from an organization-wide perspective regarding the organization's strategic goals and objectives in carrying out its core missions and business functions. The risk executive (function) ensures that managing risk is consistent throughout the organization, reflects organizational risk tolerance, and is considered along with other types of risk to ensure mission/business success. The risk executive (function) coordinates with senior leaders and executives to:

- Establish risk management roles and responsibilities;

- Develop and implement an organization-wide *risk management strategy* that provides a strategic view of security risks for the organization[120] and that guides and informs organizational risk decisions (including how risk is framed, assessed, responded to, and monitored over time);

- Provide a comprehensive, organization-wide, holistic approach for addressing risk—an approach that provides a greater understanding of the integrated operations of the organization;

- Manage threat, vulnerability, and security and privacy risk (including supply chain risk) information for organizational systems and the environments in which the systems operate;

- Establish organization-wide forums to consider all types and sources of risk (including aggregated risk);

- Identify the organizational risk posture based on the aggregated risk from the operation and use of systems and the respective environments of operation for which the organization is responsible;

- Provide oversight for the risk management activities carried out by organizations to help ensure consistent and effective risk-based decisions;

- Develop a broad-based understanding of risk regarding the strategic view of organizations and their integrated operations;

- Establish effective vehicles and serve as a focal point for communicating and sharing risk information among key stakeholders (e.g., authorizing officials and other senior leaders) internally and externally to organizations;

- Specify the degree of autonomy for subordinate organizations permitted by parent organizations regarding framing, assessing, responding to, and monitoring risk;

- Promote cooperation and collaboration among authorizing officials to include authorization actions requiring shared responsibility (e.g., joint authorizations);

- Provide an organization-wide forum to consider all sources of risk (including aggregated risk) to organizational operations and assets, individuals, other organizations, and the Nation;

- Ensure that authorization decisions consider all factors necessary for mission and business success; and

- Ensure shared responsibility for supporting organizational missions and business functions using external providers receives the needed visibility and is elevated to appropriate decision-making authorities.

The risk executive (function) presumes neither a specific organizational structure nor formal responsibility assigned to any one individual or group within the organization. Heads of agencies

---

[120] Authorizing officials may have narrow or localized perspectives in rendering authorization decisions without fully understanding or explicitly accepting the organization-wide risks being incurred from such decisions.

or organizations may choose to retain the risk executive (function) or to delegate the function. The risk executive (function) requires a mix of skills, expertise, and perspectives to understand the strategic goals and objectives of organizations, organizational missions/business functions, technical possibilities and constraints, and key mandates and guidance that shape organizational operations. To provide this needed mixture, the risk executive (function) can be filled by a single individual or office (supported by an expert staff) or by a designated group (e.g., a risk board, executive steering committee, executive leadership council). The risk executive (function) fits into the organizational governance structure in such a way as to facilitate efficiency and effectiveness.

SECURITY OR PRIVACY ARCHITECT

The *security or privacy architect* is an individual, group, or organization responsible for ensuring that stakeholder protection needs and the corresponding system requirements necessary to protect organizational missions and business functions and individuals' privacy are adequately addressed in the enterprise architecture including reference models, segment architectures, and solution architectures (systems supporting mission and business processes). The security or privacy architect serves as the primary liaison between the enterprise architect and the systems security or privacy engineer and coordinates with system owners, common control providers, and system security or privacy officers on the allocation of controls.

Security or privacy architects, in coordination with system security or privacy officers, advise authorizing officials, chief information officers, senior accountable officials for risk management or risk executive (function), senior agency information security officers, and senior agency officials for privacy on a range of security and privacy issues. Examples include establishing authorization boundaries; establishing security or privacy alerts; assessing the severity of deficiencies in the system or controls; developing plans of action and milestones; creating risk mitigation approaches; and potential adverse effects of identified vulnerabilities or privacy risks.

When the security architect and privacy architect are separate roles, the security architect is generally responsible for aspects of the enterprise architecture that protect information and information systems from unauthorized system activity or behavior to provide confidentiality, integrity, and availability. The privacy architect is responsible for aspects of the enterprise architecture that ensure compliance with privacy requirements and manage the privacy risks to individuals associated with the processing of PII. Security and privacy architect responsibilities overlap regarding aspects of the enterprise architecture that protect the security of PII.

SENIOR ACCOUNTABLE OFFICIAL FOR RISK MANAGEMENT

The *senior accountable official for risk management* is the individual that leads and manages the risk executive (function) in an organization and is responsible for aligning information security and privacy risk management processes with strategic, operational, and budgetary planning processes. The senior accountable official for risk management is the head of the agency or an individual designated by the head of the agency. The senior accountable official for risk management determines the organizational structure and responsibilities of the risk executive (function), and in coordination with the head of the agency, may retain the risk executive (function) or delegate the function to another organizational official or group. The senior accountable official for risk management is an inherent U.S. Government function and is assigned to government personnel only.

SENIOR AGENCY INFORMATION SECURITY OFFICER

The *senior agency information security officer* is an organizational official responsible for carrying out the chief information officer security responsibilities under FISMA, and serving as the primary liaison for the chief information officer to the organization's authorizing officials, system owners, common control providers, and system security officers. The senior agency information security officer is also responsible for coordinating with the senior agency official for privacy to ensure coordination between privacy and information security programs. The senior agency information security officer possesses the professional qualifications, including training and experience, required to administer security program functions; maintains security duties as a primary responsibility; and heads an office with the specific mission and resources to assist the organization in achieving trustworthy, secure information and systems in accordance with the requirements in FISMA. The senior agency information security officer may serve as authorizing official designated representative or as a security control assessor. The role of senior agency information security officer is an inherent U.S. Government function and is therefore assigned to government personnel only. Organizations may also refer to the senior agency information security officer as the senior information security officer or chief information security officer.

SENIOR AGENCY OFFICIAL FOR PRIVACY

The *senior agency official for privacy* is the senior official or executive with agency-wide responsibility and accountability for ensuring compliance with applicable privacy requirements and managing privacy risk. Among other things, the senior agency official for privacy is responsible for:

- Coordinating with the senior agency information security officer to ensure coordination of privacy and information security activities;

- Reviewing and approving the categorization of information systems that create, collect, use, process, store, maintain, disseminate, disclose, or dispose of personally identifiable information;

- Designating which privacy controls will be treated as program management, common, system-specific, and hybrid privacy controls;

- Identifying assessment methodologies and metrics to determine whether privacy controls are implemented correctly, operating as intended, and sufficient to ensure compliance with applicable privacy requirements and manage privacy risks;

- Reviewing and approving privacy plans for information systems prior to authorization, reauthorization, or ongoing authorization;

- Reviewing authorization packages for information systems that create, collect, use, process, store, maintain, disseminate, disclose, or dispose of personally identifiable information to ensure compliance with privacy requirements and manage privacy risks;

- Conducting and documenting the results of privacy control assessments to verify the continued effectiveness of all privacy controls selected and implemented at the agency; and

- Establishing and maintaining a privacy continuous monitoring program to maintain ongoing awareness of privacy risks and assess privacy controls at a frequency sufficient to ensure compliance with privacy requirements and manage privacy risks.

The role of senior agency official for privacy is an inherent U.S. Government function and is therefore assigned to government personnel only.

SYSTEM ADMINISTRATOR

The *system administrator* is an individual, group, or organization responsible for setting up and maintaining a system or specific system elements. System administrator responsibilities include, for example, installing, configuring, and updating hardware and software; establishing and managing user accounts; overseeing or conducting backup, recovery, and reconstitution activities; implementing controls; and adhering to and enforcing organizational security and privacy policies and procedures. The system administrator role includes other types of system administrators (e.g., database administrators, network administrators, web administrators, and application administrators).

SYSTEM OWNER

The *system owner* is an organizational official responsible for the procurement, development, integration, modification, operation, maintenance, and disposal of a system.[121] The system owner is responsible for addressing the operational interests of the user community (i.e., users who require access to the system to satisfy mission, business, or operational requirements) and for ensuring compliance with security requirements. In coordination with the system security and privacy officers, the system owner is responsible for the development and maintenance of the security and privacy plans and ensures that the system is operated in accordance with the selected and implemented controls.

In coordination with the information owner/steward, the system owner decides who has access to the system (and with what types of privileges or access rights).[122] The system owner ensures that system users and support personnel receive the requisite security and privacy training. Based on guidance from the authorizing official, the system owner informs organizational officials of the need to conduct the authorization, ensures that resources are available for the effort, and provides the required system access, information, and documentation to control assessors. The system owner receives the security and privacy assessment results from the control assessors. After taking appropriate steps to reduce or eliminate vulnerabilities or security and privacy risks, the system owner assembles the authorization package and submits the package to the authorizing official or the authorizing official designated representative for adjudication.[123]

---

[121] Organizations may refer to system owners as program managers or business/asset owners.

[122] The responsibility for deciding who has access to specific information within an organizational system (and with what types of privileges or access rights) may reside with the information owner/steward.

[123] The authorizing official may choose to designate an individual other than the system owner to compile and assemble the information for the authorization package. In this situation, the designated individual coordinates the compilation and assembly activities with the system owner.

SYSTEM SECURITY OR PRIVACY OFFICER

The *system security or privacy officer*[124] is an individual responsible for ensuring that the security and privacy posture is maintained for an organizational system and works in close collaboration with the system owner. The system security or privacy officer also serves as a principal advisor on all matters, technical and otherwise, involving the controls for the system. The system security or privacy officer has the knowledge and expertise to manage the security or privacy aspects of an organizational system and, in many organizations, is assigned responsibility for the day-to-day system security or privacy operations. This responsibility may also include, but is not limited to, physical and environmental protection; personnel security; incident handling; and security and privacy training and awareness.

The system security or privacy officer may be called on to assist in the development of the system-level security and privacy policies and procedures and to ensure compliance with those policies and procedures. In close coordination with the system owner, the system security or privacy officer often plays an active role in the monitoring of a system and its environment of operation to include developing and updating security and privacy plans, managing and controlling changes to the system, and assessing the security or privacy impact of those changes.

When the system security officer and system privacy officer are separate roles, the system security officer is generally responsible for aspects of the system that protect information and information systems from unauthorized system activity or behavior to provide confidentiality, integrity, and availability. The system privacy officer is responsible for aspects of the system that ensure compliance with privacy requirements and manage the privacy risks to individuals associated with the processing of PII. The responsibilities of system security officers and system privacy officers overlap regarding aspects of the system that protect the security of PII.

SYSTEM USER

The *system user* is an individual or (system) process acting on behalf of an individual that is authorized to access information and information systems to perform assigned duties. System user responsibilities include, but are not limited to, adhering to organizational policies that govern acceptable use of organizational systems; using the organization-provided information technology resources for defined purposes only; and reporting anomalous or suspicious system behavior.

SYSTEMS SECURITY OR PRIVACY ENGINEER

The *systems security or privacy engineer* is an individual, group, or organization responsible for conducting systems security or privacy engineering activities as part of the SDLC. Systems security and privacy engineering is a process that captures and refines security and privacy requirements for systems and ensures that the requirements are effectively integrated into

---

[124] Organizations may define a *system security manager* or *security manager* role with similar responsibilities as a system security officer or with oversight responsibilities for a security program. In these situations, system security officers may, at the discretion of the organization, report directly to system security managers or security managers. Organizations may assign equivalent responsibilities for privacy to separate individuals with appropriate subject matter expertise.

NIST SP 800-37, REVISION 2

RISK MANAGEMENT FRAMEWORK FOR INFORMATION SYSTEMS AND ORGANIZATIONS
A System Life Cycle Approach for Security and Privacy

systems and system elements through security or privacy architecting, design, development, and configuration. Systems security or privacy engineers are part of the development team—designing and developing organizational systems or upgrading existing systems along with ensuring continuous monitoring requirements are addressed at the system level. Systems security or privacy engineers employ best practices when implementing controls including software engineering methodologies; system and security or privacy engineering principles; secure or privacy-enhancing design, secure or privacy-enhancing architecture, and secure or privacy-enhancing coding techniques. Systems security or privacy engineers coordinate security and privacy activities with senior agency information security officers, senior agency officials for privacy, security and privacy architects, system owners, common control providers, and system security or privacy officers.

When the systems security engineer and privacy engineer are separate roles, the systems security engineer is generally responsible for those activities associated with protecting information and information systems from unauthorized system activity or behavior to provide confidentiality, integrity, and availability. The privacy engineer is responsible for those activities associated with ensuring compliance with privacy requirements and managing the privacy risks to individuals associated with the processing of PII. The responsibilities of systems security engineers and privacy engineers overlap regarding activities associated with protecting the security of PII.

APPENDIX E

SUMMARY OF RMF TASKS

RMF TASKS, RESPONSIBILITIES, AND SUPPORTING ROLES

TABLE E-1: PREPARE TASKS, RESPONSIBILITIES, AND SUPPORTING ROLES

RMF TASKS	PRIMARY RESPONSIBILITY	SUPPORTING ROLES
Organization Level		
TASK P-1 **Risk Management Roles** Identify and assign individuals to specific roles associated with security and privacy risk management.	• Head of Agency • Chief Information Officer • Senior Agency Official for Privacy	• Authorizing Official or Authorizing Official Designated Representative • Senior Accountable Official for Risk Management or Risk Executive (Function) • Senior Agency Information Security Officer
TASK P-2 **Risk Management Strategy** Establish a risk management strategy for the organization that includes a determination of risk tolerance.	• Head of Agency	• Senior Accountable Official for Risk Management or Risk Executive (Function) • Chief Information Officer • Senior Agency Information Security Officer • Senior Agency Official for Privacy
TASK P-3 **Risk Assessment—Organization** Assess organization-wide security and privacy risk and update the risk assessment results on an ongoing basis.	• Senior Accountable Official for Risk Management or Risk Executive (Function) • Senior Agency Information Security Officer • Senior Agency Official for Privacy	• Chief Information Officer • Authorizing Official or Authorizing Official Designated Representative • Mission or Business Owner
TASK P-4 **Organizationally-Tailored Control Baselines and Cybersecurity Framework Profiles (Optional)** Establish, document, and publish organizationally-tailored control baselines and/or Cybersecurity Framework Profiles.	• Mission or Business Owner • Senior Accountable Official for Risk Management or Risk Executive (Function)	• Chief Information Officer • Authorizing Official or Authorizing Official Designated Representative • Senior Agency Information Security Officer • Senior Agency Official for Privacy

Guide for Applying the Risk Management Framework to Federal Information Systems (800-37 rev 2)

RMF TASKS	PRIMARY RESPONSIBILITY	SUPPORTING ROLES
TASK P-5 **Common Control Identification** Identify, document, and publish organization-wide common controls that are available for inheritance by organizational systems.	• Senior Agency Information Security Officer • Senior Agency Official for Privacy	• Mission or Business Owner • Senior Accountable Official for Risk Management or Risk Executive (Function) • Chief Information Officer • Authorizing Official or Authorizing Official Designated Representative • Common Control Provider • System Owner
TASK P-6 **Impact-Level Prioritization** (Optional) Prioritize organizational systems with the same impact level.	• Senior Accountable Official for Risk Management or Risk Executive (Function)	• Senior Agency Information Security Officer • Senior Agency Official for Privacy • Mission or Business Owner • System Owner • Chief Information Officer • Authorizing Official or Authorizing Official Designated Representative
TASK P-7 **Continuous Monitoring Strategy—Organization** Develop and implement an organization-wide strategy for continuously monitoring control effectiveness.	• Senior Accountable Official for Risk Management or Risk Executive (Function)	• Chief Information Officer • Senior Agency Information Security Officer • Senior Agency Official for Privacy • Mission or Business Owner • System Owner • Authorizing Official or Authorizing Official Designated Representative
System Level		
TASK P-8 **Mission or Business Focus** Identify the missions, business functions, and mission/business processes that the system is intended to support.	• Mission or Business Owner	• Authorizing Official or Authorizing Official Designated Representative • System Owner • Information Owner or Steward • Chief Information Officer • Senior Agency Information Security Officer • Senior Agency Official for Privacy
TASK P-9 **System Stakeholders** Identify stakeholders who have an interest in the design, development, implementation, assessment, operation, maintenance, or disposal of the system.	• Mission or Business Owner • System Owner	• Chief Information Officer • Authorizing Official or Authorizing Official Designated Representative • Information Owner or Steward • Senior Agency Information Security Officer • Senior Agency Official for Privacy • Chief Acquisition Officer

Guide for Applying the Risk Management Framework to Federal Information Systems (800-37 rev 2)
330

RMF TASKS	PRIMARY RESPONSIBILITY	SUPPORTING ROLES
TASK P-10 **Asset Identification** Identify assets that require protection.	• System Owner	• Authorizing Official or Authorizing Official Designated Representative • Mission or Business Owner • Information Owner or Steward • Senior Agency Information Security Officer • Senior Agency Official for Privacy • System Administrator
TASK P-11 **Authorization Boundary** Determine the authorization boundary of the system.	• Authorizing Official	• Chief Information Officer • Mission or Business Owner • System Owner • Senior Agency Information Security Officer • Senior Agency Official for Privacy • Enterprise Architect
TASK P-12 **Information Types** Identify the types of information to be processed, stored, and transmitted by the system.	• System Owner • Information Owner or Steward	• System Security Officer • System Privacy Officer • Mission or Business Owner
TASK P-13 **Information Life Cycle** Identify and understand all stages of the information life cycle for each information type processed, stored, or transmitted by the system.	• Senior Agency Official for Privacy • System Owner • Information Owner or Steward	• Chief Information Officer • Mission or Business Owner • Security Architect • Privacy Architect • Enterprise Architect • Systems Security Engineer • Privacy Engineer
TASK P-14 **Risk Assessment—System** Conduct a system-level risk assessment and update the risk assessment results on an ongoing basis.	• System Owner • System Security Officer • System Privacy Officer	• Senior Accountable Official for Risk Management or Risk Executive (Function) • Authorizing Official or Authorizing Official Designated Representative • Mission or Business Owner • Information Owner or Steward • System Security Officer
TASK P-15 **Requirements Definition** Define the security and privacy requirements for the system and the environment of operation.	• Mission or Business Owner • System Owner • Information Owner or Steward • System Privacy Officer	• Authorizing Official or Authorizing Official Designated Representative • Senior Agency Information Security Officer • Senior Agency Official for Privacy • System Security Officer • Chief Acquisition Officer • Security Architect • Privacy Architect • Enterprise Architect

Guide for Applying the Risk Management Framework to Federal Information Systems (800-37 rev 2)
331

RMF TASKS	PRIMARY RESPONSIBILITY	SUPPORTING ROLES
TASK P-16 **Enterprise Architecture** Determine the placement of the system within the enterprise architecture.	• Mission or Business Owner • Enterprise Architect • Security Architect • Privacy Architect	• Chief Information Officer • Authorizing Official or Authorizing Official Designated Representative • Senior Agency Information Security Officer • Senior Agency Official for Privacy • System Owner • Information Owner or Steward
TASK P-17 **Requirements Allocation** Allocate security and privacy requirements to the system and to the environment of operation.	• Security Architect • Privacy Architect • System Security Officer • System Privacy Officer	• Chief Information Officer • Authorizing Official or Authorizing Official Designated Representative • Mission or Business Owner • Senior Agency Information Security Officer • Senior Agency Official for Privacy • System Owner
TASK P-18 **System Registration** Register the system with organizational program or management offices.	• System Owner	• Mission or Business Owner • Chief Information Officer • System Security Officer • System Privacy Officer

Guide for Applying the Risk Management Framework to Federal Information Systems (800-37 rev 2)
332

TABLE E-2: CATEGORIZATION TASKS, RESPONSIBILITIES, AND SUPPORTING ROLES

RMF TASKS	PRIMARY RESPONSIBILITY	SUPPORTING ROLES
TASK C-1 **System Description** Document the characteristics of the system.	System Owner	• Authorizing Official or Authorizing Official Designated Representative • Information Owner or Steward • System Security Officer • System Privacy Officer
TASK C-2 **Security Categorization** Categorize the system and document the security categorization results.	• System Owner • Information Owner or Steward	• Senior Accountable Official for Risk Management or Risk Executive (Function) • Chief Information Officer • Senior Agency Information Security Officer • Authorizing Official or Authorizing Official Designated Representative • System Security Officer • System Privacy Officer
TASK C-3 **Security Categorization Review and Approval** Review and approve the security categorization results and decision.	• Authorizing Official or Authorizing Official Designated Representative • Senior Agency Official for Privacy (for systems processing PII)	• Senior Accountable Official for Risk Management or Risk Executive (Function) • Chief Information Officer • Senior Agency Information Security Officer

Guide for Applying the Risk Management Framework to Federal Information Systems (800-37 rev 2)

333

TABLE E-3: SELECTION TASKS, RESPONSIBILITIES, AND SUPPORTING ROLES

RMF TASKS	PRIMARY RESPONSIBILITY	SUPPORTING ROLES
TASK S-1 **Control Selection** Select the controls for the system and the environment of operation.	• System Owner • Common Control Provider	• Authorizing Official or Authorizing Official Designated Representative • Information Owner or Steward • Systems Security Engineer • Privacy Engineer • System Security Officer • System Privacy Officer
TASK S-2 **Control Tailoring** Tailor the controls selected for the system and the environment of operation.	• System Owner • Common Control Provider	• Authorizing Official or Authorizing Official Designated Representative • Information Owner or Steward • Systems Security Engineer • Privacy Engineer • System Security Officer • System Privacy Officer
TASK S-3 **Control Allocation** Allocate security and privacy controls to the system and to the environment of operation.	• Security Architect • Privacy Architect • System Security Officer • System Privacy Officer	• Chief Information Officer • Authorizing Official or Authorizing Official Designated Representative • Mission or Business Owner • Senior Agency Information Security Officer • Senior Agency Official for Privacy • System Owner
TASK S-4 **Documentation of Planned Control Implementations** Document the controls for the system and environment of operation in security and privacy plans.	• System Owner • Common Control Provider	• Authorizing Official or Authorizing Official Designated Representative • Information Owner or Steward • Systems Security Engineer • Privacy Engineer • System Security Officer • System Privacy Officer
TASK S-5 **Continuous Monitoring Strategy—System** Develop and implement a system-level strategy for monitoring control effectiveness that is consistent with and supplements the organizational continuous monitoring strategy.	• System Owner • Common Control Provider	• Senior Accountable Official for Risk Management or Risk Executive (Function) • Chief Information Officer • Senior Agency Information Security Officer • Senior Agency Official for Privacy • Authorizing Official or Authorizing Official Designated Representative • Information Owner or Steward • Security Architect • Privacy Architect • Systems Security Engineer • Privacy Engineer • System Security Officer • System Privacy Officer

RMF TASKS	PRIMARY RESPONSIBILITY	SUPPORTING ROLES
TASK S-6 **Plan Review and Approval** Review and approve the security and privacy plans for the system and the environment of operation.	• Authorizing Official or Authorizing Official Designated Representative	• Senior Accountable Official for Risk Management or Risk Executive (Function) • Chief Information Officer • Senior Agency Information Security Officer • Senior Agency Official for Privacy • Chief Acquisition Officer

Guide for Applying the Risk Management Framework to Federal Information Systems (800-37 rev 2)

335

TABLE E-4: IMPLEMENTATION TASKS, RESPONSIBILITIES, AND SUPPORTING ROLES

RMF TASKS	PRIMARY RESPONSIBILITY	SUPPORTING ROLES
TASK I-1 **Control Implementation** Implement the controls in the security and privacy plans.	• System Owner • Common Control Provider	• Information Owner or Steward • Security Architect • Privacy Architect • Systems Security Engineer • Privacy Engineer • System Security Officer • System Privacy Officer • Enterprise Architect • System Administrator
TASK I-2 **Update Control Implementation Information** Document changes to planned control implementations based on the "as-implemented" state of controls.	• System Owner • Common Control Provider	• Information Owner or Steward • Security Architect • Privacy Architect • Systems Security Engineer • Privacy Engineer • System Security Officer • System Privacy Officer • Enterprise Architect • System Administrator

Guide for Applying the Risk Management Framework to Federal Information Systems (800-37 rev 2)
336

TABLE E-5: ASSESSMENT TASKS, RESPONSIBILITIES, AND SUPPORTING ROLES

RMF TASKS	PRIMARY RESPONSIBILITY	SUPPORTING ROLES
TASK A-1 **Assessor Selection** Select the appropriate assessor or assessment team for the type of control assessment to be conducted.	• Authorizing Official or Authorizing Official Designated Representative	• Chief Information Officer • Senior Agency Information Security Officer • Senior Agency Official for Privacy
TASK A-2 **Assessment Plan** Develop, review, and approve plans to assess implemented controls.	• Authorizing Official or Authorizing Official Designated Representative • Control Assessor	• Senior Agency Information Security Officer • Senior Agency Official for Privacy • System Owner • Common Control Provider • Information Owner or Steward • System Security Officer • System Privacy Officer
TASK A-3 **Control Assessments** Assess the controls in accordance with the assessment procedures described in assessment plans.	• Control Assessor	• Authorizing Official or Authorizing Official Designated Representative • System Owner • Common Control Provider • Information Owner or Steward • Senior Agency Information Security Officer • Senior Agency Official for Privacy • System Security Officer • System Privacy Officer
TASK A-4 **Assessment Reports** Prepare the assessment reports documenting the findings and recommendations from the control assessments.	• Control Assessor	• System Owner • Common Control Provider • System Security Officer • System Privacy Officer
TASK A-5 **Remediation Actions** Conduct initial remediation actions on the controls and reassess remediated controls.	• System Owner • Common Control Provider • Control Assessor	• Authorizing Official or Authorizing Official Designated Representative • Senior Agency Information Security Officer • Senior Agency Official for Privacy • Senior Accountable Official for Risk Management or Risk Executive (Function) • Information Owner or Steward • Systems Security Engineer • Privacy Engineer • System Security Officer • System Privacy Officer

Guide for Applying the Risk Management Framework to Federal Information Systems (800-37 rev 2)
337

RMF TASKS	PRIMARY RESPONSIBILITY	SUPPORTING ROLES
TASK A-6 **Plan of Action and Milestones** Prepare the plan of action and milestones based on the findings and recommendations of the assessment reports.	• System Owner • Common Control Provider	• Information Owner or Steward • System Security Officer • System Privacy Officer • Senior Agency Information Security Officer • Senior Agency Official for Privacy • Chief Acquisition Officer • Control Assessor

TABLE E-6: AUTHORIZATION TASKS, RESPONSIBILITIES, AND SUPPORTING ROLES

RMF TASKS	PRIMARY RESPONSIBILITY	SUPPORTING ROLES
TASK R-1 **Authorization Package** Assemble the authorization package and submit the package to the authorizing official for an authorization decision.	• System Owner • Common Control Provider	• System Security Officer • System Privacy Officer • Senior Agency Information Security Officer • Senior Agency Official for Privacy • Control Assessor
TASK R-2 **Risk Analysis and Determination** Analyze and determine the risk from the operation or use of the system or the provision of common controls.	• Authorizing Official or Authorizing Official Designated Representative	• Senior Accountable Official for Risk Management or Risk Executive (Function) • Senior Agency Information Security Officer • Senior Agency Official for Privacy
TASK R-3 **Risk Response** Identify and implement a preferred course of action in response to the risk determined.	• Authorizing Official or Authorizing Official Designated Representative	• Senior Accountable Official for Risk Management or Risk Executive (Function) • Senior Agency Information Security Officer • Senior Agency Official for Privacy • System Owner or Common Control Provider • Information Owner or Steward • Systems Security Engineer • Privacy Engineer • System Security Officer • System Privacy Officer
TASK R-4 **Authorization Decision** Determine if the risk from the operation or use of the information system or the provision or use of common controls is acceptable.	• Authorizing Official	• Senior Accountable Official for Risk Management or Risk Executive (Function) • Chief Information Officer • Senior Agency Information Security Officer • Senior Agency Official for Privacy • Authorizing Official Designated Representative
TASK R-5 **Authorization Reporting** Report the authorization decision and any deficiencies in controls that represent significant security or privacy risk.	• Authorizing Official or Authorizing Official Designated Representative	• System Owner or Common Control Provider • Information Owner or Steward • System Security Officer • System Privacy Officer • Senior Agency Information Security Officer • Senior Agency Official for Privacy

Guide for Applying the Risk Management Framework to Federal Information Systems (800-37 rev 2)

TABLE E-7: MONITORING TASKS, RESPONSIBILITIES, AND SUPPORTING ROLES

RMF TASKS	PRIMARY RESPONSIBILITY	SUPPORTING ROLES
TASK M-1 **System and Environment Changes** Monitor the information system and its environment of operation for changes that impact the security and privacy posture of the system.	• System Owner or Common Control Provider • Senior Agency Information Security Officer • Senior Agency Official for Privacy	• Senior Accountable Official for Risk Management or Risk Executive (Function) • Authorizing Official or Authorizing Official Designated Representative • Information Owner or Steward • System Security Officer • System Privacy Officer
TASK M-2 **Ongoing Assessments** Assess the controls implemented within and inherited by the system in accordance with the continuous monitoring strategy.	• Control Assessor	• Authorizing Official or Authorizing Official Designated Representative • System Owner or Common Control Provider • Information Owner or Steward • System Security Officer • System Privacy Officer • Senior Agency Information Security Officer • Senior Agency Official for Privacy
TASK M-3 **Ongoing Risk Response** Respond to risk based on the results of ongoing monitoring activities, risk assessments, and outstanding items in plans of action and milestones.	• Authorizing Official • System Owner • Common Control Provider	• Senior Accountable Official for Risk Management or Risk Executive (Function) • Senior Agency Information Security Officer • Senior Agency Official for Privacy; Authorizing Official Designated Representative • Information Owner or Steward • System Security Officer • System Privacy Officer • Systems Security Engineer • Privacy Engineer • Security Architect • Privacy Architect
TASK M-4 **Authorization Package Updates** Update plans, assessment reports, and plans of action and milestones based on the results of the continuous monitoring process.	• System Owner • Common Control Provider	• Information Owner or Steward • System Security Officer • System Privacy Officer • Senior Agency Official for Privacy • Senior Agency Information Security Officer

Guide for Applying the Risk Management Framework to Federal Information Systems (800-37 rev 2)
340

RMF TASKS	PRIMARY RESPONSIBILITY	SUPPORTING ROLES
TASK M-5 **Security and Privacy Reporting** Report the security and privacy posture of the system to the authorizing official and other organizational officials on an ongoing basis in accordance with the organizational continuous monitoring strategy.	• System Owner • Common Control Provider • Senior Agency Information Security Officer • Senior Agency Official for Privacy	• System Security Officer • System Privacy Officer
TASK M-6 **Ongoing Authorization** Review the security and privacy posture of the system on an ongoing basis to determine whether the risk remains acceptable.	• Authorizing Official	• Senior Accountable Official for Risk Management or Risk Executive (Function) • Chief Information Officer • Senior Agency Information Security Officer • Senior Agency Official for Privacy • Authorizing Official Designated Representative
TASK M-7 **System Disposal** Implement a system disposal strategy and execute required actions when a system is removed from operation.	• System Owner	• Authorizing Official or Authorizing Official Designated Representative • Information Owner or Steward • System Security Officer • System Privacy Officer • Senior Accountable Official for Risk Management or Risk Executive (Function) • Senior Agency Information Security Officer • Senior Agency Official for Privacy

APPENDIX F

SYSTEM AND COMMON CONTROL AUTHORIZATIONS
AUTHORIZATION DECISIONS AND SUPPORTING EVIDENCE

This appendix provides information on the system and common control authorization processes to include: types of authorizations; content of authorization packages; authorization decisions; authorization decision documents; ongoing authorization; reauthorization; event-driven triggers and significant changes; type and facility authorizations; and authorization approaches.

TYPES OF AUTHORIZATIONS

Authorization is the process by which a senior management official, the *authorizing official*, reviews security and privacy information describing the current security and privacy posture of information systems or common controls that are inherited by systems. The authorizing official uses this information to determine if the mission/business risk of operating a system or providing common controls is acceptable—and if it is, explicitly accepts the risk. Security and privacy information is presented to the authorizing official in an authorization package, which may consist of a report from an automated security/privacy management and reporting tool.[125] System and common control authorization occurs as part of the RMF *Authorize* step. A system authorization or a common control authorization can be an initial authorization, an ongoing authorization, or a reauthorization as defined below:

- *Initial authorization* is defined as the initial (start-up) risk determination and risk acceptance decision based on a complete, zero-based review of the system or of common controls. The zero-based review of the system includes an assessment of all implemented system-level controls (including the system-level portion of the hybrid controls) and a review of the security status of inherited common controls as specified in security and privacy plans.[126] The zero-based review of common controls (other than common controls that are system-based) includes an assessment of applicable controls (e.g., policies, operating procedures, implementation information) that contribute to the provision of a common control or set of common controls.

- *Ongoing authorization* is defined as the subsequent (follow-on) risk determinations and risk acceptance decisions taken at agreed-upon and documented frequencies in accordance with the organization's mission/business requirements and organizational risk tolerance. Ongoing authorization is a time-driven or event-driven authorization process. The authorizing official is provided with the necessary information regarding the near real-time security and privacy posture of the system to determine whether the mission/business risk of continued system

---

[125] [SP 800-137] provides information on automated security management and reporting tools. Future publications will address privacy management and reporting tools.

[126] The zero-based review of a system does not require a zero-based review of the common controls that are available for inheritance by that system. The common controls are authorized under a separate authorization process with a separate authorizing official accepting the risk associated with the provision of those controls. The review of the security and privacy plans containing common controls is necessary to understand the current state of the controls being inherited by organizational systems and factoring this information into risk-based decisions associated with the system.

operation or the provision of common controls is acceptable. Ongoing authorization is fundamentally related to the ongoing understanding and ongoing acceptance of security and privacy risk and is dependent on a robust continuous monitoring program.

- *Reauthorization* is defined as the static, single point-in-time risk determination and risk acceptance decision that occurs after initial authorization. In general, reauthorization actions may be time-driven or event-driven. However, under ongoing authorization, reauthorization is in most instances, an event-driven action initiated by the authorizing official or directed by the senior accountable official for risk management or risk executive (function) in response to an event that results in security and privacy risk above the level of risk previously accepted by the authorizing official. Reauthorization consists of a review of the system or the common controls similar to the review carried out during the initial authorization. The reauthorization differs from the initial authorization because the authorizing official can choose to initiate a complete zero-based review of the system or of the common controls or to initiate a targeted review based on the type of event that triggered the reauthorization. Reauthorization is a separate activity from the ongoing authorization process. However, security and privacy information generated from the continuous monitoring program may be leveraged to support reauthorization. The reauthorization actions may necessitate a review of and changes to the organization's information security and privacy continuous monitoring strategies which may in turn affect ongoing authorization.

AUTHORIZATION PACKAGE

The *authorization package* provides a record of the results of the control assessments and provides the authorizing official with the information needed to make a risk-based decision on whether to authorize the operation of a system or common controls.[127] The system owner or common control provider is responsible for the development, compilation, and submission of the authorization package. This includes information available from reports generated by an automated security/privacy management and reporting tool. The system owner or common control provider receives inputs from many sources during the preparation of the authorization package (e.g., senior agency information security officer; senior agency official for privacy, senior accountable official for risk management or risk executive [function]; control assessors; system security or privacy officer; and the continuous monitoring program). The authorization package[128] includes the following:

- Executive summary;
- Security and privacy plans;[129] [130]

---

[127] Authorization packages for common controls that are not system-based may not include a security or privacy plan, but do include a record of common control implementation details.

[128] The authorizing official determines what additional supporting information, artifacts, or references may be required in the authorization package. The additional documentation may include, for example, risk assessments, contingency plans, or SCRM plans.

[129] [SP 800-18] provides guidance on system security plans. Guidance on privacy plans will be addressed in a planned publication specific to privacy plans.

[130] In accordance with [OMB A-130], the information system security plan and the privacy plan may be integrated into one consolidated document.

- Security and privacy assessment reports;[131] and

- Plans of action and milestones.

The executive summary provides a consolidated view of the security and privacy information in the authorization package. The executive summary identifies and highlights risk management issues associated with protecting information systems and the environments in which the systems operate. The summary provides the essential information needed by the authorizing official to understand the security and privacy risks to the organization's operations and assets, individuals, other organizations, and the Nation. The executive summary information can be used by the authorizing official to make informed, risk-based decisions regarding the operation and use of the system or the provision of common controls that can be inherited by organizational systems.

The security and privacy plans provide an overview of the security and privacy requirements and describe the controls in place or planned for meeting those requirements.[132] The plans provide sufficient information to understand the intended or actual implementation of the controls implemented within the system and indicate the controls that are implemented via inherited common controls. Additionally, privacy plans describe the methodologies and metrics that will be used to assess the controls. The security and privacy plans may also include as supporting appendices or as references, additional documents such as a privacy impact assessment, interconnection security agreements, security and privacy configurations, contingency plan, configuration management plan, supply chain risk management plan, incident response plan, and system-level continuous monitoring strategy. The security and privacy plans are updated whenever events dictate changes to the controls implemented within or inherited by the system.

The security and privacy assessment reports, prepared by the control assessor or generated by automated security/privacy management and reporting tools, provide the findings and results of assessing the implementation of the controls identified in the security and privacy plans to determine the extent to which the controls are implemented correctly, operating as intended, and producing the desired outcome with respect to meeting security and privacy requirements. The assessment reports may contain recommended corrective actions for deficiencies identified in the controls.[133] The authorizing official reviews the reports and determines the appropriate risk response [Task R-3].

Supporting the near real-time risk management objectives of the authorization process, the assessment reports are updated on an ongoing basis whenever changes are made to the controls implemented within or inherited by the system.[134] Updates to the assessment reports

---

[131] [SP 800-53A] provides guidance on security assessment reports. Guidance on privacy assessment reports will be addressed in future publications.

[132] The information system security plan and the privacy plan may be integrated into one consolidated document.

[133] An executive summary provides an authorizing official with an abbreviated version of the security and privacy assessment reports focusing on the highlights of the assessment, synopsis of findings, and recommendations for addressing deficiencies in the security and privacy controls.

[134] Because the desired outcome of ongoing tracking and response to assessment findings to facilitate risk management decisions is the focus (rather than the specific process used), organizations can manage and update security assessment report information using any format or method consistent with internal organizational processes.

ensure that system owners, common control providers, and authorizing officials maintain an awareness of control effectiveness. The effectiveness of the controls directly affects the security and privacy posture of the system and decisions regarding explicit acceptance of risk.

The plan of action and milestones describes the measures planned to correct deficiencies identified in the controls during the assessment; and to address known vulnerabilities or security and privacy risks.[135] The content and structure of plans of action and milestones are informed by the risk management strategy developed as part of the risk executive (function) and are consistent with the plans of action and milestones process established by the organization which include any requirements defined in federal laws, executive orders, policies, directives, or standards. If the systems and the environments in which those systems operate have more vulnerabilities than available resources can realistically address, organizations develop and implement plans of action and milestones that facilitate a prioritized approach to risk mitigation and that is consistent across the organization. A prioritized and consistent approach to risk mitigation ensures that plans of action and milestones are based on:

- The security categorization of the system and security, privacy, and supply chain risk assessments;

- The specific deficiencies in the controls;

- The criticality of the control deficiencies (i.e., the direct or indirect effect the deficiencies may have on the security and privacy posture of the system and the risk exposure of the organization);[136]

- The risk mitigation approach of the organization to address the identified deficiencies in the controls; and

- The rationale for accepting certain deficiencies in the controls.

Organizational strategies for plans of action and milestones are guided and informed by the security categorization of the systems affected by the risk mitigation activities. Organizations may decide, for example, to allocate their risk mitigation resources initially to the highest-impact systems or other high value assets because a failure to correct the known deficiencies in those systems or assets could potentially have the most significant adverse effects on their missions or business functions. Organizations prioritize deficiencies using information from risk assessments and the risk management strategy developed as part of the risk executive (function). Therefore, a high-impact system would have a prioritized list of deficiencies for that system, and similarly for moderate-impact and low-impact systems.

AUTHORIZATION DECISIONS

Authorization decisions are based on the content of the authorization package. There are four types of authorization decisions that can be rendered by authorizing officials:

- Authorization to operate;

---

[135] If changes are made as a result of mitigation actions from plans of actions and milestones, system security plans are updated accordingly.

[136] In general, risk exposure is the degree to which an organization is threatened by the potential adverse effects on organizational operations and assets, individuals, other organizations, or the Nation.

- Common control authorization;

- Authorization to use; and

- Denial of authorization.

Authorization to Operate

If the authorizing official, after reviewing the authorization package, determines that the risk to organizational operations, organizational assets, individuals, other organizations, and the Nation is acceptable, an *authorization to operate* is issued for the information system. The system is authorized to operate for a specified period in accordance with the terms and conditions established by the authorizing official. An *authorization termination date* is established by the authorizing official as a condition of the authorization. The authorization termination date can be adjusted at any time by the authorizing official to reflect an increased level of concern regarding the security and privacy posture of the system. For example, the authorizing official may choose to authorize the system to operate only for a short period of time if it is necessary to test a system in the operational environment before all controls are fully in place, (i.e., the authorization to operate is limited to the time needed to complete the testing objectives).[137] The authorizing official may choose to include operating restrictions such as limiting logical and physical access to a minimum number of users; restricting system use time periods; employing enhanced or increased audit logging, scanning, and monitoring; or restricting the system functionality to include only the functions that require live testing. The authorizing official considers results from the assessment of controls that are fully or partially implemented since if the system is ready to be tested in a live environment, many of the controls should already be in place. If the system is under ongoing authorization, a time-driven authorization frequency is specified. Additionally, an adverse event could occur that triggers the need to review the authorization to operate.[138]

Common Control Authorization

A *common control authorization* is similar to an authorization to operate for systems. If the authorizing official, after reviewing the authorization package submitted by the common control provider, determines that the risk to organizational operations and assets, individuals, other organizations, and the Nation is acceptable, a common control authorization is issued. It is the responsibility of common control providers to indicate that the common controls selected by the organization have been implemented, assessed, and authorized and are available for inheritance by organizational systems. Common control providers are also responsible for ensuring that the system owners inheriting the controls have access to appropriate documentation and tools.

Common controls are authorized for a specific time period in accordance with the terms and conditions established by the authorizing official and the organization. An *authorization termination date* is established by the authorizing official as a condition of the initial common control authorization. The termination date can be adjusted at any time to reflect the level of concern by the authorizing official regarding the security and privacy posture of the common controls that are available for inheritance. If the controls are under ongoing authorization, a

---

[137] Formerly referred to as an interim authority to test.

[138] Additional information on event-driven triggers is provided below.

time-driven authorization frequency is specified. Within any authorization type, an adverse event could trigger the need to review the common control authorization. Common controls that are implemented in a system do not require a separate common control authorization because the controls receive an authorization to operate as part of the system authorization to operate.[139]

Authorization to Use

An *authorization to use* is employed when an organization (hereafter referred to as the customer organization) chooses to accept the information in an existing authorization package produced by another organization (either federal or nonfederal) for an information system that is authorized to operate by a federal entity (referred to as the provider organization).[140] The authorization to use is a mechanism to promote reciprocity for systems under the purview of different authorizing officials. An authorization to use is issued by an authorizing official from the customer organization instead of an authorization to operate. The official issuing an authorization to use has the same level of responsibility and authority for risk management as an authorizing official issuing an authorization to operate or a common control authorization.[141]

The acceptance of the information in the authorization package from the provider organization is a form of reciprocity and is based on a need to use shared systems, services, or applications. A customer organization can issue an authorization to use only after a valid authorization to operate has been issued by another federal entity (i.e., the provider organization).[142] The authorization to operate by the provider organization is a statement of acceptance of risk for the system, service, or application being provided. The authorization to use by the customer organization is a statement of the acceptance of risk in using the system, service, or application with respect to the customer's information. An authorization to use provides opportunities for significant cost savings and avoids a potentially costly and time-consuming authorization process by the customer organization.

An authorization to use requires the customer organization to review the authorization package from the provider organization as the fundamental basis for determining risk.[143] When

---

[139] In certain situations, system owners may choose to inherit controls from other organizational systems that may not be designated officially as common controls. System owners inheriting controls from other than approved common control providers ensure that the systems providing such controls have valid authorizations to operate. The authorizing official of the system inheriting the controls is also made aware of the inheritance.

[140] The term *provider organization* refers to the federal agency or subordinate organization that provides a shared system, service, or application and/or owns and maintains the authorization package (i.e., has granted an Authorization to Operate for the shared system, service, or application). The shared system, service, or application may not be owned by the organization that owns the authorization package, for example, in situations where the shared system, service, or application is provided by an external provider.

[141] Risk-based decisions related to control selection and baseline tailoring actions by organizations providing cloud or shared systems, services, or applications should consider the protection needs of the customer organizations that may be using those cloud or shared systems, services, or applications. Thus, organizations hosting cloud or shared systems, services, or applications should consider the shared risk of operating in those types of environments.

[142] A provisional authorization (to operate) issued by the General Services Administration (GSA) as part of the Federal Risk and Authorization Management Program (FedRAMP) is considered a valid authorization to operate for customer organizations desiring to issue an authorization to use for cloud-based systems, services, or applications.

[143] The sharing of the authorization package (including security and privacy plans, security and privacy assessment reports, plans of action and milestones, and the authorization decision document) is accomplished under terms and conditions agreed upon by all parties (i.e., the customer organization and the service provider organization).

reviewing the authorization package, the customer organization considers various risk factors such as the time elapsed since the authorization results were produced; the environment of operation (if different from the environment reflected in the authorization package); the impact level of the information to be processed, stored, or transmitted; and the overall risk tolerance of the customer organization. If the customer organization plans to integrate the shared system, application, or service with one or more of its systems, the customer organization considers the risk in doing so.

If the customer organization determines that there is insufficient information in the provider authorization package or inadequate controls in place for establishing an acceptable level of risk, the organization may negotiate with the provider organization and request additional controls or security, privacy, or supply chain information. Requests for additional controls may include for example, supplementing controls for risk reduction; implementing compensating controls; conducting additional or more rigorous assessments; or establishing constraints on the use of the system, application, or service provided. Requests for additional information may include, for example, information the provider organization produced or discovered in the use of the system that is not reflected in the authorization package. When the provider organization does not provide the requested controls, the customer organization may choose to implement additional controls to reduce risk to an acceptable level. The additional controls, along with any other controls for which the customer organization is responsible, are documented, implemented, assessed, authorized, and monitored.

Once the customer organization is satisfied with the security and privacy posture of the shared or cloud system, application, or service (as reflected in the current authorization package) and the risk of using the shared or cloud system, application, or service has been sufficiently mitigated, the customer organization issues an authorization to use in which the customer organization explicitly understands and accepts the security or privacy risk incurred by using the shared system, service, or application.[144] Ultimately, the customer organization is responsible and accountable for the risks that may impact the customer organization's operations and assets, individuals, other organizations, or the Nation.

The authorization to use does not require a termination date but remains in effect if the customer organization continues to accept the security and privacy risk of using the shared or cloud system, application, or service and the authorization to operate issued by the provider organization meets the requirements established by federal and organizational policies. It is incumbent on the customer organization to ensure that information from the monitoring activities conducted by the provider organization is shared on an ongoing basis and that the provider organization notifies the customer organization when there are significant changes to the system, application, or service that may affect the security and privacy posture of the provider. If desired, the authorization to use decision may specify time- or even-driven triggers for review of the security and privacy posture of the provider organization system, service, or application being used by the customer organization. The provider organization to notifies the

---

[144] In accordance with [FISMA], the head of each agency is responsible for providing information security protections commensurate with the risk resulting from unauthorized access, use, disclosure, disruption, modification, or destruction of information collected or maintained by or on behalf of the agency; and information systems used or operated by an agency or by a contractor of an agency. [OMB A-130] describes organizational responsibilities for accepting security and privacy risk.

NIST SP 800-37, REVISION 2

RISK MANAGEMENT FRAMEWORK FOR INFORMATION SYSTEMS AND ORGANIZATIONS
A System Life Cycle Approach for Security and Privacy

customer organization if there is a significant event that compromises or adversely affects the customer organization's information.[145]

Figure F-1 illustrates the types of authorization decisions that can be applied to organizational systems and common controls and the risk management roles in the authorization process.

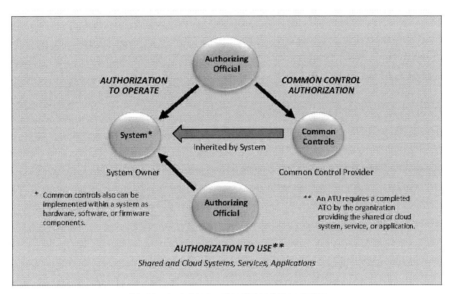

FIGURE F-1: TYPES OF AUTHORIZATION DECISIONS

Denial of Authorization

If the authorizing official, after reviewing the authorization package, including any inputs provided by the senior accountable official for risk management or risk executive (function), determines that the risk to organizational operations, organizational assets, individuals, other organizations, and the Nation is unacceptable and immediate steps cannot be taken to reduce the risk to an acceptable level, the authorization is not granted. A *denial of authorization* means that the information system is not authorized to operate and not placed into operation; common controls are not authorized to be provided to systems; or that the provider's system is not authorized for use by the customer organization. If the system is currently in operation, all activity is halted. Failure to receive an authorization means that there are significant deficiencies in the controls.

The authorizing official or designated representative works with the system owner or the common control provider to revise the plan of action and milestones to help ensure that measures are taken to correct the deficiencies. A special case of authorization denial is an

---

[145] The customer organization may develop memoranda of agreement/understanding, contracts, or other types of agreements with the provider organization to help ensure security posture information about the provided system is shared appropriately.

authorization rescission. Authorizing officials can rescind a previous authorization decision when there is a violation of federal or organizational policies, directives, regulations, standards, or guidance; or a violation of the terms and conditions of the authorization. For example, failure to maintain an effective continuous monitoring program may be grounds for rescinding an authorization decision.

AUTHORIZATION DECISION INFORMATION

The authorization decision is transmitted from the authorizing official to system owners, common control providers, and other key organizational officials. The authorization decision includes the following information:

- Authorization decision;
- Terms and conditions for the authorization;
- Time-driven authorization frequency or authorization termination date;
- Events that may trigger a review of the authorization decision (if any); and
- For common controls, the [FIPS 199] impact level supported by those controls.

The authorization decision indicates if the system is authorized to operate or authorized to be used; or if the common controls are authorized to be provided to system owners and inherited by organizational systems. The terms and conditions for the authorization provide any limitations or restrictions placed on the operation of the system that must be followed by the system owner or alternatively, limitations or restrictions placed on the implementation of common controls that must be followed by the common control provider. If the system or common controls are not under ongoing authorization, the termination date for the authorization established by the authorizing official indicates when the authorization expires and reauthorization is required. The authorization decision document is transmitted with the original authorization package to the system owner or common control provider.[146]

Upon receipt of the authorization decision and authorization package, the system owner and common control provider acknowledge, implement, and comply with the terms and conditions of the authorization. The system owner and common control provider retain the authorization decision and authorization package.[147] The organization ensures that authorization documents are available to organizational officials when requested. The contents of authorization packages, including sensitive information regarding system vulnerabilities, privacy risks, and control deficiencies, are marked and protected in accordance with federal and organizational policy. Authorization decision information is retained in accordance with the organization's record retention policy. The authorizing official verifies on an ongoing basis, that the terms and conditions established as part of the authorization are being followed by the system owner and common control provider.

---

[146] Authorization decision documents may be digitally signed to ensure authenticity.

[147] Organizations may choose to employ automated tools to support the development, distribution, and archiving of risk management information to include artifacts associated with the authorization process.

Authorization to Use Decision

The authorization to use is a streamlined version of the authorization to operate and includes:

- A risk acceptance statement; and
- Time- or event-driven triggers for review of the security and privacy posture of the provider organization shared cloud or system, application, or service (if any).

An authorization to use is issued by an authorizing official from a customer organization in lieu of an authorization to operate. The authorizing official has the same level of risk management responsibility and authority as an authorizing official issuing an authorization to operate or a common control authorization. The risk acceptance statement indicates the explicit acceptance of the security and privacy risk incurred from the use of a shared system, service, or application with respect to the customer organization information processed, stored, or transmitted by or through the shared or cloud system, service, or application.

ONGOING AUTHORIZATION

Continuous monitoring strategies[148] promote effective and efficient risk management on an ongoing basis. Risk management can become *near real-time* by using automation and state-of-the-practice tools, techniques, and procedures for the ongoing monitoring of controls and changes to systems and the environments in which those systems operate. Continuous monitoring based on the needs of the authorizing official, produces the necessary information to determine the security and privacy posture of the system[149] and highlights the risks to organizational operations and assets, individuals, other organizations, and the Nation. Ultimately, continuous monitoring guides and informs the authorizing official's decision whether to authorize the continued operation of the system or the continued use of the common controls inherited by organizational systems.

Continuous monitoring helps to achieve a state of *ongoing authorization* where the authorizing official maintains sufficient knowledge of the current security and privacy posture of the system to determine whether continued operation is acceptable based on ongoing risk determinations—and if not, which steps in the RMF need to be revisited to effectively respond to the additional risk. Reauthorizations are unnecessary in situations where the continuous monitoring program provides authorizing officials with the information necessary to manage the risk arising from changes to the system or the environment in which the system operates. If a reauthorization is required, organizations maximize the use of status reports and relevant information about the security and privacy posture of the system that is produced during the continuous monitoring process to improve efficiency.

When a system or common controls are under ongoing authorization, the system or common controls may be authorized on a time-driven and/or event-driven basis, leveraging the security and privacy information generated by the continuous monitoring program. The system and

---

[148] [SP 800-137] provides additional guidance on information security continuous monitoring. Guidance on privacy continuous monitoring will be provided in future publications.

[149] For greater efficiency, the information security continuous monitoring (ISCM) and privacy continuous monitoring (PCM) strategies may be consolidated into a single unified continuous monitoring strategy. Similarly, the ISCM and PCM programs may also be consolidated into a single unified continuous monitoring program.

common controls are authorized on a time-driven basis in accordance with the authorization frequency determined as part of the organization- and system-level continuous monitoring strategies. The system and common controls are authorized on an event-driven basis until organizational-defined trigger events occur. Whether the authorization is time-driven or event-driven, the authorizing official acknowledges the ongoing acceptance of identified risks. The organization determines the level of formality required for such acknowledgement by the authorizing official.

Conditions for Implementation of Ongoing Authorization

When the RMF has been effectively applied across the organization and the organization has implemented a robust continuous monitoring program, systems may transition from a static, point-in-time authorization process to a dynamic, near real-time ongoing authorization process. To do so, the following conditions must be satisfied:

- The system or common control being considered for ongoing authorization has received an initial authorization based on a complete, zero-based review of the system or the common controls.[150]

- An organizational continuous monitoring program is in place that monitors implemented controls with the appropriate degree of rigor and at the required frequencies specified by the organization in accordance with the continuous monitoring strategy and NIST standards and guidelines.[151]

The organization establishes and implements a process to designate that the two conditions are satisfied and the system or the common controls are transitioning to ongoing authorization. The process includes the authorizing official acknowledging that the system or common control is now being managed by an ongoing authorization process and accepting the responsibility for performing all activities associated with that process. The transition to ongoing authorization is documented by the authorizing official by issuing a new authorization decision.[152] The security and privacy information generated through the continuous monitoring process is provided to the authorizing officials and other organizational officials in a timely manner through security and privacy management and reporting tools. Such tools facilitate risk-based decision making for the ongoing authorization for systems and common controls.

Information Generation, Collection, and Independence Requirements

To support ongoing authorization, security and privacy information for controls is generated and collected at the frequency specified in the organization's continuous monitoring strategy. Security and privacy information may be collected using automated tools or other methods of assessment depending on the type and purpose of the control and desired rigor of the assessment. Automated tools may not generate security and privacy information that is

---

[150] System owners and authorizing officials leverage security and privacy information about inherited common controls from assessments conducted by common control providers.

[151] [SP 800-53] and [SP 800-53A] provide guidance regarding the appropriate degree of rigor for security assessments and monitoring. Future publications will address privacy assessments.

[152] Prior to transitioning to ongoing authorization, organizations have authorization decision documents that include an authorization termination date. By requiring a new authorization decision document, it is made clear that the system or the common controls are no longer bound to the termination date specified in the initial authorization document because the system and the common controls are now under ongoing authorization.

sufficient to support the authorizing official in making risk determinations. Automated tools may not provide sufficient support for various reasons (e.g., the tools do not generate information for every control or every part of a control, additional assurance is needed, or the tools do not generate information on specific technologies or platforms). In such cases, manual control assessments are conducted at organizationally-determined frequencies to cover any gaps in automated security and privacy information generation. The manually-generated assessment results are provided to the authorizing official in the manner deemed appropriate by the organization.

To support ongoing authorizations for moderate- and high-impact systems, the security and privacy information provided to the authorizing official, whether generated manually or in an automated fashion, is produced and analyzed by an entity that meets the independence requirements established by the organization. The senior agency official for privacy is responsible for assessing privacy controls and for providing privacy information to the authorizing official. At the discretion of the organization, privacy controls may be assessed by an independent assessor. The independent assessor is impartial and free from any perceived or actual conflicts of interest regarding the development, implementation, assessment, operation, or management of the organizational systems and common controls being monitored.

Ongoing Authorization Frequency

[SP 800-53] security control CA-6, Part c. specifies that the authorization for a system and any common controls inherited by the system be updated at an organization-established frequency. This part of the control reinforces the concept of ongoing authorization. In accordance with CA-6 (along with the security and privacy assessment and monitoring frequency determinations established as part of the continuous monitoring strategy), organizations determine a frequency with which authorizing officials review security and privacy information via the security or privacy management and reporting tool or manual process.[153] The near real-time information from the reporting tool or manual process is used to determine whether the mission or business risk of operating the system or providing the common controls continues to be acceptable. [SP 800-137] provides criteria for determining assessment and monitoring frequencies.

Under ongoing authorization, *time-driven* authorization triggers refer to the frequency with which the organization determines that authorizing officials are to review security and privacy information and authorize the system (or common controls) for continued operation as described above. Time-driven authorization triggers can be based on a variety of organization-defined factors including the impact level of the system. When a time-driven trigger occurs, authorizing officials review security and privacy information on the systems for which they are responsible and accountable to determine the ongoing organizational mission or business risk, the acceptability of such risk in accordance with organizational risk tolerance, and whether the approval for continued operation is justified. The organizational continuous monitoring process, supported by the organization's security and privacy management and reporting tools, provides

---

[153] *Ongoing authorization* and *ongoing assessment* are different concepts but closely related. To employ an ongoing authorization approach (which implies an ongoing understanding and acceptance of risk), organizations must have in place, an organization-level and system-level continuous monitoring process to assess implemented controls on an ongoing basis. The findings or results from the continuous monitoring process provides information to authorizing officials to support near-real time risk-based decision making.

the appropriate functionality to notify the responsible and accountable authorizing official that it is time to review the security and privacy information to support ongoing authorization.

In contrast to time-driven authorization triggers, *event-driven* triggers necessitate an immediate review of security and privacy information by the authorizing official. Organizations may define event-driven *triggers* (i.e., indicators or prompts that cause an organization to react in a predefined manner) for ongoing authorization and reauthorization. When an event-driven trigger occurs under ongoing authorization, the authorizing official is either notified by organizational personnel (e.g., senior agency information security officer, senior agency official for privacy, system owner, common control provider, or system security or privacy officer) or via automated tools that defined trigger events have occurred requiring an immediate review of the system or the common controls. The authorizing official may also determine independently that an immediate review is required. The event-driven trigger review is conducted in addition to the time-driven frequency review defined in the organizational continuous monitoring strategy and occurs during ongoing authorization when the residual risk remains within the acceptable limits of organizational risk tolerance.[154]

Transitioning from Static Authorization to Ongoing Authorization

The intent of continuous monitoring is to monitor controls at a frequency that is sufficient to provide authorizing officials with the information necessary to make effective, risk-based decisions, whether by automated or manual means.[155] However, if a substantial portion of monitoring is not accomplished via automation, it will not be feasible or practical to move from the current static authorization approach to an effective and efficient ongoing authorization approach. A phased approach for the generation of security and privacy information may be necessary during the transition as automated tools become available and a greater number of controls are monitored by automated techniques. Organizations may begin by generating security and privacy information from automated tools and fill in gaps by generating additional information from manual assessments. As additional automated monitoring functionality is added, processes can be adjusted.

Transitioning from a static authorization process to a dynamic, ongoing authorization process requires considerable thought and planning. One methodology that organizations may consider is to take a phased approach to the migration based on the security categorization of the system. Because risk tolerance levels for low-impact systems are likely to be greater than for moderate-impact or high-impact systems, implementing continuous monitoring and ongoing authorization for low-impact systems first may ease the transition. The phased approach starting with low-impact systems allows organizations to incorporate lessons learned as continuous monitoring and ongoing authorization processes are implemented for moderate-impact and high-impact systems. Incorporating lessons learned facilitates the consistent progression of the continuous monitoring and ongoing authorization implementation from the

---

[154] The immediate reviews initiated by specific trigger events may occur simultaneously (i.e., in conjunction) with time-driven monitoring activities based on the monitoring frequencies established by the organization and how the reviews are structured within the organization. The same reporting structure may be used for event- and time-driven reviews to achieve efficiencies.

[155] Privacy continuous monitoring means maintaining ongoing awareness of privacy risks and assessing privacy controls at a frequency sufficient to ensure compliance with applicable privacy requirements and to manage privacy risks.

lowest to the highest impact levels for the systems within the organization. Organizations may also consider employing the phased implementation approach by partitioning systems into subsystems or system elements and subsequently transitioning those subsystems or system elements to ongoing authorization one segment at a time until the entire system is ready for the full transition (at which time the authorizing official acknowledges that the system is now being managed by an ongoing authorization process).

REAUTHORIZATION

Reauthorization actions occur at the discretion of the authorizing official in accordance with federal or organizational policy.[156] If a reauthorization action is required, organizations maximize the use of security and privacy risk information produced as part of the continuous monitoring processes currently in effect. Reauthorization actions, if initiated, can be either time-driven or event-driven. Time-driven reauthorizations occur when the authorization termination date is reached (if one is specified). If the system is under ongoing authorization,[157] a time-driven reauthorization may not be necessary. However, if the continuous monitoring program is not sufficiently comprehensive to fully support ongoing authorization, a maximum authorization period can be specified by the authorizing official. Authorization termination dates are guided and informed by federal and organizational policies and by the requirements of authorizing officials.

Under ongoing authorization, a reauthorization may be necessary if an event occurs that produces risk above the acceptable organizational risk tolerance. A reauthorization may be warranted, for example, if there is a breach/incident or failure of or significant problems with the continuous monitoring program. Reauthorization actions may necessitate a review of and changes to the continuous monitoring strategy which may in turn, affect ongoing authorization.

For security and privacy assessments associated with reauthorization, organizations leverage security and privacy information generated by the continuous monitoring program and fill in gaps with manual assessments. Organizations may supplement automatically-generated assessment information with manually-generated information in situations where an increased level of assurance is needed. If the security control assessments are conducted by qualified assessors with the necessary independence, use appropriate security standards and guidelines, and are based on the needs of the authorizing official, the assessment results can be applied to the reauthorization.[158]

The senior agency official for privacy is responsible for assessing privacy controls and those assessment results can be cumulatively applied to the reauthorization. Independent assessors may assess privacy controls at the discretion of the organization. The senior agency official for privacy reviews and approves the authorization packages for information systems that process PII prior to the authorizing official making a reauthorization decision. The reauthorization action may be as simple as updating the security and privacy plans, security and privacy assessment

---

[156] Decisions to initiate a formal reauthorization include inputs from the senior agency information security officer, senior agency official for privacy, and senior accountable official for risk management/risk executive (function).

[157] An ongoing authorization approach requires that a continuous monitoring program is in place to monitor all implemented security controls with a frequency specified in the continuous monitoring strategy.

[158] [SP 800-53A] describes the specific conditions when security information can be reused to support authorization actions.

reports, and plans of action and milestones—focused only on specific problems or ongoing issues, or as comprehensive as the initial authorization.

The authorizing official signs an updated authorization decision document based on the current risk determination and acceptance of risk to organizational operations and assets, individuals, other organizations, and the Nation. In all situations where there is a decision to reauthorize a system or the common controls inherited by organizational systems, the maximum reuse of authorization information is encouraged to minimize the time and expense associated with the reauthorization effort (subject to organizational reuse policy).

EVENT-DRIVEN TRIGGERS AND SIGNIFICANT CHANGES

Organizations define event-driven *triggers* (i.e., indicators or prompts that cause a predefined organizational reaction) for both ongoing authorization and reauthorization. Event-driven triggers may include, but are not limited to:

- New threat, vulnerability, privacy risk, or impact information;
- An increased number of findings or deficiencies from the continuous monitoring program;
- New missions/business requirements;
- Change in the authorizing official;
- Significant change in risk assessment findings;
- Significant changes to the system, common controls, or the environments of operation;
- Changes in the supply chain affecting security or privacy risks to operational systems; or
- Exceeding organizational thresholds.

When there is a change in authorizing officials, the new authorizing official reviews the current authorization decision document, authorization package, any updated documents from ongoing monitoring activities, or a report from automated security/privacy management and reporting tools. If the new authorizing official finds the current risk to be acceptable, the official signs a new or updated authorization decision document, formally transferring responsibility and accountability for the system or the common controls. In doing so, the new authorizing official explicitly accepts the risk to organizational operations and assets, individuals, other organizations, and the Nation. If the new authorizing official finds the current risk to be unacceptable, an authorization action (i.e., ongoing authorization or reauthorization) can be initiated. Alternatively, the new authorizing official may instead establish new terms and conditions for continuing the original authorization, but not extend the original authorization termination date (if not under ongoing authorization).

A significant change is defined as a change that is likely to substantively affect the security or privacy posture of a system. Significant changes to a system that may trigger an event-driven authorization action may include, but are not limited to:

- Installation of a new or upgraded operating system, middleware component, or application;
- Modifications to system ports, protocols, or services;
- Installation of a new or upgraded hardware platform;

- Modifications to how information, including PII, is processed;

- Modifications to cryptographic modules or services;

- Changes in information types processed, stored, or transmitted by the system; or

- Modifications to security and privacy controls.

Significant changes to the environment of operation that may trigger an event-driven authorization action may include, but are not limited to:

- Moving to a new facility;

- Adding new core missions or business functions;

- Acquiring specific and credible threat information that the organization is being targeted by a threat source; or

- Establishing new/modified laws, directives, policies, or regulations.

The examples of changes listed above are only significant when they represent a change that is likely to affect the security and privacy posture of the system. Organizations establish criteria for what constitutes significant change based on a variety of factors (e.g., mission and business needs; threat and vulnerability information; environments of operation for systems; privacy risks; and security categorization).

Risk assessment results or the results from an impact analysis may be used to determine if changes to systems or common controls are significant and trigger an authorization action. If an authorization action is initiated, the organization targets only the specific controls affected by the changes and reuses previous assessment results wherever possible. An effective monitoring program can significantly reduce the overall cost and level of effort of authorization actions. Most changes to a system or its environment of operation can be handled through the continuous monitoring program and ongoing authorization.

TYPE AND FACILITY AUTHORIZATIONS

A *type authorization*[159] is an official authorization decision that allows for a single authorization package to be developed for an archetype (i.e., common) version of a system. This includes, for example hardware, software, or firmware components that are deployed to multiple locations for use in specified environments of operation (e.g., system installation and configuration requirements or operational security and privacy needs provided by the host organization at a specific location). A type authorization is appropriate when the system is deployed in a defined environment and is comprised of identical instances of system architecture, software, identical information types, functionally identical hardware, information that is processed in the same way, identical control implementations, or identical configurations. A type authorization is used

---

[159] Examples of type authorizations include: an authorization of the hardware and software applications for a standard financial system deployed in multiple locations; or an authorization of a common workstation or operating environment (i.e., hardware, operating system, and applications) deployed to all operating units within an organization.

in conjunction with authorized site-specific controls[160] or with a facility authorization as described below. A type authorization is issued by the authorizing official responsible for the development of the system[161] and represents an authorization to operate. At the site or facility where the system is deployed, the authorizing official who is responsible for the system at the site or facility accepts the risk of deploying the system and issues an authorization to use. The authorization to use leverages the information in the authorization packages for the archetype system and the facility common controls.

A *facility authorization* is an official authorization decision that is focused on specific controls implemented in a defined environment of operation to support one or more systems residing within that environment. A facility authorization addresses common controls within a facility and allows systems residing in the defined environment to inherit the common controls and the affected system security and privacy plans to reference the authorization package for the facility. The common controls are provided at a specified impact level to facilitate risk decisions on whether it is appropriate to locate a given system in a particular facility.[162] Physical and environmental controls are addressed in a facility authorization but other controls may also be included, for example, boundary protections; contingency plan and incident response plan for the facility; or training and awareness and personnel screening for facility staff. The facility authorizing official issues a common control authorization to describe the common controls available for inheritance by systems residing within the facility.

TRADITIONAL AND JOINT AUTHORIZATIONS

Organizations can choose from two distinct approaches when planning for and conducting authorizations. These include an authorization with a *single* authorizing official or an authorization with *multiple* authorizing officials.[163] The first approach is the traditional authorization process defined in this appendix where a single organizational official in a senior leadership position is responsible and accountable for a system or for common controls. The organizational official accepts the security and privacy risks that may adversely impact organizational operations, organizational assets, individuals, other organizations, or the Nation.

The second approach, *joint authorization*, is employed when multiple organizational officials either from the same organization or different organizations, have a shared interest in authorizing a system. The organizational officials collectively are responsible and accountable for the system and jointly accept the security and privacy risks that may adversely impact organizational operations and assets, individuals, other organizations, and the Nation. A similar authorization process is followed as in the single authorizing official approach with the essential difference being the addition of multiple authorizing officials. Organizations choosing a joint authorization approach are expected to work together on the planning and the execution of RMF tasks and to document their agreement and progress in implementing the tasks.

---

[160] Site-specific controls are typically implemented by an organization as *common controls*. Examples include physical and environmental protection controls and personnel security controls.

[161] Typically, type authorizations are issued by organizations that are responsible for developing standardized hardware and software capabilities for customers and delivered to the recipient organizations as "turn key" solutions. The senior leaders issuing such authorizations may be referred to as developmental authorizing officials.

[162] For example, if the facility is categorized as moderate impact, it may not be appropriate to locate high-impact systems or system elements in that environment of operation.

[163] Authorization approaches can be applied to systems and to common controls inherited by organizational systems.

Collaboration on security categorization, control selection and tailoring, a plan for assessing controls to determine effectiveness, a plan of action and milestones, and a system-level continuous monitoring strategy is necessary for a successful joint authorization. The terms and conditions of the joint authorization are established by the participating parties in the joint authorization including the process for ongoing determination and acceptance of risk. The joint authorization remains in effect only while there is agreement among authorizing officials and the authorization meets the specific requirements established by federal and organizational policies. [SP 800-53] controls CA-6(1), *Joint Authorization – Same Organization* and CA-6(2) *Joint Authorization – Different Organizations*, describe the requirements for joint authorizations.

Guide for Applying the Risk Management Framework to Federal Information Systems (800-37 rev 2)

APPENDIX G

AUTHORIZATION BOUNDARY CONSIDERATIONS
COMPLEX SYSTEMS, APPLICATIONS, AND THE EFFECTS OF CHANGING TECHNOLOGIES

This appendix provides additional considerations for determining authorization boundaries for complex systems and software applications. It also includes guidance on authorization boundaries when organizations use external providers for their information resources. The foundational RMF steps and tasks described in Chapter Three can be applied in all three scenarios to help organizations manage security and privacy risks and comply with the laws, executive orders, and OMB policies discussed in Chapter One.

AUTHORIZATION BOUNDARIES FOR COMPLEX SYSTEMS

The determination of authorization boundaries for complex systems can present significant challenges to organizations. A complex system can be viewed as set of individual subsystems. A subsystem is a major subdivision of a system consisting of system elements that perform one or more specific functions. Figure G-1 illustrates the concept of a complex system.

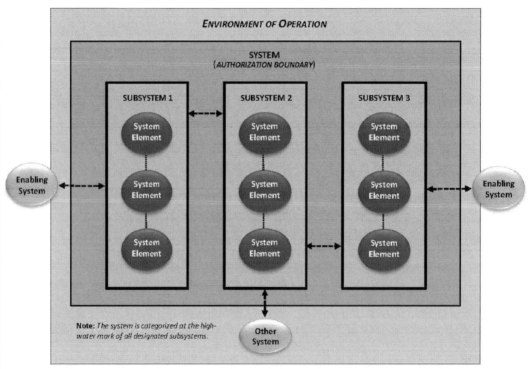

FIGURE G-1: CONCEPTUAL VIEW OF A COMPLEX SYSTEM

Organizations can employ the concept of subsystems to divide complex systems into a set of manageable system elements or identify those elements that support a similar mission, but are sufficiently distinct to be identified separately. Each subsystem has its own boundary (distinct from an authorization boundary) and can be defined within a comprehensive authorization boundary that includes all subsystems.

For example, an organization may find it useful to combine several systems that are under the same direct management control or that have similar missions or business functions into a single system to achieve the dual purposes of effective risk and resource management. An organization may also choose to develop a system composed of multiple independent systems (distributed across a widespread geographic area) supporting a set of common missions or business functions. Similarly, a system can be divided into multiple subsystems to facilitate and support management of the system and risk-based decision making (e.g., categorization decisions, tailoring decisions, and control allocation decisions).

Dividing a system into subsystems (i.e., divide and conquer) facilitates a targeted application of controls to achieve adequate security, protection of individual privacy, and a cost-effective risk management process. Dividing complex systems into subsystems also supports the important security concepts of domain separation and network segmentation, which can be significant when dealing with high value assets. When systems are divided into subsystems, organizations may choose to develop individual subsystem security and privacy plans or address the system and subsystems in the same security and privacy plans.

Information security and privacy architectures play a key part in the process of dividing complex systems into subsystems. This includes monitoring and controlling communications at internal boundaries among subsystems and selecting, allocating, and implementing controls that meet or exceed the security and privacy requirements of the constituent subsystems. One approach to control selection and allocation is to categorize each identified subsystem separately (see Task C-2). However, separately categorizing each subsystem does not change the overall categorization of the system. Rather, separately categorizing each subsystem allows the subsystems to receive a separate and more targeted allocation of controls from [SP 800-53] instead of deploying higher-impact controls across the entire system (see Task P-17 and Task S-3). Another approach is to bundle smaller subsystems into larger subsystems within the system, categorize each of the aggregated subsystems, and allocate controls to the subsystems, as needed. While subsystems within complex systems may exist as complete systems, the subsystems are, in most cases, not treated as independent entities because they are typically interdependent and interconnected.

When the security categorizations for the identified subsystems are different (e.g., low-impact versus high-impact), the organization examines the subsystem interfaces,[164] information flows, and security and privacy dependencies among subsystems and selects the appropriate controls

---

[164] The types of interfaces and couplings among subsystems may introduce inadvertent vulnerabilities in a complex system. For example, if a large organizational intranet is decomposed into smaller subsystems (e.g., severable systems such as local area network segments) and subsequently categorized individually, the specific protections at the system level may expose an attack vector against the intranet by erroneously selecting and implementing controls that are not sufficiently strong with respect to the rest of the system. To avoid this situation, organizations carefully examine the interfaces among subsystems and take appropriate actions to eliminate potential vulnerabilities in this area, thus helping to ensure that the information system is adequately protected.

for the interconnection of the subsystems to eliminate or reduce potential vulnerabilities. This helps to ensure that the system is adequately protected. Controls for the interconnection of subsystems are also employed when the subsystems implement different security and privacy policies or are administered by different authorities. The extent to which the selected controls are implemented correctly, operating as intended, and producing the desired outcome with respect to meeting the security and privacy requirements for the complex system, can be determined by combining control assessments at the system level and adding considerations addressing interface issues. The combined approach facilitates a targeted and cost-effective risk management process by scaling the level of effort of the assessment in accordance with the security categorization and allowing for reuse of assessment results at the system level.

AUTHORIZATION BOUNDARIES FOR SOFTWARE APPLICATIONS

Authorization boundaries include all system elements, including hardware, firmware, and software. Software elements include applications (e.g., database applications, customized business applications, and web applications), middleware, and operating systems. The software elements are included in authorization boundaries, either as part of the information system on which the software is hosted or as a part of an application-only system or subsystem that inherits controls from the hosting system. Software applications may depend on the resources provided by the hosting system and as such, can leverage the controls provided by the hosting system to help provide a foundational level of protection for the hosted applications. Additional application-level controls are provided by the respective software applications, as needed. Application owners coordinate with system owners to help ensure that security and privacy requirements are satisfied among applications and hosting systems. Coordination between system owners and application owners includes, for example, consideration for the selection, implementation, assessment, and monitoring of controls for the applications; the effects of changes to the applications on the security and privacy posture of the system and the organization; and the effects of changes to the system on the hosted applications.

AUTHORIZATION BOUNDARIES AND EXTERNAL PROVIDERS

While the concepts of external systems and external service providers are not new, the current pervasiveness and frequency of their invocation can present organizations with significant, new challenges. There are instances where system elements, subsystems, or perhaps the entire system may be outside of the direct control of the organization that authorizes its operation. The nature of such external systems can vary from organizations employing external cloud computing services to process, store, and transmit federal information to organizations allowing platforms under their control to host applications or services developed by some external entity.[165]

FISMA and OMB policy require external providers that process, store, or transmit federal information or operate information systems on behalf of the federal government to meet the same security and privacy requirements as federal agencies. Federal security and privacy requirements also apply to external systems storing, processing, or transmitting federal information and any services provided by or associated with the external system. Furthermore,

---

[165] The Federal Risk and Authorization Management Program (FedRAMP) operated by the General Services Administration (GSA) provides guidance on determining cloud authorization boundaries.

the assurance or confidence that the risk from using external providers is at an acceptable level depends on the trust that the organization places in the provider. In some instances, the level of trust is based on the amount of direct control the organization can exert on the provider regarding the employment of controls necessary to protect federal information and protect the privacy of individuals.

The level of trust can also be based on the evidence brought forth by the external provider or by an independent assessor as to the effectiveness of those controls. In other instances, trust can be based on other factors, such as the previous experience the organization has had with the external provider and the confidence the organization has in the provider taking the correct actions. There are a variety of factors that can complicate the level of trust with external providers:

- The delineation between what is owned by the external provider and the organization may be blurred (e.g., organization-owned platform executing external provider-developed application, software module, or firmware);

- The degree of control the organization has over the external provider may be very limited;

- The nature and content of the system, subsystem, service, or application may be subject to rapid change; and

- The system, subsystem, service, or application may be of such critical nature that it needs to be incorporated into organizational systems very rapidly.

The consequence of the above factors is that some of the traditional means organizations use to verify and validate the correct functioning of a system, subsystem, application or service and the effectiveness of implemented controls (e.g., clearly defined requirements, design analysis, testing and evaluation before deployment, control assessments and continuous monitoring) may not be feasible. As a result, organizations may be left to depend upon the nature of the trust relationships with the external provider as the basis for determining whether to issue an authorization to use or authorization to operate for the system or subsystems processing, storing, or transmitting federal information (e.g., use of GSA list of approved providers). Alternatively, organizations may allow externally provided systems or services to be used only in those instances where the exchange of information risk determined by the organization is acceptable.

Ultimately, when the level of trust in the external provider does not provide sufficient assurance, the organization employs compensating controls; accepts greater risk; contracts with a more trustworthy external provider; or does not obtain the service (i.e., conducts its missions and business operations with reduced levels of functionality or possibly no functionality at all).

LEVERAGING EXTERNAL PROVIDER CONTROLS AND ASSESSMENTS

Organizations should exercise caution when attempting to leverage external provider controls and assessment results. Controls implemented by external providers may be different than the controls in [SP 800-53] in the scope, coverage, and capability provided. NIST provides a mapping of the controls in its catalog to the [ISO 27001] security controls and to the [ISO 15408-2] and [ISO 15408-3] security requirements. However, such mappings are inherently subjective and should be reviewed carefully by organizations to determine if the controls and requirements addressed by external providers meet the protection needs of the organization. The mappings between different standards or guidelines also do not address the potential for differing scopes and purpose for each publication.

Similar caution should be exercised when attempting to use or leverage security and privacy assessment results from external providers. The type, rigor, and scope of the assessments may vary widely from provider to provider. In addition, the assessment procedures employed by the provider and the independence of the assessors conducting the assessments are critical issues that should be reviewed and considered by organizations prior to leveraging assessment results.

Effective risk decisions by authorizing officials depend on the transparency of controls selected and implemented by external providers and the quality and efficacy of the assessment evidence produced by those providers. Transparency is essential to achieve the assurance necessary to ensure adequate protection for organizational assets.

APPENDIX H

SYSTEM LIFE CYCLE CONSIDERATIONS
OTHER FACTORS EFFECTING THE EXECUTION OF THE RMF

All systems, including operational systems, systems under development, and systems that are undergoing modification or upgrade, are in some phase of the SDLC.[166] Defining requirements is a critical part of an SDLC process and begins in the *initiation* phase.[167] Security and privacy requirements are part of the functional and nonfunctional[168] requirements allocated to a system. The security and privacy requirements are incorporated into the SDLC simultaneously with the other requirements. Without the early integration of security and privacy requirements, significant expense may be incurred by the organization later in the life cycle to address security and privacy concerns that could have been included in the initial design. When security and privacy requirements are defined early in the SDLC and integrated with other system requirements, the resulting system has fewer deficiencies, and therefore, fewer privacy risks or security vulnerabilities that can be exploited in the future.

Integrating security and privacy requirements into the SDLC is the most effective, efficient, and cost-effective method to ensure that the organization's protection strategy is implemented. It also ensures that security and privacy processes are not isolated from the other processes used by the organization to develop, implement, operate, and maintain the systems supporting ongoing missions and business functions. In addition to incorporating security and privacy requirements into the SDLC, the requirements are integrated into the organization's program, planning, and budgeting activities to help ensure that resources are available when needed and program and project milestones are completed. The enterprise architecture provides a central record of this integration within an organization.

RISK MANAGEMENT IN THE SYSTEM DEVELOPMENT LIFE CYCLE

Risk management activities begin early in the SDLC and continue throughout the life cycle. These activities are important in helping to shape the security and privacy capabilities of the system; ensuring that the necessary controls are implemented and that the security and privacy risks are being adequately addressed on an ongoing basis; and ensuring that the authorizing officials understand the current security and privacy posture of the system in order to accept the risk to organizational operations and assets, individuals, other organizations, and the Nation.

Ensuring that security and privacy requirements are integrated into the SDLC helps facilitate the development and implementation of more resilient systems to reduce the security and privacy

---

[166] There are five phases in the SDLC including initiation; development and acquisition; implementation; operation and maintenance; and disposal. [SP 800-64] provides guidance on the SDLC.

[167] Organizations may employ a variety of development processes (e.g., waterfall, spiral, or agile).

[168] Nonfunctional requirements include, for example, quality and assurance requirements.

Guide for Applying the Risk Management Framework to Federal Information Systems (800-37 rev 2)
365

risks (including supply chain risks) to organizational operations and assets, individuals, other organizations, and the Nation. This can be accomplished by using the concept of integrated project teams.[169] Organizational officials ensure that security and privacy professionals are part of the SDLC activities. Such team integration fosters an increased level of cooperation among personnel responsible for the design, development, implementation, assessment, operation, maintenance, and disposition of systems and the security and privacy professionals advising the senior leadership on the controls needed to adequately mitigate security and privacy risks and protect organizational missions and business functions.

Finally, organizations maximize the use of security- and privacy-relevant information generated during the SDLC process to satisfy requirements for similar information needed for other security and privacy purposes. The reuse of security and privacy information is an effective method to reduce duplication of effort and documentation; promote reciprocity; and avoid unnecessary costs when security and privacy activities are conducted independently of the SDLC processes. Reuse promotes consistency of information in the development, implementation, assessment, operation, maintenance, and disposition of systems including security and privacy considerations.

This publication is available free of charge from: https://doi.org/10.6028/NIST.SP.800-37r2

---

[169] Integrated project teams are multidisciplinary entities consisting of individuals with a range of skills and roles to help facilitate the development of systems that meet the requirements of the organization.

THE IMPORTANCE OF ARCHITECTURE AND ENGINEERING

Security architects, privacy architects, systems security engineers, and privacy engineers can play an essential role in the SDLC and in the successful execution of the RMF. Security and privacy architects and engineers provide *system owners* and *authorizing officials* with technical advice on the selection and implementation of controls in information systems—guiding and informing risk-based decisions across the enterprise.

Security and Privacy Architects:

- Ensure that security and privacy requirements necessary to protect mission and business processes are adequately addressed in all aspects of enterprise architecture including reference models, segment and solution architectures, and the systems supporting those missions and business processes.

- Serve as the primary liaison between the enterprise architect and the systems security and privacy engineers.

- Coordinate with system owners, common control providers, and system security and privacy officers on the allocation of controls.

- Advise authorizing officials, chief information officers, senior accountable officials for risk management/risk executive (function), senior agency information security officers, and senior agency officials for privacy on a range of security and privacy issues.

Security and Privacy Engineers:

- Ensure that security and privacy requirements are integrated into systems and system elements through purposeful security or privacy architecting, design, development, and configuration.

- Employ best practices when implementing controls within a system, including the use of software engineering methodologies; systems security or privacy engineering principles; secure or privacy-enhancing design, secure or privacy-enhancing architecture, and secure or privacy-enhancing coding techniques.

- Coordinate security and privacy activities with senior agency information security officers, senior agency officials for privacy, system owners, common control providers, security and privacy architects, and system security or privacy officers.

NIST Special Publication 800-137

Information Security Continuous Monitoring (ISCM) for Federal Information Systems and Organizations

National Institute of Standards and Technology

U.S. Department of Commerce

Kelley Dempsey
Nirali Shah Chawla
Arnold Johnson
Ronald Johnston
Alicia Clay Jones
Angela Orebaugh
Matthew Scholl
Kevin Stine

INFORMATION SECURITY

Computer Security Division
Information Technology Laboratory
National Institute of Standards and Technology
Gaithersburg, MD 20899-8930

SEPTEMBER 2011

U.S. Department of Commerce
Rebecca M. Blank, Acting Secretary

National Institute of Standards and Technology
Patrick D. Gallagher, Under Secretary for Standards and Technology and Director

Reports on Computer Systems Technology

The Information Technology Laboratory (ITL) at the National Institute of Standards and Technology (NIST) promotes the U.S. economy and public welfare by providing technical leadership for the nation's measurement and standards infrastructure. ITL develops tests, test methods, reference data, proof of concept implementations, and technical analyses to advance the development and productive use of information technology. ITL's responsibilities include the development of management, administrative, technical, and physical standards and guidelines for the cost-effective security and privacy of other than national security-related information in federal information systems. The Special Publication 800-series reports on ITL's research, guidelines, and outreach efforts in information system security, and its collaborative activities with industry, government, and academic organizations.

Authority

This publication has been developed by NIST to further its statutory responsibilities under the Federal Information Security Management Act (FISMA), Public Law (P.L.) 107-347. NIST is responsible for developing information security standards and guidelines, including minimum requirements for federal information systems, but such standards and guidelines shall not apply to national security systems without the express approval of appropriate federal officials exercising policy authority over such systems. This guideline is consistent with the requirements of the Office of Management and Budget (OMB) Circular A-130, Section 8b(3), Securing Agency Information Systems, as analyzed in Circular A-130, Appendix IV: Analysis of Key Sections. Supplemental information is provided in Circular A-130, Appendix III.

Nothing in this publication should be taken to contradict the standards and guidelines made mandatory and binding on federal agencies by the Secretary of Commerce under statutory authority. Nor should these guidelines be interpreted as altering or superseding the existing authorities of the Secretary of Commerce, Director of the OMB, or any other federal official. This publication may be used by nongovernmental organizations on a voluntary basis and is not subject to copyright in the United States. Attribution would, however, be appreciated by NIST.

NIST Special Publication 800-137, 80 pages

(September 2011)

National Institute of Standards and Technology
Attn: Computer Security Division, Information Technology Laboratory
100 Bureau Drive (Mail Stop 8930) Gaithersburg, MD 20899-8930
Electronic mail: 800-137comments@nist.gov

Acknowledgements

The authors, Kelley Dempsey, Arnold Johnson, Matthew Scholl and Kevin Stine of the National Institute of Standards and Technology (NIST), Ronald Johnston of the Department of Defense Chief Information Officer, Defense-wide Information Assurance Program (DOD-CIO, DIAP), Alicia Clay Jones and Angela Orebaugh of Booz Allen Hamilton, and Nirali Shah Chawla of PricewaterhouseCoopers LLP (PwC), wish to thank their colleagues who reviewed drafts of this document and contributed to its technical content. The authors would like to acknowledge their colleagues for their keen and insightful assistance with technical issues throughout the development of the document. And finally, the authors gratefully acknowledge and appreciate the significant contributions from individuals and organizations in the public and private sectors whose thoughtful and constructive comments improved the overall quality and usefulness of this publication.

Table of Contents

EXECUTIVE SUMMARY

In today's environment where many, if not all, of an organization's mission-critical functions are dependent upon information technology, the ability to manage this technology and to assure confidentiality, integrity, and availability of information is now also mission-critical. In designing the enterprise architecture and corresponding security architecture, an organization seeks to securely meet the IT infrastructure needs of its governance structure, missions, and core business processes. Information security is a dynamic process that must be effectively and proactively managed for an organization to identify and respond to new vulnerabilities, evolving threats, and an organization's constantly changing enterprise architecture and operational environment.

The Risk Management Framework (RMF) developed by NIST,[1] describes a disciplined and structured process that integrates information security and risk management activities into the system development life cycle. Ongoing monitoring is a critical part of that risk management process. In addition, an organization's overall security architecture and accompanying security program are monitored to ensure that organization-wide operations remain within an acceptable level of risk, despite any changes that occur. Timely, relevant, and accurate information is vital, particularly when resources are limited and agencies must prioritize their efforts.

> Information security continuous monitoring (ISCM) is defined as maintaining ongoing awareness of information security, vulnerabilities, and threats to support organizational risk management decisions.

Any effort or process intended to support ongoing monitoring of information security across an organization begins with leadership defining a comprehensive ISCM strategy encompassing technology, processes, procedures, operating environments, and people. This strategy:

- Is grounded in a clear understanding of organizational risk tolerance and helps officials set priorities and manage risk consistently throughout the organization;

- Includes metrics that provide meaningful indications of security status at all organizational tiers;

- Ensures continued effectiveness of all security controls;

- Verifies compliance with information security requirements derived from organizational missions/business functions, federal legislation, directives, regulations, policies, and standards/guidelines;

- Is informed by all organizational IT assets and helps to maintain visibility into the security of the assets;

- Ensures knowledge and control of changes to organizational systems and environments of operation; and

- Maintains awareness of threats and vulnerabilities.

---

[1] See NIST Special Publication (SP) 800-37, as amended, *Guide for Applying the Risk Management Framework to Federal Information Systems: A Security Life Cycle Approach.*

An ISCM program is established to collect information in accordance with preestablished metrics, utilizing information readily available in part through implemented security controls. Organizational officials collect and analyze the data regularly and as often as needed to manage risk as appropriate for each organizational tier. This process involves the entire organization, from senior leaders providing governance and strategic vision to individuals developing, implementing, and operating individual systems in support of the organization's core missions and business processes. Subsequently, determinations are made from an organizational perspective on whether to conduct mitigation activities or to reject, transfer, or accept risk.

Organizations' security architectures, operational security capabilities, and monitoring processes will improve and mature over time to better respond to the dynamic threat and vulnerability landscape. An organization's ISCM strategy and program are routinely reviewed for relevance and are revised as needed to increase visibility into assets and awareness of vulnerabilities. This further enables data-driven control of the security of an organization's information infrastructure, and increase organizational resilience.

Organization-wide monitoring cannot be efficiently achieved through manual processes alone or through automated processes alone. Where manual processes are used, the processes are repeatable and verifiable to enable consistent implementation. Automated processes, including the use of automated support tools (e.g., vulnerability scanning tools, network scanning devices), can make the process of continuous monitoring more cost-effective, consistent, and efficient. Many of the technical security controls defined in NIST Special Publication (SP) 800-53, *Recommended Security Controls for Federal Information Systems and Organizations*, as amended, are good candidates for monitoring using automated tools and techniques. Real-time monitoring of implemented technical controls using automated tools can provide an organization with a much more dynamic view of the effectiveness of those controls and the security posture of the organization. It is important to recognize that with any comprehensive information security program, all implemented security controls, including management and operational controls, must be regularly assessed for effectiveness, even if the monitoring of such controls cannot be automated or is not easily automated.

Organizations take the following steps to establish, implement, and maintain ISCM:

- **Define** an ISCM strategy;

- **Establish** an ISCM program;

- **Implement** an ISCM program;

- **Analyze** data and **Report** findings;

- **Respond** to findings; and

- **Review and Update** the ISCM strategy and program.

A robust ISCM program thus enables organizations to move from compliance-driven risk management to data-driven risk management providing organizations with information necessary to support risk response decisions, security status information, and ongoing insight into security control effectiveness.

CHAPTER ONE

INTRODUCTION

Information security continuous monitoring (ISCM) is defined as maintaining ongoing awareness of information security, vulnerabilities, and threats to support organizational risk management decisions. [2] This publication specifically addresses assessment and analysis of security control effectiveness and of organizational security status in accordance with organizational risk tolerance. Security control effectiveness is measured by correctness of implementation and by how adequately the implemented controls meet organizational needs in accordance with current risk tolerance (i.e., is the control implemented in accordance with the security plan to address threats and is the security plan adequate). [3] Organizational security status is determined using metrics established by the organization to best convey the security posture of an organization's information and information systems, along with organizational resilience given known threat information. This necessitates:

- Maintaining situational awareness of all systems across the organization;

- Maintaining an understanding of threats and threat activities;

- Assessing all security controls;

- Collecting, correlating, and analyzing security-related information;

- Providing actionable communication of security status across all tiers of the organization; and

- Active management of risk by organizational officials.

Communication with all stakeholders is key in developing the strategy and implementing the program. This document builds on the monitoring concepts introduced in NIST SP 800-37 Rev. 1, *Guide for Applying the Risk Management Framework to Federal Information Systems: A Security Life Cycle Approach.* An ISCM program helps to ensure that deployed security controls continue to be effective and that operations remain within stated organizational risk tolerances in light of the inevitable changes that occur over time. In cases where security controls are determined to be inadequate, ISCM programs facilitate prioritized security response actions based on risk.

An ISCM strategy is meaningful only within the context of broader organizational needs, objectives, or strategies, and as part of a broader risk management strategy, enabling timely

---

[2] The terms "continuous" and "ongoing" in this context mean that security controls and organizational risks are assessed and analyzed at a frequency sufficient to support risk-based security decisions to adequately protect organization information. Data collection, no matter how frequent, is performed at discrete intervals.

[3] NIST SP 800-53A, as amended, defines security control effectiveness as "the extent to which the controls are implemented correctly, operating as intended, and producing the desired outcome with respect to meeting the security requirements for the system."

management, assessment, and response to emerging security issues. Information collected through the ISCM program supports ongoing authorization decisions.[4]

ISCM, a critical step in an organization's Risk Management Framework (RMF), gives organizational officials access to security-related information on demand, enabling timely risk management decisions, including authorization decisions. Frequent updates to security plans, security assessment reports, plans of action and milestones, hardware and software inventories, and other system information are also supported. ISCM is most effective when automated mechanisms are employed where possible for data collection and reporting. Effectiveness is further enhanced when the output is formatted to provide information that is specific, measurable, actionable, relevant, and timely. While this document encourages the use of automation, it is recognized that many aspects of ISCM programs are not easily automated.

1.1 BACKGROUND

The concept of monitoring information system security has long been recognized as sound management practice. In 1997, Office of Management and Budget (OMB) Circular A-130, Appendix III[5] required agencies to *review* their information systems' security controls and to ensure that system changes do not have a significant impact on security, that security plans remain effective, and that security controls continue to perform as intended.

The Federal Information Security Management Act (FISMA) of 2002 further emphasized the importance of continuously monitoring information system security by requiring agencies to conduct assessments of security controls at a frequency appropriate to risk, but no less than annually.

Most recently, OMB issued memorandum M-11-33, *FY 2011 Reporting Instructions for the Federal Information Security Management Act and Agency Privacy Management*.[6] The memorandum provides instructions for annual FISMA reporting and emphasizes monitoring the security state of information systems on an ongoing basis with a frequency sufficient to make ongoing, risk-based decisions.

Tools supporting automated monitoring of some aspects of information systems have become an effective means for both data capture and data analysis. Ease of use, accessibility, and broad applicability across products and across vendors help to ensure that monitoring tools can be readily deployed in support of near real-time, risk-based decision making.

1.2 RELATIONSHIP TO OTHER SPECIAL PUBLICATIONS

NIST SP 800-39, *Managing Information Security Risk: Organization, Mission, and Information System View*, describes three key organization-wide ISCM activities: monitoring for effectiveness, monitoring for changes to systems and environments of operation, and monitoring

---

[4] See OMB Memoranda M-11-33, Question #28, for information on ongoing authorization (http://www.whitehouse.gov/sites/default/files/omb/memoranda/2011/m11-33.pdf).

[5] OMB Circular A-130 is available at http://www.whitehouse.gov/omb/circulars_a130_a130trans4.

[6] OMB memorandum M-11-33 is available at http://www.whitehouse.gov/sites/default/files/omb/memoranda/2011/m11-33.pdf.

for compliance. NIST SP 800-37 describes monitoring security controls at the system level (RMF Step 6) and also includes an organization-wide perspective, integration with the system development life cycle (SDLC), and support for ongoing authorizations. The concepts presented in NIST SP 800-39 and NIST SP 800-37 are expanded upon in order to provide guidelines sufficient for developing an ISCM strategy and implementing an ISCM program.

The tiered approach herein mirrors that described in NIST SP 800-37 and NIST SP 800-39 where Tier 1 is organization, Tier 2 is mission/business processes, and Tier 3 is information systems. In NIST SP 800-39, these tiers are used to address risk management from varying organizational perspectives. In this document, the tiers are used to address perspectives for ISCM for each tier. Organization-wide, tier-specific ISCM policies, procedures, and responsibilities are included for the organization, mission/business processes, and information systems tiers. Automation is leveraged where possible, and manual (e.g., procedural) monitoring methodologies are implemented where automation is not practical or possible.

The ISCM program will evolve over time as the program matures in general, additional tools and resources become available, measurement and automation capabilities mature, and changes are implemented to ensure continuous improvement in the organizational security posture and in the organization's security program. The monitoring strategy is regularly reviewed for relevance and accuracy in reflecting organizational risk tolerances, correctness of measurements, applicability of metrics, and effectiveness in supporting risk management decisions.

1.3 PURPOSE

The purpose of this guideline is to assist organizations in the development of an ISCM strategy and the implementation of an ISCM program that provides awareness of threats and vulnerabilities, visibility into organizational assets, and the effectiveness of deployed security controls. The ISCM strategy and program support ongoing assurance that planned and implemented security controls are aligned with organizational risk tolerance, as well as the ability to provide the information needed to respond to risk in a timely manner.

1.4 TARGET AUDIENCE

This publication serves individuals associated with the design, development, implementation, operation, maintenance, and disposal of federal information systems, including:

- Individuals with mission/business ownership responsibilities or fiduciary responsibilities (e.g., heads of federal agencies, chief executive officers, chief financial officers);

- Individuals with information system development and integration responsibilities (e.g., program managers, information technology product developers, information system developers, information systems integrators, enterprise architects, information security architects);

- Individuals with information system and/or security management/oversight responsibilities (e.g., senior leaders, risk executives, authorizing officials, chief information officers, senior information security officers[7]);

---

[7] At the *agency* level, this position is known as the Senior Agency Information Security Officer. Organizations may also refer to this position as the Chief Information Security Officer.

- Individuals with information system and security control assessment and monitoring responsibilities (e.g., system evaluators, assessors/assessment teams, independent verification and validation assessors, auditors, or information system owners); and

- Individuals with information security implementation and operational responsibilities (e.g., information system owners, common control providers, information owners/stewards, mission/business owners, information security architects, information system security engineers/officers).

1.5 ORGANIZATION OF THIS SPECIAL PUBLICATION

The remainder of this special publication is organized as follows:

- Chapter 2 describes the fundamentals of ongoing monitoring of information security in support of risk management;

- Chapter 3 describes the process of ISCM, including implementation guidelines; and

- Supporting appendices provide additional information regarding ISCM including: (A) general references; (B) definitions and terms; (C) acronyms; and (D) descriptions of technologies for enabling ISCM.

CHAPTER TWO

THE FUNDAMENTALS

ONGOING MONITORING IN SUPPORT OF RISK MANAGEMENT

This chapter describes the fundamental concepts associated with organization-wide continuous monitoring of information security and the application of ISCM in support of organizational risk management decisions (e.g., risk response decisions, ongoing system authorization decisions, Plans of Action and Milestones (POA&M) resource and prioritization decisions, etc.). In order to effectively address ever-increasing security challenges, a well-designed ISCM strategy addresses monitoring and assessment of security controls for effectiveness, and security status monitoring.[8] It also incorporates processes to assure that response actions are taken in accordance with findings and organizational risk tolerances and to assure that said responses have the intended effects.

The process of implementing ISCM as described in Chapter Three is:

- **Define** the ISCM strategy;

- **Establish** an ISCM program;

- **Implement** the ISCM program;

- **Analyze** and **Report** findings;

- **Respond** to findings; and

- **Review** and **Update** ISCM strategy and program.

ISCM strategies evolve in accordance with drivers for risk-based decision making and requirements for information. These requirements may come from any tier in the organization. Organizations implement ISCM based on requirements of those accountable and responsible for maintaining ongoing control of organizational security posture to within organizational risk tolerances. The implementation is standardized across the organization to the greatest extent possible so as to minimize use of resources (e.g., funding for purchase of tools/applications, data calls, organization-wide policies/procedures/templates, etc.) and to maximize leveragability of security-related information. Upon analysis, the resulting information informs the discrete processes used to manage the organization's security posture and overall risk. ISCM helps to provide situational awareness of the security status of the organization's systems based on information collected from resources (e.g., people, processes, technology, environment) and the capabilities in place to react as the situation changes.

---

[8] Organizations implement processes to manage organizational security and metrics that provide insight into those
     processes and hence into organizational security status. Some of those security processes will align with individual
     security controls, and others will align with components or combinations of controls. Discussions of metrics can
     be found in Section 3.2.1 and in NIST SP 800-55, *Performance Measurement Guide for Information Security*, as
     amended.

ISCM is a tactic in a larger strategy of organization-wide risk management.[9] Organizations increase situational awareness through enhanced monitoring capabilities and subsequently increase insight into and control of the processes used to manage organizational security. Increased insight into and control of security processes in turn enhances situational awareness. Therefore, the process of implementing ISCM is recursive. ISCM informs and is informed by distinct organizational security processes and associated requirements for input and output of security-related information. Consider the following example:

Security-related information pertaining to a system component inventory is used to determine compliance with CM-8 *Information System Component Inventory*.[10] The information is assessed to determine whether or not the control is effective, (i.e., if the inventory is accurate). If found to be inaccurate, an analysis to determine the root cause of the inaccuracy is initiated (e.g., perhaps a process for connecting components to the network has been ignored or is out of date, asset management tools are not operating as expected, or the organization is under attack). Based on the analysis, responses are initiated as appropriate (e.g., responsible parties update inventory, update relevant organizational processes, train employees, disconnect errant devices, etc.). Additionally, security-related information pertaining to a system component inventory may be used to support predefined metrics. More accurate system component inventories support improved effectiveness of other security domains such as patch management and vulnerability management.

This example illustrates how data collected in assessing a security control is leveraged to calculate a metric and provide input into various organizational processes. It further illustrates that a problem, once detected, can trigger an assessment of one or more controls across an organization, updates to relevant security-related information, modifications to the organizational security program plan and security processes, and improved compliance to the security program and applicable system security plan. The end result is improved organization-wide risk management and continual improvement limited only by the speed with which the organization can collect information and respond to findings.

2.1 ORGANIZATION-WIDE VIEW OF ISCM

Maintaining an up-to-date view of information security risks across an organization is a complex, multifaceted undertaking. It requires the involvement of the entire organization, from senior leaders providing governance and strategic vision to individuals developing, implementing, and operating individual information systems in support of the organization's core missions and business functions. Figure 2-1 illustrates a tiered approach to organization-wide ISCM in support of risk management. Tier 1 governance, risk management goals, and organizational risk tolerance drive the ISCM strategy. Organizational risk tolerance established by senior executives/leaders as part of the risk executive (function)[11] influences ISCM policy, procedures, and implementation activities across all tiers. Data collection primarily occurs at the information systems tier. Metrics are designed to present information in a context that is meaningful for each tier. For example, ISCM data collected at Tier 3 may be aggregated to provide security status or risk scores for a single system, for a collection of systems, across a core business process, or for the entire organization. Policies, procedures, and tools may be established at any tier; however, when

---

[9]   ISCM is discussed within the larger context of organization-wide risk management in NIST SP 800-39.

[10] CM-8 is a security control from the Configuration Management family in NIST SP 800-53, Appendix F.

[11] See Section 2.4 for a discussion of roles and responsibilities of the risk executive (function).

established at Tiers 1 or 2, they facilitate the consistent implementation of ISCM across the organization and better support data reuse and judicious use of resources. Data collection, analysis, and reporting are automated where possible.[12] Through the use of automation, it is possible to monitor a greater number of security metrics with fewer resources, higher frequencies, larger sample sizes,[13] and with greater consistency and reliability than is feasible using manual processes. Organizations regularly review the ISCM strategy to ensure that metrics continue to be relevant, meaningful, actionable, and supportive of risk management decisions made by organizational officials at all tiers.

---

[12] Care must be taken in determining how best to use security-related information from individual information systems in calculating organizational metrics for security and risk. Dashboards and metrics, designed to provide organizational situational awareness of security and risk, can provide a false sense of security if used without continued assurance of the relevance of the metrics.

[13] If an organization does not have the resources or infrastructure necessary to assess every relevant object within its information infrastructure, sampling is an approach that may be useful in reducing the level of effort associated with continuous monitoring. Additional information is provided in Section 3.1.4.

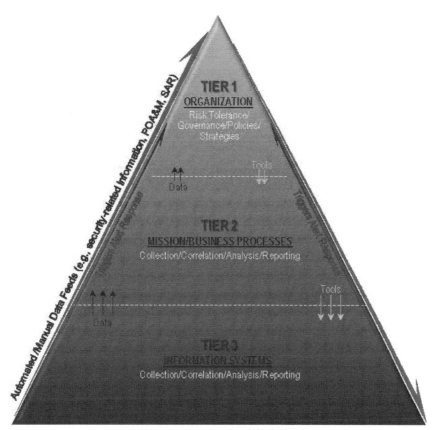

Figure 2-1. Organization-wide ISCM

An organization-wide approach to continuous monitoring of information and information system security supports risk-related decision making at the *organization* level (Tier 1), the *mission/business processes* level (Tier 2), and the *information systems* level (Tier 3).[14]

2.1.1 TIER 1- ORGANIZATION

Tier 1 risk management activities address high-level information security governance policy as it relates to risk to the organization as a whole, to its core missions, and to its business functions. At this tier, the criteria for ISCM are defined by the organization's risk management strategy, including how the organization plans to assess, respond to, and monitor risk, and the oversight required to ensure that the risk management strategy is effective. Security controls, security status, and other metrics defined and monitored by officials at this tier are designed to deliver information necessary to make risk management decisions in support of governance. Tier 1 metrics are developed for supporting governance decisions regarding the organization, its core missions, and

---

[14] NIST Special Publication 800-39, as amended, provides guidelines on the holistic approach to risk management.

its business functions. Tier 1 metrics may be calculated based on security-related information from common, hybrid, and system-specific security controls. The metrics and the frequency with which they are monitored[15] and reported are determined by requirements to maintain operations within organizational risk tolerances. As part of the overall governance structure established by the organization, the Tier 1 risk management strategy and the associated monitoring requirements are communicated throughout Tiers 2 and 3.

2.1.2 TIER 2 - MISSION/BUSINESS PROCESSES

Organizational officials that are accountable for one or more missions or business processes are also responsible for overseeing the associated risk management activities for those processes. The Tier 2 criteria for continuous monitoring of information security are defined by how core mission/business processes are prioritized with respect to the overall goals and objectives of the organization, the types of information needed to successfully execute the stated mission/business processes, and the organization-wide information security program strategy. Controls in the Program Management (PM) family are an example of Tier 2 security controls. These controls address the establishment and management of the organization's information security program. Tier 2 controls are deployed organization-wide and support all information systems. They may be tracked at Tier 2 or Tier 1. The frequencies with which Tier 2 security controls are assessed and security status and other metrics are monitored are determined in part by the objectives and priorities of the mission or business process and measurement capabilities inherent in the infrastructure.[16] Security-related information may come from common, hybrid, and system-specific controls. Metrics and dashboards can be useful at Tiers 1 and 2 in assessing, normalizing, communicating, and correlating monitoring activities below the mission/business processes tier in a meaningful manner.

2.1.3 TIER 3 - INFORMATION SYSTEMS

ISCM activities at Tier 3 address risk management from an *information system* perspective. These activities include ensuring that all system-level security controls (technical, operational, and management controls) are implemented correctly, operate as intended, produce the desired outcome with respect to meeting the security requirements for the system, and continue to be effective over time. ISCM activities at Tier 3 also include assessing and monitoring hybrid and common controls implemented at the system level. Security status reporting at this tier often includes but is not limited to security alerts, security incidents, and identified threat activities.[17] The ISCM strategy for Tier 3 also ensures that security-related information supports the monitoring requirements of other organizational tiers. Data feeds/assessment results from system-level controls (system-specific, hybrid, or common), along with associated security status reporting, support risk-based decisions at the organization and mission/business processes tiers. Information is tailored for each tier and delivered in ways that inform risk-based decision making at all tiers. Those resulting decisions impact the ISCM strategy applied at the information systems tier.[18] ISCM metrics originating at the information systems tier can be used to assess, respond,

---

[15] Monitoring organizationally defined metrics is referred to as security status monitoring throughout this document.

[16] As an organization's technical and human capital capabilities mature, monitoring capabilities increase.

[17] Threat activities include malicious activities observed on organizational networks or other anomalous activities that are indicators of inappropriate actions. See NIST SP 800-30, as amended, for more information on threats.

[18] A continuous monitoring strategy for an individual system may also include metrics related to its potential impact on other systems.

and monitor risk across the organization. The ongoing monitoring activities implemented at the information systems tier provide security-related information to authorizing officials (AOs) in support of ongoing system authorization decisions and to the risk executive (function) in support of ongoing organizational risk management.

At Tier 3, RMF Step 6 Monitor activities and ISCM activities are closely aligned. The assessment methods relevant for implemented security controls are the same whether the assessments are being done solely in support of system authorization or in support of a broader, more comprehensive continuous monitoring effort. Information systems tier officials and staff conduct assessments and monitoring, and analyze results on an ongoing basis. The information is leveraged at the organization, mission/business processes, and information systems tiers to support risk management. Though frequency requirements differ, each tier receives the benefit of security-related information that is current and applicable to affected processes. RMF Step 6 activities performed within the context of an ISCM program support information system risk determination and acceptance, i.e., authorization (RMF Step 5) on an ongoing basis.

2.2 ONGOING SYSTEM AUTHORIZATIONS

Initial authorization to operate is based on evidence available at one point in time, but systems and environments of operation change. Ongoing assessment of security control effectiveness supports a system's security authorization over time in highly dynamic environments of operation with changing threats, vulnerabilities, technologies, and missions/business processes. Through ISCM, new threat or vulnerability information is evaluated as it becomes available, permitting organizations to make adjustments to security requirements or individual controls as needed to maintain authorization decisions. The process for obtaining system authorization, and more generally, for managing information security and information system-related risk, is the RMF.[19] The RMF, illustrated in Figure 2-2, provides a disciplined and structured process that integrates information system security and risk management activities into the SDLC. The monitoring step (Step 6) of the RMF includes interactions between the three tiers as illustrated in the organizational view of ISCM in Figure 2-1. Interaction between the tiers includes data from system owners, common control providers, and authorizing officials on security control assessments and ongoing authorization of system and common controls provided to the risk executive (function).[20] There is also dissemination of updated risk-related information such as vulnerability and threat data and organizational risk tolerance from Tiers 1 and 2 to authorizing officials and information system owners. When the RMF is applied within an organization that has also implemented a robust ISCM strategy, organizational officials are provided with a view of the organizational security posture and each system's contribution to said posture on demand.

---

[19] System authorization to operate may be partially dependent on assessment/monitoring and ongoing security
      authorization of common controls. NIST SP 800-37, as amended, provides information on security authorization
      of common controls.

[20] Roles and responsibilities of organizational officials within a continuous monitoring program are discussed in
      Section 2.4. NIST SP 800-37, as amended, describes the interaction of the risk executive (function) in the context
      of the RMF.

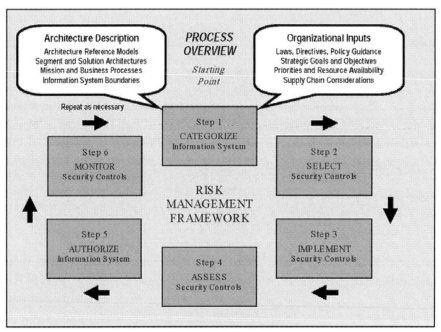

Figure 2-2. Risk Management Framework

The output of a strategically designed and well-managed organization-wide ISCM program can be used to maintain a system's authorization to operate and keep required system information and data (i.e., System Security Plan together with Risk Assessment Report, Security Assessment Report, and POA&M) up to date on an ongoing basis. Security management and reporting tools may provide functionality to automate updates to key evidence needed for ongoing authorization decisions. ISCM also facilitates risk-based decision making regarding the ongoing authorization to operate information systems and security authorization for common controls by providing evolving threat activity or vulnerability information on demand. A security control assessment and risk determination process, otherwise static between authorizations, is thus transformed into a dynamic process that supports timely risk response actions and cost-effective, ongoing authorizations. Continuous monitoring of threats, vulnerabilities, and security control effectiveness provides situational awareness for risk-based support of ongoing authorization decisions. An appropriately designed ISCM strategy and program supports ongoing authorization of type authorizations, as well as single, joint, and leveraged authorizations. [21]

ISCM in support of ongoing assessment and authorization has the potential to be resource-intensive and time-consuming. It is impractical to collect security-related information and assess every aspect of every security control deployed across an organization at all times. A more practical approach is to establish reasonable assessment frequencies for collecting security-related information. The frequency of assessments should be sufficient to assure adequate security commensurate with risk, as determined by system categorization and ISCM strategy

---

[21]   See NIST SP 800-37, as amended, for a discussion of authorization types.

requirements. Sampling of information system security objects, rather than 100 percent
inspection, can also be an efficient and effective means of monitoring, particularly in cases where
monitoring is not automated. Important considerations in determining sample sizes and
monitoring frequencies are discussed in Chapter Three.

Monitoring frequencies (e.g., annually, quarterly, monthly, daily) are not static, and they are not
uniform across all metrics. Security control assessment and monitoring frequencies, for example,
are adjusted to support changes in organizational information systems or their environments of
operation, including emerging information on security threats and vulnerabilities. The priorities
for ISCM vary and are adjusted in response to security incidents, to identify problems with
security control implementations, or to evaluate changes to systems and system components that
are determined to have a significant impact on security. An ISCM strategy can deliver dynamic
updates of security-related data to support system authorizations conducted at any interval.
Section 3.2.2 includes a more complete discussion of factors to consider when determining
monitoring frequencies.

2.3 ROLE OF AUTOMATION IN ISCM

When possible, organizations look for automated solutions to lower costs, enhance efficiency,
and improve the reliability of monitoring security-related information. Security is implemented
through a combination of people, processes, and technology. The automation of information
security deals primarily with automating aspects of security that require little human interaction.
Automated tools are often able to recognize patterns and relationships that may escape the notice
of human analysts, especially when the analysis is performed on large volumes of data. This
includes items such as verifying technical settings on individual network endpoints or ensuring
that the software on a machine is up to date with organizational policy. Automation serves to
augment the security processes conducted by security professionals within an organization and
may reduce the amount of time a security professional must spend on doing redundant tasks,
thereby increasing the amount of time the trained professional may spend on tasks requiring
human cognition.

The ISCM strategy does not focus solely on the security-related information that is easy for an
organization to collect or easy to automate. When an ISCM program is first implemented, there
will likely be several aspects of the organization's security program that are manually monitored.
Organizations' monitoring capabilities will expand and mature over time. Metrics will evolve
with lessons learned and with increased insight into organizational security status and risk
tolerance. The focus of an ISCM strategy is to provide adequate information about security
control effectiveness and organizational security status allowing organizational officials to make
informed, timely security risk management decisions. Thus, implementation, effectiveness, and
adequacy of all security controls are monitored along with organizational security status.

When determining the extent to which the organization automates ISCM, organizations consider
potential efficiencies of process standardization that may be gained with automation, and the
potential value (or lack of value) of the automated security-related information from a risk
management perspective. Additionally, organizations consider intangibles such as the potential
value of personnel reassignment and more comprehensive situational awareness.

While automation of IT security has the potential to significantly reduce the amount of time a human must spend doing certain tasks, it is not possible to fully automate all of an organization's information security program functions. The technologies discussed in Appendix D, for example, still require human analysis for implementation and maintenance of the tools as well as appropriate interpretation of findings. Similarly, these tools operate within the context of processes designed, run, and maintained by humans. If individuals carry out their responsibilities insecurely, then the effectiveness of the technologies is compromised, and the security of the systems and the mission/business or organizational processes supported by those systems is put in jeopardy.

Automation makes security-related information readily available in an environment where ongoing monitoring needs change. Therefore, during security control implementation (RMF Step 3), consideration is given to the capabilities inherent in available technology to support ISCM as part of the criteria in determining how best to implement a given control.

Consideration is given to ISCM tools that:

- Pull information from a variety of sources (i.e., assessment objects[22]);

- Use open specifications such as the Security Content Automation Protocol (SCAP);

- Offer interoperability with other products such as help desk, inventory management, configuration management, and incident response solutions;

- Support compliance with applicable federal laws, Executive Orders, directives, policies, regulations, standards, and guidelines;

- Provide reporting with the ability to tailor output and drill down from high-level, aggregate metrics to system-level metrics; and

- Allow for data consolidation into Security Information and Event Management (SIEM) tools and dashboard products.

Automation supports collecting more data more frequently and from a larger and more diverse pool of technologies, people, processes, and environments. It can therefore make comprehensive, ongoing control of information security practical and affordable. How effective the organization is in utilizing the monitoring results (obtained in a manual or automated fashion) still depends upon the organizational ISCM strategy, including validity and comprehensiveness of the metrics, as well as the processes in place to analyze monitoring results and respond to findings. Technologies for enabling automation of some ISCM tasks are discussed in greater detail in Appendix D.

2.4 ISCM ROLES AND RESPONSIBILITIES

This section describes the roles and responsibilities of key participants involved in an organization's ISCM program. Widely varying missions and organizational structures may lead to differences in naming conventions for ISCM-related roles and how specific responsibilities are allocated among organizational personnel (e.g., multiple individuals filling a single role or one

---

[22] See NIST SP 800-53A, as amended, for information on assessment objects.

individual filling multiple roles). Roles and responsibilities commonly associated with ISCM include:

Head of Agency. The agency head is likely to participate in the organization's ISCM program within the context of the risk executive (function).

Risk Executive (Function). The risk executive (function) oversees the organization's ISCM strategy and program. The risk executive (function) reviews status reports from the ISCM process as input to information security risk posture and risk tolerance decisions and provides input to mission/business process and information systems tier entities on ISCM strategy and requirements; promotes collaboration and cooperation among organizational entities; facilitates sharing of security-related information; provides an organization-wide forum to consider all sources of risk; and ensures that risk information is considered for continuous monitoring decisions.

Chief Information Officer (CIO). The CIO leads the organization's ISCM program. The CIO ensures that an effective ISCM program is established and implemented for the organization by establishing expectations and requirements for the organization's ISCM program; working closely with authorizing officials to provide funding, personnel, and other resources to support ISCM; and maintaining high-level communications and working group relationships among organizational entities.

Senior Information Security Officer (SISO). The SISO establishes, implements, and maintains the organization's ISCM program; develops organizational program guidance (i.e., policies/procedures) for continuous monitoring of the security program and information systems; develops configuration management guidance for the organization; consolidates and analyzes POA&Ms to determine organizational security weaknesses and deficiencies; acquires or develops and maintains automated tools to support ISCM and ongoing authorizations; provides training on the organization's ISCM program and process; and provides support to information owners/information system owners and common control providers on how to implement ISCM for their information systems.

Authorizing Official (AO). The AO assumes responsibility for ensuring the organization's ISCM program is applied with respect to a given information system. The AO ensures the security posture of the information system is maintained, reviews security status reports and critical security documents and determines if the risk to the organization from operation of the information system remains acceptable. The AO also determines whether significant information system changes require reauthorization actions and reauthorizes the information system when required.

Information System Owner (ISO)/Information Owner/Steward. The ISO establishes processes and procedures in support of system-level implementation of the organization's ISCM program. This includes developing and documenting an ISCM strategy for the information system; participating in the organization's configuration management process; establishing and maintaining an inventory of components associated with the information system; conducting security impact analyses on changes to the information system; conducting, or ensuring conduct of, assessment of security controls according to the ISCM strategy; preparing and submitting security status reports in accordance with organizational policy and procedures; conducting remediation activities as necessary to maintain system authorization; revising the system-level security control monitoring process as required; reviewing ISCM reports from common control providers to verify that the common controls continue to provide adequate protection for the information system; and updating critical security documents based on the results of ISCM.

Common Control Provider.[23] The common control provider establishes processes and procedures in support of ongoing monitoring of common controls. The common control provider develops and documents an ISCM strategy for assigned common controls; participates in the organization's configuration management process; establishes and maintains an inventory of components associated with the common controls; conducts security impact analyses on changes that affect the common controls; ensures security controls are assessed according to the ISCM strategy; prepares and submits security status reports in accordance with organizational policy/procedures; conducts remediation activities as necessary to maintain common control authorization; updates/revises the common security control monitoring process as required; updates critical security documents as changes occur; and distributes critical security documents to individual information owners/information system owners, and other senior leaders in accordance with organizational policy/procedures.

Information System Security Officer (ISSO). The ISSO supports the organization's ISCM program by assisting the ISO in completing ISCM responsibilities and by participating in the configuration management process.

Security Control Assessor. The security control assessor provides input into the types of security-related information gathered as part of ISCM and assesses information system or program management security controls for the organization's ISCM program. The security control assessor develops a security assessment plan for each security control; submits the security assessment plan for approval prior to conducting assessments; conducts assessments of security controls as defined in the security assessment plan; updates the security assessment report as changes occur during ISCM; and updates/revises the security assessment plan as needed.

Organizations may define other roles (e.g., information system administrator, ISCM program manager) as needed to support the ISCM process.

---

[23] Organizations may have multiple common control providers.

CHAPTER THREE

THE PROCESS

Defining an ISCM Strategy and Implementing an ISCM Program

This chapter describes the process for developing an ISCM strategy and implementing an ISCM program including activities at the organization, mission/business process, and information systems tiers. A well-designed ISCM strategy encompasses security control assessment, security status monitoring, and security status reporting in support of timely risk-based decision making throughout the organization. It also incorporates processes to assure that response actions are taken. An organization's strategy for action based on the data collected is as important (if not more important) than collecting the data. The process for developing an ISCM strategy and implementing an ISCM program is as follows:

- **Define** an ISCM strategy based on risk tolerance that maintains clear visibility into assets, awareness of vulnerabilities, up-to-date threat information, and mission/business impacts.

- **Establish** an ISCM program determining metrics, status monitoring frequencies, control assessment frequencies, and an ISCM technical architecture.

- **Implement** an ISCM program and collect the security-related information required for metrics, assessments, and reporting. Automate collection, analysis, and reporting of data where possible.

- **Analyze** the data collected and **Report** findings, determining the appropriate response. It may be necessary to collect additional information to clarify or supplement existing monitoring data.

- **Respond** to findings with technical, management, and operational mitigating activities or acceptance, transference/sharing, or avoidance/rejection.

- **Review and Update** the monitoring program, adjusting the ISCM strategy and maturing measurement capabilities to increase visibility into assets and awareness of vulnerabilities, further enable data-driven control of the security of an organization's information infrastructure, and increase organizational resilience.

This process is depicted below in Figure 3- 1.

Figure 3-1. ISCM Process

Risk tolerance, enterprise architecture, security architecture, security configurations, plans for changes to the enterprise architecture, and available threat information provide data that is fundamental to the execution of these steps and to ongoing management of information security-related risks. Security-related information is analyzed for its relevance to organizational risk management at all three tiers.

The balance of this chapter discusses the process of ISCM, providing detail on topics not covered by existing guidelines and referencing existing guidelines where appropriate. Primary roles, supporting roles, expected inputs, and expected outputs are given for each process step as a guide. Roles and responsibilities will vary across organizations as will implementation-level details of an ISCM program.

3.1 DEFINE ISCM STRATEGY

Effective ISCM begins with development of a strategy that addresses ISCM requirements and activities at each organizational tier (organization, mission/business processes, and information systems). Each tier monitors security metrics and assesses security control effectiveness with established monitoring and assessment frequencies and status reports customized to support tier-specific decision making. Policies, procedures, tools, and templates that are implemented from Tiers 1 and 2, or that are managed in accordance with guidance from Tiers 1 and 2, best support shared use of data within and across tiers. The lower tiers may require information in addition to that required at higher tiers and hence develop tier-specific strategies that are consistent with those at higher tiers and still sufficient to address local tier requirements for decision making. Depending on the organization, there may be overlap in the tasks and activities conducted at each tier.

The guidelines below, though not prescriptive, helps to ensure an organization-wide approach to ISCM that best promotes standardized methodologies and consistent practices and hence maximizes efficiencies and leveragability of security-related data. As changes occur, the ISCM strategy is reviewed for relevance, accuracy in reflecting organizational risk tolerances, correctness of measurements, and applicability of metrics. An inherent part of any ISCM strategy is the inclusion of criteria describing the conditions that trigger a review or update of the strategy, in addition to the preestablished frequency audit. Likewise, the organization defines criteria and procedures for updating the ISCM program based on the revised ISCM strategy.

3.1.1   ORGANIZATION (TIER 1) AND MISSION/BUSINESS PROCESSES (TIER 2) ISCM STRATEGY

The risk executive (function) determines the overall organizational risk tolerance and risk mitigation strategy at the organization tier.[24] The ISCM strategy is developed and implemented to support risk management in accordance with organizational risk tolerance. While ISCM strategy, policy, and procedures may be developed at any tier, typically, the organization-wide ISCM strategy and associated policy are developed at the organization tier with general procedures for implementation developed at the mission/business processes tier. If the organization-wide strategy is developed at the mission/business processes tier, Tier 1 officials review and approve the strategy to ensure that organizational risk tolerance across all missions and business processes has been appropriately considered. This information is communicated to staff at the mission/business processes and information systems tiers and reflected in mission/business processes and information systems tier strategy, policy, and procedures.

When developed at Tiers 1 and/or 2, the following policies, procedures, and templates facilitate organization-wide, standardized processes in support of the ISCM strategy:

- Policy that defines key metrics;

- Policy for modifications to and maintenance of the monitoring strategy;

- Policy and procedures for the assessment of security control effectiveness (common, hybrid, and system-level controls);

- Policy and procedures for security status monitoring;

- Policy and procedures for security status reporting (on control effectiveness and status monitoring);

- Policy and procedures for assessing risks and gaining threat information and insights;

- Policy and procedures for configuration management and security impact analysis;[25]

- Policy and procedures for implementation and use of organization-wide tools;

- Policy and procedures for establishment of monitoring frequencies;

- Policy and procedures for determining sample sizes and populations and for managing object sampling;

- Procedures for determining security metrics and data sources;

---

[24] See NIST SP 800-39, as amended, for a discussion of the risk executive (function) roles and responsibilities.

[25] See NIST SP 800-128, as amended, for more information on security-focused configuration management.

- Templates for assessing risks; and

- Templates for security status reporting (on control effectiveness and status monitoring).

Policy, procedures, and templates necessarily address manual and automated monitoring methodologies. Additionally at these tiers, organizations establish policy and procedures for training of personnel with ISCM roles. This may include training on management and use of automated tools (e.g., establishing baselines and tuning of measurements to provide accurate monitoring of operational environments). It may also include training for recognition of and appropriate response to triggers and alerts from metrics indicating risks beyond acceptable limits, as well as training on internal or external reporting requirements. This training may be included in existing role-based training requirements for those with significant security roles, or it may consist of training specifically focused on implementation of the organization's ISCM policy and procedures.

When implementing policies, procedures, and templates developed at higher tiers, lower tiers fill in any gaps related to their tier-specific processes. Decisions and activities by Tier 1 and 2 officials may be constrained by things such as mission/business needs, limitations of the infrastructure (including the human components), immutable governance policies, and external drivers.

Primary Roles: Risk Executive (Function), Chief Information Officer, Senior Information Security Officer, Authorizing Officials

Supporting Roles: Information System Owner/Common Control Provider

Expected Input: Organizational risk assessment and current risk tolerance, current threat information, organizational expectations and priorities, available tools from OMB lines of business and/or third-party vendors

Expected Output: Updated information on organizational risk tolerance, organization-wide ISCM strategy and associated policy, procedures, templates, tools

3.1.2 INFORMATION SYSTEM (TIER 3) ISCM STRATEGY

The system-level ISCM strategy is developed and implemented to support risk management, not only at the information systems tier, but at *all three tiers* in accordance with system and organizational risk tolerance. Although the strategy may be defined at Tiers 1 or 2, system-specific policy and procedures for implementation may also be developed at Tier 3. System-level security-related information includes assessment data *pertaining to* system-level security controls and metrics data *obtained from* system-level security controls. System owners establish a system-level strategy for ISCM by considering factors such as the system's architecture and operational environment, as well as organizational and mission-level requirements,[26] policy, procedures, and templates.

System-level ISCM addresses monitoring security controls for effectiveness (assessments), monitoring for security status, and reporting findings. At a minimum, all security controls, including common and hybrid controls implemented at the system level, are assessed for

---

[26] The ISCM strategy is designed, in part, to help ensure that compromises to the security architecture are managed in a way to prevent or minimize impact on business and mission functions.

effectiveness in accordance with the system security plan and the methods described in NIST SP
800-53A, as amended. System owners determine assessment frequencies of security controls
based on drivers from all three tiers. A full discussion of factors to consider when determining
assessment and monitoring frequencies can be found in Section 3.2.2. System-level security-
related information is used to determine security status at all three tiers. Use of system-level
security-related information in metrics for determining security status is addressed in Section
3.2.1.

The ISCM strategy at the information systems tier also supports ongoing authorization. Ongoing
authorization implies recurring updates to the authorization decision information in accordance
with assessment and monitoring frequencies. Assessment results from monitoring common
controls implemented and managed at the organization or mission/business process tier may be
combined with information generated at the information systems tier in order to provide the
authorizing official (AO) with a complete set of independently-generated evidence.[27] Assessment
evidence obtained from ISCM is, at a minimum, provided to AOs as often as required by
organizational policy.

Primary Roles: Information System Owner/Common Control Provider, Information System
Security Officer

Supporting Roles: Senior Information Security Officer, Authorizing Official, Security Control
Assessor

Expected Input: Organizational risk tolerance information, organizational ISCM strategy, policy,
procedures, templates, system-specific threat information, and system information (e.g., System
Security Plan, Security Assessment Report, Plan of Action and Milestones, Security Assessment
Plan, System Risk Assessment, etc.[28])

Expected Output: System-level ISCM strategy that complements the Tier 1 and 2 strategies and
the organizational security program and that provides security status information for all tiers and
real-time updates for ongoing system authorization decisions as directed by the organizational
ISCM strategy

3.1.3 PROCESS ROLES AND RESPONSIBILITIES

Tiers 1 and 2 officials have responsibilities throughout the ISCM process, including, but not
limited to, the following:

- Provide input to the development of the organizational ISCM strategy including
  establishment of metrics, policy, and procedures, compiling and correlating Tier 3 data into
  security-related information of use at Tiers 1 and 2, policies on assessment and monitoring
  frequencies, and provisions for ensuring sufficient depth and coverage when sampling
  methodologies are utilized [ISCM steps: Define, Establish, Implement].

---

[27] See NIST SP 800-53, CA-2, Control Enhancement 1, for specific assessor independence requirements. Assessors
need only be independent of the operation of the system. They may be from within the organizational tier, the
mission/business tier, or from within some other independent entity internal or external to the organization.
Results of assessments done by system operators can be used if they have been validated by independent
assessors.

[28] This system information is an outcome of the RMF. Electronic standardized templates and document management
systems readily support frequent updates with data generated by continuous monitoring programs.

- Review monitoring results (security-related information) to determine security status in accordance with organizational policy and definitions [ISCM step: Analyze/Report].

- Analyze potential security impact to organization and mission/business process functions resulting from changes to information systems and their environments of operation, along with the security impact to the enterprise architecture resulting from the addition or removal of information systems [ISCM step: Analyze/Report].

- Make a determination as to whether or not current risk is within organizational risk tolerance levels [ISCM steps: Analyze/Report, Review/Update].

- Take steps to respond to risk as needed (e.g., request new or revised metrics, additional or revised assessments, modifications to existing common or PM security controls, or additional controls) based on the results of ongoing monitoring activities and assessment of risk [ISCM step: Respond].

- Update relevant security documentation [ISCM step: Respond].

- Review new or modified legislation, directives, policies, etc., for any changes to security requirements [ISCM step: Review/Update].

- Review monitoring results to determine if organizational plans and polices should be adjusted or updated [ISCM step: Review/Update].

- Review monitoring results to identify new information on vulnerabilities [ISCM step: Review/Update].

- Review information on new or emerging threats as evidenced by threat activities present in monitoring results, threat modeling (asset- and attack-based), classified and unclassified threat briefs, USCERT reports, and other information available through trusted sources, interagency sharing, and external government sources [ISCM step: Review/Update].

Tier 3 officials have responsibilities throughout the ISCM process including, but not limited to, the following:

- Provide input to the development and implementation of the organization-wide ISCM strategy along with development and implementation of the system level ISCM strategy [ISCM steps: Define, Establish, Implement; RMF Step: Select].

- Support planning and implementation of security controls, the deployment of automation tools, and how those tools interface with one another in support of the ISCM strategy [ISCM step: Implement; RMF Step: Select].

- Determine the security impact of changes to the information system and its environment of operation, including changes associated with commissioning or decommissioning the system [ISCM step: Analyze/Report; RMF Step: Monitor].

- Assess ongoing security control effectiveness [ISCM step: Implement; RMF Steps: Assess,[29] Monitor].

- Take steps to respond to risk as needed (e.g., request additional or revised assessments, modify existing security controls, implement additional security controls, accept risk, etc.) based on the results of ongoing monitoring activities, assessment of risk, and outstanding items in the plan of action and milestones [ISCM step: Respond; RMF Step: Monitor].

- Provide ongoing input to the security plan, security assessment report, and plan of action and milestones based on the results of the ISCM process [ISCM step: Respond; RMF Step: 6].

- Report the security status of the information system including the data needed to inform Tiers 1 and 2 metrics [ISCM step: Analyze/Report; RMF Steps: Assess, Monitor].

- Review the reported security status of the information system to determine whether the risk to the system and the organization remains within organizational risk tolerances [ISCM step: Analyze/Report; RMF Steps: Authorize, Monitor].

3.1.4 DEFINE SAMPLE POPULATIONS

Organizations may find that collecting data from every object of every system within an organization may be impractical or cost-prohibitive. Sampling is a methodology employable with both manual and automated monitoring that may make ISCM more cost-effective. A risk with sampling is that the sample population may fail to capture the variations in assessment outcomes that would be obtained from an assessment of the full population. This could result in an inaccurate view of security control effectiveness and organizational security status.

NIST SP 800-53A, as amended, describes how to achieve satisfactory coverage when determining sample populations for the three named assessment methods: examine, interview, and test. The guidelines in NIST SP 800-53A for basic, focused, and comprehensive testing[30] addresses the need for a "representative sample of assessment objects" or a "sufficiently large sample of assessment objects." Statistical tools can be used to help quantify sample size.

NIST 800-53A provides guidelines to help address the general issue of sampling and particularly that of coverage. In selecting a sample population, the coverage attribute is satisfied through consideration of three criteria:

- **Types of objects** - ensure sufficient diversity of types of assessment objects;

- **Number of each type** - chose "enough" objects of each type to provide confidence that assessment of additional objects will result in consistent findings; and

- **Specific objects per type assessed** - given all of the objects of relevance throughout the organization that could be assessed, include "enough" objects per type in the sample population to sufficiently account for the known or anticipated variance in assessment outcomes.

---

[29] Prior to initial authorization, the system is not included in the organization's continuous monitoring program. This reference to RMF 4 is relevant after the system becomes operational, and is passing through Step 4 in support of ongoing authorization.

[30] See NIST SP 800-53A, as amended, Appendix D.

Sample measurements are summarized into a statistic (e.g., sample mean) and the observed value compared with the allowable value as represented by organizational risk tolerance. Statistics calculated using sampling can become less reliable predictors of the full population if the population is not randomly selected and if the sample size (i.e., objects to be tested) is small.[31] As described in the NIST Engineering Statistics Handbook, when deciding how many objects to include in sample populations, the following are considered:[32]

- Desired information (what question will the measurements help answer);

- Cost and practicality of making the assessment;

- Information already known about the objects, organization, or operating environments;

- Anticipated variability across the total population; and

- Desired confidence in resulting statistics and conclusions drawn about the total population.

Ways to achieve "increased" or "further increased grounds for confidence that a control is implemented correctly and operating as intended" across the entire organization include asking more targeted questions, increasing the types of objects assessed, and increasing the number of each type of object assessed.

Organizations may also target specific objects for assessment in addition to the random sample, using the above criteria. However, sampling methods other than random sampling are used with care to avoid introducing bias. Automated data collection and analysis can reduce the need for sampling.

Primary Roles: Information System Owner, Common Control Provider, Information System Security Officer, Security Control Assessor

Supporting Roles: Risk Executive (Function), Authorizing Official, Chief Information Officer, Senior Information Security Officer

Expected Input: Organizational- and system-level policy and procedures on ISCM strategy, metrics, and the Security Assessment Plan updated with assessment and monitoring frequencies

Expected Output: Security Assessment Plan documentation on acceptable sample sizes, security-related information

---

[31] The Central Limit Theorem is a key theorem that allows one to assume that a statistic (e.g., mean) calculated from a random sample has a normal distribution (i.e., bell curve) regardless of the underlying distribution from which individual samples are being taken. For small sample sizes (roughly less than 30), the normal distribution assumption tends to be good only if the underlying distribution from which random samples are being taken is close to normal.

[32] For detailed information on selecting sample sizes, see http://www.itl.nist.gov/div898/handbook/ppc/section3/ppc333.htm.

3.2 ESTABLISH AN ISCM PROGRAM

Organizations establish a program to implement the ISCM strategy. The program is sufficient to inform risk-based decisions and maintain operations within established risk tolerances. Goals include detection of anomalies and changes in the organization's environments of operation and information systems, visibility into assets, awareness of vulnerabilities, knowledge of threats, security control effectiveness, and security status including compliance. Metrics are designed and frequencies determined to ensure that information needed to manage risk to within organizational risk tolerances is available. Tools, technologies, and manual and/or automated methodologies are implemented within the context of an architecture designed to deliver the required information in the appropriate context and at the right frequencies.

3.2.1 DETERMINE METRICS

Organizations determine metrics to be used to evaluate and control ongoing risk to the organization. Metrics, which include all the security-related information from assessments and monitoring produced by automated tools and manual procedures, are organized into meaningful information to support decision making and reporting requirements. Metrics should be derived from specific objectives that will maintain or improve security posture. Metrics are developed for system-level data to make it meaningful in the context of mission/business or organizational risk management.

Metrics may use security-related information acquired at different frequencies and therefore with varying data latencies. Metrics may be calculated from a combination of security status monitoring, security control assessment data, and from data collected from one or more security controls. Metrics may be determined at any tier or across an organization. Some examples of metrics are the number and severity of vulnerabilities revealed and remediated, number of unauthorized access attempts, configuration baseline information, contingency plan testing dates and results, and number of employees who are current on awareness training requirements. risk tolerance thresholds for organizations, and the risk score associated with a given system configuration.

As an example, a metric that an organization might use to monitor status of authorized and unauthorized components on a network could rely on related metrics such as physical asset locations, logical asset locations (subnets/Internet protocol (IP) addresses), media access control (MAC) addresses, system association, and policies/procedures for network connectivity. The metrics would be refreshed at various frequencies in accordance with the ISCM strategy. The metrics might be computed hourly, daily, or weekly. Though logical asset information might change daily, it is likely that policies and procedures for network connectivity will be reviewed or revised no more than annually. These metrics are informative only and are not recommended metrics. They are included to assist in explaining the concept of metrics as they are applied across tiers. Organizations define their own metrics and associated monitoring frequencies. In order to calculate metrics, associated controls and/or their objects are assessed and monitored with frequencies consistent with the timing requirements expressed in the metric.

It should be noted that metrics are fundamentally flawed without assurance that *all* security controls are implemented correctly. Metrics are defined or calculated in accordance with output from the security architecture. Collecting metrics from a security architecture with security controls that have not been assessed is equivalent to using a broken or uncalibrated scale. The interpretation of metrics data presumes that controls directly and indirectly used in the metric calculation are implemented and working as anticipated. If a metric indicates a problem, the root cause could be any number of things. Without fundamental assurance of correct implementation and continued effectiveness of security controls that are *not* associated with the metric, the root cause analysis is going to be hampered, and the analysis may be inappropriately narrowed to a predetermined list, overlooking the true problem. For detailed information on establishing metrics, see NIST SP 800-55, as amended.

Primary Roles: Risk Executive (Function), Chief Information Officer, Senior Information Security Officer

Supporting Roles: Authorizing Officials, Information System Owner/Common Control Provider

Expected Input: Organizational risk assessment, organizational risk tolerance, current threat information, reporting requirements, current vulnerability information

Expected Output: Established metrics to convey security status and security control effectiveness at all three tiers, and to give recipients/users of reports visibility into assets, awareness of vulnerabilities, and knowledge of threats

3.2.2 ESTABLISH MONITORING AND ASSESSMENT FREQUENCIES

Determining frequencies for security status monitoring and for security control assessments are critical functions of the organization's ISCM program. For some organizations, dashboards and ongoing assessments are a shift away from the model of complete security control assessments conducted at a distinct point in time. For this shift to be constructive and effective from security, assurance, and resource use perspectives, organizations determine the frequencies with which *each* security control or control element is assessed for effectiveness and the frequencies with which *each* metric is monitored.

Security control effectiveness across a tier or throughout the organization can itself be taken as a security metric and as such may have an associated status monitoring frequency. Though monitoring and assessment frequencies are determined for each individual metric and control, organizations use this data of different latencies to create a holistic view of the security of each system as well as a view of the security of the enterprise architecture. As the monitoring program matures, monitoring and assessment frequencies are important in the context of how the data is used and the question *When did the system receive authorization to operate?* will become less meaningful than *How resilient is the system?*

Considerations in Determining Assessment and Monitoring Frequencies.

Organizations take the following criteria into consideration when establishing monitoring frequencies for metrics or assessment frequencies for security controls:

- **Security control volatility**. Volatile security controls are assessed more frequently, whether the objective is establishing security control effectiveness or supporting calculation of a metric.[33] Controls in the NIST SP 800-53 Configuration Management (CM) family are a good example of volatile controls. Information system configurations typically experience high rates of change. Unauthorized or unanalyzed changes in the system configuration often render the system vulnerable to exploits. Therefore, corresponding controls such as CM-6,

---

[33] Security control volatility is a measure of how frequently a control is likely to change over time subsequent to its implementation.

Configuration Settings, and CM-8, Information System Component Inventory, may require more frequent assessment and monitoring, preferably using automated, SCAP-validated tools that provide alerts and status on demand. Conversely, controls such as PS-2, Position Categorization, or PS-3, Personnel Screening, (from the NIST SP 800-53 Personnel Security family of controls) are not volatile in most organizational settings. They tend to remain static over long periods and would therefore typically require less frequent assessment.

- **System categorizations/impact levels.** In general, security controls implemented on systems that are categorized as high-impact are monitored more frequently than controls implemented on moderate-impact systems, which are in turn monitored more frequently than controls implemented on low-impact systems.[34]

- **Security controls or specific assessment objects providing critical functions.** Security controls or assessment objects that provide critical security functions (e.g., log management server, firewalls) are candidates for more frequent monitoring. Additionally, individual assessment objects that support critical security functions and/or are deemed critical to the system (in accordance with the Business Impact Analysis[35]) or to the organization may be candidates for more frequent monitoring.

- **Security controls with identified weaknesses.** Existing risks documented in security assessment reports (SARs) are considered for more frequent monitoring to ensure that risks stay within tolerance. Similarly, controls documented in the POA&M as having weaknesses are monitored more frequently until remediation of the weakness is complete. Note that not all weaknesses require the same level of monitoring. For example, weaknesses deemed in the SAR to be of minor or low-impact risk to the system or organization are monitored less frequently than a weakness with a higher-impact risk to the system or organization.

- **Organizational risk tolerance.**[36] Organizations with a low tolerance for risk (e.g., organizations that process, store, or transmit large amounts of proprietary and/or personally identifiable information (PII), organizations with numerous high-impact systems, organizations facing specific persistent threats) monitor more frequently than organizations with a higher tolerance for risk (e.g., organizations with primarily low- and moderate-impact systems that process, store, or transmit very little PII and/or proprietary information).

- **Threat information.** Organizations consider current credible threat information, including known exploits and attack patterns,[37] when establishing monitoring frequencies. For instance, if a specific attack is developed which exploits a vulnerability of an implemented technology, temporary or permanent increases to the monitoring frequencies for related controls or metrics may help provide protection from the threat.

- **Vulnerability information.**[38] Organizations consider current vulnerability information with respect to information technology products when establishing monitoring frequencies. For

---

[34] System impact levels are in accordance with FIPS 199 and NIST SP 800-60.

[35] See NIST SP 800-34, as amended, *Contingency Planning Guide for Federal Information Systems*, May 2010.

[36] See NIST SP 800-39, as amended, for more information on how to determine organizational risk tolerance.

[37] Attack patterns describe common methods for exploiting software, based on in-depth analysis of specific real-world attack examples. For more information, see the Common Attack Pattern Enumeration and Classification (CAPEC) site at http://capec.mitre.org/.

[38] For current vulnerability information, see http://www.kb.cert.org/vuls and http://nvd.nist.gov/.

instance, if a specific product manufacturer provides software patches monthly, an organization might consider conducting vulnerability scans on that product at least that often.

- **Risk assessment results.** Results from organizational and/or system-specific assessments of risk (either formal or informal) are examined and taken into consideration when establishing monitoring frequencies. For instance, if a system-specific risk assessment identifies potential threats and vulnerabilities related to nonlocal maintenance (NIST SP 800-53, MA-4), the organization considers more frequent monitoring of the records kept on nonlocal maintenance and diagnostic activities. If a risk scoring scheme is in place at the organization, the risk scores may be used as justification to increase or decrease the monitoring frequencies of related controls.

- **Output of monitoring strategy reviews.** Review and adjustment of the monitoring strategy is covered in detail in Section 3.6.

- **Reporting requirements.** Reporting requirements do not drive the ISCM strategy but may play a role in the frequency of monitoring. For instance, if OMB policy requires quarterly reports on the number of unauthorized components detected and corrective actions taken, the organization would monitor the system for unauthorized components at least quarterly.

Organizations focus on obtaining the data required at the determined frequencies and deploy their human and capitol resources accordingly. As automation capability or resources are added, organizations may consider increasing affected monitoring frequencies. Similarly, if resource availability decreases, the organization considers adjusting affected monitoring frequencies to ensure that security-related information is appropriately analyzed while continuing to meet organizational risk management requirements.

Many security controls in the NIST SP 800-53 catalog have multiple implementation requirements along with control enhancements that may also have multiple implementation requirements. It may be necessary to assess or monitor individual control requirements and/or control enhancements within a given control with differing frequencies. For instance, the control AC-2, Account Management, has ten separate requirements (a. through j.) within the base control and four control enhancements [(1) through (4)]. The monitoring frequency may vary for each requirement in accordance with the considerations discussed. For example, AC-2a involves the identification of account types. For a typical information system, once the account types have been identified and documented, they are not likely to change very often. For this reason, AC-2a is a candidate for relatively infrequent assessment. AC-2h involves the deactivation of temporary accounts and accounts of terminated or transferred users. Since personnel regularly come and go, a typical organization would most likely assess AC-2h on a more frequent basis than AC-2a. AC-2 (3) requires that the system automatically disable accounts after a specified time period of inactivity. As an automated control and one with typically high volatility, AC-2 (3) is a candidate for relatively frequent monitoring and also may serve to automate some of the base control requirements so that they can be monitored more frequently in accordance with the organizational ISCM strategy.

Organization and Mission/Business Processes Tiers.

At the mission/business processes tier, the organization establishes the minimum frequency with which each security control or metric is to be assessed or monitored. Frequencies are established across all organizational systems and common controls based on the criteria described above in this section. Common, hybrid, and system-specific security controls are addressed by organization and mission/business processes tier policy and procedures. Common controls are often inherited by a large number of organizational systems. The aggregate criticality of such controls may require more frequent assessments than would similar controls responsible for protecting a single system. Additionally, determining the frequency for assessing common controls includes the organization's determination of the trustworthiness of the common control provider. Common controls that are process-related (e.g., procedures/templates, PM controls) do not tend to be volatile and typically do not lend themselves well to automation. Still, the organization considers the volatility of such controls as well as related threat information when establishing assessment frequencies.

Primary Roles: Chief Information Officer, Senior Information Security Officer

Supporting Roles: Risk Executive (Function), Authorizing Officials, Common Control Provider, Information System Owner

Expected Input: Organizational risk assessment, organizational risk tolerance, current threat information, reporting requirements, current vulnerability information, output from monitoring strategy reviews

Expected Output: Organization-wide policies and procedures, recommended frequencies with which each security control and metric is assessed or monitored

Information Systems Tier.

At the information systems tier, system owners review the minimum monitoring/assessment frequencies established by organization and/or mission/business processes tier policy and determine if the minimum frequencies are adequate for a given information system. For some information systems, it may be necessary to assess specific controls or metrics with greater frequency than prescribed by the organization, again based on the criteria described above in this section. System owners also consider identification of specific system components that may require more frequent monitoring than other system components (e.g., public-facing servers, boundary protection devices, components deemed critical in the Business Impact Analysis).

Primary Roles: Information System Owner, Information System Security Officer

Supporting Roles: Authorizing Official, Senior Information Security Officer, Information Owner/Steward

Expected Input: Organizational strategy and procedures with minimum frequencies, current threat information, reporting requirements, current vulnerability information, output from monitoring strategy reviews, security assessment plans

Expected Output: Security assessment plans updated to reflect the frequency with which each system-specific security control is assessed and metrics are monitored

Event-Driven Assessments.

Events may occur that trigger the immediate need to assess security controls or verify security status outside of requirements expressed in the ISCM strategy. This may require an assessment that is unplanned, but of the type defined in the ISCM strategy or a customized assessment tailored to address an emerging need (e.g., a change in planned assessment or monitoring frequency). For example, if a Web application is added to a system, an existing ISCM process that includes configuration management and control, SIA, developmental vulnerability scans, etc., may be sufficient to assess controls implemented for the new Web application.

When defining criteria for event-driven assessments, organizations consider events such as incidents, new threat information, significant changes to systems and operating environments, new or additional mission responsibilities, and results of a security impact analysis (SIA) or assessment of risk.

Depending on the significance of the event, an event-driven assessment may trigger one or more system reauthorizations.

Primary Roles: Information System Owner/Common Control Provider, Authorizing Official, Information System Security Officer

Supporting Roles: Risk Executive (Function), Senior Information Security Officer, Security Control Assessor

Expected Input: Organizational risk assessment, organizational risk tolerance, current threat information, current vulnerability information, organizational priorities and expectations

Expected Output: Documented criteria and thresholds for event-driven assessments/authorizations (e.g., significant change procedures, policy and procedures on event-driven authorizations)

3.2.3 DEVELOP ISCM ARCHITECTURE

Organizations determine how the information will be collected and delivered within and between the tiers as well as external to the organization. The core requirements of an architecture implemented to support ISCM are data collection, data storage, data analysis capabilities, and retrieval and presentation (reporting) capabilities. Methodologies are standardized to facilitate efficiencies, intra- and inter-tier information exchange, correlation, and other analysis.

Organizations use automated tools, technologies, and methodologies where appropriate to allow for increased efficiencies and insight including those gained through collection, analysis and dissemination of large volumes of data from diverse sources. The architecture and associated policies and procedures are designed to minimize data calls and maximize data reuse.[39] Data feeds come from a heterogeneous mix of sources (e.g., authorization packages, training records, system logs) and accommodate different stakeholder views. Interoperable data specifications (e.g., SCAP, XML) enable data to be collected once and reused many times. Accountability for different facets of the security posture may reside with different roles or functions within an organization and hence require use of raw data in different metrics and contexts and at different

---

[39] An example of an architecture for ISCM can be found in Draft NISTIR 7756, *CAESARS Framework Extension: An Enterprise Continuous Monitoring Technical Reference Architecture (Draft)*.

intervals (e.g., security assessment and authorization, user awareness and training, and access control). Similarly, organizational missions and business functions have varied requirements for reporting and various drivers for action (e.g., changes to risk tolerance; changes in operational environments, including evolving threat activities; security architecture adjustments, security status reporting).

3.3 IMPLEMENT AN ISCM PROGRAM

ISCM is implemented in accordance with the strategy. Security-related information (data) is collected as required for predefined metrics, security control assessments are conducted, and the security-related information generated is reported in accordance with organizational policies and procedures. *All* security control classes (management, operational, and technical) and types (common, hybrid, and system-specific) are included in the organizational continuous monitoring program. Every control is monitored for effectiveness, and every control is subject to use in monitoring security status. Data sources include people, processes, technologies, the computing environment, as well as any existing relevant security control assessment reports.

Collection, analysis, and reporting of data are automated where possible. Whether manual or automated, the data collected is assembled for analysis and reported to the organizational officials charged with correlating and analyzing it in ways that are relevant for risk management activities. As indicated in the examples above, this may mean taking data from a variety of sources, collected at various points in time, and combining it in ways that are meaningful for the official receiving it at the time that it is requested. Part of the implementation stage of the continuous monitoring process is effectively organizing and delivering ISCM data to stakeholders in accordance with decision-making requirements. Tools and methodologies are chosen for the organization-wide ISCM architecture, in order to help ensure that risk-based decisions are informed by accurate, current security-related information.

Discrete security processes inform and are informed by ISCM data. Organizations also use ISCM data to inform processes that are not primarily used to control information security risk. Similarly, data from those processes can also be used to inform the ISCM program. Examples of processes that inform and are informed by ISCM include, but are not limited to, patch management, asset management, license management, configuration management, vulnerability management, and system authorization.

As described in Chapter Two, the ISCM data output from one process may serve as input to many others.

Primary Roles: Information System Owner, Common Control Provider, Information System Security Officer, Security Control Assessor

Supporting Roles: Risk Executive (Function), Authorizing Official, Chief Information Officer, Senior Information Security Officer

Expected Input: Organizational- and system-level policies and procedures on ISCM strategy, metrics, the Security Assessment Plan updated with assessment and monitoring frequencies, and automation specifications

Expected Outputs: Security-related information

3.4 ANALYZE DATA AND REPORT FINDINGS

Organizations develop procedures for analyzing and reporting assessment and monitoring results. This includes the specific staff/roles to receive ISCM reports, the content and format of the reports, the frequency of reports, and any tools to be used. Also included are requirements for analyzing and reporting results of controls that are not easily automated. It may be necessary to collect additional data to supplement or clarify security-related information under analysis or provided in initial reports. System- and mission/business-level staff receives and provides reports as required by organizational and mission/business-level policies and procedures.

3.4.1 ANALYZE DATA

Organizations analyze the security-related information resulting from ISCM. It may be necessary to collect additional data to supplement or clarify security-related information under analysis. The information to be analyzed is provided to organizational officials in a variety of ways, such as recurring reports, automated reports, ad hoc reports, data feeds, and database views.

Security-related information resulting from ISCM is analyzed in the context of stated risk tolerances, the potential impact that vulnerabilities may have on information systems, mission/business processes, and organization as a whole, and the potential impact of mitigation options. Even with real-time or near real-time organization-specific and system-specific security-related information, evolving vulnerability and threat data is always considered during the analysis. Organizational officials review the analyzed reports to determine whether to conduct mitigation activities or to transfer, avoid/reject, or accept risk. In some cases, authorizing officials may determine that accepting some specific risk is preferable to implementing a mitigating response. The rationale for such determinations may include organizational risk tolerance, negative impact to mission/business processes, or cost-effectiveness/return on investment of the implementation. Resolution of risk and the rationale for the decision is recorded in accordance with organizational policies and procedures.

Primary Roles: Risk Executive (Function), Chief Information Officer, Senior Information Security Officer; Authorization Officials, Security Control Assessors

Supporting Roles: Information System Owners, Common Control Providers, System Security Officers

Expected Input: Security-related information, organizational ISCM strategy, organizational risk tolerance, reporting requirements

Expected Output: Analysis of security status information for all tiers; updated System Security Plan, Security Assessment Report, and Plan of Action and Milestones; revised organizational risk management decisions

3.4.2 REPORT ON SECURITY CONTROL ASSESSMENTS

Organizations report on assessments of all implemented security controls for effectiveness in accordance with organizational requirements. Security-related information from assessments may be conveyed in templates or spreadsheets or collected and reported in an automated fashion. At the system level, security-related information from assessments directly supports ongoing authorization decisions and plans of action and milestones creation and tracking. Some security controls or elements of security controls, by definition, are security metrics (e.g., SI-4

Information System Monitoring). Hence, assessing the effectiveness of these controls results in monitoring the security status of the related metric.

Staff report assessment results in accordance with organizational policies and procedures. Reporting on additional metrics and/or assessment results may be required by higher-level organizations such as OMB. Organizations define security status reporting requirements in the ISCM strategy. This includes the specific staff/roles to receive ISCM reports, the content and format of the reports, the frequency of reports, and any tools to be used.

Tier 3 officials report on findings, document any system-level mitigations made, and/or provide recommendations to officials at Tiers 1 and 2. Organizational officials at Tiers 1 and 2 review Tier 3 findings to determine aggregate security status and the effectiveness and adequacy of *all controls* in meeting mission/business and organizational information security requirements. Information contained within a report will vary based on its recipient, frequency, purpose, supported tool sets, and metrics used. For example, the risk executive (function) may receive a general report on all systems annually and a detailed report on specific high-impact systems quarterly. The reports provided to the CIO and SISO may contain more granular technical data on all systems quarterly, and the AO may receive monthly comprehensive reports on the systems for which s/he is responsible. The computer incident response team (CIRT) lead may receive exception reports when alerts are generated, and network administrators may review dashboards showing network activity that is updated every minute, with summary metrics that are updated hourly or daily.[40] Organizations may consider more frequent reports for specific controls with more volatility or on controls for which there have been weaknesses or lack of compliance.

Organizations also define requirements for reporting results of controls, such as PM controls, that are not easily automated. Organizations develop procedures for collecting and reporting assessment and monitoring results, including results that are derived via manual methods, and for managing and collecting information from POA&Ms to be used for frequency determination, status reporting, and monitoring strategy revision.

Primary Roles: System Owner, Common Control Provider, System Security Officer, Security Control Assessor

Supporting Roles: Risk Executive (Function), Chief Information Officer, Chief Information Security Officer, Authorizing Official

Expected Input: Security-related information (assessment results); organizational ISCM policies and procedures; reporting requirements from the Authorizing Official, Chief Information Officer, Chief Information Security Officer, and/or Risk Executive (Function)

Expected Output: Reports on assessment results as required by organizational ISCM policies and procedures and by the Authorizing Official in support of ongoing authorization (or reauthorization)

3.4.3   REPORT ON SECURITY STATUS MONITORING

Organizations develop procedures for reporting on security status monitoring. Security status data is derived from monitoring the predefined metrics across the organization using output generated

---

[40]   Reporting frequencies noted here are for illustrative purposes only.

by organization-wide tools (often implemented as common controls). The organization-wide tools may be part of a specific system or systems, but the security-related information generated may not be system-specific.

Primary Roles: System Owner, Common Control Provider, System Security Officer, Security Control Assessor

Supporting Roles: Risk Executive (Function), Chief Information Officer, Chief Information Security Officer, Authorizing Official

Expected Input: Security-related information (security status data); organizational ISCM policies and procedures; reporting requirements from the Authorizing Official, Chief Information Officer, Chief Information Security Officer, and/or Risk Executive (Function)

Expected Output: Reports on security status as required by organizational ISCM policies and procedures and by the Authorizing Official in support of ongoing authorization (or re-authorization)

3.5   RESPOND TO FINDINGS

Security-related information obtained from monitoring is analyzed and met with appropriate responses. Response to findings at all tiers may include risk mitigation, risk acceptance, risk avoidance/rejection, or risk sharing/transfer, in accordance with organizational risk tolerance.[41]

Responses are coordinated with appropriate security management activities such as the security-focused configuration management program. At Tier 1, response to findings may result in changes to security policies around organizational governance. Tier 1's response may be constrained by the mission/business needs and the limitations of the enterprise architecture (including the human components), immutable governance policies, or other external drivers. At Tier 2, response to findings may include requests for additional security-related information, new or modified metrics, changes in mission/business processes, or Tier 3 reporting requirements, and/or additions or modifications to common control implementations. The Tier 2 response may be constrained by organizational governance policies and strategies as well as mission/business goals and objectives and limitations of organizational resources and infrastructure. At Tier 3, mitigation strategies have a direct and immediate impact on system-level risk and responses to findings may include implementation of additional controls, modifications to previously implemented controls, removal of systems' authorization to operate, changes to the frequency of monitoring, and/or additional or more detailed analysis of security-related information. System-level mitigations are made within constraints set by Tier 1 and 2 policies, requirements, and strategies, to ensure that organizational processes are not negatively affected.

Response strategies may be implemented over a period of time, documenting implementation plans in the system's Plan of Action and Milestones. As weaknesses are found, response actions are evaluated and any mitigation actions are conducted immediately or are added to the POA&M. Other key system documents are updated accordingly. Security controls that are modified, enhanced, or added as part of the response step of the continuous monitoring process are assessed

---

[41]   For a detailed description of risk responses, see NIST SP 800-39, as amended.

to ensure that the new or revised controls are effective in their implementations.[42] Going forward, new or revised controls are included in the overall continuous monitoring strategy.

Primary Roles: System Owner, Common Control Provider, System Security Officer

Supporting Roles: Authorizing Official, Senior Information Security Officer, Information Owner/Steward

Expected Input: Reports on security status, reports on assessment results (e.g., Security Assessment Reports), organizational- and system-level risk assessments, Security Assessment Plans, System Security Plans, organizational procedures and templates

Expected Output: Decisions on risk responses, updated system security information (e.g., System Security Plans, POA&Ms, Security Assessment Reports), updated security status reports

3.6   REVIEW AND UPDATE THE MONITORING PROGRAM AND STRATEGY

ISCM strategies and programs are not static. Security control assessments, security status metrics, and monitoring and assessment frequencies change in accordance with the needs of the organization. The continuous monitoring strategy is reviewed to ensure that it sufficiently supports the organization in operating within acceptable risk tolerance levels, that metrics remain relevant, and that data is current and complete. The strategy review also identifies ways to improve organizational insight into security posture, effectively supports informed risk management decision making/ongoing authorizations, and improves the organization's ability to respond to known and emerging threats.

The organization establishes a procedure for reviewing and modifying all aspects of the ISCM strategy, including relevance of the overall strategy, accuracy in reflecting organizational risk tolerance, accuracy/correctness of measurements, and applicability of metrics, reporting requirements, and monitoring and assessment frequencies. If any of the data collected is not required for reporting purposes or found to be not useful in maintaining or improving the organization's security posture, then the organization considers saving resources by discontinuing that particular collection. Factors precipitating changes in the monitoring strategy may include, but are not limited to:

- Changes to core missions or business processes;

- Significant changes in the enterprise architecture (including addition or removal of systems);

- Changes in organizational risk tolerance;

- Changes in threat information;

- Changes in vulnerability information;

- Changes within information systems (including changes in categorization/impact level);

- Increase/decrease in POA&Ms related to specific controls;

---

[42] Changes to security controls are made after being fully tested, vetted, and reviewed in a test environment.

- Trend analyses of status reporting output;

- New federal laws or regulations; and/or

- Changes to reporting requirements.

Officials examine consolidated POA&M information to determine if there are common weaknesses/deficiencies among the organization's information systems and propose or request solutions. The aggregate POA&M information is used to allocate risk mitigation resources organization-wide and to make adjustments to the monitoring strategy. Similarly, status reports and metrics are analyzed to determine if there are any security trends that suggest changes to the monitoring strategy may be necessary. For instance, if weekly assessments of component inventories over a six-month period indicate that very few changes are being made in a given week and changes that *were* made are accurately reflected in the inventories, the organization may wish to reduce the frequency of monitoring component inventories to biweekly or monthly. Conversely, if biweekly audit record analyses over a six-month period indicate increases in anomalous events, the organization may wish to increase the frequency of audit record reviews to weekly.

An organization's ISCM strategy also changes as the organization's security program(s) and monitoring capabilities mature. In a fully mature program, security-related information collection and analysis are accomplished using standardized methods across the organization, as an integral part of mission and business processes, and automated to the fullest extent possible. In this case, the security program is mature enough to ensure that sufficient processes and procedures effectively secure the enterprise architecture in accordance with organizational risk tolerances, and to collect, correlate, analyze, and report on relevant security metrics.[43]

ISCM is a recursive process in the sense that the monitoring strategy is continually refined as the steps of the process repeat. Further, the organization-wide application of ISCM is accomplished through smaller or more narrowly focused instances of the similar efforts at the mission/business processes and systems tiers. In other words, the output of ISCM at Tier 3 is input to the implementation of the ISCM programs at Tiers 1 and 2. Working from the top of the pyramid in Figure 2-1 (Tier 1) to its bottom (Tier 3), upper-tier monitoring strategies set the parameters for lower-tier monitoring programs, and observations made at the lower tiers may result in changes to upper-tier monitoring strategies. The ISCM program itself must be monitored so that it can evolve with changes in organizational missions and objectives, operational environments, and threats.

Primary Roles: Senior Information Security Officer, Authorizing Official, Information System Owner/Common Control Provider

Supporting Roles: Risk Executive (Function), Chief Information Officer, Information System Security Officer

Expected Input: Trend analyses from existing monitoring; organizational risk tolerance information; information on new laws, regulations, reporting requirements; current threat and vulnerability information; other organizational information as required, updates to automation specifications

---

[43] See NIST SP 800-55, as amended, for more information on security metrics.

Expected Output: Revised ISCM strategy or a brief documented report noting review details and that modifications to the strategy were not necessary (in accordance with the established review process)

Information Security Continuous Monitoring (ISCM) for Federal Info Systems & Orgs (800-137)

411

APPENDIX A

REFERENCES

LEGISLATION

1. E-Government Act [includes FISMA] (P.L. 107-347), December 2002.

POLICIES, DIRECTIVES, INSTRUCTIONS

1. Office of Management and Budget, Circular A-130, Appendix III, Transmittal Memorandum #4, *Management of Federal Information Resources*, November 2000.

2. Office of Management and Budget Memorandum M-02-01, *Guidance for Preparing and Submitting Security Plans of Action and Milestones*, October 2001.

3. Cyber Security Research and Development Act of 2002.

GUIDELINES

1. National Institute of Standards and Technology Special Publication 800-12, *An Introduction to Computer Security: The NIST Handbook*, October 1995.

2. National Institute of Standards and Technology Special Publication 800-34, Revision 1, *Contingency Planning Guide for Federal Information Systems*, May 2010.

3. National Institute of Standards and Technology Special Publication 800-37, Revision 1, *Guide for Applying the Risk Management Framework to Federal Information Systems: A Security Life Cycle Approach*, February 2010.

4. National Institute of Standards and Technology Special Publication 800-39, *Managing Information Security Risk: Organization, Mission, and Information System View*, March 2011.

5. National Institute of Standards and Technology Special Publication 800-40, Version 2, *Creating a Patch and Vulnerability Management Program*, November 2005.

6. National Institute of Standards and Technology Special Publication 800-53, Revision 3, *Recommended Security Controls for Federal Information Systems and Organizations*, August 2009.

7. National Institute of Standards and Technology Special Publication 800-53A, *Guide for Assessing the Security Controls in Federal Information Systems and Organizations: Building Effective Security Assessment Plans*, June 2010.

8. National Institute of Standards and Technology Special Publication 800-55, Revision 1, *Performance Measurement Guide for Information Security*, July 2008.

9. National Institute of Standards and Technology Special Publication 800-92, *Guide to Computer Log Management*, September 2006.

10. National Institute of Standards and Technology Special Publication 800-126, Revision 1, *The Technical Specification for the Security Content Automation Protocol (SCAP): SCAP Version 1.1*, February 2011.

11. National Institute of Standards and Technology Special Publication 800-128, *Guide for Security-Focused Configuration Management of Information Systems*, August 2011.

12. National Institute of Standards and Technology Interagency Report 7756, DRAFT, *CAESARS Framework Extension: an Enterprise Continuous Monitoring Technical Reference Architecture*, February 2011.

OTHER

1. Common Vulnerabilities and Exposures (CVE), http://cve.mitre.org/about/index.html.

2. Common Vulnerability Scoring System (CVSS), http://www.first.org/cvss/.

APPENDIX B

GLOSSARY

COMMON TERMS AND DEFINITIONS

This appendix provides definitions for security terminology used within Special Publication 800-137. The terms in the glossary are consistent with the terms used in the suite of FISMA-related security standards and guidelines developed by NIST. Unless otherwise stated, all terms used in this publication are also consistent with the definitions contained in the CNSS Instruction 4009, *National Information Assurance Glossary.*

Activities [NISTIR 7298]	An assessment object that includes specific protection-related pursuits or actions supporting an information system that involve people (e.g., conducting system backup operations, monitoring network traffic).
Adequate Security [OMB Circular A-130, Appendix III]	Security commensurate with the risk and the magnitude of harm resulting from the loss, misuse, or unauthorized access to or modification of information. This includes assuring that systems and applications used by the agency operate effectively and provide appropriate confidentiality, integrity, and availability, through the use of cost-effective management, personnel, operational, and technical controls.
Advanced Persistent **Threats** [NIST SP 800-39]	An adversary with sophisticated levels of expertise and significant resources, allowing it through the use of multiple different attack vectors (e.g., cyber, physical, and deception) to generate opportunities to achieve its objectives, which are typically to establish and extend footholds within the information technology infrastructure of organizations for purposes of continually exfiltrating information and/or to undermine or impede critical aspects of a mission, program, or organization, or place itself in a position to do so in the future; moreover, the advanced persistent threat pursues its objectives repeatedly over an extended period of time, adapting to a defender's efforts to resist it, and with determination to maintain the level of interaction needed to execute its objectives.
Agency	See *Executive Agency.*

Allocation [NISTIR 7298]	The process an organization employs to determine whether security controls are defined as system-specific, hybrid, or common.
	The process an organization employs to assign security controls to specific information system components responsible for providing a particular security capability (e.g., router, server, remote sensor).
Application [NISTIR 7298]	A software program hosted by an information system.
Assessment	See *Security Control Assessment*.
Assessment Findings [NISTIR 7298]	Assessment results produced by the application of an assessment procedure to a security control or control enhancement to achieve an assessment objective; the execution of a determination statement within an assessment procedure by an assessor that results in either a *satisfied* or *other than satisfied* condition.
Assessment Method [NISTIR 7298]	One of three types of actions (examine, interview, test) taken by assessors in obtaining evidence during an assessment.
Assessment Object [NISTIR 7298]	The item (specifications, mechanisms, activities, individuals) upon which an assessment method is applied during an assessment.
Assessment Objective [NISTIR 7298]	A set of determination statements that expresses the desired outcome for the assessment of a security control or control enhancement.
Assessment Procedure [NISTIR 7298]	A set of assessment *objectives* and an associated set of assessment *methods* and assessment *objects*.
Assessor	See *Security Control Assessor*.
Assurance [NISTIR 7298]	The grounds for confidence that the set of intended security controls in an information system are effective in their application.
Assurance Case [NISTIR 7298]	A structured set of arguments and a body of evidence showing that an information system satisfies specific claims with respect to a given quality attribute.
Authentication [FIPS 200]	Verifying the identity of a user, process, or device, often as a prerequisite to allowing access to resources in an information system.

Authenticity [CNSSI 4009]	The property of being genuine and being able to be verified and trusted; confidence in the validity of a transmission, a message, or message originator. See *Authentication*.
Authorization (to operate) [CNSSI 4009]	The official management decision given by a senior organizational official to authorize operation of an information system and to explicitly accept the risk to organizational operations (including mission, functions, image, or reputation), organizational assets, individuals, other organizations, and the Nation based on the implementation of an agreed-upon set of security controls.
Authorization Boundary [NIST SP 800-37]	All components of an information system to be authorized for operation by an authorizing official and excludes separately authorized systems, to which the information system is connected.
Authorizing Official (AO) [CNSSI 4009]	A senior (federal) official or executive with the authority to formally assume responsibility for operating an information system at an acceptable level of risk to organizational operations (including mission, functions, image, or reputation), organizational assets, individuals, other organizations, and the Nation.
Availability [44 U.S.C., Sec. 3542]	Ensuring timely and reliable access to and use of information.
Categorization	See *Security Categorization*.
Chief Information Officer (CIO) [PL 104-106, Sec. 5125(b)]	Agency official responsible for: 1) Providing advice and other assistance to the head of the executive agency and other senior management personnel of the agency to ensure that information technology is acquired and information resources are managed in a manner that is consistent with laws, Executive Orders, directives, policies, regulations, and priorities established by the head of the agency; 2) Developing, maintaining, and facilitating the implementation of a sound and integrated information technology architecture for the agency; and 3) Promoting the effective and efficient design and operation of all major information resources management processes for the agency, including improvements to work processes of the agency.
Chief Information Security Officer	See *Senior Agency Information Security Officer*.

Common Control [CNSSI 4009]	A security control that is inherited by one or more organizational information systems. See *Security Control Inheritance*.
Common Control Provider [NISTIR 7298]	An organizational official responsible for the development, implementation, assessment, and monitoring of common controls (i.e., security controls inherited by information systems).
Compensating Security Controls [NISTIR 7298]	The management, operational, and technical controls (i.e., safeguards or countermeasures) employed by an organization in lieu of the recommended controls in the low, moderate, or high baselines described in NIST Special Publication 800-53, that provide equivalent or comparable protection for an information system.
Comprehensive Testing [NISTIR 7298]	A test methodology that assumes explicit and substantial knowledge of the internal structure and implementation detail of the assessment object. Also known as white box testing.
Computer Incident Response Team (CIRT) [CNSSI 4009]	Group of individuals usually consisting of Security Analysts organized to develop, recommend, and coordinate immediate mitigation actions for containment, eradication, and recovery resulting from computer security incidents. Also called a Computer Security Incident Response Team (CSIRT) or a CIRC (Computer Incident Response Center, Computer Incident Response Capability, or Cyber Incident Response Team).
Confidentiality [44 U.S.C., Sec. 3542]	Preserving authorized restrictions on information access and disclosure, including means for protecting personal privacy and proprietary information.
Configuration Control (or Configuration Management) [CNSSI 4009]	Process for controlling modifications to hardware, firmware, software, and documentation to protect the information system against improper modifications before, during, and after system implementation.
Continuous Monitoring	Maintaining ongoing awareness to support organizational risk decisions. See *Information Security Continuous Monitoring*, *Risk Monitoring*, and *Status Monitoring*.
Controlled Interface [CNSSI 4009]	A boundary with a set of mechanisms that enforces the security policies and controls the flow of information between interconnected information systems.
Countermeasures [CNSSI 4009]	Actions, devices, procedures, techniques, or other measures that reduce the vulnerability of an information system. Synonymous with security controls and safeguards.

Coverage [NISTIR 7298]	An attribute associated with an assessment method that addresses the scope or breadth of the assessment objects included in the assessment (e.g., types of objects to be assessed and the number of objects to be assessed by type). The values for the coverage attribute, hierarchically from less coverage to more coverage, are basic, focused, and comprehensive.
Data Loss	The exposure of proprietary, sensitive, or classified information through either data theft or data leakage.
Depth [NISTIR 7298]	An attribute associated with an assessment method that addresses the rigor and level of detail associated with the application of the method. The values for the depth attribute, hierarchically from less depth to more depth, are basic, focused, and comprehensive.
Domain [CNSSI 4009]	An environment or context that includes a set of system resources and a set of system entities that have the right to access the resources as defined by a common security policy, security model, or security architecture. See *Security Domain*.
Environment of Operation [NISTIR 7298]	The physical surroundings in which an information system processes, stores, and transmits information.
Examine [NISTIR 7298]	A type of assessment method that is characterized by the process of checking, inspecting, reviewing, observing, studying, or analyzing one or more assessment objects to facilitate understanding, achieve clarification, or obtain evidence, the results of which are used to support the determination of security control effectiveness over time.
Executive Agency [41 U.S.C., Sec. 403]	An executive department specified in 5 U.S.C., Sec. 101; a military department specified in 5 U.S.C., Sec. 102; an independent establishment as defined in 5 U.S.C., Sec. 104(1); and a wholly owned Government corporation fully subject to the provisions of 31 U.S.C., Chapter 91.
Expected Output	Any data collected from monitoring and assessments as part of the ISCM strategy.
Federal Agency	See *Executive Agency*.
Federal Information System [40 U.S.C., Sec. 11331]	An information system used or operated by an executive agency, by a contractor of an executive agency, or by another organization on behalf of an executive agency.
High-Impact System [FIPS 200]	An information system in which at least one security objective (confidentiality, integrity, or availability) is assigned a FIPS 199 potential impact value of high.

Hybrid Security Control [CNSSI 4009]	A security control that is implemented in an information system in part as a common control and in part as a system-specific control.
	See *Common Control* and *System-Specific Security Control*.
Incident [FIPS 200]	An occurrence that actually or potentially jeopardizes the confidentiality, integrity, or availability of an information system or the information the system processes, stores, or transmits or that constitutes a violation or imminent threat of violation of security policies, security procedures, or acceptable use policies.
Individuals [NISTIR 7298]	An assessment object that includes people applying specifications, mechanisms, or activities.
Information [FIPS 199]	An instance of an information type.
Information Owner [CNSSI 4009]	Official with statutory or operational authority for specified information and responsibility for establishing the controls for its generation, collection, processing, dissemination, and disposal.
Information Resources [44 U.S.C., Sec. 3502]	Information and related resources, such as personnel, equipment, funds, and information technology.
Information Security [44 U.S.C., Sec. 3542]	The protection of information and information systems from unauthorized access, use, disclosure, disruption, modification, or destruction in order to provide confidentiality, integrity, and availability.
Information Security Architect [NISTIR 7298]	Individual, group, or organization responsible for ensuring that the information security requirements necessary to protect the organization's core missions and business processes are adequately addressed in all aspects of enterprise architecture including reference models, segment and solution architectures, and the resulting information systems supporting those missions and business processes.
Information Security Continuous Monitoring (ISCM)	Maintaining ongoing awareness of information security, vulnerabilities, and threats to support organizational risk management decisions.
	[Note: The terms "continuous" and "ongoing" in this context mean that security controls and organizational risks are assessed and analyzed at a frequency sufficient to support risk-based security decisions to adequately protect organization information.]

Information Security Continuous Monitoring (ISCM) Program	A program established to collect information in accordance with preestablished metrics, utilizing information readily available in part through implemented security controls.
Information Security Continuous Monitoring (ISCM) Process	A process to: • Define an ISCM strategy; • Establish an ISCM program; • Implement an ISCM program; • Analyze data and Report findings; • Respond to findings; and • Review and Update the ISCM strategy and program.
Information Security Program Plan [NISTIR 7298]	Formal document that provides an overview of the security requirements for an organization-wide information security program and describes the program management controls and common controls in place or planned for meeting those requirements.
Information Security Risk [NIST SP 800-39]	The risk to organizational operations (including mission, functions, image, reputation), organizational assets, individuals, other organizations, and the Nation due to the potential for unauthorized access, use, disclosure, disruption, modification, or destruction of information and /or information systems. See *Risk*.
Information System [44 U.S.C., Sec. 3502]	A discrete set of information resources organized for the collection, processing, maintenance, use, sharing, dissemination, or disposition of information.
Information System Boundary	See *Authorization Boundary*.
Information System Owner (or Program Manager) [NISTIR 7298]	Official responsible for the overall procurement, development, integration, modification, or operation and maintenance of an information system.
Information System Security Engineer [CNSSI 4009]	Individual assigned responsibility for conducting information system security engineering activities.
Information System Security Engineering [CNSSI 4009]	Process that captures and refines information security requirements and ensures that their integration into information technology component products and information systems through purposeful security design or configuration.

Information System-related Security Risks	Risks that arise through the loss of confidentiality, integrity, or availability of information or information systems and consider impacts to the organization (including assets, mission, functions, image, or reputation), individuals, other organizations, and the Nation. See *Risk*.
Information System Security Officer (ISSO) [CNSSI 4009]	Individual with assigned responsibility for maintaining the appropriate operational security posture for an information system or program.
Information Technology [40 U.S.C., Sec. 1401]	Any equipment or interconnected system or subsystem of equipment that is used in the automatic acquisition, storage, manipulation, management, movement, control, display, switching, interchange, transmission, or reception of data or information by the executive agency. For purposes of the preceding sentence, equipment is used by an executive agency if the equipment is used by the executive agency directly or is used by a contractor under a contract with the executive agency which: (i) requires the use of such equipment; or (ii) requires the use, to a significant extent, of such equipment in the performance of a service or the furnishing of a product. The term *information technology* includes computers, ancillary equipment, software, firmware, and similar procedures, services (including support services), and related resources.
Information Type [FIPS 199]	A specific category of information (e.g., privacy, medical, proprietary, financial, investigative, contractor sensitive, security management) defined by an organization or in some instances, by a specific law, Executive Order, directive, policy, or regulation.
Integrity [44 U.S.C., Sec. 3542]	Guarding against improper information modification or destruction, and includes ensuring information non-repudiation and authenticity.
Interview [NISTIR 7298]	A type of assessment method that is characterized by the process of conducting discussions with individuals or groups within an organization to facilitate understanding, achieve clarification, or lead to the location of evidence, the results of which are used to support the determination of security control effectiveness over time.
Intrusion Detection and Prevention System (IDPS) [NISTIR 7298]	Software that automates the process of monitoring the events occurring in a computer system or network and analyzing them for signs of possible incidents and attempting to stop detected possible incidents.

Malware [NISTIR 7298]	A program that is inserted into a system, usually covertly, with the intent of compromising the confidentiality, integrity, or availability of the victim's data, applications, or operating system or of otherwise annoying or disrupting the victim.
Management Controls [FIPS 200]	The security controls (i.e., safeguards or countermeasures) for an information system that focus on the management of risk and the management of information system security.
Mechanisms [NISTIR 7298]	An assessment object that includes specific protection-related items (e.g., hardware, software, or firmware) employed within or at the boundary of an information system.
Metrics [NISTIR 7298]	Tools designed to facilitate decision making and improve performance and accountability through collection, analysis, and reporting of relevant performance-related data.
National Security System [44 U.S.C., Sec. 3542]	Any information system (including any telecommunications system) used or operated by an agency or by a contractor of an agency, or other organization on behalf of an agency—(i) the function, operation, or use of which involves intelligence activities; involves cryptologic activities related to national security; involves command and control of military forces; involves equipment that is an integral part of a weapon or weapons system; or is critical to the direct fulfillment of military or intelligence missions (excluding a system that is to be used for routine administrative and business applications, for example, payroll, finance, logistics, and personnel management applications); or (ii) is protected at all times by procedures established for information that have been specifically authorized under criteria established by an Executive Order or an Act of Congress to be kept classified in the interest of national defense or foreign policy.
Operational Controls [FIPS 200]	The security controls (i.e., safeguards or countermeasures) for an information system that are primarily implemented and executed by people (as opposed to systems).
Organization [FIPS 200, Adapted]	An entity of any size, complexity, or positioning within an organizational structure (e.g., a federal agency, or, as appropriate, any of its operational elements).
Organizational Information Security Continuous Monitoring	Ongoing monitoring sufficient to ensure and assure effectiveness of security controls related to systems, networks, and cyberspace, by assessing security control implementation and organizational security status in accordance with organizational risk tolerance – and within a reporting structure designed to make real-time, data-driven risk management decisions.

Patch Management [CNSSI 4009]	The systematic notification, identification, deployment, installation, and verification of operating system and application software code revisions. These revisions are known as patches, hot fixes, and service packs.
Penetration Testing [NISTIR 7298]	A test methodology in which assessors, using all available documentation (e.g., system design, source code, manuals) and working under specific constraints, attempt to circumvent the security features of an information system.
Plan of Action & Milestones (POA&M) [OMB Memorandum 02-01]	A document that identifies tasks needing to be accomplished. It details resources required to accomplish the elements of the plan, any milestones in meeting the tasks, and scheduled completion dates for the milestones.
Potential Impact [FIPS 199]	The loss of confidentiality, integrity, or availability could be expected to have: (i) a *limited* adverse effect (FIPS 199 low); (ii) a *serious* adverse effect (FIPS 199 moderate); or (iii) a *severe* or *catastrophic* adverse effect (FIPS 199 high) on organizational operations, organizational assets, or individuals.
Records [CNSSI 4009]	The recordings (automated and/or manual) of evidence of activities performed or results achieved (e.g., forms, reports, test results), which serve as a basis for verifying that the organization and the information system are performing as intended. Also used to refer to units of related data fields (i.e., groups of data fields that can be accessed by a program and that contain the complete set of information on particular items).
Resilience [NIST SP 800-39, Adapted]	The ability to continue to: (i) operate under adverse conditions or stress, even if in a degraded or debilitated state, while maintaining essential operational capabilities; and (ii) recover to an effective operational posture in a time frame consistent with mission needs.
Risk [FIPS 200, Adapted]	A measure of the extent to which an entity is threatened by a potential circumstance or event, and typically a function of: (i) the adverse impacts that would arise if the circumstance or event occurs; and (ii) the likelihood of occurrence.
	[Note: Information system-related security risks are those risks that arise from the loss of confidentiality, integrity, or availability of information or information systems and reflect the potential adverse impacts to organizational operations (including mission, functions, image, or reputation), organizational assets, individuals, other organizations, and the Nation. Adverse impacts to the Nation include, for example, compromises to information systems that support critical infrastructure applications or are paramount to government continuity of operations as defined by the Department of Homeland Security.]

Information Security Continuous Monitoring (ISCM) for Federal Info Systems & Orgs (800-137)
423

Risk Assessment [CNSSI 4009]	The process of identifying risks to organizational operations (including mission, functions, image, reputation), organizational assets, individuals, other organizations, and the Nation, resulting from the operation of an information system. Part of risk management, incorporates threat and vulnerability analyses, and considers mitigations provided by security controls planned or in place. Synonymous with risk analysis.
Risk Executive (Function) [CNSSI 4009]	An individual or group within an organization that helps to ensure that: (i) security risk-related considerations for individual information systems, to include the authorization decisions, are viewed from an organization-wide perspective with regard to the overall strategic goals and objectives of the organization in carrying out its missions and business functions; and (ii) managing information system-related security risks is consistent across the organization, reflects organizational risk tolerance, and is considered along with organizational risks affecting mission/business success.
Risk Management [FIPS 200, Adapted]	The program and supporting processes to manage information security risk to organizational operations (including mission, functions, image, reputation), organizational assets, individuals, other organizations, and the Nation, and includes: (i) establishing the context for risk-related activities; (ii) assessing risk; (iii) responding to risk once determined; and (iv) monitoring risk over time.
Risk Monitoring	Maintaining ongoing awareness of an organization's risk environment, risk management program, and associated activities to support risk decisions.
Risk Response [NIST SP 800-39]	Accepting, avoiding, mitigating, sharing, or transferring risk to organizational operations (mission, functions, image, or reputation), organizational assets, individuals, other organizations, and the Nation.
Risk Tolerance [NISTIR 7298]	The level of risk an entity is willing to assume in order to achieve a potential desired result.
Safeguards [CNSSI 4009]	Protective measures prescribed to meet the security requirements (i.e., confidentiality, integrity, and availability) specified for an information system. Safeguards may include security features, management constraints, personnel security, and security of physical structures, areas, and devices. Synonymous with security controls and countermeasures.
Security Authorization	See *Authorization*.

Security Automation Domain	An information security area that includes a grouping of tools, technologies, and data.
Security Categorization [CNSSI 1253, FIPS 199]	The process of determining the security category for information or an information system. Security categorization methodologies are described in CNSS Instruction 1253 for national security systems and in FIPS 199 for other than national security systems.
Security Control Assessment [CNSSI 4009, Adapted]	The testing and/or evaluation of the management, operational, and technical security controls in an information system to determine the extent to which the controls are implemented correctly, operating as intended, and producing the desired outcome with respect to meeting the security requirements for the system.
Security Control Assessor [NISTIR 7298]	The individual, group, or organization responsible for conducting a security control assessment.
Security Control Baseline [FIPS 200, Adapted]	One of the sets of minimum security controls defined for federal information systems in NIST Special Publication 800-53 and CNSS Instruction 1253.
Security Control Effectiveness	The measure of correctness of implementation (i.e., how consistently the control implementation complies with the security plan) and how well the security plan meets organizational needs in accordance with current risk tolerance.
Security Control Inheritance [CNSSI 4009]	A situation in which an information system or application receives protection from security controls (or portions of security controls) that are developed, implemented, assessed, authorized, and monitored by entities other than those responsible for the system or application; entities either internal or external to the organization where the system or application resides. See *Common Control*.
Security Controls [FIPS 199]	The management, operational, and technical controls (i.e., safeguards or countermeasures) prescribed for an information system to protect the confidentiality, integrity, and availability of the system and its information.
Security Domain [CNSSI 4009]	A domain that implements a security policy and is administered by a single authority.
Security Impact Analysis [NIST SP 800-53]	The analysis conducted by an organizational official to determine the extent to which changes to the information system have affected the security state of the system.
Security Incident	See *Incident*.

Security Management Dashboard [NIST SP 800-128]	A tool that consolidates and communicates information relevant to the organizational security posture in near real-time to security management stakeholders.
Security Objective [FIPS 199]	Confidentiality, integrity, or availability.
Security Plan [NISTIR 7298]	Formal document that provides an overview of the security requirements for an information system or an information security program and describes the security controls in place or planned for meeting those requirements. See *System Security Plan* or *Information Security Program Plan*.
Security Policy [CNSSI 4009]	A set of criteria for the provision of security services.
Security Posture [CNSSI 4009]	The security status of an organization's networks, information, and systems based on IA resources (e.g., people, hardware, software, policies) and capabilities in place to manage the defense of the organization and to react as the situation changes.
Security Requirements [FIPS 200]	Requirements levied on an information system that are derived from applicable laws, Executive Orders, directives, policies, standards, instructions, regulations, procedures, or organizational mission/business case needs to ensure the confidentiality, integrity, and availability of the information being processed, stored, or transmitted.
Security Status	See *Security Posture*.
Senior (Agency) Information Security Officer (SISO) [44 U.S.C., Sec. 3544]	Official responsible for carrying out the Chief Information Officer responsibilities under the Federal Information Security Management Act (FISMA) and serving as the Chief Information Officer's primary liaison to the agency's authorizing officials, information system owners, and information system security officers. [Note: Organizations subordinate to federal agencies may use the term *Senior Information Security Officer* or *Chief Information Security Officer* to denote individuals filling positions with similar responsibilities to Senior Agency Information Security Officers.]
Senior Information Security Officer	See *Senior Agency Information Security Officer*.

Specification [NISTIR 7298]	An assessment object that includes document-based artifacts (e.g., policies, procedures, plans, system security requirements, functional specifications, and architectural designs) associated with an information system.
Status Monitoring	Monitoring the information security metrics defined by the organization in the information security ISCM strategy.
Subsystem [NISTIR 7298]	A major subdivision of an information system consisting of information, information technology, and personnel that performs one or more specific functions.
System	See *Information System*.
System Development Life Cycle (SDLC) [CNSSI 4009]	The scope of activities associated with a system, encompassing the system's initiation, development and acquisition, implementation, operation and maintenance, and ultimately its disposal.
System Development Life Cycle (SDLC) [CNSSI 4009, Adapted]	The scope of activities associated with a system, encompassing the system's initiation, development and acquisition, implementation, operation and maintenance, and ultimately its disposal that instigates another system initiation.
System Security Plan [FIPS 200]	Formal document that provides an overview of the security requirements for an information system and describes the security controls in place or planned for meeting those requirements.
System-Specific Security Control [CNSSI 4009]	A security control for an information system that has not been designated as a common security control or the portion of a hybrid control that is to be implemented within an information system.
Tailoring [CNSSI 4009]	The process by which a security control baseline is modified based on: (i) the application of scoping guidance; (ii) the specification of compensating security controls, if needed; and (iii) the specification of organization-defined parameters in the security controls via explicit assignment and selection statements.
Technical Controls [FIPS 200]	The security controls (i.e., safeguards or countermeasures) for an information system that are primarily implemented and executed by the information system through mechanisms contained in the hardware, software, or firmware components of the system.
Test [NISTIR 7298]	A type of assessment method that is characterized by the process of exercising one or more assessment objects under specified conditions to compare actual with expected behavior, the results of which are used to support the determination of security control effectiveness over time.

Information Security Continuous Monitoring (ISCM) for Federal Info Systems & Orgs (800-137)
427

Threat [CNSSI 4009, Adapted]	Any circumstance or event with the potential to adversely impact organizational operations (including mission, functions, image, or reputation), organizational assets, individuals, other organizations, or the Nation through an information system via unauthorized access, destruction, disclosure, modification of information, and/or denial of service.
Threat Information [CNSSI 4009, Adapted]	Analytical insights into trends, technologies, or tactics of an adversarial nature affecting information systems security.
Threat Source [FIPS 200]	The intent and method targeted at the intentional exploitation of a vulnerability or a situation and method that may accidentally trigger a vulnerability. Synonymous with threat agent.
Vulnerability [CNSSI 4009]	Weakness in an information system, system security procedures, internal controls, or implementation that could be exploited or triggered by a threat source.
Vulnerability Assessment [CNSSI 4009]	Formal description and evaluation of the vulnerabilities in an information system.
White Box Testing	See *Comprehensive Testing*.

APPENDIX C

ACRONYMS

COMMON ABBREVIATIONS

AO	Authorizing Official
CAPEC	Common Attack Pattern Enumeration & Classification
CIO	Chief Information Officer
CIRT	Computer Incident Response Team
COTS	Commercial Off-The-Shelf
CVSS	Common Vulnerability Scoring System
CVE	Common Vulnerabilities and Exposures
CWE	Common Weakness Enumeration
CWSS	Common Weakness Scoring System
DLP	Data Loss Prevention
FDCC	Federal Desktop Core Configuration
FISMA	Federal Information Security Management Act of 2002
IDPS	Intrusion Detection and Prevention System
ISCM	Information Security Continuous Monitoring
ISO	Information System Owner
ISSO	Information System Security Officer
IT	Information Technology
NCP	National Checklist Program
NVD	National Vulnerability Database
OCIL	Open Checklist Interactive Language
OMB	Office of Management and Budget
OVAL	Open Vulnerability and Assessment Language
PII	Personally Identifiable Information
PM	Program Management
POA&M	Plan Of Action & Milestones
RMF	Risk Management Framework
SAR	Security Assessment Report
SCAP	Security Content Automation Protocol
SDLC	System Development Life Cycle

SIA	Security Impact Analysis
SIEM	Security Information and Event Management
SISO	Senior Information Security Officer
SP	Special Publication
SwAAP	Software Assurance Automation Protocol
USGCB	United States Government Configuration Baseline
XCCDF	eXtensible Configuration Checklist Description Format
XML	Extensible Markup Language

APPENDIX D

TECHNOLOGIES FOR ENABLING ISCM

Organizations can make more effective use of their security budgets by implementing technologies to automate many of the ISCM activities in support of organizational risk management policy and strategy, operational security, internal and external compliance, reporting, and documentation needs. Organizations may choose to follow a reference architecture, such as NIST CAESARS Framework Extension, to implement ISCM technologies.[44] There are a variety of tools and technologies available that an organization can use to efficiently and effectively gather, aggregate, analyze, and report data ranging from continuously monitoring the security status of its enterprise architecture and operating environment(s) down to components of individual information systems. These tools and technologies can enable and assist automated monitoring in support of a variety of organizational processes including but not limited to:

- Ongoing assessments of security control effectiveness;

- Reporting of security status at the appropriate level of granularity to personnel with security responsibilities;

- Management of risk and verification and assessment of mitigation activities;

- Assurance of compliance with high-level internal and external requirements; and

- Analysis of the security impact of changes to the operational environment.

The tools and technologies discussed in this appendix leverage the strategies, policies, and roles and responsibilities of the overall ISCM program, and can assist organizations in their efforts to automate the implementation, assessment, and monitoring of many NIST SP 800-53 security controls. Though these tools and technologies lend themselves primarily to the continuous monitoring of technical security controls that can be automated, they can provide evidence, in an automated manner, to support the existence and effectiveness of nontechnical security controls or parts of technical security controls that cannot be easily automated. Automation is achieved through a variety of commercial off-the-shelf (COTS) and government off-the-shelf (GOTS) products, built-in operating system capabilities, and custom tools and scripting that use standardized automation specifications.

It is important to understand and appreciate the need to assess the effectiveness of all security controls, particularly nontechnical security controls, periodically. Data collected from automated tools may not provide feedback on the existence and the effectiveness of nontechnical security controls. It may be possible in some cases to make certain inferences about the effectiveness of nontechnical security controls based on data collected from automated tools. While it may not be possible to use automated tools and technologies to monitor adherence to policies and procedures, it may be possible to monitor associated security objectives in an automated fashion.

---

[44] For more information, please refer to DRAFT NISTIR 7756, as amended, *CAESARS Framework Extension: An Enterprise Continuous Monitoring Technical Reference Architecture.*

The Open Checklist Interactive Language (OCIL), discussed in Section D.3.1, may be used to partially automate certain controls that require human interaction and can be verified in a question and answer type format. For example, it may be possible to create an automated questionnaire to gather information related to annual security awareness training.

The validity of the security-related information collected continuously or on demand from automated tools assumes the continued effectiveness of the underlying management and operational security controls. As such, the value of automated tools and technologies, including those that perform direct data gathering and aggregation and analysis of data, is dependent upon the operational processes supporting their use. For organizations to realize the operational security benefits and for the tools and technologies to provide an accurate security status, knowledgeable staff should select, implement, operate, and maintain these tools and technologies, as well as all underlying security controls, interpret the monitoring data obtained, and select and implement appropriate remediation.

This appendix discusses the role of tools and technologies in automating many ISCM activities. It discusses common tools, technologies, and open specifications used to collect, analyze, and meaningfully represent data in support of continuous monitoring of an organization's security posture, including providing visibility into the information assets, awareness of threats and vulnerabilities, and status of security control effectiveness. Examples of security controls that can be automated using the various technologies are included. This is not an exhaustive set of examples. New products and technologies continue to reach the market. Controls commonly automated but that do not appear as examples associated with the technologies named below include those where automation is achieved through capabilities built into operating systems, custom tools and scripts, or a combination of several tools and capabilities.[45]

D.1 TECHNOLOGIES FOR DATA GATHERING

Data gathering technologies are those that provide the capability to observe, detect, prevent, or log known security threats and vulnerabilities, and/or remediate or manage various aspects of security controls implemented to address those threats and vulnerabilities. These technologies are primarily implemented at the information systems level (Tier 3). However, they can be configured to support an organization's ongoing security monitoring needs up through mission/business processes and information security governance metrics. Implementing a tool across an organization allows systems within that organization to inherit and leverage said capability.

A security automation domain is an information security area that includes a grouping of tools, technologies, and data. Data within the domains is captured, correlated, analyzed, and reported to present the security status of the organization that is represented by the domains monitored. Security automation provides standardized specifications that enable the interoperability and flow of data between these domains. Monitoring capabilities are achieved through the use of a variety of tools and techniques. The granularity of the information collected is determined by the organization, based on its monitoring objectives and the capability of the enterprise architecture to support such activities.

---

[45] Examples of such controls that lend themselves to full or partial automation through security engineering or the use of proprietary/third party software and log management tools include account management, security training records, incident reporting, and physical access control.

This section describes the tools and technologies within eleven security automation domains that support continuous monitoring:

- Vulnerability Management;

- Patch Management;

- Event Management;

- Incident Management;

- Malware Detection;

- Asset Management;

- Configuration Management;

- Network Management;

- License Management;

- Information Management; and

- Software Assurance.

The domains are pictured in Figure D-1.

Figure D-1. Security Automation Domains

D.1.1 VULNERABILITY AND PATCH MANAGEMENT

A vulnerability is a software flaw that introduces a potential security exposure. The number of vulnerabilities discovered and patches developed to address those vulnerabilities continues to grow, making manual patching of systems and system components an increasingly difficult task. To the extent possible, organizations should identify, report, and remediate vulnerabilities in a coordinated, organization-wide manner using automated vulnerability and patch management tools and technologies.

Vulnerability scanners are commonly used in organizations to identify known vulnerabilities on hosts and networks and on commonly used operating systems and applications. These scanning tools can proactively identify vulnerabilities, provide a fast and easy way to measure exposure, identify out-of-date software versions, validate compliance with an organizational security policy, and generate alerts and reports about identified vulnerabilities.

Patch management tools scan for vulnerabilities on systems and system components participating in an organization's patching solution, provide information regarding needed patches and other software updates on affected devices, and allow an administrator to decide on the patching implementation process. Patch management tools and utilities are available from various vendors to assist in the automated identification, distribution, and reporting of software patches. It is critical to understand the impact of patches before applying and to deploy them within the context of a defined patch management policy, providing assurance that systems will not lose critical functionality due to an unintended side effect of a patch. In some cases where a patch cannot be deployed, other compensating security controls may be necessary.

The implementation and effective use of vulnerability assessment and patch management technologies[46] can assist organizations in automating the implementation, assessment, and

---

[46] For more information, please refer to NIST SP 800-40, as amended, *Creating a Patch and Vulnerability*

continuous monitoring of several NIST SP 800-53 security controls including SI-2, Flaw
Remediation; CA-2, Security Assessments; CA-7, Continuous Monitoring; CM-3, Configuration
Change Control; IR-4, Incident Handling; IR-5, Incident Monitoring; MA-2, Controlled
Maintenance; RA-5, Vulnerability Scanning; SA-11, Developer Security Testing; and SI-11,
Error Handling. Vulnerability assessment and patch management technologies may also provide
supporting data to assist organizations in responding to higher-level reporting requirements in the
areas of configuration and vulnerability management.

D.1.2 EVENT AND INCIDENT MANAGEMENT

Event management involves monitoring and responding to as necessary, observable occurrences
in a network or system. A variety of tools and technologies exist to monitor events, such as
intrusion detection systems and logging mechanisms. Some tools may detect events based on
known attack signatures, while others detect anomalies in behavior or performance that could
indicate an attack. Certain events may signal that an incident has occurred, which is a violation or
imminent threat of violation of computer security policies, acceptable use policies, or standard
computer security practices. Incident management tools may assist in detecting, responding to,
and limiting the consequences of a malicious cyber attack against an organization.

A log is a record of the events occurring within an organization's systems and networks. Logs are
composed of log entries; each entry contains information related to a specific event that has
occurred within a system or system component. Many logs within an organization contain records
related to computer security. These computer security logs can be generated by many sources,
including security software such as malware protection software, firewalls, and intrusion
detection and prevention systems, operating systems on servers, workstations, networking
equipment, and applications.[47]

The number, volume, and variety of security logs have increased greatly, which has created the
need for information system security log management – the process of generating, transmitting,
storing, analyzing, and disposing of security log data. Log management is essential for ensuring
that security records are stored in sufficient detail for an appropriate period of time. Logs are a
key resource when performing auditing and forensic analysis, supporting internal investigations,
establishing baselines, and identifying operational trends and long-term problems. Routine log
analysis is beneficial for identifying security incidents, policy violations, fraudulent activity, and
operational problems, and as such, supports an ISCM capability.

The implementation and effective use of logging and log management tools and technologies can
assist organizations in automating the implementation, assessment, and continuous monitoring of
several NIST SP 800-53 security controls including AU-2, Auditable Events; AU-3, Content of
Audit Records; AU-4, Audit Storage Capacity; AU-5, Response to Audit Processing Failures;
AU-6, Audit Review, Analysis, and Reporting; AU-7, Audit Reduction and Report Generation;
AU-8, Time Stamps; AU-12, Audit Generation; CA-2, Security Assessments; CA-7, Continuous
Monitoring; IR-5, Incident Monitoring; RA-3, Risk Assessment; and SI-4, Information system
Monitoring.

Intrusion detection is the process of monitoring the events occurring in a computer system or
network and analyzing them for signs of possible incidents, which are violations or imminent

Management Program.

[47] For more information, please refer to NIST SP 800-92, *Guide to Computer Security Log Management.*

threats of violation of computer security policies, acceptable use policies, or standard security practices. *Intrusion prevention* is the process of performing intrusion detection and attempting to stop possible incidents as they are detected. Intrusion detection and prevention systems (IDPSs)[48] are focused primarily on identifying possible incidents, logging information about them, attempting to stop them, and reporting them to security administrators for further analysis and action.

IDPSs typically are used to record information related to observed events, notify security administrators of important observed events, and automatically generate reports, with remediation actions performed manually after human review of the report. Many IDPSs can also be configured to respond to a detected threat using a variety of techniques, including changing security configurations or blocking the attack.

Within the context of an ISCM program, IDPSs can be used to supply evidence of the effectiveness of security controls (e.g., policies, procedures, and other implemented technical controls), document existing threats, and deter unauthorized use of information systems. The implementation and effective use of IDPSs can also assist organizations in automating the implementation, assessment, and continuous monitoring of several NIST SP 800-53 security controls including AC-4, Information Flow Enforcement; AC-17, Remote Access; AC-18, Wireless Access; AU-2, Auditable Events; AU-6, Audit Review, Analysis, and Reporting; AU-12, Audit Generation; AU-13, Monitoring for Information Disclosure; CA-2, Security Assessments; CA-7, Continuous Monitoring; IR-5, Incident Monitoring; RA-3, Risk Assessment; SC-7, Boundary Protection; SI-3, Malicious Code Protection; SI-4, Information System Monitoring; and SI-7, Software and Information Integrity. IDPSs may also provide supporting data to assist organizations in meeting US-CERT incident reporting requirements and in responding to OMB and agency CIO reporting requirements in the areas of system and connections inventory, security incident management, boundary protections, and configuration management.

D.1.3 MALWARE DETECTION

Malware detection[49] provides the ability to identify and report on the presence of viruses, Trojan horses, spyware, or other malicious code on or destined for a target system. Organizations typically employ malware detection mechanisms at information system entry and exit points (e.g., firewalls, email servers, Web servers, proxy servers, remote access servers) and at endpoint devices (e.g., workstations, servers, mobile computing devices) on the network to detect and remove malicious code transported by electronic mail, electronic mail attachments, Web accesses, removable media or other means, or inserted through the exploitation of information system vulnerabilities.

Malware detection mechanisms can be configured to perform periodic scans of information systems, as well as real-time scans of files from external sources as the files are downloaded, opened, or executed in accordance with organizational security policy. Malware detection mechanisms can frequently take a predetermined action in response to malicious code detection.

---

[48] For more information, please refer to NIST SP 800-94, as amended, *Guide to Intrusion Detection and Prevention Systems (IDPS).*

[49] For more information, please refer to NIST SP 800-83, as amended, *Guide to Malware Incident Prevention and Handling.*

In addition to malware detection, a variety of technologies and methods exist to limit or eliminate the effects of malicious code attacks. Used in conjunction with configuration management and control procedures and strong software integrity controls, malware detection mechanisms can be even more effective in preventing execution of unauthorized code. Additional risk mitigation measures, such as secure coding practices, trusted procurement processes, and regular monitoring of secure configurations, can help to ensure that unauthorized functions are not performed.

The implementation and effective use of malware detection technologies can assist organizations in automating the implementation, assessment, and continuous monitoring of several NIST SP 800-53 security controls, including CA-2, Security Assessments; CA-7, Continuous Monitoring; IR-5, Incident Monitoring; RA-3, Risk Assessment; SA-12, Supply Chain Protection; SA-13, Trustworthiness; SI-3, Malicious Code Protection; SI-4, Information System Monitoring; SI-7, Software and Information Integrity; and SI-8, Spam Protection. Malware detection technologies may also provide supporting data to assist organizations in meeting US-CERT incident reporting requirements and in responding to OMB and agency CIO reporting requirements related to incident management, remote access, and boundary protections.

D.1.4 ASSET MANAGEMENT

Asset management tools help maintain inventory of software and hardware within the organization. This can be accomplished via a combination of system configuration, network management, and license management tools, or with a special-purpose tool. Asset management software tracks the life cycle of an organization's assets and provides tools such as remote management of assets and various automated management functions.

The implementation and effective use of asset management technologies can assist organizations in automating the implementation, assessment, and continuous monitoring of several NIST SP 800-53 security controls including CA-7, Continuous Monitoring; CM-2, Baseline Configuration; CM-3, Configuration Change Control; CM-4, Security Impact Analysis; CM-8, Information System Component Inventory; and SA-10, Developer Configuration Management.

D.1.5 CONFIGURATION MANAGEMENT

Configuration management tools allow administrators to configure settings, monitor changes to settings, collect setting status, and restore settings as needed. Managing the numerous configurations found within information systems and network components has become almost impossible using manual methods. Automated solutions may lower the cost of configuration management efforts while enhancing efficiency and improving reliability.

System configuration scanning tools provide the automated capability to audit and assess a target system to determine its compliance with a defined secure baseline configuration. A user may confirm compliance with, and identify deviations from, checklists appropriate for relevant operating systems and/or applications.

If an information system or system component is unknowingly out of synchronization with the approved secure configurations as defined by the organization's baseline configurations and the System Security Plan, organization officials and system owners may have a false sense of security. An opportunity to take actions that would otherwise limit vulnerabilities and help protect the organization from attack would subsequently be missed. Monitoring activities offer the organization better visibility into the state of security for its information systems, as defined by the security metrics being monitored.

Identity and account configuration management tools allow an organization to manage identification credentials, access control, authorization, and privileges. Identity management systems may also enable and monitor physical access control based on identification credentials. Identity and account configuration management tools often have the ability to automate tasks such as account password resets and other account maintenance activities. These systems also monitor and report on activities such as unsuccessful login attempts, account lockouts, and resource access.

There are a wide variety of configuration management tools available to support an organization's needs. When selecting a configuration management tool, organizations should consider tools that can pull information from a variety of sources and components. Organizations should choose tools that are based on open specifications such as SCAP; that support organization-wide interoperability, assessment, and reporting; that provide the ability to tailor and customize output; and that allow for data consolidation into SIEM tools and management dashboards.

The implementation and effective use of configuration management technologies can assist organizations in automating the implementation, assessment, and continuous monitoring of several NIST SP 800-53 security controls including AC-2, Account Management; AC-3, Access Enforcement; AC-5, Separation of Duties; AC-7, Unsuccessful Login Attempts; AC-9, Previous Logon (Access) Notification; AC-10, Concurrent Session Control; AC-11, Session Lock; AC-19, Access Control for Mobile Devices; AC-20, Use of External Information Systems; AC-22, Publicly Accessible Content; CA-2, Security Assessments; CA-7, Continuous Monitoring; CM-2, Baseline Configuration; CM-3, Configuration Change Control; CM-5, Access Restrictions for Change; CM-6, Configuration Settings; CM-7, Least Functionality; IA-2, Identification and Authentication (Organizational Users); IA-3, Device Identification and Authentication; IA-4, Identifier Management; IA-5, Authenticator Management; IA-8, Identification and Authentication (Non-Organizational Users); IR-5, Incident Monitoring; MA-5, Maintenance Personnel; PE-3, Physical Access Control; RA-3, Risk Assessment; SA-7, User Installed Software; SA-10, Developer Configuration Management; and SI-2, Flaw Remediation. Organization-wide security configuration management and engineering technologies may also provide supporting data to assist organizations in responding to higher-level compliance reporting requirements in the areas of configuration and asset management.

D.1.6 NETWORK MANAGEMENT

Network configuration management tools include host discovery, inventory, change control, performance monitoring, and other network device management capabilities. Some network configuration management tools automate device configuration and validate device compliance against pre-configured policies. Network management tools may be able to discover unauthorized hardware and software on the network, such as a rogue wireless access point.

The implementation and effective use of network management technologies can assist organizations in automating the implementation, assessment, and continuous monitoring of several NIST SP 800-53 security controls including AC-4, Information Flow Enforcement; AC-17, Remote Access; AC-18, Wireless Access; CA-7, Continuous Monitoring; CM-2, Baseline Configuration; CM-3, Configuration Change Control; CM-4, Security Impact Analysis; CM-6, Configuration Settings; CM-8, Information System Component Inventory; SC-2, Application Partitioning; SC-5, Denial of Service Protection; SC-7, Boundary Protection; SC-10, Network Disconnect; SC-32, Information System Partitioning; and SI-4, Information System Monitoring.

D.1.7 LICENSE MANAGEMENT

Similar to systems and network devices, software and applications are also a relevant data source for ISCM. Software asset and licensing information may be centrally managed by a software asset management tool to track license compliance, monitor usage status, and manage the software asset life cycle. License management tools offer a variety of features to automate inventory, utilization monitoring and restrictions, deployment, and patches for software and applications.

The implementation and effective use of license management technologies can assist organizations in automating the implementation, assessment, and continuous monitoring of several NIST SP 800-53 security controls including CA-7, Continuous Monitoring; CM-8, Information System Component Inventory; and SA-6, Software Usage Restrictions.

D.1.8 INFORMATION MANAGEMENT

There are vast quantities of digital information stored across the myriad of systems, network devices, databases, and other assets within an organization. Managing the location and transfer of information is essential to protecting the confidentiality, integrity, and availability of the data.

Data loss is the exposure of proprietary, sensitive, or classified information through either data theft or data leakage. Data theft occurs when data is intentionally stolen or exposed, as in cases of espionage or employee disgruntlement. Data leakage is the inadvertent exposure of data, as in the case of a lost or stolen laptop, an employee storing files using an Internet storage application, or an employee saving files on a USB drive to take home.

An effective data loss prevention (DLP) strategy includes data inventory and classification; data metric collection; policy development for data creation, use, storage, transmission, and disposal; and tools to monitor data at rest, in use, and in transit. There are a variety of tools available for DLP. Typical network and security tools such as network analysis software, application firewalls, and intrusion detection and prevention systems can be used to monitor data and its contents as it is transmitted. Specially purposed DLP software also exists with features such as port and endpoint control, disk and file encryption, and database transaction monitoring. These tools may be specialized network traffic monitors or software agents installed on desktops, laptops, and servers. DLP tools have built-in detection and mitigation measures such as alerting via email, logging activities, and blocking transmissions.

The implementation and effective use of DLP technologies can assist organizations in automating the implementation, assessment, and continuous monitoring of several NIST SP 800-53 security controls including AC-4, Information Flow Enforcement; AC-17, Remote Access; CA-3, Information System Connections; CA-7, Continuous Monitoring; CM-7, Least Functionality; SC-9, Transmission Confidentiality; and SI-12, Information Output Handling and Retention.

D.1.9 SOFTWARE ASSURANCE

The NIST Software Assurance Metrics and Tool Evaluation (SAMATE) project defines software assurance as the "planned and systematic set of activities that ensures that software processes and products conform to requirements, standards, and procedures from NASA Software Assurance Guidebook and Standard to help achieve:

- Trustworthiness – No exploitable vulnerabilities exist, either of malicious or unintentional origin

- Predictable Execution – Justifiable confidence that software, when executed, functions as intended."

There are several automation specifications that can assist with continuous monitoring of software assurance, including the emerging Software Assurance Automation Protocol (SwAAP) that is being developed to measure and enumerate software weaknesses and assurance cases. SwAAP uses a variety of automation specifications such as the Common Weakness Enumeration (CWE), which is a dictionary of weaknesses that can lead to exploitable vulnerabilities (i.e., CVEs) and the Common Weakness Scoring System (CWSS) for assigning risk scores to weaknesses. SwAAP also uses the Common Attack Pattern Enumeration & Classification (CAPEC), which is a publicly available catalog of attack patterns with a comprehensive schema and classification taxonomy, to provide descriptions of common methods for exploiting software and the Malware Attribute Enumeration & Characterization (MAEC), which provides a standardized language for encoding and communicating information about malware based upon attributes such as behaviors, artifacts, and attack patterns.

There are a number of software assurance tools and technologies that are now incorporating many of these automation specifications to provide software security throughout the software development life cycle. The implementation and effective use of software assurance technologies can assist organizations in automating the implementation, assessment, and continuous monitoring of several NIST SP 800-53 security controls including CA-7, Continuous Monitoring; SA-4, Acquisitions; SA-8, Security Engineering Principles; SA-11, Developer Security Testing; SA-12, Supply Chain Protection; SA-13, Trustworthiness; SA-14, Critical Information System Components; and SI-13, Predictable Failure Prevention.

D.2 TECHNOLOGIES FOR AGGREGATION AND ANALYSIS

Aggregation and analysis technologies are those that have the capability to collect raw data from one or more security controls or other direct data gathering technologies and correlate, analyze, and represent the raw data in a way that provides a more meaningful perspective on the effectiveness of security control implementation across part or all of an organization than would data from any single technology.

This section discusses common types of aggregation and analysis technologies and their role in supporting an ISCM capability. They include SIEM and management dashboards.

D.2.1 SECURITY INFORMATION AND EVENT MANAGEMENT (SIEM)

To enhance the ability to identify inappropriate or unusual activity, organizations may integrate the analysis of vulnerability scanning information, performance data, network monitoring, and system audit record (log) information through the use of SIEM tools. SIEM tools are a type of centralized logging software that can facilitate aggregation and consolidation of logs from multiple information system components. SIEM tools can also facilitate audit record correlation and analysis. The correlation of audit record information with vulnerability scanning information is important in determining the veracity of the vulnerability scans and correlating attack detection events with scanning results.

SIEM products usually include support for many types of audit record sources, such as operating systems, application servers (e.g., Web servers, email servers), and security software, and may even include support for physical security control devices such as badge readers. An SIEM server analyzes the data from all the different audit record sources, correlates events among the audit record entries, identifies and prioritizes significant events, and can be configured to initiate responses to events.

For each supported audit record source type, SIEM products typically can be configured to provide functionality for categorization of the most important audit record fields (e.g., the value in field 12 of application XYZ's logs signifies the source IP address) which can significantly improve the normalization, analysis, and correlation of audit record data. The SIEM software can also perform event reduction by disregarding those data fields that are not significant to information system security, potentially reducing the SIEM software's network bandwidth and data storage usage.

The implementation and effective use of SIEM technologies can assist organizations in automating the implementation, assessment, and continuous monitoring of several NIST SP 800-53 security controls including AC-5, Separation of Duties; AU-2, Auditable Events; AU-6, Audit Review, Analysis, and Reporting; AU-7, Audit Reduction and Report Generation; CA-2, Security Assessments; CA-7, Continuous Monitoring; IR-5, Incident Monitoring; PE-6, Monitoring Physical Access; RA-3, Risk Assessment; RA-5, Vulnerability Scanning; and SI-4, Information System Monitoring.

D.2.2 MANAGEMENT DASHBOARDS

A security management dashboard (or security information management console) consolidates and communicates information relevant to the organizational security status in near real-time to security management stakeholders. Personnel with responsibility for information security range from a technical system administrator, to the SISO, to the risk executive (function). The security management dashboard presents information in a meaningful and easily understandable format that can be customized to provide information appropriate to those with specific roles and responsibilities within the organization.

To maximize the benefits of management dashboards, it is important to obtain acceptance and support from upper-level management, define useful and quantifiable organization-specific performance metrics that are based on information security policies and procedures, and ensure the availability of meaningful performance data.

The implementation and effective use of management dashboards can assist organizations in automating the implementation, assessment, and continuous monitoring of several NIST SP 800-53 security controls including AC-5, Separation of Duties; CA-6, Security Authorization, CA-7, Continuous Monitoring; PM-6, Information Security Measures of Performance; PM-9, Risk Management Strategy; RA-3, Risk Assessment; and SI-4, Information System Monitoring.

D.3 AUTOMATION AND REFERENCE DATA SOURCES

Managing the security of systems throughout an organization is challenging for several reasons. Most organizations have many systems to patch and configure securely, with numerous pieces of software (operating systems and applications) to be secured on each system. Organizations need to conduct continuous monitoring of the security configuration of each system and be able to determine the security posture of systems and the organization at any given time. Organizations may also need to demonstrate compliance with security requirements expressed in legislation, regulation, and policy. All of these tasks are extremely time-consuming and error-prone because there has been no standardized, automated way of performing them. Another problem for organizations is the lack of interoperability across security tools; for example, the use of proprietary names for vulnerabilities or platforms creates inconsistencies in reports from multiple tools, which can cause delays in security assessment, decision making, and vulnerability remediation. Organizations need standardized, automated approaches to overcoming these challenges.

Automation is an efficient way to enable ISCM within and across domains to capture, correlate, analyze, and report the overall security status of the organization. Automation specifications and standardized formats enable the interoperability and flow of data between these domains. Just about every security tool provides some sort of automated capability as part of its functionality, including importing and exporting data and performing other pre-configured, unassisted operations. Some of these automated capabilities rely on proprietary methods and protocols, while others use standardized specifications and methods. When using a tool that automatically configures devices or changes settings, the new configurations are first tested in a test environment. Some examples of security automation activities include:

- Scanning for vulnerabilities and automatically applying the appropriate patches;

- Automatically enabling security configurations based on a checklist of security settings;

- Scanning for compliance against a pre-configured checklist of security settings; and

- Collecting security metrics from tools and reporting them to a management console in a standardized format.

These are just a few of the many security activities that can be automated. The tools and technologies discussed in this publication leverage a variety of supporting protocols, specifications, and resources to provide the standardization and interoperability necessary to enable ISCM.

The automation specification movement is a community-driven effort to standardize the format and nomenclature for communicating security and IT related information. These data exchange standards create the foundation for automating activities across disparate vendor tool sets, as well as interoperability across domain boundaries. The most mature and widely used set of specifications is the Security Content Automation Protocol (SCAP), which is used to standardize the communication of software flaws and security configurations. This section discusses how SCAP, the National Vulnerability Database (NVD), and security configuration checklists are used to represent and communicate data in a standardized format for performing security automation capabilities and their roles in supporting an ISCM program.

D.3.1 SECURITY CONTENT AUTOMATION PROTOCOL (SCAP)

SCAP is a suite of specifications[50] that standardizes the format and nomenclature by which security software products communicate security flaw and security configuration information. SCAP is a multipurpose protocol that supports automated vulnerability and patch checking,

---

[50] For more information, please refer to NIST DRAFT SP 800-126, as amended, *The Technical Specification for the Security Content Automation Protocol (SCAP): SCAP Version 1.1.*

security control compliance activities, and security measurement. Goals for the development of
SCAP include standardizing system security management, promoting interoperability of security
products, and fostering the use of standard expressions of security content. SCAP can be used for
maintaining the security of organizational systems, such as automatically verifying the
installation of patches, checking system security configuration settings, and examining systems
for signs of compromise.

What Can Be Automated With SCAP

There are many readily available tools that can be used to automate ISCM activities using SCAP.
The SCAP Product Validation Program[51] is designed to test the ability of products to use the
features and functionality available through SCAP and its component standards.

The SCAP validation program validates two types of vulnerability and patch scanners:
authenticated and unauthenticated. Authenticated vulnerability and patch scanners provide the
capability to scan a target system using target system logon privileges, to locate and identify the
presence of known vulnerabilities, and evaluate the software patch status to determine the
ongoing security status of the system based on an organization's defined patch policy.
Unauthenticated vulnerability scanners provide the capability to determine the presence of known
vulnerabilities by evaluating the target system over the network without authenticated access.
SCAP-enabled vulnerability scanners can be configured to scan connected systems at regular
intervals, thus providing a quantitative and repeatable measurement and scoring of software flaws
across systems. The use of SCAP-validated vulnerability scanners enables interoperability among
vulnerability scanners and reporting tools to provide consistent detection and reporting of these
flaws and supports comprehensive remediation capabilities.

While patching and vulnerability monitoring and remediation can often appear an overwhelming
task, consistent mitigation of system software vulnerabilities can be achieved through a tested and
integrated patching process. A mature patch and vulnerability management program that
embraces security automation technologies will help the organization to be more proactive than
reactive with regard to maintaining appropriate levels of security for their systems.

Vulnerability assessment and patch management technologies focus primarily on testing for the
presence of known vulnerabilities in common operating systems and applications. For custom
software and applications and in discovering unknown, unreported or unintentional vulnerabilities
in commercial off-the-shelf (COTS) products, vulnerability assessment and analysis may require
the use of additional, more specialized techniques and approaches, such as Web-based application
scanners, source code reviews, and source code analyzers. These tools, coupled with security
control assessment methodologies such as red team exercises and penetration testing, provide
additional means for vulnerability identification.

The SCAP Validation Program evaluates the capabilities of configuration scanners that can audit
and assess a target system to determine its compliance with a defined secure baseline
configuration. Examples of secure baseline configurations include the Federal Desktop Core

---

[51]   For more information on the SCAP Validation Program, please refer to http://scap.nist.gov/validation/.

Configuration (FDCC)[52] and profiles created under the United States Government Configuration
Baseline (USGCB)[53] initiative.

How to Implement SCAP

To implement SCAP for ISCM, SCAP-validated[54] tools and SCAP-expressed checklists are used
to automate secure configuration management and produce assessment evidence for many NIST
SP 800-53 security controls. SCAP-expressed checklists can be customized as appropriate to
meet specific organizational requirements. SCAP-expressed checklists can also map individual
system security configuration settings to their corresponding security requirements. For example,
mappings are available between Windows XP secure baseline configurations and the security
controls in NIST SP 800-53. These mappings can help demonstrate that the implemented settings
provide adequate security and adhere to requirements. The mappings are embedded in SCAP-
expressed checklists which allow SCAP-validated tools to generate assessment and compliance
evidence automatically. This can provide a substantial savings in effort and cost of configuration
management. If SCAP-validated tools are not available or are not currently deployed within an
organization, organizations should consider implementing SCAP-expressed checklists for their
secure baseline configurations in order to be well-positioned when SCAP-validated tools become
available and/or are deployed.

To automate continuous monitoring of known software vulnerabilities, SCAP-expressed
checklists and SCAP-validated tools can be used to assess the software assets installed and derive
a mitigation strategy for known vulnerabilities based on risk severity. By performing regularly
scheduled scans of the enterprise architecture with the latest available SCAP-expressed security-
related information, a security officer and/or system administrator can attain on-demand
situational awareness of the security of their networked systems in terms of configuration settings
and mitigation of known software vulnerabilities.

Partially Automated Controls

The implementation, assessment, and monitoring of some security controls may not be automated
by existing tools; however, they may be partially automated using the Open Checklist Interactive
Language (OCIL). OCIL defines a framework for expressing a set of questions to be presented to
a user and corresponding procedures to interpret responses to these questions. OCIL may be used
in conjunction with other SCAP specifications such as eXtensible Configuration Checklist
Description Format (XCCDF) to help handle cases where lower-level checking languages such as
Open Vulnerability and Assessment Language (OVAL) are unable to automate a particular check.
OCIL provides a standardized approach to express and evaluate manual security checks. For
example, a system user may be asked, "Do you have a safe to store documents?" The OCIL
specification provides the ability to define questions, define possible answers to a question from
which the user can choose, define actions to be taken resulting from a user's answer, and
enumerate the result set. One of the benefits of OCIL is that the answers can be returned in a
standardized format, allowing statistical analysis and other calculations to be performed in an
automated manner.

---

[52]   For more information on the FDCC, please refer to http://fdcc.nist.gov.

[53]   For more information on the USGCB, please refer to http://usgcb.nist.gov.

[54]   For more information on SCAP-validated products, please refer to http://nvd.nist.gov/scapproducts.cfm.

D.3.2 REFERENCE DATA SOURCES

NIST provides the two data repositories, the NVD and security configuration checklists, to support both automated and manual ISCM efforts.

National Vulnerability Database (NVD)

The NVD is the U.S. government repository of standards-based vulnerability management data represented using the SCAP specifications. This data enables automation of vulnerability management, security measurement, and compliance. The NVD includes security checklists, security-related software flaws, misconfigurations, product names, and impact metrics.

The content in the NVD is dynamic; for example, vulnerabilities are updated with new information such as patch content, checklists are updated, and new checklists are added. As information becomes available in the NVD, systems are rescanned to reassess risk and mitigate any new vulnerabilities. To facilitate a standardized distribution of the data, vulnerability content in the form of XML data feeds is available and updated at two-hour intervals. Organizations can leverage this standardized data for ISCM automation by configuring scheduled scans of systems and evaluating changes that may have occurred and any associated security risks from the changes.

Security Configuration Checklists

The Cyber Security Research and Development Act of 2002[55] tasked NIST to "develop, and revise as necessary, a checklist setting forth settings and option selections that minimize the security risks associated with each computer hardware or software system that is, or is likely to become widely used within the Federal Government." The National Checklist Program (NCP)[56] is the U.S. government repository of publicly available security checklists. The use of such checklists within the context of an overarching information security program can markedly reduce the vulnerability exposure of an organization.

A security configuration checklist, sometimes referred to as a lockdown guide, hardening guide, or benchmark configuration, is essentially a document that contains instructions or procedures for configuring an information technology (IT) product to a baseline level of security. Checklists can be developed not only by IT vendors, but also by consortia, academia, and industry, federal agencies and other governmental organizations, and others in the public and private sectors.

The NCP provides checklists both in prose format and in SCAP-expressed format. The SCAP-expressed checklists allow SCAP-validated tools to process the checklists and scan systems automatically. A subset of checklists also provides embedded Common Configuration Enumerations (CCEs) mapped to the NIST SP 800-53 security controls that allow for checklist results to be returned in the context of NIST SP 800-53 control requirements. A checklist might include any of the following:

- Configuration files that automatically set various security settings (e.g., executables, security templates that modify settings, scripts);

---

[55] The Cyber Security Research and Development Act of 2002 is available at http://csrc.nist.gov/drivers/documents/HR3394-final.pdf

[56] For more information on the NCP, see http://web.nvd.nist.gov/view/ncp/repository.

- Documentation (e.g., text file) that guides the checklist user to manually configure software;

- Documents that explain the recommended methods to securely install and configure a device; and

- Policy documents that set forth guidelines for such activities as auditing, authentication security (e.g., passwords), and perimeter security.

Not all instructions in a security configuration checklist are for security settings. Checklists can also include administrative practices for an IT product that go hand in hand with improvements to the product's security. Often, successful attacks on systems are the direct result of poor administrative practices such as not changing default passwords or failure to apply new patches.

A checklist comparison can also be performed as part of auditing and continuous monitoring of deployed systems' security, to ensure that the baseline configurations are maintained. It is not normally sufficient to configure a computer once and assume that the settings will be maintained; settings may change as software is installed, upgraded, and patched, or as computers are connected and disconnected from domains. Users might also alter security settings, such as in the case of a user who feels that a locking screen saver is inconvenient and hence turns the feature off.

D.4 REFERENCE MODEL

Organizations can use the technologies, specifications, and reference data sources discussed in Appendix D in an integrated manner to architect an ISCM technical implementation that maximizes the use of security-related information and promotes consistency in the planning and implementation of ISCM. Where possible, this ISCM technical implementation automates the collection, aggregation and analysis, and reporting and presentation of data that is necessary to support organization-defined metrics.

However, organizations face significant challenges in integrating these technologies to enable ISCM. Organizations typically use a diverse set of security products from multiple vendors. Thus it is necessary to extract security-related information (ideally in the form of raw system state data) from these tools and to normalize that data so that it is comparable (at tier 3 level and at tiers 2 and 1). A tier 3 capability is created to enable querying and reporting on the data aggregated from multiple tools covering multiple ISCM security automation domains. Since there are often many local tier 3 repositories covering different parts of a large enterprise, the tier 3 ISCM repositories regularly report data to tier 2 repositories, likely following a hierarchical architecture. The tier 2 repositories in turn report data to tier 1 repositories that may report data to even higher level users. As this data is passed up the ISCM hierarchy, it is abstracted since it is not usually possible or advisable to replicate all low level security-related information at all tiers in the hierarchy. Higher tier users query the lower level tiers to retrieve data. One challenge is the need for a technical mechanism to allow a higher tier query to be passed to lower tier ISCM instances for fulfillment. Another challenge is that in conducting query fulfillment, the lower tier ISCM instances may need to perform analysis of raw data to generate the results. These results may be findings (comparison of raw data against policy) or scores (numerical evaluation of a set of findings) and so a mechanism in the query by which to convey the desired analysis that is to be performed is needed. Ideally, if the requested data is not available at tier 3, then the tier 3 ISCM instance tasks its diverse security tools to collect the requested data.

These challenges can be met through the use of a reference model that describes the types of tools needed, their relationships, and their required roles in fulfilling ISCM functionality. The model either leverages or provides interface specifications that enable integration of these tools in order for an organization to compose an ISCM technical implementation. The model also provides specifications for each tool type so that the tools perform their roles appropriately in implementing organization wide ISCM.

One example of an ISCM reference model that promotes this consistent integration is the CAESARS Framework Extension, described in NIST Interagency Report (NISTIR) 7756, *CAESARS Framework Extension: An Enterprise Continuous Monitoring Technical Reference Architecture (Draft)*. NISTIR 7756 provides a foundation for a continuous monitoring reference model that aims to enable organizations to aggregate collected data from across a diverse set of security tools, analyze that data, perform scoring, enable user queries, and provide overall situational awareness.

The model is based on a set of high level workflow that describe necessary data movement within an ISCM technical implementation. These workflow are realized through the model's subsystem specifications (i.e., requirements for types of tools) and interface specifications for tool communication. One ability to leverage the model is dependent in part on the available infrastructure and the maturity of the organization's measurement program.[57] The functional capabilities of an architecture implemented to support ISCM include data collection, storage, querying, analysis, retrieval, propagation to higher tiers, and presentation.

In the model, data is collected (for predefined metrics or in response to a user query) to include those related to security control implementation and effectiveness. The types of data sources include people, processes, technologies, and the computing environment, (including security control assessment results). A variety of methods, both automated and manual, can be used to collect data. Organizations consider utilizing standards-based methods within tools for performing data collection to reduce integration costs, to enable interoperability of diverse tools and technologies, and to enable data to be collected once and reused many times. Data generated by humans can be collected using mechanisms that use automation and that leverage standardized methods. Collection methodologies are standardized and automated where possible to enable intra- and inter-tier information exchange, correlation and analysis.

Collected data is tagged with metadata when stored in ways that maximize reuse of collected data. Data is normalized for purposes of aggregation, correlation, and consistent use in metrics. Care is taken to store data that has been normalized or otherwise processed with its relevant attributes so as to minimize the possibility of contamination of one metric by cleansing algorithms used in support of another.

The model enables an ISCM infrastructure that has retrieval, analysis, and presentation capabilities sufficient to support reporting and risk-based decision making at all tiers. Metrics are calculated in accordance with the ISCM strategy and the established program. All security-related information is presented to those with ISCM roles and responsibilities as well as other stakeholders including consumers of monitoring information who use it to control operations within organizational risk tolerances in accordance with ISCM strategy (e.g., individuals

---

[57] See NIST SP 800-55, as amended, for more information on measurement programs.

responsible for patch management, security control assessment, security awareness and training).
Data presentation is flexible enough to satisfy diverse data display needs across all tiers.

Figure D-2 provides a high-level view of an ISCM implementation that depicts a sample flow of
security-related information from source data collection, through aggregation and analysis, to
reporting of data to users at all tiers. The ISCM data needs of users vary by tier. For example,
system administrators at Tier 3 may be interested in technical details to support system-level
actions (e.g. configuration changes), whereas management officials at Tier 1 may be more
interested in aggregated data to enable organization-wide decision making (e.g. changes in
security policies, an increase in resources for security awareness programs, or modifications to
the security architecture). Careful design of ISCM capabilities provides each user with the data
content in the *format* they need and with the *frequency* of data collection they require to make
effective decisions. More detailed information on ISCM reference models is available in NIST
Interagency Report 7756.

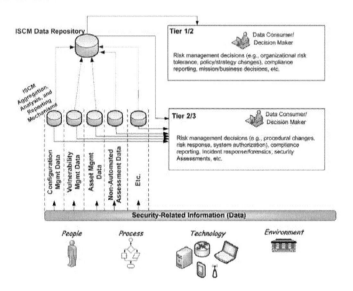

Figure D-2. Sample ISCM Implementation

Printed in Great Britain
by Amazon